Operating Systems Principles

Lubomir F. Bic
University of California, Irvine

Alan C. Shaw
University of Washington, Seattle

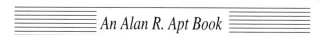

An Alan R. Apt Book

PEARSON EDUCATION, INC.
Upper Saddle River, New Jersey 07458

Library of Congress Cataloging-in-Publication Data

Bic, Lubomir

Operating Systems Principles / Lubomir F. Bic, Alan C. Shaw.

p. cm.

Includes bibliographical references and index.

ISBN 0-13-026611-6

1. Operating systems (Computers) I. Title.

QA76.76.063 B525 2002

005.4′3–dc21   2002029025

Vice President and Editorial Director, ECS: *Marcia J. Horton*

Publisher: *Alan R. Apt*

Associate Editor: *Toni D. Holm*

Editorial Assistant: *Patrick Lindner*

Vice President and Director of Production and Manufacturing, ESM: *David W. Riccardi*

Executive Managing Editor: *Vince O'Brien*

Assistant Managing Editor: *Camille Trentacoste*

Production Editor: *Joan Wolk*

Director of Creative Services: *Paul Belfanti*

Creative Director: *Carole Anson*

Art director: *Jayne Conte*

Cover Designer: *Geoffrey Cassar*

Art Editor: *Greg Dulles*

Manufacturing Manager: *Trudy Pisciotti*

Manufacturing Buyer: *Lynda Castillo*

Marketing Manager: *Pamela Shaffer*

Marketing Assistant: *Barrie Reinhold*

© 2003 by Pearson Education, Inc.

Pearson Education, Inc.

Upper Saddle River, New Jersey 07458

The author and publisher of this book have used their best efforts in preparing this book. These
efforts include the development, research, and testing of the theories and programs to determine their
effectiveness. The author and publisher make no warranty of any kind, expressed or implied, with
regard to these programs or the documentation contained in this book. The author and publisher shall
not be liable in any event for incidental or consequential damages in connection with, or arising out
of, the furnishing, performance, or use of these programs.

Printed in the United States of America

10 9 8 7 6 5 4 3 2

ISBN 0-13-026611-6

Pearson Education LTD., *London*

Pearson Education Australia PTY, Limited, *Sydney*

Pearson Education Singapore, Pte. Ltd

Pearson Education North Asia Ltd, *Hong Kong*

Pearson Education Canada, Ltd., *Toronto*

Pearson Educación de Mexico, S.A. de C.V.

Pearson Education—Japan, *Tokyo*

Pearson Education Malaysia, Pte. Ltd

Pearson Education, Inc., *Upper Saddle River, New Jersey*

To Zuzana and Alexander
Lubomir Bic

To Elizabeth
Alan Shaw

Preface

Operating systems bridge the gap between the hardware of a computer system and the user. Consequently, they are strongly influenced by hardware technology and architecture, both of which have advanced at a breathtaking pace since the first computers emerged in the 1940s. Many changes have been quantitative: the speed of processors, memories, and devices has been increasing continuously, whereas their size, cost, and power consumption have been decreasing. But many qualitative changes also have occurred. For example, personal computers with sophisticated input, output, and storage devices are now omnipresent; most also are connected to local area networks or the Internet. These advances have dramatically reshaped the world within which operating systems must exist and cooperate. Instead of managing a single processor controlling a collection of local memories and I/O devices, contemporary operating systems are required to manage highly parallel, distributed, and increasingly more heterogeneous configurations.

This book is an introduction to operating systems, appropriate for computer science or computer engineering majors at the junior or senior level. One objective is to respond to a major paradigm shift from single-processor to distributed and parallel computer systems, especially in a world where it is no longer possible to draw a clear line between operating systems for centralized environments and those for distributed ones. Although most of the book is devoted to traditional topics, we extend and integrate these with basic ideas in distributed computing.

The authors express their sincere appreciation to Gary Harkin, Montana State University; Mukkai Krisnimoorthy, Rensselaer Polytechnic Institute; Scott Cannon, Utah State University; John Hartman, University of Arizona; Gopal Lakhani, Texas Tech; Herb Mayer, Portland State University; and Chung Kuang-Shene, Michigan Technological University for their review of the book.

CONTENTS

After the introductory chapter, the book is organized into four main sections: Process Management and Coordination, Memory Management, File and I/O Management, and Protection and Security. At the end of each chapter, there is a list of the key concepts, terms, and abbreviations defined in the chapter; the back of the book contains a glossary.

Processes and Threads

Processes and, more recently, threads, are the basis of concurrency and parallelism, and have always been prominent parts of the study of operating systems. This area can be subdivided into two components: the creation of processes or threads, and their coordination. In Chapters 2 and 3, we treat the topic from the programming point of view, presenting a spectrum of constructs for expressing concurrency and for coordinating the execution of the resulting processes or threads. This includes the coordination of processes in a distributed environment, which must be based ultimately on message-passing rather than shared variables. In Chapters 4 and 5, we examine the problem from the implementation point of view by presenting the necessary data structures and operations to implement and manage processes and threads at the operating systems level. This discussion also includes issues of process and threads scheduling, interrupt handling, and other kernel functions. Chapter 6 is concerned with the important problem of deadlocks in both centralized and distributed systems.

Main Memory

Main memory has always been a scarce resource, and much of the past operating systems research has been devoted to its efficient use. Many of these results have become classical topics of operating systems; these are covered in Chapters 7, 8, and 9. Among these topics are techniques for physical memory allocation, implementation of virtual memory using paging or segmentation, and static and dynamic sharing of data and code. We also present the principles of distributed shared memory, which may be viewed as an extension of virtual memory over multiple computers interconnected by a communication network.

File Systems and I/O

Files were devised in the early days of computing as a convenient way to organize and store data on secondary storage devices. Although the devices have evolved dramatically, the basic principles of files have not. In Chapter 10, we discuss file types and their representations on disks or tapes. We also present ways of organizing and implementing file directories. In recent years, the most significant developments in the file systems area have been driven by the proliferation of networking. Many systems today do not maintain their own file systems on local drives. Instead, a more typical configuration is a network of machines, all accessing dedicated file servers. Frequently, the file systems are distributed over multiple servers or multiple networks. The last section of the chapter addresses file systems issues in such distributed environments.

Hiding the details of individual I/O devices by supporting higher-level abstractions has always been one of the main tasks of operating systems. Modern systems must continue to provide this essential service, but with a larger variety of faster and more sophisticated devices. Chapter 11 is devoted to this topic, presenting the principles of polling, interrupts, and DMA, as employed by various device drivers. Also discussed are device-independent aspects of I/O processing, including buffering and caching, error-handling, and device scheduling.

Protection and Security

Protecting a computing facility from various attacks requires a broad spectrum of safeguards. Chapter 12 focuses on the protection and security interface of the system, which guards the system access. This requires authentication of users, remote services, and clients. Despite many technological breakthroughs, user authentication still relies largely on passwords presented by users at the time of login. But the existence of computer networks has again stimulated the most dramatic developments in protection and security: the vulnerability of communication lines makes it necessary to employ techniques in secret or public key cryptography. We discuss the application of cryptographic methods both to protect information transmitted between computers and to verify its authenticity.

Once a user has entered the system, the system must control the set of resources accessible to that user. This is accomplished by hardware mechanisms at the instruction level and by access or capability lists at the software level. In addition, mechanisms to prevent unauthorized flow of information among different users also must be provided. Chapter 13 discusses such internal protection mechanisms.

EXERCISES AND PROGRAMMING PROJECTS

Each chapter ends with a set of exercises reflecting the presented topics. The exercises have been chosen carefully to satisfy the needs of different teaching styles. Each exercise set contains both analytical and constructive exercises, where students must apply conceptual knowledge acquired from the chapter to solve specific problems. We also have included questions that lend themselves to discussion or speculative analysis. A solutions manual is available to professors; they can obtain a copy from their local Prentice-Hall representative.

The set of five large programming projects and several smaller programming exercises at the end of the book are designed to complement the conceptual understanding gained from the book with practical hands-on experience. They may be used selectively as term projects or can serve as the basis for a separate laboratory component in operating systems.

APPROACH AND PHILOSOPHY

As expected, we provide in-depth coverage of all standard topics in the field of operating systems. A conventional approach typically also includes separate chapters on operating systems support for distributed network-based environments, usually appearing at the end of the text. The problem with this organization is that it makes an artificial distinction between centralized and distributed systems. In reality, there is often no clear demarcation line between the two, and they have many issues in common. Concurrency and parallelism have always been a major topic of operating systems. Even the earliest mainframes of the 1950s and 1960s attempted to overlap CPU execution with I/O processing to achieve better utilization of both. Advanced programming techniques of the 1970s and 1980s made it necessary to support concurrent processes at the user level, leading operating systems designers to provide new process synchronization and scheduling techniques, many of which also apply to networked environments. The last two decades have forced software manufacturers to seriously consider networking and physical distribution, and to integrate the necessary tools and techniques into their operating systems products.

We have chosen to preserve the natural relationship and overlap between centralized and distributed operating systems issues by integrating them within each chapter. The main distributed operating systems topics presented include message-based synchronization and remote procedure calls, distributed deadlocks, distributed shared memory, distributed file systems, and secure communication using cryptography.

Following the above philosophy, we also have refrained from presenting case studies of existing operating systems in separate chapters. Instead, we have distributed and integrated all case studies—from Unix, Linux, Windows, and many other influential operating systems—throughout the chapters. They illustrate the relevance of each concept at the time of its presentation.

Lubomir Bic

September 2002

Alan Shaw

Contents

Part Two   Memory Management   **205**

Part Five   Programming Projects   475

C H A P T E R 1

Introduction

1.1 THE ROLE OF OPERATING SYSTEMS
1.2 ORGANIZATION OF OPERATING SYSTEMS
1.3 OPERATING SYSTEM EVOLUTION AND CONCEPTS

We begin by examining the gap between the requirements and expectations placed on computer systems by the user community and the low-level capabilities of existing hardware. This gap is bridged by the operating system (OS) and other utility and support programs. We then outline the overall organization of OS, including interfaces to the hardware, the application programs, and the user. The remainder of the chapter traces the evolution of key OS concepts in the context of changing technology and the increasing diversity and sophistication of the user community.

1.1 THE ROLE OF OPERATING SYSTEMS

1.1.1 Bridging the Hardware/Application Gap

Most computer systems today are based on the principles of a "stored-program computer" formulated by mathematician John von Neumann and others in the late 1940s. The basic components of a computer and their interconnections are shown schematically in Figure 1-1 in the form of a high-level block diagram. At the heart of this system is the computational engine consisting of a **central processing unit (CPU)** and executable **main memory**. The memory is a linear sequence of directly addressable cells; it holds programs (lists of executable machine instructions) and data. The CPU continuously repeats the following basic hardware cycle:

- Fetch the instruction pointed to by a special register called the program counter.

- Increment the program counter.

- Decode the current instruction, held in a special instruction register, to determine what must be done.

- Fetch any operands referenced by the instruction.

- Execute the instruction.

This cycle forms the basis of all computations on present-day computers.

For this computational scheme to be of any practical value, two fundamental components must be included. The first is a set of **communication devices** to allow data and commands to be exchanged between the user and the machine or between one computer

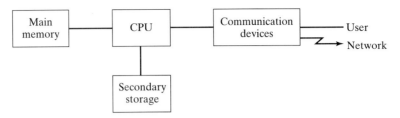

FIGURE 1-1. Main components of a computer system.

and another. It consists of **input/output (I/O) devices** (e.g., a keyboard and display terminal) and network interface devices. The second component is **secondary storage** to hold programs and data that are not currently loaded in main memory or that are only partially or temporarily loaded. This storage is needed because the system's main memory is volatile and thus loses its contents when power is turned off, and because it is also much smaller in size than secondary storage.

Sometimes the distinction between communication and storage devices is clear cut. For example, a CD-ROM drive is strictly an input device, whereas a hard disk is clearly a storage device. However, there are also common cases where such a distinction cannot be made easily. For example, a removable diskette can be viewed as storage, but it also can be used as an I/O device when moving information between different systems. From an operating system's perspective, CD-ROM, hard disk, diskette, and other devices are similar in nature, and many of the same techniques are employed to service them. We will refer to secondary storage and communication devices jointly as I/O devices.

Another degree of complexity is added when the computer system consists of more than one CPU. This can take several different forms, depending on the sharing level of the system's hardware components. Figure 1-2 shows three possible architectures that extend the basic single-CPU architecture of Figure 1-1 in different ways. In the first case (Fig. 1-2a), the two CPUs share a common main memory. The secondary storage and communication devices are typically shared. The presence of multiple CPUs poses new challenges for the OS. One of these is caching. If each CPU maintains its own local memory cache, the system must ensure that two caches do not contain different values for the same memory element. With a shared memory, this problem, referred to as **cache coherence**, is handled by the hardware and is transparent to the OS. Another important problem is the scheduling of processes. With a single CPU, scheduling is a matter of controlling the order in which processes execute. With multiple CPUs, the OS (or the application) also must decide on which CPU a given task should run. Synchronization and communication among processes running on different CPUs is performed through the shared memory; the approaches are similar to those for coordinating processes on a single CPU.

Figure 1-2b shows an architecture where each CPU has its own main memory. The secondary storage and other devices could still be shared. However, the communication subsystem must include an interconnection network that allows the CPUs to interact with each other, since no shared memory is available. There is a broad range of interconnection networks, ranging from a simple shared bus to dedicated connections arranged in a

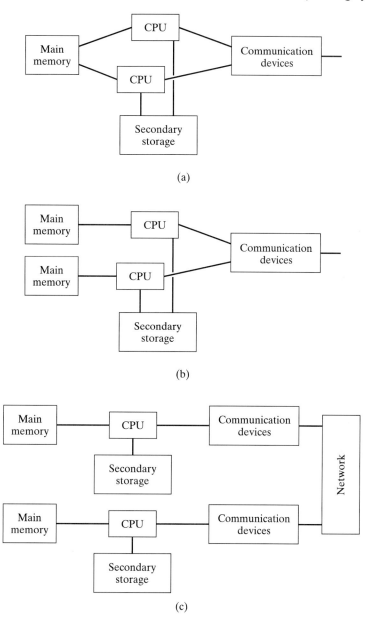

FIGURE 1-2. Systems with multiple CPUs: (a) Shared-memory multiprocessor; (b) Distributed-memory multiprocessor; and (c) Multicomputer.

variety of topologies. In the absence of shared memory, both scheduling and process coordination become more complicated. Scheduling involves not only the assignment of processes to different CPUs but also the assignment of data, some of which may be needed by multiple processes, to the disjoint local memory modules. Given that such architectures are intended primarily for high-performance scientific computing, many scheduling issues are delegated to the applications rather than handled transparently by the OS. However, the system must provide the primitives necessary to support process synchronization and communication. These are based on messages sent between the different CPUs through the interconnection network. Depending on the sophistication of the network, the system also may have to be involved in solving the cache coherence problem.

The architectures of both Figure 1-2a and b are generally referred to as **multiprocessors**. They provide multiple CPUs and possibly multiple main memory modules, but other hardware components are shared. Thus the system can still be viewed as a single computer. Figure 1-2c shows a different type of architecture, generally referred to as a **multicomputer**, where each CPU has not only its own local memory but also its own set of storage and communication devices. Among the communication devices are special **network controllers**, which allow each computer to send and receive data to/from other computers through the network. Thus, a multicomputer is viewed as a collection of complete autonomous computers, interacting with each other via the network.

There are many network types, distinguished by their size, topology, speed of data transmission, reliability, and other attributes. One popular way for two computers to communicate is through already existing telephone lines. These lines have been designed to carry analog voice data. To transmit digital data on a telephone line, each of the communicating computers uses a **modem**—a device designed to transform digital data into analog at the sender site, and analog back into digital at the receiver site. The modem is connected to an I/O bus just like any other device controller.

Faster and more reliable connections can be achieved with communication lines that are specifically designed to interconnect two or more computers. For a small number of computers, colocated in the same room or building, a **local area network (LAN)** is typically used. Figure 1-3 illustrates the two most common topologies of LANs: the **ring network** and the **broadcast bus**. The ring connects each computer to two neighbors. Data is passed along the ring in one direction from the sender to the receiver via the intermediate nodes. The broadcast bus is similar to the internal system buses. The most common type is the **Ethernet** bus. Each computer connects to the bus via a specialized network controller, an Ethernet card. All such controllers "listen to the bus," i.e., monitor it for any data placed on it. A computer wishing to send a message to another computer places the message on the bus, preceded by the receiver's address. All nodes listening to the bus examine the address, and the one whose address it matches reads the body

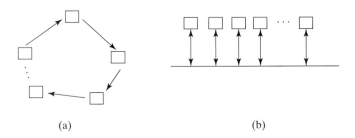

(a)   (b)

FIGURE 1-3. LAN network topologies. (a) ring network (b) broadcast bus.

of the message. The controllers also implement a protocol for resolving **collisions**—the simultaneous placement of data on the bus by two or more computers.

Local area networks are limited by the number of computers they can support and their physical distance. To interconnect large numbers of computers over long distances, a **wide area network (WAN)** is used. This employs a variety of hardware devices that repeat and amplify the signals as they travel across long distances. With WANs, it is no longer practical to establish point-to-point communication channels among all communicating computers. Instead, a message is broken into multiple **packets**, each of which is routed through switches and nodes of the WAN, and reassembled at the destination. This requires sophisticated and complex **communication protocols** that govern all aspects of the transmissions, so that large numbers of heterogeneous computers and local area subnetworks can cooperate and compete. The ultimate example of a very large heterogeneous network is the Internet, which interconnects millions of computers worldwide.

Unfortunately, there is still a long way to go from the architectural schemes depicted in Figures 1-1 and 1-2 to a practical computer system. The main problem is that the hardware operates at a very low level of abstraction relative to the problems that must be solved at the user level. Consequently, a significant amount of support software must be provided before a user application is able to take advantage of the machine's hardware. Let us consider the individual components in turn:

- The **machine instructions** executed by a CPU perform only very simple tasks: read or write a value from/to a register or a main memory location; perform an arithmetic or logical operation on binary numbers; compare two bit-strings; or set the program counter to alter the sequence of instruction execution. The programmer developing an application, on the other hand, thinks in terms of high-level data structures (e.g., arrays) and the corresponding operations to manipulate these (e.g., matrix multiplication or Fast Fourier Transform). The resulting semantic gap must be bridged by software.

- The **main memory** is a linear sequence of simple cells that hold executable programs and their data. The programmer, in contrast, manages a diverse collection of entities of various types, sizes, or shapes, including executable programs, modules, procedures, or functions; and data structures such as arrays, trees, lists, stacks, or queues, each accessed by different operations. The semantic gap between the programmer's heterogeneous collections of entities, some of which may be created and destroyed at runtime, and their machine representations in the simple sequential hardware main memory, must be bridged by software.

- The most common **secondary storage** devices are magnetic disks. These are two-dimensional structures that organize data in concentric rings, called tracks, each consisting of multiple blocks. To access a block of data requires a physical movement of the read/write head (a seek operation), waiting for the desired block to pass under the read/write head, and finally transferring the block to/from memory. Programmers who use the disk for storage of programs or data do not care about the disk's internal organization and operation. They wish to treat an entire program or data collection as a single abstract entity—a file—that can be created, destroyed, copied, and transferred between different locations using only a small set of high-level commands. These high-level abstractions must be created by software to close this semantic divide.

- The hardware interface to communication and **I/O** devices generally consists of registers that must be written and read using specific instruction sequences to cause the device to perform its functions. These sequences tend to be very complex, requiring a deep understanding of the specific device's operation. In contrast, most programmers would like to have simple, uniform interfaces and high-level operations that do not require a detailed understanding of the devices. Similarly, users would like to send messages to processes on other computers without worrying about the underlying network topologies, transmission errors, or network congestion problems. This semantic gap must again be bridged by software in the form of specialized device drivers and communication protocols.

In summary, it is the responsibility of the system's software to reduce the large divide between the capabilities of a computer's hardware components and the needs and expectations of programmers. Assemblers, compilers, and interpreters address the problem of the low-level instruction set. They permit programmers to develop code and data structures using high-level languages, which are then automatically translated into equivalent programs in the low-level machine language. Other system software, such as linkers, editors, or debuggers, contribute indirectly to reducing the semantic gap by facilitating the program development process and providing various support functions.

The remaining gaps between the hardware's capabilities and the programmers' needs are bridged by the OS.

1.1.2 Three Views of Operating Systems

Three key concepts permeate the design and organization of an OS. Each of these results in a different view of an OS and its role:

1. **Abstraction** is applied to handle *complexity*. It allows us to hide the complexity and low-level features of the hardware by building a layer of software on top of it. Abstraction also is used to define and construct multiple layers of software, each hiding the complexity of the level below.

2. **Virtualization** helps us to support *sharing* of computer resources among different users or applications. It also permits resource sharing within a single application or user. Virtualization allows us to create the illusion of multiple dedicated resources that do not need to be shared.

3. **Resource management** addresses the problem of *efficiency*. It aims at maximizing overall *performance* of the system while addressing the needs of individual users and their applications.

These three ideas give rise to three views of the nature of an OS: extended machines, virtual machines, and resource managers.

Operating Systems as Extended Machines

Imagine for a moment using a computer system without any I/O support. To read a data item from disk, the programmer must first face the challenging task of understanding the disk's low-level interface. Instead of issuing a single read operation to get the desired data block, he or she must write dozens of low-level instructions that move the read/write head into position, supervise the transfer of the appropriate data block, and handle a multitude of possible errors. The problem is aggravated further because no widely accepted standards for the operation of I/O devices exist; different sequences of instructions are usually required not only for each major device class (e.g., laser printers) but also for each individual device model within that class.

To liberate the programmer from the low-level details and complexity of I/O processing, the OS applies the concept of *abstraction*—one of the main techniques in computer science that handle complexity. The basic idea is to package sequences of lower-level instructions into functions that can be invoked as single higher-level operations. The collection of such functions extends the underlying instruction set, thus creating the illusion of a more powerful **extended machine**.

Operating systems make extensive use of abstraction at many levels. Generally, all I/O operations (e.g., reading or writing a block of data) are implemented as functions provided by the OS. Figure 1-4 illustrates the abstraction idea with a specific example. It shows a high-level *read* operation that specifies the file to be accessed ($f1$), the logical block number within the file (*lblk*), and the main memory offset at which the data block should be deposited (*mm*). The underlying I/O routines implement the high-level read by performing the necessary lower-level operations, such as moving the read/write arm to the appropriate position on the disk and checking for possible errors. These lower-level operations are, in turn, abstractions of the actual machine-level sequences that interact directly with the device by reading and writing specific registers of the device controllers. The programmer can treat the high-level read instruction as a single primitive operation, similar to a machine instruction, without worrying about the specific sequence of any lower-level instructions executed.

Similarly, operations to manipulate files are viewed as primitives, without knowing anything about the thousands of machine instructions executed to implement each high-level file operation. The file operations may, in turn, use the abstract I/O operations to perform their function. Thus, abstraction can be applied repeatedly to create *multiple levels* of extended machines.

Another example of abstraction is the command language through which users control the system's operation. A command, for example, to load and run a program,

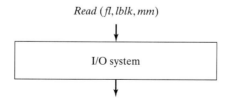

Read ($fl, lblk, mm$)

I/O system

Compute position of *lblk* on disk
Move read/write a run to corresponding disk track
Check for seek errors
Read physical block
Check for read errors
Copy block to *mm*

FIGURE 1-4. Principle of abstraction.

or to retrieve information about the system status, typically involves many lower-level operations by the system. From the user's point of view, however, the OS appears as an extended machine with the set of commands as its "machine" language.

Operating Systems as Virtual Machines

Operating systems manage and control the sharing of hardware resources by multiple users. Although some applications must cooperate with one another, most simply compete for the available resources. Ideally, each application would like the entire computer system for its own use, without handling presence of other processes using the system concurrently. The concept of *virtualization* permits this sharing. It creates the illusion of having multiple copies of the same physical resource or a more powerful form of a given physical resource.

Similar to abstraction, virtualization is applied heavily by an OS at many levels, including CPU management, memory management, and device management. In a time-sharing system, the CPU time is sliced into small time intervals. Each process is allowed to run for only a short time interval, at which time the CPU is taken away from it and assigned to another process. The switching is done completely transparently to the processes, giving each process the illusion of having the CPU for itself. Thus, all processes continue making progress concurrently, albeit at a slower rate than if each had the actual hardware CPU entirely for itself. The time-slicing of the physical CPU implements a **virtual CPU** for each process.

The prime example of applying virtualization to create a more powerful resource than the physically available one is **virtual memory**. Whenever a given program exceeds the available memory space, it must somehow be partitioned into smaller segments that are then loaded into memory when needed. If no virtualization is used, i.e., the physical memory is visible at the program level, the programmer is responsible for determining which parts of the program are to reside in main memory at any given time. Modern OSs have liberated the programmer from this burden by implementing virtual memory, which supports the illusion of large contiguous storage regions. The OS accomplishes this by automatically transferring those program segments relevant to the current computation between main memory and secondary storage.

Virtualization also is applied to I/O devices. For example, rather than interacting with an actual hardware printer, an application writes its output to a virtual printer, implemented as a file. When the output is complete, it is sent to the actual printer without having to block the process. This **spooling** technique[1] allows multiple processes to "print" concurrently, because each has its own set of **virtual devices**.

Figure 1-5 illustrates the principles of virtualization. The system hardware consists of a CPU, main memory, and a printer. Each hardware component is replicated into multiple virtual components by the OS and allocated to an application. Thus, each application runs as if it had its own dedicated CPU (created by transparent context switching), its own private memory (created by transparent memory management routines), and its own printer (created by spooling).

---

[1] The acronym "spool" stands for "simultaneous peripheral operations on-line." The idea originated in the late 1950s on the IBM 7070 computer system, where it was first recognized that I/O-intensive jobs involving slow peripheral devices, such as printers, could be performed indirectly through secondary storage and in parallel with computational tasks. The concept was an important precursor to multiprogramming, introduced later in this chapter.

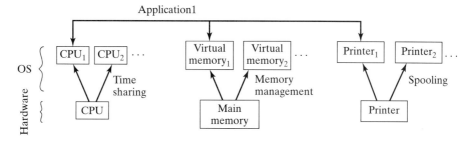

FIGURE 1-5. Principles of virtualization.

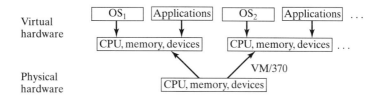

FIGURE 1-6. IBM's virtual machine concept.

IBM pushed virtualization to its limit in the 1970s with the VM/370 OS. It applied the concept uniformly at the lowest possible level by creating multiple virtual machines that are exact replicas of an entire physical machine. Figure 1-6 shows the basic organization. The VM/370 runs on bare hardware. Rather than selectively virtualizing the CPU, the main memory, or the devices for different applications, it creates the illusion of multiple copies of a *complete* hardware system. Each of these complete virtual machines can then run its own OS. This system only needs to support a single user, who then has the entire (virtual) machine to himself, and thus can be considerably simpler than a general-purpose, time-sharing system.

Operating Systems as Resource Managers

A typical application executes code stored in main memory, reads data from some input device (e.g., a keyboard or a disk), and outputs results to a printer or disk. The performance of the application, even when run in isolation, depends greatly on the efficient use of various devices. In addition, it is affected by the presence of other applications that are running on or occupying the system simultaneously. One of the main tasks of an OS is to optimize the use of all its computational resources to ensure good overall application performance, while satisfying the needs and constraints imposed by specific applications, such as guaranteeing acceptable response time for interactive processes or meeting specific deadlines of time-critical tasks.

To ensure that a given application makes good progress, the OS must grant it sufficient resources. In particular, the OS must implement scheduling policies such that each process gets a fair share of the CPU. A process also requires an adequate amount of main memory to run efficiently. This is especially critical in systems with virtual memory, where processes frequently wait for the relevant portions of their program or data space to be loaded from disk by the OS. The overhead of moving information between main memory and disk can be substantial and must be minimized. Finally, the OS should try to reduce the time that a process is waiting for its input to be ready or output to be processed. In the case of output, providing virtual devices can solve the problem of waiting. To speed up input, the OS may implement read-ahead strategies that get some data into memory in anticipation of read operations.

The overall performance of all applications can be improved by exploiting the potential parallelism opportunities in the system. Specifically, the OS should strive to keep the CPU, the main memory, and all its storage and I/O devices busy at all times by overlapping their operation whenever possible. Given the potentially large number of different devices, and the great discrepancies in speeds and capabilities, this task is a major challenge for any OS. To gain a better appreciation of the problem, briefly consider the major characteristics of different hardware components.

The CPU is normally the fastest component of a computer. Its speed is measured in CPU cycles, which typically range in hundreds of megahertz (MHz). The actual number of instructions executed per unit of time, however, is highly dependent on the CPU's architecture, including the degree of pipelining, parallelism, and the amount of on-chip memory.

The speed of instruction execution is bounded by the speed of main memory; it takes approximately 10 nanoseconds or less to perform one read or write operation. Thus, main memory is an order of magnitude slower than the CPU. Since the discrepancy occurs at very low-level instruction execution, it cannot be resolved by any software mechanisms; rather, additional hardware in the form of faster (but smaller and more expensive) memory is necessary. Fast registers hold the current instruction, the program counter, intermediate data values, and various control and status values; caches hold the most recently accessed blocks of instructions and data, with the expectation that these will be accessed again in the future. Both registers and caches have short access times of approximately 1 nanosecond or less.

For nonvolatile secondary storage, most systems provide magnetic disks (hard disks or removable floppies) or tapes. The most important characteristics that differentiate between different device types are their **capacity** (i.e., the amount of data they can hold), their **block size** (i.e., the granularity at which information may be accessed), and their **access time**, which determines how long it takes (on average) to access a data item. Typical hard disk capacities are in the dozens of gigabytes, whereas tapes can hold several times as much. Block sizes for both range in the hundreds of bytes, but the access time for the disk is significantly shorter, typically 10 milliseconds or less. Furthermore, tapes only can be accessed sequentially, which makes them unsuitable for many applications.

Common I/O devices to allow users to communicate with their applications and the system include keyboards, display terminals, pointing devices (e.g., mouse, light pen), and a variety of printers. The most important quantitative characteristic of the different I/O devices is their speed, i.e., the rate at which they can transfer data to or from the system.

The different components of a computer system are interconnected via **buses**. These are sets of parallel communication links that allow the components to exchange data with each other. In the simplest case, a single bus may interconnect all components. Figure 1-7 shows a more typical architecture, where multiple buses with different speeds of data transmission and different protocols form a hierarchy. The **memory bus** allows the CPU

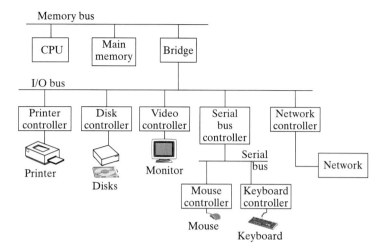

FIGURE 1-7. Hardware organization.

to access main memory. A hardware bridge connects the memory bus with the **I/O bus**; this allows the CPU to communicate with devices such as disks, printers, and terminals. These are attached to the bus via **device controllers**—specialized hardware components that provide a register-based interface to the CPU. Since the number of *slots* or places where a device controller may be attached to a bus is limited, multiple devices may share a single controller or have their own low-level bus. In the figure, two disks share a single controller. The slowest, character-oriented devices, such as the keyboard or the mouse, also are connected via a single controller that manages its own serial bus.

1.2   ORGANIZATION OF OPERATING SYSTEMS

Operating systems are large complex collections of software. To be maintainable, extendible, and comprehensible, they must be organized coherently according to general principles. We examine the organization of an OS from several points of view. The first is its **structure**, which describes how the different functionalities are grouped together and interact with each other. The second aspect, closely related to the system's internal structure, is the set of **interfaces** that the OS presents to the outside world. The third view is the system's **runtime organization**, which defines the types of entities that exist during execution.

1.2.1   Structural Organization

Any large software system is designed as a collection of functions that call each other. Those functions visible to the outside constitute the system's programming and user interface; they form the extension of the underlying hardware by exporting a set of high-level abstract operations that applications may invoke.

If we impose no further restrictions on the internal organization of various functions, we end up with a **monolithic** structure—a single-level extension of bare hardware that provides a set of new functionalities. Any modification to such a structure requires a recompilation and reinstallation of the complete system.

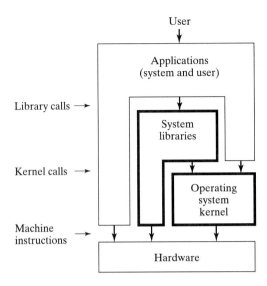

FIGURE 1-8. Structural organization of an operating system.

Monolithic systems are not only very difficult to maintain from the software engineering point of view, but also are very limited in their extensibility and adaptability to different situations. Thus, most modern OSs are designed as subsystem collections, each consisting of sets of functions but each having its own internal interface that facilitates a modular composition of the system. Furthermore, the functions are organized into multiple **layers**, such that functions at one level of the hierarchy may invoke functions at lower levels to perform their tasks. Thus, each layer may be viewed as a further extension of the ones below, i.e., a different abstract machine.

Figure 1-8 shows the simplest but most common organization of OSs, where the OS functions are split into two main layers. The lower layer, usually called the OS **kernel**, contains the most fundamental functions necessary to manage the systems resources. These are extended by a layer of **system library** routines that provide a greatly expanded suite of functionalities to meet application demands. The kernel and library functions are compiled into native code, i.e., instructions that execute directly on the machine hardware—the lowest layer of any computer system.

The application layer takes advantage of all three underlying layers. Most of an application program is compiled directly into machine instructions. Any library functions needed or invoked by the program are linked to the application so that the relevant (compiled) functions execute as part of the application. The application also may take advantage of the OS services by issuing calls directly to the system's kernel.

1.2.2 The Hardware Interface

The lowest-level interface of the OS is between the hardware and the software; it consists of the machine instructions provided by the CPU. The OS is compiled into these machine instructions and runs entirely on the bare machine hardware. The system's libraries and applications are compiled into machine instructions and thus run on the machine hardware, but the transitions between the user code and the system code must be carried out in a controlled manner that requires hardware support. In addition, the OS must respond quickly to events occurring asynchronously as the system executes. Modern CPUs support two hardware mechanisms that are essential for the above tasks, and thus allow the OS to fulfill its duties as a resource manager and supervisor. These are (1) interrupts and traps, and (2) multiple modes of instruction execution. Let us examine these in turn.

Interrupts and Traps

An important responsibility of an OS is the management of all the storage and communication devices. Efficient operation implies the ability to respond quickly to any change in the state of these devices. Such fast responses are generally accomplished by means of interrupt-driven processing.

An **interrupt** is a hardware signal issued to the CPU from some *external* device. Whenever an interrupt occurs, the CPU completes the current machine instruction, but, instead of fetching the next instruction specified by the program counter, it transfers control to a predetermined location. A special routine of the OS, the **interrupt handler**, is stored at this location. The interrupt handler analyzes the cause of the interrupt and takes appropriate actions. In the simplest case, control is then returned to the interrupted application. Figure 1-9a illustrates the basic principle. It shows how the normal flow of instruction execution is interrupted by the arrival of the external signal and temporarily diverted to the OS. The interrupt is transparent to the application.

There are two main applications of the interrupt mechanism:

- **Process management**. When multiple applications use the system concurrently, the CPU is switched between them according to scheduling policies. To allow the OS to periodically seize control of the CPU, a **time-out** interrupt can be generated

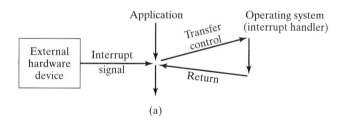

(a)

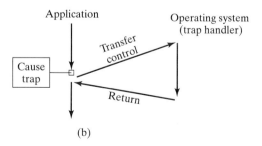

(b)

FIGURE 1-9. Principles of (a) interrupts and (b) traps.

by a timer device. The OS then invokes a scheduler, which reevaluates the overall situation and decides which tasks to run next.

- **Device management**. Most I/O devices are very slow compared with the CPU. Hence, the CPU can execute other programs while devices are moving data between external sources, main memory, or buffer registers. Whenever a device completes its operation, it generates an interrupt. This immediately alerts the OS which can then assign the next task to the device.

There are other situations that require the OS's immediate attention, yet are not caused by external devices. Such events are handled through internal interrupt mechanisms called *traps*. Similar to an external interrupt, a trap also sets a bit internal to the CPU, which is automatically tested as part of every machine instruction. When it is set, the CPU suspends the execution of the current program and temporarily diverts control to the OS. The trap idea is sketched in Figure 1-9b. Both traps and interrupts transfer control to the OS—its interrupt or trap handler. The main difference is the source of the interruption: for interrupts, the event that triggers the transfer is external to the CPU, whereas for traps, it is internal.

A typical example of an event causing a trap is the overflow or underflow of an arithmetic operation. The current application cannot proceed beyond this point. Its execution is suspended (or terminated) and the OS is invoked to handle the situation. Another example occurs as part of main memory management. Large programs are sometimes partitioned into smaller chunks called pages or segments. An OS does not always keep all pages of an application resident in memory. Instead, it loads them only when they are actually needed, i.e., on demand. The loading of a page is handled by traps. When the application references a page that is currently not in main memory, the current instruction automatically sets a trap bit, and control is transferred to the OS to load the missing page.

Traps that are triggered by arithmetic errors or memory management are implicit. But traps also are used to cause a voluntary, explicit transfer to the OS. These are necessary whenever an application requests a service, such as an I/O operation, from the OS. The transfer is accomplished by a special machine instruction, a **supervisor call (SVC)**, that sets a trap and forces control to be immediately transferred to the OS. A parameter supplied with each SVC identifies the particular service that the OS must perform when the SVC is issued. SVCs are used to implement all kernel calls and form the basic interface between the OS kernel and the rest of the software.

Modes of Instruction Execution

There are certain machine instructions that should not be executed by ordinary applications. These include instructions that control I/O devices, set system registers or flags in the CPU, manipulate system tables, or modify external timers. Misuse of such instructions could jeopardize the security of the system, cause serious malfunction, or simply impede overall progress. To ensure that only trusted system programs execute such instructions, the instruction set is partitioned into multiple classes. In the simplest case, the instructions are divided into **privileged** and **nonprivileged** classes. To execute a privileged instruction, the CPU must be in a privileged **mode**, represented by a special bit within the CPU; if this bit is not set, an attempt to execute a privileged instruction causes a trap, invoking the OS to handle the violation. The privileged mode bit can be set implicitly as part of interrupts or traps, or explicitly by issuing an SVC instruction. Because the SVC instruction immediately transfers control to the OS, no user program can switch to the privileged mode without also transferring to the OS at the same time.

1.2.3   The Programming Interface

As shown in Figure 1-8, a set of libraries extends the OS kernel, which, in turn, provides the basic functionalities of the system. From the application point of view, the difference between kernel and library functions is not very significant. In fact, some OSs, such as MS Windows, do not even disclose the exact list of existing kernel calls. Instead, the application program interface (API) defines only library functions, which invoke the appropriate kernel functions. The advantage of hiding the kernel from the application is that the kernel may be modified without affecting the correctness of any existing applications. In contrast, the UNIX philosophy is to publicize both the library functions and the available kernel calls. Jointly, the two layers define an extended machine, consisting of the nonprivileged instruction set and a set of functions that application programs may invoke as primitive operations.

From the implementation point of view, however, the two function sets are quite different. Kernel functions execute in the privileged mode, which gives them access to instructions and resources that ordinary user programs are not allowed to use. By restricting itself to only sensitive tasks, the kernel can be relatively small, and thus easier to test, verify, and maintain. All other functions are implemented as library functions that run in the nonprivileged user mode.

Figure 1-10 traces calls on both library and kernel functions. Figure 1-10a shows the control flow when an applications invokes a library function, *lib_func()*. For example, all mathematical or string-manipulating functions fall into this category. These are handled entirely through the normal function call mechanisms. The application code pushes the parameters on the calling stack and transfers control to the compiled function body. The body carries out the desired service and returns to the caller. After popping the calling stack, the application continues with the code following the function call.

Figure 1-10b traces the control flow when an application uses a kernel service that must execute in privileged mode. For example, most I/O operations fall into this class. The application issues a call to a function corresponding to the desired service, *kern_func()*. This is a library function just like *lib_func()* of Figure 1-10a. However, it does not perform the service directly; it only serves as an intermediary between the application and the kernel. Its main role is to set up the necessary parameters for an SVC call in specific registers and to issue the SVC. The actual service is carried out within the kernel in privileged mode. When this is accomplished, the nonprivileged mode is restored and control returns to the library function. The latter, in turn, returns to the application, which pops the stack pointer and continues executing.

The specific function sets provided by a given OS kernel and its libraries vary greatly between different OSs. The following classes of system calls (kernel or library) are generally available; each includes a broad range of functions to support the needs of different applications.

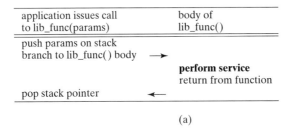

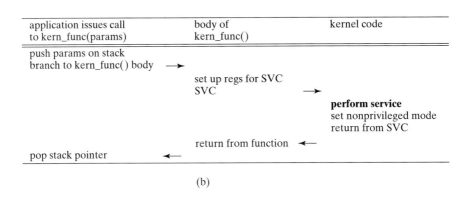

FIGURE 1-10. Invoking system services (a) nonprivileged library service and (b) privileged kernel service.

- Process management:

    - create/destroy, suspend/activate process

    - send signal or message to process

    - wait for event or signal

- Memory management:

    - allocate/deallocate region of main memory

    - increase/decrease size of allocated region

- File management:

    - create/destroy, open/close, move, rename file

    - append data to file or concatenate files

    - display content of file or directory

    - display/change file attributes

- Input/output:

    - read/write character or block of data from a file or device

    - control/check status of a device

- Miscellaneous services:

  - get current date and time
  - schedule an alarm to occur
  - apply mathematical or string-manipulation functions
  - generate various system diagnostics

1.2.4   The User Interface

The application layer (Fig. 1-8) contains both system and user programs. The distinction between the two is not strict; applications that aid in the development and use of other applications are generally considered system programs. These include *compilers, assemblers, interpreters* (e.g., the java virtual machine), *text processors, Internet browsers*, and other *utilities* typically provided by a computer facility.

Each application has its own interface through which the user may interact with it; for example, by supplying parameters and obtaining results of the computation. However, the system must provide one common interface that is ready when the system is initially booted up and which remains available at all times so that users can launch, use, monitor, and manage applications and files. This top-level user interface can have one of two forms: a **text-based** interface, generally referred to as the **shell**, or a **graphics-based** interface, commonly called a **GUI** ("graphics user interface").

The Shell

A shell is a **command interpreter** that accepts and interprets statements (commands) issued by the user through the keyboard, mouse, or other pointing devices. A typical multiuser system would provide commands to perform the following tasks:

- Execute and manage programs

- Manipulate files

- Obtain system information

Not surprisingly, many shell commands are similar to the functions that make up the programming interface discussed earlier. For example, creating/destroying a file or spawning a new task can be done from within a running program or from a user terminal. The format used by a shell, however, is not that of a function call. Instead, the user types in the command name followed by a list of arguments. The command is sent to the shell when the user presses the ENTER or RETURN key.

Let us examine commands in each of the above categories in turn. The primary task of any computer is to develop or execute various application programs. Thus any command language contains statements directing the OS to load and execute programs, including system applications such as assemblers, compilers, interpreters, editors, debuggers, and other utility programs. Typical commands in this domain are those to *link* separately compiled modules together, *load* executable programs into memory, and start their *execution*. Each such command usually includes a wide range of optional parameters, for example, to control the format of the output or the amount of feedback generated, or to support testing and debugging.

The second category of commands relates to file management. These include various commands to *create, delete, move, copy, append, print,* or *rename* files and directories (folders), and to change their protection status.

The last class of commands are inquiries into the current state of the system and the state of the user's applications. Information regarding the system that may be of interest to a particular user includes the current date and time of day, the number of users presently logged in, the system load, memory and device utilization, the system configuration, description of individual devices, and resource availability. Examples of information pertaining to the user's process are the CPU time used so far, the connect time, files currently open, devices assigned to the process, and other runtime statistics.

In addition to user commands, the shell also may define a number of constructs that make it a complete programming language. This enables the user to write programs, called **shell scripts**, that tie together different commands and execute them, without the user's help. The constructs and features supported by a shell fall into several categories:

- **Local variables.** The shell maintains a state during its execution, consisting of system-defined and user-defined variables, usually of type integer and string.

- **Iterative statements.** Constructs such as *while* or *until-do* allow the creation of loops.

- **Conditionals.** *if-then-else statements* permit different commands to be invoked based on runtime information.

- **Arithmetic and logical operators.** Variables, strings, or constants may be combined or compared in different ways.

- **Wildcards.** Names can be compared for partial matches; for example, in one standard notation, *sect** matches any string beginning with *sect*, such as *section*; *sect?* matches any string beginning with *sect* followed by exactly one more character, such as *sect9* but not *sect10*; and *[sS]ect** matches any string beginning with *sect* or *Sect*, followed by any other characters.

- **Connectors.** Multiple commands can be combined to execute sequentially or in parallel; their inputs or outputs may be connected to files, the user terminal, or to each other.

- **Automatic name completion.** Command and file names need not be typed completely; instead, the user types only the first few leading characters and the system completes the rest as soon as the name becomes unambiguous.

CASE STUDY: THE UNIX SHELL

The idea of turning the command language into a powerful programming language—the shell—was pioneered in the UNIX operating system. When a user logs into the system, the shell is started and a prompt is displayed. Statements of the following form are then expected:

command$_1$ arg1$_1$ ... arg1$_k$; ...; command$_n$ argn$_1$ ... argn$_{k'}$

The semicolon functions as a RETURN or ENTER key: it allows multiple commands to be issued using a single command line. Proceeding from left to right, the shell interprets each *command$_i$* as a program to be executed. It searches the file system directory and, if a file with the name *command$_i$* is found, it creates a new process that then executes the program with its arguments *argi$_1$* .... When all commands in the sequence have been processed, control returns to the shell, which is ready to interpret the next sequence. Examples of simple commands supported by the shell include:

TABLE 1-1. Examples of simple commands

command	effect
who	Generate a list of all users currently logged in.
pwd	Print the name of the current working directory.
cd f	Set the current working directory to be the file *f*.
ls	List in alphabetical order all files recorded in the current directory; several arguments may be specified to modify the basic *ls* command; for example, `ls -t` lists the files according to their last modification date.
du	Return information about the current disk usage; an argument may be specified to determine the disk usage for only a certain subtree of the current file hierarchy.
cat f1 f2	Concatenate the two files *f1* and *f2* and type them on the user terminal.
lpr f	Send the file named *f* to the printer; additional parameters maybe supplied to specify the desired printer, number of copies to print, page layout, handling of special characters, and other options.
wc f	Count the number of lines, words, and characters in the file *f*.
man c	Print on-line manual pages pertaining to the command *c*.

Multiple commands can be submitted simultaneously; the semicolon indicates sequential processing of commands. The shell also permits several tasks, each started by a different command, to execute concurrently. This is accomplished by including the character "&" as the last argument of a command. In this case, the shell does not wait for the termination of the corresponding process but immediately proceeds with the next command. For example, the sequence:

$$\text{command}_1 \ldots \& ; \text{command}_2 \ldots$$

starts two concurrent processes, executing the files *command$_1$* and *command$_2$*. When both terminate, the shell returns to the user with a prompt to accept the next line of commands.

In comparison, the sequence:

$$\text{command}_1 \ldots \& ; \text{command}_2 \ldots \&$$

CASE STUDY: THE UNIX SHELL (*continued*)

---

also starts two processes concurrently; however, it does not wait for their termination but returns to the user immediately. In this way, background processes may be started and continue executing while the user is free to further use the shell.

Shell facilities also are available for directing the I/O of programs to various devices, files, and other programs. Each time a shell is started for a user, two files, named **standard input** and **standard output**, are automatically opened. Any user input statement receives data from the standard input, whereas any output is sent to the standard output. Normally, these standard I/O files are associated with the user terminal, thus permitting the user to communicate directly with the currently running program. However, the shell also permits the standard input and standard output to be reassigned to other files or devices. This is accomplished by specifying one or both of the arguments:

<code><in_file, >out_file</code>

where *in_file* and *out_file* become the I/O files, respectively. The symbols '<' and '>' indicate the direction of the data flow, i.e., 'from' *in_file* and 'to' *out_file*. The assignment is valid for the duration of the command. For example, the following command line uses a temporary file to pass the output of one program (*command$_1$*) to be used as the input to another program (*command$_2$*):

<code>command₁ > temp_file; command₂ < temp_file</code>

The shell offers a more elegant solution to passing temporary data between programs; it permits the standard output of a program to be directed into the standard input of another program without the use of a temporary file. The two programs are connected using a construct called the **pipe**, for example:

<code>command₁ | command₂</code>

Unlike the previous solution, both processes are started concurrently, with the standard output from *command$_1$* becoming the standard input to *command$_2$*. They may be viewed as a producer and a consumer, respectively, with the pipe serving as a virtually unbounded buffer. The necessary synchronization is performed internally by the system.

The following code is a simple shell script illustrating the use of shell variables and control statements.

```
COUNT='who|wc -l'
if test $COUNT -lt 8
then echo $COUNT users logged in
else echo too many users
fi
```

When this code is placed into an executable file, e.g., *check_users*, then typing the command *check_users* on the command line will display the number of users currently on the system. The script works as follows. The system utility *who* generates a line for each user currently on the system. This is piped into the *wc* utility, which, given the flag *-l*, counts the number of lines produced by *who*. The result is stored in the new shell variable *COUNT*. The next line checks the value of *COUNT*; the $-sign refers to the variable's content, rather than its name. If *COUNT* is less than 8, the script displays (using the *echo* command) the message "*N users logged in*," where *N* is the actual number of users; if *COUNT* is greater than or equal to 8, the script displays the message "*too many users*" instead.

A Graphics User Interface

Using the system through a text-oriented shell requires considerable expertise. To cater to the increasing numbers of casual users, Apple introduced a graphics-based user interface (GUI) in the mid-1980s that was based on seminal work done earlier at the Xerox PARC research laboratory. Instead of typing previously memorized complex command and file names, users click on graphical representations of commands, called **icons**, to invoke applications. Since then, many systems have adopted the graphics-oriented approach to their user interfaces. Figure 1-11 contains several commonly used icons. Each corresponds to an application that the user can start by simply double-clicking on the corresponding icon. Some of these applications are specific to a given OS. For example, the *Windows Explorer* icon starts the File Manager of the Microsoft (MS) Windows OS. Other icons, such as *America Online* or *Netscape Communicator*, represent independently developed products.

When an application is started, a new area or **window** of the display is created for its execution. The user can manipulate windows by changing their size, shape, screen position, and visibility relative to other windows. The user also can control the actions taken when the mouse cursor is placed on a particular portion of a window or when a mouse button is pressed. Typically, pressing the right mouse button displays a drop-down menu (a small window listing a number of commands that can be performed by selecting them with the mouse cursor). For example, in MS Windows—an OS that took its name from the windowing concept—pressing the right mouse button on the initial start-up screen or "desktop" displays a drop-down menu with commands that allow the user to arrange the icons on the screen in different ways, create new folders and objects, or find out the properties of the display.

My Computer.lnk

Windows Explorer.lnk

Microsoft Word.lnk

Microsoft PowerPoint.lnk

Netscape Communicator.lnk

America Online.lnk

FIGURE 1-11. Commonly used icons.

An important feature of a GUI is the ability to move objects around by dragging them, i.e., by clicking on an object and then moving the mouse while depressing the button. For example, with this feature, icons can be arranged on the desktop manually, and files can be moved between different folders. A file or an icon also can be easily deleted by dragging it over a special icon; for example, in MS Windows, the icon is named the *Recycle Bin*.

The main attraction of an icon and menu-oriented GUI over a text-based shell is its visual approach that makes many common tasks more intuitive and thus easier to perform. By establishing simple overall conventions, such as starting all applications by double-clicking a mouse button or displaying drop-down menus with the right mouse button, the GUI enables a user to navigate through the system without prior knowledge of any command and file names. Not surprisingly, GUIs are supported by virtually all OSs today. However, text-based interfaces have not become obsolete. Expert users and programmers require greater control over the system's resources and must be closer to the system code than is possible with an icon- and menu-based interface. Consequently, UNIX, Linux, and other systems continue to provide a shell, but even these are generally used via a graphics interface such as X Windows. Such a system offers the flexibility of multiple windows on the display, but allows the use of a text-based shell via typed commands and file names within any window.

CASE STUDY: WINDOWS EXPLORER VS. THE UNIX SHELL

To illustrate the difference between a text-based and a graphics-based user interface, we contrast the GUI of the MS Windows OS with the UNIX shell. In both cases, we consider the task of managing files.

The file manager of MS Windows, *Windows Explorer*, has the GUI of Figure 1-12. It is divided into two panels containing file information and a number of buttons and drop-down menus through which the files are managed. The left panel shows the directory structure, starting with the highest file directory (folder), the *Desktop*. The latter consists of the directory *My Computer* that lists the available disk drives, such as a *3 1/2 Floppy (A:)*, an internal hard disk *(C:)*, and a *CD-ROM drive (D:)*. Each directory is preceded by a box containing a plus or minus sign. Clicking on a minus sign expands the directory to show the next level. In the figure, the hard-disk directory *C:* is expanded, showing a number of subdirectories: *Adobeapp, Aladdin, America Online 5.0, Documents and Settings*, and so on. The directory *America Online 5.0* is expanded further to show its subdirectories, *Aoltemp, backup*, and so on.

The right panel shows the contents of one directory in the structure on the left—the one selected with a mouse click or a cursor key. In the figure, the directory *backup* is selected (highlighted in the structure); it contains a subdirectory *Temp* and two files, *Global.org* and *main.idx*.

Browsing files and directories. Windows Explorer has a very convenient way to browse through existing directories. Using the plus/minus signs and the sliding bars of the panels, the user can quickly examine the directory structure and obtain important information about existing files, their sizes, types, and other properties. In contrast, a UNIX user must be familiar with several commands. The *pwd* (print working directory) command is used to determine the current directory (the one corresponding to the highlighted one in the Windows Explorer). The *ls* (list) command lists the contents of

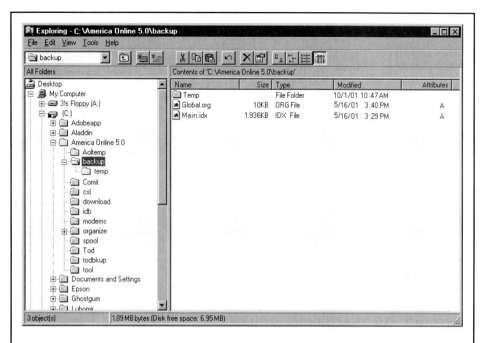

FIGURE 1-12. File Manager in Microsoft Windows.

the current directory; this corresponds to the content of the right panel in the Windows Explorer. The directory hierarchy can be navigated with the *cd* (change directory) command; Windows Explorer accomplishes this by browsing and selection as above.

Creating and deleting files and directories. These operations are menu driven in Windows Explorer. The user selects the *File* menu, which lists commands to *Create, Delete*, or *Rename* files and directories. In UNIX, the user must be familiar with the available commands, such as *rm* to remove a file or *mkdir* to create a new directory.

Moving files and directories. With Windows Explorer, one simply selects the appropriate file or directory with the mouse and drags it to the new destination directory. UNIX users use the *mv* (move) command, specifying as parameters the file or directory to be moved and the new directory.

Displaying file contents. Each file in MS Windows may be associated with an application that handles the specific file type. To view text files (ASCII characters), the user invokes a text editor, such as *Notepad*, designed to handle text files without inserting any formatting information. In contrast, UNIX provides a single powerful command to handle text files, denoted *cat* (for concatenate). Typing *cat* followed by a file name displays the file's content on the user terminal. But *cat* also can be used to create new files, to append text to existing ones, or to combine (concatenate) existing files. For example:

```
cat f1, f2, f3 > fnew
```

combines the contents of the three files *f1* through *f3* and writes their contents into the newly created file *fnew*.

CASE STUDY: WINDOWS EXPLORER VS. THE UNIX SHELL (*continued*)

The above comparisons between common operations under MS Windows and UNIX demonstrate how a graphics-oriented user interface offers a more convenient, intuitive way to manage files and directories. Thus most systems, especially those aimed at nonprogrammers and casual users, have a GUI as their high-level OS interface. A text-based shell, however, is still essential to satisfy the needs of many programmers and expert users. Commands can be combined into complex scripts, allowing the efficient and convenient invocation of frequently used sequences. A text-based interface is also more flexible and expressive because each command can specify a wide range of parameters and control flags. For example, the *rmdir* (remove directory) command of UNIX lets a user recursively delete all files and subdirectories of a given directory; while doing so, the user may choose an interactive mode, requiring a confirmation of certain file deletions. The user also may control the level of diagnostic feedback displayed during the operation. Other commands, such as *ls* (list), have dozens of optional flags and parameters that can control which file types to display, the format of the display, the level and extent of the attributes shown, and other options. A menu-driven interface is just not powerful enough to capture all the combinations and nuances needed by expert users.

1.2.5 Runtime Organization

Structurally, any OS is organized as a collection of functions as described in Section 1.2.1. At runtime, we have two fundamental choices of how to invoke any given function. To illustrate the differences, consider for example a simple service function, *time()*, that returns the current time of day to its caller. This function can be implemented as a library function or a kernel call if privileged execution was necessary (Section 1.2.3). Any application needing the service can simply call the function, which then executes as part of the invoking process. This choice is sketched in Figure 1-13a. Any OS service that

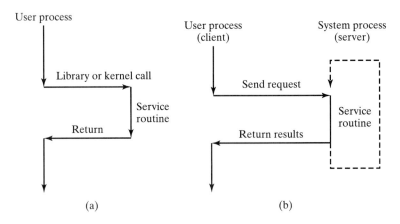

FIGURE 1-13. Runtime organization of an operating system (a) service as a subroutine and (b) service as a process.

is called explicitly by an application can be handled in this manner, i.e., as *subroutines* of the user processes. Only services invoked by hardware interrupts are handled by a special OS process.

The second option is to provide OS services as separate autonomous *system processes*. For the time-of-day service, a timer-server process can be part of the OS. Its task is to accept requests from other processes in the form of messages, execute the *time()* function for each such request, and return the result to the caller, again in the form of a message. Under this implementation, shown graphically in Figure 1-13b, the process providing the service is generally referred to as a **server** and the calling process termed a **client**.

The disadvantage of the client-server implementation of system services is that the OS must maintain a number of permanent server processes that listen and respond to various requests. But the client-server approach has important benefits:

- It is suitable for a *distributed system* where a collection of separate machines is connected through a network, and integrated with a single system and set of user interfaces. Here, a given service may be implemented on a separate dedicated machine and invoked remotely by different clients. A network file server is a typical example of such an organization.

- The organization is convenient for many different types of services, not only for those provided by the OS directly. The various services offered over the Internet are examples.

- It has a greater degree of fault tolerance than an organization based on function calls. When a server process (or its machine) crashes, other services of the OS may continue functioning. In contrast, when services are implemented as subroutines invoked as part of the calling processes, a crash generally brings down the entire OS, which must be restarted.

- A client-server organization enforces a strict segregation of functionalities, which makes them easier to understand, debug, and maintain, than large homogeneous collections of functions calling each other.

Most modern OSs use a combination of the two approaches to runtime organization. Services that maintain a global view of resources and that must be constantly available are normally implemented as autonomous concurrent processes, whereas other services are constructed as subroutines invoked as part of existing processes. For example, the UNIX scheduler, which selects the next process to run on the CPU, runs as a separate process, whereas many other UNIX services execute as subroutines.

1.3 OPERATING SYSTEM EVOLUTION AND CONCEPTS

Operating systems have been evolving steadily since their first appearance in the 1950s, driven in part by advances in technology and by growing demands of the user community. Some early developments have become obsolete, but many are still present. Here, we introduce the most important concepts that make up the field and examine their evolution by identifying the main driving forces and the solutions that have emerged in response to the new challenges.

1.3.1 Early Systems

From about 1949, when the first stored-program digital computer actually began executing instructions, until the mid 1950s, the basic organization and mode of operation for computers remained relatively constant. The classical von Neumann architecture implied strictly sequential instruction execution, including I/O operations. To run a program, the users would work at a dedicated systems terminal, called the console, which was generally the only direct (online) connection to the machine. Users would interact with their computations, one at a time on the machine and at the lowest machine level, by manually examining and setting machine registers, stepping through instructions, and looking at contents of memory locations. Programs were written in absolute machine language (using a decimal or octal notation) and loaded into the machine by an absolute loader, which required the user to specify the exact physical memory locations for all code and data.

In these early years of computing, programming aids were either nonexistent or minimal; the most advanced installations featured assemblers to liberate the user from the lowest-level machine language programming, and a few rudimentary library routines to handle the most tedious and repetitive tasks. As the importance of symbolic programming was recognized and assembly systems came into more widespread use, a standard operating procedure evolved: A loader would read an assembler into main memory and transfer control to it. The assembler would read the user source program and library routines, generally from punched cards or paper tape, and then assemble these into executable machine code. Because main memory was very small, the executable code would be written to a magnetic tape or punched cards as it was being produced by the assembler. A loader would again be invoked to read the complete assembled program into main memory, which would then be executed. Any output generated by the program was either written to tape or cards, or printed by a line printer.

A difficulty faced by even the earliest systems was **initial startup**. The CPU could only execute instructions in main memory, but main memory was volatile—it lost all information when power was turned off. (Older core memories were not volatile, but were small and continually being overwritten.) Thus, the problem was how to get a program, for example, the initial loader capable of loading other programs, into main memory when power was turned on. To accomplish that task, a special hardware mechanism was used to transfer a minimal amount of code into memory and cause it to be executed. This initial program then loaded larger programs into memory, until the entire OS was resident and ready to control the system.

The above approach to solve the initial system startup problem has been described by a metaphor—a person attempting to pull himself up by his own shoe laces or boot straps. Thus, initializing a system after power is turned on was widely termed **bootstrapping** and later simply **booting**.

Bootstrapping in older systems was typically done from disk. Turning on power would cause a special hardware circuitry to copy one data record from a predefined disk location into a fixed set of main memory locations, and set the program counter so that the CPU would begin executing this initial program. This program would then incrementally load the complete OS from the disk. In present-day computers, the bootstrapping problem has greatly been simplified by the availability of nonvolatile executable memory, typically in the form of read-only memory (*ROM*) that can hold the initial startup software. For example, most personal computers (PCs) contain a set of basic I/O functions, called the basic input output system (*BIOS*), in nonvolatile memory. It starts automatically when the system is turned on or when the reset button is pressed. BIOS examines the existing hardware configuration and then attempts to "boot" the system, i.e., to load the actual OS. It first tries to read it from a diskette drive, giving the user the opportunity to boot the system from a chosen diskette. If no diskette is present, BIOS attempts to boot from the CD-ROM drive or from the hard disk.

1.3.2   Batch Operating Systems

The first generation of OSs, built in the late 1950s, was motivated by the inefficiencies of the early systems. Because the latter required manual assistance from an operator at each of the steps of loading, assembly, and execution of a program, they consumed a great deal of time and resulted in the inefficient use of the very expensive hardware.

The solution was to automate the standard load/translate/load/execute sequence with a central control program that would find and load required system programs—assemblers, compilers, linkers, or library subroutines—and handle the job-to-job transitions automatically. This permitted submitting multiple jobs to the system for processing at the same time, typically in batches of punched cards. The control program became known as a **batch operating system**.

The development of these systems was greatly accelerated by new hardware technologies. First, vacuum tubes were replaced by transistors, which made machines considerably smaller, more reliable, and cheaper. Input/output processing also was improved significantly. One of the most important hardware innovations was the **I/O processor** or **I/O channel**, a processor similar to the CPU but with a much smaller instruction set specialized for I/O processing. An I/O processor frees the main processor—the CPU—from frequent low-level interactions with I/O devices. On receiving a high-level I/O request from a CPU, an I/O processor executes a specialized program to carry out the high-level operation. The CPU is involved only when the operation has been completed. The I/O processor made it possible to efficiently overlap the operation of the CPU and many I/O devices, thus improving overall system performance through parallelism.

Initially, the CPU would periodically interrogate the status of the I/O processor to determine if it was still busy or had encountered some error. But it soon became clear that the system could operate more efficiently if one could find a mechanism that permitted the I/O processor to inform the CPU as soon as it needed its attention, either to report a problem or to accept a new command. The solution was the introduction of **interrupts**—hardware signals that the I/O processor could send to the CPU to get its immediate attention. Interrupts were later expanded to allow the CPU to respond quickly to a variety of different conditions, such as a division by zero, invalid opcode, memory protection violation, and a host of others.

To further streamline the operation of batch systems, compilers were written to produce **relocatable** rather than absolute code. Linking loaders were then provided so that separately compiled programs, including library routines, could be combined without recompilation. As a result, services from the human user were needed only to manage the I/O batches, to set up nonstandard jobs, and to take corrective action in case of system failure. The programmer was gradually banished from the machine room, which became the exclusive domain of a new specialist, the computer operator.

The term *batch* is still widely used today but its meaning has evolved to refer to noninteractive computing. A **batch job** is one that does not require any user interaction; it is submitted to the system with the understanding that it will be executed at a time chosen by the system as the most convenient. For example, the system will generally execute a batch job at a lower priority than interactive jobs. It may also choose to postpone its execution until it has spare capacity or until it has accumulated a suitable collections of jobs to run. Alternatively, the user may schedule the job's execution to commence at a later time (e.g., at night).

1.3.3 Multiprogramming Systems

The introduction of interrupts, I/O processors, and controllers with direct access to memory enabled the CPU to keep many devices operating simultaneously and, at the same time, perform other computations. A single program, however, is rarely able to exploit this potential. Rather, a typical program alternates between phases of input, computation, and output, and limits itself to using just a few of the existing devices.

Consider, for example, a simple program which reads a file, performs some computation on the data, and outputs the results. Even with the most sophisticated interrupt and I/O processing hardware, the overlap between CPU and devices is limited to that of Figure 1-14. Clearly, the CPU is drastically underutilized during the I/O phase; the system is said to be **I/O bound** during this phase. Conversely, all devices are idle during the compute phase; in this interval, the system is said to be **compute bound**. Furthermore, even when the CPU and the I/O devices are kept busy most of the time, the use of other computer resources is often poor; for example, if the program is small, much of main memory remains unused.

A solution is to run several programs or jobs in an apparently simultaneous manner by storing them in main memory at the same time and interleaving their executions. This is the basic idea underlying **multiprogramming**; the OS controlling this kind of virtual parallelism is termed a **multiprogramming system**. This strategy not only decreases the amount of idle resources, but also improves the system throughput and turnaround time for individual programs.

A particularly good choice of programs to run simultaneously is an I/O-bound program, such as one updating a large data file, and a compute-bound program, such as one solving a set of partial differential equations. While the I/O-bound program is waiting for I/O, the compute-bound program can compute. On I/O completion, control is switched back to the I/O-bound program. Figure 1-15 illustrates the execution of two such programs in both a single-programmed and a multiprogrammed environment. The time saved by multiprogramming is evident in this example. The total time to execute both programs is reduced by eliminating some of the idle times of both the CPU and the I/O device.

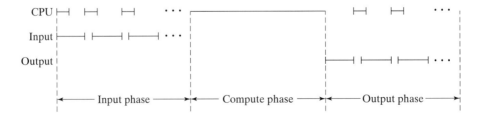

FIGURE 1-14. CPU and I/O overlap in a single program.

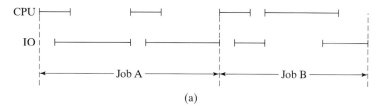

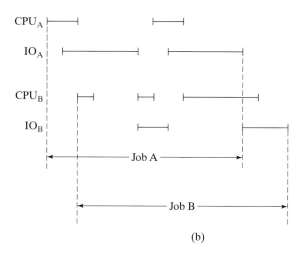

FIGURE 1-15. CPU and I/O overlap under (a) sequential execution and (b) multi-programming.

Note that multiprogramming involves the **sharing of time** on processors and the **sharing of space** in main memory, and the potential sharing of other resources. An additional space-saving benefit accrues from the ability to *share code* resident in main memory. If several programs require the same language translator or request the same system service, a single copy of these routines may be kept in memory and used by all. Sharing hardware and software resources through multiprogramming is beneficial to users in another important way—it makes it economically possible to provide a wider variety of services.

To support multiprogramming, the underlying computer hardware should include several key components, and the OS must be extended to efficiently and transparently manage the system resources in this complex environment. A multiprogramming system attempts to hide the fact that resources are shared among different processes or users. Except for the slower speed at which services are performed, each user should have the illusion of having the system entirely for himself. With this kind of environment, three new and important issues must be addressed:

Protection

Since the system is shared by many different users, an OS must ensure its own integrity and the integrity of user processes from accidental or malicious damage. In addition, privacy should be guaranteed, i.e., information must be protected against snooping by unauthorized user programs. Finally, ownership of data, programs, or services also must be respected, which means that the OS prevents unauthorized execution of programs or invocation of services.

Process Synchronization and Communication

In a multiprogramming system, different processes may be executing concurrently. In many situations, two or more processes may compete for a common resource that they need to read or modify. A shared file is a good example: to preserve the integrity of the file's content, it may be necessary to impose an order in which the file may be accessed. Similarly, processes may wish to cooperate by exchanging information at various stages of their execution. The OS provides synchronization and communication primitives that facilitate correct programming for such competition and cooperation.

Dynamic Memory Management

When a program waits for a lengthy event, such as the completion of an I/O operation, it may be desirable to remove it temporarily from main memory so that other programs can use the otherwise wasted space. As a practical matter, when **swapping** programs in and out of main memory, it should be possible to load a given program into different locations each time it is returned to main memory. Furthermore, a program should be permitted to only partially reside in main memory. This not only improves memory utilization but also permits execution of programs whose total size exceeds the size of main memory. Thus, effective management of main memory under multiprogramming is a major challenge for the OS.

As a consequence of all of the software and hardware requirements for multiprogramming, computers of the 1960s grew considerably in size, frequently filling entire rooms. The descendents of such computers or **mainframes** are still in use today, mainly employed as central servers of very large databases, libraries, or Internet servers. Significantly, the techniques and issues of multiprogramming still underlie all contemporary OSs.

1.3.4 Interactive Operating Systems

The main focus of early OSs was performance, especially as measured by job throughput. Given the high cost of the underlying hardware and software, the overriding concern was maximizing the number of jobs processed per unit of time. By using interrupt mechanisms, I/O processors, and devices with direct memory access, batch systems were able to free the CPU from most of the low-level I/O processing while permitting different I/O devices to operate concurrently. The objective of multiprogramming is to generate sufficient workload so that much of the available CPU and device time could be exploited. The success in meeting this objective is certainly one of its great benefits.

A second major benefit is the ability to simultaneously share a machine's resources so that more than one online user may interact with the system simultaneously. However, to make this approach practical, it is necessary to guarantee some acceptable **response time** to each user at his terminal. This implies that even programs that display an ideal behavior in terms of a balanced resource utilization must not be permitted to run for extensive periods of time if other programs are waiting. Rather, all active processes must receive a fair share of the available resources, especially the CPU time. One common system policy is to serve all active processes cyclically by assigning to each a small portion or **quantum** of the available CPU time, for example, $1/n$th of a second every second for n users. This **time-sharing** concept employs the basic principles of multiprogramming to create the illusion of a separate **virtual machine** for each user. Conceptually, each of these virtual machines is an exact image of the actual machine, except for its speed which is divided by the number of currently active users.

One of the first successful time-sharing systems was Compatible time-sharing system (CTSS) developed at MIT in the early 1960s. This was followed by the pioneering Multiplexed information and computing service project (Multics), which yielded many techniques in memory and process management that are still in use today.

Although mainframes continued to be popular as large-scale interactive systems, a new line of smaller computers, known as **minicomputers**, emerged in the late 1960s and began to dominate the market in the 1970s. These computers were many times more affordable than mainframes, making it possible for smaller organizations and units within organizations to acquire their own computers. The smaller size of minicomputers led to scaled-down versions of the large time-sharing OSs. One prominent example is the UNIX system. Since its creation in the late 1960s, it has gone through many variations and extensions, and remains a favorite in its modern incarnations.

1.3.5   Personal Computer and Workstation Operating Systems

During the 1970s and early 1980s, technology continued to develop at a rapid pace. Large-scale integration (LSI) and very large-scale integration (VLSI) made it possible to manufacture large quantities of powerful hardware components at very low cost. This caused a new major trend in the computer marketplace: the emergence of **personal computers** (PCs) and **workstations**. LSI made it possible to manufacture such computers as powerful as many of the earlier mainframe computers but at a fraction of their cost, and thus affordable to individual users.

Because of their relatively simple hardware and single-user mode of operation, no major innovations in OS technology were necessary; rather, most of the principles governing OSs for earlier large computers could still be applied. The main significant innovation was the development of GUIs (Section 1.2.4). These interfaces make computers more accessible, especially for the average consumer and professional user, where the main goal is to run existing applications, such as word processors, Internet browsers, or computer games (in the case of consumers), and specific applications for professionals in engineering and research organizations.

Early OSs for PCs, such as DOS, were not only single-user systems but also single-program systems, similar to those of early-generation mainframes. Some were later extended to support multiprogramming, but only in a greatly simplified form where the user is responsible for manually switching between the active tasks. This form of *explicit multiprogramming* does not improve performance by overlapping CPU and I/O execution, but it greatly improves the system's usability by allowing the user to work with multiple applications concurrently. For example, while querying a database or debugging a program, the user may wish to keep a word processor open to record notes or to save important pieces of information for later use. The switching between the concurrent tasks is not initiated by the OS, but explicitly by the user (e.g., by clicking the mouse on the window he or she wishes to work with).

More recent PC OSs (e.g., MS Windows 3.x) support *implicit multiprogramming* (called multitasking) where the switching among concurrent tasks happens automatically and transparently to the user. But the tasks must all cooperate in this effort by periodically releasing the CPU so that another task could get its turn; a renegade task that refused to yield would block all other tasks from making any progress. Hence, this form of multiprogramming is referred to as **cooperative multiprogramming**.

True **preemptive multiprogramming** requires that any computation be periodically interrupted and the control given to the OS, which is then able to assign the CPU to different tasks to preserve fairness. This form of multiprogramming, supported by IBM's OS/2 operating system and MS Windows 95 and later versions, is transparent not only to the interactive user but to the applications themselves.

In the workstation world, more sophisticated OSs were necessary and available from the start, commonly based on UNIX. The systems for the Sun and Dec workstations are good examples. Modern PC and workstation OSs are equally sophisticated and essentially indistinguishable.

In addition to rapidly declining hardware costs, another major driving force responsible for the proliferation of PCs and workstations was the development of networking technologies. Local area networks made it possible to share costly resources by multiple users and to support efficient communication among them. They also made it possible to dedicate individual machines to specific functions, such as maintaining file systems for other machines on the network. Such functional specialization leads to better utilization of resources, increased flexibility in configuring the system, and scalability. A related result was the development of distributed OSs, introduced in Section 1.3.7.

Wide area networks, notably the Internet, allow the sharing and dissemination of information and services on an unprecedented scale, providing even more motivation for many users to acquire computers. From the OS point of view, one major challenge in such highly distributed environments is to cope with rapid change. This forces them to be highly modular and extensible to rapidly incorporate new functionalities, at the same time guaranteeing adequate protection vis-a-vis an increasingly unpredictable and open-ended environment.

1.3.6   Real-Time Operating Systems

A large class of computer systems is devoted to **real-time** applications where the purpose is to monitor, respond to, or control some external process or environment (Shaw 2001). Examples include complete stand-alone systems, such as air traffic control, medical patient monitoring, power plant control, and military command and control systems, and **embedded** systems that are a component of some larger system, such as an automobile control system or a cell phone. Real-time systems have existed since the first days of computers, and their operating software has evolved in tandem with that for general-purpose systems.

However, there are some important differences between the requirements of real-time and conventional software. First, real-time systems must satisfy timing constraints that are imposed upon them by the external world to which they are attached, most commonly in the form of deterministic **deadlines**. Failure to meet a constraint generally means that the system fails. **Concurrency** is another distinguishing feature; external signals arrive asynchronously and sometimes simultaneously, and must be handled in parallel to meet constraints. Many applications have strict *fault tolerance and* *reliability* requirements; failures can cause mission, money, property, and even human life losses. These systems also are exceptionally difficult to *test and certify* because of their complexity and the high cost of failure; live debugging usually is not an option.

Most of the technology for conventional general-purpose OSs has been adapted and extended for the real-time domain. For example, there are many variations of real-time UNIX, and Linux has been modified for real-time use. The three ideas of abstraction, virtualization, and resource management still dominate real-time OS design, as they do for standard OSs. But there are several critical distinctions, related to the unique requirements of real-time processing described above.

Much of the difference follows from the need for predictability. Operating system functions, while supporting high-level abstractions for the application's programmer, should have bounded and known execution times. The allocation or scheduling of CPUs to various OS and applications processes must ultimately be under the control of the user, and usually based on time so that deadlines are met. Main memory management, even with virtual memories, cannot involve asynchronous and unpredictable swapping of pages or segments. Instead, the allocation should be preplanned. Predictable and usually contiguous placement of file contents on secondary storage also is necessary to avoid lengthy and essentially nondeterministic file operations, such as seek operations to dynamically determined disk cylinders. Finally, a real-time OS provides user handles for inevitable errors, such as missed deadlines, which are guaranteed to occur in any practical system. Particularly important system services are accurate and controllable clocks and timers.

1.3.7   Distributed Operating Systems

Probably the most significant recent trend in OSs is distributed systems that run over multiple machines connected through one or more networks (Tanenbaum 1995). Virtually all computers are attached or attachable to a communications network. The complete system—machines, network, and software—may be **loosely coupled** or **tightly coupled**. Loosely coupled systems are those where each node is relatively independent, communicates at a level not much higher than message passing, and may be connected over long distances, e.g., over a WAN. The other extreme, a very tightly coupled system, is much more integrated, typically in a LAN or multicomputer configuration, and often supports higher-level communication on top of message passing, usually remote-procedure call. In both cases, the OS on each machine or cluster of machines is responsible for handling communication, in much the same way that it supports other I/O.

A client-server software architecture works well for loosely coupled systems. Servers (e.g., file servers, printer servers, special-purpose computational servers, or timer servers) can be implemented on separate nodes of a network with a separate and independent OS kernel in each node. A common communications framework (e.g., transmission protocol and data coding) will ensure coherent client-server interactions. However, the system complexity increases dramatically when the servers themselves are distributed over several nodes. Tightly coupled environments offer a more transparent interface to the user. Ideally, the user should not even be aware of the distributed nature of the underlying system, which still typically uses a client-server approach.

Generally, several new problems arise when designing distributed OSs. One important issue is **time**. It is a critical part of many applications; for example, time stamps may identify the most recent version of a file or determine the sending or arrival order of messages. To use time correctly, it is imperative that clocks on different machines be synchronized, accurate, and monotonic increasing—characteristics that are extremely difficult to achieve and maintain in a distributed system. Networks are normally much less reliable than single systems, and individual machines occasionally crash. Fault tolerance considerations lead to protocols and higher-level software that includes extensive checking, reconfiguring, checkpointing, and restarting or retransmitting.

Distributed file systems can be especially interesting. Files and directories may be located on more than one machine and throughout the network. At any time, several copies of a file could exist, each located at a different machine and each undergoing various update or read operations. There is the thorny problem of ensuring that each user views the same coherent version of a file and the directory system. Additionally, there is the difficulty in creating a file-naming scheme that is location independent.

Starting in the late 1970s and early 1980s, many distributed OSs were built. Examples that emphasize small kernels and efficient message passing include the V distributed system (Cheriton 1988) and Mach (Accetta et al. 1986). The Amoeba system (Tanenbaum et al. 1990) is an object-oriented OS that presents complete distribution transparency to the user. All three systems, V, Mach, and Amoeba, offer UNIX-like interfaces or directly emulate UNIX.

•••

THE END OF THE BEGINNING

This ends our introduction and overview. We now start from the "bottom-up" and delve into the details of OS design, analysis, and construction. Part I, Chapters 2, 3, 4, 5, and 6, are concerned with the management and coordination of processes: the fundamental computational units that are controlled by an OS. The problems and techniques of main memory management are presented next in Part II, consisting of Chapters 7, 8, and 9. File and I/O Management then follow in Part III, Chapters 10 and 11. The last part of the book, Part IV (Chapters 12 and 13), studies protection and security, two related issues with important social and technical components.

CONCEPTS, TERMS, AND ABBREVIATIONS

The following concepts have been introduced in this chapter. Test yourself by defining and discussing each keyword or phrase.

Batch processing	Multiprogramming
Bootstrap	Network
Channel	Operating system (OS)
Client-server	Personal computer (PC)
Central processing unit (CPU)	Real-time system
Distributed system	Shell
Execution mode	Spooling
Graphics user interface (GUI)	Time-sharing
Interrupt	Trap
Input-output (I/O)	Virtual machine
Kernel	Wide area network (WAN)
Local area network (LAN)	

EXERCISES

1. Give examples of semantic gaps that must be bridged by software, including the OSs at the following levels: CPU (instruction) level, main memory level, secondary storage level, I/O device level.

2. What do abstraction and virtualization have in common? How are they different? Give an example of each.

3. What do traps and interrupts have in common? How are they different? Give an example of each.

4. Display a list of all commands supported by your UNIX system. Estimate what fraction of these are related to file processing. (Hint: Executable commands usually are in the system directory */bin*.)

5. Compare the convenience and expressiveness of the online help provided by a text-based interface, e.g., using the *man* command of UNIX, with the online help of a graphics-based interface, e.g., the *Help* button of the Windows OS. Assume you are not very familiar with these systems and attempt to find out the following:
   (a) How to find all files containing the strings "unix," "UNIX," but not "Unix."
   (b) How to make a file read-only for other system users.
   (c) How to open and display a file on the screen (a) from the keyboard and (b) from within a running program (application).
   (d) How to format a floppy disk.
   (e) How much disk space if being used by your files.

6. Determine how many key strokes, mouse clicks, and mouse moves are required for each of the following tasks using (a) the UNIX shell, (b) the Windows GUI:
   (a) Move a file from one directory (folder) to another
   (b) Delete a file
   (c) Locate and display a file
   (d) Create a new directory
   (e) Start a file editor

7. Simplify the shell script on page 20 such that it always displays the number of users currently on the system. Do you still need to use the variable *COUNT*?

8. What do multiprogramming and time-sharing have in common? How are they different? Is multiprogramming possible without interrupts? Is time-sharing possible without interrupts?

PART ONE

PROCESS MANAGEMENT AND COORDINATION

C H A P T E R   2

Basic Concepts: Processes and Their Interactions

2.1 THE PROCESS NOTION
2.2 DEFINING AND INSTANTIATING PROCESSES
2.3 BASIC PROCESS INTERACTIONS
2.4 SEMAPHORES
2.5 EVENT SYNCHRONIZATION

2.1 THE PROCESS NOTION

When developing a large and complex system, it is of utmost importance to use some structuring method to guide and manage the design. The system must be decomposed into manageable software parts and subsystems that perform well-defined functions and interact with one another via well-defined interfaces. Many such systems, particularly operating systems (OSs), have additional challenges due to their high degree of non-determinism and their logical and physical parallelism.

Consider first the presence of nondeterminism: Many functions or services are invoked in response to particular events. These may occur at unpredictable times and with a varying degree of frequency. We can order the events informally according to their typical frequency of occurrence. At the highest level are requests from communication and storage devices needing attention from the CPU. The next frequency level consists of requests for resources such as physical devices, blocks of memory, or software components. Finally, at the lowest of the three levels, we have commands entered by interactive users or the operator via terminals, and possible hardware or software errors. All these events typically arrive at unpredictable times and may require that different modules or subsystems of the OS be invoked.

An OS also must handle a high degree of parallelism. The parallel activities causing the nondeterministic events, the parallel execution of user and OS programs, and the parallel operation of computer components.

The notion of a **sequential process** is introduced as a way to cope elegantly with the structuring problem, the highly nondeterministic nature of the environment, and the parallel activities. Informally, a sequential process (sometimes also called **task**) is the activity resulting from the execution of a program by a sequential processor (CPU). A process consists of a **program** and a **data area**, both of which reside in main memory. It also contains a **thread of execution**, which is represented by the program counter and the stack. The program counter points at the currently executing instruction and the stack captures the sequence of nested function invocations. Some systems allow multiple threads of execution to exist within a single process. Each such thread is represented by its own program counter and stack.

Conceptually, each thread of execution has its own CPU and main memory. In reality, the number of physical CPUs is much smaller than the number of processes or threads ready to run. Many computers are equipped with only a single CPU. Thus, many processes are forced to share the same CPU. To treat each process as an autonomous unit of execution, the details of CPU sharing must be invisible to the processes. This is accomplished by the lowest level of the operating system, usually referred to as the **kernel**; a principal task of the kernel is to "virtualize" the CPU, i.e., to create the illusion of a separate CPU for each running process. The kernel also may provide a separate storage—a virtual memory—for each process. Under these assumptions, each process may be viewed in isolation; it interacts with other processes only via a limited number of primitives provided by the kernel.

In systems with only one processor, the achieved concurrency among processes is a *logical* one since only one process may be executing at any given time. In the case of multiprocessors or multicomputers where more than one processing element is dedicated to general computation, or in systems equipped with specialized I/O coprocessors, *physical* concurrency is also possible.

Regardless of whether the concurrency is logical or physical, the OS and the user applications are viewed as a collection of processes, all running concurrently. These processes operate almost independently of one another, *cooperate* by sharing memory or by sending messages and synchronization signals to each other, and *compete* for resources. Each process is dedicated to a specific function, and its interactions with other processes are limited to only a few well-defined interfaces.

The process notion is invaluable for addressing the problems of distributing computation to the available processors. In both uniprocessor and multiprocessor environments, each process is treated as an autonomous entity, and each of its threads may be scheduled for execution on a CPU.

By examining the logic of processes and ignoring the number of physical processors and the details of physical memory allocation, it is possible to develop hardware-independent solutions to several systems and application problems. The solutions will ensure that a system of processes cooperate correctly, regardless of whether or not they share physical resources. The process model has several other implications in OSs. It has permitted the isolation and specification of many primitive OS tasks, has simplified the study of the organization and dynamics of an OS, and has led to the development of useful design methodologies.

In summary, the process concept is one of the fundamental notions in OSs. Using the idea of processes and its variants, both user applications and OSs consist of logically and physically concurrent programs. This chapter covers the basic methods, operations, and issues of concurrent programming with processes, with special emphasis on applications to OSs. For the purposes of this chapter, we will use the term *process* to refer primarily to its thread of execution. Thus creating a new process means starting a new thread of execution, with its own program counter and stack. Depending on the implementation, the new thread may share the memory with its creator, or it may get its own copy of the program and data areas. The details of implementing processes and threads—which is one of the main functions of an OS kernel—are treated in Chapter 4.

2.2 DEFINING AND INSTANTIATING PROCESSES

Traditionally, only the OS itself was permitted (and able) to create new processes. It was assumed that application programmers had neither the need nor the expertise to handle concurrency. This view has changed in modern computer systems. Typically, users may now employ sophisticated process mechanisms to create their own subsystems consisting of many concurrent processes.

Depending on the sophistication of the system, process creation may be done either *statically* or *dynamically*. In the first case, all processes are predeclared and activated when the system begins execution. More flexibility is attained when processes may be spawned (and terminated) dynamically during execution. The most advanced systems treat processes as first-class programming elements, similar to functions, procedures, modules, data types, objects, and classes.

2.2.1 Precedence Relations Among Processes

Programming constructs for creating and terminating processes should be able to implement a variety of precedence relations. These relations define when processes start and stop executing relative to one another. For example, each interactive user in a simple system might start a session with an initialization or login process followed in sequence by a command interpreter process; during the session a mail process might run concurrently with a date and time process, and with the command interpreter.

Figure 2-1 illustrates some of the precedence constraints that are possible among processes. The execution of a process p_i is represented by a directed edge of a graph. Each graph in the figure denotes an execution-time trace of a set of processes, and the graph connectivity describes the start and the finish precedence constraints on the processes. These graphs will be called **process flow graphs**. Any directed acyclic graph may be interpreted as a process flow graph.

An important class of process flow graphs are those that are properly nested. Let $S(p_1, \ldots, p_n)$ denote the serial execution of processes p_1 through p_n and let $P(p_1, \ldots, p_n)$ denote the parallel execution of processes p_1 through p_n. Then a process flow graph is *properly nested* if it can be described by the functions S and P, and only function composition.[1]

EXAMPLES: Process Flow Graphs

1. The graphs in Figure 2-1a, b, and c, respectively, can be described by the following expressions:

$$S(p_1, p_2, p_3, p_4),$$

$$P(p_1, p_2, p_3, p_4), \text{ and}$$

$$S(p_1, P(p_2, S(p_3, P(p_4, p_5)), p_6), P(p_7, p_8)).$$

2. *Evaluation of arithmetic expressions.* Many subexpressions of arithmetic expressions are independent and can be evaluated in parallel; the amount of parallelism

---

[1]This property is very similar to the "proper nesting" of block structure in programming languages and of parentheses within expressions.

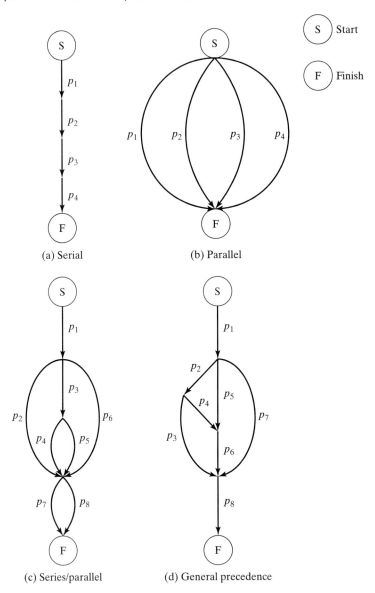

FIGURE 2-1. Precedence relations among processes: (a) serial; (b) parallel; (c) serial/parallel; and (d) general precedence.

that can occur is limited by the depth of the expression tree. Figure 2-2 shows an example of an arithmetic expression and the corresponding expression tree. (Edges are labeled by the code executed by the corresponding process). Many problems in which the primary data structure is a tree can be logically described in terms of parallel computations.

3. *Sorting.* During the ith pass in a standard two-way merge sort, pairs of sorted lists of length 2^{i-1} are merged into lists of length 2^i; each of the merges can be

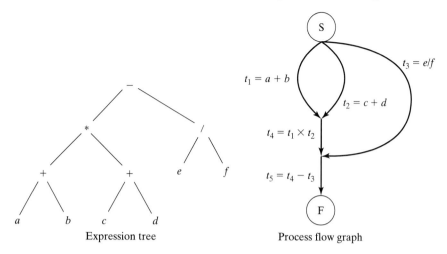

Expression tree   Process flow graph

FIGURE 2-2. Process flow graph.

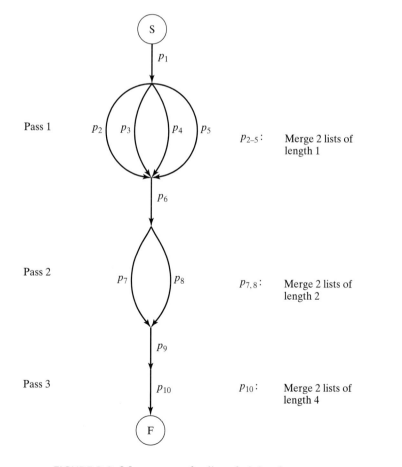

FIGURE 2-3. Merge-sort of a list of eight elements.

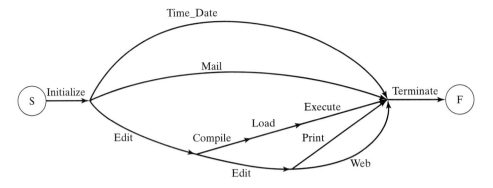

FIGURE 2-4. User session at a workstation.

performed in parallel within a pass (Fig. 2-3). This kind of parallelism where each of the processes executes the same code but on a different portion of the data is termed **data parallelism** (see example 1 on page 46).

4. *Workstation interactions.* Figure 2-4 illustrates the relations among a set of processes created during a typical user session. After initialization, three processes are established in parallel: one that continually displays the time and date, a second that permits sending and reading mail, and a third for editing. On termination of the first edit process, another edit process is created in parallel with a sequence of three processes: compile, load, and execute; the second edit is followed by a print and Web search.

The general precedence graph of Figure 2-1d is *not* properly nested. We prove this by first observing that any description by function composition must include at the innermost level an expression of the form $S(p_{i_1}, \ldots, p_{i_n})$ or $P(p_{i_1}, \ldots, p_{i_n})$ for $n \geq 2$ and $1 \leq i_j \leq 8$ ($1 \leq j \leq n$). The expression $P(p_{i_1}, \ldots, p_{i_n})$ cannot appear, since Figure 2-1d does not contain any subgraph of this form (i.e., a graph similar to Fig. 2-1b.) The expression $S(p_{i_1}, \ldots, p_{i_n})$ also cannot appear for the following reason. All serially connected processes p_i and p_j have at least one other process p_k that starts or finishes at the node between p_i and p_j; thus for any $S(\ldots, p_i, p_j, \ldots)$ in the expression, the connection of p_k to p_i or p_j could not be described without repeating p_i or p_j in a separate expression. This is not allowed, since the process would have to appear in the graph twice. Therefore, $S(p_{i_1}, \ldots, p_{i_n})$ cannot appear in the expression, and a properly nested description is not possible. Consequently, to describe this more general interaction pattern among processes, another mechanism is necessary.

2.2.2 Implicit Process Creation

By convention, program statements that are separated by semicolons or controlled by a loop iterator are executed in sequence. To specify possible parallel execution of blocks of code, we must introduce other separator or controlling symbols. Each sequential code section within a parallel construct then can be treated naturally as a process.

Specifying Parallelism with the *cobegin // coend* Constructs

The *cobegin* and *coend* primitives, originally called *parbegin* and *parend* (Dijkstra 68), specify a set of program segments that may be executed concurrently. They are used in conjunction with the separator "//" to describe concurrency. The general form is:

```
cobegin C1 // C2 // ...// Cn coend
```

where each *Ci* is a block of code. It results in the creation of a separate concurrent computation for each *Ci*, executing independently of all other processes within the *cobegin-coend* construct. Nesting of sequential and parallel blocks is normally permitted so that any *Ci* could contain other *cobegin-coend* statements.

Note that, although the *specification* of the concurrent computations is *explicit*, the actual *creation* of the corresponding underlying processes is *implicit*; it is up to the system to decide how and when to create these.

The *cobegin-coend* primitives correspond in a straightforward way to the S and P functions defined in Section 2.2.1 for describing properly nested process flow graphs. The above *cobegin-coend* construct corresponds to the following expression:

$$P(C_1, C_2, \ldots C_n)$$

Similarly, a sequential code segment,

```
C1; C2; ...; Cn;
```

can be expressed as:

$$S(C_1, C_2, \ldots C_n)$$

EXAMPLE: Use of cobegin/coend

Consider again the workstation example of the last section (Fig. 2-4). Assuming that code segments are represented by their corresponding process names, the system can be specified by the following program:

```
Initialize;
    cobegin
    Time_Date // Mail //
        { Edit; cobegin
                { Compile; Load; Execute } //
                { Edit; cobegin Print // Web coend }
                coend
        }
    coend;
Terminate
```

CASE STUDY: OCCAM/CSP

A construct semantically similar to *cobegin-coend* is used in Occam, a concurrent language based on the distributed programming language CSP (Hoare 1978). In Occam 2 (e.g., Burns 1988), the keyword *PAR* denotes that the subsequent list of code blocks may be executed in parallel; similarly, *SEQ* precedes a sequential list of statements. Indentation is used for grouping purposes. The arithmetic expression computation in Figure 2-2 can be written as:

```
SEQ
    PAR
        SEQ
            PAR
                t1 = a + b
                t2 = c + d
            t4 = t1 * t2
        t3 = e / f
    t5 = t4 - t3
```

Data Parallelism: The *forall* Statement

Another natural form of concurrency is a parallel analog of iteration. It occurs when the same body of code is executed on different parts of a data structure, usually an array—hence, the name *data parallelism*. The merge sort example of Section 2.2.1 is typical. This type of concurrency occurs frequently in scientific computation.

We illustrate the idea with a *forall* construct, modeled loosely after the *FORALL* statement defined in the current version of ISO Fortran and used in an earlier version of the high performance Fortran language (HPF) (e.g., Andrews 2000). The syntax of the *forall* statement is:

$$forall \ (\ parameters \ ) \ statements$$

where the *parameters* field specifies a set of data elements, typically through a list of indices, each of which is bound to a separate concurrent instantiation of the code given by *statements*—the loop body. Each such code instance corresponds implicitly to a concurrent process.

EXAMPLES: Merge-Sort and Matrix Multiplication

1. *Merge-Sort*. Consider again the merge sort described in Section 2.2.1 (Fig. 2-3). Let there be 2^k elements in the list to be sorted. This gives rise to k passes in a two-way merge sort. During each pass i, 2^{k-i} merging processes can be created and executed in parallel. Following is the code for the main part of a concurrent program for the sort. It assumes the existence of a function *Merge(s,n)*, which merges two lists of size s; the first list starts at index n and the other starts at index $n + s$:

```
for ( i=1; i<=k; i++ ) {
    size = pow(2, i-1 );
```

```
        forall ( j:0..(pow(2, k-i)-1) )
            Merge(size, j*size*2);
}
```

The notation $(j : 0..(pow(2, k - i) - 1)$ binds j to each element in the set $\{0, \ldots, (pow(2, k - i) - 1)\}$.

2. *Matrix multiplication.* On performing the matrix multiplication $A = B \times C$, all elements of the product A can be computed simultaneously. Let B be an n by r matrix and C be a r by m matrix. Then, the product can be computed concurrently by the code:

```
forall ( i:1..n, j:1..m ) {
        A[i][j] = 0;
        for ( k=1; k<=r; ++k )
            A[i][j] = A[i][j] + B[i][k]*C[k][j] ;
}
```

2.2.3 Explicit Process Creation with *fork* and *join*

The primitives *fork* and *join* provide a more general means for explicitly spawning parallel activities in a program. They may also be used in a straightforward way to implement the *cobegin-coend* and *forall* constructs, used to denote independent and thus potentially parallel computations. We will start with the early, low-level form (Conway 1963; Dennis and Van Horn 1966), and then discuss several recent versions supported by contemporary systems.

A process p executing the instruction:

```
fork x
```

creates a new process q, which starts executing at the instruction labeled x; p and q then execute concurrently. The instruction:

```
join t,y
```

decrements t by 1 and, if t equals zero, transfers control to the location y. The following statements describe the effect of the *join* instruction:

```
t = t-1;
if (t==0) goto y;
```

The execution of the *join* instruction must be *atomic*. That is, the two statements must be executed as a single indivisible instruction without interruption and interference from any other process.

In addition to the *fork* and *join* instructions, the instruction *quit* is provided, which allows a process to terminated itself.

To illustrate the use of *fork/join/quit*, consider the following program segment for evaluating the expression of Figure 2-2:

```
                    n = 2;
                    fork L3;
                    m = 2;
                    fork L2;
                    t1 = a+b; join m,L4; quit;
            L2:     t2 = c+d; join m,L4; quit;
            L4:     t4 = t1*t2; join n,L5; quit;
            L3:     t3 = e/f; join n,L5; quit;
            L5:     t5 = t4-t3;
```

This program first forks two child processes, $L3$ and $L2$, to compute the values of $t3$ and $t2$, respectively. In the meantime, the parent process computes the value of $t1$. It then joins with the child process $L2$ as follows. Both execute the same *join* statement. The process that executes the *join* first, finds m equal to 1 (after decrementing it) and terminates itself by executing the *quit* statement following the *join*. The other process finds m equal to 0 (after decrementing it) and continues executing at $L4$. It then joins with $L3$ in an analogous manner, and the survivor of the join executes the final statement at $L5$.

To create private or local copies of variables within parallel processes, variables may be declared as "private" to a process by the declaration:

$$\text{private: x1,x2, ..., xn;}$$

The variables xi then only exist for the process executing the private declarations; in addition, any new process created by the latter (using a *fork*) will receive its own copy of the private variables of the parent process.

To illustrate the use of private variables, consider the following example from image processing. We are given an array $A[0..n+1, 0..n+1]$ consisting of zeros and ones representing a digitized image. It is desired to "smooth" the image by replacing each interior point $A[i, j]$ by 1 if the majority of $A[i, j]$ and its immediate eight neighbors are 1, and by 0 otherwise. This procedure is called *local averaging* and is logically a parallel computation. We assume that the smoothed image is stored in a new array, B.

```
    Local_average( int A[][], int n, int B) {
    int t,i,j; private: i,j;
        t = n*n;
        for (i=1; i<=n; ++i)
        for (j=1; j<=n; ++j)
            fork e;
        quit;
    e:  if (A[i-1][j-1]+A[i-1][j]+A[i-1][j+1]
           +A[i][j-1]+A[i][j]+A[i][j+1]+A[i+1][j-1]
           +A[i+1][j]+A[i+1][j+1] >= 5) B[i][j] = 1;
        else B[i][j] = 0;
        join t,r;
        quit;
    r:  return;
    }
```

The main virtue of the statements *fork, join* and *quit* is their high expressive power. They are sufficient to describe any process flow graph. Below is a program for the graph of Figure 2-1d, which is not properly nested:

```
        t1 = 2; t2 = 3;
        p1; fork L2; fork L5; fork L7; quit;
L2:     p2; fork L3; fork L4; quit;
L5:     p5; join t1,L6; quit;
L7:     p7; join t2,L8; quit;
L3:     p3; join t2,L8; quit;
L4:     p4; join t1,L6; quit;
L6:     p6; join t2,L8; quit;
L8:     p8; quit;
```

The main disadvantages of these primitives are that they are low level and may be used indiscriminately anywhere within a program. When invoked inside of loops or other control statements, the program structure may become rather obscure. However, various higher-level forms and derivatives of *fork* and *join* are implemented in many OSs and languages. The following five examples are representative.

CASE STUDY: PROCESS CREATION WITH FORK **and** JOIN

1. *UNIX fork.* The UNIX OS employs a variant of the *fork* primitive that has the form:

$$procid = fork()$$

Execution of this statement causes the current process, called the *parent*, to be simply replicated. The only distinction between the parent and the newly created process, called *child*, is the variable *procid*; in the parent it contains the process number of the child as its value, whereas in the child its value is zero. This permits each of the two processes to determine its identity and to proceed accordingly. Typically, the next statement following *fork* will be of the form:

```
if (procid==0) do_child_processing;
else do_parent_processing;
```

One of the processes, say the child, may overlay itself by performing the call *exec()* as part of the *do_child_processing* clause. This function specifies a new program as one of its parameters; the new program then continues executing as the child process.

2. *Linux clone.* The Linux OS provides a system call:

$$procid = clone(params)$$

This is similar to the UNIX *fork*, but the parameters supp' ed to the function allow the caller to control what is shared between the caller (the parent) and

---

CASE STUDY: PROCESS CREATION WITH FORK **and** JOIN ***(continued)***

---

the child process. In particular, the child can get its own copy of the program and data space. In this case, the *clone* functions as the UNIX *fork*. Alternately, the child can share its program and data space with the parent. In this case, the child becomes only a new thread within the same parent process.

3. *UNIX/Linux join*. Both UNIX and Linux provide a construct similar to a *join*:

$$procid = waitpid(pids, *stat\_loc, ...)$$

The calling process specifies the identifications of one or more of its children in the parameter *pids*. The *waitpid* call then suspends the calling process until one of the specified children terminates (using the call *exit()*, which corresponds to the statement *quit*.) Upon awakening, the parent process may examine the child's status in the variable **stat_loc*. The difference between *waitpid* and *join* is that the latter is symmetric—two or more processes execute the same *join* statement, and all may continue executing after the *join*. With *waitpid*, only one process—the parent—may wait and then continue, whereas the child must always terminate.

4. *Orca*. In the examples 1 and 2 above, the *fork* and *clone* statements were part of the OS interface. Frequently, such primitives are incorporated directly in a programming language. One interesting example is the Orca parallel programming language (Bal, Kaashoek, and Tanenbaum 1992). In Orca, a new process can be generated with the statement:

```
fork pname(params) on cpu;
```

pname is the name of a previously declared process, *params* are any parameters associated with the process, and *cpu*, which is optional, identifies the machine on which the new forked process is to run.

5. *Java join*. The concurrency facility offered by the Java language (Naughton and Schildt 1997) has a *join* method for synchronizing with the termination of a thread. The call:
```
thread_id.join();
```
causes the caller to wait until the thread named *thread_id* completes before it continues execution.

6. *Mesa fork/join*. The Mesa language (Lampson and Redell 1980) is an influential concurrent programming language that has been used for implementing OSs. It permits *any* procedure $q(...)$ to be invoked as a separate process. The two statements used to spawn and coordinate concurrent processes have the following form:

```
p = fork q(...);
var_list = join p;
```

The *fork* statement creates a new process which begins executing the procedure *q* concurrently with the parent process. In Mesa, each process is considered an *object*, and it may be assigned to a variable. In the above statement, the variable *p* represents the child process. Note that, unlike the *procid* variable in UNIX, the variable *p* contains not just a process identifier but also the process object itself. This permits processes to be treated as any other variable; for example, a process may be passed to another procedure as a parameter.

To synchronize the termination of a child process with the parent's computation, the *join* primitive is used. It forces the parent process to wait for the termination of the child process *p*. Each procedure in Mesa must explicitly specify a list of values to be returned as the result of the procedure's computation. When a child process terminates, the results of the corresponding procedure may be transmitted to the parent process by assigning them to variables listed as part of the *join* statement. In the above example, the results returned from the procedure *q* executed by the child process *p* are assigned to the variables listed in *var_list* upon *p*'s termination. At that point, the parent process resumes its execution with the next instruction following the *join*.

2.2.4   Process Declarations and Classes

Some languages have combined the virtues of both *fork-join* and *cobegin-coend* by providing mechanisms that designate segments of code to be separate processes or classes of separate processes, but permit their invocation and instantiation to be controlled during execution. A process is declared using the following syntax:

```
process p {
    declarations_for_p;
    executable_code_for_p;
}
```

The keyword *process* designates the segment of code between the curly braces as a separate unit of execution named *p*. The list of declarations preceding the executable code typically contains local variables, functions, procedures, and other process declarations. As soon as the process *p* is activated, all processes defined within the declaration portion of *p* are activated as well. This mechanism represents a *static* creation of processes.

To provide more flexibility, processes may be created *dynamically* by replacing the keyword *process* by the phrase *process type*. This can be interpreted as defining a process class or template, instances of which may be created dynamically during execution by using a special command *new*. The following program skeleton illustrates the distinction between static and dynamic process creation:

```
process p {
    process p1 {
        declarations_for_p1;
        executable_code_for_p1;
    }
```

```
                    process type p2 {
                        declarations_for_p2;
                        executable_code_for_p2;
                    }
                    other_declarations_for_p;
                    . . .
                    q = new p2;
                    . . .
            }
```

The process *p1* is declared statically within the declaration part of *p* and will be activated as soon as the process *p* begins execution. The process *p2*, on the other hand, is declared as a process type, and an instance of *p2* will be created only as a result of the explicit call *new p2*, performed during the execution of the body of process *p*. The new instance of *p2* will be named *q*.

CASE STUDY: PROCESS DECLARATIONS AND CLASSES

1. *Ada*. The Ada language (Ada 1995) supports both static and dynamic process creation as described above. The processes in Ada are called *tasks*.

2. *Java*. The Java language supports concurrency through a class named *Thread*. The Java *join* method, discussed in Example 5 of Section 2.2.3, is part of this class. A Java thread can be created or instantiated using the *new* primitive, which is similar to the one discussed above. To start the actual execution of a created thread—to put the thread on a ready list for the CPU scheduler of the OS—the *start* method may be used, for example:

```
                    thread_id.start();
```

Process declarations permit any number of processes to be declared and spawned at arbitrary times and in arbitrary order during execution. However, they do not permit processes to interact with one another in any way. For example, a process cannot delay itself to await the termination of some other process. When compared with the *fork-join* primitives, the term *new* acts as a *fork* and the *end* statement is similar to a *quit*; however, there is no construct corresponding to the primitive *join*. This implies that additional mechanisms must be provided if more controlled interactions such as those depicted in Figure 2-1c and 2-1d are to be enforced.

2.3 BASIC PROCESS INTERACTIONS

2.3.1 Competition: The Critical Section Problem

When several processes may asynchronously access a common data area, it is necessary to protect the data from simultaneous change by two or more processes. If this protection is not provided, the updated area may be left in an inconsistent state.

There is also a *distributed* version of the problem where the goal again is to ensure that only one process at a time can access a data area or resource. However, the processes and resource may be on different nodes of a distributed network, and do not directly share memory. We will consider the distributed problem is Section 3.2.3. This section assumes the shared memory version.

Consider two processes p_1 and p_2, both asynchronously incrementing a common variable x representing, say, the number of units of a resource:

```
cobegin
p1:   ...
        x = x + 1;
        ...
      //
p2:   ...
        x = x + 1;
        ...
coend
```

Each of the two high-level instructions `x = x + 1;` is normally translated into several machine-level instructions. Let us assume that these instructions are:

1. load the value of x into some internal register ($R = x;$).
2. increment that register ($R = R + 1;$).
3. store the new value into the variable x ($x = R;$).

Assume that p_1 and p_2 run on two separate CPUs, each having its own set of registers but sharing the main memory. Given that the two processes are asynchronous and may proceed at arbitrary pace, either of the two execution sequences shown below could occur over time.

Sequence 1:

```
p1:   R1 = x; R1 = R1 + 1; x = R1;  ...
p2:   ...                           R2 = x; R2 = R2 + 1; x = R2;  ...
```

Sequence 2:

```
p1:   R1 = x; R1 = R1 + 1; x = R1;  ...
p2:   ...     R2 = x; R2 = R2 + 1; x = R2;  ...
```

Let x contain the value v at the time execution begins. At the time of completion, x should contain $v + 2$. This will be the case if the execution follows sequence 1, which executes the instructions sequentially. However, the value of x is $v + 1$ if execution follows sequence 2. The reason is that $R1$ and $R2$ both receive the *same* initial value v, and both later store the same value $v + 1$ into x.

The same problem can occur even on a uniprocessor system, where p_1 and p_2 are time-sharing the same CPU with control switching between the processes by means of interrupts. This is true even if both processes use the same register to load and update the value of x. The reason is that registers are saved and restored during every process switch, and each process has its own copy of all register contents. For example, the following interleaved sequence of execution produces the same incorrect result as Sequence 2 above:

Sequence 3:

```
p1:  R = x;  ...                       R = R + 1; x = R;  ...
p2:     ...     R = x; R = R + 1; x = R;  ...
```

The loss of one of the updates of the variable x by Sequence 2 and 3 is clearly unacceptable. To solve this problem, we must prevent the interleaving or concurrent execution of the three machine instructions corresponding to the high-level instruction $x = x + 1$. In general, any segment of code involved in reading and writing a shared data area is called a **critical section** (CS).

The CS problem now can be stated more precisely as follows. We are given n sequential processes ($n \geq 2$), which can communicate with each other through a shared data area. Each process contains a code section—its *CS*—in which read and write accesses to the common data are made. The processes are cyclic, each executing in an infinite loop. During each iteration, a process p_i needs to execute its CS, CS_i. It also executes other code, denoted as *program$_i$*, which does not involve any of the shared data. The following code skeleton shows the overall organization of the competing processes:

```
cobegin
p1: while (1) {CS1; program1;}
         //
p2: while (1) {CS2; program2;}
         //
         ⋮
         //
pn: while (1) {CSn; programn;}
coend
```

We make the following additional assumptions about the system:

1. Writing into a variable and reading from a variable are each indivisible operations. Thus simultaneous access to the same memory location by more than one process results in a sequential access in an unknown order. For example, when two or more processes attempt to simultaneously write to the same location, one of the values (chosen at random) is stored; the others are lost.

2. CSs do not have priorities associated with them.

3. The relative speeds of the processes are unknown. Thus processors of different speeds may be used and the interleaving of instructions on a single processor may be arbitrary.

4. A program may halt only outside of its CS.

The CS problem is then to implement the processes so that, at any point in time, at most one of them is in its CS; once a process p enters its CS, no other process may do the same until p has left its CS. This property is called **mutual exclusion**, since CSs must be executed in a mutually exclusive fashion with respect to each other.

At the same time, **mutual blocking** of processes must be avoided. We can distinguish the following types of blocking:

1. A process operating well outside its CS, i.e., a process that is not attempting to enter its CS, must not be preventing another process from entering its CS.
2. It must not be possible for one of the processes to repeatedly enter its CS while the other process never gets its chance; i.e., the latter process cannot **starve**.
3. Two processes about to enter their CSs must not enter infinite waiting loops or blocking statements that would cause them to wait forever. Such a condition is referred to as a **deadlock**
4. Two processes about to enter their CSs must not repeatedly yield to each other and indefinitely postpone the decision on which one actually enters. Such a condition is referred to as a **livelock**.

Software Solution

In this section, we will present a solution to the CS problem that does not require any special machine instructions or other hardware. Before presenting this solution, we will illustrate some of the difficulties and pitfalls that exist when solving this seemingly simple problem. In fact, solving CS and other synchronization problems are among the most difficult and error-prone tasks in concurrent programming.

We restrict the system initially to only two processes as illustrated in Figure 2-5. The primary goal is to prevent p_1 and p_2 from executing in their respective CSs together (mutual exclusion) while avoiding all forms of mutual blocking.

The problem is easily solved if we insist that p_1 and p_2 enter their CSs alternately; one common variable, *turn*, can keep track of whose turn it is. This idea is implemented in the first algorithm.

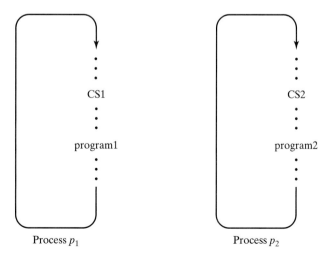

FIGURE 2-5. Two processes with critical sections.

```
/* CS Algorithm: Try #1 */
int turn = 1;
cobegin
p1:   while (1) {
            while (turn==2) ; /*wait loop*/
            CS1; turn = 2; program1;
      }
      //
p2:   while (1) {
            while (turn==1) ; /*wait loop*/
            CS2; turn = 1; program2;
      }
coend
```

Initially, *turn* is set to 1, which allows p_1 to enter its CS. After exiting, the process sets *turn* to 2, which now allows p_2 to enter its CS, and so on.

Unfortunately, if *program1* were much longer than *program2* or if p_1 halted in *program1*, this solution would hardly be satisfactory. One process well outside its CS can prevent the other from entering its CS, violating the requirement 1 stated above.

To avoid this type of blocking, two common variables, *c1* and *c2*, may be used as flags to indicate whether a process is inside or outside of its CS. A process p_i wishing to enter its CS indicates its intent by setting the flag c_i to 1. It then waits for the other flag to become 0 and enters the CS. Upon termination of the CS it resets its flag to 0, thus permitting the other process to continue. Our second try below follows this logic.

```
/* CS Algorithm: Try #2 */
int c1 = 0, c2 = 0;
cobegin
p1:   while (1) {
            c1 = 1;
            while (c2) ; /*wait loop*/
            CS1; c1 = 0; program1;
      }
      //
p2:   ... /*analogous to p1*/
coend
```

Mutual exclusion is guaranteed with this solution but mutual blocking of the third type is now possible. Both *c1* and *c2* may be set to 1 at the same time and the processes would loop forever in their *while* statements, effectively deadlocked. The obvious way to rectify this is to reset *c1* and *c2* to 0 after testing whether they are 1, leading to our third try at an algorithm for solving the CS problem.

```
/* CS Algorithm: Try #3 */
int c1 = 0, c2 = 0;
cobegin
p1:   while (1) {
            c1 = 1;
```

```
            if (c2) c1 = 0;
                else {
                    CS1; c1 = 0; program1;
                }
        }
        //
    p2: ...
    coend
```

Unfortunately, this solution may lead to both the second and fourth type of blocking. When the execution timing is such that one process, say p_2, always tests the $c1$ flag just after it was set to 1 by p_1 and, as a result, sets $c2$ to 0 before it is tested by p_1, p_1 will always succeed in entering its critical section, while p_2 is forced to wait.

The fourth type of blocking occurs when both processes begin execution at the same time and proceed at exactly the same speed. They will keep setting and testing their mutual flags indefinitely, without ever entering their CSs. Note, however, that such indefinite postponement is much less likely to occur here than with the previous solution, since both processes must maintain the same speed indefinitely; if one becomes slower than the other, the mutual blocking is resolved. With the previous solution (Try #2), both processes remained in their respective *while*-loops forever, regardless of speed.

The above three attempts at solving the CS problem illustrate some of the subtleties underlying process synchronization. In 1981, G. L. Peterson proposed a simple and elegant algorithm, which we now present as the final complete software solution to the CS problem.

```
/* CS Algorithm: Peterson Solution */
int c1 = 0, c2 = 0, will_wait;
cobegin
p1: while (1) {
        c1 = 1;
        will_wait = 1;
        while (c2 && (will_wait==1)) ; /*wait loop*/
        CS1; c1 = 0; program1;
    }
    //
p2: while (1) {
        c2 = 1;
        will_wait = 2;
        while (c1 && (will_wait==2)) ; /*wait loop*/
        CS2; c2 = 0; program2;
    }
coend
```

A process indicates its interest to enter the CS by setting its flag c_i to 1. To break possible race conditions, the algorithm uses the variable *will_wait*; by setting this variable to its own identifier, a process indicates its willingness to wait if both processes are trying to enter their CS at the same time. Since *will_wait* can contain the identifier of only one process at any time, the one who sets it last will be forced to wait.

The solution guarantees mutual exclusion and prevent all forms of blocking. Consider first the problem of mutual blocking. If it were possible, at least one of the processes, e.g., p_1, must somehow circle through its *while* loop forever. This is not possible for the following reason. When p_1 is in its loop, the second process p_2 may be doing one of three general things: (1) not trying to enter its CS, (2) waiting in its own *while* loop, or (3) repeatedly executing its own complete loop. In the first case, p_1 detects that $c2$ is 0 and proceeds into its CS. The second case is impossible because *will_wait* is either 1 or 2, which permits one of the processes to proceed. Similarly, the third case is impossible since p_2 will set *will_wait* to 2, and, consequently, not pass through its *while* statement test. It will not be able to proceed until p_1 has executed its CS.

To show that the solution guarantees mutual exclusion, assume that p_1 has just passed its test and is about to enter its CS. At this time, $c1$ must be 1. Let us examine if there is any way for p_2 to enter *CS2*, thus violating the mutual exclusion requirement. There are two cases to consider:

1. p_1 has passed its test because $c2$ was 0. This implies that p_2 is currently not trying to enter its CS, i.e., it is outside of the segment of code delimited by the instructions $c2 = 1$; and $c2 = 0$;. If it now tries to enter, it must first set *will_wait* to 2. Since $c1$ is 1, it will fail its test and will have to wait until p_1 has left its CS.

2. p_1 has passed its test because *will_wait* was equal to 2. This implies that, regardless of where p_2 is at this time, it will find $c1$ equal to 1 and *will_wait* equal to 2 when it reaches its test, and will not be permitted to proceed.

The CS problem is concerned with the most basic requirements when independent processes may access the same resource or data. Mutual exclusion is also the basis for many other more complex types of process interactions and resource sharing. The solutions to these and other resource allocation scenarios are discussed in the remainder of this chapter and in Chapter 3.

2.3.2   Cooperation

The CS problem described above is a situation in which processes *compete* for a resource that may not be accessed by more than one process at any given time. Note that each process could exist without the other—their interaction is needed only to resolve simultaneous access to the resource. A different situation arises when two or more processes **cooperate** in solving a common goal. In this case, each of them is aware of, and usually depends on, the existence of the other. Similar to concurrent processes with CSs, cooperating processes have a need to exchange information with one another. In the simplest cases, only synchronization signals are necessary. In more general scenarios, processes must pass data to each other, which may be done through shared memory or by sending messages.

One general example of cooperation occurs in the implementation of precedence relations among processes (Section 2.2.1). The activation of some processes is synchronized with the termination of others. A similar application, appearing frequently in scientific computations, is *barrier* synchronization, which is required when a group of processes must all arrive at a particular point before continuing.

Processes engaged in what is typically characterized as a **producer/consumer** relationship also fall into this category. Figure 2-6 describes this situation for one *Consumer* and one *Producer* process that communicate via a shared *Buffer* storage that can hold a

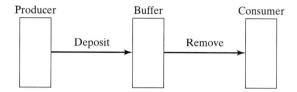

FIGURE 2-6. A producer and a consumer communicating through a buffer.

finite number of data elements. The *Producer*'s task is to generate (produce) one or more new elements of data, which it deposits in the buffer. These are removed (consumed) from the buffer by the *Consumer* process.

Different buffering scenarios occur throughout the I/O system, the file system, and various network components. For example, a main application process may be producing output data and placing them into available buffer slots, while, asynchronously, an output process is removing them from the buffer and printing them. Alternately, the *Producer* could be an input process, and the *Consumer* is the main application process using the input data.

Since both processes run concurrently at varying speeds, we must guarantee that the *Producer* does not overwrite any data in the buffer before the *Consumer* can remove it. Similarly, the *Consumer* must be able to wait for the *Producer* when the latter falls behind and does not fill the buffer on time. Hence the two processes must be able to exchange information about the current state of the shared buffer—specifically, the number of data elements present.

Process cooperation is also necessary in distributed systems, where the processes do not share any memory. For example, OS services such as file or directory servers, are frequently implemented as separate processes running on dedicated machines. Other processes make use of such a service by sending it the necessary input data in the form of messages. Upon performing the desired computations with the received data, the service returns the results to the calling process in the form of reply messages. Such cooperating processes are referred to as **communicating** processes, and this form of interaction is called a **client-server** architecture. It requires a general interprocess communication facility to allow processes to establish logical channels with one another, through which arbitrary messages can be exchanged. We will discuss the principles of message passing in Chapter 3. In the remainder of this chapter, we introduce the principles of *semaphores*. In reality, semaphores are devices for signaling or conveying information by changing the position of a light, flag, or other signal. Semaphores in OSs are an analogy to such signaling devices. They offer an elegant, universal, and popular scheme that can be used as a foundation for programming both process competition and process cooperation in uniprocessor or shared-memory multiprocessor systems.

2.4 SEMAPHORES

There are several unappealing features of the software solution to the CS problem that was presented earlier:

1. The solution is difficult to understand and verify. Enforcing mutual exclusion for even two processes results in complex and awkward additions to programs.

Extending the solution to more than two processes requires even more code to be generated.

2. The solution applies to only competition among processes. To address the problem of cooperation, entirely different solutions must be devised.

3. While one process is in its CS, the other process continues running but is making no real progress—it is repeatedly accessing and testing some shared variables. This type of waiting steals memory cycles from the active process; it is also consuming valuable CPU time without really accomplishing anything. The result is a general slowing down of the system by processes that are not doing any useful work.

Dijkstra (1968) introduced two new primitive operations, called P and V, that considerably simplified the coordination of concurrent processes. The operations are universally applicable to competition and cooperation among any number of processes. Furthermore, P and V may be implemented in ways that avoid the performance degradation resulting from waiting.

2.4.1   Semaphore Operations and Data

The P and V primitives operate on *nonnegative integer* variables called **semaphores**.[2] Let s be a semaphore variable, initialized to some nonnegative integer value. The operations are defined as follows:

- $V(s)$: Increment s by 1 in a single *indivisible* action; i.e, the fetch, increment, and store of s cannot be interrupted, and s cannot be accessed by another process during the operation.

- $P(s)$: If $s > 0$ then decrement s and proceed; otherwise (i.e., when $s == 0$), the process invoking the P operation must wait until $s > 0$. The successful testing and decrementing of s also must be an indivisible operation. In Chapter 4, we discuss in detail how the waiting is accomplished when s is zero. In brief, the invoking process can be suspended or it can execute a "busy-wait" loop continually testing s.

In addition to the indivisibility of the P and V operations, we make the following assumptions:

- If several processes simultaneously invoke a P or V operation on the same semaphore, the operations will occur sequentially in an arbitrary order;

- If more than one process is waiting inside a P operation on the same semaphore and the semaphore becomes positive (because of the execution of a V), one of the waiting processes is selected arbitrarily to complete the P operation.

The P and V operations are used to synchronize and coordinate processes. The P primitive includes a potential wait of the calling process, whereas the V primitive may possibly activate some waiting process. The indivisibility of P and V assures the integrity of the values of the semaphores and the atomicity of the test and decrement actions within each P operation.

[2] P and V are the first letters of Dutch words that mean "pass" and "release," respectively.

2.4.2 Mutual Exclusion with Semaphores

Semaphore operations allow a simple and straightforward solution to the CS problem. Let *mutex* (which stands for *mut*ual *ex*clusion) be a semaphore variable used to protect the CS. A program solution for *n* processes operating in parallel is as follows:

```
semaphore mutex = 1;
cobegin
p1:  while (1) { P(mutex); CS1; V(mutex); program1; }
     //
pi:  while (1) { P(mutex); CS2; V(mutex); program2; }
     //
       ⋮
     //
pn:  while (1) { P(mutex); CSn; V(mutex); programn; }
coend;
```

The value of *mutex* is 0 when any process is in its CS; otherwise *mutex* is 1. The semaphore has the function of a simple lock. Mutual exclusion is guaranteed, since only one process can decrement *mutex* to zero with the *P* operation. All other processes attempting to enter their CSs while *mutex* is zero will be forced to wait by *P(mutex)*, and execution of *P(mutex)* by multiple processes simultaneously selects one of them at random. Mutual blocking (through a deadlock or indefinite postponement) is not possible, because simultaneous attempts to enter CSs when *mutex* is 1 must, by our definition, translate into *sequential P* operations. The starvation of a process wishing to enter its CS is, however, possible. This depends on how the semaphores are implemented. Starvation may in fact be desirable in some cases, for example, when processes are serviced on a priority basis; but servicing *P* operations in a first-come/first-served order eliminates any possibility of starvation.

When a semaphore can take only the values 0 or 1, it is called a **binary** semaphore; otherwise—when the semaphore can take any nonnegative integer value—it is referred to as a **counting** semaphore. An important and widespread application of binary semaphores is the implementation of mutual exclusion locks, such as in the above CS problem: *P* locks a data structure for exclusive use, and a later *V* unlocks it. This, and nested versions of it, are such common scenarios that systems provide special operations for just the locking and unlocking of CSs, in addition to counting semaphores.

CASE STUDY: SEMAPHORE PRIMITIVES

1. *Solaris.* The Solaris OS offers both binary and counting semaphores through thread libraries. The binary semaphore is called a *mutex* and may be defined for interprocess or intraprocess synchronization. In the first case, the mutex variable is local to a process and may be used to synchronize threads within that process. The second type allows threads belonging to different processes to synchronize with each other. Mutex synchronization supports the following function:

   - *mutex_init():* creates and initializes a mutex;
   - *mutex_destroy():* destroys an existing mutex;

CASE STUDY: SEMAPHORE PRIMITIVES (*continued*)

- *mutex_lock():* locks a mutex; when another thread tries to lock the same mutex, it is blocked until the original locking thread unlocks it;
- *mutex_trylock():* this is a nonblocking version of the *mutex_lock*; it tries to lock the mutex but if the mutex is already locked, it returns an error value, instead of blocking;
- *mutex_unlock():* unlocks a mutex.

Counting semaphores may take on any nonnegative integer value, and function exactly as described in this section. They support five function, analogous to those for mutexes:

- *sema_init():* creates and initializes a semaphore;
- *sema_destroy():* destroys an existing semaphore;
- *sema_wait():* decrements the semaphore if its value is greater than 0; otherwise the operation blocks;
- *sema_trylock():* this is a nonblocking version of the *sema_wait*; it tries to decrement the sempahore but if this is zero, it returns an error value, instead of blocking;
- *sema_post():* increments the semaphore.

2. *Linux.* Linux offers two types of synchronization primitives. The first, referred to as *kernel semaphores*, are general counting semaphores, and may be used on both uniprocessor and multiprocessor systems. The two main functions, corresponding to *P* and *V*, are *down()* and *up()*, respectively.

The other type of primitive are binary semaphores, called *spin locks* (because of their implementation as waiting loops; see Chapter 4). They are controlled through several macros, notably, *spin_lock*, which locks a given binary semaphore, *spin_unlock*, which unlocks it, and *spin_trylock*, which is the nonblocking variant of *spin_lock*. In addition to these exclusive binary semaphores, Linux defines a second type, called *read/write spin locks*. Such locks are controlled using the following macros:

- *read_lock:* locks the semaphore in read-only mode; other threads may apply the same *read_lock* to the semaphore and proceed concurrently; *read_lock* blocks only when the semaphore is already locked using the *write_lock*;
- *write_lock:* locks the semaphore in exclusive (read/write) mode; if the semaphore is already locked (for either reading or writing), the operation blocks;
- *read_unlock:* this removes one of the previously placed read locks, thus decrementing the number of concurrent readers;
- *write_unlock:* this removes a previously placed write lock.

2.4.3 Semaphores in Producer/Consumer Situations

Processes in computer systems request and release various resources. Access to non-sharable resources is generally protected by CSs as described above. In addition, processes may be *producing* resources, such as messages, signals, or data items, which are *consumed* by other processes. Semaphores can be used to maintain resource counts, synchronize processes, and lock out CSs.

For example, a process can block itself by a *P* operation on a semaphore *s* to wait for a certain condition, such as a new data item becoming available. It can be awakened by another process executing *V* on *s* when this condition becomes satisfied. The following code skeleton illustrates this type of interaction among processes:

```
semaphore s = 0;
cobegin
p1:  { ...; P(s); ... }     /* Wait for signal from p2.*/
     //
p2:  { ...; V(s); ... }     /* Send wakeup signal to p1.*/
coend
```

In this scenario, *p1* may also be viewed as consuming units of the resource represented by the semaphore *s* through the instruction *P(s)*, while *p2* produces units of *s* through *V(s)*.

EXAMPLE: The Bounded-Buffer Problem (Dijkstra 68)

Probably the best known and practical producer/consumer situation is the bounded buffer scenario introduced in Section 2.3.2. A *Producer* process generates data elements and adds them to a shared buffer. Concurrently, a *Consumer* process removes data elements from the buffer and processes them. The buffer is a shared data area. At any point in time, it will contain zero or more full data elements (deposited but not yet removed) and a number of empty slots.

Let the buffer consist of *n* equal-sized slots, each capable of holding one data element. We use two resource counters:

- *e* denotes the number of empty buffer slots; these are currently available to the *Producer*;

- *f* denotes the number of full buffer slots; these are currently available to the *Consumer*.

Incrementing and decrementing *e* and *f* must be indivisible, or their values could be in error as a result of possible race conditions (Section 2.3.1). Thus, instead of implementing *e* and *f* as ordinary variables and treating their changes as CSs, they are implemented as semaphores. The *P* and *V* operations then guarantee that all changes are atomic. Furthermore, the *P(e)* ensures that the *Producer* does not proceed unless an empty buffer slot is available; similarly, *P(f)* guarantees that the *Consumer* waits until at least one full buffer slot exists.

Assume that adding elements to and taking elements from the buffer constitute CSs. We use a binary semaphore, *b*, for mutual exclusion. The processes then may be described as follows:

```
semaphore e = n, f = 0, b = 1;
cobegin
Producer:  while (1) {
                  Produce_next_data_element;
```

```
                    /* Deposit data element. */
                    P(e); P(b); Add_to_buffer; V(b); V(f);
                }
                //
    Consumer:   while (1) {
                    /* Remove data element. */
                    P(f); P(b); Take_from_buffer; V(b); V(e);
                    Process_data_element;
                }
    coend
```

If the buffer was implemented as an array, mutual exclusion, enforced by the semaphore *b*, might not be necessary. The reason is that the *Producer* and the *Consumer* always refer to different buffer elements. However, if linked lists of buffers are employed or if the program is generalized to *m* producers and *n* consumers ($m, n \geq 1$), mutual exclusion is necessary. The reason is both processes could be manipulating pointers linking together adjacent list elements or pointers designating the next empty or full slot.

2.5 EVENT SYNCHRONIZATION

An **event** designates some change in the state of the system that is of interest to a process. An event is usually considered to take zero time. In computer systems, events are generated principally through hardware interrupts and traps, either directly or indirectly. For example, the end of an I/O operation, the expiration of a timer or clock, a machine error, or a programming error such as overflow or an invalid address, are all considered events that must trigger an action. Events, implemented by software interrupts, also are used for process interactions, e.g., for one process to interrupt and terminate another, or for general interprocess synchronization.

Many systems provide facilities to define and handle specific events. We can differentiate between two type of events: **synchronous** and **asynchronous**. In the first case, a process blocks itself to wait for the occurrence of a specific event or set of events, generated by another process. This is similar to the consumer/producer situation discussed earlier, and, consequently, the primitives to handle synchronous events are similar to binary semaphores.

Generally, support for synchronous events includes ways to define event types, generate or post events, and wait for events. An operation, such as *E.wait*, can be used as an explicit wait for an event, *E*, to occur. An instance of this event is generated by an explicit command, e.g., *E.post*. If there are any processes or threads waiting on *E*, one or more is awakened by the *E.post* operation.

In their simplest form, events can be implemented using binary semaphores. However, there is no consistent definition of events, and a variety of schemes with differing semantics are in use. One common variant that clearly distinguishes events from binary semaphores has no "memory" of posted events. If there are no waiting processes when an event is posted (signaled), then the instance of that event simply disappears. In contrast, the effect of a *P* or *V* operation is reflected in the new value of the semaphore. Some implementations of events also allow the *broadcasting* of an event to a group of waiting processes or to wake up only a single waiter.

Asynchronous events also must be defined and explicitly posted using a *E.post* operation. However, a process does not explicitly block itself to await the occurrence of an asynchronous event. Instead, it only indicates its interest in specific types of events and specifies the actions to be taken when a particular event occurs. This is commonly done by providing **event handlers** for different types of events. Each handler is a section of code that is to be executed automatically and asynchronously with the current process whenever the event is posted. Thus, asynchronous events are similar to interrupts.

CASE STUDY: EVENT SYNCHRONIZATION

1. *UNIX signals.* UNIX allows processes to signal various conditions to each other using asynchronous events. Such signals are sent using the function *kill(pid, sig)*, where *pid* is the receiving process and *sig* is the type of signal sent. The function name, *kill*, is a misnomer—it does not necessary kill the receiving process, even though that is the default.

   There are certain predefined types of signals. For example, *SIGHUP* signals that the phone line the process was using has been hung up, *SIGILL* signals an illegal instruction, *SIGFPE* signals a floating point error, *SIGKILL* signals that the process is to be terminated, and *SIGUSR1* and *SIGUSR2* are intended for application-specific signals defined by the user.

   The receiving process may specify, using the function *sigaction()*, what should happen when a signal arrives. If nothing is specified, the process is killed. If the process specifies that a signal is to be ignored, the signal is simply lost. Alternately, the process may catch a signal by specifying a signal handler, which is invoked automatically whenever a signal of the specified type arrives. Certain types of signals, such as *SIGKILL* cannot be ignored or caught by any process. This is necessary to guarantee that any process can be killed, for example, to prevent runaway processes.

   Signals also may be used in a synchronous manner. A process may issue the call *pause()*, which will block it until the next signal arrives.

2. *Windows 2000 Synchronization.* Windows 2000 provides a broad spectrum of synchronization options, which it unifies in a common framework of *dispatcher objects*. Each dispatcher object may be in one of two possible states: *signaled* or *nonsignaled*. A process may block itself to wait on an nonsignaled object using the function *WaitForSingleObject*; it is resumed when some other project changes the state of that object to signaled. A process may also block itself on multiple objects using the function *WaitForMultipleObjects*. It is resumed when all the objects have been signaled.

   The possible object types include processes, threads, files, events, semaphores, timers, mutexes, and queues. The change from nonsignaled to signaled depends on the type of object. The following list summarizes the possible causes and actions:

   - A *process* object is signaled when its last thread terminates; all waiting threads are woken up;

CASE STUDY: EVENT SYNCHRONIZATION   (*continued*)

- A *thread* object is signaled when it terminates; all waiting threads are woken up;
- A *semaphore* object is signaled when the semaphore value is decremented; a single thread is woken up;
- A *mutex* object is signaled when a thread releases the mutex lock; a single thread is woken up;
- An *event* object is signaled when a thread explicitly posts this event; there are two version of this object: one wakes up all waiting threads while the other wakes up only one thread;
- A *timer* object is signaled when a timer expires; similar to an event object, a timer object may wake up all waiting threads or just one;
- A *file* object is signaled when on I/O operation on that file terminates; all waiting threads are woken up;
- A *queue* object is signaled when an item is placed on the queue; a single thread is woken up.

CONCEPTS, TERMS, AND ABBREVIATIONS

The following concepts have been introduced in this chapter. Test yourself by defining and discussing each keyword or phrase.

Bounded buffer	P and V operations
Cobegin-coend statements	Process
Critical section	Process flow graph
Event	Producer-consumer
Forall statement	Semaphore, general and binary
Fork-join statements	Starvation
Mutual exclusion	

EXERCISES

1. Show the process flow graph for the following expressions:

$$S(p_1, P(p_2, S(P(S(p_3, p_4), p_5), P(p_6, p_7))))$$

$$S(P(S(p_1, P(p_2, p_3)), p_4), p_5)$$

2. Rewrite the program below using *cobegin/coend* statements. Make sure that it exploits maximum parallelism but produces the same result as the sequential execution. Hint: Draw first the process flow graph where each line of the code corresponds to an edge. Start with the last line.

```
W = X1 * X2;
V = X3 * X4;
Y = V * X5;
Z = V * X6;
```

```
Y = W * Y;
Z = W * Z;
A = Y + Z;
```

3. The following expression describes the serial/parallel precedence relationship among six processes p_1 through p_6:

$$P(S(P(p_3, S(p_1, P(p_6, p_5))), p_2), p_4)$$

Transform this expression into a program using:
(a) *cobegin/coend*
(b) *fork, join, quit* primitives

4. Rewrite the matrix multiplication example of Section 2.2.2 to reduce the degree of parallelism as follows:
   (a) The elements of each row i are computed in parallel, but the rows are computed sequentially one at a time
   (b) The elements of each column j are computed in parallel, but the columns are computed sequentially one at a time
   Under what circumstances would either of the above versions of the program be preferable to the one given in the text, where all elements of the matrix are computed in parallel?

5. The following function sorts the elements of an array $A[n]$ in place using a recursive two-way merge-sort. Assume that the function *merge()* merges the two subranges $A[lo, mid]$ and $A[mid + 1, hi]$ of the array A.

```
void mergesort(int A[], int lo, int hi) {
    int mid;
    if (lo < hi) {
        mid = (lo + hi) / 2;
        mergesort(A, lo, mid);
        mergesort(A, mid+1, hi);
        merge(A, lo, mid, mid+1, hi);
    }
}
```

   Rewrite the function using *fork, join, quit* such that the two invocations of *mergesort()* are executed in parallel.

6. Why must most of the *join* operation be indivisible?

7. Consider the CS problem of Section 2.3.1. Show all possible interleavings of the three machine instructions executed on a uniprocessors by the processes p_1 and p_2 that result in an incorrect value of x.

8. Consider the last software solution to the mutual exclusion problem (Section 2.3.1).
   (a) Assume process $p1$ is inside $CS1$. What are the values of $c1$, $c2$, and *will_wait* that prevent $p2$ from entering its critical section?
   (b) Assume that both processes have just entered the while-loop immediately preceding their respective critical sections. What are the values of $c1$, $c2$, and *turn* at that point? What guarantees that exactly one process will be able to proceed?
   (c) Assume process $p1$ terminates. What are the values of $c1$, $c2$, and *turn* that allow $p2$ to continue entering its critical section repeatedly?

9. Consider the last software solution to the mutual exclusion problem (Section 2.3.1). Assume that process p_1 sets the *will_wait* flag to 2 (instead of 1), indicating that

p_2 should wait if necessary. Similarly, p_2 sets the *will_wait* flag to 1 (instead of 2), indicating that p_1 should wait if necessary. No other changes are made to the program. Will this still prevent mutual exclusion?

10. Generalize the last software solution to the mutual exclusion problem (Section 2.3.1) to work with three processes. (Hint: Use two stages. During the first stage, one of the three processes is held back. During the second stage, the remaining two processes compete with each other and one is held back.)

11. Use semaphores to describe the synchronization of the eight processes in the general precedence graph of Figure 2-1d.

12. What is the effect of interchanging:
    (a) $P(b)$ and $P(e)$ or
    (b) $V(b)$ and $V(f)$
    in the producer process in the Bounded Buffer example of Section 2.4.3?

13. A simple batch OS may be described as a set of three processes interacting as follows:

```
process BATCH_OS;
 ...
    process reader;
    begin
        while(1)
            read record from input device;
            deposit record in input_buffer
    end;

    process main;
    begin
        while(1)
            fetch record from input_buffer;
            process record and generate output line;
            deposit line in output_buffer
    end;

    process printer;
    begin
        while(1)
            fetch line from output_buffer;
            print line on output device
    end
end
```

Modify and augment the batch OS above using semaphore operations to properly buffer the input data that flows from the reader to the main function, and the output data that flows from main to the printer.

14. The following code spawns $n - 1$ concurrent processes. Each process i repeatedly updates the elements $A[i]$ and $B[i]$ of two shared arrays.

```
int A[n], B[n];
A[0] = init();
forall (i:1..(n-1)) {
    while (not_done) {
        A[i] = f(A[i], A[i-1]);
```

```
                B[i] = g(A[i])
            }
        }
```

Since computing $A[i]$ uses $A[i-1]$, each process i must wait for its predecessor process $i-1$ to complete the computation of $A[i-1]$. Insert the necessary semaphore operations into the code to guarantee that processes wait for each other to guarantee the correctness of the program, but allow for as much overlap between the computations as possible. Also show the initial values of all semaphores used. Hint: Declare an array of semaphores $s[n-1]$.

15. Consider the following two functions, where A and B are arbitrary computations:

```
f1() {                          f2() {
    P(s1);                          P(s2);
    c1 = c1 + 1;                    c2 = c2 + 1;
    if (c1 == 1) P(d);             if (c2 == 1) P(d);
    V(s1);                          V(s2);
    A;                              B;
    P(s1);                          P(s2);
    c1 = c1 - 1;                    c2 = c2 - 1;
    if (c1 == 0) V(d);             if (c2 == 0) V(d);
    V(s1);                          V(s2);
}                               }
```

Initially: s1=s2=d=1; c1=c2=0;
Assume that an unbounded number of processes are invoking either of the functions $f1()$ or $f2()$.

(a) How many invocations of the computation A can proceed concurrently? What are the values of $s1$, $c1$, and d at that time?

(b) While A is running, how many invocations of B can proceed concurrently? What are the values of $s2$, $c2$, and d at that time?

(c) Can A or B starve? Explain why or why not.

16. Simulate the traffic at an intersection of two one-way streets using semaphore operations. In particular, the following rules should be satisfied:

• Only one car can be crossing at any given time;

• When a car reaches the intersection and there are no cars approaching from the other street, it should be allowed to cross;

• When cars are arriving from both directions, they should take turns to prevent indefinite postponement of either direction.

C H A P T E R 3

Higher-Level Synchronization and Communication

3.1 SHARED MEMORY METHODS
3.2 DISTRIBUTED SYNCHRONIZATION AND COMMUNICATION
3.3 OTHER CLASSIC SYNCHRONIZATION PROBLEMS

The main objections to semaphores and events—the synchronization mechanisms introduced in the last chapter—are that they are too low level and do not support the elegant structuring of concurrent programs. For example, they do not permit a segment of code to be designated explicitly as a critical section (CS). Rather, the effect of a CS must be enforced by correctly using the semaphore operations, i.e., by enclosing the desired segment between a pair of P and V operations and presetting the corresponding semaphore to 1, or by employing a *mutex_lock* and *mutex_unlock* pair correctly. Violating any of these rules will destroy the desired effect.

Since P and V operations may be used anywhere in a program, the task of understanding and verifying the desired behavior of programs becomes very difficult. One common error that is usually extremely difficult to detect is the omission of a required V operation from a program or its mere bypassing when execution follows some unexpected path; this could result in a situation where processes are blocked forever—a situation commonly referred to as **deadlock**. Equally dangerous and common is an unintentional execution of a V operation, permitting, e.g., more than one process to enter a CS.

The first part of the chapter presents several constructs that are used as alternatives to the low-level semaphore and event operations. These are based on ideas from abstract data types and objects. The aim is to concentrate and encapsulate all accesses to a shared resource, including any required synchronization. These mechanisms assume that processes *share* parts of main memory.

However, it is not always desirable or possible that processes share some portion of memory. For example, it is sound software engineering practice to encapsulate program entities, including processes, as a way to improve understanding, analysis, and reusability. Shared memory is in conflict with this principle. For security reasons, processes often must run in isolation, each in its own logical space, with all interactions under strict control of the participating process. Another reason for alternatives to shared memory constructs is the increasing importance and use of distributed systems. In such environments, each processor may have only its own local memory; consequently, there can be no direct data sharing among processes running on different processors. For these reasons, distributed schemes for interprocess communication (IPC) and synchronization are commonly available.

The most common distributed approaches, message passing and procedure-based interactions, are the subjects of the second part of this chapter. The distributed schemes we discuss are usable and frequently used on shared memory architectures; conversely, shared memory methods are often simulated on distributed architectures. The final sections of this chapter describe and solve several famous and classical synchronization problems.

3.1 SHARED MEMORY METHODS

The two most interesting, useful, and popular constructs for higher-level, shared memory synchronization are **monitors** and **protected types**.

3.1.1 Monitors

Hoare Monitors

The monitor concept (Hoare 1974; Brinch Hansen 1973b) follows the principles of abstract data types. For any distinct data type, there is a well-defined set of operations through which, and *only* through which, any instance of that data type is manipulated. Following this idea, a monitor is defined as a collection of data representing the state of the resource controlled by the monitor, and a set of procedures to manipulate that resource data.

The implementation of the monitor construct must guarantee the following:

1. Access to the resource is possible only via one of the monitor procedures.
2. Procedures are mutually exclusive; i.e., at any given time, only one process may be executing a procedure within a given monitor. The jargon is that only one process or thread may be *inside* a given monitor at a time. During that time, other processes calling a procedure of this same monitor are delayed until the process leaves the monitor.

A monitor, as defined above, is sufficient to implement a CS by preventing simultaneous access to a resource. However, it does not provide any means for processes to communicate or synchronize with one another. For this purpose, monitors introduce a special type of variable called a **condition variable**. Two operations, *wait* and *signal*, operate on condition variables and can only be used inside monitor procedures.

An operation *wait* on a condition variable c will be denoted as:

```
c.wait.
```

It causes the executing process to be suspended (blocked) and placed on a queue associated with the condition variable c. The blocked process releases the mutual exclusion lock of the monitor so that some other process can now execute a procedure of that monitor, i.e., "enter" the monitor. Performing the *signal* operation on c, written as:

```
c.signal,
```

wakes up one (if any) of the processes waiting on c, placing it on a queue of processes wanting to reenter the monitor and resume execution after the *wait*. Here, we assume that the process that has waited the longest will be awakened. If no processes are waiting, a *signal* acts as a null operation, much like a memoryless *post* of an event.

Condition variables are not variables in the classical sense, i.e., there is no value associated with one. Rather, each condition variable may be viewed as a *name* chosen by the programmer to refer to a specific event, state of a computation, or assertion. To illustrate this idea, assume that a process may proceed only when some variable, e.g., *X*, has a value greater than zero. We can define a condition variable, e.g., *X_is_positive*, and use it to exchange information about the truth value of the expression "*X* > 0" among different processes. Whenever a process, e.g., *p*, finds this value to be *false*, it performs the operation *X_is_positive.wait*, which suspends that process on a queue associated with *X_is_positive*. Figure 3-1a illustrates the effect of *wait*. When another process, e.g., *q*, changes the content of *X* to a positive value, it may inform the suspended process of this event by performing the operation *X_is_positive.signal*. Figure 3-1b shows this situation. Note that the condition variable *X_is_positive* does not actually contain the value *true* or *false* of the expression *X* > 0; the logic of the monitor code must explicitly test for the desired condition.

There is one important issue surrounding the meaning or semantics of the *signal* operation. Since it is used to indicate that a condition associated with some condition variable *c* on which some process *p* may be suspended, is now satisfied, there may be

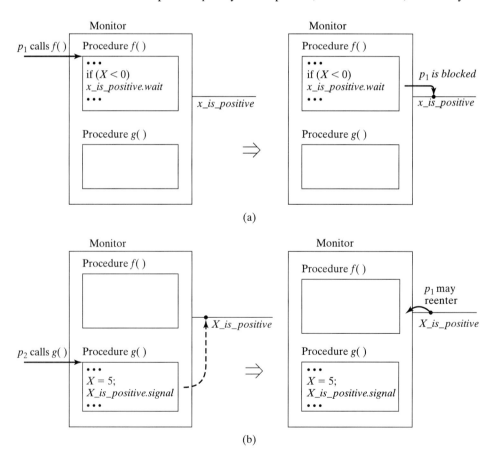

FIGURE 3-1. A monitor (a) effect of *wait*; and (b) the effect of *signal*.

two processes eligible to run inside the monitor after a *signal* is issued: (1) the process executing the *signal* (process *q* in Fig. 3-1), and (2) process *p* that previously issued the *wait* and is now selected for reactivation. By the monitor definition, only one process may be active inside a monitor at any one time; thus, one of the two processes must wait. In the original proposal, Hoare defined the semantics of the *signal* operation such that the process executing *signal* is suspended and *p* immediately reenters the monitor where it last left off (i.e., immediately after the *wait*). The suspended process *q* is then assigned the highest priority and reenters the monitor as soon as the previously reactivated process *p* leaves the monitor, either through a normal exit or by blocking itself with a *wait* operation.

The rationale behind the above choice is that *p* is waiting because some condition *B* or assertion, such as $X > 0$, is not satisfied, and the signaling process sets *B* to *true* immediately before issuing the *signal*. Consequently, *p* can be assured that nothing will change *B* between the time of the signal and the time it regains control of the monitor. Many other alternatives to implementing condition signaling exist. We will examine one popular choice in the next section.

EXAMPLE: Monitor Solution to the Bounded-Buffer Problem

Consider the bounded-buffer problem described in the last chapter. Let each element of the buffer be a single character, and implement the shared data area as an array of characters. The monitor, called *Bounded_Buffer*, exports two operations, *deposit* and *remove*, which insert and remove, respectively, one character. The synchronization conditions are represented by the condition variables *notempty* and *notfull*; these refer to the state of the buffer: not empty and not full, respectively. Thus, for example, a *deposit* will not be permitted to proceed until the buffer is not full.

```
monitor Bounded_Buffer {
    char buffer[n];
    int nextin=0, nextout=0, full_cnt=0;
    condition notempty, notfull;

deposit(char c) {
    if (full_cnt==n) notfull.wait;
    buffer[nextin] = c;
    nextin = (nextin + 1) % n;
    full_cnt = full_cnt+1;
    notempty.signal;
}

remove(char c) {
    if (full_cnt==0) notempty.wait;
    c = buffer[nextout];
    nextout = (nextout + 1) % n;
    full_cnt = full_cnt - 1;
    notfull.signal;
}
}
```

The two monitor procedures may be invoked by any process through the calls *Bounded_Buffer.deposit(data)* and *Bounded_Buffer.remove(data)*, respectively, where *data* is a variable of type *char*. If *full_cnt* is zero when *remove* is called, the process will block on the *notempty.wait*, and remain blocked until another process deposits a character and issues a *notempty.signal*. Similarly, a process calling *deposit* when *full_cnt* equals *n* will wait on *notfull.wait* until another process later does a *remove* thereby issuing *notfull.signal*. (The percent sign denotes a modulo *n* operation.)

Priority Waits

When more than one process is waiting on the same condition, a *signal* will cause the longest waiting process to be resumed. (This is the usual implementation.) There are many cases where simple first-come/first-served scheduling is not adequate. To give a closer control over scheduling strategy, Hoare (1974) introduced a **conditional** (or scheduled) *wait*, which includes a priority for the waiting process. This has the form:

$$c.\text{wait}(p)$$

where *c* is the condition variable on which the process is to be suspended, and *p* is an integer expression defining a priority. When the condition *c* is signaled and there is more than one process waiting, the one which specified the *lowest* value of *p* is resumed.

EXAMPLE: Alarm Clock

The following example of an alarm clock illustrates the use of priority waits. *Alarm_Clock* enables a process to delay itself for a specified number of clock "ticks," by calling the procedure *wakeme*. A second operation, *tick*, updates the clock and signals *wakeme*.

```
monitor Alarm_Clock {
    int now=0;
    condition wakeup;

wakeme(int n) {
    int alarmsetting;
    alarmsetting = now + n;
    while (now<alarmsetting) wakeup.wait(alarmsetting);
    wakeup.signal;    /* In case more than one process is to */
                      /* wake up at the same time. */
}

tick() {
    now = now + 1;
    wakeup.signal;
}
}
```

The *wakeme* procedure presets the wakeup time to *now+n* and suspends the calling process until the current time *now* is equal to or exceeds *alarmsetting*. The priority associated with the suspended process provides the basis for the alarm-setting value.

The *tick* function is assumed to be invoked automatically by hardware (e.g., through an interrupt) at regular intervals. It increments the value of the current time *now*, and wakes up the process with the lowest alarm setting time. The awakened process compares the time with its *alarmsetting*. If *now* is less than *alarmsetting*, it goes back to sleep by executing the same *wait* operation; otherwise, it performs a *signal* operation to wake up the next process in the queue, which might have its alarm preset to the same time.

Mesa and Java Monitors

The *signal* operation as defined above causes the current process to be suspended immediately whenever another process is awakened. A simple variant of *signal* is the *notify* primitive, defined for the programming language Mesa (Lampson and Redell 1980). *Notify* does not suspend the current process (the notifier). It only indicates to a waiting process, without actually activating it, that the corresponding condition has been satisfied; *notify* does this by inserting the waiting process on a queue ready to reenter the monitor. The waiting process is resumed sometime after the current process exits the monitor.

In this scheme, however, a process suspended because of a particular condition *B* was found *false* cannot be guaranteed that the condition will still be *true* when the process resumes execution. To understand why such a guarantee cannot be given, consider two processes, p_1 and p_2, both of which are currently blocked as a result of executing the statements:

```
if (!B1) c1.wait;
```

and:

```
if (!B2) c2.wait;
```

respectively. Assume that the process currently executing inside the monitor causes both conditions to become *true* and indicates this fact by executing the statements *c1.notify* and *c2.notify*. When it exits the monitor, one of the waiting processes, e.g., p_1, will be permitted to reenter the monitor. During its execution and *after* the *notify* was issued, p_1 may modify the contents of any variable inside the monitor, possibly making the condition *B2 false* again. It is also possible that another process enters the monitor after p_1 leaves. Consequently, when p_2 is permitted to reenter, it cannot assume *B2* to be *true*. Rather, it must reevaluate *B2* to determine its current value and, if *false*, suspend itself again.

In general, *wait* statements should be enclosed in a loop of the form:

```
while (!B) c.wait;
```

instead of writing:

```
if (!B) c.wait;
```

as would be done in monitors using *signal*. While apparently more complex than the Hoare *signal* semantics, the *notify* definitions admit to a more efficient implementation, may result in fewer context switches, and also can be used without explicit condition variables. The cost is decreased performance, due to looping and testing.

Another version of *notify* appears as part of the monitorlike facility defined in the popular Java language (Lea 1997). To control the sharing of data within an object, the particular methods or operations on the object are declared *synchronized*. Threads that access an object through "synchronized" methods do so in a mutually exclusive fashion, much like monitor procedures. Within synchronized object methods, *wait* and *notify* primitives may be employed for synchronization. However, there are no condition variables in Java; equivalently, each object can be viewed as having one (implicit) condition variable.

Both Mesa and Java also have a *broadcast* form of *notify* that awakens *all* threads that are blocked, instead of just one. Another useful feature available in both languages is a *timeout* parameter that may be associated with a *wait*. If a thread fails to be "notified" by the specified time, it still unblocks. Such timeouts are very useful for detecting errors, such as deadlocks or runaway processes.

3.1.2 Protected Types

The synchronization primitives of monitors, *wait* and *signal* or *notify*, may be distributed throughout the procedure code. It is also necessary to insert explicit tests before each *wait*. However, in almost all applications, the test and *wait* occur, if at all, in the first executed statement of a monitor procedure. A *signal* or *notify*, if issued, occurs as the last-executed statement. Protected types, as defined in the Ada95 language (ADA 1995), are an attractive alternative to monitors that take advantage of this common behavioral pattern. They do so by factoring out the waiting condition at the start of a procedure and providing an implicit signal at the end. The ideas underlying protected types are a combination of those appearing in monitors and conditional critical regions (Hoare 1972; Brinch Hansen 1973).

A protected type is an encapsulated object with public access procedures called *entries*. Each procedure (entry) may have an associated Boolean **guard**, which is a condition that must evaluate to *true* before the procedure is eligible for execution. A condition is reevaluated when a procedure exits a protected type and only if there are one or more tasks queued or blocked on that condition. Like monitor procedures, protected-type procedures are also mutually exclusive; only one procedure at a time can be executed.

EXAMPLE: Bounded Buffer

To illustrate these notions, we use the standard example of a bounded buffer, as specified in the last section. An object is defined in two parts: a specification that declares the exported procedures and data, and an implementation that lists the code or *body* of the object.

For the bounded buffer, the specification part describes the *deposit* and *remove* interfaces, and the internal or *private* data of the *Bounded_Buffer* object:

```
protected Bounded_Buffer {
    entry deposit(char data);
    entry remove(char data);
private
    char buffer[n];
    int nextin=0,nextout=0,full_cnt=0;
}
```

In the implementation part, each entry starts with the keyword *when*. For example, the condition for *deposit* is the expression *when (full_cnt < n)*; thus, a call on *deposit* will not be permitted to proceed until *full_cnt < n*. The body of the protected type is:

```
protected body Bounded_Buffer {

    entry deposit(char c)
        when (full_cnt < n) {
            buffer[nextin] = c;
            nextin = (nextin + 1) % n;
            full_cnt = full_cnt + 1;
        }

    entry remove(char c)
        when (full_cnt > 0) {
            c = buffer[nextout];
            nextout = (nextout + 1) % n;
            full_cnt = full_cnt - 1;
        }

}
```

In addition to procedures, protected types also support functions. The distinction is significant. Procedures may modify the private variables and must be executed under mutual exclusion. Functions, on the other hand, only return values. They have no side effects, i.e., they cannot modify any variables private to the protected type. Consequently, they can be executed in parallel. This constraint—concurrent function execution, one-at-a-time procedure execution, and mutual exclusion between function and procedure executions—is called a *readers/writers* constraint. (This type of problem is discussed further in Section 3.3.1.)

3.2   DISTRIBUTED SYNCHRONIZATION AND COMMUNICATION

The synchronization mechanisms presented so far assume that processes share some portion of memory. For centralized systems where process isolation and encapsulation is desirable (e.g., for security reasons and for distributed systems where processes may reside on different nodes in a network), IPC typically occurs through either message passing or remote procedure calls. Both techniques are described in the following sections. Section 3.2.3 covers the important application of distributed mutual exclusion.

3.2.1   Message-Based Communication

Probably the most common form of IPC is message passing, with some variant of *send* and *receive* operations. Unlike shared-memory primitives, such as the *P* and *V* operations on semaphores, there is not a universally accepted definition of *send* and *receive*. Depending on a particular system, many different interpretations may be found. A generic form of these two primitives is:

```
send(p, m)

receive(q, m)
```

The operation *send()* causes the message, stored in or pointed to by the variable *m*, to be transmitted to the process *p*. The *receive()* operation is used to obtain a message. It names the process *q* from which a message is expected; when the message arrives, it is deposited in the variable *m*. Generally, the message could be arbitrary data, such as a string of binary bits, or it could be a strongly typed object. Some implementations permit the parameters *p* or *q* to be omitted.

One way to extract and understand the many possibilities for defining *send* and *receive* is to answer some fundamental questions:

1. When a message is emitted, must the sending process wait until the message has been accepted by the receiver or can it continue processing immediately after emission?

2. What should happen when a *receive* is issued and there is no message waiting?

3. Must the sender name exactly one receiver to which it wishes to transmit a message or can messages be simultaneously sent to a group of receiver processes?

4. Must the receiver specify exactly one sender from which it wishes to accept a message or can it accept messages arriving from any member of a group of senders?

There are two possible answers to the first question. If the sending process is blocked until the message is accepted, the *send* primitive is called **blocking** or **synchronous**. On the other hand, the process may proceed while the message is being transferred to the destination process, the *send* is said to be **nonblocking** or **asynchronous**.

The second question distinguishes two types of *receive* operations, analogous to the blocking and nonblocking *send*. In the first case, if a *receive* is issued and there is no message waiting, the process is blocked; such a *receive* is called *blocking* or *synchronous*. The second alternative is to permit the receiving process to continue when no messages are waiting; this variant of *receive* is called *nonblocking* or *asynchronous*.

The last two questions address the problem of naming. A process may wish to transmit a message nonselectively to any of a number of processes that may wish to receive it. This operation is usually referred to as **broadcasting** or *send* with **implicit naming**, because there may be many potential receiving processes and they are not named explicitly. A restricted but widespread form of broadcast is the **multicast** *send* that transmits a message to all members of a named group of processes. Similarly, a process may receive messages from any of a number of possible senders, depending on their order of arrival. A *receive* with *implicit naming* is used for this purpose.

The semantics of various *send/receive* primitives can be summarized as follows (Shatz 1984):

send	blocking	nonblocking
explicit naming	Send message m to receiver r. Wait until message is accepted.	Send message m to receiver r.
implicit naming	Broadcast message m. Wait until message is accepted.	Broadcast message m.

receive	blocking	nonblocking
explicit naming	Wait for message from sender s.	If there is a message from sender s, then receive it; otherwise proceed.
implicit naming	Wait for message from any sender.	If there is a message from any sender, then receive it; otherwise proceed.

Combinations of the above primitives may be provided to implement a variety of different facilities for process interactions. Blocking *send/receive* primitives are powerful mechanisms for solving a variety of process coordination problems. This is because both the sender and receiver are fully synchronized at the point of communication. The receiving process knows that the sender will continue *only* after the message has been accepted; the sender knows that at its continuation point, the message has been safely received. In the case of *send*, the blocking version with implicit naming is of little practical use because of the complexities of synchronizing a broadcasted *send* with *all* possible receivers; hence, broadcasting is usually done in the nonblocking form. On the other hand, the blocking versions of *receive* are both very useful and much more common than their nonblocking forms. For example, consider a server process such as a printer, a stand-alone buffer processes, or a file server, which accepts service request messages from clients. The natural form of *receive* is blocking with implicit naming, since the server should accept messages from any of a group of clients, perhaps not known in advance.

CASE STUDY: SYSTEM V

The V distributed system (Cheriton 1988) is one example that includes blocking operations for IPC. Their basic scheme involves a pair of synchronous *send/receive* operations of short fixed-length messages (32 bytes). A client outputs a message using a blocking *send*; a server accepts a message with a blocking *receive* and later transmits a *reply* message. The client issues a *receive* operation and remains blocked until it receives the reply. This sequence of events occurs most commonly in the higher-level *remote procedure call* interaction that we present in the next section. System V also supports prominently a multicast facility.

The nonblocking operations with explicit naming are also important and have many applications. However, they are at a higher level than the blocking ones since they require a form of built-in buffering to hold all sent messages not yet requested by a receiving process. Here, the bounded-buffer problem is solved implicitly within the primitives themselves. Because, by definition, there is no waiting with the nonblocking *send* and *receive*, these operations do not have the flavor of synchronization primitives but provide the functions of a more general "mailing" facility. Both types of problem—synchronization and the asynchronous exchange of messages—are important in a general-purpose computing facility; thus many operating systems (OS) provide several different versions of *send* and *receive* to satisfy the needs of different users.

Message Channels, Ports, and Mailboxes

Several indirect forms of message passing exist, wherein processes communicate through a named intermediary rather than directly. One common form uses **named channels** as the intermediary. These are abstractions of wires or other media (e.g., radio waves) that may connect processes. A process communicates with another by sending a message over a particular channel, and a receiver obtains a message from a specific channel. In general, there may be many channels connecting processes; the channels could be unidirectional or bidirectional, and the communications could be synchronous or asynchronous. In the latter case, the channel requires some memory to act as a buffer.

The best known example of a named-channel system is the implementation of Hoare's *communicating sequential processes* (CSP) in the Occam language (Hoare 1978, 1984; Inmos 1984, 1988). In CSP/Occam, channels are unidirectional, messages are typed, and communication is synchronous.

For example, suppose that channel *ch1* connects process p_1 to p_2, and can carry messages of type *char*. p_1 could send the character "a" to p_2 with the command[1]:

$$\texttt{send(ch1, ''a'');}$$

p_2 accepts the message with the command:

$$\texttt{receive(ch1, x);}$$

using a variable *x* of type *char*. p_1 will wait until p_2 is ready to receive, and p_2 waits until p_1 is ready to send. Communication occurs instantaneously, if and when it occurs. At that point, *x* is assigned the value *"a"*, and both processes continue in execution.

To simplify the use of the communication primitives, receive statements may be implemented in the form of **guarded commands** (Dijkstra 1975). These are similar to the *when* clauses defined with protected types (Section 3.1.2). The syntax of the guarded commands is:

$$\texttt{when (C) S}$$

where *C* is an arbitrary Boolean expression and *S* is a set of executable statements. The expression *C* is called the **guard**. As with protected types, the statements in *S* are executed only when the expression *C* evaluates to *true*. The difference is that *C* also may contain *receive* statements. These evaluate to *true* only if the sending process is ready to execute the corresponding *send* on the same channel. Several guarded input commands may be enabled at the same time and are potentially executable. One is selected arbitrarily; the others have no effect. This feature of CSP is a form of a "selective input," similar to the selective accept statement of Ada presented in the next section. It permits processes to communicate in a nondeterministic fashion, depending on the availability of input data at run time. The CSP/Occam ideas are illustrated with our bounded-buffer example.

EXAMPLE: Bounded Buffer with CSP/Occam

Since all send and receive primitives are blocking, we have the following problem: When the buffer is completely full, it can only send data to the consumer. Similarly, when the

---

[1]We use a different syntax than that of CSP or Occam, mainly because their syntax is relatively unusual.

buffer is completely empty, it can only receive data from the producer. The problem occurs when the buffer is partially filled. In this case, its action depends on whether the producer is ready to send more data or the consumer is ready to receive any data. Determining whether the producer is ready can be solved by embedding the receive statement in a guarded clause. Determining whether the consumer is ready can be done only by asking the consumer to first send a request to the buffer, followed by the data-receiving statement. The buffer may then detect the presence of a request by embedding its request-receiving statement in a guarded clause.

The complete protocol is as follows: We define three channels, *deposit, request*, and *remove*, named to reflect their purpose. They are used as follows: The producer process inserts an element named *data* into the buffer by sending it on the channel named *deposit* to the process *Bounded_Buffer*:

```
send(deposit, data);
```

The consumer process requires two communications to perform its function. First, it sends a request to *Bounded_Buffer* on the channel named *request* and follows this by a *receive* command on the *remove* channel.

```
send(request);
receive(remove, data);
```

Note that the *send* has an empty message; it is sufficient that *Bounded_Buffer* just receives a signal on the *request* channel. The received message is stored in the variable *data*.

The buffer process takes the following form:

```
process Bounded_Buffer {
    message buffer[n];
    int nextin=0, nextout=0, full_cnt=0;
    while (1) {
        when ((full_cnt < n) && receive(deposit, buffer[nextin])) {
            nextin = (nextin + 1) % n;
            full_cnt = full_cnt + 1;
        }
        or
        when ((full_cnt > 0) && receive(request)) {
            send(remove, buffer[nextout]);
            nextout = (nextout + 1) % n;
            full_cnt = full_cnt - 1;
        }
    }
}
```

The two *when* clauses separated by *or* indicate possible nondeterministic selection. If *full_cnt* is neither 0 nor *n*, and *send*s are pending on both the *request* and *deposit* channels, then one of the *send*s is selected arbitrarily, and the code following the guard is executed.

In the absence of *receive* primitives with *implicit* naming or the guarded input commands used in CSP/Occam, a process is limited to only one potential source of messages at any given time. If the *receive* is nonblocking, it can be embedded into a "busy-wait" loop to simulate the effect of implicit naming. However, this solution is quite inefficient. A common way to avoid the limitations of explicit naming which does not suffer from the performance problem of busy-waiting is to use *indirect* communication with queues or buffers. The basic idea is to make visible to the processes those queues holding messages between senders and receivers. That is, a *send* primitive does not use the name of a process as its destination; rather, it addresses the queue to which the message is to be appended. Similarly, a receiving process names the queue from which a message is to be accepted.

A queue that can be named by more than one sender and more than one receiver process is called a **mailbox**. This scheme is illustrated in Figure 3-2a. Mailboxes provide the most general communication facility, because any of the *n* senders may emit messages that may be intercepted by any of the *m* receivers. Unfortunately, in a distributed environment, the implementation of the *receive* operation can be costly, because *receives* referring to the same mailbox may reside on different computers. Therefore, a limited form of a mailbox, usually called a **port**, is frequently implemented. A port is associated with only one receiver. Messages that come from different processes but address the same port are sent to one central place associated with the receiver, as shown in Figure 3-2b.

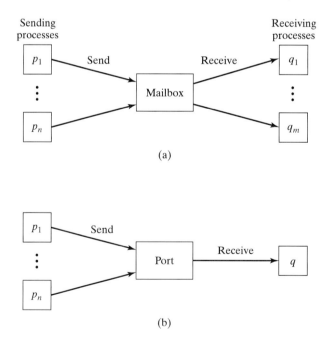

FIGURE 3-2. Indirect process communication: (a) through a mailbox; and (b) through a port.

CASE STUDY: UNIX IPC

Pipes are the standard IPC scheme on uniprocessors in UNIX systems (e.g., [Lefler et al. 1989]). A pipe may be used to connect two or more processes into a sequence of the form:

$$p1 \ | \ p2 \ | \ \ldots \ | \ pn$$

where each vertical bar represents a pipe. It connects the standard input of the process on the left to the standard output of the process on the right. Thus, a pipe can be interpreted as an unnamed communication channel with memory that handles variable-length messages of byte streams.

The more elaborate facilities that are defined for distributed UNIX systems employ **sockets**. Sockets are named endpoints of a two-way communication channel that may be established between two processes running on different machines. To establish a channel, one of the processes acts as a server, whereas the other acts as a client. The server first binds its socket to the IP address of its machine and a port number; this becomes the incoming communication channel on which the server listens. By issuing an *accept* statement, the server blocks until the client issues a corresponding *connect* statement. The *connect* statement supplies the client's address and port number to complete the two-way communication channel. Both processes may then send data to each other via this dynamically established connection.

3.2.2 Procedure-Based Communication

One problem with the *send/receive* primitives is their low level. The programmer is forced to abandon the structuring concepts of procedures and other high-level modules, and use these message passing primitives in much the same way as one uses P and V operations on semaphores. **Remote Procedure Calls** (RPC) and **rendezvous** have been proposed as higher-level mechanisms for process communication to overcome this problem. They also provide a natural way to program client/server interactions, which are the basis of many distributed applications. A client requests a service by invoking an RPC or performing a rendezvous with a service procedure, which may reside on another machine or node of a network.

As far as the calling process is concerned, both RPC and rendezvous have the same effect as regular procedure calls. Each transfers control to another procedure while suspending the caller; a return statement executed by the called procedure then transfers control back to the caller, where execution continues with the instruction following the call. Consequently, the called procedure may be viewed as a service invoked by the caller, i.e., the client.

Ideally, the caller should not be aware of the fact that the called procedure is remote. However, the fact that the caller and the procedure are on different machines cannot be made completely transparent. The main distinction between regular procedures and remote procedures is the inability to pass pointers as parameters to the remote procedure. This is because the client and the server do not share any memory. To exchange information, the calling procedure must pass copies of all input parameters to the called procedure. Similarly, results are returned to the caller as explicit copies of the values.

At the implementation level, remote procedures are quite different from regular procedures. Since a remote procedure executes in a separate address space on a different computer, it cannot become part of the calling process. Rather, a separate process must execute the called procedure. This process may be created dynamically at each call or statically as a dedicated service.

Assume that a client issues the call:

$$res = f(params)$$

where f is a remote procedure. In the simplest implementation, a permanent process, e.g., *RP_server*, contains the code for the remote procedure f and repeatedly executes this embedded code for each call. Coordination of the caller and callee processes can be accomplished using the low-level *send/receive* primitives. Each remote call by a client is implemented as a pair of synchronous *send* and *receive* statements. The client initiates the call by transmitting the function name and the necessary input parameters (*params*) to the server; the server executes the specified function, f, locally, and returns the results (*res*) to the client. This implementation is illustrated by the following code skeleton:

```
Calling Process:                    Server Process:

                                    process RP_server {
...                                     while (1) {
send(RP_server, f,params);                  receive(caller, f,params);
...                                         res = f(params);
receive(RP_server, results);                send(caller, res);
...                                     }
                                    }
```

Now consider how such procedure-based communications can be incorporated into a high-level language. Doing so greatly expands the applicability of remote procedures. With the RPC scheme as described so far, the interaction is always asymmetric: a dedicated server must be set up, whose sole purpose is to accept calls from clients and to execute their remote procedure requests. In contrast, allowing any process to accept remote calls from other processes results in a general IPC and coordination mechanism. The receiving process is able to perform arbitrary computations on its own, prior to or following any calls. It may also maintain its own state between any calls. Finally, the mechanism is fully symmetrical: Any process may play the role of a client by invoking a remote procedure in another process, and any process may play the role of a server by accepting remote calls.

To implement such a scheme, generally referred to as *rendezvous*, we must provide mechanisms for clients to issue remote procedure calls and for servers to accept them. We describe the approach taken in Ada (Ada 1995), which pioneered the rendezvous concept. From the calling process perspective, calling a remote procedure is similar to calling a local procedure; the main differences are the inability to pass pointers to a different machine and the possibility of remote machine failure. However, the receiving process must be able to express its willingness to accept a call. In the simplest case, an *accept* statement is used. This statement defines a procedure that may be invoked remotely by another process. It has the following form:

```
accept  f(params) S
```

where *f* is the procedure name, *params* are its parameters, and *S* is the procedure body. Its counterpart in the calling program is a procedure call of the form:

```
q.f(params)
```

where *q* is the name of the remote process, and *params* are the actual parameters passed to the *accept* statement.

To understand the semantics of a rendezvous, assume that *p* is the process issuing the call, and *q* is the process executing the corresponding *accept* statement.

1. If the process *p* issues the call before process *q* has reached the corresponding *accept*, *p* becomes blocked. When *q* executes the *accept* statement, it proceeds by executing the procedure body, *S*. After completion of this rendezvous, both processes continue their execution concurrently. This is illustrated in Figure 3-3a.

2. If process *q* reaches the *accept* statement before the procedure call has been issued by *p*, *q* becomes blocked. As soon as a call is made, the rendezvous takes place and *q* resumes execution. While *q* executes the procedure body *S*, process *p* is suspended. As in the first case, both processes continue concurrently upon termination of *S*. Figure 3-3b illustrates this case.

In this fully exposed form, the *accept* statement suffers from the same problem as a blocking *receive* with explicit naming. It does not permit the process executing this statement to wait selectively for the arrival of one of several possible requests. This would make sharing the code limited to a predetermined order of arrivals.

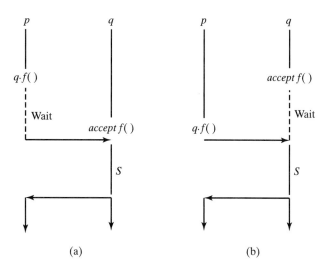

(a)   (b)

FIGURE 3-3. Execution of a rendezvous: (a) calling process is delayed; and (b) called process is delayed.

CSP/Occam solved this problem by introducing nondeterministic selective input. Similarly, Ada provides a *select* statement that permits several *accept*s to be active simultaneously. A Boolean guard also may be associated with each *accept*, which prevents its execution when its value is *false* at the time the *select* statement is executed. The *accept* statements are embedded into a *select* statement as follows[2]:

```
select {
    [when B1:]
        accept E1(...) S1 ;
    or
    [when B2:]
        accept E2(...) S2 ;
    or
    ...
    [when Bn:]
        accept En(...) Sn ;
    [else R]
}
```

The construct has the following semantics: The *when* clause, associated with each *accept* statement, is optional, as indicated by the square brackets. When omitted, its value is assumed to be *true*.

Execution of the *select* statement causes one of the embedded *accept*s to be executed. To be selected, the corresponding *when* clause must yield the value *true*, and there must be at least one pending procedure call to that *accept* statement performed by another (currently blocked) process. If there is more than one such eligible *accept* statement, the system chooses among these according to a fair internal policy. On the other hand, if none of the *accept* statements is eligible, the *else* clause containing the statement *R* is executed.

The *else* clause is optional. If it is omitted, the *select* statement behaves as follows: If none of the *when* clauses evaluates to *true*, an *error* is generated. Otherwise, the process is suspended until a call to one of the *accept* statements is performed for which the *when* clause evaluates to *true*. At this time, the body *Si* of that *accept* statement is executed and both processes continue concurrently.

EXAMPLE: Bounded Buffer

We present a solution to the Bounded Buffer problem using a selective *accept* statement. The buffering system is implemented as a separate server process:

```
process Bounded_Buffer {
...
while(1) {
    select {
        when (full_cnt < n):
            accept deposit(char c) {
                buffer[nextin] = c;
```

---

[2]We have modified the original syntax using a C-like approximation.

```
                    nextin = (nextin + 1) % n;
                    full_cnt = full_cnt + 1;
                }
        or
        when (full_cnt > 0):
            accept remove(char c) {
                c = buffer[nextout];
                nextout = (nextout + 1) % n;
                full_cnt = full_cnt - 1;
            }
        }
    }
}
```

The two operations on the buffer may be invoked by other client processes issuing the procedure calls:

Bounded_Buffer.deposit(data)

and

Bounded_Buffer.remove(data),

respectively. This code is at the same high level as the analogous version used in protected types and is slightly more abstract than the CSP/Occam version, both described in previous sections.

In summary, procedure-based communication can be considered as closing the gap between procedure-oriented synchronization schemes, such as monitors and protected types, and distributed methods based on message passing. From the programmer's point of view, remote procedures are high-level objects that fit well into the philosophy of block-structured programming languages. On the other hand, their implementation in terms of simple message-passing primitives makes them suitable to distributed environments.

3.2.3 Distributed Mutual Exclusion

The CS problem, discussed in the last chapter within the context of a shared memory architecture, also has a distributed version. In this case, we have a set of processes that share a resource in a mutually exclusive fashion, but the processes can communicate only through message passing or remote procedures. There are no shared memory, no shared clock, and possibly significant message delays. Consequently, different solution techniques are required.

The distributed CS problem arises in different situations. Several processes or nodes in a network could share some hardware resource, such as a printer, a satellite or GPS link, a special-purpose processor, or another expensive or rare piece of equipment. Similarly, some expensive software resource, such as a database or filing system, may be used by several distributed processes. The processes require mutually exclusive access to the resource. One reason is to preserve the integrity of the shared data. A less-obvious reason arises in systems where software resources, especially files, are replicated over a network so that each user process can efficiently access a nearby copy. A read access may be done using any replica, but a write request must be propagated to all replicas. One way to ensure consistency of the replicas is to enforce the mutual exclusion constraints on all write accesses.

There are several approaches to ensure distributed mutual exclusion. Perhaps the most straightforward involves a **centralized controller**. Whenever a process requires the resource, i.e., wants to enter a CS, it sends a request to the controller and waits for its request to be granted. After using the resource, it informs the controller, which then may allocate it to another waiting process. One disadvantage of this approach is that it relies on the correct operation of the controller. If the controller fails, the resource allocation fails, thus eliminating one of the benefits of distribution—resilience on failures of individual nodes. Another disadvantage of a centralized allocator is that it is potentially a performance bottleneck. Simultaneous requests by many processes can slow down the entire system.

The other extreme is a **fully distributed** approach where a process that needs the resource must engage in a lengthy arbitration involving all processes. The problems with this scheme include the large amount of message passing, a requirement for accurate time stamps on messages, and the difficulty of managing node or process failures. A practical and elegant compromise is the **token ring** method that we now develop in detail (LeLann 1977).

Assume n processes, p_0 to p_{n-1}, where each process p_i continuously loops through a critical section CS_i and a noncritical part, $program_i$. The idea of the token ring is to define a separate controller process, $controller_i$, associated with each p_i. The controllers are arranged in a circle and repeatedly pass a token from neighbor to neighbor (Fig. 3-4). The token represents the opportunity for a controlled process to enter its CS. If a process p_i wishes to enter its CS_i, it sends a request message (*Request_CS*) to $controller_i$; the controller grants the request when it receives the token, and it keeps the token while p_i

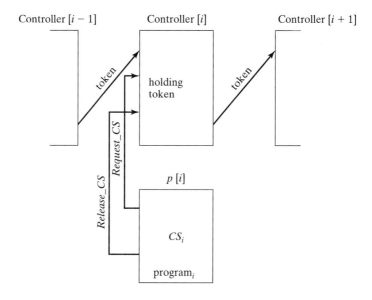

FIGURE 3-4. Distributed mutual exclusion with a token ring.

is in CS_i. The process informs its controller that it has left CS_i using a second message (*Release_CS*). The controller then passes the token on to its neighbor.

The controller algorithm and p_i skeleton are described using the selective accept statements as follows:

```
process controller[i] {
    while(1) {
        accept Token;
        select {
            accept Request_CS() {busy=1;}
            else null;
        }
        if (busy) accept Release_CS() {busy=0;}
        controller[(i+1) % n].Token;
    }
}

process p[i] {
    while(1) {
        controller[i].Request_CS();
            CSi;
        controller[i].Release_CS();
        programi;
    }
}
```

The system is represented by two arrays of processes, *p[n]* and *controller[n]*. The code for the process is straightforward. Prior to entering its CS, it issues the blocking call *Request_CS()* to its controller; after exiting the CS, it informs the controller using the call *Release_CS()*. Note that neither call has any parameters or executable body of code. Their sole purpose is to serve as synchronization signals between the process and the controller.

The passing of the token around the ring is implemented using the pairs of statements *accept Token* and *controller[(i+1) % n].Token*. Note than no real data item (token) is passed between the controllers. Instead, the token is represented by the current locus of control. At any moment in time, only one controller is active; all others are blocked on their accept Token calls.

When the controller receives the token, it checks if its process wishes to enter the CS. This is accomplished using the selective *accept* of *Request_CS*. If no call is pending, the controller executes the else clause, which is empty. The controller then immediately passes the token to its neighbor. If a call is pending, the controller accepts it and sets its *busy* flag to 1. As a result, it blocks itself by executing the statement *accept Release_CS()* until the process leaves the CS.

Mutual exclusion is clearly satisfied, because only the controller currently holding the token may grant CS entry; all others are blocked. Starvation is also not possible; once a process has issued the request, it waits for at most one complete round of the token through the other controllers, but then its controller will accept this request. The principal disadvantages are the overhead resulting from the additional controller processes and the need for continuous message passing around the token ring, even when there is no demand for a CS. Note also that a failure of a single controller will make the system inoperable. Extensions to the algorithm exist that make it more resilient against such failures.

3.3   OTHER CLASSIC SYNCHRONIZATION PROBLEMS

In the previous sections, we have used the CS problem and the bounded-buffer problem to study various approaches to process synchronization and communication, as well as the capabilities of different synchronization mechanisms. These problems are also important in their own right in concurrent programming and in OSs. In this section, we present four well-known problems that have been used extensively in the literature and are abstractions of important OS applications.

3.3.1   The Readers/Writers Problem

This problem, first formulated and solved by Courtois, Heymans, and Parnas (1971), arises when two types of processes, referred to as *readers* and *writers*, must share a common resource, such as a file. Writers are permitted to modify the state of the resource and must have exclusive access. On the other hand, readers only can interrogate the resource state and, consequently, may share the resource concurrently with an unlimited number of other readers. In addition, fairness policies must be included, for example, to prevent the indefinite exclusion or starvation of readers, writers, or both. Depending on fairness requirements, there are several different variants of the basic readers/writers problem.

In the original paper, two solutions using semaphore *P* and *V* operations were given. The first adopts the policy that readers have priority over writers. That is, no reader should be kept waiting unless a writer has already obtained the permission to use the resource. Note that this policy will result in an indefinite postponement (starvation) of writers if there is a continuous stream of read requests (see exercise 12).

CASE STUDY: READERS AND WRITERS IN LINUX

The read/write spin locks of Linux, discussed in Section 2.4.2, implement this policy. The *read_lock* macro is allowed to proceed concurrently with others, unless the resource is already locked for writing. Thus, new readers are admitted indefinitely, whereas the *write_lock* macro remains blocked until the number of readers drops to zero.

The second policy gives priority to writers. When a writer arrives, only those readers already granted permission to read will be allowed to complete their operation. All new readers arriving after the writer will be postponed until the writer's completion. This policy will result in the indefinite postponement of read requests when there is an uninterrupted stream of writers arriving at the resource.

With these two priority policies, one of the process types has absolute priority over the other. To prevent this from occurring, Hoare (1974) proposed a fairer policy, defined by the following rules:

1. A new reader should not be permitted to start during a read sequence if there is a writer waiting.

2. All readers waiting at the end of a write operation should have priority over the next writer.

We show this solution in the form of a monitor. For this problem and many others, it is convenient to add yet another function to our monitor primitives. If c is a condition variable, then the Boolean function *empty(c)* returns *false* whenever there are one or more processes waiting on the c queue as a result of a *c.wait*; it returns *true* otherwise.

The monitor provides four procedures, used by reader and writer processes as follows:

1. *start_read*: Called by a reader that wishes to read.

2. *end_read*: Called by a reader that has finished reading.

3. *start_write*: Called by a writer that wishes to write.

4. *end_write*: Called by a writer that has finished writing.

The resource itself is not part of the monitor. The monitor only guarantees that it can be accessed safely by a reader between the calls to *start_read* and *end_read*, and by a writer between the calls *start_write* and *end_write*. The monitor is implemented as follows:

```
monitor readers/writers {
    int read_cnt=0, writing=0;
    condition OK_to_read, OK_to_write;

start_read() {
    if (writing || !empty(OK_to_write)) OK_to_read.wait;
    read_cnt = read_cnt + 1;
    OK_to_read.signal;
}

end_read() {
    read_cnt = read_cnt - 1;
    if (read_cnt == 0) OK_to_write.signal;
}


start_write() {
    if ((read_cnt != 0) || writing) OK_to_write.wait;
    writing = 1;
}

end_write() {
    writing = 0;
    if (!empty(OK_to_read)) OK_to_read.signal;
    else OK_to_write.signal;
}
}
```

The variable *read_cnt* keeps track of the number of processes currently reading the resource data, whereas *writing* indicates whether a writer is currently using the resource. The Boolean condition in the first statement of *start_read* guarantees that rule 1 of the priority policy is obeyed. That is, a new reader is not admitted if there is a writer currently writing or waiting to write. The reader is blocked on the *OK_to_read* queue. The *OK_to_read.signal* in *end_write* wakes up the first waiting reader on this queue.

The *OK_to_read.signal* in *start_read* ensures that once one reader is permitted entry, all other waiting readers will follow immediately one after the other. Thus, rule 2 of the priority policy also is satisfied.

3.3.2 The Dining Philosophers Problem

To illustrate the subtleties of deadlock and indefinite postponement in process synchronization, Dijkstra (1968) formulated and proposed a solution to a toy problem that became known as the dining philosophers problem.

Five philosophers, p_i ($1 \le i \le 5$), sit around a table in the middle of which is a bowl of spaghetti. There is a plate in front of each philosopher and there are five forks, f_i ($1 \le i \le 5$), on the table, one between each two plates, as illustrated in Figure 3-5. At unspecified times, each of the philosophers may wish to eat. To do that, a philosopher p_i must first pick up the two forks f_i and $f_{(i+1)\%5}$ next to p_i's plate. Only then is p_i allowed to start eating. When p_i is finished (after a finite time), p_i places the forks back on the table. The problem is to develop a fork acquisition protocol so that none of the philosophers starve because of the unavailability of forks.

There are three main concerns when developing a solution to this problem:

1. *Deadlock:* A situation must be prevented where each philosopher obtains one of the forks and is blocked forever waiting for the other to be available.
2. *Fairness:* It should not be possible for one or more philosophers to conspire in such a way that another philosopher is prevented indefinitely from acquiring its fork.

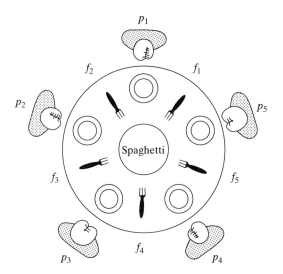

FIGURE 3-5. Five dining philosophers.

3. *Concurrency:* When one philosopher, e.g., p_1, is eating, only its two immediate neighbors (p_5 and p_2) should be prevented from eating. The others (p_3 and p_4) should not be blocked; one of these must be able to eat concurrently with p_1.

Assume that each philosopher is a process and each fork is a resource. A process $p(i)$ ($1 \le i \le 5$) loops through two phases, a thinking phase *think(i)* and an eating phase *eat(i)*, as shown in the following code skeleton:

```
p(i) {
    while (1) {
        think(i);
        grab_forks(i);
        eat(i);
        return_forks(i);
    }
}
```

The action is in the entry and exit protocols for eating, *grab_forks(i)* and *return_forks(i)*, respectively. Let us develop a solution using semaphores. The forks are represented by an array of binary semaphores $f[1], f[2], \ldots, f[5]$. The most obvious scheme has each process acquiring its left fork and then its right fork in sequence:

```
grab_forks(i): P(f[i]); P(f[(i + 1) % 5]);
return_forks(i): V(f[i]); V(f[(i + 1) % 5]);
```

This solution guarantees fairness as long as processes blocked on the same semaphore are serviced in an unbiased order, i.e., using first-in/first-out (FIFO) or a random order. Under this assumption, a philosopher blocked on a semaphore will eventually acquire this semaphore and may proceed. Concurrent execution of nonneighboring philosophers is also possible. Unfortunately, this solution can easily lead to a deadlock situation. Suppose that each process moves from its "think" phase to its "eat" phase at approximately the same time and obtains its left fork, i.e., successfully passes through its $P(f[i])$. Then they each attempt to acquire their right fork ($P(f[(i+1) \% 5])$); they will all block, waiting for their right neighbor (also blocked) to release its fork. The release will never happen, because for a process to release a fork, it must first acquire both. The processes are blocked forever; deadlock has occurred.

To avoid this deadlock, we must ensure that the circular wait described above can never occur. One easy solution is to implement a global counter (e.g., a semaphore) that allows at most $n - 1$ philosophers (i.e., 4 in the above example) to compete for their forks.

Another solution, which does not require a global semaphore, is to have one process, e.g., $p(1)$, pick up its *right* fork first instead of the left fork first. This breaks the circular condition, since two of the philosophers ($p(1)$ and $p(2)$) will be competing for the same fork $f(2)$ first, before attempting to acquire the other. Since only one will win this competition, the other will not be able to continue, and hence its other fork will remain free. Unfortunately, this solution violates the concurrency requirement: As one philosopher, e.g., $p(1)$ is eating, all others could be blocked in a chain of requests to get their respective left forks. A better solution that avoids this problem is to divide all philosophers into odd- and even-numbered ones. One group, e.g., the odd-numbered philosophers, pick up their right fork before the left; the even-numbered ones pick up their left fork first. This way, pairs of neighboring philosophers compete for the same fork, which avoids the unbounded chain of blocked processes waiting for each other.

3.3.3   The Elevator Algorithm

Consider an elevator in a multistory building. We present a monitor that governs the motion of the elevator in response to requests by people wishing to travel to other floors. (In Chapter 11, we will see how the same algorithm may be used to schedule the motion of the read/write head of a magnetic disk.)

Figure 3-6 shows the basic organization of the elevator. There are n floors, 1 being the lowest and n the highest. There are two types of control buttons. At each floor, a

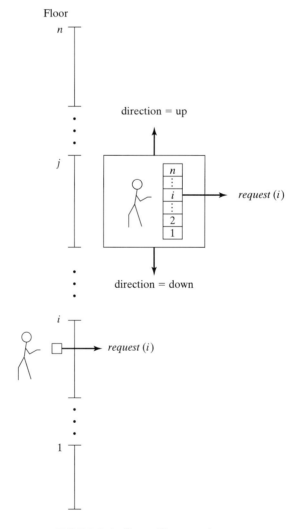

FIGURE 3-6. Controlling an elevator.

person may press a *call button* to indicate she wishes to use the elevator. (We ignore the fact that most modern elevators provide two such call buttons, one to go up and one to go down; see exercise 17.) Inside the elevator cage, a panel with buttons numbered 1 through *n* allows the person to specify which floor she wishes to move to.

The algorithm controlling the elevator is as follows. At any point in time, the elevator has a current direction of motion (up or down). It maintains this direction for as long as there are requests for floors in that direction. When there are no such requests, the current direction is reversed, and the elevator begins to service (stop at) floors in the opposite direction.

We implement this algorithm as a monitor, which accepts the following calls from the elevator hardware:

- Pressing the call button at floor *i* or pressing one of the buttons labeled *i* inside the elevator both invoke the function *request(i)*;

- Whenever the elevator door closes, the function *release()* is automatically invoked.

The monitor code is then as follows:

```
monitor elevator {
    int direction=1, up=1, down=-1, position=1, busy=0;
    condition upsweep,downsweep;

request(int dest) {
    if (busy) {
        if ((position<dest) ||
        ((position==dest) && (direction==up)))
            upsweep.wait(dest);
        else downsweep.wait(-dest);
    }
    busy = 1;
    position = dest;
}

release() {
    busy = 0;
    if (direction==up) {
        if (!empty(upsweep)) upsweep.signal;
        else {
            direction = down;
            downsweep.signal;
        }}
    else if (!empty(downsweep)) downsweep.signal;
        else {
            direction = up;
            upsweep.signal;
        }
}
```

The monitor uses the following variables:

- *position* records the current floor of the elevator (1 through *n*);

- *direction* records the current direction in which the elevator is moving (up or down);

- *busy* records the current state of the elevator; *busy==0* means the elevator is not moving, and there are no pending requests (no buttons have been pressed); *busy==1* means the elevator is servicing a request (the door is open), or it is moving to a new floor.

Whenever any button is pressed and the elevator is not busy, the *busy* flag is set to 1 and *position* is set to the requested destination floor, *dest*. The function then exits, which is interpreted by the elevator hardware as a permission to move to the new floor. If the elevator is busy when a button is pressed, the request is placed on one of two queues, *upsweep* or *downsweep*. The decision on which queue the request is placed depends on the current elevator position, the destination, and the direction of the current sweep. The following rules apply:

- When the elevator is below the requested destination, then, regardless of the current direction of motion, the request will be placed on the *upsweep* queue and served during an upsweep.

- Analogously, when the elevator is above the requested destination, the request is placed on the *downsweep* queue;

- When the elevator is at the requested destination, it should be serviced immediately, i.e., during the current stop. For example, when a person presses the button *i* when the elevator is on floor *i*, the door should open immediately, rather than waiting for the elevator to return to the same floor during the next sweep. To guarantee this, the request must be placed on the queue currently being serviced—if the direction is up, the request is placed on the *upsweep* queue; if the direction is down, it is placed on the *downsweep* queue.

Within each queue, all requests must be ordered according to the direction of travel. This is accomplished by specifying a priority for each queued request as follows:

- On the *upsweep* queue, lower-numbered floors have precedence over higher-numbered ones because they are closer to the current position; thus, the priority is given by the destination, i.e., *downsweep.wait(dest)*;

- On the downsweep, higher-numbered floors have precedence over lower-numbered ones; thus, the priority is given by the inverse of the destination *dest*, i.e., *downsweep.wait(-dest)*.

The function *release* signals one of the waiting requests (if any) to proceed. If the elevator is moving up and the *upsweep* queue is not empty, the process with the smallest priority on that queue is enabled. Similarly, on a downsweep, the smallest priority process from the *downsweep* queue is enabled. The direction of the sweep is reversed whenever the corresponding queue is empty. The Boolean function *empty(c)* is used to test whether the queue associated with the condition variable *c* is empty.

3.3.4   Event Ordering with Logical Clocks

A clock service is a fundamental component of any computer. One major difference between centralized and distributed systems is that there is no single global clock in the latter. Generally, each node in a distributed system has its own clock. These clocks may be synchronized so that their values are reasonably close to each other, but they will rarely have identical values because of various systematic errors that appear in all clock hardware, notably errors resulting from clock drift.

A particularly important application of clocks is the determination of the **causality** of events by **time-stamping**, i.e., labeling each event with its time of occurrence. An event could be, for example, the start of the execution of a program segment, allocation of a resource, sending or receiving a message, an interrupt, updating of a file, or the activation of a process. The problem is to label the events of interests so that for any two events e_1 and e_2, it is possible to tell whether e_1 preceded e_2, or vice versa, or neither.

Such a labeling is easy to do in a centralized system. We can simply attach the current clock value to the event of interest; then, if $C(e)$ is the time of event e, $C(e_1) < C(e_2)$ is true whenever e_1 precedes e_2.[3] We wish to provide such a labeling to events in a distributed system. The following example shows that a straightforward use of the clocks at each node does not always produce a correct labeling.

EXAMPLE: Labeling with Physical Clocks

Suppose that a file user U and a file server FS each reside on a separate node. The user process has a clock C_U and the server has a (different) clock C_{FS}. U updates a file by sending changes *delta1* and *delta2* to FS using an asynchronous *send* command, such as:

```
send(FS, delta1)
```

FS employs a blocking *receive*, such as:

```
receive(U, changes)
```

These processes and a set of hypothetical clock values are illustrated in Figure 3-7.

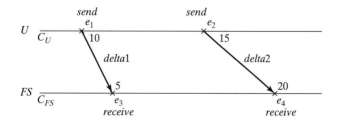

FIGURE 3-7. Distributed file updates.

---

[3]Note that the clock is assumed to be monotonically increasing; thus, it is never set back (resetting from daylight saving to standard time would destroy this monotonicity) and is never called twice in a row before it has a chance to tick at least once.

Difficulties occur because the clock values differ on the two nodes. In particular, assume that $C_U(send(FS, delta1)) = 10$ and $C_{FS}(receive(U, delta1)) = 5$. Thus, from the perspective of an external observer, the *receive* event e_3 seems to have happened before the *send* event e_1, which is not only counterintuitive, but can easily lead to errors. For example, suppose that the system was being debugged or it crashed, and a rerun or recreation was necessary. A common debugging or recovery technique assumes that a history or *log* of all significant events with their clock values is kept. Then, one essentially executes this log starting from a previous correct version of the system. Using the clock values for ordering events, our log would contain the event sequence $< e_3, e_1, e_2, e_4 >$, instead of either $< e_1, e_3, e_2, e_4 >$ or $< e_1, e_2, e_3, e_4 >$, making it impossible or extremely difficult to execute correctly.

A very simple but clever solution was developed by Lamport (1978). Time-stamping is still employed, but not using the real clocks at each node. Instead, integer counters, called **logical clocks**, provide the event-ordering labels. Associated with each process p is a logical clock L_p that is incremented when events occur. More precisely, the clock is incremented between any two successive events e_i and e_{i+1} within a given process p, thus assuring that $L_p(e_i) < L_p(e_{i+1})$. Usually, the chosen increment value is one. Thus, incrementing the clock between the two events follows the rule:

$$L_p(e_{i+1}) = L_p(e_i) + 1$$

The tricky part is to handle events that are associated with the interaction of processes on different nodes. We assume that processes interact only through message-passing using the *send* and *receive* primitives, defined as in the example above. A *send* by a process p to another process q is treated as an event, say e_s, within p. Its time-stamp is:

$$L_p(e_s) = L_p(e_i) + 1$$

where $L_p(e_i)$ is the time-stamp of the last event within p.

The corresponding *receive* is an event, say e_r, within the process q. To guarantee that this event has a greater time-stamp than e_s, process p attaches its local time-stamp $L_p(e_s)$ to the message. The receiving process, instead of just incrementing the value of its last event, derives the time-stamp for the *receive* event using the following rule:

$$L_q(e_r) = max(L_p(e_s), L_q(e_i)) + 1$$

where $L_q(e_i)$ is the time-stamp of the last event within q.

This scheme yields a partial ordering of events with respect to a relation called **happened-before**. This relation, denoted by "$\rightarrow$", captures the *flow of information* through the system. In particular, given two events e_i and e_j, the relation $e_i \rightarrow e_j$ holds if the following two conditions are satisfied:

1. e_i and e_j belong to the same process and e_i occurred before e_j (in real time);
2. e_i is the event of sending a message and e_j is the event of receiving the same message.

EXAMPLE: Using Logical Clocks

Figure 3-8 shows how the logical clocks change for three processes, p_1, p_2, and p_3, as events occur and messages are passed. Events are denoted by ×-marks on a vertical logical clock line. The arrows indicate message communications. The clocks of all three processes start at 0. After 3 internal events, p_1 sends a message to process p_2 with the time-stamp of $L_{p1}(u) = 4$. p_2's clock is still at 1 (event j) when the message arrives. Thus p_2 advances its clock for the *receive* event to $L_{p2}(v) = max(4, 1) + 1 = 5$.

When p_2 sends a message to p_3 at time 6, p_3's clock is already at 12. Thus the new time-stamp assigned to the *receive* event in p_3 is $L_{p3}(x) = max(6, 12) + 1 = 13$.

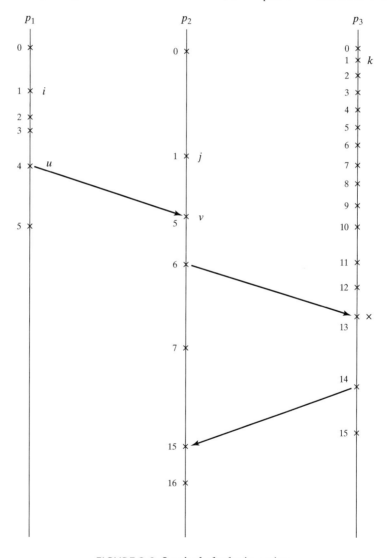

FIGURE 3-8. Logical clocks in action.

Time-stamps of several events could be identical in the scheme described so far. For example, in Figure 3-8, $L_{p1}(i) = L_{p2}(j) = L_{p3}(k) = 1$. If nodes and/or processes have unique identifiers, we can obtain a unique global time-stamp for each event by just concatenating this identifier with the logical clock value; the causality ordering will not be changed. For example, assume the unique IDs of processes p_1, p_2, and p_3 are 1, 2, and 3, respectively. Then $L_{p1}(i) = 1.1$, $L_{p2}(j) = 1.2$, and $L_{p3}(k) = 1.3$ would yield three unique time-stamps.

There are many applications of Lamport's logical clocks. The time-stamping of events allows the simulation or replay of a distributed set of interacting programs, as was illustrated by the file server example above. Some algorithms for solving the distributed mutual exclusion problem, for implementing distributed semaphores, for ordering messages broadcast (multicast) by different processes, and for detecting deadlocks in distributed systems also rely on logical clocks in a central way.

Yet another application area is transaction processing, an important part of database systems (e.g., [Bernstein and Lewis 1993]). A **transaction** is a unit of execution that accesses and possibly updates a database using a sequence of read, write, and computational operations. A standard example is a banking system transaction where a customer accesses and withdraws money from one account and transfers it to another; the customer and each of the accounts may reside at different computer sites. The entire sequence of operations starting from the access of the first account to the completion of the update of the second is defined as a single transaction. The banking system must service many of these transactions at the same time for reasons of cost and speed.

Generally, there is a possibility that the transaction may crash or deadlock before completion, leaving the database in an inconsistent state unless properly handled. Consequently, an "all-or-nothing" approach is required: either all the operations of a transaction are completed correctly or none of them may have any effect. This property of transactions is called **atomicity**. In addition, concurrent or interleaved execution of transactions must have the same effect as if all transactions had been executed sequentially one at a time. This requirement is referred to as **serializability** of transactions.

Note that the problem of concurrent or interleaved execution is similar to the CS problem discussed in Chapter 2; however, unlike CS, transactions must be allowed to proceed concurrently for reasons of speed and efficiency. The system must detect inconsistent interleavings of operations at runtime and abort, undo, and redo all affected transactions.

One set of techniques for providing atomicity and serializability in a distributed environment involves the use of unique time-stamps, such as those definable with logical clocks, for each transaction. Transactions may then be ordered by their relative age. This information may be used to decide which transaction should be aborted and redone, or which transactions depend causally on other transactions and result in additional abort, undo, and redo operations.

CONCEPTS, TERMS, AND ABBREVIATIONS

The following concepts have been introduced in this chapter. Test yourself by defining and discussing each keyword or phrase.

Alarm clock	Monitor, Hoare monitor,
Asynchronous communications	Java monitor, Mesa monitor
Broadcast	Notify
Condition variable	Priority wait
Communicating Sequential Processes	Protected type
programming language (CSP)	Readers/writers problem
Dining philosophers problem	Remote procedure call (RPC)
Distributed mutual exclusion	Rendezvous
Elevator algorithm	Send/Receive operations
Entry guard or barrier	Signal
Guarded command	Timeout
Interprocess communication (IPC)	Time-stamp
Logical clock	Token ring
Mailbox	Transaction
Message port	

EXERCISES

1. Consider the following monitor pseudocode:

```
       monitor m() {
           int x=10, y=2;
           condition c;

       A() {
(1)        x++;
(2)        c.signal;
(3)        y = x-2; }

       B() {
(4)        if (x>10)
(5)            x--
(6)            else {c.wait;
(7)                   x--;} }

       }
```

Assume that after the monitor is initialized, functions A and B are called in the following sequence by various processes:

m.A(); m.A(); m.B(); m.B(); m.B(); m.B(); m.A(); m.A();

Using the line numbers in the code, trace the sequence of instruction execution. Show values of x and y at the end of each instruction.

2. Rewrite the code of Exercise 14, Chapter 2 (forall code with arrays A[] and B[]) using a monitor with priority waits to enforce the proper synchronization of the processes. Hint: Define a monitor with two functions. One is called to request permission to update element A[i]; the other is called when the update is done.

3. Write a monitor that implements a bounded stack, *b_stack*, i.e., a stack of at most *max* elements. The push and pop operations behave as follows:
- *b_stack.push(x)*: if the stack is not completely full, the operation pushes the new element *x* on top of the stack; otherwise, the operation has no effect and the value of *x* is discarded.
- *b_stack.pop(x)*: if the stack is not completely empty, the operation removes the value currently on top of the stack and returns it in the variable *x*; if the stack is empty, the operation waits until a value has been pushed on the stack and then completes by popping and returning this value.

4. Let a *bounded semaphore* *s* be a general semaphore that cannot exceed a given value $smax > 0$. The corresponding operations *PB* and *VB* are defined as:
- $PB(s)$: wait until $s > 0$; then decrement s by 1;
- $VB(s)$: wait until $s < smax$; then increment s by 1.

Write a monitor, named *s*, such that the calls $s.PB()$ and $s.VB()$ emulate the operations on bounded semaphores.

5. Repeat the previous exercise using protected types.

6. Modify and augment the simple batch OS (Exercise 13, Chapter 2) using each of the synchronization mechanisms below:
- **(a)** Monitors
- **(b)** Protected types
- **(c)** Send/Receive primitives
- **(d)** Rendezvous with selective accept statements

7. There are two processes, c_1 and c_2, which at unpredictable times call another process p. The task of p is to count how many times it has been called by each c_i process. Once in a while, a fourth process q calls p to get the accumulated counts for the c_i processes. When the counts are reported to q, p resets both counters to 0. Write the code for process p using rendezvous with selective accept statements.

8. Consider the following rendezvous code:

```
while (1) {
  select {
    when a==TRUE :
      accept A() { f1; b=FALSE }
    when b==TRUE :
      accept B() { f2; a=FALSE }
    else { a=TRUE; b=TRUE }
  }
}
```

Assume that there are no outstanding calls to A or B when the select statement is executed for the first time. Thereafter, the following calls arrive in the given order:

$$A(), B(), B(), A(), A(), B()$$

- **(a)** In which order will the calls be accepted (processed)?
- **(b)** Can caller of A (or B) starve?

9. Two concurrent processes, p and q, interact as follows:
- p and q start concurrently;
- while p computes "$x1 = some\_computation$," q computes "$y1 = some\_compu$-$tation$";
- a rendezvous takes place during which p computes "$y2 = y1 + x1$";

- while p computes "$x2 = some\_computation$," q computes "$y3 = y2 + some\_computation$";
- a second rendezvous takes place during which p computes "$y4 = y3 + x2$".

Write the pseudocode for the two processes p and q using rendezvous.

10. Consider the solution to the readers/writers problem (Section 3.3.1). Assume the first request is a writer W_1. While W_1 is writing, the following requests arrive in the given order:

$$W_2, R_1, R_2, W_3, R_3, W_4$$

   (a) In which order will these requests be processed? Which groups of readers will be reading concurrently?

   (b) Assume that two new readers R_4 and R_5 arrive while W_2 is writing. For each, indicate when it will be processed (i.e., following which write request)?

11. Consider the solution to the readers/writers problem (Section 3.3.1). Assume that there is only a single-writer processes. That is, the function *start_write* will never be invoked until the preceding *end_write* has terminated. Simplify the code accordingly.

12. The following solution to the readers/writers problem was proposed by Courtois, Heymans, and Parnas (1971):

```
reader() {                          writer() {
    P(mutex);                           P(w);
    read_cnt++;                         WRITE;
    if (read_cnt==1) P(w);              V(w)
    V(mutex);                       }
    READ;
    P(mutex);
    read_cnt--;
    if (read_cnt==0) V(w);
    V(mutex);
}

Initially: mutex=1; read_cnt=0; w=1;
```

Does this solution satisfy the basic requirements of the readers/writers problem? Is starvation of readers or writers possible?

13. Consider the analogy of a tunnel with only a single lane. To avoid a deadlock, cars must be prevented from entering the tunnel at both ends simultaneously. Once a car enters, other cars from the same direction may follow immediately. Ignoring the problem of starvation, write the code using semaphores to solve this problem. (Hint: Consider the readers/writers code given in the previous exercise. The tunnel problem is a variation of the readers/writers problem where multiple readers or multiple writers are allowed to enter the critical region.)

14. Write a solution for the tunnel problem of the previous exercise, but this time guarantee that cars from neither direction will wait indefinitely (no starvation). (Hint: Write a monitor similar to the readers/writers problem.)

15. Assume that each of the five philosophers, i, in the dining philosophers problem execute the following segment of code:

```
P(mutex);
    P(fork[i]);
    P(fork[i+1 % 5]);
V(mutex);
```

```
                eat;
            V(fork[i]);
            V(fork[i+1 % 5])
```

(a) Does this code satisfy all requirements of the dining philosophers problem?

(b) Would the solution improve or get worse if the V(mutex) statement was moved:

- after the second *V()* operation;

- between the two *P()* operations.

16. Consider the Elevator algorithm in Section 3.3.3. Assume we replace the line:

```
    if ((position<dest) || ((position==dest) &&
                    (direction==up)))
```

with either of the following simpler conditions:

(a) `if (position<dest)`

(b) `if (position<=dest)`

Will the algorithm still work? In what way will its behavior change?

17. Extend the elevator algorithm in Section 3.3.3 to have two separate call buttons—UP and DOWN—on each floor. The elevator should stop at the floor only if it is traveling in the requested direction.

18. Consider the three processes in Figure 3-8.

(a) For each of the following pairs of logical clocks (L_i, L_j) indicate whether:

- $(L_i \rightarrow L_j)$ (L_i happened before L_j);

- $(L_i \leftarrow L_j)$ (L_i happened after L_j);

- neither (L_i is concurrent with L_j).

The subscripts indicate which process the clock value belongs to:

$$(1_a, 1_c), (1_a, 10_c), (1_a, 14_c), (5_a, 1_c), (5_a, 14_c), (1_a, 7_b), (16_b, 10_c),$$

(e) Assume another message was sent from process *c* to process *a*. The message was sent at time 10 according to *c*'s clock and received at time 2 according to *a*'s clock. Update the values of all the logical clocks affected by the new message in the figure.

C H A P T E R   4

The Operating System Kernel: Implementing Processes and Threads

The process model is fundamental to operating system (OS) design, implementation, and use. Mechanisms for process creation, activation, and termination, and for synchronization, communication, and resource control form the lowest level or **kernel** of all OS and concurrent programming systems. Chapters 2 and 3 described these mechanisms abstractly from a user's or programmer's view, working at the application level of a higher level of an OS. However, these chapters did not provide details of the internal structure, representations, algorithms, or hardware interfaces used by these mechanisms.

In this chapter, we present a more complete picture, discussing, for example, how a process is blocked and unblocked. We start with an overview of possible kernel functions, objects, and organizations. The remaining sections are concerned with implementation aspects of the kernel.

First, we outline the various queue data structures that are pervasive throughout OSs. The next two sections elaborate on the most widely used adaptation of processes, namely, **threads**, and show how processes and threads are built. Internal representations and code for important interaction objects, including semaphores, locks, monitors, and messages are then discussed; a separate subsection on the topic of timers also appears. The last section presents the lowest-level kernel task, *interrupt handling*, and illustrates how this error-prone, difficult function can be made to fit naturally into the process model.

4.1 KERNEL DEFINITIONS AND OBJECTS

The OS kernel is a basic set of objects, primitive operations, data structures, and processes from which the remainder of the system may be constructed. In one appealing view, the purpose and primary function is to transform the computer hardware into an OS's "machine"—a computer that is convenient for constructing OSs. Thus, in a layered functional hierarchy (Chapter 1), the kernel is the lowest level of software, immediately above the hardware architectural level.

Compatible with this view is the notion that the kernel should define or provide *mechanisms* from which an OS designer can implement a variety of *policies* according to application or client desires. The mechanism-policy distinction is important. For example, semaphores and monitors are generally considered mechanisms, whereas resource-allocation schemes that use these mechanisms, such as storage or buffer allocators, are OS policies. A scheduler that allocates CPUs to processes according to given priorities is a mechanism; how and on what basis to select the process priorities are policy decisions. The difference between the two ideas is not always unambiguous. An example is the queue removal operation for a semaphore *mechanism*; it normally also incorporates a *policy* decision, such as either first-come/first-served or priority-based.

What constitutes a kernel is a matter of definition. In one view, the part of the OS that resides permanently in main memory is called the kernel. Because the OS must be protected from user programs, most of it, especially the kernel, runs under a form of hardware protection, such as supervisor mode. This leads to another pragmatic definition of the kernel as that part of the OS that runs in a protected mode. Yet another variation combines both of the above definitions. In this view, the kernel includes any part of the system that resides permanently in main memory and runs in a supervisory mode.

The set of possible functions and objects in a kernel can be divided into four classes:

1. *Process and thread management:* Process creation, destruction, and basic interprocess communication and synchronization.

2. *Interrupt and trap handling:* Responding to signals triggered by various system events; among these are the termination of a process, completion of an I/O operation, a timer signal indicating a timeout or clock tick, request for a service to be performed by the OS, an error caused by a program, or hardware malfunctioning.

3. *Resource management:* Primitives for maintaining, allocating, and releasing units of resources such as CPUs, timers, main memory, secondary storage, I/O devices, or files.

4. *Input and output:* Read, write, and control operations for initiating and supervising the transfer of data between I/O devices and main memory or registers.

OS kernels can be quite small, so-called **microkernels**, consisting of most of the first two classes and some limited resource management, usually processor scheduling and low-level virtual memory allocation. Windows NT (Solomon 1998) and Mach (Accetta et al. 1986) are examples of systems with such microkernels. At the other extreme, almost all of the functions listed in the four classes above can be incorporated into a very large kernel. Most versions of UNIX, as well as Linux, have monolithic kernels.

In this chapter, we are concerned primarily with the first two types of kernel operations, i.e., those for process and thread management, and interrupt handling; the next chapter covers CPU scheduling. The discussion of I/O and the management of other important resources is the subject of later chapters.

A highest-level user process is usually established in response to a request expressed in the system's control or command language; a standard request of this sort is a "login" command. We will assume that such a highest-level supervisory or "envelope" process, say p_j, is created for each user j. In many systems, this is actually the case. Where it is not, it is still convenient conceptually to assume the existence of such a process, even though its function may be performed centrally by a systems process. The process p_j has the responsibility for initiating, monitoring, and controlling the progress of j's work through the system as well as for maintaining a global accounting and resource data structure for the user. The latter may include static information such as user identification, maximum time and I/O requirements (for batch processing), priority, type (e.g., interactive, batch, real-time), and other resource needs. It also may include dynamic information related to resource use and other processes created as children.

In general, p_j will create a number of such child processes, each corresponding to a requested unit of work. These processes may in turn create additional ones, either in sequence or in parallel. Thus, as a computation progresses, a corresponding tree hierarchy of processes grows and shrinks. The processes are not totally independent, but interact with each other and parts of the OS such as resource managers, schedulers, and file system components, using synchronization and communication primitives provided by the kernel.

These ideas are illustrated in Figure 4-1, where an OS process p_s has created user processes $p_1, \ldots, p_n$, and the process p_j, in turn, has created the processes $q_1, \ldots, q_m$, and so on. All processes use the primitives provided by the underlying kernel. The remainder of

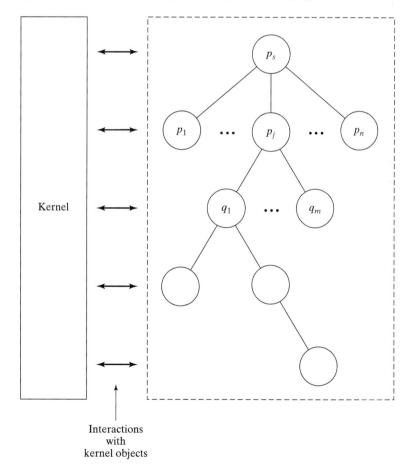

FIGURE 4-1. A process creation hierarchy.

this chapter will discuss the internal representation of processes and the implementation of operations on processes and resources.

4.2   QUEUE STRUCTURES

Every kernel and higher-level object in an OS is normally represented by a data structure containing its basic state, identification, accounting, and other information. Thus, there are data structures for each active object, such as a process or a thread, for each hardware and software resource, and for each synchronization element. These data structures are referred to as system **control blocks** or **descriptors**. Collectively, they represent the state of the OS and, as such, are accessed and maintained by systems routines. Later sections and chapters discuss the possible organizations and contents of particular object descriptors. This section focuses on queues—their central role at the kernel and higher OS level, and their implementations.

4.2.1   Resource Queues in an Operating System

A popular practical view considers an OS to be a queue processor. The active objects of the system move from one resource queue to another, triggered by interrupts and requests for service. A user entity might originate in a long-term queue, eventually being served by a long-term scheduler that activates or swaps in the object, sending it to a short-term scheduling queue. The latter is typically a **ready list** of processes waiting for allocation of a CPU by a scheduler.

During execution, an object will request other resource elements, and enqueue itself on servers or allocators for that resource. Thus, there are queues associated with managers of hardware such as main memory and secondary storage, I/O devices, and clocks. There are also queues for shared software components, such as files, buffers, and messages, and queues for low-level synchronization resources such as semaphores, locks, and monitors. In fact, it is no exaggeration to say that queues are the primary generic data structures of OSs. Many of these queues appear at the kernel level and are the descriptor representations for the kernel objects.

A variety of schemes or servicing policies are needed. The simplest, most efficient, and most common is *first-come/first-served* (FIFO); requests are considered and satisfied in the order of arrival. The bounded-buffer example developed throughout Chapter 3 uses a queue with exactly this policy. At the other extreme are *priority-based* schemes. Typically, a numerical priority is attached to each object in a queue, and the queue is serviced in priority order. For example, processes may be given different priorities according to their importance: Processes that are CPU-bound often have a lower priority for the CPU than processes that are I/O-bound. Processes with short time deadlines typically have higher CPU priorities than those with longer deadlines. Objects waiting on CSs, semaphores, or monitors might require priority waits, such as in the elevator algorithm described in Chapter 3. Priority-based queues are a very general and versatile mechanism, and subsume many other simpler schemes as special cases. For example, FIFO queues are also priority-based, where the priority depends directly on arrival time. But for pragmatic reasons—ease of implementation or areas of applicability—they are typically viewed as distinct structures.

Specific examples of OS queues are presented in the remainder of the book. The next section describes basic queue implementations usable by kernels and higher-level OS objects.

4.2.2   Implementations of Queues

We consider the two basic types of queues mentioned above: FIFO and priority based. To maintain these queues, at least two operations are needed, one to append a new element x to a queue Q and one to remove the first element from a given queue. Common forms for these operations are:

`insert(queue Q, element x)`

and

`remove(queue Q, element x).`

These are similar to the *deposit* and *remove* commands defined for the bounded buffer. (An alternative for the *remove* defines it as a function that returns an element, with the side effect of deleting the element from the queue; functions with side effects are generally not considered good programming practice.)

It is also convenient to provide a test for emptiness of a given queue; its form is:

`int empty(queue Q)`

This returns 1 if the queue is empty and 0 otherwise. Sometimes, it is also useful to define operations that insert an element into or remove an element from an arbitrary place in a queue structure, violating the basic queue properties. This is a practical compromise for those situations where a data structure is a queue most of the time, but not always. For simplicity, we will use the same notation *insert/remove* for such operations.

In addition to the queue elements themselves, most queues also contain a **header** or more global descriptive data. This may include some generic information about the queue, such as its name, length, and history of use, as well as application- or resource-specific data. Examples of the latter might be maximum and minimum message lengths in a message queue, the number of free and allocated blocks of memory for a memory queue, a list of allowed users of the queue, and the maximum amount of time allocated to all processes waiting in a ready list (queue) for a CPU.

Single-Level Queues

A bounded array is often the most convenient and efficient way to construct a FIFO queue, especially at the kernel level. A diagram of a typical implementation appears in Figure 4-2a. The queue elements are stored in a "circular" array of size n, with two moving pointers, *front* which points to the head of the queue (the first element to be removed) and *rear* (the last element that was deposited). Both pointers are advanced to the right, modulo n, which implements the circular nature of the queue. This is essentially the data structure assumed for the bounded buffer in Chapter 3.

Operations on the array implementation are fast and deterministic. However, there are two negative features. The first is the boundedness. We must know, or check at every *deposit* call, that the queue does not overflow beyond its capacity of n. Similarly, we must check at every *remove* that the queue does not underflow below zero. An additional problem with arrays is that it is an awkward form if we must insert or delete an element at an arbitrary place in the structure.

A linked list implementation is more flexible but not as efficient. A singly linked version is sketched in Figure 4-2b. Such a list is, in principle, unbounded in length,

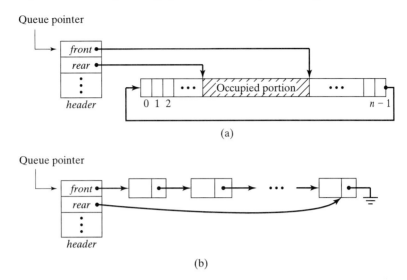

(a)

(b)

FIGURE 4-2. FIFO queues: (a) circular array implementation; and (b) linked list implementation.

and thus, able to accommodate long bursts of insertions. However, length checking may be necessary, since kernel space is usually limited and node storage must be obtained dynamically. Insertions and deletions at arbitrary spots are also easy to handle, especially if each node is doubly linked.

Priority Queues

A priority queue combines several simple queues into one common data structure. In addition to its application data, each queue element contains a priority associated with the corresponding object. Typically, the priorities are positive integers with lower numbers treated as higher or lower priorities, depending on the implementation. The *remove* operation is obligated to delete and return the highest-priority queue element.

A common case is when there are a *fixed* and relatively small number of priorities, say n, numbered from 0 to $n - 1$. One particularly convenient organization starts with an **array of n headers** of FIFO queues, one header for each priority. As shown in Figure 4-3a, each header points to a linked list of elements queued at that priority; alternatively, and at greater storage cost, each queue could be represented as a circular array. In either case, inserting an element with a given priority can be accomplished quickly in constant time. Similarly, a removal is implemented by just scanning the header array from the top down for the first nonempty queue. By keeping the number of the highest-priority, nonempty queue in the global header, a removal can be performed more quickly. With the linked-list version, it is also relatively easy to insert or delete an element at an arbitrary location in the queue, or to change the priority of some entry.

A data structure that works well when priorities are not fixed but can range over a large domain of values is the **binary heap** (e.g., [Weiss 1993]). Examples of such priorities are those that are directly based on time, such as deadlines, or on space, such as storage addresses (e.g., disk cylinder) or numbers of memory blocks. A binary heap

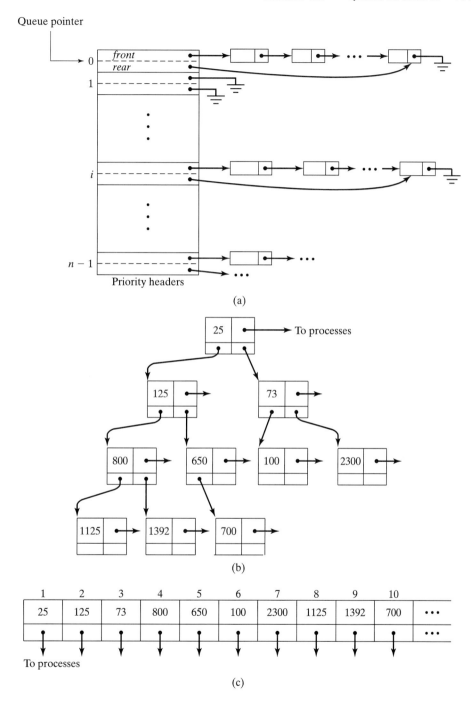

FIGURE 4-3. Priority queues: (a) array indexed by priority; (b) binary heap of priorities; and (c) array implementation of binary heap.

is a complete binary tree where the value (priority number in our case) at the root of any subtree is always smaller than the value of any other node in the subtree. Figure 4-3b shows an example of a binary heap with 10 different priority values. Each element in the heap consists of the priority value, the two pointers to its left and right subtree, and a pointer to the process (or list of processes) at that priority level.

A binary heap is also suitable for kernel-level priority queues because it can be implemented efficiently as an array. The tree root is placed at index 1 of the array. The left and right subtrees are stored recursively using the following rule: The left subtree of any node i starts at index $2i$, and the right subtree starts at index $2i + 1$. Figure 4-3c shows the array representation of the binary heap of Figure 4-3b.

Insertions and removals each take $O(\log n)$ time; thus, these operations are slightly less deterministic and efficient than the corresponding ones in a fixed-priority array implementation. However, the range of possible priority value is open-ended.

4.3 THREADS

The normal implementation of processes, especially traditional UNIX processes where each process has a single thread of execution, results in much runtime overhead—creation, termination, synchronization, and context-switching are all lengthy operations. To alleviate this problem, various user-level packages have been developed that allow multiple "lightweight" scheduling units to be implemented within a process. These units share the same resources as their host process; notably, they have the same address space. But they can be created, scheduled, and synchronized more efficiently.

A similar approach also allows resource sharing among concurrent entities but implements their scheduling as part of the OS rather than a user package. The most extreme version appeared in the Pilot OS, an early and influential single-user system that contained one process but many schedulable threads of control (Redell et al. 1980). Pilot

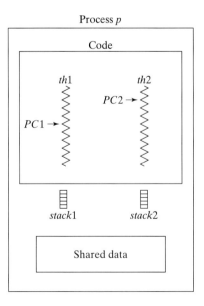

FIGURE 4-4. Threads within a process.

was written in the Mesa language and was probably the first commercial OS written using monitors. The Mesa form of threads was called a "lightweight process."

The general idea of efficiently sharing resources, especially address spaces, among related scheduling blocks was so successful that most contemporary systems provide this facility. The scheduling units are known as **threads**. Processes still exist, but these are now *passive resource holders* for threads. In this popular model, a process contains one or more active threads.

Figure 4-4 illustrates the relationship between processes and threads. It shows two threads, $th1$ and $th2$, executing within the same code segment of a process p. Each thread is uniquely characterized by its own program counter (PC_i) and function-calling stack ($stack_i$). The process data area is shared by the two threads.

CASE STUDY: USER-LEVEL AND KERNEL-LEVEL THREAD FACILITIES

Windows NT (Solomon 1998), the POSIX interface prescribed for UNIX (POSIX, 1993), and the Mach OS (Accetta et al. 1986), all support threads. The Windows NT approach is particularly interesting because it supports both kernel- and user-level threads. An NT process consists of the executable program code, data, address space, resources such as files and semaphores, and at least one kernel-level thread. Each thread is an active executable object whose state or context is maintained by the kernel. The state consists of the current values of its CPU registers, a user- and kernel-level stack, and a private systems storage area. NT threads are scheduled by the OS kernel according to the priority specified by their owning process.

Because each context switch between threads requires a call to the kernel, these threads are still relatively expensive. To solve the problem, Windows NT also supports a user-level version of threads, called **fibers**. Each kernel-level thread may define any number of fibers, and each fiber may be scheduled for execution. But the context switch between fibers is not visible to the kernel; it must be done explicitly by a function call *SwitchToFiber*, which causes the currently executing fiber to give up the CPU to the new fiber specified in the call.

Because the threads in a process share resources, they can communicate efficiently, for example, through shared memory. Threads within the same group can be created, terminated, preempted, blocked, and scheduled quickly. However, the price paid for this performance gain is a loss of protection. Standard traditional processes that do not share resources with other active objects have hardware and software guards that automatically check against or prevent accidental or malicious interferences. For example, a process cannot normally access the address space of another process. In contrast, threads belonging to the same process can easily interfere with one another since they do share the same virtual (and real) space.

It is also the case that some applications lend themselves more readily to tightly coupled threads than to more independent processes. Good examples appear in data or file sharing. Here, two related objects that must access the same data more or less concurrently can conveniently be represented by two threads; this might occur in a parallel compiler where a lexical analyzer and a syntax analyzer both use a common symbol table. Similarly, a popular service, such as a file server, can be parallelized conveniently with threads since each concurrent object shares the same file space and, often, the same code.

Operations on threads are analogous, and in many cases, identical to those discussed for pure processes. Thus, an OS typically offers services or commands to:

- Create a new thread;

- Initiate or make a thread ready;

- Destroy or terminate a thread;

- Delay or put a thread to sleep for a given amount of time;

- Synchronize threads through semaphores, events, or condition variables;

- Perform lower-level operations, such as blocking, suspending, or scheduling a thread.

4.4 IMPLEMENTING PROCESSES AND THREADS

As noted in Section 4.2, every process and thread is represented by a data structure containing its basic state, identification, and accounting information. These system control blocks or descriptors are accessed and maintained by OS routines and collectively represent part of the state of the OS. As such, they are accessed and maintained by systems routines. This section describes the contents and organization of these descriptors, followed by the design of their operations.

4.4.1 Process and Thread Descriptors

First assume that we are dealing with a system composed solely of processes; much of the discussion will also apply to threads. A process descriptor or **process control block** (PCB) is constructed at process creation and represents the process during its existence. Process descriptors are used and modified by basic process and resource operations, interrupt routines, and schedulers. They also may be referenced during performance monitoring and analysis. Figure 4-5 shows a possible descriptor data set for a process p in a general purpose OS. Each entry may be viewed as an element of a structure, where each element type is given inside the box. The access to any element of a given descriptor is accomplished via a conventional selection mechanism. For example, p->*Memory* refers to the *Memory* field of the PCB of process p. We have grouped the items comprising the process descriptor into five categories according to their primary purpose as follows:

Identification

Each process is uniquely identified by its descriptor. Pointers to PCBs are maintained by the system. In addition, a process p often has a system-wide unique identification p->*ID* supplied by the user or the system. Its purpose is to allow convenient and explicit interprocess references. To eliminate conflicts arising from the use of the same ID for more than one process, we assume that the system assigns a new unique ID to every process at the time of its creation. New process IDs are obtained using the function:

```
pid = Get_New_PID()
```

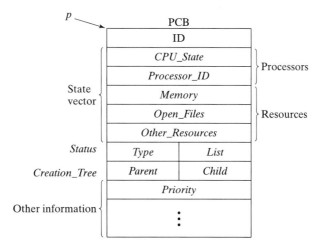

FIGURE 4-5. Structure of process descriptor.

Since all pointers to process descriptors are maintained by the system, we also assume the existence of a function:

$$p = \text{Get\_PCB}(pid)$$

that takes a unique *pid* as argument and returns the pointer *p* to the process descriptor.

State Vector

The execution of a process or a thread *p* can be described as a sequence of **state vectors** $s_0, s_1, \ldots, s_i, \ldots$, where each state vector s_i contains the address of the current program instruction to be executed and the values of all variables of the program. It also comprises the state of the processor executing *p*, the allocated address space, and any other resources currently associated with *p*. In other words, a state vector of a process *p* is that amount of information required by a processor to run *p* or restart *p* after it has been interrupted. The state vector can be changed either by the execution of *p* or by the execution of other objects sharing state vector components with *p*.

The state vector portion in Figure 4-5 comprises the five components following *ID*, and may be subdivided further into information about the processor(s) and the global resources.

Processors

CPU_State contains copies of all hardware registers and flags of the CPU. This includes the program counter, instruction and data registers, and protection and error flags. In general, *CPU_State* contains the information stored in a typical machine state-word; this data is saved automatically by the hardware when an interrupt occurs. Thus, as long as a process is running, its *CPU_State* field is meaningless—it contains obsolete values saved during the last interrupt. When the process is not running, its *CPU_State* contains the necessary data to restart the process at the point of its last interruption.

The *Processor_ID* field identifies the CPU that is executing *p*. This is meaningful only in a multiprocessor system; in a uniprocessor, it is omitted.

Resources

The *Memory* field gives the main memory map for the process. It describes its real address space and, in case of a virtual memory (see Chapter 8), the mapping between the virtual name space and physical memory locations. Thus, *Memory* could contain upper- and lower-bounds registers for a contiguous partition in main memory, a list of memory blocks allocated to the process, or a pointer to a page or segment table.

The next component *Open_Files* specifies all files that are currently open. Typically, it points to a list of open file descriptors that record such information as file type, disk location, current reading or writing position, and buffer state. The last field, *Other_Resources*, represents jointly all other interesting resources owned by the process. These might be resources such as peripherals, secondary storage space, or files.

Status Information

The status of a process p may be described by a structure with two components: *Status.Type* and *Status.List*. *Status.Type* is one of **ready**, **running**, or **blocked**. The meaning of each of these values is given by Table 4-1.

Generally, the status of a *running* process changes to *blocked* if the process issues a resource *Request* that cannot be met. A *blocked* process becomes *ready* as a result of the *Release* of the resource it is waiting for. The changes between *ready* and *running* are the results of scheduling the process for execution.

The field *Status.List* points to one of several possible lists on which the process may reside. When the process is running or ready to run, it has an entry on the *Ready List* of the process scheduler. When the process blocks on a resource, this entry is moved from the *Ready List* to the *Waiting List* associated with that resource. When the process acquires the resource, its entry is moved back to the *Ready List*. The field *Status.List* points to either the *Ready List* or one of the *Waiting Lists*, depending on the process status. This information is essential for efficiency. For example, when the process is to be destroyed, we must be able to find quickly the list on which the process resides.

The three basic status types—*running, ready*, and *blocked*—can handle many situations, but there are some applications for which a finer division is desirable. Consider the following two examples:

- A user is interactively debugging a running program. Often, the user wishes to suspend execution to examine the state of the computation, possibly make some changes, and either continue or terminate the execution.

TABLE 4-1. Status type of process

running	p is currently running on a processor (the one designated by p->*Processor_ID*).
ready	p is ready to run, waiting for a processor.
blocked	p cannot logically proceed until it receives a particular resource for example, a lock, file, table, message, I/O device, or semaphore.

- An internal process might wish to suspend the activity of one or more other processes to examine their state or modify them. The purpose of the suspension may be, for example, to detect or prevent a deadlock, to detect and destroy a "runaway" process, or to temporarily swap the process out of main memory.

In both cases, we could explicitly block the process to achieve the suspension. However, a process could be already blocked when the suspension is desired. Unless we wish to allow a process to be blocked at the same time for more than one reason, a new "suspended" status is required. We define it as follows.

A process is either **active** or **suspended**. If active, it may be running, ready, or blocked, denoted by a *Status.Type* of *running, ready_a*, or *blocked_a*, respectively. When the process is suspended, the *Status.Type* is *ready_s* or *blocked_s*. The possible status changes of a given process *p* are shown in Figure 4-6. Each change is the result of an operation performed by either the process *p* itself (e.g., request a resource) or another process (e.g., *suspend/activate* process *p*). The implementation of these operations will be discussed in detail in Section 4.4.2.

Creation Tree

Earlier in this chapter, the concept of spawning hierarchies of processes was briefly introduced and illustrated in Figure 4-1. Each process *p* has a creator, typically called **parent**, which created the process, and owns and controls any of its offsprings. When the system is first started, one initial process is typically created, which becomes the root of the creation tree. The parent of any process (except the root) is recorded in the field *Creation_Tree.Parent*, usually and conveniently as a pointer to the parent's descriptor. Similarly, every process may create other processes. The *Creation_Tree.Child* field identifies all direct offsprings of a process, say, by pointing to a linked list of their descriptors. This list can be implemented efficiently by distributing the list elements over the PCBs, instead of maintaining it as a separate dynamically allocated list (see the Linux case study below.)

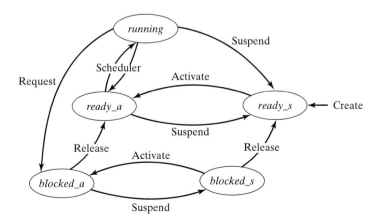

FIGURE 4-6. Process status changes.

Other Information

The *Priority_ID* field indicates the importance of the process relative to other processes. This information is used by the scheduler when deciding which process should be running next. In the simplest case, *Priority* could be a single-integer value, assigned to the process at the time of creation. More typically, the priority of a process consists of two components: a statically assigned **base** priority and a dynamically changing **current** priority. The latter can be derived using a complex function of the base priority, the resource demands of the process, and the current state of the environment, i.e., other processes and resources in the system. (The topic is discussed in detail in Chapter 5.)

The last part of the process descriptor also may contain a variety of other fields that are useful for scheduling, accounting, resource allocation, and performance measurement. Typical elements include CPU time used by the process, time remaining (according to some estimate), resources used, resources claimed, resource quotas, and the number of I/O requests since creation.

CASE STUDY: LINUX PROCESS DESCRIPTOR

The basic data structure for processes in Linux, called the *process descriptor*, contains essentially the information presented above (e.g., [Bovet and Cesati 2001]). We outline some of the differences and more interesting features.

- Linux distinguishes the following main states of a process p:

running	p is either using or waiting for the CPU; Thus this state jointly represents the two states we defined as *running* and *ready_a*; the distinction is implied by the assignment of the CPU
interruptible	p is blocked on a resource; this corresponds to our *blocked_a* state; when the resource becomes available, p is moved to the *running* state
stopped	p has been explicitly suspended; this corresponds jointly to our two states *ready_s* and *blocked_s*
zombie	p has terminated its execution but its PCB is kept active so that its parent can obtain information about p's status

- There are multiple lists linking the PCBs together. A *process lists* links *all* existing PCBs together; a *running list* (corresponding to our *Ready List*) links the PCBs of running processes. These two lists are embedded within the PCBs. That is, each PCB contains two pairs of pointers. Each pair points to the predecessor and the successor PCB on each of the two lists. In addition, there are multiple waiting lists (called wait queues), one for each resource a process may be blocked on. These are implemented as separate linked lists, where each list element points to a PCB.

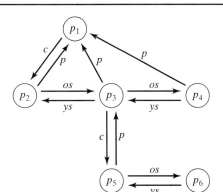

FIGURE 4-7. Representing process creation hierarchy.

- The creation tree of processes also is distributed throughout the PCBs. Each PCB contains four pointers: one for its parent, one for its first child, one for its younger sibling, and one for its older sibling. Figure 4-7 illustrates this scheme for six processes. The pointer labels p, c, ys, and os correspond to the four possible pointer types. The parent, p_1 points to its youngest child p_2 (pointer c). The three processes p_2, p_3, and p_4 are all children of p_1 and point to it using parent pointers. They also point to each other using the sibling pointers. p_3 has two children of its own, p_5 and p_6, linked to it in an analogous manner.

Several other features of the Linux PCBs are worth mentioning:

- In addition to open files, the working directory of the process is also accessible through the descriptor.
- A *signal* component stores the set of signals that have been sent to the process, as well as other related information such as how they should be handled.
- Scheduling data includes the priority and the policy to be executed, such as round-robin or FIFO. Fields are also available for quotas on various resources; examples are file size, stack size, and execution time quotas.

The full descriptor is a complex and lengthy object, leading to a heavyweight process. Linux provides creation of lightweight versions of these with sharing of different components, i.e., the equivalent of threads through the *clone* operation discussed in Chapter 2.

Let us now consider a system that implements multiple threads within each process. Each process and each thread will have its own descriptor. The thread data structure is essentially the *CPU_State*, the *Status*, and the *Priority* fields of the PCB of Figure 4-5. The state changes shown in Figure 4-6 now apply separately to each individual thread. The execution stack of a thread is part of its private, nonshared, space and is pointed to from the descriptor. In addition, there is a pointer to the thread's host process. A process PCB in the threaded environment contains essentially the information about the shared resources, i.e., the memory, files, and other resource fields of Figure 4-5. It also keeps a record of its corresponding threads.

CASE STUDY: THREAD AND PROCESS DATA STRUCTURES IN WINDOWS NT

The record for an NT thread includes its name, priority options, runable processor list, execution times in user and kernel mode, and the basic CPU and stack data. The descriptor for a process object contains the standard information already discussed, as well as a security field with an *access token* that defines the resources accessible by the process.

4.4.2   Implementing Operations on Processes

In Section 2.2, we specified a variety of language mechanisms for creating, activating, and terminating processes and threads. Some of the underlying operations were implicit, and some were explicit. These included *cobegin/coend, forall, fork, join, quit*, explicit process declarations and instantiations through a *new* operation, *PAR*, and *thread_name.start*. Here, we show how a representative set of these primitive operations can be implemented.

We view processes and threads as basic OS objects that can be represented by abstract data types. These consist of private data structures—the process descriptors—and the interface operations that manipulate these descriptors. The primitives are considered indivisible CSs and are protected by a common "busy wait" or "spinning" type lock. This kind of lock and its construction are discussed in the next section. For clarity, we omit the locks in the following descriptions; error and protection checking also are omitted. These topics are addressed separately in Chapter 13.

We define four operations on processes:

1. *Create:* Establish a new process.
2. *Destroy:* Remove one or more processes.
3. *Suspend:* Change process status to "suspended."
4. *Activate:* Change process status to "active."

Figure 4-6, introduced in the last section, traces the status changes caused by these operations.

Create

To create a new child process, the parent process calls the *Create* primitive with the input parameters: initial CPU state *s0*, initial main memory *m0*, and priority *pi*. The *m0* field could be a fairly complex structure, for example, encompassing real and virtual space for programs, data, and stacks. The initial status will be *ready_s—ready* because the new process should be in position to proceed without waiting for any resources and *suspended* because it may be desirable to create a process well before its activation. The *Create* primitive returns the unique id (*pid*) of the new process as an output parameter.

```
Create(s0, m0, pi, pid) {
    p = Get_New_PCB();
    pid = Get_New_PID();
    p -> ID = pid;
    p -> CPU_State = s0;
```

```
p -> Memory = m0;
p -> Priority = pi;
p -> Status.Type = 'ready_s';
p -> Status.List = RL;
p -> Creation_Tree.Parent = self;
p -> Creation_Tree.Child = NULL;
insert(self -> Creation_Tree.Child, p);
insert(RL, p);
Scheduler(); }
```

The first instruction creates a new instance of the process descriptor (Fig. 4-5) with *p* pointing to that instance. The next two instructions create and assign a unique ID to the new process. Subsequent instructions fill the individual fields of the descriptor using given parameters. We assume that any process is able to obtain the pointer to its *own* descriptor, either through an agreed-upon register or through a kernel call; the name *self* designates this pointer. *Create* adds *p* to *self*'s child list and inserts *p* on the Ready List *RL*. The initial resources—here only main memory—are usually shared resources for the new process and, typically, must be a subset of those belonging to the parent process. The parent may share any of its resources with other child processes in a similar manner. The created process, in turn, can share its resources with any children it creates. At the end, the scheduler is called to select the process to run next.

Suspend

A process is generally permitted to suspend only its descendants. Suspension could be treated in two different ways. A call, *Suspend(pid)*, could suspend only the named process, or it could suspend all its descendants; both these options may be desirable. The latter possibility is somewhat tricky, since a descendent may already have been suspended by their ancestors (which are descendants of *pid*). For example, the RC4000 system (Brinch Hansen 1970) suspends in this manner but, as a consequence, requires more complex process status types (see Exercise 3). For simplicity, our solution permits suspension of only one process at a time.

```
Suspend(pid) {
    p = Get_PCB(pid);
    s = p -> Status.Type;
    if ((s == 'blocked_a') || (s == 'blocked_s'))
        p -> Status.Type = 'blocked_s';
    else p -> Status.Type = 'ready_s';
    if (s == 'running') {
        cpu = p -> Processor_ID;
        p -> CPU_State = Interrupt(cpu);
        Scheduler();
    }
}
```

This function obtains a pointer *p* to the descriptor of the process with the unique identifier *pid* and sets the *Status.Type* to suspended. If the process was running, the processor executing the process is stored in the variable *cpu* and the machine is interrupted.

We assume that the *Interrupt(cpu)* function returns the current state of the CPU, which is saved in the *CPU_State* field of the PCB. The interrupt also tags the CPU as free. The *Scheduler* is called at the end to allocate the CPU to another *ready_a* process. The suspended process remains linked within the list it occupied prior to its suspension, i.e., the ready list or one of the waiting lists.

Activate

Process activation is straightforward, involving a status change to active and a possible call on the scheduler. The latter permits the option of preemption scheduling if the activated process becomes *ready_a*. A process may activate any of its known descendants, in particular, its child.

```
Activate(pid) {
    p = Get_PCB(pid);
    if (p -> Status.Type == 'ready_s') {
        p -> Status.Type = 'ready_a';
        Scheduler();
    }
    else p -> Status.Type - 'blocked_a';
}
```

Destroy

For destroying a process, the same alternatives are possible as for the *Suspend* operation—we can either remove a single process (a descendant) or remove that process and all of its descendants. If the first policy is selected, the process hierarchy can easily fragment, potentially leaving isolated processes in the system with no control over their behavior. We therefore require that *Destroy* removes the named process and *all* its descendants.

```
Destroy(pid) {
    p = Get_PCB(pid);
    Kill_Tree(p);
    Scheduler();
}

Kill_Tree(p) {
    for (each q in p -> Creation_Tree.Child) Kill_Tree(q);
    if (p -> Status.Type == 'running') {
        cpu = p -> Processor_ID;
        Interrupt(cpu);
    }
    Remove(p -> Status.List, p);
    Release_all(p -> Memory);
    Release_all(p -> Other_Resources);
    Close_all(p -> Open_Files);
    Delete_PCB(p);
}
```

The function is invoked by the call *Destroy(pid)*, where *pid* is the ID of the root process of the subtree to be removed. The procedure obtains the pointer to this process and calls the routine *Kill_Tree(p)*, which recursively eliminates the entire tree. It calls *Kill_Tree(q)* for each process *q* on the current process child list. For each process in the tree, *Kill_Tree* proceeds as follows. If the process is currently running, it is stopped by interrupting its CPU and marking it as free. The procedure then removes the process from the list pointed to by *Status.List*. This is the ready list if the process was running or ready, and otherwise a waiting list associated with the resource upon which the process was blocked. Next, the procedure releases all resources currently allocated to the process and closes all files opened by the process. This potentially unblocks other processes waiting for the released resources. Finally, the process descriptor is deleted and its space returned to the system. When the entire tree is eliminated and *Kill_Tree(p)* returns to *Destroy(pid)*, the process scheduler is called to determine which process(es) should be running next. This may include the current process—the one who issued the *Destroy* command—and any number of processes that may have become unblocked as a result of the *Destroy* operation.

4.4.3 Operations on Threads

Now consider the case of a process/thread framework. A *Create_Process* operation typically establishes the resources for a set of yet-to-be-defined threads, and creates one initial thread. Thus, both a new process descriptor and a new thread descriptor are created. Other resources are shared by future threads within the process. Thread execution may be controlled by four operations analogous to those for processes: *Create_Thread*, *Activate_Thread*, *Suspend_Thread*, and *Destroy_Thread*.

CASE STUDY: POSIX THREADS

The POSIX thread library provides a function *pthread_create()*, which corresponds to the above *Create_Thread* primitive. It starts a new thread that executes a function specified as a parameter. To destroy a thread, the function *pthread_cancel* (and several related ones) are provided. This corresponds to *Destroy_Thread* but cancels only the named thread; its descendants all continue running. Another important distinction is that a *pthread* may control whether and at which points it may be canceled. For example, it may prevent its cancellation while executing in a CS. This capability is similar to the signal-handling options of UNIX processes described in Section 2.5, where a process may ignore or catch a signal, rather than being killed.

4.5 IMPLEMENTING SYNCHRONIZATION AND COMMUNICATION MECHANISMS

Chapter 3 presented a large variety of mechanisms by which processes and threads interact to synchronize, communicate, and share resources. Here, we outline some standard methods for implementing many of these schemes. Most are used primarily at the OS kernel level, but many also can be used at higher OS levels and by user programs. In particular, we introduce basic techniques for building semaphores, locks, monitors, timer services, and message-passing.

Semaphores, locks, monitors, messages, time, and other hardware and software objects can be viewed as resources that are requested and released by processes or threads. These *Request* and *Release* operations may cause a process or thread to change its status between *blocked* and *ready*, as indicated in Figure 4-6. We outline a generic version of the *Request/Release* primitives, that is applicable to a single-unit reusable resource, such as a lock, table, I/O device, or memory area. The following pseudocode outlines the necessary actions:

```
Request(res) {
    if (Free(res))
        Allocate(res, self)
    else {
        Block(self, res);
        Scheduler();
    }
}

Release(res) {
    Deallocate(res, self);
    if (Process_Blocked_on(res, pr)) {
        Allocate(res, pr);
        Unblock(pr, res);
        Scheduler();
    }
}
```

The *Request* function first checks whether or not the specified resource *res* is free. If yes, *res* is allocated to the invoking process (*self*); if not, the process is blocked on the resource and the *Scheduler* is called to give the CPU to a *ready* process. When a process no longer needs resource *res*, it does a *Release*. The resource is then deallocated, i.e., removed from the calling process (*self*). If a process, say *pr*, is blocked waiting for *res*, the resource is allocated to that process, and the process is unblocked, which involves changing its status from *blocked* to *ready*, and moving its PCB from the waiting list of *res* to the ready list. Finally, the *Scheduler* is invoked to decide which process should continue.

There are many implementations and forms of the above generic *Request* and *Release* functions, depending on the resource type and the system. They could be calls to the OS kernel for specific resources, for example, *Request_Memory(number_of_blocks)*. Alternately, they could be implemented as library functions to extend the basic functionality of the kernel. In the remainder of this section, we present four specific instantiations of *Request/Release*: 1) as *P* and *V* operations on semaphores (Section 4.5.1); 2) as operations embedded as monitor procedures (Section 4.5.2); 3) as calls to manage clocks, timers, delays, and timeouts (Section 4.5.3); and 4) as *send/receive* operations (Section 4.5.4).

4.5.1 Semaphores and Locks

Few, if any, computers have hardware instructions, such as *P* and *V* operations, which directly address mutual exclusion locks, binary semaphores, or general semaphores.

However, it is not difficult to program the logical equivalents of these objects, provided that our computer has an instruction that can do two things as a global CS. The most common form of such an instruction is to **test and set** a memory location in *one indivisible, atomic* operation.

Let our version of such an instruction be designated $TS(R,X)$. The operand R is a CPU register, and the operand X is an arbitrary memory location that can contain either a 0 *(false)* or a 1 *(true)*. Thus, we treat X as a Boolean variable. $TS(R,X)$ performs the following two actions indivisibly, i.e., without interruption or interleaving with any other operations:

$$R = X ;$$
$$X = 0 ;$$

Thus $TS(R,X)$ always sets its operand X to 0 and stores the previous value of X in the register R where it can later be accessed.

In other words, the value of R indicates whether a change has been made to the value of X.

Spinning Locks on Binary Semaphores

First consider a restricted version of the semaphore operations, one that operates only on **binary** semaphores, i.e., semaphores that may only have the value 0 or 1. We denote such restricted operations as Pb and Vb. They are defined as follows:

1. *Pb(sb)*: If sb is 1 then set it to 0 and proceed; otherwise, i.e., if sb is already 0, wait until it becomes 1, then complete the operation.
2. *Vb(sb)*: Set sb to 1; note that Vb has no effect if the semaphore already is 1.

These operations may be implemented using the TS instruction as follows:

```
Pb(sb) is equivalent to:    do TS(R,sb) while (!R);/*wait loop*/
Vb(sb) is equivalent to:    sb = 1;
```

When the semaphore sb has the value *false*, a process attempting to execute Pb will wait by repeatedly executing the *while*-loop. This form of waiting is referred to as **spinning** or **busy waiting**, since the process consumes memory cycles and processor time while executing the loop. Note that R is a register and thus each process has its own private copy of its content. The execution of TS is atomic and thus only a single process is able to pass the busy-wait loop.

These spinning operations are used extensively for mutual exclusion locks, where $Pb(sb)$ is a lock request, say *mutex_lock(sb)*, and $Vb(sb)$ is an unlock, say *mutex_unlock(sb)*. They appear especially in multiprocessor synchronization where several processors may compete for the same lock, and as a means for implementing higher-level methods including the general semaphore algorithms outlined next.

General Semaphores with Spinning Locks

The P and V operations on a **general** semaphore s may be implemented using the above Pb and Vb operations with two binary semaphores, say *mutex_s* and *delay_s*. The lock *mutex_s* assures the logical indivisibility of the code while *delay_s* provides for a busy-wait when necessary on a *P*. Initially, *mutex_s = 1* and *delay_s = 0*.

The *P* operation is defined as:

```
P(s) {
    Pb(mutex_s);
    s = s-1;
    if (s < 0) {Vb(mutex_s); Pb(delay_s);}
    Vb(mutex_s);
}
```

The *V* operation is defined as:

```
V(s) {
    Pb(mutex_s);
    s = s+1;
    if (s <= 0) Vb(delay_s); else Vb(mutex_s);
}
```

The locking semaphore *mutex_s* guarantees that only one process at a time will be able to access and manipulate the semaphore variable *s*. Initially, *s* is set to the desired semaphore value and is decremented with each *P* operation and incremented with each *V* operation. Since *s* may become negative, it serves a *dual purpose*. As long as it is greater or equal zero, it corresponds to the actual semaphore value; whenever it becomes negative, it represents the number of processes blocked or waiting on that semaphore.

A process executing a *P* or *V* should be protected from processor preemption, for example, by inhibiting interrupts for the duration of these operations. This is necessary, even though the semaphore variable *s* is protected by the *mutex_s* semaphore. Without inhibiting the interrupts, the following undesirable situation could occur. Assume that a process executing in the middle of a *P* or *V* operation is preempted and the processor is assigned to another higher-priority process. Suppose that the latter now attempts to execute a *P* or *V* operation on the same semaphore. It would find *mutex_s* equal to 0 and, as a result, remain in the corresponding *while* loop of the *Pb* operation forever. Infinite loops of this type are a form of **deadlock** and must be avoided.

On a uniprocessor system, inhibiting interrupts would normally be sufficient to prevent other processes from simultaneously executing operations on any semaphore. In this case, the *P(mutex_s)* and *V(mutex_s)* operations are not necessary. On a multi-processor, however, inhibiting interrupts on one processor does not prevent processes running on another processor from accessing the semaphore. This is achieved by the *Pb(mutex_s)* operation, which guarantees that at most one *P* or one *V* is acting upon any given semaphore.

When a process executes a *P* operation and finds the semaphore value less than zero, it blocks itself by executing *P(delay)*. Note that this implements a busy-wait—the process continues running in a wait loop while another process is in the CS. Busy-waits for CSs are acceptable if the CS is short. Frequently, this is the case. CSs should be designed to have this property if at all possible. But in an environment involving lengthy CSs and synchronizations—for example, when a process is waiting for an I/O operation to be completed, for a hardware resource to become available, or for a message from another process that can arrive at any arbitrary time—busy waits are unsatisfactory. They can degenerate a multiprogrammed system into a uniprogrammed one, as well as increase the response time for real-time events to intolerable levels.

Avoiding the Busy-Wait

The alternative to busy-waiting which avoids the above problems is to *block* processes on unsuccessful *P* operations and provide for the possible activation of processes on *V* operations. Such a blocking policy is employed for most OS applications and for most synchronization and resource allocation mechanisms, including semaphores. We develop one implementation of this general strategy in this section.

The *P* operation is defined as:

```
P(s) {
    Inhibit_Interrupts;
    Pb(mutex_s);
    s = s-1;
    if (s < 0) {      /*Context Switch*/
        Block(self, Ls);
        Vb(mutex_s);
        Enable_Interrupts;
        Scheduler();
    }
    else {
        Vb(mutex_s);
        Enable_Interrupts;
    }
}
```

The operation always decrements *s*. As long as *s* remains nonnegative, the invoking process or thread proceeds as in the case of busy-waits: It releases the *mutex_s* semaphore, enables interrupts, and continues executing the next instruction. When *s* falls below zero, the process cannot proceed. Instead, it blocks itself by invoking the procedure *Block(self, Ls)*. This first saves the current state in the field *CPU_State* of the process descriptor. This information is necessary to restart the process at a later time. The procedure then inserts the process (a pointer to its PCB) on a **blocked list** *Ls* associated with the semaphore *s*. It also updates the *Status.Type* and *Status.List* fields of the descriptor to reflect these changes. Next, the scheduler is invoked, which selects another ready process from a ready list (*RL*) of processes and transfers control to it. Thus, the new process continues executing on the processor instead of the original process. Such a process reassignment is called a **context switch**.

The *V* operation is defined as:

```
V(s) {
    Inhibit_Interrupts;
    Pb(mutex_s);
    s = s+1;
    if (s <= 0) {
        Unblock(q, Ls);
        Vb(mutex_s);
        Enable_Interrupts;
        Scheduler();
    }
    else {
        Vb(mutex_s);
        Enable_Interrupts;
    }
}
```

The operation first increments *s*. If *s>0*, there are no processes blocked on this semaphore, and the operation simply exits by releasing *mutex s* and enabling interrupts. Otherwise, the operation must unblock the process, *q*, at the head of the list *Ls* associated with *s*. The *Unblock* operation moves the process *q* from the *Ls* list to the *RL* and changes its status accordingly. The scheduler is again called to resume the unblocked process *q*. If there is a free processor, *q* will be started immediately; otherwise, it remains on the RL. Note that, depending on the scheduling policy and the relative priorities of the processes, *q* also could preempt the process that called *V(s)* or another running process.

Since interrupts are inhibited and a busy-wait exists inside the *Pb* operation, it is important that the above code for *P* and *V* operations be short and efficient for the same reasons discussed earlier. The main improvement of this implementation of *P* and *V* over the previous one is that a process busy-waits only when another process is inside a *P* and *V* operation, but not for the entire duration of the CS. This permits CSs to be of arbitrary length, without causing any performance degradation as a result of busy-waiting.

4.5.2 Monitor Primitives

Request/Release operations on resources may be implemented as monitor procedures. There are two main advantages of such an implementation. First, the resource is encapsulated within the monitor as an abstract data type. Second, monitors may be implemented at the user level. The blocking and wake-up of processes or threads is enforced elegantly through the monitor *wait/signal* operations, without modifying the kernel. (Note that monitors are used most naturally in a shared-memory environment, and the active objects are threads in most contemporary systems. We will continue to use the word *process* to mean either process or thread.)

A monitor implementation must enforce mutual exclusion among all monitor procedures. It also must implement the *wait* and *signal* operations. Thus to implement a basic monitor facility, it is necessary to construct code sequences for:

- *Entering* a given monitor: This code is inserted in front of every procedure body within the monitor;

- *Leaving* a monitor: This code is inserted at the end of every monitor procedure;

- *Waiting* on a given condition variable *c*: This code replaces every *c.wait* operation;

- *Signaling* a condition variable *c*: This code replaces every *c.signal* operation.

We assume Hoare monitors and show in detail how they may be implemented using semaphores. Recall the basic semantics of Hoare monitors:

- All procedures or functions must be executed under mutual exclusion.

- Executing a *c.wait* immediately blocks the process on a queue associated with *c*.

- When a *c.signal* is executed, the monitor must determine whether any processes are waiting on the condition *c*. If so, the current process, i.e., the one executing the *signal*, is suspended, and one of the waiting processes is reactivated. Usually, the selection of the process is based on FIFO, but it also could be based on process priorities. If there are no waiting processes, the signaling process continues.

- Whenever a process exits a monitor or issues a *wait*, there may be processes waiting to enter or reenter the monitor. Processes that were suspended earlier as a result of *signal* operations are chosen over those that are queued on initial monitor entry.

To enforce the above semantics, we use three types of semaphores:

- *mutex:*   This is used to enforce the mutual exclusion requirement among procedures.

- *condsem_c:* One such semaphore is defined for each condition variable *c* to block processes executing *c.wait*. An associated integer counter *condcnt_c* keeps count of the number of processes currently blocked on *condsem_c*.

- *urgent:*   This semaphore is used for blocking processes executing a *c.signal*. An integer counter *urgentcnt* keeps count of the number of processes currently blocked on the semaphore *urgent*.

Initially, *mutex* = *1*; *condsem_c* = *0* and *condcnt_c* = *0* for all *c*; and *urgent* = *0* and *urgentcnt* = *0*.

The body of each procedure is then surrounded by entry and exit codes to provide mutual exclusion and priority to suspended processes as follows.

```
P(mutex);
procedure_body;
if (urgentcnt) V(urgent); else V(mutex);
```

The *if-statement* checks for processes currently on the *urgent* queue (as a result of an earlier *c.signal* operation). If so, one of them is re-admitted (*V(urgent)*); otherwise, the *V(mutex)* allows a new process to enter one of the monitor procedures by executing the corresponding *P(mutex)*.

Each *c.wait* within a procedure body is coded as:

```
condcnt_c = condcnt_c + 1;
if (urgentcnt) V(urgent); else V(mutex);
P(condsem_c); /* The process waits here. */
condcnt_c = condcnt_c - 1;
```

The process entering this code is about to block itself on *P(condsem_c)*. Prior to doing so, it takes two actions. First, it increments the number of processes blocked on this semaphore. Second, it admits another process into the monitor. The choice is analogous to the statement following each procedure body. If the *urgent* queue is not empty, one of these processes is readmitted; otherwise, a new process is admitted.

After the process wakes up from the *P(condsem_c)* operation, it decrements the count of blocked processes and continues its execution within the monitor procedure.

Every *c.signal* in a monitor is replaced by the code:

```
if (condcnt_c) {
    urgentcnt = urgentcnt + 1;
    V(condsem_c); P(urgent);
    urgentcnt = urgentcnt - 1;
}
```

This code blocks the executing process on *P(urgent)* if the queue associated with condition *c* is not empty. Prior to blocking itself, it increments the *urgentcnt*, which is tested by every exiting procedure and every *c.wait* operation to determine which process to readmit.

The implementation of monitors can be simplified when various restrictions are placed on the use of *wait* and *signal* (see Exercise 15). For example, a *signal*, if it appears at all, is often the last executed statement in a monitor procedure. All the examples in Chapter 3 were of this nature. Given this restricted use of signals, there is no need for *urgent* and *urgentcnt*. It is also the case that a *wait*, if it appears at all, is almost always the first executed statement of a monitor procedure, perhaps guarded by a Boolean expression. In fact, this feature is directly employed in protected types (see Section 2.6.2). Simpler implementations are also possible with other monitor versions, particularly Mesa and Java monitors, which employ a *notify* instead of a *signal*.

Finally, we emphasize the central use of semaphores in implementing monitors, taking advantage of the state-saving, queuing, blocking, and scheduling that are already built into semaphores. A more direct approach may be more efficient, but hardly as clear.

4.5.3 Clock and Time Management

OS and user programs require facilities to access, wait on, and signal **time**—both relative time intervals and absolute "wall-clock" or calendar time. Applications for the OS include performance measurement, processor scheduling, time-stamping events such as I/O and file systems calls, and deadlock and other fault detection.

Current computers provide time support through a variety of mechanisms ranging from a straightforward periodic clock interrupt to a fairly complex clock chip that implements many timer functions and can be controlled by operating software. For our discussion, we assume the availability of a hardware **ticker** that issues an interrupt at a fixed period. A typical tick interval might be one millisecond. The *Alarm_Clock* monitor presented in Chapter 3 shows how such a tick interrupt is interfaced to a time service.

Another basic timer module that is found in most computers is a hardware **countdown timer**. This device has a program-settable register that is decremented by one at each clock tick; when the register value reaches zero, an interrupt is issued. The tick granularity here can be quite small—on the order of microseconds. In Section 4.6, we discuss in some detail methods and models for connecting interrupts, for example, from clocks, countdown timers, and I/O devices, to OS software.

Given a periodic hardware clock signal and a countdown timer, the goal is to build higher-level clock and timer services for use by the OS and applications. Many of these services appear in the kernel because they are used by other kernel services, must be protected from errors or abuse, and require indivisible execution at a high priority to produce correct results.

Wall Clock Timers

The principal function of a computer's wall clock service is to maintain and return an *accurate* **time of day**. Because computer clocks, like most of those on our wrists, are ultimately controlled by a periodic quartz crystal, they drift over time. For example, a typical crystal might lose or gain up to 10^{-5} μsec per second, which roughly equals one second per day. To maintain accuracy, the clocks are synchronized periodically with accurate standard clocks, such as universal coordinated time (UTC), which can be obtained through GPS receivers or over a network.

The OS and applications also rely on the **monotonicity** of clock values—for two successive clock readings, the value returned by the second reading should be greater or equal to that from the first reading. For example, time-stamps on file updates are commonly employed to determine the most recent update. Monotonicity is violated if a clock is reset back in time during synchronization (or when daylight saving time is reset back to standard time). When a backward change is required, a solution that maintains monotonicity continues running the clock forward but at a *slower* rate until the change catches up.

EXAMPLE: Maintaining Monotonicity

Suppose that a computer clock reads 3:00 P.M., but should be set back one hour to the correct time of 2:00 P.M. If we run the clock at a slower rate, say at one-half the real-time rate, computer time and correct real-time will meet at 4:00 P.M., while the clock is always increasing monotonically. Running the clock at one-half the real-time rate means essentially ignoring every other tick interrupt. At 4:00 P.M., the clock rate of the computer is reset to its normal real-time rate.

An object implementing a wall clock service typically offers three functions:

1. *Update_Clock*: The current time, say *tnow*, is updated. This function is invoked on each clock tick interrupt and must be tightly coupled to it. The update must occur as a CS and, generally, without interruption. The value of *tnow* is typically a single

positive integer indicating the number of clock ticks since some known starting time, making the *Update_Clock* function very fast and deterministic.

2. *Get_Time*: The current clock value is returned. This can be the integer value *tnow*, or it might involve a computation. For example, *Get_Time* could return the current time in the form of a sextuple [month, year, day, hour, minutes, seconds], where the individual components are derived from the value *tnow*.

3. *Set_Clock(tnew)*: The current time is explicitly set to a new value *tnew*.

Countdown Timers

Another basic set of timer functions is related to **alarm clocks**. A process or thread requires a *timeout* signal at some specified time in the future. In its purest form, the process wishes to delay, sleep, or block until awakened by the timer signal event. Thus the basic function provided by a countdown timer is:

- *Delay(tdel)*: block the invoking process for the period of time specified by the parameter *tdel*; this is typically a nonnegative time interval relative to the current time *tnow*; i.e., the process remains blocked until the wall clock time reaches *tnow+tdel*.

To implement this function, assume first that a dedicated countdown timer is allocated to each process. The following function is provided to operate this counter:

- *Set_Timer(tdel)*: The timer is set to the starting countdown value *tdel*. When the value reaches zero, an interrupt is generated, which invokes a function *Timeout()*

Using the above countdown timer, we can implement the *Delay* function as follows:

```
Delay(tdel) {
  Set_Timer(tdel);
  P(delsem); /* Wait for interrupt. */
}

Timeout() {
  V(delsem);
}
```

The *Delay* function simply loads the hardware timer with the *tdel* value and blocks the calling process on a binary semaphore, say *delsem*, associated with the hardware timer and initialized to zero. When the counter reaches zero, the interrupt routine *Timeout* wakes up the blocked process by performing a *V* operation on the semaphore *delsem*.

In most realistic cases, hardware timers are shared among a group of processes or threads. Each process has its own logical timer, just as each process has its own logical CPU. More generally, a process may desire several logical timers. This leads to the following operations defined for a logical countdown timer object:

1. *tn = Create_LTimer()*: Creates a new timer, returning its identifier in *tn*.
2. *Destroy_LTimer(tn)*: Destroys the logical timer identified by *tn*.

3. *Set_LTimer(tn, tdel)*: This is the logical equivalent to the *Set_Timer(tdel)* function defined for a single hardware timer. It loads the timer *tn* with the value *tdel*. When the value reaches zero, *Timeout()* is invoked by the interrupt. Loading the time with a value of zero disables the timer, no interrupt is generated.

The main question is then how to implement *multiple logical* timers using a *single hardware* timer. We present two possible approaches to this problem.

Using a Priority Queue with Absolute Wakeup Times

The first approach uses both a countdown timer and a wall clock timer. The wakeup times of the blocked processes are kept in a priority queue. This could be implemented as a sorted list or a binary heap (see Section 4.2.2). Let the priority queue be designated *TQ* and each element contain a triple *(p, tn, wakeup)*, where *p* is a process identifier, *tn* is a logical countdown timer, and *wakeup* is a future time value until which the process *p* wishes to delay itself. The priority queue orders elements such that lowest *wakeup* values have highest priority.

EXAMPLE: Priority Queue with Absolute Wakeup Times

Figure 4-8a shows an example of such a priority queue, organized as a simple linked list. (We show only the process names and their *wakeup* times; the names of the logical clocks are omitted for clarity.) The figure shows entries for four processes: p_1 wishes to wake up at wall clock time 115, p_2 at time 135, and so on. The figure also shows the current value of the wall clock (103) and the current value of the countdown timer (12). The next interrupt will occur 12 time units later, at time 115.

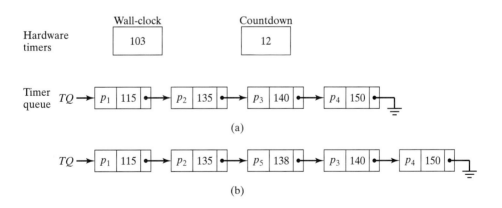

FIGURE 4-8. Timer queue.

The following algorithm then implements the *Set_LTimer* function for logical clocks:

```
Set_LTimer(tn, tdel) {
    wnew = Get_Time() + tdel;
    wold = first(TQ)->wakeup;
```

```
                         /* Get wakeup value of first element.*/
        if ( wnew < wold ) Set_Timer(tdel);
        insert(TQ, (*, tn, wnew));
                    /* Insert current process (*) into TQ */
                    /* in the order determined by the wakeup field. */
    }
```

The algorithm uses the computer wall clock to obtain the current time (*Get_Time*). The delay value *tdel* is added to the current time to determine where to place the new entry within the list. If *wnew* is less than the wakeup value of the first element in the queue (*wold*), the new element becomes the head of the queue. In this case, the countdown timer must be set to the new delay interval *tdel* using the *Set_Timer(tdel)*. The new element is then inserted into *TQ* according to the *wakeup* value.

Due to the time-sensitive nature of the operations, the function is executed as a CS. In particular, interrupts from the timer are inhibited during *Set_LTimer*.

EXAMPLE: Effect of `Set_LTimer`

To illustrate the above code, consider the state of the system in Figure 4-8a and assume that a new process p_5 issues the call *Set_LTimer(tn, 35)*. The value of *wold* is 115; the value of *wnew* is $103 + 35 - 138$. The new element is inserted as shown in Figure 4-8b, and the value of the countdown timer remains unchanged. In contrast, a new element created with the call *Set_LTimer(tn, 5)* would become the current head of the queue and the timer would be set to 5.

The *Delay* function can now be implemented using logical timers in the same way as hardware timers. It loads the logical timer with *tdel* value using the above function *Set_LTimer(tn, tdel)*. It then blocks the invoking process on a *P* operation.

When the value in the physical countdown timer reaches zero, the interrupt routine services the first element in the queue *TQ*. It removes this element and wakes up the corresponding process using a *V* operation. It also sets the timer to a new value, computed as the difference between the *wakeup* value of the next element in the queue and the current time, *Get_Time*, i.e.:

```
        Set_LTimer(tn, first(TQ)->wakeup - Get_Time())
```

EXAMPLE: Effect of Timer Expiration

In Figure 4-8, when the countdown timer reaches zero, the wall clock time reads 115. The first element of TQ is removed, process p_1 is woken up, and the time is set to $135 - 115 = 20$, to wake up process p_2 20 time units later.

Using a Priority Queue with Time Differences

The previous solution made no assumptions about the implementation of TQ. Figure 4-8 shows an implementation as a sorted linked list, but TQ also could be implemented as a binary heap to speed up insertion or another form of priority queue. A linked-list implementation is suitable when the number of logical timers is relatively small, say on the order of 20 or less. In that case, a more efficient variant is possible which uses only the countdown

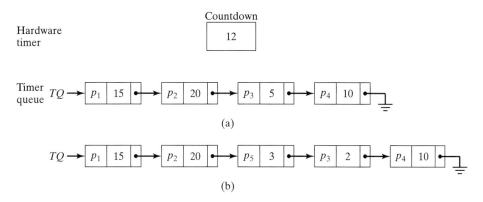

FIGURE 4-9. Timer queue with differences.

timer; no wall clock is required. The idea is to record only the **differences** between wakeup times in successive elements, rather than the absolute wakeup time values.

Figure 4-9a illustrates this idea for the same four processes of Figure 4-8a. Process p_1 is at the head of the queue and so it will wake up when the countdown timer reaches 0, i.e., after 12 time units. p_2 is to wake up 20 time units after p_1, p_3 is to wake up 5 time units after p_2, and so on. Thus, the interrupt routine is quite simple: Whenever the time expires and the process at the head of the queue is removed, the countdown timer is set to the value stored in the next element. In Figure 4-9a, when p_1 is removed, the counter is loaded with the value 20.

The *Set_LTimer(tn, tdel)* is more complicated. Its main task is to find the two elements, say *left* and *right*, between which the new request is to be inserted. It does so by adding the differences in the entries, starting with the current value of the countdown timer, until the *tdel* value is reached. The difference currently stored in the *right* element is then divided into two portions. One is stored in the new element and represents the difference between the left and the new element. The other is stored in the right element and represents the difference between the new and the right element.

EXAMPLE: Priority Queue with Time Differences

At the time represented by Figure 4-9a, process p_4 is scheduled to wake up in $12 + 20 + 5 + 10 = 47$ time units. Suppose that a *Set_LTimer(tn, 35)* is executed at this time by a process p_5. The effect is shown in Figure 4-9b. The entry for p_5 is inserted between p_2 and p_3 since p_5's wakeup time lies between two processes: $(12 + 20) = 32 < 35 < (12 + 20 + 5) = 37$. The original difference in p_3, (5), is divided into $3 + 2$, where 3 is stored in the new element p_5, and 2 is stored in its right neighbor, p_3.

The main purpose of countdown timers is to generate **timeout** signals. Synchronization primitives that involve possible blocking or waiting, such as those defined in semaphores, message-passing, or rendezvous, often have built-in timeouts. For example, instead of a regular *P* operation on a semaphore, it is also common to support a *P* with timeout. Such an operation might have the form:

```
int P(sem, dt)
```

which returns 1 for a normal *P* operation on the semaphore *sem*, and 0 if the calling process is still blocked after *dt* time units have expired.

4.5.4 Communication Primitives

We introduce the implementation principles of building centralized and distributed communications. The most basic form involves **message-passing** and is often directly supported at the kernel level. More abstract mechanisms, such as rendezvous and RPC, can be realized with message-passing operations, as was illustrated in Section 3.2.2. Message-passing is most natural with processes or threads executing on separate machines or with separate address spaces that wish to communicate or synchronize.

A generic form of message-passing primitives includes the following two basic operations:

- *send(p, m)*: Send message *m* to process *p*.

- *receive(q, m)*: Receive a message *m* from process *q*.

Either operation could be blocking or nonblocking, and it could be selective or nonselective (i.e., name a specific process *p* or send to/receive from any process).

Consider first a shared-memory system with one or more processors. To implement any form of the send/receive operations, we need two **buffers**: one in the user space of the sender to hold the message while it is being sent, and the other in the user space of the receiver to hold the received copy of the message. Figure 4-10a illustrates the situation. The parameter *m* of the *send* operations points to the sender's buffer, *sbuf*, which holds the message to be sent. Similarly, the *receive* operation identifies a receiving buffer, *rbuf*. When *send* is invoked, the system copies the message from *sbuf* to *rbuf*, where it may be retrieved by the *receive* operation.

There are two important issues that must be resolved with the above simple scenario:

1. How does the sender process know that *sbuf* has been copied and may be reused?
2. How does the system know that the contents of *rbuf* are no longer needed by the receiver process and may be overwritten?

There are two possible solutions to the first problem. One is to block the process inside the *send* operation until *sbuf* has been copied. This results in a *blocking send*. If the *receive* also is blocking, the communication is completely synchronous; both processes must reach their respective send/receive points before either one may continue.

Such tight synchronization is not always necessary or even desirable. For example, the sender may not wish to reuse *sbuf* and need not be blocked. To permit the sender to continue, the system could provide a flag associated with *sbuf* to indicate whether *sbuf* has already been copied. This results in a *nonblocking send*; however, the need to explicitly poll the flag is awkward. Alternately, an interrupt could be generated when the buffer has been copied to inform the sender, but the resulting nondeterminism makes programming very difficult.

A similar difficulty arises at the receiver's site (Question 2 above). A possible solution is to associate a flag with *rbuf* to inform the system that *rbuf* is no longer needed. But this flag must be explicitly set by the receiving process and repeatedly tested by the system. Consequently, such mechanisms are not very convenient.

A more elegant solution to the synchronization problems at both ends is to use additional intermediate buffers, rather than attempting to copy *sbuf* directly to *rbuf*. Figure 4-10b shows the general organization. A pool of **system buffers** is used at each end. The *send* operation simply copies the message from the user buffer *sbuf* to one of the system buffers. For selective sends, it also includes the name of the receiving process. Once the copy is made, the sender is free to proceed; thus, the send becomes *nonblocking*, and with a sufficiently large pool of system buffers, allows the sender to continue generating and sending messages. The system copies each full buffer, along

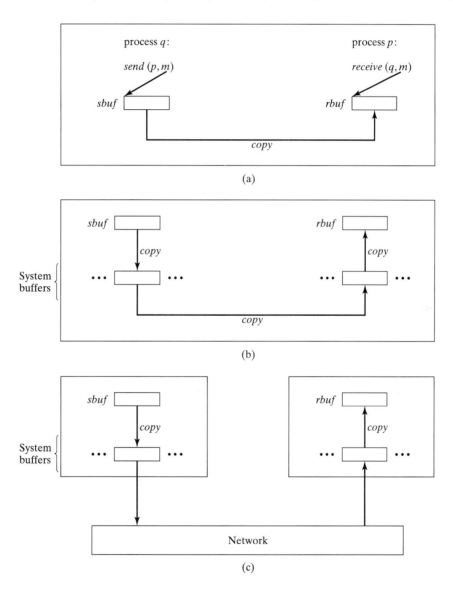

FIGURE 4-10. Send/receive buffers; (a) copying user buffers; (b) copying through system buffers; and (c) copying across network.

with the sender's name, into a corresponding empty system buffer at the receiver's end. (Or it simply reallocates the full buffer to the receiver, avoiding one copy operation.) Thus, the set of system buffers acts as a message port for receiving messages.

Each *receive* operation then simply copies the next system buffer into the *rbuf* of the receiver, and the system buffer is freed. It is up to the receiver to determine when *rbuf* is no longer needed; it will be overwritten whenever the process issues the next *receive* operation.

Using this scheme, *receive* also may be implemented as *blocking* or *nonblocking*. In the first case, the operation blocks if no system buffer contains any data for the process. It is awakened when a message arrives and is copied into *rbuf*. A nonblocking version only checks the availability of full system buffers. If none are available, a corresponding error condition is returned, instead of blocking the process.

CASE STUDY: RC4000 PRIMITIVES

The multiprogramming system for the RC4000 computer (Brinch Hansen 1970) was an early influential OS that pioneered the use of processes. An interesting and elegant set of message transmission operations was defined, consisting of an asynchronous *sendmessage*, a blocking *receivemessage*, an asynchronous *sendanswer*, and a blocking *waitanswer*. Under normal conditions, a sender issues a *sendmessage*, followed later by a *waitanswer*; a receiver's sequence is *waitmessage*, followed by *sendanswer*. Each process has a message queue, essentially a set of buffers linked together in the order of message sends, to store received messages and answers.

The basic *send/receive* scheme described above works provided that the processes and communication channels are error-free. In reality, common errors include issuing a *send* to a nonexistent process, transmitting bursts of many *send*s to the same process, resulting in buffer overflows and deadlocks where a *receive* might be blocked forever. The system will attempt to hide errors from the application, for example, by automatic retransmissions and the use of error-correcting codes. However, some errors cannot be handled fully transparently. A common approach to error detection is to return a *success/fail* flag (or an error code) on each function call, and let the process take appropriate actions. Another mechanism is to add a timeout parameter to the blocking primitives (here, the blocking *receive*) and indicate to the process (by an error code) whether the operation succeeded or timed out.

The use of system buffers is particularly important in multiprocessor or multicomputer systems, where no shared memory is available between different machines and the delays in message transmissions are large. Figure 4-10c shows such a system with two machines communicating with each other through a network—LAN or WAN.

The copying of the system buffers involves much additional processing, generally performed by a specialized communications (sub)kernel to handle the I/O across the network. The kernel is typically responsible for breaking messages into fixed-size transmission packets, routing the packets through the network, reassembling them into messages at the destination, and handling a variety of transmission errors. Thus, the copying of each message buffer between different machines passes through multiple layers of communication protocols. For example, the Open Systems Interconnection Reference Model (OSI), developed by the International Standards Organization, specifies seven different layers, interfaces, and protocols for communications: physical, data link, network, transport, session, presentation, and application. Another international standard, promoted by telephone companies as a means to handle both voice and data messages, is Asynchronous Transfer Mode (ATM). This layered protocol is a suitable choice for multimedia applications.

4.6   INTERRUPT HANDLING

The term *interrupt* generally refers to an event occurring at an unpredictable time that forces a transfer of control out of the normal processing sequence of a computer. One insightful view is that the purpose of interrupt handling is to remove the notion of asynchronous events from higher levels of the kernel, the OS, and applications. Ultimately, it is through interrupts that the abstraction of processes—almost independent activities operating logically in parallel—is implemented. The asynchrony of events, such as I/O completion, also is hidden by the interrupt handling mechanisms.

As described briefly in Section 1.2.2, interrupts are often classified as **internal** or **external**, depending on their source. External interrupts are generated by hardware that is extraneous to a computer and essentially runs in parallel with it. The standard examples of this extraneous hardware are, of course, I/O devices and controllers (see Chapter 11). Through interrupts, they signal events such as the end of an I/O read or write, the arrival of a message, or an error during I/O. Other external interrupt sources are timers, other processors in a multiprocessor system, and machine-monitoring systems that check for hardware errors.

Internal interrupts or traps are those that occur directly as a consequence of the current computation. These also are called **exceptions** because they identify some exceptional, usually error, condition associated with the current instruction. By nature, exceptions occur synchronously with the current computation. Similarly, traps to the supervisor, such as SVC instructions, are also synchronous. Our discussion in this section pertains primarily to external interrupts, which represent asynchronous events produced by physically concurrent hardware.

Interrupts from the same source are generally treated as a class in terms of their hardware access, shared data, and operations. The different classes are sorted by their importance. Common operations on classes of interrupts include the following:

- *Enable*: Activate the interrupts. Any pending (previously inhibited) interrupts are now processed and future interrupts are processed immediately.

- *Disable*: Deactivate the interrupts. All future interrupts are ignored. Note that some critical classes of interrupts, such as a power failure, cannot be disabled.

- *Inhibit*: Delay the processing of interrupts. The interrupts are kept pending until the class is again enabled using the above operation.

When an interrupt occurs, further interrupts from classes at the same or lower priority level are normally automatically inhibited until a special instruction, often called *return_from_interrupt*, is executed. Built-in hardware priorities permit handlers of high-priority events to preempt those of lower priority, much in the same way as a CPU scheduler ensures that high-priority processes preempt lower-priority ones.

Regardless of the source and type of interrupt, the OS goes through a standard interrupt-handling sequence whenever the CPU is interrupted:

1. Save the state of the running process or thread so that it can be restarted later. Most of this is done automatically by the CPU interrupt hardware.

2. Identify the type of interrupt and invoke an *interrupt service routine*, generally called the **interrupt handler** (IH), associated with this type of interrupt.

3. Execute the IH, which services the interrupt. Because the IH is considered to be a CS, every effort is made to keep it short.

4. Restore the state of the interrupted process on the CPU, which resumes its execution at the point of the interruption. Alternatively, another process could be selected for execution on the interrupted CPU. This is frequently the case, because the IH may have awakened processes that were waiting for the interrupt-causing event to occur.

Figure 4-11a illustrates the use of this interrupt-handling sequence in the design of a hardware/software interface. We assume the existence of an external hardware device. To use this device, a process p invokes a procedure, Fn, which initiates the device, passes parameters to it from the calling process, and, when the device terminates, returns results to the process. The procedure Fn, after initiating the device, blocks itself to await the completion of the device operation. The OS takes over and selects another process to run in the meantime. When the device terminates, it generates an interrupt, which saves the state of the currently running process and invokes the IH. The IH services the interrupt, unblocks process p, and issues the *return_from_interrupt* instruction, which transfers control back to the OS. The scheduler now selects the next process to run, and restores its state. We assume that the original process p is restarted. This allows the procedure Fn to complete and return to its caller.

This example illustrates some of the main difficulties in developing interrupt-handling mechanisms to address asynchronous events. First, the procedure Fn must be able to block itself on a given event. If this procedure is to be written by the user, this requires knowledge (or possibly even a modification) of the OS kernel. Second, the IH must be able to unblock a process associated with the event. Third, the IH must be able to "return" from the interrupt, i.e., pass control to the OS. These issues must be addressed by specially designed kernel mechanisms, even if application programmers are allowed to develop their own interrupt-handling facilities. Designing the interfaces among the hardware, the kernel routines, and the rest of the system coherently and without error has always been a major challenge. We present one model that provides a framework for building these interfaces in a more uniform abstract manner.

The solution is to extend the process model down into the hardware itself, so that interrupts and their handlers are somehow included. At the same time, we replace the blocking and wakeup facilities by standard interprocess synchronization constructs, such as P/V, *send/receive*, or monitor operations, which do not require any knowledge of or extension to the kernel.

Figure 4-11b shows the modified organization corresponding to the situation of Figure 4-11a. We view the hardware device as a separate process, which is started (at least conceptually) by the *Init* operation issued by the procedure Fn. The procedures Fn and IH, which are designed to operate the hardware, are implemented in the form

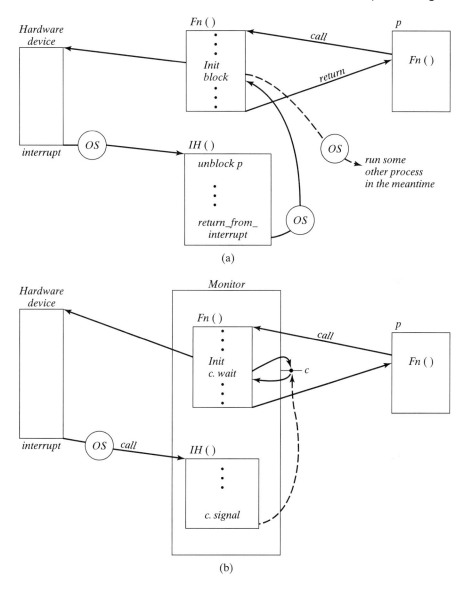

FIGURE 4-11. Using a hardware device; (a) basic interrupt sequence; and (b) using a monitor.

of a monitor placed between the hardware and the process p. The process uses the hardware by invoking Fn as before. Fn initiates the hardware process and blocks itself using $c.wait$, where the condition c is associated with the device. When the hardware terminates, the interrupt is implemented as a call to the IH function of the monitor. This services the interrupt and issues a $c.signal$ to wake up the function Fn.

The main advantages of this solution over that in Figure 4-11a are the following. The procedures Fn and IH require no knowledge of the OS kernel; they interact purely through the monitor primitives and may be written at the application level. The blocking, which also involves the OS and causes another process to execute in the meantime, is completely transparent to *Fn*. The *Init* procedure is a process-creation call to the hardware process, similar to a *fork*, or a wakeup message to the hardware process. The interrupt is a procedure call to a monitor procedure, rather than special signal. The hardware must still save the state of the interrupted process, but from *p*'s perspective, *IH* is just like any other procedure of the monitor.

Note that some of the procedures (e.g., *Fn*) are called by the software process, whereas others (e.g., *IH*) are called by the hardware process. Thus, the monitor serves as a uniform hardware/software interface. It provides CS protection, it allows the hardware to signal the arrival of data when appropriate (by calling *IH*), and allows the processes to wait for data or events when logically necessary.

An interesting question is then: To which process does the *IH* procedure belong? One answer that fits in well with our abstractions and leads to straightforward and efficient code is: Let *IH* belong to the hardware process. Thus, the monitor is shared by the process *p* and by the hardware process.

EXAMPLE: Simple Clock Server

Consider a simple clock server with three procedures, *Update_Clock*, *Get_Time*, and *Set_Clock*, as described in Section 4.5.3. *Update_Clock* is directly connected to a periodic hardware ticker, whereas the other two procedures are used by processes to access and set the current time (Fig. 4-12). The code for the monitor is outlined below:

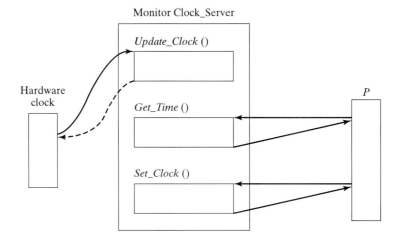

FIGURE 4-12. Using a timer through a monitor.

```
monitor Clock_Server {
. . .
Update_Clock() {
. . .
    tnow = tnow + 1;
    /* Perhaps update time structure also.*/
}
```

```
int Get_Time() {
    . . .
    return(tnow);
    /* Perhaps return some more complex time structure
        instead. */
}

Set_Clock(int tnew) {
    . . .
    tnow = tnew;
}
}
```

Each clock tick is generated by a hardware process that calls *Update_Clock*. In the underlying implementation, the clock interrupt mechanism automatically saves the currently running process state and calls the *Update_Clock* procedure. When it exists, the interrupt handler restores the state of the original process.

CONCEPTS, TERMS, AND ABBREVIATIONS

The following concepts have been introduced in this chapter. Test yourself by defining and discussing each keyword or phrase.

Activate a process	Process control block (PCB)
Asynchronous Transfer Mode (ATM)	Priority queue
Binary heap	Process descriptor
Blocked list	Process state vector
Busy wait	Process status
Clock server	Queue
Context switch	Ready list (RL)
Control block	Release operation
Countdown timer	Request operation
Descriptor	Spinning lock
Exception	Suspend a process
Interrupt handler (IH)	Test and set instruction (TS)
Kernel	Thread
Nucleus	Thread descriptor
Open Systems Interconnection	
Reference Model (OSI)	

EXERCISES

1. Consider a producer/consumer situation where the producer must never be blocked. To avoid the overhead of implementing the buffer as a linked list, the following scheme is used. The buffer is implemented as fixed size array, $A[n]$, where n is large enough most of the time. In the case where the producer finds the buffer full, the array size n is temporarily extended to accommodate the spike in the production. The

extension is removed when the number of elements falls again below n. Compare the effectiveness of this scheme with a linked list implementation, given the following values:

- tl is the time to perform one insert or remove operation in a linked list implementation;
- ta is the time to perform one insert or remove operation in the proposed array implementation;
- oh is the overhead time to temporarily extend the array;
- p is the probability that any given insert operation will overrun the normal array size n.

(a) Derive a formula for computing the value of p below which the proposed scheme will outperform the linked list implementation.

(b) What is the value of p when $tl = 10 \times ta$ and $oh = 100 \times ta$?

2. Assume that each resource is represented by a data structure called RCB (resource control block). This contains information about the resource and a waiting queue for processes blocked on this resource. Consider a single-processor system with currently four processes p_1 through p_4, and two resources, r_1 and r_2. Process p_1 has created p_2 and p_3; process p_3 has created p_4. Presently, p_1 is *running*, p_2 is *ready*, and p_3 and p_4 are both *blocked* on the resource r_2. The ready list is a simple linked list of pointers to processes. Show the details of all process descriptors and their interconnections (pointers) reflecting the above system state.

3. Suppose that the *Suspend* and *Activate* operations are similar to *Destroy* in that they suspend not only the named process but also its descendants. Modify *Suspend* and *Activate* accordingly. To simplify the solution, assume that a process may only suspend and activate a process it has created as its direct child process (see Exercise 4).

Note that processes lower in the hierarchy may already be suspended. Make sure that any suspended descendant process is activated only by the process that originally suspended that process. (*Hint:* Extend the process control block to keep track of who suspended the process.)

When devising your algorithms, consider what should happen when a process attempts to suspend an already suspended child processes, or activate an already active child process.

4. In the previous exercise, it was assumed that a process may suspend and activate only its immediate child processes.

(a) What difficulties would arise if a process was allowed to suspend and activate any of its descendants (i.e., child, grandchild, grand-grandchild, etc.)? (Hint: Consider what should happen if two processes attempt to suspend and later activate the same process.)

(b) What difficulties would arise if a process was allowed to suspend itself (or possibly one of its ancestors)?

5. Can a process apply the function *Destroy()* to itself to successfully terminate its own execution? If not, what changes must be made?

6. Simplify the *Create, Destroy, Suspend*, and *Activate* operations for a system with only a single CPU.

7. Consider a system with only three possible process states: running, ready, and blocked, i.e., there is no distinction between *active* and *suspended*. Modify the process state diagram (Fig. 4-5) to reflect the simplification.

8. Consider a machine instruction, *SWAP*, which swaps the contents of a memory location, M, with the contents of a register, R, in a single indivisible operation. That is,

SWAP is defined as follows:

$$\text{SWAP}(\text{R, M})\{\texttt{temp} = \text{R; R} = \text{M; M} = \texttt{temp; ; }\}$$

Implement the *Pb* and *Vb* operations on binary semaphores using *SWAP*. (Hint: Use the fact that the memory location *M* is shared, and each process has a private copy of the register *R*.)

9. Consider a machine instruction, *TSB*, which performs the following function as a single indivisible operation:

$$\text{TSB}(\text{X, L}) \ \{\texttt{if}(\text{X} == 0) \ \texttt{goto L else X} = 0; \}$$

That is, *TSB* tests the variable *X*. Depending on the outcome of the test, the instruction either branches to an address *L*, or it sets *X* to zero, and execution continues with the next instruction following *TSB*.
Implement the *Pb* and *Vb* operations on binary semaphores using *TSB*.

10. Is the implementation of the general semaphore operations using spinning locks (Section 4.5.1) still correct if one of the following changes are made:
    (a) The *Pb(mutex_s)* statement is moved after the $s = s - 1$ statement in the *P* operation.
    (b) The *Vb(mutex_s)* statement is moved in front of the *if (s < 0)* {...} statement in the *P* operation.

11. The UNIX OS has no general interprocess communication or synchronization scheme. Instead, binary semaphore operations can be simulated by creating and deleting a known file. Find out how files are created and what happens when an already existing file is "created." Show how this idea can be implemented.

12. Consider the following synchronization primitives:
    - *ADVANCE(X)*: increments the variable *X* by 1;
    - *AWAIT(X,C)*: blocks the process executing this instruction until $X \geq C$.

    Using these primitives, develop a solution to the bounded-buffer problem.

13. Assume that the following function is part of a monitor body:

```
f(x) {
    if (x) c1.wait;
    x++;
    c2.signal;
    x = 0;
}
```

Translate this code using *P* and *V* operations to implement the *wait* and *signal* operations and the mutual exclusion as required by the definition of Hoare monitors.

14. Demonstrate that monitors and semaphores have equal expressive power. (Hint: Consider the implementation of monitors given in the text. Then write a monitor that emulates P/V operations on general semaphores.)

15. Under each of the following assumptions, the code implementing a monitor (see Section 4.5.2) may be simplified. Show the new code for each case:
    (a) The monitor contains no *wait* or *signal* operations.
    (b) The last instruction of the monitor body is *signal*. (Other *signal* operations may occur earlier in the body.)
    (c) The use of *signal* is restricted such that it may occur *only* as the last instruction of any monitor.

16. Show how Mesa monitors (see Section 4.5.2) can be implemented using P and V operations on general semaphores.

17. Modify the *Set_LTimer()* function of Section 4.5.3 such that it blocks the invoking process until an absolute wall clock time *tabs*, i.e., the function has the format *Set_LTimer(tn, tabs)*. What should happen when the specified wakeup time *tabs* is already in the past?

18. Consider the *Delay(tdel)* function in Section 4.5.3. Implement an analogous function, *Delay(tn,tdel)*, which uses a logical countdown timer *tn* instead of a physical one. Show the pseudocode for the function and the associated *Timeout()* function.

19. Assume at time 500 there are four processes, p_1 through p_4, waiting for a timeout signal. The four processes are scheduled to wake up at time 520, 645, 695, 710.

    (a) Assuming the implementation using a priority queue with time differences (see Section 4.5.3), show the queue and the content of the countdown timer at time 500.

    (b) After p_1 wakes up, it immediately issues an another call *Set_LTimer(tn,70)*. Assuming that processing the call takes no time, show the priority queue after the call.

    (c) Assume p_1 issues the same call again (*Set_LTimer(tn,70)*) immediately after it wakes up for the second time. Show the new priority queue.

C H A P T E R   5

Process and Thread Scheduling

5.1   ORGANIZATION OF SCHEDULERS
5.2   SCHEDULING METHODS
5.3   PRIORITY INVERSION
5.4   MULTIPROCESSOR AND DISTRIBUTED SCHEDULING

One of the major tasks performed by an operating system (OS) is to allocate ready processes or threads to the available processors. This task may usefully be divided into two parts. The first part, referred to as **process scheduling**, embodies decision-making policies to determine the order in which active processes should compete for the use of processors. The actual binding of a selected process to a processor, which involves removing the process from the ready queue, changing its status, and loading the processor state, is performed by a **process dispatcher**. Scheduling and dispatching are typically done by different modules of the OS. Frequently, these modules are part of the kernel, but they also could appear at higher OS levels and in applications code. In a more complex fashion, different elements of the system may even have their own schedulers so that scheduling is distributed throughout. Unless explicitly distinguished, we will refer to both components jointly as the **scheduler** and to both tasks jointly as **scheduling**.

The next section is concerned primarily with the general design of schedulers, with particular emphasis on priority-based systems. Following that is a detailed description and evaluation of common scheduling strategies used for batch, interactive, and real-time applications. The reminder of this chapter presents the priority inversion problem and discusses scheduling for multiprocessor and distributed systems.

5.1   ORGANIZATION OF SCHEDULERS

5.1.1   Embedded and Autonomous Schedulers

A scheduler may be shared by processes in the system in the same manner that the kernel operations developed in Chapter 4 are shared—the scheduler is invoked by a function or procedure call as an indirect result of a kernel operation. The kernel and the scheduler are then contained in the address space of all processes and execute within any process. They are *embedded* as functions or procedures of currently running processes.

A second method is to centralize the scheduler, possibly with a centralized kernel. Conceptually, this type of scheduler is considered a separate and *autonomous process*,

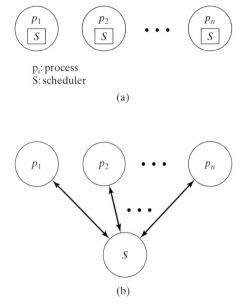

p_i: process
S: scheduler

(a)

(b)

FIGURE 5-1. Organization of schedulers. (a) shared scheduler (b) autonomous scheduler.

running on its own processor. It can continuously poll the system for work, or it may be driven by wakeup signals. The autonomous and the shared alternatives are illustrated in Figure 5-1.

A shared approach offers a number of advantages. Because shared-kernel components are automatically included in every process, they are independent of the number of available processors and need not be permanently associated with any particular one. The view that the kernel really defines a set of machine operations necessary to transform a standard computer into an OS machine leads naturally to a shared organization. A final point is that different groups of processes may in principle have different OSs controlling them. Here, several different schedulers may coexist simultaneously, each attached to (shared by) a different set of processes.

The autonomous approach may be preferable in multiprocessor and distributed systems where one processor can be permanently dedicated to scheduling, kernel, and other supervisory activities such as I/O and program loading. In such a master/slave organization, the OS (i.e., the master) is, at least in principle, cleanly separated from user processes (i.e., the slaves). Even if a separate processor is not dedicated exclusively to executing parts of the OS, the autonomous scheduler approach is still possible in both uniprocessor and multiprocessor configurations. A logical difficulty, however, arises in these situations—namely, who dispatches the scheduler process? One solution is to automatically transfer control to the scheduler whenever a process blocks, is interrupted, or is awakened. In a time-sharing system, the scheduler is typically invoked at the end of a quantum interrupt, i.e., when a process has run for a predefined period time (i.e., the quantum) or has voluntarily given up the CPU. The scheduler dispatches the next process and resets the timer to count down the next quantum.

CASE STUDIES: ORGANIZATION OF SCHEDULERS

1. *UNIX*. UNIX is an example of a system where the scheduler (dispatcher) is a separate process. It runs every other time, i.e., between any two other processes. It also serves as the "dummy" or idle process which runs when no other process is ready, as mentioned earlier in Section 3.5.1. A detailed example of a shared scheduler will be presented shortly.

2. *Windows 2000*. Windows 2000 uses an embedded scheduler (dispatcher), consisting of a set of routines invoked when any of the following events occur:

    - A new thread is created.
    - A previously blocked thread is awakened.
    - A thread uses up its time quantum.
    - A thread blocks itself.
    - A thread terminates.
    - A thread's priority changes.
    - The preferred processor of a thread in a multiprocessor system (called the processor affinity) changes.

5.1.2 Priority Scheduling

Virtually all schedulers use the concept of **priority** when deciding which process should be running next. We will define the notion of priority formally in Section 5.2.1. For now, assume that priority is a numeric value, denoted as P and derived for each process p by a specific function $P = Priority(p)$. Depending on the function used, the value of P may be **static**; i.e., it remains constant for the lifespan of the process. Or it can be **dynamic**, i.e., it is recomputed every time the scheduler is invoked. Regardless of how the priorities are derived for each process, they divide all processes into multiple **priority levels**. The priority levels are generally implemented as a data structure, referred to as the **ready list** (*RL*). Processes at a given level $RL[i]$ have precedence over all processes at lower levels $RL[j]$, $j < i$. Processes at the same priority level are ordered according to additional criteria, such as their order of arrival in the system. Section 4.2 presented several options for implementing priority queues.

The scheduler is invoked either periodically or as the results of events that can affect the priorities of the existing processes. The role of the scheduler is then to guarantee that, at the time it terminates, the *np* highest-priority processes are running, where *np* is the number of processors in the system. In other words, the priority of any *running* process must always be greater than or equal to that of any *ready_a* process.

We now present a concrete example of a priority scheduler/dispatcher that implements the above principles. The implementation follows the embedded design, where the *Scheduler()* function is invoked at the end of other kernel operations described in Chapter 4. These operations generally change the current state of the system. In particular, CPUs become inactive as a result of a *Suspend*, a *Destroy*, or a blocking operation, such as a *P* operation on semaphores, requesting a currently unavailable resource; processes become *ready_a*, possibly resulting in preemption, due to a wakeup operation on a resource, such as a *V* operation, or an *Activate*.

The ready list *RL* is structured as a multilevel priority list, shown in Figure 4-3a; it contains all processes having *Status.Type* ∈ {*running, ready_a, ready_s*}. The basic algorithm of *Scheduler* is as follows:

```
Scheduler() {
    do {
        Find highest priority ready_a process p;
        Find a free cpu;
        if (cpu != NIL) Allocate_CPU(p,cpu);
    } while (cpu != NIL);
    do {
        Find highest priority ready_a process p;
        Find lowest priority running process q;
        if (Priority(p) > Priority(q)) Preempt(p,q);
    } while (Priority(p) > Priority(q));
    if (self->Status.Type != 'running') Preempt(p,self);
}
```

During the first do-loop, the scheduler allocates the highest-priority processes to free CPUs, if any are available. The function *Allocate_CPU* dispatches each process to the CPU and adjusts its descriptor to reflect its new *running* status. During the second do-loop, the scheduler tries to preempt running processes. This must happen whenever the priority of a currently running process is lower than the priority of another ready process; such a condition occurs when a new process is created or an existing one is unblocked.

Preemption is accomplished by the *Preempt* function which performs the same tasks as *Allocate_CPU* but does this after preempting the current (lower-priority) running process. This involves stopping the process and saving its current CPU state in its PCB (Fig. 4-5). The CPU state of the process to be restarted is loaded into the CPU instead.

Special care must be taken if the process to be preempted is the one currently running the scheduler. In this case, the actual preemption must be postponed to permit the scheduler to complete its task. Only when there are no other lower-priority running processes to be preempted does the running process give up the CPU by preempting itself.

There is one other condition under which preemption is necessary—namely when the state of the currently running process (self) is not "running." This can happen, for example, when the scheduler is called from a request operation that could not be satisfied. As a result, the state of the invoking process was already changed to "blocked" by the time the scheduler function was invoked. When the scheduler finds this to be the case (last if-statement in the above code), the current process (the one running the scheduler) must give up the CPU.

The scheduler, while manageable, can nevertheless be simplified if some of the underlying assumptions are relaxed. The common situation in which only a single central processor is available ($np = 1$) leads to a much less complex scheduling algorithm. In this case, neither *Suspend* nor *Destroy* would ever call *Scheduler*; and, at most one process switch could occur. Another possibility is to limit resource allocators so that at most *one* process is ever taken off a blocked list (awakened) at any time, for example, by not supporting a *broadcast* version of a synchronization operation or by releasing resources one at a time.

5.2   SCHEDULING METHODS

In a typical state of execution, the number of active processes able to run will exceed the number of available processors. The task of a scheduler is to examine the current allocation of processes to processors and, when appropriate, perform a reallocation according to some scheduling policy. It is usually desirable to employ different strategies for different types of processes. For example, we might wish to discriminate between processes associated with batch jobs and those of interactive users, between system and user processes, or between processes dealing directly with I/O and those engaged in purely internal activities. With a general priority mechanism and the careful use of timers, a uniform organization can be designed to handle a broad spectrum of such strategies. We present a general framework for possible scheduling strategies, which formalizes the notion of priority scheduling introduced in the preceding section. Within this framework, we discuss a variety of common scheduling strategies. Such strategies can be incorporated into actual schedulers, such as the one presented in the last section.

5.2.1   A Framework for Scheduling

A scheduler can be specified within the following general framework (Ruschitzka and Fabry 1977), which asks two fundamental questions:

- *When* to schedule, i.e., when the scheduler should be invoked. This decision is governed by the **decision mode**.

- *Who* to schedule, i.e., how to choose a process (or thread) among the currently active processes. This is governed jointly by a **priority function** and an **arbitration rule**.

At certain points in time, specified by the *decision mode*, the scheduler evaluates the *priority function* for all active processes in the system. For each process, the priority function yields a value, referred to as the *current priority*. The processes with the highest priorities are assigned to the existing CPUs. The *arbitration rule* is applied in the case of ties when there is more than one process with the same priority. Depending on the particular decision mode, priority function, and arbitration rule, different scheduling disciplines may be defined.

The Decision Mode

The decision mode specifies the points in time at which process priorities are evaluated and compared, and at which processes are selected for execution. The allocation of processes to CPUs cannot change between two consecutive decision times.

There are two basic types of decision modes: **nonpreemptive** and **preemptive**. In the first case, a process, once started, is always allowed to run when logically possible; i.e., scheduling decisions are made only when a process terminates or blocks itself by requesting a service from the OS, or when a newly arriving process finds an idle CPU. Although they are more economical, nonpreemptive algorithms are usually not adequate in real-time or time-shared systems. Rather, a preemptive decision mode must be used. This permits a currently running process to be stopped and the CPU assigned to another process with higher priority.

The decision to attempt a preemption may be made when a new process arrives or when an existing process is awakened as a result of a message or interrupt. Preemption also may be performed periodically each time a process has executed for a period of q milliseconds. In this case, the algorithm is called **quantum-oriented**, with q as its quantum size. Preemption also may occur whenever the priority of a ready process rises above the priority of a currently running process. This could occur in systems that dynamically change the relative priorities of existing processes.

Preemptive scheduling policies are usually more costly than nonpreemptive ones because of process switching times, the additional logic in the scheduler itself, and the possible swapping of programs and data between primary and secondary memories. Many systems use a combination of both strategies. For example, a critical part of an OS process, such as a kernel routine, may be nonpreemptive, whereas most user processes are preemptive.

The Priority Function

The priority function when applied to a process p generates a numeric value, P, that represents p's current priority. The function may use different attributes of the process or the system as a whole to generate the value. The most common attributes applicable to a given process are the following:

- attained service time;

- real-time in system;

- total service time;

- deadline;

- periodicity;

- external priority;

- memory requirements.

The first three time-related parameters have two possible interpretations. In *long-term* scheduling, also referred to as **job scheduling**, where the scheduler's task is to choose among possible *batch* jobs to be included in the ready list, the times relate to the entire run of the job (process). That means, its **arrival** in the system is defined as the point during which its status changed to *ready_s* for the first time, and its **departure** from the system is the time at which the process terminates or is destroyed.

In **process scheduling**, where the scheduler's (dispatcher's) task is to select among the currently ready processes to run next on the CPU, the times relate to the period between two consecutive blocking operations. That means, the **arrival** of a process is the time when its status changes from *blocked* to *ready* as the result of a wakeup operation. Its **departure** is the time when it status changes from *running* to *blocked*, as a result of a request operation. Between its arrival and departure time, the process' status can switch many times between *running* and *ready*.

In this section, we are concerned primarily with process scheduling, but some of the algorithms presented are applicable also to long-term job scheduling.

- The **attained service time** is the amount of time during which the process was using the CPU since its arrival and is often the most important parameter for scheduling.

- The **real time in system** is the actual time the process has spent in the system since its arrival. It is composed of the *attained service time* and the *waiting time* during which the process was ready but not running. Note that the attained service time increases at the rate of the actual (real) time when the process is running and remains constant when the process is waiting for the CPU.

- The **total service time** is the CPU time the process will consume during its lifetime, i.e., before it departs (terminates or blocks on a request). Note that, at the point the process departs, its total service time is equal to the attained service time. Some systems assume that the total service time is known in advance. This is usually true of repetitive service tasks, such as the processing of a stream of signals or messages. In other cases, the total service time frequently can be predicted based on the most recent behavior of the process: A process that performs long computations without I/O or other systems services will block infrequently, resulting in long total service times. A process performing a lot of I/O operations will have short total service time requirements. Since processes tend to remain processor-bound or I/O-bound for significant periods of time, we can devise a function that predicts the next total service time period based on the most recent periods.

- A **deadline** is a point in real time by which a task must be completed. The need for such a requirement arises in situations where the results of a computation are time-sensitive in that their usefulness or value decreases with time. As an extreme example, the results of a weather forecast are useless after the date for which the prediction is made. Deadlines are specially important in real-time applications. For example, the transmission of a video or audio signal can be seriously distorted if deadlines for most data packets are not met. In safety- and mission-critical applications, computations that are not completed in time may lead to extremely costly or life-threatening situations. In these systems, priorities often correspond directly with deadlines; the shorter the deadline, the higher the priority.

- **Periodicity** refers to the repetition of a computation. In many real-time applications, the same, usually very short, computation is repeated at fixed intervals. Many other applications that are not normally considered as real-time also use periodic processes. One example is an email system that checks periodically for mail or message arrivals. Even event-driven processes that are not periodic are often handled as periodic processes by polling for events at a suitable frequency.

  A fixed period automatically imposes an implicit deadline: The current computation must be completed before the start of the next period. The converse, however, is not generally true. Deadlines may be imposed for reasons other than periodic computations.

- **External priorities** are values assigned explicitly to processes. They may be used as base priorities to differentiate between different classes of processes. One common policy, for example, is to assign the highest priorities to real-time processes, the next lower priorities to interactive processes, and the lowest to batch processes. In a business organization, the priority of a user process may correspond to the user's position in the company hierarchy. Historically, when computers were more expensive than people, a cost based on the type of resources employed was frequently associated with each priority level. This setup permits users to select the priority for their processes which provides adequate service (response) at a price they can afford. For example, a process with a given priority P could be charged a dollar amount $f_1(P)$ for each second of processor time, $f_2(P)$ for each block of main memory per second, $f_3(P)$ for each second of terminal connect time, and $f_4(P)$ for each I/O operation.

- The **memory requirements** specify the amount of main memory the process needs for its execution. This serves as a major scheduling criterion in batch OSs. In interactive systems, it is also important since it is a good measure of swapping overhead. However, other criteria, typically those related to time, are usually more important.

In addition to the process-specific attributes discussed above, the priority function can consider various attributes of the system as a whole. Notably, the overall **system load** is an important parameter, since it has a significant effect on system response. Under heavy load, some schedulers would attempt to maintain good response to high-priority processes by discriminating more strongly among external priorities. Thus, the distinction between the "rich" and the "poor" becomes even more pronounced when resources become scarce. Others take a more egalitarian point of view by attempting to increase the overall system throughput, for example by reducing swapping overhead through the use of larger quantum sizes. This idea improves the general conditions for all participants uniformly.

The Arbitration Rule

This rule resolves conflicts among processes with equal priority. If the likelihood of two or more processes having the same priority is low because of the nature of the priority function, the choice could be performed at *random*. In quantum-oriented preemptive scheduling algorithms, processes with equal highest priority are usually assigned quanta in a *cyclic* (round-robin [RR]) manner. In most other schemes, the *chronological* ordering of process arrivals serves as the arbitration rule; i.e., processes with equal priority are dispatched on a FIFO basis.

5.2.2 Common Scheduling Algorithms

The scheduler framework presented in the previous section is very general: Many scheduling algorithms may be expressed by specifying a decision mode, a priority function of various parameters, and an arbitration rule. In the following two sections, we describe and compare the most widely used methods in terms of these three concepts that govern when and who to schedule. We will use a simple example to illustrate the main features of each algorithm. This assumes there are two processes, p_1 and $p2$; p_1 arrives at time 0 and needs five units of CPU time to complete its task; $p2$ arrives at time 2 and needs two units of CPU time. A scheduling decision is to be made at time 2. Figure 5-2 illustrates this scenario.

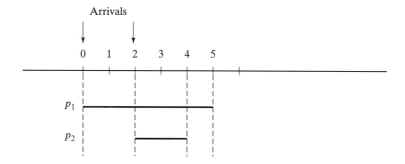

FIGURE 5-2. Example of two processes to be scheduled.

First-In/First-Out

The FIFO strategy dispatches processes according to their arrival time; the earlier the arrival, the higher the process priority. Thus, the current priority, P, of a process depends only on the real time, r, the process has spent in the system since its arrival: The larger the value of r, the higher the process priority. The priority function then may be expressed as $P = r$. The decision mode of FIFO is nonpreemptive, whereas its arbitration rule assumes a random choice among processes arriving at exactly the same time.

EXAMPLE: FIFO Algorithm

Assume that at time 2 (Fig. 5-2), neither process has been started yet. The priority of process p_1 at that time is $r_{p1} = 2$; the priority of process p_2 is $r_{p2} = 0$. Thus, p_1 starts, and it executes until it fishes its task. Then p_2 is allowed to run.

Shortest-Job-First

The shortest-job-first (SJF) policy is a nonpreemptive strategy that dispatches processes according to their total service time, t. The priority varies inversely with the service time: The larger the value of t, the lower the current priority. Thus, the priority function may be expressed as $P = -t$. Either a chronological or a random ordering is normally employed as the arbitration rule for processes with the same time requirements.

EXAMPLE: SJF Algorithm

Assume again that at time 2, neither process has been started yet. The priority of process p_1 at that time is $t_{p1} = -5$; the priority of process p_2 is $t_{p2} = -2$. Thus p_2 starts. However, if p_1 had already started at time 2, it would be allowed to finish its task before p_2 could run, since SJF is nonpreemptive.

Shortest-Remaining-Time

The shortest-remaining-time (SRT) policy may be viewed as the preemptive and dynamic version of SJF. It assigns the highest priority to the process that will need the least amount of time to complete, i.e., the remaining time $t - a$. The priority is dynamic, increasing as a process runs and its time to completion becomes smaller. Thus, the priority function has the form $P = -(t - a)$. The same arbitration rule as in SJF is usually employed.

EXAMPLE: SRT Algorithm

Assume that p_1 started executing immediately upon its arrival, i.e., at time 0. Then at time 2, the priorities of the two processes are as follows: The priority of p_1 is $-(t_{p1} - a_{p1}) = -(5 - 2) = -3$, whereas the priority of p_2 is $-(t_{p2} - a_{p2}) = -(2 - 0) = -2$. Since $-2 > -3$, p_2 preempts process p_1, which resumes its execution after p_2 terminates.

Round-Robin

The round-robin (RR) scheduling discipline imposes a fixed-time quantum q, also referred to as a *time slice*, on the amount of *continuous* CPU time that may be used by any process. If a process has run for q continuous time units, it is preempted from its processor and placed at the end of the process list waiting for the processor. Note that all processes have the same priority, i.e., $P = 0$. The RR behavior is enforced by using a quantum-oriented decision mode that causes the assignment of processes to processors to be reevaluated every q time units. Since the priorities of all processes are the same, the cyclic arbitration rule is applied at that time.

The time quantum q may be constant for long periods of time, or it may vary with the process load. If the time Q for one complete RR of all active processes is kept constant, q can be computed dynamically every Q seconds as $q = Q/n$, where n is the number of active processes competing for the CPU. Methods based on the RR scheme are used by most time-sharing systems for handling interactive processes.

EXAMPLE: RR Algorithm

Assume a time quantum of 0.1 time units. At time 2 in Figure 5-2, the CPU begins to switch between the two processes every 0.1 time units. Thus, both processes run concurrently but at half their normal speed. Assuming the context switching adds no overhead, p_2 is finished at time 6. Thereafter, p_1 is allowed to run to completion.

Multilevel Priority

The multilevel priority (ML) scheme uses a fixed set of priorities, 1 through n, where 1 is the lowest and n is the highest priority. Every process is assigned an external priority value, e, which is recorded in the process descriptor and determines the process' current priority. The assignment of the priority may occur once, at the time the process is created, or it may be changed explicitly at runtime by authorized kernel calls. Thus, the priority function may be expressed as $P = e$.

The ML discipline is typically preemptive in that a newly arriving process preempts the currently running one if its priority is greater than that of the current process. Within each priority queue, scheduling may be preemptive or nonpreemptive. In the first case, RR scheduling is applied within each priority level. That means, processes at the highest-priority level are cycled through the CPU at each quantum interrupt until they all terminate or block. Then the next priority level is serviced in the same RR manner, and so on.

With the nonpreemptive decision mode, FIFO is used within each level. That means, processes at the highest-priority level are started in the order of their arrival and allowed to run until they terminate or block. When the current priority level becomes empty, the next level is serviced in the same way.

EXAMPLE: ML Algorithm

Assume that p_1 (Fig. 5-2) runs at priority level $e_{p1} = 15$, and p_2 runs at priority level $e_{p2} = 14$. Then p_1 will run to completion before p_2 is started. If both priority levels were equal, i.e., $e_{p1} = e_{p2}$, the decision mode would determine the sequence of execution. With a preemptive decision mode, the two processes would run as under the RR policy. With a nonpreemptive mode, they would run as under the FIFO policy.

Multilevel Feedback

Similar to ML, the multilevel feedback (MLF) scheduling policy also provides n different priority levels. However, processes do not remain at the same priority level but gradually migrate to lower levels as their attained service time increases. With each priority level P we associate a time t_P, which is the maximum amount of processor time any process may receive at that level. If a process exceeds t_P, its priority is decreased to $P - 1$. One possible scheme is to choose a constant value, T, for the highest priority level and double that value for each lower priority level. That means, $t_P = T$ for $P = n$, and $t_P = 2 \times t_{P+1}$ for $1 \le P < n$.

The organization of the MLF queues is shown in Figure 5-3. A newly arrived process or a process awakened from a blocking operation is queued at the highest-priority level n, where it must share the processor with all other processes at the same level. When it has received the maximum of T units of CPU time, it is moved to the next lower-priority queue, $n - 1$, where it can consume up to $2T$ units of CPU time, and so on. When it reaches the lowest level 1, it remains there for a period of $2^{n-1}T$ time units. Exceeding this time is interpreted as an error, i.e., a runaway process. The CPU is always serving the highest-priority nonempty queue. Thus, a process at a level P will receive service only when the queues at the levels n through $P + 1$ are empty.

Similar to ML, the decision mode of MLF may be preemptive or nonpreemptive within each priority queue. In the first case, processes at each level are sharing the processor in a RR fashion. Usually, each of the times t_P is a multiple of the basic quantum q; thus, a process at level P will receive t_P/q time quanta before it is moved to the next lower-priority queue. If the nonpreemptive mode is used, each level follows the FIFO discipline: The process at the head of the highest-priority nonempty queue P is assigned a processor and it executes until it runs to completion or it exhausts the maximum time t_P, at which time it is moved to the next lower-priority queue. The next process at the same level P then continues.

The priority function for the MLF scheduling discipline is a function of the attained service time a and can be derived as follows. The priority of a process changes from P to $P - 1$ whenever its total attained service time exceeds the sum of all times attained at levels n through P. Assuming the scheme where the maximum time at each level is twice that of the previous level, we observe the following pattern: $a < T$ at priority level n, $a < T + 2T$ at priority level $n - 1$, $a < T + 2T + 4T$ at priority level $n - 2$,

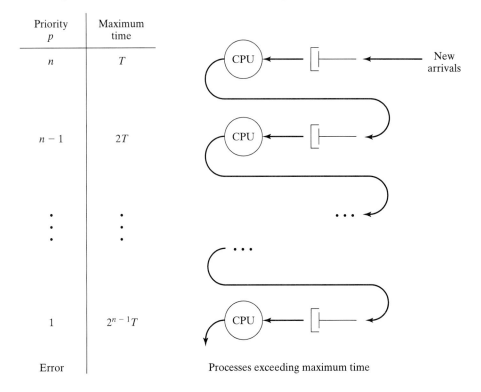

Priority p	Maximum time
n	T
$n-1$	$2T$
$\vdots$	$\vdots$
1	$2^{n-1}T$
Error	

FIGURE 5-3. Organization of queues within MLF scheduling.

and so on. In general, $a < (2^{i+1} - 1)T$ at priority level $n - i$. Thus, to determine the priority $P = n - i$ of a process given its attained service time a, we must find the smallest integer i such that the condition $a < (2^{i+1} - 1)T$ holds. Solving this inequality for i yields the expression $i = \lfloor lg_2(a/T + 1) \rfloor$. Thus, the priority function for MLF is $P = n - i = n - \lfloor lg_2(a/T + 1) \rfloor$.

With this expression, $P = n$ when $a < T$. As a increases, P steps through the values $n - 1$ through 1. When a exceeds the value $(2^n - 1)T$, the priority P becomes zero, indicating an error.

EXAMPLE: MLF Algorithm

Assume that the maximum time a process may spend at the highest-priority level is $T = 2$. Both processes p_1 and p_2 start at the highest-priority level, n, where each is allowed to use 2 units of time. p_2 will finish at that level, whereas p_1 will migrate to level $n - 1$, where it is allowed to spend up to $2T = 4$ time units. Thus, p_1 will terminate its task at that level.

Rate Monotonic

In real-time systems, processes and threads are frequently *periodic* in nature so that computations are repeated at fixed intervals. Typically, the deadline for each computation is the beginning of the next period. Thus, if a process has a period d, it is activated every d units of time, and its computation (total service time t) must be completed before the start of the next period, i.e., within d time units.

The rate monotonic (RM) method is a preemptive policy that dispatches according to period length; the shorter the period, d, the higher the priority. The priority function has the form $P = -d$. For example, a computation that is repeated every second has a higher priority than one repeated every hour. The arbitration rule is either random or chronological.

EXAMPLE: RM Algorithm

To illustrate the use of RM, assume that both p_1 and p_2 are periodic processes with the following respective periods: $d_1 = 9$ and $d_2 = 8$. Thus, the priority of p_2 is always higher than the priority of p_1. Consequently, at time 2, process p_2 will preempt the currently executing process p_1, which will resume its execution at time 4, i.e., when the current execution of p_2 terminates.

Earliest-Deadline-First

The earliest-deadline-first (EDF) method is a preemptive and dynamic scheme, used primarily for real-time applications. The highest priority is assigned to the process with the smallest remaining time until its deadline. As in the RM case above, we assume that all processes are periodic and that the deadline is equal to the end of the current period. The priority function can be derived as follows. If r is the time since the process first entered the system and d is its period, then $r \div d$ is the number of completed periods and the remainder of this division, $r \% d$ (i.e., r modulo d) is the already expired fraction of the current period. The time remaining until the end of this period is then $d - r \% d$. Thus, the priority function has the form $P = -(d - r \% d)$. For an arbitration rule, either a random or a chronological policy is defined typically.

EXAMPLE: EDF Algorithm

Assume again the same periods for the two processes, $d_1 = 9$ and $d_2 = 8$. At time 2, the priority of p_1 is $-(d_1 - r_1 \% d_1) = -(9 - 2 \% 9) = -(9 - 2) = -7$, and the priority of p_2 is $-(d_2 - r_2 \% d_2) = -(8 - 0 \% 8) = -(8 - 0) = -8$. Since $-7 > -8$, p_1 will continue executing, whereas p_2 is delayed until time 5, when p_1 terminates.

Figure 5-4 summarizes the main characteristics of the scheduling methods in terms of the decision mode, the priority function, and the arbitration rule.

5.2.3 Comparison of Methods

The first three algorithms discussed above—FIFO, SJF, and SRT—have been developed primarily for batch processing systems. FIFO is the simplest to implement, since processes are maintained in the order of their arrival on a queue. On the other hand, SJF requires that processes are serviced in the order defined by their time requirement, implying either a more complex priority queue data structure or lengthy sorting and searching operations.

Scheduling algorithm	Decision mode	Priority function	Arbitration rule
FIFO	Nonpreemptive	r	Random
SJF	Nonpreemptive	$-t$	Chronological or random
SRT	Preemptive	$-(t - a)$	Chronological or random
RR	Preemptive	0	Cyclic
ML	Preemptive Nonpreemptive	e (same)	Cyclic Chronological
MLF	Preemptive Nonpreemptive	$n - \lfloor lg_2(a/T + 1) \rfloor$ (same)	Cyclic Chronological
RM	Preemptive	$-d$	Chronological or random
EDF	Preemptive	$-(d - r \% d)$	Chronological or random

a – attained service time e – external priority
r – real time in system n – number of priority levels
t – total service time T – maximum time at highest level
d – period

FIGURE 5-4. Charactcristics of scheduling methods.

In the case of SRT, a similar implementation is necessary. In addition, preemption of the currently running process may be performed whenever a new process enters the system.

If the total service times are known (or can be predicted), SJF or SRT are generally preferable to FIFO, because both favor shorter computations over long-running ones. This is important for two reasons. First, users will not be satisfied unless they receive fast service for short tasks. (Supermarkets have long recognized this elementary fact by providing special checkout counters for customers with few items.) The second reason derives from a theoretical consideration: The order in which processes are executed has no effect on the total time required to complete all processes. The preferential treatment of shorter processes, however, reduces the average time a process spends in the system. This time is referred to as the **average turnaround time** and is the most important metric used to compare many scheduling algorithms.

The average turnaround time for a set of processes is defined as the value of the expression $(\sum_{i=1}^{n} r_i)/n$, where r_i is the real time each process i spends in the system during its lifetime and n is the total number of active processes. Generally, average turnaround time is shortest using SJF and SRT. For example, if two processes, p_1 and p_2, have total service times t_1 and t_2, respectively, with $t_1 < t_2$, and they both arrive at the same time, then an SJF policy selects process p_1 to run first. Thus for p_1, $r_1 = t_1$. process p_2 must wait for t_1 time units and then runs for t_2 time units. Thus, $r_2 = t_1 + t_2$; the average turnaround time is $\frac{t_1+(t_1+t_2)}{2}$. This is less than a policy that executes process p_2 first, resulting in the average turnaround time of $\frac{t_2+(t_2+t_1)}{2}$.

EXAMPLE: FIFO, SJF, and SRT

Consider three batch processes, p_1, p_2, and p_3, with the following arrival times and total service times:

	arrival	service
p_1	t	4
p_2	t	2
p_3	$t+3$	1

Figure 5-5 shows a timing diagram for completing the three processes under FIFO, SJF, and SRT scheduling disciplines.

- **FIFO:** Since both p_1 and p_2 arrived at the same time, we assume that p_1 is started first. p_2 and p_3 then follow in the order of their arrival.

- **SJF:** p_2 has a shorter service time than p_1 and is started first. When it terminates, p_1 is the only process waiting and is started. Finally, p_3, which arrived in the meantime, is processed.

- **SRT:** p_2 and p_1 begin at the same respective times as under SJF. However, when p_3 arrives, its remaining time is only 1 unit of time whereas the remaining time of p_1 is 3. Thus p_1 is preempted and must wait for the completion of p_3.

Figure 5-6 shows the turnaround times for each process, computed as the sum of the waiting time and the total service time. The last column shows the average

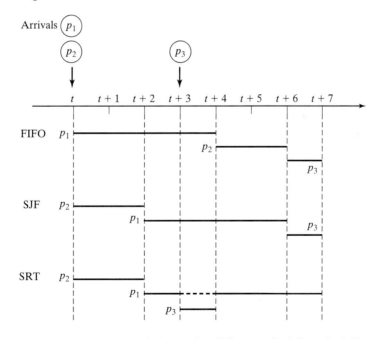

FIGURE 5-5. Process completion under different scheduling disciplines.

	p_1	p_2	p_3	Mean
FIFO	0 + 4	4 + 2	3 + 1	14/3 = 4.66
SJF	2 + 4	0 + 2	3 + 1	12/3 = 4.00
SRT	3 + 4	0 + 2	0 + 1	10/3 = 3.33

FIGURE 5-6. Process turnaround times.

turnaround time for all three processes. FIFO gives the largest turnaround time, whereas SRT produces the shortest.

In time-shared systems, where a number of users interact with the system in the form of a dialog, a scheduler should guarantee an acceptable **response time** for each user. This implies the use of a preemptive algorithm with preemption of processes at definite time intervals predetermined by the system. Of the methods presented above, only RR and MLF satisfy this requirement. RR is the simplest to implement, and therefore it is relied on heavily in many existing systems. It divides the CPU time evenly among all active processes according to the quantum size q, which becomes the most important parameter of this class of algorithms. Ideally, all processes may be viewed as running simultaneously at the speed cpu_speed/n, where cpu_speed is the speed of the CPU and n is the number of active processes sharing this CPU. If q is large, process switching is less frequent, and overhead is reduced; response time will, of course, deteriorate. In the extreme case, where $q \rightarrow \infty$, processes are never preempted, and the RR algorithm turns into a FIFO discipline. At the other extreme, where $q \rightarrow 0$, the overhead associated with process switching dominates and no work is done.

CASE STUDY: QUANTUM SIZE IN WINDOWS 2000

Windows 2000. The quantum is controlled by an entry in the internal database, the registry. The first choice is between a short and a long quantum. A short quantum lasts two clock ticks (or around 20 ms on an Intel 486 processor) and is usually used by general-purpose computer systems. A long quantum lasts 12 clock ticks. This reduces the context-switching overhead; thus, the long quantum is the preferred choice for servers, where high throughput is more important than high responsiveness.

In addition to selecting the length, the quantum may be set as fixed for all threads, or it may be different for background and foreground processes. In the latter case, the quanta are selected from a table of possible combinations, which range between two and 12 clock ticks (in increments of 2).

Frequently, more sophisticated preemption schemes are needed that discriminate among different groups of processes based on priorities. The criteria for assigning priorities may be based on a variety of parameters, including external values; more often, they are based on measurements of process behavior rather than a priori declarations. The static ML discipline uses a fixed classification of all processes. Most of the dynamic schemes are designed to move interactive and I/O-bound processes to the top of the priority queues and to let CPU-bound processes drift to lower levels. The MLF policy accomplishes this objective by always placing new processes and those awakened as a result of I/O completion into the highest-priority queue. Processes with short computation phases between I/O operations will not exhaust the maximum times associated with the top levels and will tend to retain higher priority over processes with few I/O operations.

CASE STUDIES: APPROACHES TO SCHEDULING

1. *VAX/VMS*. A popular system of an earlier generation, VAX/VMS, has an elegant scheduling scheme that combines the principles of several disciplines discussed earlier (DIGITAL 1982). It supports 32 priority levels divided into two groups of 16. As illustrated in Figure 5-7a, priorities 31-16, where 31 is the highest, are reserved for *real-time* processes. Other processes, referred to as *regular*,

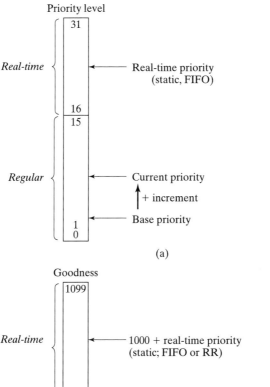

(a)

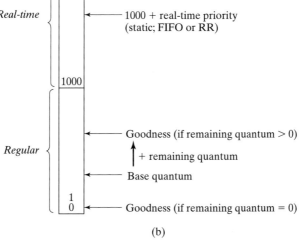

(b)

FIGURE 5-7. Priority levels (a) VAX/VMS; and (b) Linux.

CASE STUDIES: APPROACHES TO SCHEDULING   (*continued*)

---

occupy priority levels 15-0. Processes are dispatched according to their current priority. This guarantees that real-time processes have precedence over regular processes; thus, a regular process will be scheduled only when no real-time process is awaiting execution.

The priority assigned to a real-time process is fixed for the duration of that process. Thus the top 15 priority levels are processed according to the ML scheme (without feedback). On the other hand, priorities of regular processes float in response to various events occurring in the system. A *base* priority is assigned to each such process when it is created; this specifies its minimum priority level. The *current* priority of the process then varies dynamically with its recent execution history according to the following rules. Each system event has an assigned priority *increment* that is characteristic of the event cause. For example, terminal read completion has a higher increment value than terminal write completion, which, in turn, has a higher value than disk I/O completion. When a process is awakened as a result of one of these events, the corresponding increment is added to its current priority value, and the process is enqueued at the appropriate level. When the process is preempted after receiving its fair share of CPU usage, its current priority is decremented by one, which places it into the next lower-priority queue. Thus the priority of a regular process fluctuates between its base priority and the value 15, which is the maximum priority for any regular process.

Preemption of a currently running process from the CPU may be caused by a number of events. A real-time process is preempted only when it blocks itself, for example, by issuing an I/O instruction or when a higher-priority process arrives or is awakened; otherwise, it is permitted to run to completion. A regular process is preempted for the same reasons. In addition, it also is preempted when it exceeds a quantum assigned for the current priority level. When this occurs, the process is stopped and placed into the next lower-priority queue. Thus, regular processes are prevented from monopolizing the CPU.

Note that the scheduling algorithm for regular processes (levels 15-0) is a variant of the MLF discipline. The two main distinctions are:

(a) Under MLF, processes always start at the highest-priority level and, if not blocked, propagate toward the lowest level. The VMS scheduler restricts the priority range within which a process may float. The lowest level is given by the process base priority, whereas the highest level depends on the type of event that caused the reactivation of the process.

(b) A quantum is associated with a process rather than with a priority level, which permits the scheduler to discriminate among individual processes.

2. *Windows 2000*. The basic scheduling principles of Windows 2000 are very similar to those of the VAX/VMS. The main difference is that VAX/VMS schedules *processes*, whereas Windows 2000 schedules *threads* within processes. A *base priority* is assigned to each process at creation. Threads within each process inherit this base priority as the default. Then, whenever a thread wakes up, it gets a boost according to the event it was waiting for. For example, a thread waiting for disk I/O will get a boost of 1, whereas a thread waiting for a mouse or keyboard interrupt gets a boost of 6. Thus, a thread enters the system at the *current priority*, which is equal to the thread's base priority plus the current boost. As it continues executing, its current priority is decreased by one each time it exhausts the quantum until it again reaches the base priority. As in the case of VAX/VMS, real-time threads have a static priority; no boosts are added.

3. *Minix.* The Minix OS is a small version of UNIX and predecessor of Linux that is user-compatible with UNIX but with a different internal design (Tannen-baum and Woodhull 1997). The scheduler employs a ML discipline with three priority levels, called *task*, *server*, and *user* levels. A queue of ready processes is associated with each level.

   The highest-priority processes are kernel processes at the task level. These consist primarily of I/O driver processes, for example, for the disk, clock, and Ethernet, and a system task that interfaces with servers. The server processes are assigned the middle priority. These implement higher-level OS functions such as memory, file, and network management. User processes have the lowest priority.

   At the task and server levels, processes are run nonpreemptively until they block or terminate. User processes are scheduled using RR with a 100-ms quantum. If the three queues are all empty, an idle process is dispatched.

4. *Linux.* Linux employs a very elaborate scheduling scheme. One of its distinguishing features is that it does not maintain processes or threads sorted in a special priority queue. Instead, it orders them according to a dynamically computed value, referred to as the *goodness* of a thread. Although no explicit priority data structure exists, it is still convenient to visualize the threads arranged in a list sorted by their goodness. Figure 5-7b shows such a structure. Note that the goodness of a thread is similar to what other systems call current priority; it determines the importance of a thread relative to others.

   The threads in Linux are divided into two basic classes, *real-time* and *regular*. Each real-time thread has a static priority assigned to it at the time of creation. This is an integer recorded in its PCB, which is added to the base value of 1000 to derive the thread's goodness. This guarantees that the goodness of any real-time thread is always higher than that of a regular thread.

   Real-time threads are subdivided further into FIFO and RR threads. This information also is recorded in the PCB of each thread. A FIFO thread always runs until completion. A RR thread is preempted when its current quantum expires but its goodness does not change. Thus, RR threads with the same goodness share the CPU in a RR fashion.

   The goodness of a regular thread fluctuates between a base value and a current value. This is similar to the dynamic priorities of the VAX/VMS and Windows

---

CASE STUDIES: APPROACHES TO SCHEDULING *(continued)*

2000. However, the base and current goodness values are directly tied to the quantum. That means, a quantum is not a fixed amount of CPU time associated with a given priority level. Instead, each thread has its own variable-length quantum, which, similar to a countdown timer, is decremented as the process executes. Specifically, the following rules apply:

- Each thread is assigned a *base quantum*, *bq*, at the time of creation. This value (also referred to as the thread's priority) may be modified by an explicit call to the function *nice()* but otherwise remains constant.
- Each thread has a counter that keeps track of its *remaining quantum*, *rq*.
- The current *goodness*, *g*, of the thread is computed using the following two rules:

$$\text{if } (rq == 0) \; g = 0;$$

$$\text{if } (rq > 0) \; g = bq + rq.$$

As a result, threads that have exhausted their current quantum are not permitted to run. The remaining threads are ordered by their goodness, which considers both their base quantum (base priority) and their remaining quantum.

Another distinguishing feature of the Linux scheduler is that it divides time into periods called *epochs*. An epoch ends when no threads are able to run. This happens when all threads have either exhausted their current quantum or are blocked. At this point, the scheduler resets the quanta of all threads, which starts the next epoch. The quanta are reset according to the following formula:

$$rq = bq + (rq/2)$$

That means, each thread gets its base quantum plus half of its remaining quantum from the previous epoch. This naturally favors I/O-bound threads. A CPU-bound thread will have exhausted its quantum and thus only gets its base quantum for the next epoch. On the other hand, an I/O-bound thread gets to keep half of its unused quantum, in addition to getting a new base quantum.

Many processes, especially those that monitor or control signals from an external environment, must meet deterministic timing constraints, particularly deadlines. For such *real-time* processes, it is often important to know *before* their execution whether or not deadlines will be met. An assignment of processes to processors, called a **schedule**, is said to be **feasible** if all deadlines are satisfied. A scheduling method is defined as **optimal** if the schedule resulting from the use of the method meets all deadlines whenever a feasible schedule exists. In other words, an optimal algorithm produces a feasible schedule if one exists. (A more detailed discussion of real-time scheduling appears in [Shaw 2001]).

Each periodic process uses a fraction of the CPU. Specifically, a process p_i will use t_i/d_i of the CPU time, where d_i is the period length and t_i is the total service time for process i for one period. For n processes, we define the overall CPU utilization as:

$$U = \sum_{i=1}^{n} \frac{t_i}{d_i}$$

Then scheduling is feasible using EDF as long as $U \leq 1$. This is the best that any algorithm can do, since it is impossible to produce a schedule if $U > 1$. With $U = 1$ the CPU is fully saturated. With RM, scheduling is feasible whenever U is less than approximately 0.7. The actual value depends on the particular set of processes. Furthermore, the condition is sufficient but not necessary; i.e., feasible schedules may still be possible for $U > 0.7$, but RM is not guaranteed to always find them.

EXAMPLE: RM vs. EDF

Let process p_1 have a period $d_1 = 4$ and service time $t_1 = 1$, and process p_2 have a period $d_2 = 5$ with service time $t_2 = 3$. Figure 5-8a shows the periods and service times for the two processes for the first 24 time units. On a uniprocessor, the two processes cannot run in parallel. The sequential schedule produced by RM is shown in Figure 5-8b. p_1 has a shorter period and always has a higher priority than p_2. Note that p_1 preempts p_2 whenever its new period begins (at times 12 and 16 in this example). The schedule meets all deadlines for both processes.

Figure 5-8c shows the schedule produced by EDF. For the first 12 time units the two schedules are identical, because p_1's remaining time until the next deadline is shorter than p_2's remaining time. At time 12, the situation changes. p_1's remaining time until the next deadline is 4; p_2's remaining time until the next deadline is 3. According to the priority function, p_1's priority is -4 and p_2's priority is -3; thus, p_2 continues, whereas p_1 must wait until time 13. An analogous situation occurs at time 16, where p_1 does not preempt p_2 but waits until time 18.

To illustrate that EDF always produces feasible schedules and RM does not, consider the same processes p_1 and p_2 but assume that p_1's service time is extended to $t_1 = 1.5$. The utilization of the system is $U = t_1/d_1 + t_2/d_2 = 1.5/4 + 3/5 = 0.975$. This is less than 1, and the processes are in principle schedulable. Figure 5-9 shows the two schedules. RM fails at time 5 where p_2 has not been able to complete its computation

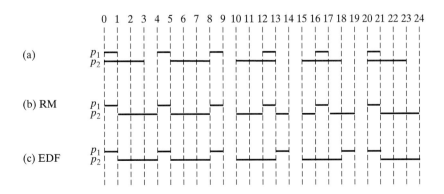

FIGURE 5-8. Scheduling using RM and EDF.

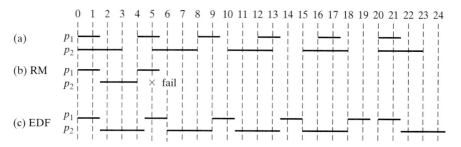

FIGURE 5-9. Failure of RM.

before its next deadline. In contrast, EDF produces a valid schedule where both processes meet all deadlines. Note that the entire cycle repeats at time 20, when the arrival of both processes coincide again as at time 0.

5.3 PRIORITY INVERSION

Most scheduling mechanisms in OSs are preemptive and priority-based, or can be transformed into or viewed as such. When employing these systems in realistic environments that include CSs and other resource interactions, a common problem occurs that conflicts with the intent of priorities: higher-priority processes or threads can be delayed or blocked, often unnecessarily, by lower-priority ones. This situation, called the **priority inversion problem**, was first publicized with respect to the Pilot OS and Mesa language (Lampson and Redell 1980), and later thoroughly investigated for real-time OSs (Sha, Rajkumar, and Lehocsky 1990).

The problem is best illustrated through a standard example. Consider three processes, p_1, p_2, and p_3, such that p_1 has the highest priority, p_3 the lowest, and p_2 has priority between the other two. Suppose that p_1 and p_3 interact through CSs locked by a common semaphore *mutex*, and p_2 is totally independent of p_1 and p_3. The code skeletons follow.

```
p1:  . . . P(mutex); CS_1; V(mutex); . . .

p2:  . . . program_2; . . . /* independent of p1 and p3 */

p3:  . . . P(mutex); CS_3; V(mutex); . . .
```

One possible execution history for a single processor is illustrated in Figure 5-10. p_3 starts first and enters its CS, *CS_3*. At time a, p_2 is activated and preempts p_3 because it has a higher priority. Process p_1 becomes ready and preempts p_2 at point b. When p_1 attempts to enter *CS_1* at c, it blocks on *P(mutex)* because the semaphore is still held by the lowest-priority process p_3. Process p_2 therefore continues its execution until it terminates at d. Then, p_3 finishes its CS, releases *mutex* waking up p_1, and is therefore preempted by p_1 at time e.

This scenario is certainly logically correct; it does not violate the specification of the scheduler given in Section 5.1.2. But the behavior is counterintuitive because the highest-priority process is blocked, perhaps for an inordinately long time. The problem

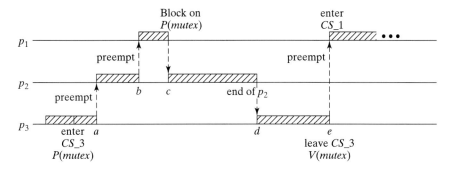

FIGURE 5-10. Priority inversion example.

is not that p_3 is blocking p_1; that is unavoidable since they both compete for the same resource, probably at unknown times. The problem is that the intermediate process p_2, which is totally independent of p_1 and p_3, is prolonging the blocked state of p_1. In fact, the blocking of p_1 by p_2 may in general last an unbounded and unpredictable amount of time. The highest-priority process is essentially blocked by an unrelated process of lower priority. Such a priority inversion is undesirable in general-purpose OSs and intolerable in real-time systems.

There are several solutions that avoid the inversion. One possibility is to make CSs nonpreemptable. This may be practical if CSs are short and few. However, it would not be satisfactory if high-priority processes often found themselves waiting for lower-priority processes, especially unrelated ones. A more practical solution is to execute CSs at the highest priority of any process that *might* use them. Using this policy in our example, process p_3 would execute CS_3 at p_1's priority, thus blocking p_1 for the time it takes to complete its CS. This simple technique, however, suffers from overkill and leads to other forms of priority inversion; higher-priority processes now cannot preempt lower-priority ones in their CSs, even when the higher ones are not currently trying to enter the CS. For example, p_1 might not try to enter CS_1 until well after p_3 has exited its CS, but p_1 still would not be able to preempt p_3 while p_3 is inside CS_3. Similarly, p_2 would not be able to preempt p_3 while p_3 is inside CS_3.

A practical set of methods that does not have the above disadvantages is based on **dynamic priority inheritance** (Sha, Rajkumar, and Lehocsky 1990). In its purest form, priority inheritance supports the following protocol. Whenever a process p_1 attempts to enter a CS and is blocked by a lower-priority process p_3 that is already in a CS (locked by the same lock or semaphore), then p_3 inherits p_1's priority and keeps it until it leaves the CS, releasing the lock. The execution of Figure 5-10 is repeated in Figure 5-11, only this time with priority inheritance. At point c when process p_1 blocks, p_3 inherits p_1's high priority and resumes execution until it exits from CS_3. Priorities then revert to normal, and p_1 runs to completion at e, followed by resumption of p_2.

The protocol works for any number of higher-priority processes becoming blocked on the same lock. The lock holder keeps inheriting the priority of the highest-priority blocked process. It also is applicable to nested CSs. Blocking times for the higher-priority processes are bounded by the CS execution times of lower-priority processes. The protocol can be implemented relatively efficiently as part of locking and unlocking

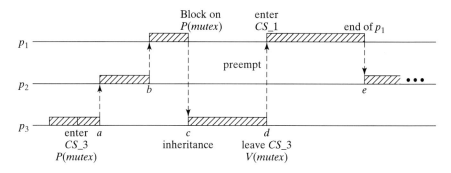

FIGURE 5-11. Priority inheritance.

operations, such as operations on *mutual exclusion* semaphores, since blocked processes are normally linked directly through a semaphore or lock data structure.

Priority inheritance methods are supported in a number of systems, and are compulsory requirements in real-time OSs. As examples, many of the real-time versions of UNIX conform to the IEEE POSIX standard and its real-time extensions.

CASE STUDIES: PREVENTING PRIORITY INVERSION

1. *POSIX.* POSIX supports two mechanisms for preventing priority inversion. The simpler one allows the user to associate a *ceiling* attribute with a mutex semaphore. The ceiling is an integer, specified using the function *pthread_mutexattr_setprioceiling.* The corresponding protocol to use this ceiling is specified as *POSIX_THREAD_PRIO_PROTECT.* Then, when a thread locks this mutex, its priority is automatically raised to the value of the ceiling. Thus, all threads using this mutex will run at the same level and will not preempt each other.

   The second mechanism is the actual priority inheritance, as described in this section. The user must specify the use of the protocol as *POSIX_THREAD_PRIO_INHERIT.* Then, no thread holding the mutex can be preempted by another thread with a priority lower than that of any thread waiting for the mutex.

2. *Windows 2000.* Windows 2000 addresses the priority inversion problem indirectly, through scheduling. A routine called the *balance set manager* scans all ready threads every second. If it finds a thread that has been idle for more than approximately 3 seconds, it boosts its priority to 15 (the highest nonreal-time priority) and doubles its quantum. This prevents starvation of even the lowest-priority thread. Thus, no thread will be postponed indefinitely because of a possibly unrelated higher-priority thread; it will be able to complete its CS, which indirectly avoids the priority inversion problem.

5.4   MULTIPROCESSOR AND DISTRIBUTED SCHEDULING

We consider scheduling and dispatching issues for shared-memory multiprocessors and for tightly coupled distributed systems, such as LANs. There are two principal approaches to scheduling processes and threads on multicomputers:

- *Use a single scheduler.* All CPUs are in the same resource pool, and any process can be allocated to any processor.

- *Use multiple schedulers.* The computers are divided into sets of separately scheduled machines, and each process is preallocated permanently to a particular set. Each set has its own scheduler.

In the previous sections, the first approach was assumed. Whenever a scheduling decision was to be made, a single mechanism considered all CPUs and all eligible processes or threads. Generally, this approach is most applicable to multiprocessor clusters, where all machines have the same features. One of the main goals is to evenly distribute the load over the machines—a technique called **load balancing**—for which many different algorithms have been developed. The second approach (using multiple schedulers), is often the choice for nonuniform multiprocessors, where different CPUs have different characteristics and functions. For example, there might be separate machines and associated schedulers for conventional I/O, filing, data acquisition, fast Fourier transforms, matrix computations, and other applications. Users and applications also have greater control over performance when there is support for more than one scheduler.

CASE STUDIES: MULTIPROCESSOR SCHEDULING

1. *The Mach Scheduler.* The Mach OS for multiprocessors employs the second approach (Black 1990). Each machine set has a global RL of schedulable threads. In addition, each CPU has a local ready queue for those threads permanently assigned to that CPU. Dedicating specific threads to a given processor may be necessary for UNIX compatibility or because the threads work only for a particular machine. Threads that handle I/O on devices attached to a particular CPU fit into the latter category. Dispatching occurs by selecting the highest priority thread from the local queue. If the local queue is empty, the highest-priority thread is dispatched from the global list. An idle thread associated with each CPU is executed when both lists are empty.

2. *Windows 2000.* For multiprocessor systems, Windows 2000 implements a form of scheduling called **affinity scheduling**. It maintains two integers associated with every thread: the *ideal processor* and the *last processor*. The ideal processor is chosen at random when a thread is created. The last processor is the one on which the thread ran last. The two numbers are used as follows:

   - When a thread becomes ready, it looks for a currently idle processors in the following order: 1) the ideal processor; 2) the last processor; 3) the processor currently running the scheduler; and 4) any other processor. If there is no idle processor, the scheduler tries to preempt a currently running thread, using the above order of desirability when examining the processors.
   - When a processor becomes idle (because a thread terminates or blocks), the scheduler looks for a thread to run on that processor. It makes the

---

CASE STUDIES: MULTIPROCESSOR SCHEDULING   (*continued*)

---

selection using the following order: 1) the thread that last ran on the processor; and 2) the thread for which this is the ideal processor. If neither of these threads is ready, the scheduler selects a thread based on current priorities.

The main objective of affinity scheduling is to keep a thread running on the same processor as possible. This increases the chances that the cache still contains relevant data and improves performance.

Distributed systems normally have separate schedulers at each site (cluster), where either of the above two approaches are used at the local level, depending on the application and configuration. Processes are usually preallocated to clusters, rather than scheduled across the network using a single scheduler, for several reasons. First, communication is costly in time, and scheduling across a network inevitably requires much message traffic. A second reason is applications with shared address spaces as implemented by threads. Although distributed shared-memory and migrating threads are practical ideas, their realization is still slow compared with a conventional architecture. Hence, for performance reasons, threads that share memory are scheduled on the same multiprocessor set. Distributed systems also frequently have functional distribution, leading to different schedulers. Thus, in a typical client/server environment, different server nodes might exist for filing, email, printing, and other services, each using its own scheduler.

For real-time systems, neither RM nor EDF are optimal for multiprocessors. However, they are often satisfactory heuristics, in that they typically produce feasible schedules when they exist and when machines are not too heavily loaded. Thus, for distributed real-time systems, preallocation of processes to nodes is most common because of the complexity of trying to meet real-time constraints.

CONCEPTS, TERMS, AND ABBREVIATIONS

The following concepts have been introduced in this chapter. Test yourself by defining and discussing each keyword or phrase.

Deadline	Priority ceiling
Dispatcher	Priority inheritance
Distributed systems scheduling	Priority inversion
Earliest-deadline-first (EDF)	Rate monotonic (RM)
Feasible schedule	Round-robin (RR)
First-in, first-out (FIFO)	Scheduler
Load balancing	Service time
Multilevel feedback (MLF)	Shortest-job-first (SJF)
Multiprocessor scheduling	Shortest-remaining-time (SRT)
Optimal schedule	Time quantum
Preemptive scheduling	

EXERCISES

1. The scheduler of Section 5.1.2 is invoked as part of every *Suspend, Activate,* and *Destroy* operation on processes. For each of the three operations, determine how many times the function *Allocate_CPU()* and the function *Preempt()* would be invoked, assuming that at the time the scheduler is called there are:
   (a) 3 free CPUs
   (b) 0 free CPUs

2. Simplify the scheduler of Section 5.1.2 for the following cases:
   (a) There is only a single CPU
   (b) Processes are never preempted; a process gives up the CPU only when it blocks on a request or terminates (assume that termination changes the process status to "terminated")
   (c) Both restrictions (a) and (b) are combined

3. Consider the following set of five processes where *arrival* is the time the process became ready, t is the total service time, and e is the external priority.

process	arrival	t	e
$p0$	0	80	9
$p1$	15	25	10
$p2$	15	15	9
$p3$	85	25	10
$p4$	90	10	11

   Assume that execution starts immediately at time 0 and there is no context switch overhead. For the following scheduling disciplines, draw a time diagram showing when each of the five processes executes. (In the case of a tie, assume that the process with the lower process number goes first.)
   (a) FIFO
   (b) SJF
   (c) SRT
   (d) RR (quantum $= 1$)
   (e) ML (with FIFO at each priority level)
   (f) MLF (with $n = 5$, $T = 10$, and FIFO at each priority level)

4. For each of the scheduling disciplines in the previous exercise, determine the average turnaround time for the five processes.

5. Assume that at time t_0, there are three processes $p0$, $p1$, and $p2$, in the system. Their arrival times, total service times (t), external priorities (e), and periods (d) are listed in the table below. Execution of $p0$ started immediately at its arrival. For each scheduling discipline, give the numerical priority (as defined by the appropriate priority function) of each of the three processes at time t_0.

process	arrival	t	e	d
$p0$	$t_0 - 20$	50	0	160
$p1$	$t_0 - 10$	60	1	200
$p2$	t_0	20	2	150

   (a) FIFO
   (b) SJF
   (c) SRT
   (d) RR
   (e) ML

(f) MLF (with $n = 5$, $T = 2$, and $t_P = 2 \times t_{P+1}$)

(g) RM

(h) EDF

6. Consider n processes sharing the CPU in a RR fashion.

   (a) Assuming that each context switch takes s milliseconds, determine the quantum size q such that the overhead resulting from process switching is minimized but, at the same time, each process is guaranteed to get its turn at the CPU at least every t seconds.

   (b) If $n = 100$, $t = 1$, and $s = 0.001$, what would be the size of q? What if s increased to 0.01?

7. Consider a system using RR scheduling with a fixed quantum q. Every context switch takes s milliseconds. Any given process runs for an average of t milliseconds before it blocks or terminates.

   (a) Determine the fraction of CPU time that will be wasted because of context switching for each of the following cases:

   i. $t < q$

   ii. $t \gg q$ (i.e., t is much greater than q)

   iii. q approaches 0

   (b) Under what condition will the wasted fraction of CPU time be exactly 50%?

8. Consider a system with an MLF scheduling policy, where $n = 5$, $T = 2$, $t_P = 2 \times t_{P+1}$ for all $1 \le P \le 5$, and FIFO is used within each priority level. At time 0, three processes $p0$, $p1$, and $p2$ arrive in the highest-priority queue in that order. Their respective times until the next I/O request are 3, 8, and 5 time units. When a process reaches its I/O request, it remains blocked (not competing for the CPU) for 5 time units, after which it reenters the highest-priority queue. The required CPU times until the next I/O request are again 3, 8, and 5.

   Using a timing diagram, show for the first 40 time units of execution (a) which process will be running during each time unit and (b) at which priority level.

9. Repeat the previous exercise, assuming that $t_P = 2$ (i.e., constant) for all priority levels.

10. Derive an expression for the priority function of a MLF scheduling discipline where $t_P = T$ for all $1 \le P \le n$, i.e., the maximum time a process can spend at any priority level is constant.

11. Consider three processes, $p0$, $p1$, and $p2$. The following tables show three different sets of values for the total service time (t) and period (d) of each process.

	t	d		t	d		t	d
$p0$	3	50	$p0$	15	50	$p0$	5	20
$p1$	70	1000	$p1$	5	10	$p1$	7	10
$p2$	5	40	$p2$	1	4	$p2$	4	100

   (a) Determine for which of the three cases a feasible schedule is likely to be generated by:

   i. RM

   ii. EDF

   (b) For each case, show a timing digram for the first 25 time units.

12. Consider four processes, $p0$ through $p3$. The diagram below shows the timing of each process when executed in isolation.

   That means, process $p0$ arrives at time 0; after one time unit it executes a $P(s)$ operation (s is initially 1); after 3 more time units it executes a $V(s)$ operation and

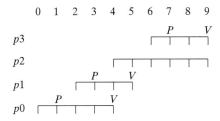

terminates. Processes $p1$ and $p3$ are similar. Process $p2$ does not execute any P or V operations. Assume that the execution of P and V is instantaneous, i.e., takes 0 time. Any context switch is also instantaneous. The priorities of the four processes are as follows: priority($p0$)<priority($p1$)<priority($p2$)<priority($p4$). Determine the start and end time of each of the four processes when executing concurrently on a single-processor system.

(a) without priority inheritance
(b) with priority inheritance
(c) without priority inheritance but making all CSs noninterruptible
(Hint: Draw timing diagrams similar to those in Figures 5-7 and Figure 5-8.)

13. Assume two processes compete for a CS implemented using simple spinning locks (Section 4.5.1). Prior to entering the CS, the process executes the statement

```
do TS(R, sb) while (!R);
```

After exiting the CS, it executes the statement:

```
sb = 1;
```

Show how this solution may lead to a deadlock under priority scheduling, whereas RR scheduling does not suffer from this problem.

14. Consider the following solution to the bounded-buffer problem (Section 2.4.3):

```
semaphore e = n, f = 0, b = 1;
cobegin
Producer:  while (1) {
    while (record_not_available) ;
    P(e); P(b); Add_record_to_buffer; V(b); V(f);
  }
  //
Consumer:  while (1) {
    P(f); P(b); Take_record_from_buffer; V(b); V(e);
    while (record_not_processed) ;
  }
coend
```

Note that the producer has a busy-wait loop to wait for the next record to become available. Similarly, the consumer has a busy-wait loop to wait for the current record to be processed. Simplify this code under the assumption that it will be running on a single-processor system with nonpreemptive scheduling. A process runs until it voluntarily gives up the CPU by executing the function *yield()*. (Hint: There is no need for any semaphores; instead, the consumer and producer processes yield the CPU to each other so that both make progress while preserving the integrity of the buffer.)

C H A P T E R   6

Deadlocks

We have already introduced the notion of deadlock informally with the dining philosophers problem in Section 3.3.2. In our solution, it is possible to reach a state where each philosopher acquires one fork and waits—indefinitely—for the other fork to become free. In general, whenever a process is blocked on a resource request that can never be satisfied because the resource is held by another blocked process, the processes are said to be *deadlocked*. This condition can only be resolved by an explicit intervention from the operating system (OS) or the user. Such intervention involves either the pre-emption of some of the resources held by the deadlocked processes, or the termination of one or more of the processes.

Why are deadlock studies important? It is clear that some action must be taken either to prevent deadlocks from occurring or to handle them whenever they do occur. If ignored, the deadlocked processes would exist indefinitely in a blocked state, never performing any useful work and wasting memory space and other resources, which cannot be used by other processes.

Since deadlocks are quite rare, yet difficult to manage efficiently, many general-purpose computing facilities simply ignore them. They are viewed as only an inconvenience, causing possible delays or interruption in service, and are handled when a user notices a system problem. However, deadlocks may become critical in a number of real-time applications, where any delay could result in loss of data or endanger human life. This includes, for example, real-time data communication, computer-aided manufacturing and process control, automated vehicle monitoring and control, and medical therapy and life-support systems in hospitals. Similarly, autonomous systems, such as those on board spacecraft, cannot always rely on timely human intervention. Thus, it is important that deadlocks be either prevented or resolved automatically.

This chapter contains a relatively formal treatment of the deadlock problem, based notably on the model of Holt (1971, 1972). Dijkstra (1968) was one of the first and most influential contributors in the area. More recently, the problem has been studied in the context of database and distributed systems. Following some examples and definitions, deadlock detection, recovery, and prevention are discussed within a uniform graph model.

6.1 DEADLOCK WITH REUSABLE AND CONSUMABLE RESOURCES

Each resource element in the system can be identified with a given class, where the number of resource classes is fixed and depends on the particular system. For the purposes of deadlock modeling, it is sufficient to assume that individual units within each resource class are indistinguishable. For example, one resource class could be disk storage. Individual disk drives or even individual disk blocks represent the indistinguishable units within that resource class. We can divide all resource classes into two fundamentally different types: conventional nonshared objects and message-like objects, referred to as **reusable** and **consumable resources**, respectively.

6.1.1 Reusable and Consumable Resources

Reusable resources are permanent objects with the following properties:

1. The number of units within a class is constant; i.e., processes cannot create or delete units at runtime.
2. Each unit is either available, or is allocated to one and only one process; there is no sharing.
3. A process must first request and acquire a resource unit before it can release that unit.

The above definition captures the essential features of most conventional, nonshared, software and hardware resources that processes may use during their lifetimes. For example, hardware components, such as main memory, secondary storage, I/O devices, or processors, and software components, such as data files, tables, or semaphores, are considered reusable resource classes.

Consumable resources are produced and consumed dynamically, and have the following properties:

1. The number of units within a class varies at runtime; it may be zero and is potentially unbounded.
2. A process may increase the number of units of a resource class by releasing one or more units into that class; i.e., processes create new resources at runtime without acquiring them first from the class.
3. A process may decrease the number of units of a resource class by requesting and acquiring one or more units of that class. The units are not returned to the resource class but are consumed by the acquiring process.

Many types of data generated by either hardware or software have the above characteristics of consumable resources. The most prominent example are interprocess messages, which are generated by one process and consumed by another. Other examples include various types of synchronization and communication signals, interrupts, events, or data structures handed from one process to another. Although consumable resources are important, they are more difficult to manage than reusable resources, and there are fewer formal results that may be used for deadlock detection or prevention. With the exception of an example in the next section, the remainder of this chapter covers exclusively reusable resources.

6.1.2 Deadlocks in Computer Systems

Deadlocks may occur with either reusable of consumable resources. The following two cases illustrate some differences.

EXAMPLES: Deadlocks with Files and Messages

1. *File Sharing.* Consider two processes p_1 and p_2, both of which must write to two files, f_1 and f_2. The files are considered reusable resources. Suppose that p_1 opens f_1 first and then f_2, and p_2 opens the files in the reverse order, as illustrated in the following code:

```
    p1:                    p2:
         ⋮                      ⋮
      open(f1, w);           open(f2, w);
      open(f2, w);           open(f1, w);
         ⋮                      ⋮
```

   The two processes are assumed to execute concurrently, but we do not know anything about their relative speed. As long as p_1 opens both files before p_2 begins opening the first, or vice versa, there is no problem. Let's say p_1 succeeds in opening both files. It will use and eventually close them. In the meantime, p_2 will be blocked on its first *open* statement, since the files must be opened in exclusive mode for writing (w). When p_1 closes the files, p_2 will reopen them and proceed unhindered.

   The problem occurs when p_1 opens f_1 while, concurrently, p_2 opens f_2. This could happen easily in a time-sharing environment. For example, control could switch from p_1 to p_2 after p_1 opened f_1; p_2 would then open f_2. At this point, both processes are deadlocked. Each is holding one of the files open while trying to open the other. Since this will never be closed, the processes will wait indefinitely.

2. *Message-Passing.* Consider three processes, p_1, p_2, and p_3. Assume that the processes send messages (m) to each other along a ring, and that the *receive* operations are blocking. After an initial *send* from p_1 to p_2, each process repeatedly receives a message from its left-hand neighbor and sends a message to its right-hand neighbor. As long as the condition C is true and the initial *send* is performed, the above cycle continues indefinitely. However, if C is false, all three processes are blocked forever on their *receive* operations, waiting for a message that will never be sent.

```
    p1:                    p2:                    p3:
         ⋮                      ⋮                      ⋮
    if (C) send(p2,m);
    while (1) {            while (1) {            while (1) {
```

```
        receive(p3,m);          receive(p1,m);          receive(p2,m);
            ⋮                       ⋮                       ⋮
        send(p2,m);             send(p3,m);             send(p1,m);
    }                       }                       }
```

Deadlock, Starvation, and Livelock

A deadlock is a state where two or more processes are blocked indefinitely, waiting for each other. A process is considered blocked when it executes a synchronization or communication operation, such as $P(s)$, or a blocking receive, and the requested resource (the semaphore s or the message) is currently not available. In Section 4.5.1, we described two ways to block a process within such an operation: busy-waiting or placing the process on a wait queue. In the first case, the process continues to run, whereas in the second case it is stopped. However, for the purposes of deadlocks both implementations are treated equally. A process is considered blocked until it leaves the synchronization or communication operation.

A condition related to deadlocks was already introduced in Section 2.3.1, where the third solution to the CS problem could result in indefinite postponement of both processes competing for the CS. This can occur if both processes proceed at exactly the same pace. Neither is blocked, yet they still make no real progress, since both keep asking for permission to enter the CS indefinitely. Such an "active" form of deadlock, commonly referred to as a **livelock**, leads to the **starvation** of both processes in the same way as an actual deadlock. Livelocks are similar to deadlocks where the blocking operation uses busy-waiting. In both cases, the processes consume CPU resources but make no progress.

However, deadlock and starvation are very different. Deadlock *always* leads to starvation of at least two processes, but starvation may have other causes. Processes may starve in a livelock fashion as above, or they can starve by being blocked for an unbounded amount of time, waiting for a resource that could be made available but never is. The latter case is not a deadlock situation. To illustrate these points, we present two memory allocation examples, one with deadlock and one with starvation.

EXAMPLES: Deadlock vs. Starvation

1. *Deadlock on Memory Blocks*

Suppose that two processes, p_1 and p_2, are competing for a memory resource containing four blocks. Let their code requests follow the sequences:

```
        p1:                         p2:

            ⋮                           ⋮
        a: Get_Mem(2);              c: Get_Mem(1);
        b: Get_Mem(2);              d: Get_Mem(2);
            ⋮                           ⋮
```

The function *Get_Mem(n)* requests *n* blocks of memory. Now, if p_1 and p_2 call the statements at labels *a* and *c* at the same time, three of the four memory units are allocated, leaving only one available unit. Deadlock occurs when the processes execute the subsequent statements at labels *b* and *d*. Both processes become blocked, waiting for two units to become free. There is no legitimate sequence of operations that can break the deadlock; system or user intervention is necessary.

2. *Starvation on Memory Blocks*

   Real deadlocks involve at least two processes, but starvation (indefinite postponement) could happen to even a single process. Consider a system with 200 MB of main memory, and assume that any process requires either 100 MB or 200 MB to execute. Suppose further that two 100-MB processes are currently running, and that the ready queue always contains 100-MB processes. Then, whenever a process terminates, the system could always choose to load another 100-MB process, since that is how much memory is available. The 200-MB process will never get a chance to run, unless the scheduler postpones the loading of another 100-MB process. A similar situation occurs with schedulers that give highest priority to short processes; the scheduling of a long-running process could be postponed indefinitely. In both cases, the blocked process is not deadlocked, since the system does not need to starve them. For example, the system above could choose not to load the next 100-MB process and wait until 200 MB are available.

6.2 APPROACHES TO THE DEADLOCK PROBLEM

Some systems choose to completely ignore deadlocks, assuming that possible deadlocks can always be resolved by explicit user interaction. For example, killing processes that do not seem to be making any progress or rebooting all or part of the entire system are typical responses. This "practical" approach usually involves *timeouts* on waits for a resource. If a process is blocked for too long a time, a possible error, including deadlock, is indicated. It is then up to the programmer to provide code to handle each timeout; for example, by repeating the request at a later time or by taking a different course of actions.

In the many cases where the above strategies are not acceptable, we must implement mechanisms to explicitly handle the problem. The following options are possible:

1. **Detection and recovery**. Using this approach, we allow a deadlock to occur, but implement methods for detecting its presence and subsequently eliminating it.

2. **Avoidance**. This refers to dynamic schemes, where the system screens all resource requests. If granting a request would take the system into a state where deadlock could occur, the request is delayed until it become safe to grant it.

3. **Prevention**. This term is used for static techniques, where the rules governing the requests and acquisitions of resources are restricted in such a way that deadlock could never occur.

In the following sections, we present specific methods to implement the above three options for reusable resources.

6.3 A SYSTEM MODEL

We first present a graph model as a convenient notation for the process-resource state of a system, for the changes that occur as a result of resource requests, allocations, and releases, and for defining specific deadlock-related states. Our deadlock algorithms are directly based on the model.

6.3.1 Resource Graphs

To be able to reason about deadlocks, we must have a representation for processes, resources, and their relationships in the system. We will represent the state of the system by a directed graph, called the **resource graph**. All processes and resource classes are represented as vertices, and allocations and requests are represented as directed edges. Thus, at any given point in time, a resource graph captures all current allocations of resources to processes, and all current requests by processes for resources. The graph consists of the following components:

- **Processes**. Each process p_i $(1 \leq i \leq n)$ is a vertex represented as a circle. For example, the graph in Figure 6-1 shows a system consisting of three processes, p_1, p_2, and p_3.

- **Resources**. Each resource class R_j $(1 \leq j \leq m)$ is a vertex represented as a rectangle. Each individual (indistinguishable) resource unit within that class is represented as a small circle inside the rectangle. The sample graph in Figure 6-1 shows two resource classes, R_1 and R_2; R_1 consists of two units, and R_2 consists of three.

- **Resource requests**. A request by a process p_i for a unit of a resource R_j is represented as a directed edge $(p_i \rightarrow R_j)$; this is called a **request edge**. Process p_1 of Figure 6-1 has no current requests, process p_2 is requesting two units of R_2, and process p_3 is requesting one unit of R_1.

- **Resource allocations**. An allocation of a resource unit of class R_j to a process p_i is represented as a directed edge $(R_j \rightarrow p_i)$; this is called an **allocation edge**. Each allocation edge is connected to one of the circles within the class to indicate that the unit is currently unavailable to other processes. In Figure 6-1 process p_1 holds one unit of each resource class, p_2 holds one unit of R_1, and process p_3 holds two units of R_2.

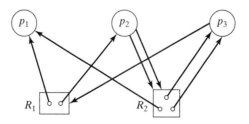

FIGURE 6-1. A resource graph.

6.3.2 State Transitions

Each resource graph represents a particular state of the system. It captures all current allocations and pending requests by all processes. The system state changes to a new state whenever a process *requests, acquires,* or *releases* a resource. These are the only possible operations, since no other action can affect the system with respect to deadlock. The three operations are defined as follows:

1. **Request**. Any process p_i in a given state may request additional resource units of any resource class R_j. The request operation changes the state of the system to a new state that contains the additional request edges $(p_i \rightarrow R_j)$.

    Any request is subject to the following restrictions:

    -   The requesting process p_i currently has no request edges from p_i to any resource classes. This condition represents the fact that a process is blocked from the time it issues a request until the request is granted. Consequently, the process cannot execute *any* operations during that time.

    -   The number of edges between p_i and R_j (both request and allocation edges) must never exceed the total number of units in R_j. Otherwise, the request could never be satisfied and the process would be blocked forever.

    Figure 6-2 illustrates the effect of a request operation. The leftmost resource graph shows a system consisting of two processes, p_1 and p_2, and a single resource class R with three resource units. In the system state S_0, process p_2 is holding one unit of R; no requests are pending. The transition to the new state S_1 is caused by a request of p_1 for two units of R. The state S_1 shows the corresponding request edges.

2. **Acquisition**. A process p_i in a given state may acquire previously requested resources. The acquisition operation changes the state of the system to a new state where the direction of all request edges $(p_i \rightarrow R_j)$ of p_i is reversed to $(R_j \rightarrow p_i)$ to reflect the allocations. Note that (unlike request and release) the

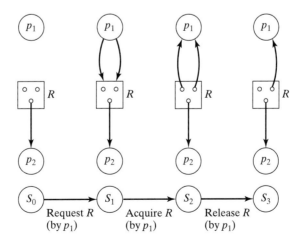

FIGURE 6-2. State transitions by process operations.

acquisition operation is not issued by the process p_i itself, but rather represent the request granting action taken by the resource manager. In fact, p_i is blocked from the time it issues a request until the acquisition is completed.

Any acquisition is subject to the following restriction:

- All outstanding requests of p_i must be satisfiable. That means, there must be a free resource (small circle inside R_j) for every request edge $(p_i \rightarrow R_j)$. This guarantees that the process gets all its requested resources, or it remains blocked. The reason for disallowing partial allocations is that it simplifies the deadlock detection algorithms.

Consider again Figure 6-2. It shows that in state S_2, the process p_1 acquires the two previously requested units of R; the two request edges in S_1 change to allocation edges in the new state S_2.

3. **Release.** A process p_i in a given state may release any previously acquired resource units. The release operation changes the state of the system to a new state where the allocation edges $(R_j \rightarrow p_i)$ corresponding to the released resource units are deleted. Any release is subject to the following restrictions:

- The process p_i currently has no request edges from p_i to any resource class. This is the same condition as in the case of the request operation.

- The process can release only those units it is currently holding; i.e., there must be an allocation edge $(R_j \rightarrow p_i)$ for any resource units being released.

The last part of Figure 6-2 illustrates the effect of a release operation. Process p_1 releases one of the previously acquired units of R.

6.3.3 Deadlock States and Safe States

Consider again the three state transitions shown in Figure 6-2. Note that these do not represent the only possible sequence of state changes for this system. The set of possible states the system can enter depends on the operations the processes can perform in a given state. For example, in state S_0 of Figure 6-2, p_2 could release the unit of R it is holding, leading to a new state with no edges. Alternately, p_1 could choose to request only one unit of R, or possibly all three; each choice would lead to a new system state. We do not generally know which path a given process may take through its code. We also do not know the order in which processes will be interleaved. But there is a finite set of state the system may potentially enter. Our ultimate goal is to identify (or prevent) those states containing deadlocked processes. We first define the following key terms:

- A process is **blocked** in a given state if it cannot cause a transition to a new state; i.e., the process can neither request, acquire, or release any resources in that state, because some of the restrictions imposed on these operations are not satisfied. Assume, for example, that process p_1 in state S_0 of Figure 6-2 requests three units of R instead of just two. It would become blocked in the new state until p_2 released the one unit it is currently holding.

- A process is **deadlocked** in a given state S if it is blocked in S and if no matter what operations (state changes) occur in the future, the process remains blocked. Assume, for example, that in the state S_3 of Figure 6-2, process p_1 requests two more units or R, and in the next transition, process p_2 also requests two more units or R. Both processes would become blocked and remain blocked forever, i.e., deadlocked.

- A state is called a **deadlock state** if it contains a deadlocked process. Note that a *cycle* in the resource graph is a necessary condition for deadlock.

- A state S is a **safe state** if for all states S' that can be reached from S using any sequence of valid request, acquire, and release operations, S' is not a deadlock state.

EXAMPLE: Reachable States of a System

Consider again the example of Section 6.1.2 where two processes p_1 and p_2 each must write to two files. Let us represent these files as two resources classes, R_1 and R_2, each containing one resource unit. Assume that p_1 always requests R_1 before R_2, and it releases R_2 before R_1. The sequence for p_2 is analogous, except that it requests and releases the resources in the reverse order.

Figure 6-3 illustrates the system state transitions if we consider only p_1 in isolation. The top portion shows the individual resource graphs, whereas the bottom portion shows possible state changes. In S_0, the resource graph has no edges; in S_1, p_1 is requesting R_1; in S_2, p_1 has acquired R_1; at this point it can release R_1, which takes it to back to S_0, or it can request R_2, which takes it to S_3; when it acquires R_2, the system is in S_4, where p_1 is holding both resources; releasing R_2 takes it back to S_2, an so on.

The state transitions of p_2, when considered in isolation, result in an analogous state transition diagram. If we now combine the processes, assuming that both can be running concurrently, we obtain the two-dimensional state transition diagram for all reachable states of the system, as shown in Figure 6-4. Each horizontal transition from a state $S_{i,j}$ to $S_{i+1,j}$ represents an operation by p_1. Each vertical transition from a state $S_{i,j}$ to $S_{i,j+1}$ represents an operation by p_2. For example, in $S_{1,1}$, each process has a request edge for one of the resources; in $S_{2,2}$, each process has an allocation edge for one of the resources; in $S_{3,3}$, each process has both an allocation edge for one of the resources and a request edge for the other resource. Figure 6-4 shows the resource graph for the state $S_{3,3}$, which is a deadlock state.

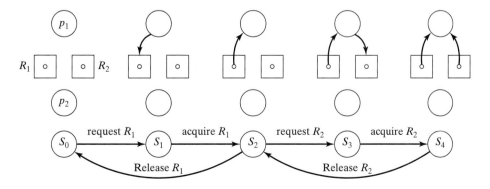

FIGURE 6-3. State transitions caused by process p_1.

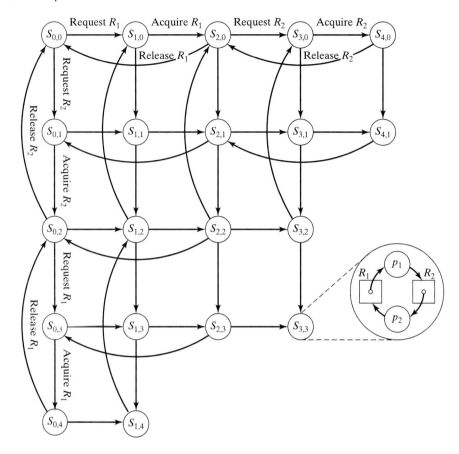

FIGURE 6-4. State transitions caused by p_1 and p_2.

The state transition diagram in Figure 6-4 also illustrates the other concepts introduced above:

- p_1 is blocked (but not deadlocked) in $S_{3,2}$ and $S_{1,4}$; there is no horizontal transition leading from these states. Similarly, p_2 is blocked (but not deadlocked) in $S_{2,3}$ and $S_{4,1}$.

- Both processes are deadlocked in $S_{3,3}$, since there is no transition, horizontal or vertical, leading from this state; i.e., $S_{3,3}$ is a deadlock state.

- No state is safe, since the deadlock state $S_{3,3}$ is reachable from any other state.

6.4 DEADLOCK DETECTION

To detect whether a given state S is a deadlock state, it is necessary to determine whether the processes that are blocked in S will remain blocked forever. This can be accomplished using a technique called **graph reduction**, which mimics the following execution scheme:

First, all requests satisfiable in state S for unblocked processes are granted, and the requesting processes continue to completion without requesting any further resources. Prior to termination, they release all their resources. These actions may wake up previously blocked processes, which then proceed to completion in the same manner. This is repeated until there are either no processes left, i.e., all processes have been terminated, or all remaining processes are blocked. In the latter case, the original state S is a deadlock state.

We now consider the graph reduction algorithm in more detail.

6.4.1   Reduction of Resource Graphs

Given a resource graph representing a system state, repeat the following steps until there are no unblocked processes remaining:

1. Select an unblocked process p.
2. Remove p, including all its request and allocation edges.

A resource graph is called **completely reducible** if, at the termination of the above reduction sequence, all process nodes have been deleted. We can now obtain the following important results in deadlock detection:

- *S is a deadlock state if and only if the resource graph of S is not completely reducible.*

- *All reduction sequences of a given resource graph lead to the same final graph.* That means, in step 1 of the reduction sequence above, it does not matter which unblocked process is selected.

The two results lead to an efficient algorithm for deadlock detection. They imply that, given a resource graph for a state S, we can apply *any* sequence of reductions. If, at the end, the graph is not completely reduced, S is a deadlock state.

EXAMPLE: Graph Reduction

To illustrate the graph reduction algorithm, consider the resource graph in Figure 6-5a. The only unblocked process in this state is p_1. Figure 6-5b shows the graph after reducing it by p_1. This unblocks p_2 and p_4, which can be removed in either order. The resulting state, shown in Figure 6-5c is irreducible, since both p_3 and p_5 are blocked. Hence, the original state was a deadlock state.

6.4.2   Special Cases of Deadlock Detection

The general results of the last section can be used to produce more efficient detection algorithms by taking advantage of a number of practical restrictions.

Testing for a Specific Process

On some occasions, we may be interested in determining only whether a specific process p is deadlocked, rather than testing the entire system state. This can be achieved by applying the graph reduction algorithm until one of the following occurs: 1) the graph

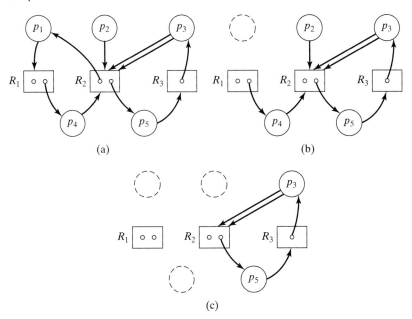

FIGURE 6-5. Graph reduction.

can be reduced by p, which implies that p is not blocked and hence not deadlocked; and 2) the graph is irreducible, in which case p is deadlocked. In both cases, the algorithm stops at this point.

Continuous Deadlock Detection

Testing for deadlock can be accomplished more efficiently if it is done on a *continuous* basis. If we know that the current state S is not deadlocked, then the next state S' is a deadlock state if and only if the operation that caused the transition was a request, and the process p that performed the operation is deadlocked in S'. In other words, a deadlock in S' can only be caused by a request that cannot be granted immediately. Thus, we only must check the specific process p; if p can be reduced, S' is not a deadlock state.

Immediate Allocations

Some resource allocators adopt the simple policy that all satisfiable requests are always granted immediately. If this is the case, a resource graph never contains any satisfiable request edges, since these are immediately turned into allocation edges. Such system states are referred to as **expedient**. For example, the state of Figure 6-5a is not expedient because p_1 is not blocked, and its request can be granted immediately. If we allocate a unit of R_1 to p_1, the state then becomes expedient. This yields a simpler condition for deadlock detection:

If a system state is expedient, then a knot in the corresponding resource graph implies a deadlock.

A **knot** in a directed graph is defined as a subset of nodes that satisfy the following two conditions: 1) Every node within the knot is reachable from every other node within the knot; and 2) a node outside the knot is not reachable from any node inside the knot. For example, consider Figure 6-5a again. If we delete the edge $R_2 \rightarrow p_1$, the graph has a knot $\{R_2, p_3, R_3, p_5\}$. If we also change the edge $p_1 \rightarrow R_1$ to $R_1 \rightarrow p_1$, the state becomes expedient, and it contains a deadlock.

To understand the intuition behind the above deadlock-detection condition, consider a resource graph containing a knot K. All processes within K must have pending requests, because each node must have an outgoing edge. Furthermore, they may only be requesting resources within K, since no edges may lead outside of K. If the state is expedient, none of the pending requests can be satisfiable, and hence all the processes must be deadlocked. Note that a knot is sufficient for deadlock, but not a necessary condition. The expedient state that we produced from Figure 6-5a by reversing the edge $p_1 \rightarrow R_1$, for example, does not have a knot but is still deadlocked.

Single-Unit Resources

In many situations, all resource classes are limited to having only a single unit. Common examples are files and locks. With this restriction, the existence of a simple *cycle* in the resource graph implies a deadlock. Thus, in this case, a cycle is both a necessary and sufficient condition for deadlock.

To show why this condition is sufficient, assume that the graph contains a cycle C. Since every process within C must have an entering and exiting edge, it must have an outstanding request for a resource in C and must hold resources in C. Therefore, every process in C is blocked on a resource in C that can be made available only by another process in C. Hence, all the processes in the cycle are deadlocked.

Thus, to detect a deadlock in systems with single-unit resources, we only must test the resource graph for cycles. There are well-known algorithms that can accomplish that in $O(n^2)$ time, where n is the number of nodes.

A single-unit resource class can have only a single allocation edge attached to it. This allows us to present the resource graph in a simplified form. We omit all resource classes and, instead, point all request edges directly at the process currently holding the resource. Such a graph is called a **wait-for graph** because an edge $(p_i \rightarrow p_j)$ indicates that process p_i is blocked on a resource currently held by p_j; i.e., p_i is waiting for p_j to release the resource. Then, more simply, a cycle in the wait-for graph is a necessary and sufficient condition for deadlock.

EXAMPLE: Wait-For Graph

Figure 6-6 illustrates the concept. In Figure 6-6a, processes p_1 and p_2 are requesting a resource currently held by p_3. In turn, p_3 is requesting a resource currently held by p_4. Figure 6-6b shows the corresponding wait-for graph: p_1 and p_2 are waiting for p_3, which is waiting for p_4.

6.4.3   Deadlock Detection in Distributed Systems

Wait-for graphs as defined in the previous section are the basis of deadlock detection in distributed systems restricted to single-unit resources. The added difficulty is that no single machine has a complete picture of all resource requests or allocations. Thus, the

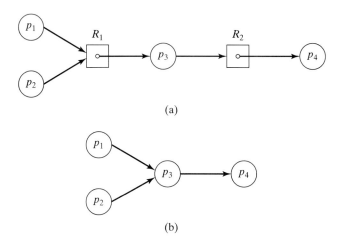

FIGURE 6-6. A wait-for graph.

wait-for graph itself is distributed; some edges cross the boundary between different machines.

Let each machine have its own local coordinator, responsible for maintaining the local portion of the wait-for graph. To detect deadlock, we must check for cycles in the global wait-for graph. But since cycles can span multiple machines, the coordinators must cooperate by exchanging information with one another to detect such global cycles. This can be done in two different ways, either through a central coordinator or in a distributed approach.

Central Coordinator Approach

The simplest way to detect cycles in the global wait-for graph is to mimic a centralized system. One of the local coordinators is designated as the **central coordinator**. It collects the local wait-for graphs from all other coordinators, assembles them into a complete global graph, and analyzes the global graph for the presence of cycles. The local graphs can be sent to the global coordinator whenever an edge is added or removed, or (less frequently) by grouping together multiple changes to reduce message traffic.

The centralized approach to deadlock detection, although straightforward to implement, has two main drawbacks. First, the global coordinator becomes a performance bottleneck and a single point of failure. Second, it is prone to detecting nonexisting deadlocks, referred to as **phantom deadlocks**. To illustrate how this can happen, consider a system with two machines, $M1$ and $M2$, each holding two processes. Figure 6-7a shows the global wait-for graph. This indicates that p_1 is currently holding a resource that p_2 is requesting; p_2, in turn, is holding a resource that p_3 (on machine $M2$) is requesting; and p_3 is holding a resource that p_4 is requesting. Assume now that p_1 requests a resource held by p_4, which adds the edge $(p_1 \rightarrow p_4)$. Concurrently, p_3 on $M2$ times out on its wait, which removes its waiting edge for p_2, i.e., $(p_3 \rightarrow p_2)$. If the global coordinator receives the update from $M1$ first, it will construct the graph shown in Figure 6-7b, and, consequently, it will report a deadlock. In reality, no deadlock exists, since the actual wait-for graph does not contain the phantom edge $(p_3 \rightarrow p_2)$.

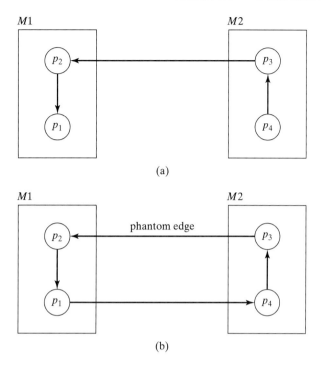

FIGURE 6-7. A phantom deadlock.

Distributed Approach

A fully distributed deadlock-detection algorithm attempts to find cycles in the global wait-for graph by tracing the different paths through the graph without gathering it in one central location. The basic idea is to send a special message, called a **probe**, which replicates itself along all outgoing edges. If one of the replicas reaches the original destination of the probe, a cycle, and thus a deadlock, has been detected. There are many different implementations of this basic concept, referred to as **edge-chasing** or **path-pushing** approaches. What distinguishes them is the type and amount of information carried by the probe, and the type and amount of information that must be maintained by each local coordinator.

Let us consider the conceptually simplest approach, where each probe is the concatenation of edges it has traversed so far. The initial probe is launched by a process p_i when it becomes blocked on a request for a resource currently held by another process p_j. The local coordinator extends the probe by adding to it the edge $(p_i \rightarrow p_j)$ and replicates it along all edges emanating from p_j. If there are no such edges, indicating that the current process is not blocked, the probe is discarded. A cycle is detected whenever the process appears on the probe twice, indicating that the probe must have returned to an already-visited process.

EXAMPLE: A Probe

Figure 6-8 illustrates the above algorithm using seven processes distributed over four different machines. Assume that p_1 requests a resource held by p_2. Process p_1 creates the

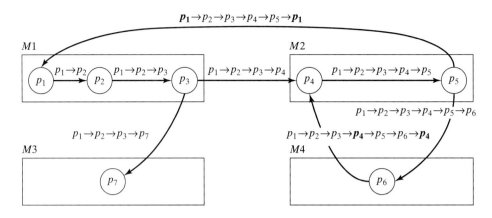

FIGURE 6-8. A probe to detect cycles.

initial probe containing the edge $p_1 \rightarrow p_2$. Since p_2 waits for p_3, the probe is extended to $p_1 \rightarrow p_2 \rightarrow p_3$. p_3 is waiting for p_4 and p_7, and consequently, replicates the probe along the two different paths, as shown. The one carrying $p_1 \rightarrow p_2 \rightarrow p_3 \rightarrow p_7$ is discarded on machine M_3, since p_7 is not blocked. On the other hand, the other probe continues through p_4 to p_5. At p_5, the probe is again replicated. The one containing $p_1 \rightarrow p_2 \rightarrow p_3 \rightarrow p_4 \rightarrow p_5 \rightarrow p_1$ closes the cycle upon reaching machine M_1. p_1 appears twice on the path—once as the initiator of the original probe and a second time as its recipient. Thus, the coordinator on M_1 detects a deadlock. In a similar manner, the coordinator on M_2 can detect the other cycle in the graph by noticing that p_4 appears twice on the probe $p_1 \rightarrow p_2 \rightarrow p_3 \rightarrow p_4 \rightarrow p_5 \rightarrow p_1 \rightarrow p_4 \rightarrow p_4$.

The main drawback of the above implementation is that the probe's length is unbounded. That may not be a serious problem in practice, since the paths in the wait-for graphs are typically short. Nevertheless, there are approaches where the probe length can be kept constant at the expense of maintaining additional information about the already-known dependencies by each local coordinator (Chandy, Misra, and Haas 1983).

6.5 RECOVERY FROM DEADLOCK

A deadlock always involves a cycle of alternating process and resource nodes in the resource graph. The two general approaches to recovery are process termination and resource preemption. In the first case, nodes and edges of the resource graph are eliminated. The second strategy involves edge deletions only. In both cases, the goal is to break the deadlock cycle.

6.5.1 Process Termination

The simplest and crudest recovery algorithms terminate *all* processes involved in the deadlock. This approach is unnecessarily wasteful, since, in most cases, eliminating a single process is sufficient to break the deadlock. Thus, it is better to terminate processes one at a time, release their resources, and at each step check if the deadlock still persists.

This is repeated until the deadlock is eliminated, or, in the worst case, until all but one of the originally deadlocked processes must be liquidated.

With this incremental method, we must decide on the order in which the processes will be terminated. Picking the processes at random is the easiest solution, but it is more rational to consider the cost of terminating different processes. Termination cost may involve a combination of the following:

1. **The priority of the process.** This metric is similar to that used for process scheduling. It may involve the process type (e.g., real-time, interactive, or batch), its CPU or memory requirements, and other metrics.

2. **The cost of restarting the process.** Many processes maintain very little state and can easily be restarted. This includes most interactive processes, such as the user shell, Internet browsers, or even text editors (provided the edited files are being saved periodically). In contrast, other applications cannot be "resumed" but must be repeated from the beginning. This includes, for example, scientific computations, which may run for hours or even days in batch mode. Terminating such applications is not only costly but also frustrating for the users.

3. **The current state of the process.** Many processes cooperate with others in a variety of ways, thus killing one process may seriously impact others that depend on it. For example, killing the consumer or the producer process in a producer-consumer scenario will leave the other process hanging. Similarly, killing a process in the middle of a CS will deadlock other processes that compete for the same CS. Finally, some operations are not idempotent, i.e., cannot be repeated without side effects. For example, appending data to a file cannot simply be repeated by rerunning a killed process.

In general, choosing the best sequence of processes to terminate is highly dependent on the particular system and its applications.

6.5.2   Resource Preemption

Resource preemption means taking away the contested resources from one or more of the deadlocked processes. This can be done in one of two ways. First, some resources may lend themselves to **direct preemption**; i.e., the system temporarily deallocates the resource, lets other processes use it, and gives it back to the original process. Few resources can be handled in this way transparently. For example, temporarily reallocating a printer in the middle of a print job would result in interleaved pages from multiple processes. Main memory is one of the few resources that can be preempted transparently, by temporarily swapping a process or some of its data to disk, and reloading it later when memory is again available.

An *indirect* form of resource preemption is achieved by **process rollback**. Some systems take periodic snapshots of processes, called **checkpoints**, to achieve fault tolerance. In the case of a crash, the process does not need to be restarted from its beginning. Instead, the process can be rolled back by restoring its last checkpoint and resuming its execution from there. We can use the same mechanism for resource preemption. To take away a resource from a process, we can roll it back to a checkpoint during which it had not acquired this resource yet. After resuming execution from this point, the process would repeat the earlier request for the resource, which, in the meantime, could be used by other processes.

6.6 DYNAMIC DEADLOCK AVOIDANCE

The previous section focused on detecting deadlocks and eliminating them once they occur. An entirely different strategy is to prevent deadlocks from developing in the first place. When this is done through rules checked and enforced at runtime, the approach is referred to as **deadlock avoidance**.

6.6.1 Claim Graphs

The basic principle of deadlock avoidance is to delay the acquisition of resources that might cause the system to enter a deadlock state in the future. This can be determined if information about future process resource needs is available. Generally, processes do not know which resources they will need in the future. However, they can specify an upper bound on their needs, called the **maximum claim**. This is the largest number of units of each resource that the process will ever need at any one time.

The maximum claim of a process can be represented as a **claim graph**, which is an extension of the general resource graph used for deadlock detection. A claim graph, in addition to showing processes, resources, request edges, and allocation edges, contains a set of *potential request edges*. In the initial system state, the number of such edges ($p_i \rightarrow R_j$) represent the maximum number of units of resource R_j that process p_i will ever need.

Each potential request edge may, in the future, be transformed into an actual request edge and, subsequently, into an assignment edge. But the total number of edges between the process p_i and resource class R_j (i.e., the sum of request, allocation, and claim edges) will always remain the same.

EXAMPLE: Claim Graph

Figure 6-9 shows an example of a claim graph in the initial system state S_0, and its transformation into other states as the result of operations by the two processes. The request and allocation edges are shown as before; the added claim edges are represented by dashed lines.

The graph shows that process p_1 may request, at most, two units of R at any given time, whereas p_2 may request all three. The first operation is a request by p_2 for one unit of R. The new state S_1 shows one of the claim edges transformed into an actual request edge. The request is granted, resulting in state S_2. The next operation is a request by p_2 for two units of R (in state S_3), which is also granted (in state S_4). At this point, p_2 could request one of two more units of R, which would block the process until the units were released by p_1.

6.6.2 The Banker's Algorithm

Claim graphs may be used for dynamic deadlock avoidance. This is achieved by disallowing any *acquisition* operations unless the resulting claim graph is completely reducible. The fact that the claim graph can be completely reduced means that the worst case of all

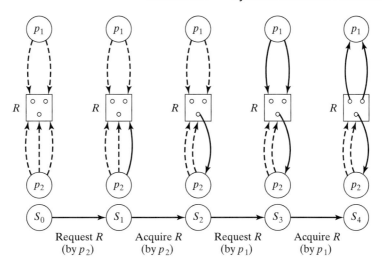

FIGURE 6-9. State transitions using claim graphs.

possible future requests could be handled. That means, even if all processes requested the remainders of their claims, all requests could still be satisfied. The following theorem has been proven formally:

If acquisition operations that do not result in a completely reducible claim graph are prohibited, any system state is safe.

This theorem is the basis of deadlock-avoidance algorithms, the best known of which is the **banker's algorithm** (Dijkstra 1968). It takes its name from an analogy to banking systems, where resource classes correspond to currencies, allocations correspond to loans, and maximum claims are considered the credit limits. Deadlock prevention is accomplished by the "banker," which grants or delays any request in a given state S as follows:

1. Assume the request in state S is granted, i.e., temporarily change the request edge(s) into the corresponding acquisition edge(s); the new tentative state is S'.
2. Reduce the claim graph of S'. That means, treat all claim edges in S' as actual request edges and reduce the resulting graph.
3. If the graph is completely reducible, grant the original request, i.e., accept S' as the new state and continue; otherwise, delay the acquisition, i.e., revert to the original state S and keep the request as pending.

EXAMPLE: The Banker's Algorithm

To illustrate the working of the banker's algorithm, consider the claim graph in Figure 6-10a, which shows the state of the same system as Figure 6-1, but at an earlier time. The requests by p_1 and p_2 for one unit of R_1 each have not been granted yet. Thus, all three processes have pending requests for one unit of R_1. The original resource graph also has been augmented by the claim edges of each process, shown as dashed lines. The task of the banker's algorithm is to decide which of the three pending requests for R_1 can safely be granted.

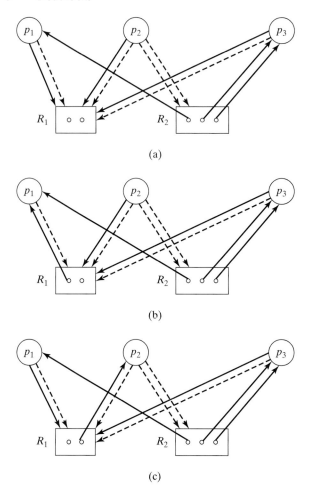

FIGURE 6-10. Deadlock avoidance using the banker's algorithm.

Figure 6-10b shows the new graph should p_1's request be granted. The resulting graph is completely reducible (first by p_1, then by p_3, and finally by p_2). Hence, this request could be granted in this state. The request by p_3 also results in a completely reducible graph and may be granted. On the other hand, the request by p_2 results in the graph shown in Figure 6-10c. If we interpret all claim edges as actual request edges, then all three processes are blocked, and the graph is not reducible. To prevent such a situation from developing, the request by p_2 must be delayed until it becomes safe to grant it.

Special Case: Single-Unit Resources

When all resource classes contain only a single unit, the reducibility of the claim graph can be tested much more efficiently. This is based on the following observation: a claim graph becomes irreducible only when an acquisition creates a cycle in the claim graph. Thus, a simple path-tracing algorithm from the acquiring process can be employed for deadlock prevention.

EXAMPLE: Single-Unit Resources

Figure 6-11a illustrates this idea using a simple system of two processes and two resources. The pending request by p_2 for R_1 must not be granted, since doing so would close the (directed) cycle $p_1 \rightarrow R_1 \rightarrow p_2 \rightarrow R_2 \rightarrow p_1$.

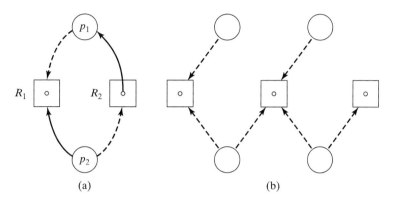

(a)   (b)

FIGURE 6-11. Deadlock avoidance with single-unit resources.

We also can easily test for safeness of states in single-unit resource graphs. This is based on the following observation: a directed cycle can develop only if the graph contains an *undirected* cycle. In other words, if we disregard the direction of all edges and determine that the graph contains no undirected cycles, then no directed cycle will develop in such a claim graph. Consequently, in this situation, *all* states are safe, and there is no possibility of deadlock. Note that this only must be checked once, when the claim graph is first created. Thus, dynamic deadlock avoidance turns into a single static test.

EXAMPLE: Safe States

Figure 6-11b illustrates a system where all states are safe. If we ignore the direction of the claim edges, we see that no cycle can be formed, since the claim edges are a superset of all possible future request or acquisition edges.

6.7 DEADLOCK PREVENTION

Dynamic deadlock avoidance relies on *runtime checks* to ensure the system never enters an unsafe state. These are performed by the system (the resource manager) that is responsible for granting or delaying any given request. On the other hand, deadlock prevention relies on imposing additional rules or conditions on the system so that all states are safe. Thus, prevention is a *static* approach, where all processes must follow certain rules for requesting or releasing resources.

By examining the general form of a resource graph, we can identify the following three structural conditions that must hold for deadlock to occur:

1. **Mutual exclusion**. Resources are not sharable; i.e., there is, at most, one allocation edge from any resource unit to a process in the resource graph.

2. **Hold and wait**. A process must be holding a resource and requesting another; i.e., there must be an allocation edge from a resource unit to a process p_1, and a request edge from p_1 to another resource unit. The two units can be within the same resource class or within different classes.

3. **Circular wait**. At least two processes must be blocked waiting for each other; i.e., the graph must contain a cycle involving at least two processes and at least two resource units, such that each process holds one of the units and is requesting another.

The elimination of any of these three conditions would make it structurally impossible for deadlock to occur.

6.7.1 Eliminating the Mutual-Exclusion Condition

If all resources could be shared (accessed concurrently), no process would block on a resource, and no deadlock would occur. Some resources that might be used nonexclusively in a shared fashion are pure program code, read-only data files or databases, and clocks. Unfortunately, mutual exclusion is a fundamental requirement for correct use of many resource types, and this condition cannot generally be eliminated. For example, files cannot usually be written into by multiple processes at the same time in a meaningful way. Similarly, database transactions require exclusive access to records to ensure data consistency.

In some instances, it is possible to circumvent the mutual exclusion requirement by transforming *nonsharable* resources into *sharable* ones. The prime example is spooling of output, which was briefly discussed in the Introduction. Printers or other output devices always must be accessed by only one process at a time to prevent interleaving of output. To avoid unnecessary blocking of processes waiting for output, many OSs provide *virtual devices*, implemented as software files, into which processes may direct their output. When the complete output sequence is available, it is sent to the actual hardware printer, and the process continues without blocking.

6.7.2 Eliminating the Hold-and-Wait Condition

The simplest way to eliminate this condition is to insist that every process *requests all resources it will ever need at the same time*. A process with resources already allocated to it will never be blocked because it cannot make any further requests. It will eventually release all its resources (not necessarily at the same time), which may unblock other processes. But a given process will have either assignment edges or request edges, but never both together. Deadlock is therefore impossible, and every state is safe.

The main drawback of this simple policy is poor resource utilization—resources must be allocated well ahead of their actual use and be unavailable to other processes for possibly long periods of time. Resources also may be requested unnecessarily in anticipation of a use that does not materialize.

A more flexible approach is allow processes to request resources as they need them, but to always *release all resources they are currently holding, prior to making any new request*. This may result in having to repeatedly request and release frequently used resources. Assume, for example, that a process needs either resources R_1 and R_2, or

R_1 and R_3, but never R_2 and R_3 together. To eliminate the hold-and-wait condition, the processes cannot simply release and request R_2 or R_3 as needed, while keeping R_1. Instead, the process must release both R_1 and R_2, prior to requesting R_1 and R_3, and vise versa.

Yet a third alternative is to give each process the ability to test whether a needed resource R is currently available. If not, the process must *release all other resources it is currently holding, prior to waiting for the unavailable resource R* to become free. None of these alternatives is really satisfactory.

6.7.3   Eliminating the Circular-Wait Condition

A cycle in the resource graph can develop only when processes request the same resources but in a different order. This can be prevented if all processes request all resources in the same order. Since it is not known, generally, which resources will be needed by which process, we assign a sequential ordering, SEQ, to all existing resource classes, such that $SEQ(R_i) \neq SEQ(R_j)$ for all $i \neq j$. In other words, any process can test whether a given resource precedes or succeeds another resource according to the ordering SEQ. Processes are then allowed to request any subset of the existing resources as in the general case, but they must *request them in the order prescribed by SEQ*. When a process already holds a resource R_i, it may only request resources R_j with a higher sequence number, i.e., resources where $SEQ(R_i) < SEQ(R_j)$.

EXAMPLE: Ordered Resources Policy

Assume a system with four resource classes, R_1, R_2, R_3, and R_4, where $SEQ(R_1) < SEQ(R_2) < SEQ(R_3) < SEQ(R_4)$. Figure 6-12 shows three processes competing for these three resource classes. Process p_1 has no outstanding requests and could request units from any of the four classes. Process p_2 is already holding a unit from the highest class, R_4, and is not allowed to make further requests. Process p_3 holds units from R_1, R_2, and R_3; thus, the only additional resources it could request are from class R_4.

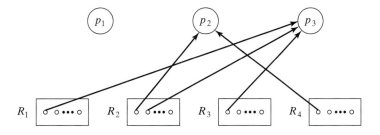

FIGURE 6-12. Ordered resources policy.

By assigning the most expensive or scarce resources to the highest classes, the requests of the most valuable resources can be deferred until they are actually needed. Nevertheless, the overall resource utilization of this ordered resources policy is still not very high, because some resources must be allocated well in advance of their need. This policy was originally devised by Havender (1968) for the IBM OS called OS/360. It also is used to prevent deadlock on monitor locks when using nested monitors, i.e., when a procedure within one monitor calls a procedure within another monitor. These monitors must be called in a given order (Lampson and Redell 1980).

CONCEPTS, TERMS, AND ABBREVIATIONS

The following concepts have been introduced in this chapter. Test yourself by defining and discussing each keyword or phrase.

Banker's algorithm	Knot
Central coordinator	Livelock
Checkpoint	Maximum claim
Circular wait	Ordered resource policy
Claim graph	Phantom deadlock
Consumable resource	Probe message
Continuous detection	Reachable state
Deadlock	Reducible graph
Deadlock avoidance	Resource graph
Deadlock detection	Reusable resource
Deadlock prevention	Rollback
Deadlock recovery	Safe state
Deadlock state	Single-unit resource
Distributed detection	Starvation
Graph reduction	State of a system
Hold and wait	Wait-for graphs

EXERCISES

1. Consider the dining philosophers problem of Section 3.3.2. Assume there are three philosophers, p_1, p_2, and p_3 using three forks, f1, f2, and f3. The philosophers execute the following code:

```
p1() {                p2() {                p3() {
while (1) {            while (1) {            while (1) {
   P(f1);                P(f1);                P(f3);
   P(f3);                P(f2);                P(f2);
   eat;                  eat;                  eat;
   V(f3);                V(f2);                V(f2);
   V(f1) }               V(f1) }               V(f3) }
}                     }                     }
```

(a) Is deadlock possible in this system?

(b) Would deadlock be possible if we reversed the order of the P operations in process p_1, p_2, or p_3?

(c) Would deadlock be possible if we reversed the order of the V operations in process p_1, p_2, or p_3?

2. Consider the following reusable resource graph:

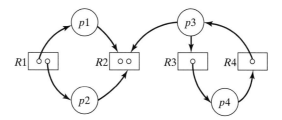

   (a) Which processes are blocked?
   (b) Which processes are deadlocked?
   (c) Is the state a deadlock state?
   (d) Does the graph contain a knot? If so, list the nodes constituting the knot.

3. Consider three processes, p_1, p_2, and p_3, executing asynchronously the following sequences of code:

p1	p2	p3
:	:	:
P(x)	P(y)	P(z)
:	: ←	:
P(z) ←	P(y)	P(x) ←
:	:	:
V(x)		V(z)
:	:	:
V(z)		V(x)

   The arrow in each line indicates which instruction the corresponding process is currently executing. All semaphores were initially set to 1.
   (a) Draw a reusable resource graph describing the above situation where each semaphore is interpreted as a resource, and *P* and *V* operations represent *requests* and *releases* of the resources.
   (b) Reduce the graph as much as possible; does it represent a deadlock state?
   (c) If you could increase the number of units of any of the three resources, which increase (if any) would resolve the deadlock?

4. Using the definitions of Section 6.3.3, show that safeness of a state and deadlock are not complementary; i.e., the statement "*S* is not a deadlock state" does *not* imply that "*S* is a safe state."

5. The basic graph-reduction algorithm given in Section 6.4.1 is very inefficient. The first step—finding an unblocked process during each iteration—requires a number of operations proportional to the number of processes. Develop a more efficient algorithm that maintains a list of unblocked processes. At each iteration, a process is selected from this list and removed from the graph. This reduction may, in turn, unblock other processes, which are added to the list. Thus, finding an unblocked process is always a single constant operation. (Hint: Maintain a counter for each process that records the number of resource classes the process is blocked on.)

6. Modify the state transition diagram of Figure 6-4 to reflect the following changes:
   (a) A process may release both resources at the same time.
   (b) A process will not release its first resource until it has acquired the second. Both resources are then released at the same time.
   (c) Process p_1 only needs resource R_2.
   (d) Would the changes in (a), (b), or (c) eliminate the possibility of deadlock?

7. Two processes, p_1 and p_2, both need two single-unit resources, R_1 and R_2. The processes repeatedly execute the following sequences (at unknown speeds):

```
p1:                        p2:
while(1) {                 while(1) {
    request R1;                request R2;
    request R2;                request R1;
    release R1;                release R2;
    release R2;                release R1;
      :                          :
      :                          :
}                          }
```

   (a) Assume first that process p_2 is not executing. Draw the state transition diagram, similar to Figure 6-3, where each state S_i corresponds to the state i of p_1. In which state(s), if any, is p_1 blocked and/or deadlocked?
   (b) Now draw the state transition diagram for both processes, similar to Figure 6-4. Each system state $S_{i,j}$ represents the state i of p_1 and the state j of p_2. In which state(s), if any, is p_1 blocked and/or deadlocked? In which state(s), if any, is p_2 blocked and/or deadlocked?
   (c) For the state transition diagram of point (b) above, draw the resource graphs corresponding to the states $S_{1,0}$, $S_{1,1}$, $S_{1,2}$, $S_{1,3}$, $S_{1,4}$, $S_{1,5}$, $S_{2,3}$, $S_{3,3}$.

8. Consider the same two processes and resources as in Exercise 7, but assume now that both processes request R_1 before R_2. Draw the state transition diagram for the two processes, similar to Figure 6-4. In which state(s), if any, is p_1 blocked and/or deadlocked? In which state(s), if any, is p_2 blocked and/or deadlocked?

9. Consider a system of three processes and a single-resource class with four units. Each process needs at most two units. Show that the system is deadlock free, i.e., all states are safe.

10. Consider a generalization of Exercise 9 where the system consists of n processes and a single-resource class with m units. Show that the system is deadlock free if the sum of all maximum needs of all processes is less than $n + m$ units.

11. Prove the following by counterexamples:
   (a) A cycle is not a sufficient condition for deadlock.
   (b) A knot is not a necessary condition for deadlock in expedient state graphs.

12. Consider five processes, each running on a different machine. The wait-for graph contains the following edges: $p1 \rightarrow p2$, $p2 \rightarrow p3$, $p3 \rightarrow p4$, $p1 \rightarrow p5$, $p5 \rightarrow p4$.
   (a) Does this represent a deadlock state?
   (b) Assume process $p5$ times out, which removes the edge $p5 \rightarrow p4$ from the graph. At the same time, $p4$ requests a resource currently held by $p1$.
      i. Is the new state a deadlock state? If not, could a centralized coordinator approach produce a phantom deadlock?
      ii. With a distributed algorithm, what probes could $p4$ receive in response to making its request?
   (c) Repeat the previous problem, assuming that instead of $p5$, process $p1$ times out, which removes its two edges from the graph.

13. Consider a system that uses process rollback for recovery from deadlocks.
    (a) What are all the possible pieces of information that must be saved as part of a process checkpoint?
    (b) Can the process be restarted completely transparently from a checkpoint? If not, which actions performed or initiated by the process may be irreversible?
14. Show that resource graphs never contain directed cycles in the following two cases:
    (a) Every process must request all resources at one time.
    (b) Processes must request all resources according to a fixed ordering of all resources (Section 6.7.3).
15. Consider the following maximum claims graph:

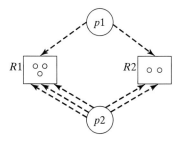

    (a) Show a sequence of operations leading from the given state to a deadlock state.
    (b) Show how the above deadlock could have been prevented using the banker's algorithm (see Section 6.6.2).
16. Consider a banking system with many different accounts. Processes may transfer money between any two accounts, A_i and A_j, by executing the following transaction:
      lock A_i; lock A_j; update A_i; update A_j; unlock A_i; unlock A_j;
    (a) Show how a deadlock can occur in such a system.
    (b) How can the ordered resource policy (see Section 6.7) be implemented to prevent deadlock if the set of possible accounts is not known a priori or changes dynamically?
17. Consider two processes, p_1 and p_2. Process p_1 needs resources R_1, R_2, R_3, R_4; process p_2 needs resources R_2, R_3, R_4, R_5. If the processes are allowed to request the resources in any order, deadlock can occur. Give five permutations of the requests that may result in deadlock, and five permutations that will never result in a deadlock.

PART TWO

MEMORY MANAGEMENT

CHAPTER 7

Physical Memory

7.1 PREPARING A PROGRAM FOR EXECUTION
7.2 MEMORY PARTITIONING SCHEMES
7.3 ALLOCATION STRATEGIES FOR VARIABLE PARTITIONS
7.4 MANAGING INSUFFICIENT MEMORY

While the cost of main memory—the memory that can be directly accessed as data or instructions by the processor—has been decreasing steadily over the past several decades, memory still constitutes one of the most critical resources of a computer system. The speed at which memory can access a data item is much slower than the speed at which the processor can process the data, and new technologies are only further widening this gap. This difference can be partially alleviated by caches and other high-speed memories. Nevertheless, effective management of main memory remains one of the most important issues in operating systems (OS) design. In this chapter, we examine the principal software techniques for managing main memory when there is no virtual memory support.

7.1 PREPARING A PROGRAM FOR EXECUTION

Most application, OS, and utility programs are written in some user-oriented, high-level language, or less frequently, in assembly language. Each such program must undergo a series of transformation before it can be executed by the machine hardware.

7.1.1 Program Transformations

Figure 7-1 illustrates the stages of a program as it is being prepared for execution. The first step in this series of transformations is a translation of the **source modules**—the code as written by the programmer—into a machine-specific version in which all symbolic instructions, operands, and addresses are converted into numerical values. In the case of high-level languages this translation process is referred to as **compilation**. The term **assembly** is used with lower-level languages that simply provide a more convenient symbolic form of the underlying machine language. The resulting program is called the **object module**.

Software systems of any substantial size cannot be developed as one monolithic entity. Instead, modules reflecting different functions of the system are designed separately, possibly by different programmers, and then interconnected into one complex system using **linking**.

At the time a source program is translated into an object module, it contains external references, i.e., operand addresses referring to data or instructions within other modules.

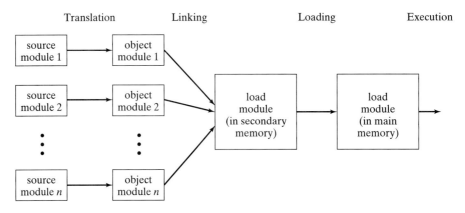

FIGURE 7-1. Program transformations.

These cannot be resolved at compile time. Instead, the compiler only records where such references occur in the program to facilitate the subsequent task of the linker. For that purpose, the compiler generates an **external symbol table** for each module, which lists all external references used in that module. The main task to be performed during linking is to resolve the external references. The resulting module is referred to as the **load module**. As shown in Figure 7-1, each source module is translated into the corresponding object module independently of other modules.

Note that resolving an external reference does not necessarily imply **binding** or assigning that reference to a physical location. It only implies that a common address space has been assigned to all modules linked together and that all references, internal and external, refer to locations within that common space. Thus, *linking* translates external symbolic references to corresponding numeric references. These can still be logical addresses, which must be translated into physical addresses before they can be accessed. When all external references are resolved before execution of the program begins, the linking is referred to as **static**. The linking is **dynamic** when external references are kept is their symbolic form until execution and are resolved during execution.

The final step in the series of transformations is the actual **loading** of the load module from secondary memory to main memory. The module can be transferred all at once or different parts of it can be transferred at different times during execution.

7.1.2 Logical-to-Physical Address Binding

Before a program can be executed, it must be loaded into main memory. This requires choosing the physical locations in which the program instruction and data will reside, and adjusting the program references to point to the appropriate locations. For example, store or load instructions must be adjusted such that their address fields refer to the current locations of the operands they are to access. Similarly, branch instructions must contain the current addresses of their destination instructions.

The assignment or binding of actual *physical* addresses to program instructions and data can take place at different points during a program life cycle. These include the time of program development, compilation, linking, loading, or execution. In the first four cases, where the binding takes place prior to execution, the binding is called **static**. If the binding takes place when the program is already running, it is called **dynamic**.

Until the binding takes place, the programmer, the compiler, the linker, or possibly the loader must work within an assumed **logical address space** when creating or transforming a module. Typically, symbolic names are used by programmers to refer to data or branch locations, which the compiler, the linker, and the loader transform into numerical values, assuming a hypothetical starting address, such as zero. When the actual physical locations are assigned, all operand and branch addresses within the module must be adjusted according to this assignment. In other words, the program is "moved" from the logical to the physical address space. It is for this reason that the binding of logical addresses to physical address also is referred to as program **relocation**. In particular, a program is called **relocatable** or dynamically relocatable if it can be moved into different areas of memory *without any transformations*. Let us examine the issues of address binding and relocation in more detail.

Static Binding

The earliest possible moment at which physical memory address can be assigned is at the time of writing the program. Some assemblers and compilers permit the specification of an absolute (physical) address thus providing for this possibility. Such **programming-time binding**, however, is used relatively infrequently, for example, at the lowest kernel level of an OS, in many real-time and embedded systems, or when the programmer must control a special hardware component. In most other cases, symbolic names are used at the programming level, and must be translated into a physical address by the compiler and linker.

To perform the translation, the compiler must be given the starting address of the program. If this is the actual physical address, the resulting program can execute only when loaded into the specific preassigned memory space; it is not relocatable. Such early **compile-time binding** of programs to physical memory locations is very restrictive and thus rarely used. It is more practical to postpone the binding until at least the time of linking. At this time, all modules to be linked together are known, permitting both internal and external references to be resolved.

With **link-time binding**, the load module is still not relocatable, i.e., it must be loaded into main memory starting with the location assumed by the linker. Consequently, the task of the loader is simply to copy the load module into memory, without any further transformations. In this case, the linker and the loader may usefully be combined into one subsystem called the **linking loader**. This approach is used widely in smaller, single-user systems.

Separating the linker from the loader offers more flexibility in that the starting address need not be known at the time of linking. Only when the module is actually to be executed are physical addresses bound by relocating the complete load module. Hence, the load module may be loaded into a different region of memory without relinking each time. However, it is still not (dynamically) relocatable.

To permit the relocation of a module at the time of linking or loading, compilers and assemblers must indicate which operands and data variables are relocatable. In general, an operand can be a register name, an immediate operand (constant), an offset to a base register, an absolute memory address, or a relative memory address. Only relative memory addresses are relocatable; all others remain unchanged. Data variables are treated in a similar manner. If they represent relative addresses, then they must be relocated; otherwise, they remain unchanged.

Assuming that an object module is to be loaded into contiguous memory starting at location x and it has been translated relative to some assumed location y, then all references within the program must be incremented by $k = x - y$, which is referred to as the **relocation constant**. In most cases, y is assumed zero, and the relocation constant k is simply the module's starting address, x.

EXAMPLE: Program Transformation Under Static Binding

Figure 7-2 shows the successive transformation of an internal and an external reference as a program is prepared for execution. The source module S contains an assignment statement, $i = \ldots$, and a function call, $f()$. The compiler is given zero as the starting address for the object module. Assuming that the integer variable, i, resides at the offset 20, the store instruction produced by the compiler as part of the assignment statement will have 20 as its operand address. The address of the function f is still unknown at this time, so it remains in its symbolic form. For simplicity, the figure shows f as the address of the branch instruction. In reality, the symbolic name f would be kept in an *eternal symbol table*, and it would point to the corresponding branch instruction.

The external references are resolved at the time of linking, when the starting addresses of all object modules are known to the linker. Let's assume that the function f is 100 words long and that it precedes S in the linking sequence. The linker, assuming zero as the starting address for the load module, adjusts the addresses as shown in the figure. That means, the operand of the store instruction is incremented by 100, which is the relocation constant for the module S. The external reference to f is set to zero, the starting address of function f.

At the time of loading, the physical starting address for the load module is known. Assuming this address to be 1000, the figure shows the final modification of the code. For both the store and branch instruction, the operand is incremented by 1000—the relocation constant for the load module.

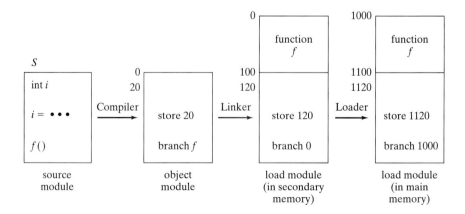

FIGURE 7-2. Transformations of a sample program under static binding.

It is worth noting that, in the above example, both the linker and the loader must modify operand addresses. In other words, all modules are relocated twice, once by the linker and a second time by the loader. With a linking loader, the two phases would have been combined, resulting in a single relocation.

Dynamic Binding

The previous section described static address binding, where all address transformations are completed *before* the program starts executing. More flexibility is gained when the binding occurs at runtime, i.e., *immediately* preceding each memory reference. This delays the binding of the program to the machine until the latest possible moment.

With such dynamic binding, the loader does not need to transform the program in any way. All memory references are still the logical addresses set up by the compiler and the linker, but they must be translated into a physical addresses before being presented to the memory. This translation is performed each time an instruction is fetched from memory and each time an operand is read from or written to memory. Since this occurs at runtime as part of each instruction execution cycle, it must be supported by hardware for reasons of efficiency.

Figure 7-3a illustrates the principles of dynamic relocation. The processor generates a logical address whenever it must fetch an instruction or access a memory operand. This address passes through a translation mechanism, called **address_map**, which performs the **logical-to-physical** address mapping. The resulting physical address is then presented to the memory, which either reads or writes the corresponding data item, based on the type of memory operation. Thus the *address_map* mechanism implements the following address translation function:

$$\texttt{physical\_address = address\_map(logical\_address)}$$

Depending on the type of memory management supported by the system, the *address_map* can be implemented entirely in hardware, or it may require complex interaction between parts of the OS and specialized hardware support.

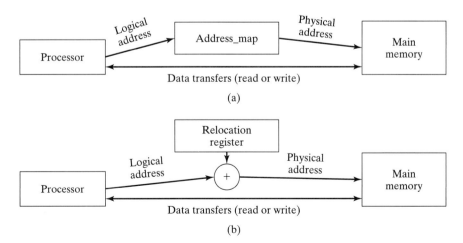

FIGURE 7-3. Dynamic address translation with (a) general address map; and (b) relocation register.

The simplest form of dynamic address binding is to use a special purpose register, called the **relocation register (RR)**, which contains the starting memory address of the currently running program. The contents of this register is then simply added to every logical address before it is presented to the memory. Formally, the *address_map* then performs the following function:

$$\texttt{physical\_address} = \texttt{logical\_address} + \texttt{RR}$$

Figure 7-3b illustrates the use of a RR.

In systems using multiprogramming, the content of the RRs becomes part of each process control block. When a context switch is performed, the RRs of the currently running process are saved along with the program counter and other registers, and the register contents of the process to be restarted are restored from the values saved in its control block. Thus, the process resumes its computation at the point of its last interruption and using the same values it had at that point in time.

The main advantage of dynamic address binding is that programs may be swapped in and out of different areas of memory easily, without having to change any of their operand addresses. Only the program's address mapping must be changed, e.g., the starting address in a relocation register.

EXAMPLE: Program Transformation Under Dynamic Binding

Figure 7-4 shows the transformations of a program in a system with dynamic binding. The tasks performed by the compiler and linker are the same as in Figure 7-2. The loader, however, does *not* change the program in any way when it loads it into memory. That means, the store instruction still contains the address zero, and the branch instruction contains the address 120. The necessary relocation constant 1000 is added to these addresses by the *address_map* mechanism each time the instructions are executed.

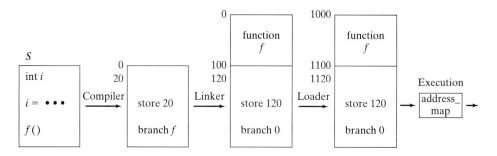

FIGURE 7-4. Transformations of a sample program under dynamic binding.

7.2   MEMORY PARTITIONING SCHEMES

Given that main memory remains a critical resource in most computer systems, we must address two important problems resulting from this limitation. One is that the size of many applications simply exceeds the amount of physical memory available in a given system. To solve this problem, programs must somehow be divided into smaller blocks and loaded into memory only as needed. The second problem arises in multiprogramming systems, where several active processes must share main memory at the same time. In this section, we introduce simple schemes for partitioning main memory to permit such sharing and coping with its limited size.

7.2.1   Fixed Partitions

The simplest memory management appears in single-programmed systems, i.e., systems where only one user program resides in memory at any one time. Here, the memory only must be divided into two parts—one for the OS and the other for the user program and its data. By convention, the OS can occupy either the lower or the upper portion of the available memory. Most PCs and other smaller computers have used this form of memory management.

In multiprogrammed OSs, memory management becomes significantly more complex. The memory manager must arbitrate among the needs of many processes that are simultaneously competing for this resource. A natural extension of the above two-part scheme is to further subdivide the portion available for user programs into multiple partitions. If the sizes of these partitions are determined at the time the OS is initialized and cannot be changed at runtime, the scheme is called **fixed-memory partitioning**. Typically, partitions have different sizes to accommodate the needs of different programs.

Choosing appropriate partition sizes has a strong impact on the system performance. Unfortunately, it is very difficult to estimate the demands that will be placed on a system at future times. Bad choices may lead to a severe underutilization of main memory or other resources.

A problem closely related to partition sizes is process scheduling for each of the partitions. Two possible schemes, depicted in Figure 7-5a and b, can be employed. In the first, a separate queue of processes exists for each partition. Typically, a process would be scheduled for the smallest partition that satisfies its memory requirements—a scheme referred to as "best-fit." This scheme is very simple to implement, provided the memory requirements are specified a priori by each process. Unfortunately, this is not always the case because most programs grow and shrink dynamically. There are two reasons for this. The first is the use of a function (procedure) calling **stack**, whose size increases with the depth of nested function calls. The second is the use of dynamically acquired memory, for example using the *malloc* command in UNIX, which permits a program to acquire additional pieces of memory in a structure called the **heap**. If a process size grows beyond the size of its current partition, it must be moved to a larger partition; to make this efficient requires dynamic relocation capabilities.

The main disadvantage of using separate queues for each partition is that some partitions may remain unused if no processes of the appropriate sizes are available. To eliminate this problem, more complex management of the queues would be necessary such that processes scheduled for a smaller partition can be moved down into a large partition if the corresponding queue becomes empty.

The second scheme, depicted in Figure 7-5b, employs a single queue for all arriving processes. The assignment to partitions is made by the OS dynamically. Each time a process leaves a partition, the OS must search the queue for the next most suitable candidate. Although more complicated to implement, this scheme offers a greater flexibility for the system to adapt to the current workload. For example, when no process with

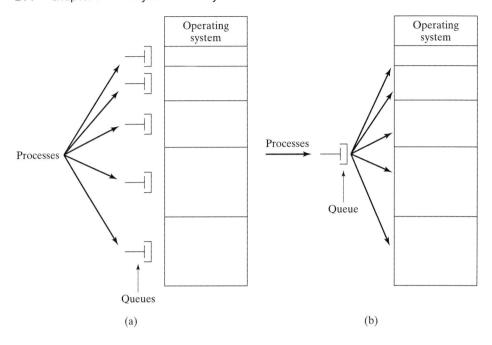

FIGURE 7-5. Scheduling of processes into fixed partitions: (a) using a separate queue for each partition; and (b) using a common queue.

the appropriate size is available for a given partition, the OS may decide to assign to it another process with smaller memory requirements, rather than leaving it completely idle.

The main advantage of fixed partitioning, regardless of the scheduling employed, is its simplicity. The partitions are set up at the time the system is initialized, and only a minimum amount of software is necessary to perform the necessary scheduling at runtime. But fixed partitions suffer from two serious drawbacks. First, the maximum size of a program that can run in such a system is limited by the largest partition. Overlays, as discussed in Section 7.4, can alleviate this problem, but the solution is burdensome for the programmer. The second problem is that some portion of memory is always wasted. That is because any given program will rarely fit its partition perfectly. The difference between the partition size and the program size results in memory that cannot be used for anything else. This problem is called **internal fragmentation**; it is "internal" because it occurs within each partition. We will revisit this problem in the context of paging in Chapter 8. Fixed partitions were used heavily in earlier mainframe computers, such as the IBM OS/MFT (*M*ultiprogramming with *F*ixed Number of *T*asks), but, because of the above limitations, have largely been replaced by more advanced memory management schemes.

7.2.2 Variable Partitions

Instead of deciding on the partition sizes at system initialization, the memory manager can postpone the decisions until runtime, when the actual sizes of programs that must be resident are known. Such a scheme is called **variable memory partitioning**. As new processes arrive, the OS assigns to each the exact amount of space requested.

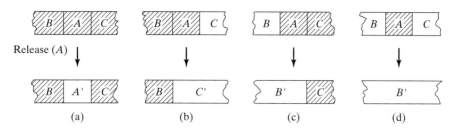

FIGURE 7-6. Hole coalescing on a release.

However, processes do not normally terminate in the order of their arrival. Whenever a process either terminates or leaves the memory because it is waiting for the completion of an event, such as the completion of an I/O operation, it will create an area of free memory space. Thus over time, memory will consist of a sequence of variable size blocks, alternating between blocks occupied by active processes and free blocks, generally termed **holes**. Hence, the main task of the OS is to keep track of the holes and to assign these to newly arriving processes.

A major part of the memory management is to **coalesce** adjacent holes released by terminating processes into larger blocks. Without coalescing, the holes would get progressively smaller. Eventually, all free memory would consist of many adjacent holes, but each too small to accommodate any request.

Figure 7-6 illustrates the four different cases that can arise when a block A is released. In the first case, the two neighboring blocks B and C are both occupied, so block A is simply turned into a new hole A'; no coalescing is necessary. The cases (b) and (c) show the two symmetrical situations where one of block A's neighbor is a hole. The hole created by releasing A must be coalesced with the neighboring hole, resulting is a single large hole, C' or B'. In the fourth scenario, block A is surrounded by holes on both sides. Coalescing combines all three areas into a single hole B'.

Requests to allocate or free memory areas are a frequent operation. When presented with a request for a given number of words or bytes, the OS must be able to quickly find a suitable hole. Similarly, when a block is returned because it is no longer needed, the OS must be able to efficiently coalesce it with any surrounding holes and include it in its inventory of free spaces. There are two basic approaches to keeping track of the available spaces. One uses a linked list and the other uses a bitmap.

Linked List Implementation

In this approach, all holes are tied together using a linked list. However, since the linked list itself requires dynamically managed memory, the question arises: Where do we keep the linked list? The best solution is to take advantage of the unused space within the holes and to distribute the list throughout the holes themselves. That means, each hole contains the pointers to its successor hole on the list.

Unfortunately, a singly linked list does not allow efficient coalescing. When a block is freed, we must be able to find its two neighbors quickly to see if they are occupied or free. One way to achieve that is to use a doubly linked list. Figure 7-7a shows an example of such an implementation. Each block starts with a header consisting of two tags. The first indicates whether the block is free (a hole) or occupied. The second gives

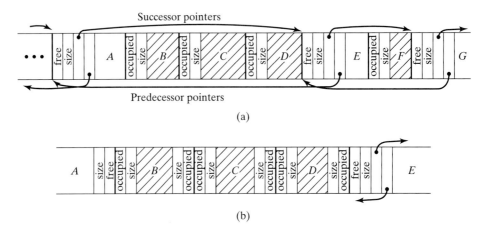

FIGURE 7-7. Holes as linked list: (a) with tags only at one end; and (b) tags at both ends.

the block size. Each hole also contains two pointers—one to its predecessor and one to its successor on the list of holes. Assume first that the list of holes is maintained **sorted** by memory addresses.

When a given block, say C in Figure 7-7a, is to be released, we need to check both its neighbors for possible coalescing. Finding the beginning of the right-hand neighbor, D, is easy since the size of the current block C is known. Since D is occupied, no coalescing is necessary. Finding the beginning of the left-hand neighbor of C is more difficult. To avoid having to scan the entire list of holes from the beginning, we can start from the first hole to the right of the current block C. In this example, this is the hole E, which we can find by skipping over any intervening occupied blocks using their size tags. Here, we skip over the block D. From the hole E, we can find the first hole to the left of C using E's predecessor pointer. This is the hole A. Using A's size tag, we determine that A is not C's immediate neighbor, and no coalescing takes place on this side either.

Having to search for the left-hand neighbor makes the above scheme unnecessarily cumbersome. The situation become even more difficult when the holes are not maintained in a sorted order by memory addresses. In this case, finding the left-hand neighbor possibly requires examining the entire list of holes. A simple solution that greatly simplifies checking of both neighbors while keeping the holes unsorted, is to repeat the tag that records the block status (free or occupied) and its size at *both* the beginning and at the end of each block (Knuth 1968).

Figure 7-7b illustrates this solution for the same block C as before. When this is to be released, we can find its immediate right-hand neighbor, D, by using C's size tag as before. To check C's left-hand neighbor is equally simple. We only need to examine the bytes immediately preceding the block C itself; these contain the size and status tags of the neighboring block B. Since both B and D are occupied, no coalescing is necessary in this case. The released block C is just inserted into the list of holes as a new element. And since the list is not maintained in sorted order, C can simply be appended to the end (or head) of that list.

Bitmap Implementation

The second approach to implementing variable partitions is to use a bitmap, where each bit represents some portion of memory and indicates whether it is free or occupied. Maintaining a separate bit for each word of memory would be wasteful, but if memory is allocated in contiguous sequences of fixed-size blocks, a bitmap may be more efficient than a linked list implementation. Assume that memory is broken into 1-KB blocks for allocation purposes and there is 1 MB of main memory. Then the allocation state of memory can be represented by a string of 1024 bits (1 $KB \times 1024$). This string is called the a **bitmap**, $B = b_0 b_1 \ldots b_{1023}$, where $b_i = 0$ or 1, depending on whether block i is free or used, respectively.

Since few modern programming languages support bit strings explicitly, B can be implemented as an array of characters, integers, or other variables. If we use characters, then an array $B[128]$ could be used, where each $B[i]$ represents 8 bits. To illustrate the use of such a bitmap, consider the blocks of Figure 7-7, and assume that the lengths of blocks A, B, C, D, and E are 3 KB, 2 KB, 5 KB, 1 KB, and 5 KB, respectively. Figure 7-8 shows the beginning of the corresponding bitmap. That means, the first three bits are zeros since the corresponding block A is a hole, the next two bits are ones since block B is occupied, and so on.

The main advantage of using a bitmap over a linked list is that all memory-management operations can be implemented efficiently using Boolean bit manipulations. Specifically, a memory-*release* operation can be performed by applying a bitwise AND to the appropriate portion of the bitmap $B[i]$ and a bit mask, which contains zeros in the positions corresponding to the blocks to be released and ones in the position to remain unchanged. For example, releasing block D in the above example is accomplished by the operation:

```
B[1] = B[1] & '11011111';
```

Notice that, unlike the list representation, the bitmap does not require any explicit coalescing of holes. Any contiguous sequence of zeros represents a hole of the corresponding size.

The *allocation* of a hole can be done using a bitwise OR operation between the appropriate portion of B and a bit mask containing ones in the positions to be allocated. For example, the following operation would allocate the first 2 KB of the hole A, leaving a remaining hole of 1 KB:

```
B[0] = B[0] | '11000000';
```

A *search* for k contiguous 1-KB blocks requires finding k contiguous zeros within B, and can be implemented using logical shifts and bitwise AND operations. Let's assume

B [0]	B [1]	
0 0 0 1 1 1 1 1	1 1 1 0 0 0 0 0	• • •

FIGURE 7-8. Bitmap representation for holes.

we start the search with $B[0]$. The operation:

$$\text{TEST} = B[0] \ \& \ \text{`10000000'};$$

can be used to test the leftmost bit of $B[0]$. The variable *TEST* contains a zero if that bit was zero, and it contains a one if the bit being tested was one. We then shift the mask by one bit to the right and repeat the AND operation. This will test the next bit of $B[0]$ in the same manner. We repeat the right-shift and AND operation until one of the following occurs:

(1) k consecutive zeros are found.

(2) The end of $B[0]$ is reached.

(3) A one is encountered.

In case 1, we found a hole of the desired size and can stop the search. In case 2, we continue the search with the next byte $B[1]$. If we reach the last byte of B without finding k consecutive bytes, the search has failed. Finally, in case 3, we search for the next zero in the bitmap and restart the search from there.

7.2.3 The Buddy System

The buddy system is a compromise between fixed and variable partitions. In its most common *binary* form, there is a fixed number of possible hole sizes, each of which is a power of two. This implies the basic principle of the buddy system: Any hole of size 2^i can be divided into two holes of size 2^{i-1}. These two holes are called **buddies** and can be combined into the original hole of size 2^i.

Assume that memory is allocated in fixed-size units. The unit could be a single word, but, more commonly, it is a fixed sequence of words (e.g., 1 KB or even larger). Assume further that the total memory comprises 2^m of the basic allocation units. Then the largest possible hole is the entire memory, or 2^m units, the next smaller hole size is 2^{m-1}, the next smaller hole size is 2^{m-2}, and so on. The smallest possible hole is 1 unit (2^0).

To keep track of the holes, the buddy system maintains an array H of $m + 1$ list headers, one for each hole size. That means, $H[i]$ links together all holes of size 2^i. A request for n units of memory is then processed as follows. First, the system finds the smallest hole size such that $n \le 2^i$. If the list of holes of this size is not empty, the system removes a hole from the list and allocates it to the requesting process. If this list is empty, the system considers increasingly larger hole sizes until a nonempty list is found. The first hole on this list, say $H[i]$, is removed and divided into two holes of half the size; let's call these two halves the l and r holes. The r hole is placed on the next-lower list $H[i-1]$. If the size of l is the smallest possible size for the request, the hole l is allocated to the process. If l is still too large, the process is repeated recursively. That means, l is divided into two holes of half the size, one of the holes is placed on the list of next smaller holes, and the other half is considered for allocation.

When a previously allocated block of size 2^i is released, the process is reversed. The system checks if the buddy of the released block is occupied. If so, the new hole is added to the list of holes of size 2^i. If the buddy is free, it is removed from the list of holes of size 2^i and the two holes are coalesced into a hole of size 2^{i+1}. This is repeated until the largest possible hole is created.

EXAMPLE: Memory Requests and Releases Under the Buddy System

Figure 7-9 illustrates the above principles. We assume a memory of 16 allocation units. The list H has five entries, representing the possible hole sizes of 1, 2, 4, 8, and 16. The initial configuration (Figure 7-9a) shows that the memory currently contains three occupied blocks and three holes. The holes of size 2 are linked together at $H[1]$, and the hole of size 4 is on the list at $H[2]$.

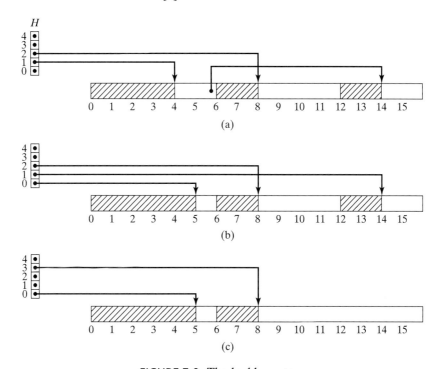

FIGURE 7-9. The buddy system.

Assume that a request for a block of size 1 is now made. The list at $H[0]$ is empty and the system considers the next larger hole size at $H[1]$. The first hole on this list (at address 4) is removed and split into two buddies. One of these is allocated to the requesting process, and the other is placed on the list $H[1]$. Figure 7-9b shows the memory after the allocation.

Next assume that the block at addresses 12 and 13 is to be released, creating a hole of size 2. The buddy corresponding to this new hole is also free (addresses 14 and 15), and a hole of size 4 is created (starting at address 12). The buddy of this larger hole is free as well (addresses 8 through 11), resulting in a hole of size 8, which is entered into the list $H[3]$. Figure 7-9c shows the memory at the end of the release operation.

The buddy system as presented so far works in principle, but the release operation is quite inefficient. Finding the buddy for a given block, which is necessary for coalescing, requires sequentially searching the list of holes at the given hole size. To speed up this operation, a set of bitmaps may be provided, one for each hole size. Then, at the time of release, the system can quickly find the bits corresponding to the released block and check is the neighboring blocks are also free.

CASE STUDY: THE BUDDY SYSTEM IN LINUX

Linux implements a paged memory, which, as will be explained in Chapter 8, does not require contiguous allocation of memory units (pages). However, some parts of the Linux OS, notably I/O operations, which move data directly between the disk and main memory, bypass the paging mechanisms. Consequently, memory must be allocated in contiguous sequences. Linux uses the buddy system for this purpose. It maintains lists of 10 different hole sizes, ranging from $2^0 = 1$ to $2^9 = 512$, which are used in the manner illustrated by the previous example (Fig. 7-9). It also maintains a set of bitmaps, one for each hole size. A bit at level i represents the state of two buddies at that level (i.e., size 2^i). The bit is 0 if both buddies are either free or both are occupied, and it is 1 if one of the buddies is free. Thus, a release operation must check the one bit representing the released block and its buddy; if this bit is 1, the buddies are coalesced and the bit at the next higher level is checked.

7.3 ALLOCATION STRATEGIES FOR VARIABLE PARTITIONS

When the memory manager is presented with a request for a block of memory of a certain size, it must find a sequence of free locations (a hole) that can accommodate that request. In general, there will be more than one hole that is large enough, so the manager must choose which hole to allocate.

Several different allocation strategies are possible, each differing in their performance characteristics. In addition, there are two related issues to consider. The first is memory **utilization**—the strategy should attempt to minimize the production of holes that are too small to be used. The latter is referred to as **external fragmentation**. It is called "external" because the wasted space occurs outside of the allocated blocks, i.e., the variable-size partitions, whereas internal fragmentation occurs within the (fixed-size) partitions. One of the main goals of the memory manager is to minimize external fragmentation, which, in turn, will maximize the number of requests that can be satisfied.

At the same time, the manager must minimize **search time**—the time it takes to find an appropriate hole. Regardless of whether we keep track of the holes using a linked list or bitmap, the manager must scan the holes sequentially and examine their sizes. The following are the most common allocation strategies:

1. **First-Fit.** This strategy always starts the search from the beginning of the list (or bitmap). It stops as soon as it finds the *first* hole large enough to accommodate the given request.

2. **Next-Fit.** Because first-fit always starts its search from the beginning of the memory, it tends to cluster the smaller holes near the top of the list. With time, it takes progressively longer on average before finding a hole of adequate size. A simple modification of the first-fit strategy is to start each search at the point where the previous search stopped, i.e., with the hole following the previous allocation. This

scheme, called **rotating-first-fit** or *next-fit*, keeps the hole sizes more uniformly distributed over the list and decreases the average search time. Unfortunately, simulations show that it results in a slightly worse memory utilization than first-fit.

3. **Best-Fit.** The intuitive idea behind this strategy is to improve memory utilization by always selecting the hole with the closest fit, i.e., the smallest hole that is still large enough to satisfy a given request. Unfortunately, the intuition fails us. Simulations have shown that the best-fit strategy results in a worse memory utilization than first-fit or next-fit. The reason is excessive memory fragmentation. Since the hole with the closest fit is selected, the remaining fragment is usually too small to be of any use. Consequently, best-fit tends to generate large numbers of very small holes, which increases memory fragmentation. Unlike first-fit or next-fit, best-fit also has a long search time because it must examine *all* holes to find the best one. This search is further exacerbated by the presence of many small holes. Thus best-fit, despite its name, is the worst choice among the three strategies.

4. **Worst-Fit.** Given that best-fit leads to such an excessive memory fragmentation, another idea is to do just the opposite. That means, use the largest currently available hole for any given request. The rationale behind this strategy, called worst-fit, is that the remaining hole will always be large enough to accommodate other requests, rather than just wasting space. Unfortunately, simulations have shown that the performance of worst-fit is not better than that of first-fit or next-fit, which are the easiest to implement.

The general conclusion that first-fit is the best choice among the four strategies of an allocation algorithm is based on simulations performed at different times and assuming different technologies (Knuth 1968, Shore 1975, Bays 1977). Other, more complex strategies, known as *optimal-fit* algorithms, have been developed to combine the benefits of the basic strategies. The choice for a particular system should be made based on its intended application domain, which determines a number of parameters crucial to performance, such as distributions of request size, request arrival times, and the residency time of blocks in memory.

7.3.1   Measures of Memory Utilization

It is possible to obtain general measures of the external fragmentation and use of main memory. To perform this analysis, we assume that the system has reached an equilibrium state where, on average, the number of requests is the same as the number of releases per unit of time. Thus, the average number of holes is constant.

Let n and m be the average number of holes and occupied blocks, respectively, at equilibrium. Consider Figure 7-6, which shows the effect of releasing a block A. There are four possible cases, depending on whether A is surrounded by free or occupied blocks. Let a, b, c, and d be the average number of occupied blocks of each type in memory during equilibrium. That means, a block of type a is surrounded by occupied blocks on both sides. A block of type b is surrounded by an occupied block on its left side and a hole on its right, and so on. The total number m of occupied blocks is then the sum of all four types:

$$m = a + b + c + d \tag{7.1}$$

The number of holes is derived as follows: For a block of type a, there are no neighboring holes; for each block of type b or c, there is one neighboring hole; and for each block of type d, there are two neighboring holes. Since a hole is always between two blocks, it must not be counted twice; thus, the total number is divided by 2:

$$n = \frac{2d + b + c}{2} \qquad (7.2)$$

We also know that every consecutive sequence of occupied blocks consists of zero or more blocks of type a, surrounded by one block of type b and one block of type c on each side. Thus, $b = c$. Substituting this into Equation 7.2, we obtain:

$$n = d + b \qquad (7.3)$$

As illustrated in Figure 7-6, the number of holes increases by 1 in (a), decreases by 1 in (d), and remains constant in (b) and (c) as a result of the release. Thus, the probability that *n increases by 1* at any change in memory allocation is:

$$Prob(release) \times \frac{a}{m} \qquad (7.4)$$

where *Prob(release)* is the probability that a memory operation is a release.

The probability that *n decreases by 1* consists of two components. When the operation is a release, n decreases if a block of type d is being released. When the operation is a request, n decreases by one but only when the request is an exact match (otherwise the hole is only reduced in size). Let q be the probability of finding an exact hole size for a given request and $p = 1 - q$. Then the probability that n decreases by 1 at any change in memory allocation is:

$$Prob(release) \times \frac{d}{m} + Prob(request) \times (1 - p) \qquad (7.5)$$

where *Prob(release)* and *Prob(request)* are the relative probabilities of memory requests and releases.

The equilibrium condition implies that $(7.4) = (7.5)$. It also implies that $Prob(request) = Prob(release)$. This yields:

$$\frac{a}{m} = \frac{d}{m} + (1 - p)$$

$$a = d + (1 - p)m \qquad (7.6)$$

Substituting (7.3) and (7.6) in (7.1), we have:

$$m = d + (1 - p)m + b + c + d = (1 - p)m + 2b + 2d = (1 - p)m + 2n$$

which gives the final result:

$$n = 0.5\ pm$$

This measure of memory fragmentation was originally derived by Knuth (1968), who called it the *50% rule*, since n tends to 50% of m as p approaches 1. In other words, when the probability p of not finding an exact match approaches 1, one-third of all the memory partitions are holes and two-thirds are occupied blocks.

The 50% rule only makes a statement about the relative *numbers* of holes and occupied blocks, but not about their relative *sizes*. Knowing these would permit us to make a statement about memory *utilization*, i.e., what fraction of memory is used by blocks and how much is wasted in holes.

Denning (1970) obtained the following result on memory utilization: Let the average hole size be $h = kb$, where b is the average occupied block size and $k > 0$ is a constant. k is the ratio between the average hole size and the average occupied block size. If we let p, the probability used in the 50% rule, be 1, then the fraction f of memory occupied by holes in an equilibrium state is given by the following equation:

$$f = \frac{k}{k + 2}$$

This can be derived by using the 50% rule with $p = 1$ as follows. Let M be the memory size. Since $M = nh + mb$, the hole size h can be expressed as:

$$h = \frac{M - mb}{n} = \frac{M - mb}{0.5\ m}$$

Since $h = kb$, we obtain:

$$kb = \frac{M - mb}{0.5\ m}$$

$$M = 0.5\ kmb + mb = mb(0.5\ k + 1)$$

The fraction f of memory M occupied by holes is then:

$$f = \frac{nh}{M} = \frac{0.5\ mh}{M} = \frac{0.5\ mkb}{mb(0.5\ k + 1)} = \frac{k}{k + 2}$$

The intuition behind this result is that k, the ratio between the average hole size h and the average occupied block size b, must be small; otherwise, much of memory will be unused. For example, with $k = 1$, i.e., when holes and occupied blocks are of the same size, $f = 1/3$. This is consistent with the 50% rule, which states that one-third of memory are holes. To reduce f, k must be made smaller. But how do we know what k is in a given situation, and how can we influence it?

Simulations by Knuth (1968) provide an answer. The ratio k depends on the average block size b *relative* to the total memory size M. For example, when b is below approximately one-tenth of M, i.e., $b \leq M/10$, then $k = 0.22$. This then results in $f \simeq 0.1$, i.e., only approximately 10% of total memory remains unoccupied.

In contrast, when b is large relative to M, say about $M/3$, k becomes 2, and f rises to 0.5. That means, when requests are large on average, one-half of the total memory space is taken up by holes, where the average hole size is twice that of an occupied block. The obvious conclusion is that M must be large relative to b, otherwise much of main memory will remain unused.

7.4   MANAGING INSUFFICIENT MEMORY

The amount of main memory available in a given computer system has been increasing steadily over past decades. Yet, regardless of how much memory a system has, there are always situations when it is not sufficient. In time-sharing systems, a part of the programs of all active users must be resident in memory. When a new process arrives while memory is full, space must somehow be created; otherwise, the process would have to wait. In batch systems, jobs can be delayed, but this may waste CPU time unnecessarily. Since I/O devices are much slower than the CPU, it is frequently the case that all currently resident processes are blocked, waiting for I/O completion or another event. During this time, the CPU would be idle, unless additional ready processes can be loaded into memory. Finally, the size of even a single program can exceed the size of the largest partition, which in the case of variable-size partitions is the entire memory (minus the portion occupied by the OS). There are several different ways to address these problems.

7.4.1   Memory Compaction

When a request cannot be satisfied because there is no block of free space large enough to accommodate the request, memory compaction may be considered. This involves consolidating smaller holes dispersed throughout the memory into a single larger hole.

There are several approaches to the problem. To illustrate the differences, assume that memory is occupied as shown in Figure 7-10a and that a request for a block of size 10 is to be satisfied. The most straightforward way to accomplish this is to move all currently occupied blocks to one end of the memory, thus creating a single free space of size 20 (Fig. 7-10b).

Note, however, that there is no need to reorganize the entire memory to create a free space of size 10. Instead of moving all the blocks at once, the compaction procedure could start moving occupied blocks to one end of the memory as in the previous case, but stop when a free space of sufficient size is created. Figure 7-10c shows the memory at that point. This approach saves time since, in general, only a small fraction of the blocks may be moved.

Finally, more sophisticated versions of the above strategies have been devised in an attempt to minimize the total amount of work to be performed. These include various heuristics to move only those blocks that are likely to generate the most space. For example, in Figure 7-10d, only the block $p2$ was relocated to free the necessary space. Such algorithms, however, are quite complex and not widely used.

The main limitation of all memory compaction schemes is that they are very costly. Even with dynamic relocation capabilities, which make it possible to move programs into different locations without any modifications to code or data, compaction requires each word of memory to be read from and written into memory. Depending on the size and type of memory, this may take as much as several seconds to accomplish. Due to this high overhead, few contemporary systems implement memory compaction.

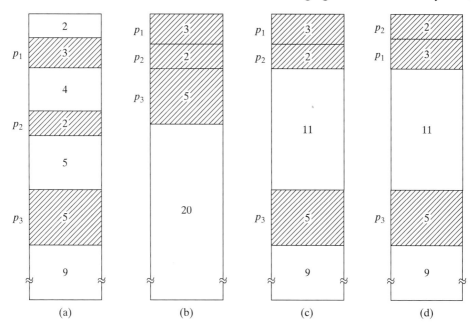

FIGURE 7-10. Memory compaction: (a) initial state; (b) complete compaction; (c) partial compaction; and (d) minimal data movement.

Swapping

When a new program must be loaded into memory—either because a new user is joining a time-sharing system or because all currently resident processes are blocked—we can create new space by selecting one of the resident processes and temporarily evicting it to secondary storage. This exchange is generally called **swapping**.

To make swapping efficient, it is important to decide where to keep the swapped-out process on disk. First, some portions of the process address space are already on the disk and there is no need to create new copies of these areas. This is true of all code areas, which have been loaded from executable files when the process was first started. As long as the process cannot modify its code, these areas do not need to be saved to disk—they are simply reloaded from the original code files when the process is swapped back in.

Data areas (both stack and heap) are created and modified at runtime. To save these on disk, the OS can use the file system and save the areas as special files. To avoid the overhead associated with file management, some systems designate a special area (partition) of the disk as the **swap space**. This consists of consecutive cylinders (tracks), which the OS can access efficiently by using low-level disk read/write operations.

In a batch system, swapping is typically triggered at the time when all current processes are blocked. In a time-sharing system, swapping can be conveniently integrated with scheduling, and performed at the end of each time quantum. Before restarting the next process, the scheduler can initiate the loading of one of the swapped-out processes so that it is ready to run when it becomes its turn. This process would replace one of the currently resident processes, possibly the one that just exhausted its time quantum, or one with a low priority. The swapping, an I/O-bound sequence of operations, proceeds concurrently with the execution of other processes and does not cause any significant disruption in the service.

Swapping is more general and more efficient than memory compaction. First, memory compaction cannot guarantee to create a hole large enough to accommodate a request. With swapping, we can always evict as many resident processes as is necessary. Swapping also affects only one or a small number of processes each time, thus requiring fewer memory accesses. Unlike compaction, swapping requires accesses to secondary memory, but these can be overlapped with the executing of other processes. Finally, swapping can be used with both fixed and variable size partitions, whereas memory compaction is applicable to only variable partitions.

CASE STUDIES: SWAPPING

1. *UNIX.* Most versions of UNIX prior to the Berkeley 3BSD used swapping to manage an appropriate load of processes in main memory. Swapping is implemented by a special process called the **swapper**. This is invoked in the following situations:

   - when a new process is created (using *fork*);
   - when the memory demands of an existing process increase; this is the case when the process explicitly increases its data area (using *brk* or *sbrk*) or when the process stack grows beyond its originally assigned stack area;
   - periodically, every 4 seconds, to guarantee that no process remains swapped out for too long.

   In all cases, it may be necessary to swap out one or more of the currently resident processes. If that is the case, the swapper first considers blocked processes. If no such processes exist, ready processes are considered. Within each type, the swapper considers various attributes of the processes, such as the amount of CPU time used and the time a process has been resident in memory, when making the selection of the victim. In addition, every process is guaranteed a minimum residency time (e.g., 2 seconds) to prevent a situation called **thrashing**, where much of the time is spent on moving processes repeatedly between the disk and main memory, and no real work gets accomplished by any process.

   If no process must be removed, the swapper attempts to swap additional processes back into memory. Again, it considers various characteristics of the processes, notably the time they have been swapped out, when making the selection.

2. *Windows 2000.* Windows 2000 uses swapping to remove idle threads and processes from main memory until they must run again. A system thread called the **swapper** is woken up ever 4 seconds. It looks for threads that have been idle for more than a certain length of time (3 seconds on small memory systems and 7 seconds on large memory systems). All such threads, i.e., their kernel stacks, are swapped out. When all threads of a given process have been swapped out, the remainder of the process, which includes code and data shared by the threads, is also removed from memory. The entire processes is then considered as swapped out.

Overlays

Memory compaction and swapping address the problem of insufficient memory caused by the presence of other programs. This shortage of memory is only temporary. But neither technique can do anything about the inability to run programs that exceed the total size of physical memory or, in the case of fixed partitions, the size of the largest partition. This shortage of memory is permanent and can only be addressed by dividing the program into smaller parts that can be loaded into memory and executed separately.

The simplest solution is **overlaying**, where different portions of the program replace (overlay) each other in memory as execution proceeds. The programmer is required to specify those parts of the program that must reside in memory simultaneously. Such a specification may be obtained from the calling structure (tree) of the program, which describes the dependencies among functions and the data they access.

EXAMPLE: Overlays

Consider a program consisting of five functions A, B, C, D, and E. The calling structure depicted in Figure 7-11a shows the function A as the parent (caller) of the two functions B and C, and C as the caller of D and E. Since B and C do not call each other, they need not reside in memory at the same time. The same is true of the functions D and E; furthermore, their presence is needed only when C is resident. Based on this information, the OS can allocate memory as shown graphically in Figure 7-11b. The two functions B and C have the *same* starting address $k1$, whereas $k2$ is the common starting address of D and E. The compiler inserts a special piece of code at the common addresses $k1$ and $k2$, which causes the overlay manager to be invoked. Thus, each time A calls either B or C, the manager is invoked, it determines which of the two functions is to be executed, and, if the needed function is not present, it loads and transfers control to it. The same principle applies when C calls D or E.

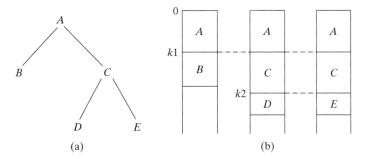

FIGURE 7-11. Program overlays: (a) function call hierarchy; and (b) address assignments.

The main drawback of overlays is that it places the burden of memory management on the programmer, who must plan and design all programs according to the available physical memory space. As a result, manual overlays are rarely used in modern systems. The main reason for discussing them in this chapter is that they represent a natural precursor for automated techniques known as virtual memory. In the next chapter, we present the concept of virtual memory, which liberates the programmer from the limits of physical memory by shifting the burden of memory management entirely to the OS.

CONCEPTS, TERMS, AND ABBREVIATIONS

The following concepts have been introduced in this chapter. Test yourself by defining and discussing each keyword or phrase.

Address map	Linking loader
Address space	Load module
Best-fit memory allocation	Next-fit memory allocation
Binding of addresses	Object module
Bit map	Overlaying
Buddy system	Partitioning memory
Coalescing holes	Relocatable program
Compacting memory	Relocation constant
Fifty-percent rule	Relocation register (RR)
First-fit memory allocation	Source module
Fragmentation	Swapping
Holes in memory	Variable partitions
Linking	Worst-fit memory allocation

EXERCISES

1. Consider the examples in Figure 7-2 and Figure 7-4. Assume that another function, occupying 50 memory words, is linked in front of function f. Assume further that the final load module will be loaded into memory starting at location 1500. Show how the various addresses will be changed in the two cases.

2. Consider a request for n bytes of memory using variable partitions. A hole of size m (where $m > n$) is chosen to satisfy the request. Is it better to allocate the first n bytes or the last n bytes of the hole? Justify your choice.

3. Consider a variable partition scheme where tags are replicated at the beginning and at the each of each block and each hole (Fig. 7-7b). Draw a diagram showing the layout of main memory after each of the following operations:

    (a) memory is initialized to empty; the total memory size is 64 MB
    (b) three blocks (A, B, C), each of size 1 MB, are requested and allocated in the given sequence
    (c) block B is released
    (d) block A is released
    (e) block C is released

4. An implementation of a variable partitions scheme using linked lists can make the following choices:

    - the list of holes is singly linked or doubly linked
    - the list of holes is kept sorted by memory addresses or unsorted
    - the tags (size and type of each block) is kept only at the beginning of each block or it is replicated at both ends.

    For each of the eight possible combinations of design choices, describe advantages and disadvantages with respect to:

    (a) searching for a hole of a given size

(b) allocating a hole (or a portion of a hole) to satisfy a request
(c) releasing a block

5. Consider a buddy system with 5 different hole sizes (2^0 through 2^4).
   (a) Assume a sequence of requests of the following sizes is made: 1, 2, 4, 2. Show the memory layout, including the header array H, after all requests have been accommodated.
   (b) Assume that the four blocks (each of size 1) at addresses 4, 5, 6, and 7 are released one at a time. Show the memory layout, including the header array H, after each release.

6. Assume a request for 1 byte of memory. How many holes will be visited by each of these schemes:
   (a) first fit
   (b) next fit
   (c) best fit
   (d) worst fit

7. Assume that memory contains three holes of 10 MB each. A sequence of 14 requests for 1 MB each is to be processed. For each of the memory allocation methods listed below, determine the sizes of the remaining holes after all 14 requests have been satisfied:
   (a) first fit
   (b) next fit
   (c) best fit
   (d) worst fit

8. Assume that the list of holes in a variable partitions memory system contains the following entries (in the given order): 190 KB, 550 KB, 220 KB, 420 KB, 650 KB, 110 KB. Consider the following sequence of requests (in the given order): A = 210 KB, B = 430 KB, C = 100 KB, D = 420 KB. Determine which holes would be allocated to which request by each of the following schemes:
   (a) first fit
   (b) next fit
   (c) best fit
   (d) worst fit
   What is the average hole size for each scheme at the end of the allocation sequence?

9. Consider a system with 640 KB of main memory. The following blocks are to be requested and released:

block	A	B	C	D	E	F
size (KB)	200	200	150	80	80	240

   Obviously, not all blocks may be accommodated at the same time. We say an allocation failure occurs when there is no hole large enough to satisfy a given request. Devise a sequence of requests and releases that results in an allocation failure under:
   (a) the first fit policy, but not the best fit policy
   (b) the best fit policy, but not the first fit policy
   For each of the two situations, draw a diagram that shows what parts of memory are allocated at the time of failure. (Hint: There is no systematic approach to this problem; you simply must experiment with different sequences.)

10. Consider a 16-MB main memory using variable partitions. Assume that (1) *hole_size* = *block_size* = 1 KB, and (2) the 50% rule holds. Determine the following:
    (a) Total number of holes

  (b) Total number of occupied blocks

  (c) Amount of space occupied by all holes

11. Consider a memory with variable partition memory. Assume that 1) *hole_size* = *block_size*; and 2) the 50% rule holds. If one-half of all occupied blocks are released in a single operation, how will the total number of holes change? How will the average hole size change?

12. Compare the overhead of using a bitmap versus a linked list to keep track of memory allocation. The bitmap approach allocates memory in chunks of c bytes. For the linked list implementation, assume that the average size of both occupied blocks and holes is 16 KB. The size of each of the tags is 2 bytes, and they are replicated at both ends of each block/hole. Determine the value of c for which the two approaches have the same overhead.

13. Consider a memory organized into variable partitions and make the following assumptions. If holes are organized using a linked list, the overhead is 8 bytes per block to store the type and size tags. If a bit map is used, one bit is needed for every 128-byte block. Determine the average size of an occupied block such that the overhead of both methods is the same for the following two cases:

  (a) $k = \frac{hole\_size}{block\_size} = 1$

  (b) $k = \frac{hole\_size}{block\_size} = .5$

  (Hint: Use the 50% rule with $p = 1$.)

14. Consider a 256-MB memory organized into variable partitions. Assume that 1) *hole_size* = *block_size* = 1 KB; and 2) the 50% rule holds. How long will it take to compact the entire memory if reading or writing of one 32-bit word takes 10 ns?

15. Consider a system with 4.2 MB of main memory using variable partitions. At some point in time, the memory will be occupied by three blocks of code/data as follows:

starting address	length
1,000,000	1 MB
2,900,000	.5 MB
3,400,000	.8 MB

  The system uses the best-fit algorithm. Whenever a request fails, memory is compacted using one of the following schemes:

  • All blocks are shifted toward address zero (see Fig. 7.10b)

  • Starting with the lowest-address block, blocks are shifted toward address zero until a hole big enough for the current request is created (see Fig. 7.10c)

  Assume that three new blocks with the respective sizes 0.5 MB, 1.2 MB, and 0.2 MB are to be loaded (in the given sequence).

  (a) Show the memory contents after all three requests have been satisfied under the two different memory compaction schemes.

  (b) How many bytes of memory had to be copied in each case?

16. When a memory request fails, a larger hole may be created by:

  • moving one or more blocks within main memory (compaction);

  • moving one or more blocks to the disk (swapping).

  What are the main advantages and drawbacks of each scheme?

C H A P T E R   8

Virtual Memory

8.1   PRINCIPLES OF VIRTUAL MEMORY
8.2   IMPLEMENTATIONS OF VIRTUAL MEMORY
8.3   MEMORY ALLOCATION IN PAGED SYSTEMS

Managing main memory, especially if it must be shared among multiple concurrent tasks or even different users, is a challenging problem. Although the size of memory has been increasing steadily, and modern CPUs now use long address fields capable of generating very large address spaces, the amount of memory available and actually installed in most computers remains a limiting factor. This situation is not likely to change anytime soon as new applications, especially those using sound, graphics, and video, are capable of utilizing all the memory available. Virtual memory addresses the problems of sharing limited memory through architectural and operating system (OS) software mechanisms that hide the presence of physical memory and present instead an abstract view of main memory to all applications. In this chapter, we describe the concept of virtual memory and the main implementation schemes.

8.1   PRINCIPLES OF VIRTUAL MEMORY

The basic idea of virtual memory is to hide the details of the real physical memory available in a given system from the user. In particular, virtual memory conceals the fact that physical memory is not allocated to a program as a single contiguous region and also conceals the actual size of available physical memory. The underlying implementation creates the *illusion* that each user has one or more contiguous address spaces, each beginning at address zero. The sizes of such virtual address spaces may, for most practical purposes, be assumed unlimited. The illusion of such a large amount of memory is created by subdividing the virtual memory into smaller pieces, which can be loaded into physical memory whenever they are needed by the execution.

The principle is illustrated in Figure 8-1, where different portions of two virtual spaces VM1 and VM2 are mapped onto physical memory. Two distinct portions of VM1 and the beginning portion of VM2 are currently present in main memory and thus accessible by the processor. The address mapping mechanisms, **address_map**, translate logical addresses, generated by the processor, to physical addresses, presented to the actual memory.

Several different forms of virtual memory exist, depending on the view presented to the user and the underlying implementation. From the user's perspective, there are two main organizations. The first presents virtual memory as a single contiguous linear space, corresponding to our conventional view of physical memory. In this organization, virtual memory is considered a large, linearly addressed sequence of n cells (words, bytes, or,

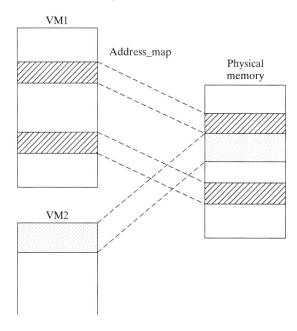

FIGURE 8-1. Principles of virtual memory.

less frequently, individual bits), which are referenced using addresses in the range from zero to $n - 1$. As with physical memory, n is usually a power of 2, i.e., $n = 2^k$ for some integer k. We call this a **single segment** address space. In the implementation, the virtual memory is subdivided into **fixed-sized** portions, called **pages**, which can be loaded into noncontiguous portions of physical memory, called **page frames**.

A **multiple segment** virtual memory divides the virtual address space into a set of segments, where each segment is a contiguous linear space and can vary in size. A **segment** is a user-defined entity that can be treated as an independent logical unit, for example, a function or a data structure. In common implementations of this second organization, each segment can be loaded as a single unit into a contiguous portion of memory, or it can be subdivided further into fixed-size pages.

For both methods—a single segment or a multiple segment virtual memory—there are several important issues that must be addressed by an implementation:

- **Address Mapping Mechanisms**. There are many different ways to define the conceptual *address_map* function that translates logical addresses to their physical equivalents. Since such a translation must be performed one or more times for every instruction executed, it is crucial to performance that it is done with minimal overhead. Section 8.2 presents the principal schemes that are used.

- **Placement Strategies.** To access any portion of the virtual memory space, it must reside in main memory. Thus, the implementation must provide a placement or memory allocation strategy, which determines *where* to load the needed portions of the virtual memory. When the virtual memory is subdivided into variable-size segments, the memory manager can employ the allocation strategies developed for variable-size partitions, such as first-fit or best-fit, which were already discussed in Section 7.3. With fixed-size pages, placement become greatly simplified, because all memory holes (page frames) are of fixed size, and a given page will fit into any free frame.

- **Replacement Strategies.** When a new portion of a virtual memory needs to be loaded into main memory and there is not enough free space available, the system must create more space. In multiprogrammed systems, this can be done by swapping out one of the current processes. Alternately, the system could evict only some portion, i.e., a single page or a segment, of one of the currently resident virtual spaces. The particular page or segment removed from executable memory affects performance critically. We will consider various solutions to this problem in Section 8.3.

- **Load Control.** A static loading policy transfers all of a process's virtual memory into main memory prior to execution. But this automatically restricts the number of processes that can be active simultaneously. It may also waste a lot of memory and I/O bandwidth when only a small portion of the virtual memory is actually used. A more flexible approach is to load different portions of virtual memory dynamically, i.e., at the time they are actually needed. This is called **demand paging** or **demand segmentation**, depending on the virtual memory organization. Its main disadvantage is that processes may run very inefficiently if they only have a relatively small amount of memory. Load control addresses the problem of *how much* of a given virtual space should be resident in memory at any given time. Section 8.3.3 discusses the various solutions and trade-offs.

- **Sharing.** There are important reasons for allowing two or more processes to share the same portion (code or data) of main memory. Both paging and segmentation permit sharing. However, since segments correspond to logical entities into which the user chose to divide the program, they are a natural basis for sharing. In contrast, pages represent an arbitrary subdivision of the virtual space, which makes sharing more difficult. The next chapter explores the trade-offs in detail.

8.2   IMPLEMENTATIONS OF VIRTUAL MEMORY

We start by describing the architecture of paging systems, present the basics of segmentation, and then discuss the common combination of the two—paging with segmentation. Paging of OS tables is treated next. The final topic of the section is the use of translation look-aside buffers for improved performance.

8.2.1   Paging

In a paging implementation, the virtual address space is divided into a sequence of equal-sized contiguous blocks called **pages**; for P pages, these are numbered consecutively p_0, p_1, ..., p_{P-1}. The most common page size is between 1 KB to 16 KB. Similarly, the available physical memory is divided into a number of equal-sized contiguous blocks called **page frames**, numbered f_0, f_1, ..., f_{F-1}, where F is the total number of frames. The page size is identical to the page frame size.

A virtual address va is then interpreted as a pair (p, w), where p is a **page number** and w is a **word number**, i.e., an **offset** or **displacement**, within the page p. Let us

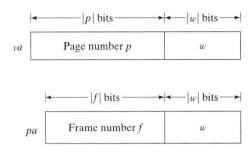

FIGURE 8-2. Form of virtual and physical address.

denote the number of bits used to represent p as $|p|$, and the number of bits used to represent w as $|w|$. A virtual address va is then a string of $|p| + |w|$ bits, resulting in a virtual memory size of $2^{|p|+|w|}$ words. The first $|p|$ bits of va are interpreted as the page number p, while the remaining $|w|$ bits give the word number w. The top portion of Figure 8-2 shows the relationships between the numbers p, w, and their bit-lengths. As an example, a 32-bit address could be divided into $|p| = 22$ and $|w| = 10$, resulting in $2^{22} = 4,194,304$ pages of $2^{10} = 1024$ words each.

A physical memory address pa is similarly interpreted as a pair (f, w), where f is the page **frame number** and w is a word number within the frame f. When pa is a string of $|f| + |w|$ bits, resulting in a physical memory of $2^{|f|+|w|}$ words, the first $|f|$ bits are interpreted as the frame number f, whereas the remaining $|w|$ bits give the word number w. The bottom portion of Figure 8-2 shows the relationships between the numbers f, w, and their bit-lengths. For example, a 16-bit address could be divided into $|f| = 6$ and $|w| = 10$, resulting in 64 frames of 1024 words each. Note that $|w|$ is the same in both va and pa because the size of a page must be the same as the size of a page frame.

At runtime, any page can reside in any frame of the physical memory. The task of the *address_map* is to keep track of the relationship between pages and their current page frames, and to translate virtual memory addresses $va = (p, w)$ generated by the processor into the corresponding physical memory addresses $pa = (f, w)$, as illustrated in Figure 8-3. Since the w component is the same in both addresses, the translation amounts to finding the frame f holding the page p. Once f is known, the physical address pa is formed in one of the following two ways, depending on the underlying hardware support.

Assume that f and w are kept in separate registers. The physical address can then be computed by the formula $pa = f \times 2^{|w|} + w$, where $2^{|w|}$ is the page size. This computation can be done efficiently in hardware by shifting f to the left by $|w|$ positions and then adding w to it. The second method is even simpler: the two registers holding f and w are simply *concatenated* into one number, pa. For the remainder of this chapter, we will use $f + w$ to denote the addition or the concatenation of the two components f and w.

The remaining question now is how the *address_map* should keep track of the mapping between the page numbers p and the frame numbers f. There are two basic mechanisms to achieve that, one using frame tables and the other using page tables.

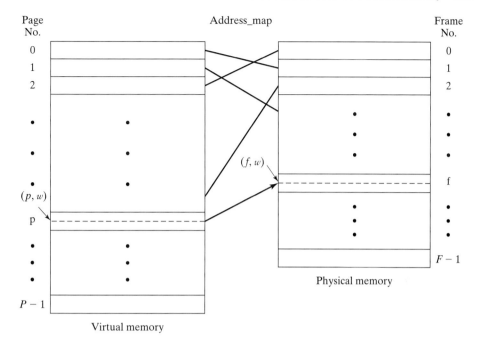

FIGURE 8-3. Paged virtual memory.

Frame Tables

The first approach to maintaining the correspondence between page numbers and frame numbers is to implement a table of length F, where each entry corresponds to a frame and contains the number of the page currently residing in that frame. With multiprogramming, the situation is more complicated because several resident processes can be using the *same* page number, each corresponding to a *different* frame; consequently, the same page number p, belonging to different processes, can be found in more than one entry of the table. Thus, in order to distinguish among the entries, we also must record the process *ID* as part of each entry.

Let us represent this **frame table** as an array $FT[F]$, where each entry $FT[f]$ is a two-component structure: $FT[f].pid$ records the process *ID* whose page is stored in frame f, and $FT[f].page$ contains the number of the page stored in that frame. Assuming that each addressed page of the current process is in main memory, the function of the *address_map* can be written conceptually as follows:

```
address_map(id, p, w) {
    pa = UNDEFINED;
    for (f = 0; f < F; f++)
        if (FT[f].pid == id && FT[f].page == p) pa = (f+w);
    return pa;
}
```

A sequential search through the table *FT* would be too inefficient since the mapping must be performed on every memory reference. One way to make this approach practical is to store the table in an **associative memory**, where the cells are referenced by their *content* rather than their address. A familiar example will clarify the idea. To find a phone number for an individual in a phone directory, it is necessary to search the directory for a *(last name, first name)* match; this task is not difficult *only* because the entries have been sorted in alphabetical order by name. If, however, one starts with a phone number and wishes to find the name or address of the party with that number, the task is hopelessly time-consuming. Storing the telephone book in a general associative memory would permit access of any entry using either a name or an address or a phone number as the search key; i.e., any field in an entry can be used and the search occurs by content.

Hardware implementations of associative memories are not quite this general and normally only provide one search field for each entry. But this is sufficient to implement the frame table FT. Each entry of FT can hold the tuple (ID, p), where p is a page number belonging to a process identified by ID. When a process generates a virtual address (p, w), the concatenation of its ID and the page number p is presented to the associative memory, which searches the frame table for a match. The search is performed entirely in hardware by examining all entries $FT[f]$ in parallel. If a match is found, the index f of the matching entry concatenated with the word offset w, which yields the physical memory address $pa = (f, w)$. The entire translation process is illustrated graphically in Figure 8-4.

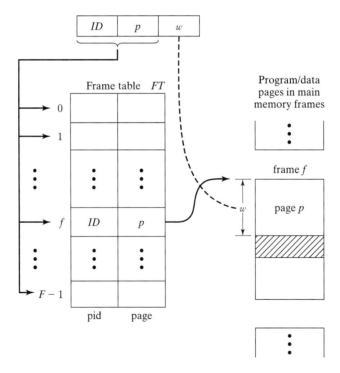

FIGURE 8-4. Address translation using frame table.

CASE STUDY: USE OF FRAME TABLES

Paging can be credited to the designers of the ATLAS computer, who employed an associative memory for the address mapping (Kilburn et al. 1962). For the ATLAS computer, $|w| = 9$ (resulting in 512 words per page), $|p| = 11$ (resulting in 2048 pages), and $f = 5$ (resulting in 32 page frames). Thus a 2^{20}-word virtual memory was provided for a 2^{14}-word machine. But the original ATLAS OS employed paging solely as a means of implementing a large virtual memory; multiprogramming of user processes was not attempted initially, and thus no process IDs must be recorded in the associative memory. The search for a match was performed only on the page number p.

In later systems, the frame table organization has gradually been displaced by a page table structure. As will be described in more detail in the next section, a page table keeps track of all frames that hold pages belonging to a given process. Thus a separate page table is needed for each process. But, recently, the virtues of frame tables have been rediscovered in a number of modern systems, including certain IBM and Hewlett-Packard workstations. The main attraction is that only a single frame table must be maintained for all processes. Such a frame table is commonly referred to as an **inverted page table**, since it stores the same information as page tables but is sorted by frame number, rather than process ID and page number.

The main problem with implementing frame tables is that, due to the increasingly larger memory sizes, frame tables tend to be quite large and cannot be kept in associative memories in their entirety, as was the case with the original ATLAS design. The solution is to use a fast implementation in software, which can be achieved using hash tables. This still requires at least one extra memory access. To minimize this overhead, associative memories are used as **translation look-aside buffers** to bypass the access to the tables most of the time.

Another problem is sharing of pages in main memory. To allow two or more processes to use the same copy of a page in main memory, the frame table would have to be extended to keep track of multiple processes for each frame entry. This further complicates the design of the frame table and increases its cost.

Page Tables

A **page table** keeps track of the current locations of all pages belonging to a given process. The p'th entry in the page table identifies the page frame containing that page. In most systems, a special page table register, *PTR*, contains the starting address of the page table of the currently running process. The translation performed by the function *address_map* is then:

```
address_map(p, w) {
    pa = *(PTR+p)+w;
    return pa;
}
```

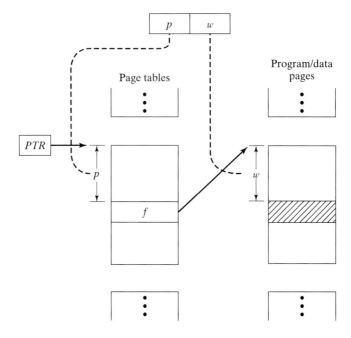

FIGURE 8-5. Address translation using page tables.

$PTR + p$ points to the page table entry for page p; the content $*(PTR + p)$ of this entry is the frame number f. Adding the offset w to f then yields the physical address pa. Figure 8-5 presents this mapping in graphical form.

EXAMPLE: Use of Page Table

Suppose that the page table for the current process is located starting at address 1024 and has the contents as shown in Figure 8-6.

...	...
1024	21504
1025	40960
1026	3072
1027	15360
...	...

FIGURE 8-6. Page table contents.

Assuming a page size of 1024 words, the virtual address $(2, 100)$ maps dynamically into $pa = *(1024 + 2) + 100 = *(1026) + 100 = 3072 + 100 = 3172$.

Note that *two* memory accesses must be made to read or write any memory word during a virtual memory operation—one access to the page table and the second to the actual page. To avoid the first access most of the time, it is common to use translation look-aside buffers to hold the most recently used parts of the page tables in associative memory.

Demand Paging

Paging greatly simplifies the problem of placement, since any page can be loaded into any free page frame. But paging also can be used to solve the problem of limited memory size so that programs larger than the available main memory could be executed without requiring the programmer to specify an overlay structure. This is accomplished by implementing dynamic memory allocation mechanisms, where pages are loaded at the time they are actually needed rather than statically before program execution. This approach is called **demand paging**.

It requires a mechanism that signals a "missing page" when reference is made to a page currently not resident in main memory. Such a missing page event is called a **page fault**. It invokes the OS; in a lengthy procedure, the OS finds the desired page, loads it into a selected frame, and restarts the process that caused the page fault.

The following extension of the *address_map* function illustrates the principles of demand paging. The function *resident(m)* returns the value *true* if *m* designates a currently resident page and the value *false* if the page is missing from memory.

```
address_map(p, w) {
    if ( resident(*(PTR+p)) ) {
        pa = *(PTR+p)+w;
        return pa; }
    else page_fault;
}
```

If no free frame is available at the time of the page fault, the OS can either block the faulting process, or it may create a free frame. The latter is accomplished by evicting one of the currently resident pages to secondary memory, or by evicting an entire process, i.e., all its resident pages, to secondary memory. Deciding which page or process to remove is governed by the load control and page replacement schemes employed.

The main drawback of pure paging is that the user is restricted to a single contiguous address space into which all program and data must be placed in some sequence. This single space presents some difficulty with dynamic data structures that may grow and shrink at runtime. Since they all share the same address space, the user (or the compiler) must decide where to place them so that they have sufficient room to expand without running into each other.

CASE STUDY: UNIX MEMORY LAYOUT

UNIX assigns a single contiguous address space to each process. A UNIX process consists of three main parts (segments): 1) the **code** segment; 2) the **data** segment; and 3) the **stack** segment. All three must be placed into the single shared address space. Fortunately, only the last two segments can vary in size—the code segment remains constant. The data segment, which contains the process' variables, can grow and shrink as the program allocates and frees data in heap memory. That means, the

---

CASE STUDY: UNIX MEMORY LAYOUT   (*continued*)

area reserved for the heap may be increased or decreased explicitly (using a system call *brk*). The stack segment grows and shrinks as a result of function invocations and returns. To allow both segments to grow independently, UNIX places them at opposite ends of the shared address space. That means, one end of the memory contains the (fixed-size) code segment, followed by the data segment. The other and contains the stack. Thus both may expand toward the middle.

8.2.2 Segmentation

There are many instances where a process consists of more than the three basic segments: code, data, and stack. For example, a process with multiple threads needs a separate stack for each thread, where each stack grows and shrinks independently. Similarly, files may be mapped temporarily into the address space of a process to simplify accessing their contents. (This will be discussed in Chapter 10.) Such files also may grow and shrink as the process executes. Placing multiple dynamically changing entities into a single address space is a difficult problem.

Segmentation solves the problem in an elegant way. It implements virtual memory as a collection of address spaces, each of which is termed a **segment** and may be a different size. This organization permits the system to mirror the organization of a given application by using a separate segment for each logical component, such as a function, a module comprising multiple functions, an array, a table, or a stack. Each such component has a name by which it is identified by the programmer.

These logical names are translated by the linker or loader into numbers, called **segment numbers**, each of which uniquely identifies one of the segments. An offset within each segment then identifies a specific word. Thus, similar to a page implementation of virtual memory, a virtual address *va* using segmentation also consists of two components, (s, w), where s is the segment number and w is the offset. The main difference is that segment numbers correspond to logical components of the program while page numbers bear no relationship with the program structure.

There are two different schemes for building a segmented virtual memory. One treats the segment as the basic unit for memory allocation and assumes that memory can be dynamically allocated and relocated in variable size blocks. The second employs paging as a means of allocating space for a segment. That is, each segment is itself subdivided into fixed-size pages to facilitate allocation.

Contiguous Allocation per Segment

Segmentation was pioneered by the Burroughs Corporation in the 1960s, where it was employed in the B5500 and B6500 computers (Burroughs 1964, 1967). These were stack machines oriented toward the efficient compilation and execution of block-structured languages.

Like a page table, a **segment table** is used for each active process to keep track of its current segments. Typically, segments are numbered sequentially with the ith entry in the segment table ($i = 0, 1, \ldots$) corresponding to segment number i. Each entry in the table contains the starting location of the segment in physical memory. It also contains protection information, to be discussed later in Chapter 13. The segment table itself is treated as a segment by the system. The starting point of the segment table of the currently running process is usually maintained in a dedicated register, the **segment table register**, *STR*. The *STR* is analogous to the *PTR* described in the last section. A virtual address (s, w) is then mapped to a physical memory address *pa* as follows:

```
address_map(s, w) {
    if ( resident(*(STR+s)) ) {
        pa = *(STR+s)+w;
        return pa; }
    else segment_fault;
}
```

The function *resident* serves the same purpose as with demand paging; if the referenced segment is currently not resident in memory, a **segment fault** invokes the operating system to take the necessary actions.

The main advantage of segmentation over paging is that it divides programs into variable-size components that correspond to their logical components, providing, for example, natural protection, debugging, and portability boundaries. Its drawbacks are a complex placement and, in the case of demand segmentation, a complex replacement scheme. Segmentation also suffers from external fragmentation, similar to the simple memory scheme discussed in Section 7.3, resulting in wasted memory space. In recent years, systems using pure paging or paging combined with segmentation have become much more common than those using pure segmentation. As an example, the Intel 286 processor had pure segmentation but later models, such as the 386 or Pentium processor, support a combination of segmentation and paging.

8.2.3 Paging with Segmentation

To provide a multisegment address space for each process and, at the same time, permit a simple placement algorithm, the principles of paging and segmentation have been combined into one memory management scheme. Under this scheme, memory is organized in variable-size segments, and, from the user's perspective, there is not much difference between pure segmentation and segmentation with paging. From the point of view of the operating system, however, segments are not contiguous portions of memory. Rather, each segment is subdivided into pages of fixed-size.

The implementation of segmentation with paging requires the use of both segment tables and page tables, and results in two levels of indirection in the logical-to-physical address translation. As with pure segmentation, a segment table register *STR* points to a segment table for the current process. Each of the segment table entries points to the page table for the corresponding segment. Each page table then keeps track of the pages belonging to that segment.

As a consequence of the two levels of indirection, a virtual memory address *va* is interpreted as a triple (s, p, w), where s is the segment number, p is the page number within the segment, and w is the offset within the page. That is, p and w together specify a word within the segment s. The resulting *address_map*, illustrated graphically in Figure 8-7, performs the following function.

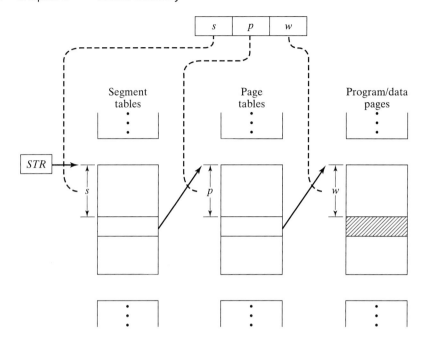

FIGURE 8-7. Address translation using segment and page tables.

```
address_map(s, p, w) {
    pa = *(*(STR+s)+p)+w;
    return pa;
}
```

This is the simplest form of the address map: it assumes that the segment table, the page tables, and the pages are all resident in memory. If this requirement is relaxed (as is frequently done to permit more efficient utilization of main memory), each reference may potentially produce a page fault. Hence, the *address_map* must be extended to ensure that a page is resident before the access is made.

With the above scheme, each segment table and page table is considered to be a page. Demand paging is attractive under this organization; it permits an efficient use of memory and allows dynamic changes in segment size. The disadvantages of paging with segmentation are the extra memory required for the tables, the overhead of administrating memory in such a complex system, and the inefficiency of two additional memory references at each mapping. Again, fast associative registers are used to avoid extra references (Section 8.2.5).

8.2.4 Paging of System Tables

The sizes of the segment and page tables of a virtual memory system are determined by the lengths of the s and p address components, respectively. Depending on the number of bits uses to represent a virtual address, these tables may become potentially very large. To illustrate the problem, consider a 48-bit address and assume that the page size is 4 KB, i.e., requiring 12 bits for the offset w. That leaves $48 - 12 = 36$ bits to be split

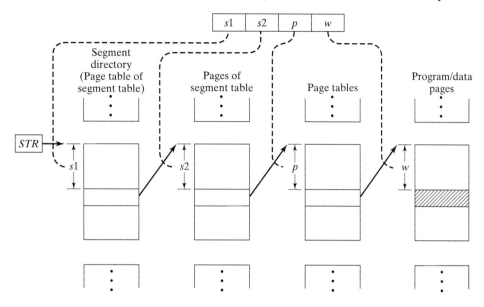

FIGURE 8-8. Address translation with paged segment table.

between s and p. One philosophy, assumed by many older systems, is to make s large while keeping p relatively small. For example, keeping p to the same size as w would leave $|s| = 36 - 12 = 24$, resulting in a very large segment table size of 2^{24} or 16 MB. Alternatively, we could keep s small while allocating the remaining address bits to p. This would yield a small number of very large segments—a philosophy that has been adopted in many recent systems due to the need to support multimedia applications, which require potentially very large objects. For example, assigning $|s| = 12$ would result in 4 K segments per process, each segment consisting of up to 2^{24} or 16 MB of individual pages of 4 KB each.

In both of the above scenarios, the resulting tables comprising megabytes of data are too large to be kept permanently resident in main memory. The solution is to subdivide each table into pages and load only those currently needed by the execution. Let us illustrate how this may be accomplished in the case of a large segment table. The s component of the virtual address is divided into two parts, say $s1$ and $s2$. The segment table is then broken into pages of size $2^{|s2|}$, where $|s2|$ is the number of bits comprising $s2$.

To keep track of the pages comprising the segment table, we need a new page table, as shown in Figure 8-8. To avoid confusion between the new page table of the segment table and the actual page tables, we will refer to the former as the **segment directory**. The $s1$ component is used to index this segment directory which, at runtime, is pointed to by the register *STR*. The individual pages comprising the segment table are indexed by $s2$, while p and w are used as before. Assuming that all tables are in memory, the address map for a virtual address ($s1, s2, p, w$) can be described as:

```
address_map(s1, s2, p, w) {
    pa = *(*(*(STR+s1)+s2)+p)+w;
    return pa;
}
```

244 Chapter 8 Virtual Memory

CASE STUDIES: PAGING OF SYSTEM TABLES

1. *MULTICS.* The s component in the MULTICS OS is 18 bits long, resulting in a segment table of 2^{18} or 262,144 entries (segments). This table is divided into pages of 1,024 words, resulting in $|s2| = 10$ and $|s1| = |s| - |s2| = 8$. Hence the segment directory (i.e., page table of the segment table) has 256 entries.

2. *Pentium.* The Intel Pentium implements an elegant memory management scheme that can support either pure segmentation or segmentation with paging. The virtual address (called the logical address in the Pentium literature) is 48 bits long, where 2 bits are used for protection, 14 bits are used for the segment

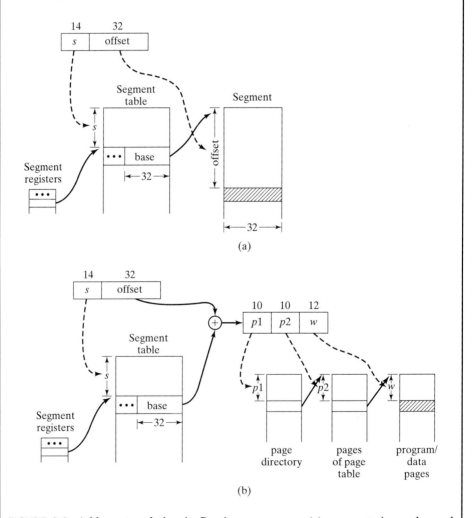

FIGURE 8-9. Address translation in Pentium processor: (a) segmentation only; and (b) segmentation with paging.

number and the remaining 32 bits are the offset within the segment. The segment table is divided into two parts of 4 K entries each. One is called the *local descriptor table* (LDT) and contains entries for segments private to the process; the other is called the *global descriptor table* (GDT) and holds descriptors for segments shared by all processes, notably, segments comprising the operating system. Each LDT or GDT entry contains the starting address of the segment, its length, and several other bits that facilitate the address translation and protection.

Figure 8-9a illustrates the address translation mechanism when pure segmentation is used. The segment number s first selects one of the segments from the segment table (i.e., the LDT or GDT), and a pointer to that segment entry is loaded into one of six special-purpose *segment registers*. Note that this is slightly different from the scheme discussed earlier (e.g. Fig. 8-7), where the starting address of the segment table itself is kept in a register (STR) and the segment number s is added to it during each address translation. The starting address (32 bits in length) of the selected segment is fetched from the segment table entry and is added to the 32-bit offset from the virtual address. The resulting address is used to access the word in the segment.

Figure 8-9b illustrates the address translation mechanism when paging is enabled. In this case, the segment descriptor is fetched from the segment table (LDT or GDT) using s as before, and the offset from the virtual address is again added to the segment base address. The resulting 32-bit quantity is however not interpreted as a physical memory address. Instead, it is divided into a 20-bit page number p and a 12-bit offset w within a page. This results in a 4-K page size ($2^{12} = 4\ K$) and a page table size of over 1 million entries (2^{20}). Since this is too large to keep in memory, the page table is subdivided further into 4-KB pages. That is, p is split into two 10-bit components, $p1$ and $p2$; the physical address is then derived as shown in the Figure 8-9b.

8.2.5   Translation Look-Aside Buffers

Virtual memory architectures offer a number of advantages over systems that make physical memory visible to programs. However, one main drawback is the increased number of physical memory operations necessary for each virtual address reference. In the simplest case of pure paging or pure segmentation, one additional memory read is necessary to access the page or segment table. If both approaches are combined, two additional memory reads are needed—one to the segment table and a second to the page table. Finally, when segment or page tables are themselves paged, the number of additional references increases to three. In all cases, each reference also possibly generates a page fault.

To alleviate this problem, special high-speed memories, usually called **translation look-aside buffers (TLB)**, are often provided to aid the address translation. The basic idea is to keep the most recent translations of virtual to physical addresses readily available for possible future use. An associative memory is employed as a buffer for this purpose. When a given virtual page is accessed several times within a short time interval, the address translation is performed only during the first reference. Subsequent accesses

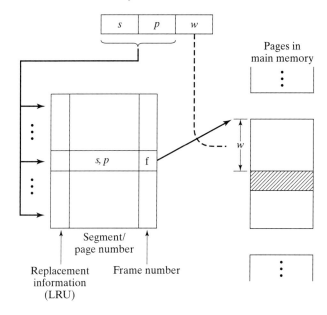

FIGURE 8-10. A translation look-aside buffer.

bypass most of the translation mechanisms by fetching the appropriate frame number directly from the associative buffer.

Figure 8-10 shows the organization of such a TLB for a system with both segmentation and paging. The first column contains entries of the form (s, p), where s is a segment number and p is a page number. When a virtual address (s, p, w) is presented to the memory system, the buffer is searched associatively (in parallel) for the occurrence of the pair (s, p). If found, the number f in the second column of the buffer gives the frame number in which the corresponding page currently resides. By adding the offset w to f, the addressed word is found. Note that only one access to main memory is necessary in this case—the segment and page table are bypassed by searching the buffer.

Only when the search for (s, p) fails, need the complete address translation be performed. The resulting frame number is then entered, together with the pair (s, p), into the buffer for possible future references to the same page. This normally requires the replacement of a current buffer entry. The most common scheme is to replace the *least recently used* (LRU) such entry, as determined by a built-in hardware mechanism. (More detail on this scheme is given in Section 8.3.)

Note that a TLB is different from a data or program *cache*, which may be used in conjunction with the translation look-aside buffer. The difference is that the buffer only keeps track of recently translated *page numbers*, while a cache keeps copies of the actual recently accessed *instructions* or *data values*.

8.3   MEMORY ALLOCATION IN PAGED SYSTEMS

One of the main advantage of paging is that it greatly simplifies placement algorithms, since, because of their uniform size, any page can be stored in any free frame in memory.

Thus an unordered list of free frames is sufficient to keep track of available space. This is true of both *statically* and *dynamically* allocated memory systems. In the former, all pages belonging to a process must be in memory before it can execute. When not enough free page frames are available, the process must wait. Alternatively, we can swap out one or more of the currently resident processes to make enough space.

When memory is allocated dynamically, the situation is more complicated. The set of pages resident in memory is constantly changing as processes continue to execute. Each process causes new pages to be loaded as a result of page faults. When no free page frames are available, the system can choose to suspend the faulting process or to swap out some other resident process, as in the case of static allocation. But with dynamic allocation it has a third option. It can choose to evict a single page (belonging either to the faulting process or to another unrelated process) to create space for the new page to be loaded.

Deciding which page to evict is determined by the **replacement** policy. An algorithm for page replacement falls into one of two general classes, depending on the choices for eviction candidates:

1. A **global** page replacement algorithm assumes a *fixed number of page frames* shared by all processes. If free frames are needed, the algorithm considers all currently resident pages as possible candidates for eviction, regardless of their owners.

2. A **local** page replacement algorithm maintains a separate set of pages, called the *working set*, for each process. The size of the working set varies over time, and thus, each process requires a *variable number of page frames*. A local page replacement algorithm automatically evicts those pages from memory that are no longer in a process current working set.

The next two sections present the most common page replacement algorithms from each category. To evaluate the performance of the various algorithms, we introduce a model that captures the behavior of a paging system independently of the underlying hardware or software implementation. The model represents the execution time trace of a particular program in the form of a **reference string (RS)**:

$$r_0 r_1 \ldots r_t \ldots r_T$$

where r_t is the number of the *page* referenced by the program at its tth memory access. The subscripts in the reference string can be treated as time instants. Thus, the string represents $T + 1$ consecutive memory references by the program.

Assume that the program represented by RS is allocated a main memory area of m page frames, where $1 \leq m \leq n$ and n is the number of *distinct* pages in RS. An allocation policy defines for each instant of time t the set of pages IN_t that are loaded into memory at time t and the set of pages OUT_t that are removed or *replaced* at time t during the processing of RS.

There are two important measures of goodness for a given replacement policy. The first is the *number of page faults* generated for a given reference string RS. The main reason for adopting this measure is that page faults are very costly and must be kept to a minimum. Each page fault involves a context switch to the OS, which must analyze the nature of the interrupt, find the missing page, check the validity of the request, find a free frame (possibly by evicting a resident page), and supervise the transfer of the page to a free frame. The page transfer from the disk to memory is the most costly of all these tasks, requiring milliseconds of disk access time. When we compare this to the access time to main memory, which is in the nanoseconds range, we see that the page fault rate must be kept to less than one in several millions of memory accesses to prevent any noticeable degradation in performance due to paging.

The second measure of goodness for a page replacement policy is the *total number of pages*, $IN_{TOT}(RS)$, loaded into memory when RS is processed.

$$IN_{TOT}(RS) = \sum_{k=0}^{T} |IN_t|$$

Note that $IN_{TOT}(RS)$ is not necessarily equal to the number of page faults; it depends on the size of IN_t, i.e., the number of pages loaded at each page fault. Thus choosing an appropriate value for IN_t is an important consideration in devising efficient replacement algorithms. Loading several pages during one operation is more cost-effective than loading them one at a time. That is because the cost of I/O follows the formula $c_1 + c_2 k$, where c_1 and c_2 are constants, and k is the amount of data being transferred. c_1 represents the fixed start-up overhead of the I/O operation and $c_2 k$ is the cost directly proportional to the number of bytes transferred. For example, the cost of loading three pages at a time is $c_1 + 3c_2$, while the cost of loading the same three pages one at a time is $3(c_1 + c_2) = 3c_1 + 3c_2$.

The main problem with loading multiple pages at each page fault is deciding which pages to load, i.e., which pages the program is likely to reference next. If the guess is incorrect, the pages will have been brought into memory in vain and put unnecessary overhead on the memory system.

CASE STUDY: PRELOADING OF PAGES

Windows 2000 employs the following **clustered paging** policy. When a page fault occurs, it loads not only the page being requested but also several pages immediately *following* the requested page. In the case of a code page, 3 to 8 additional pages are loaded, depending on the size of physical memory. In the case of data pages, 2 to 4 additional pages are loaded. The expectation is that execution will exhibit some degree of locality, and thus the preloaded pages will be accessed without causing additional page faults.

Because of the difficulty to predict the program's future behavior, most paging system implement a *pure demand paging scheme*, where only a *single page*—the one causing the page fault—is brought into memory at each page fault.

In the remainder of this chapter, we will be concerned with only pure demand paging algorithms. Since only a single page is loaded during each page fault, $|IN_t| = 1$ if a page fault occurs at time t, and $|IN_t| = 0$ if no page fault occurs. Consequently, the total number of pages, $IN_{TOT}(RS)$, is equal to the number of page faults for a given reference string:

$$IN_{TOT}(RS) = \sum_{k=0}^{T} |IN_t| = number\ of\ page\ faults$$

We will use this measure in comparing the relative performance of the different page replacement algorithms.

8.3.1   Global Page Replacement Algorithms

During normal operation of a multiprogramming system, pages belonging to different processes will be dispersed throughout the frames of main memory. When a page fault occurs and there is no free frame, the OS must select one of the resident pages for replacement. This section discusses page replacement algorithms where all currently resident pages are considered as possible candidates for replacement, regardless of the processes they belong to.

Optimal Replacement Algorithm (MIN)

For later comparisons and to provide insight into practical methods, we first describe a theoretically **optimal** but unrealizable replacement scheme. It has been proven that the following replacement strategy is optimal in that it generates the smallest number of page faults for any reference string RS (Belady 1966; Mattson et al. 1970; Aho et al. 1971):

> *Select for replacement that page which will not be referenced for the longest time in the future.*

More formally, this strategy can be expressed as follows. If a page fault requiring a replacement occurs at time t, select a page r such that:

$$r \neq r_i, \qquad \text{for } t < i \leq T \tag{8.1}$$

or if such an r does not exist, select:

$$r = r_k, \quad \text{such that } t < k \leq T, k - t \text{ is a maximum, and}$$
$$r \neq r_{k'}, \quad \text{where } t < k' \leq k \tag{8.2}$$

Equation 8.1 chooses an r that will not be referenced again in the future. If no such r exists, then the subsequent equation (8.2) chooses the r that is farthest away from t.

EXAMPLE: MIN Replacement

Consider the reference string $RS = cadbebabcd$ and assume the number of page frames to be $m = 4$. Assume further that at time 0, memory contains the pages $\{a, b, c, d\}$. With the optimal replacement algorithm, the memory allocation changes as illustrated in the following table:

Time t	0	1	2	3	4	5	6	7	8	9	10
RS		c	a	d	b	e	b	a	b	c	d
Frame 0	a	a	a	a	a	a	a	a	a	a	d
Frame 1	b	b	b	b	b	b	b	b	b	b	b
Frame 2	c	c	c	c	c	c	c	c	c	c	c
Frame 3	d	d	d	d	d	e	e	e	e	e	e
IN_t						e					d
OUT_t						d					a

Two page faults occur while processing RS. The first, at time 5, causes the replacement of page d, since d will not be referenced for the longest time in the future. For the second page fault, at time 10, any of the pages a, b, or c can be chosen, since none of them will be referenced again as part of RS; we arbitrarily chose page a.

Random Replacement and the Principle of Locality

Program reference strings are virtually never known in advance. Thus practical page replacement algorithms must be devised which can make the necessary decisions without a priori knowledge of the reference behavior. The simplest scheme one might consider is a **random** selection strategy where the page to be replaced is selected using a random number generator. This strategy would be useful if no assumption about the program behavior could be made.

Fortunately, most programs display a pattern of behavior called the **Principle of Locality**. According to this principle, a program that references a location at some point in time is likely to reference the same location and locations in its immediate vicinity in the near future. This statement is quite intuitive if we consider the typical execution patterns of a program:

1. Except for branch instructions, which in general constitute an average of only approximately 10% of all instructions, program execution is sequential. This implies that, most of the time, the next instruction to be fetched will be the one immediately following the current instruction.

2. Most iterative constructs (i.e., for-loops and while-loops) consist of a relatively small number of instructions repeated many times. Hence, computation is confined to a small section of code for the duration of each iteration.

3. A considerable amount of computation is spent on processing large data structures such as arrays or files of records. A significant portion of this computation requires sequential processing; thus, consecutive instructions will tend to reference neighboring elements of the data structure. (Note, however, that the way data structures are stored in memory plays an important role in locality behavior. For example, a large two-dimensional array stored by columns but processed by rows might reference a different page on each access.)

Since moving pages between main memory and secondary memory is costly, it is obvious that a random page replacement scheme will not yield as effective an algorithm as one that takes the principle of locality into consideration.

First-In/First-Out Replacement Algorithm (FIFO)

A FIFO strategy always selects the page for replacement that has been resident in memory for the longest time. In terms of implementation, the algorithm views the page frames as slots of a FIFO queue. A new page is appended to the end of the queue, and, at a page fault, the page at the head of the queue is selected for replacement.

More precisely, assume a physical memory size of m page frames. Let the identity of all resident pages be stored in a list, $P[0]$, $P[1]$, ..., $P[m-1]$, such that $P[i+1 \% m]$ has been loaded after $P[i]$ for all $0 \le i < m$. A pointer k is also maintained to index the least recently loaded page, $P[k]$. On a page fault, page $P[k]$ is replaced

---

EXAMPLE: FIFO Replacement

For the reference string $RS = cadbebabcd$ and physical memory size $m = 4$, we obtain the following changes in memory occupancy:

Time t	0	1	2	3	4	5	6	7	8	9	10
RS		c	a	d	b	e	b	a	b	c	d
Frame 0	→a	→a	→a	→a	→a	e	e	e	e	→e	d
Frame 1	b	b	b	b	b	→b	→b	a	a	a	→a
Frame 2	c	c	c	c	c	c	c	→c	b	b	b
Frame 3	d	d	d	d	d	d	d	d	→d	c	c
IN_t						e		a	b	c	d
OUT_t						a		b	c	d	e

We have assumed that the pages resident in memory at time 0 had been loaded in the order a, b, c, d; i.e., a is the oldest and d is the youngest resident. This causes a to be replaced first (at time 5) when the first page fault occurs. The pointer, k, represented by the small arrow, is advanced to point to b. This page is replaced at the next page fault at time 7, and so on. The algorithm results in a total of 5 page faults for the given string RS.

The main attraction of the FIFO replacement strategy is its simple and efficient implementation: A list of m elements and a pointer, incremented each time a page fault occurs, is all that is required. The list does not even have to be implemented explicitly. The pointer can simply cycle through the physical page frames in an ascending or descending address order.

Unfortunately, the FIFO strategy assumes that pages residing the *longest* in memory are the least likely to be referenced in the future and, as a consequence, it exploits the principle of locality only to some degree. It will favor the more recently loaded pages, which are likely to be referenced again in the near future. However, it is unable to address the fact that the program may return to pages referenced in the more distant past and start using those again. The FIFO algorithm will remove these pages because it only considers their absolute age in memory, which is unaffected by access patterns. Thus, the principle of locality is often violated. Moreover, FIFO can also exhibit a strange, counterintuitive behavior, called **Belady's anomaly** (Belady et al. 1969): increasing the available memory can result in more page faults! (See Exercise 14.)

Least Recently Used Replacement Algorithm (LRU)

The LRU algorithm has been designed to fully comply with the principle of locality, and it does not suffer from Belady's anomaly. If a page fault occurs and there is no empty frame in memory, it will remove that page which has not been referenced for the longest time. To be able to make the correct choice, the algorithm must keep track of the relative order of all references to resident pages. Conceptually, this can be implemented by maintaining an ordered list of references. The length of this list is m, where m is the number of frames in main memory. When a page fault occurs, the list behaves as a simple queue. The page at the head of the queue is removed and the new page is appended to the end of the queue. Hence, the queue length m remains constant. To maintain the chronological history of page references, the queue must, however, be reordered upon each reference—the referenced page is moved from its current position to the end of the queue, which gives it the greatest chance to remain resident.

EXAMPLE: LRU Replacement

The following table shows the current memory contents for the reference string $RS = cadbebabcd$ and $m = 4$ as in the previous examples. Below the memory, the queue is shown at each reference.

Time t	0	1	2	3	4	5	6	7	8	9	10
RS		c	a	d	b	e	b	a	b	c	d
Frame 0	a	a	a	a	a	a	a	a	a	a	a
Frame 1	b	b	b	b	b	b	b	b	b	b	b
Frame 2	c	c	c	c	c	e	e	e	e	e	d
Frame 3	d	d	d	d	d	d	d	d	d	c	c
IN_t						e				c	d
OUT_t						c				d	e
Queue end	d	c	a	d	b	e	b	a	b	c	d
	c	d	c	a	d	b	e	b	a	b	c
	b	b	d	c	a	d	d	e	e	a	b
Queue head	a	a	b	b	c	a	a	d	d	e	a

We assume that the pages were referenced in the order a, b, c, d, resulting in a being at the head and d at the end of the queue at time 0. During the next four references, the queue is reordered as each of the currently referenced pages is moved to the end of the queue (indicated by arrows). At time 5, a page fault occurs, which replaces page c—the current head of the queue—with the new page e. The latter is appended to the end of the queue while the former is removed. The next three references do not cause any page faults, however, the queue is reordered on each reference as shown. The next page fault at time 9 causes the removal of page d which, at that time, was the head of the queue and the least recently referenced one. Similarly, the page fault at time 10 replaces the least recently referenced page e, thus bringing the total number of page faults produced by this algorithm to 3.

The implementation of LRU as a software queue is impractical because of the high overhead with reordering the queue upon each reference. Several methods implemented directly in hardware to reduce this overhead have been developed. One implements a form of **time-stamping**. Each time a page is referenced, the current content of an internal clock maintained by the processor is stored with the page frame. At a page fault, the page with the lowest time-stamp is the one that has not been referenced for the longest time, and this is selected for replacement.

A similar scheme employs a **capacitor** associated with each memory frame. The capacitor is charged upon each reference to the page residing in that frame. The subsequent exponential decay of the charge can be directly converted into a time interval which permits the system to find the page which has not been referenced for the longest time.

Yet another technique uses an **aging register** R of n bits for each page frame:

$$R = R_{n-1} R_{n-2} \dots R_1 R_0$$

On a page reference, R_{n-1} of the referenced page is set to 1. Independently, the contents of all aging registers are periodically shifted to the right by one bit. Thus, when interpreted as a positive binary number, the value of each R decreases periodically unless the corresponding page is referenced, in which case the corresponding R contains the largest number. Upon a page fault, the algorithm selects the page with the smallest value of R to be replaced, which is the one that has aged the most.

Second-Chance (Clock) Replacement Algorithm

Due to the high cost of implementing LRU directly, even in hardware, a more economical alternative was developed. The Second-Chance Replacement scheme approximates the LRU scheme at a fraction of its cost. The algorithm maintains a circular list of all resident pages and a pointer to the current page in much the same way as the FIFO scheme described earlier. In addition, a bit u, called the **use** bit (or *reference* bit or *access* bit), is associated with each page frame. Upon each reference, the hardware automatically sets the corresponding use bit to 1.

To select a page for replacement the second-chance algorithm operates as follows. If the pointer is at a page with $u = 0$, then that page is selected for replacement and the pointer is advanced to the next page. Otherwise, the use bit is reset to 0 and the pointer is advanced to the next page on the list. This is repeated until a page with $u = 0$ is found, which in principle could take a complete pass through all page frames if all use bits were set to 1.

The name "second-chance" refers to the fact that a page with $u = 1$ gets a second chance to be referenced again before it is considered for replacement on the next pass. The algorithm is also frequently called the **clock replacement algorithm**, because the pointer that cycles through the circular list of page frames may be visualized as scanning the circumference of a dial of a clock until a page with $u = 0$ is found.

EXAMPLE: Second-Chance Replacement

For $RS = cadbebabcd$ and $m = 4$, the memory occupancy under the second-chance algorithm changes as follows:

Time t	0	1	2	3	4	5	6	7	8	9	10
RS		c	a	d	b	e	b	a	b	c	d
Frame 0	→a/1	→a/1	→a/1	→a/1	→a/1	e/1	e/1	e/1	e/1	→e/1	d/1
Frame 1	b/1	b/1	b/1	b/1	b/1	→b/0	→b/1	b/0	b/1	b/1	→b/0
Frame 2	c/1	c/1	c/1	c/1	c/1	c/0	c/0	a/1	a/1	a/1	a/0
Frame 3	d/1	d/1	d/1	d/1	d/1	d/0	d/0	→d/0	→d/0	c/1	c/0
IN_t						e		a		c	d
OUT_t						a		c		d	e

The current value of the use bit is shown as a zero or one following each page. Initially, we have assumed all pages to have the use bit set. At the time of the first page fault (time 5), the pointer is at page a. Its use bit is reset and the pointer is advanced to the next page, b. b's use bit also is reset, and the pointer is advanced to c. The same reset operation is applied to c and then to d, thus reaching the page a once more. Unless a has been referenced again in the meantime, its use bit is zero, causing that page to be replaced by the new page e. The pointer is advanced to page b. The next page fault at time 7 does not replace b because its use bit has again been set (at time 6). The search algorithm only resets b's use bit and proceeds by replacing the following page c. The last two page faults occur when c and d are rereferenced at time 9 and 10, respectively. The total number of page faults is 4.

The second-chance algorithm approximates LRU in that frequently referenced pages will have their use bit set to one and will not be selected for replacement. Only when a page has not been referenced for the duration of a *complete* cycle of the pointer through all page frames, will it be replaced.

The Third-Chance Algorithm

A replaced page must be written back onto secondary memory if its contents have been changed during its last occupancy of main memory; otherwise, the replaced page may simply be overwritten. A page that has been written into is frequently referred to as a **dirty** page. To be able to distinguish between the two types of pages, the hardware provides a **write** bit, w, associated with each page frame. When a new page is loaded, the corresponding write bit is 0; it is set to 1 when the information in that page is modified by a store instruction.

The pair of bits u (use bit) and w (write bit), associated with each page frame, is the basis for the third-chance algorithm. As was the case with the second-chance algorithm, a circular list of all pages currently resident in memory, and a pointer, are maintained. When a page fault occurs, the pointer scans the list, until it finds a page with both bits u and w equal to 0; this page is selected for replacement. Each time the pointer is advanced during the scan, the bits u and w are reset according to the rules shown in Table 8-1.

One additional complication is introduced by the fact that the two combinations $(0, 1)$ and $(1, 0)$ both yield the same combination $(0, 0)$. But in the first case, the page has been modified whereas in the second it has not. The algorithm must record this difference so that, prior to replacement, the modified page is written back onto secondary memory. The asterisk in Table 8-1 is used to indicate the modification, and can be implemented by an additional bit maintained for each frame.

TABLE 8-1. Changes of u and w bits under third-chance algorithm.

Before	After
u w	u w
1 1	0 1
1 0	0 0
0 1	0 0 *
0 0	select

The name third-chance derives from the fact that a page that has been written into will not be removed until the pointer has completed *two* full scans of the list. Thus, compared to a page that has not been modified, it has one additional chance to be referenced again before it is selected for removal.

EXAMPLE: Third-Chance Replacement

For this algorithm, in addition to specifying the reference string, $RS = cadbebabcd$, and the memory size, $m = 4$, we also must know which references are write requests. For the sake of this example, we assume that the references at time 2, 4, and 7 are write requests, as indicated by the superscript w. The memory changes are then as follows:

Time t	0	1	2	3	4	5	6	7	8	9	10
RS		c	a^w	d	b^w	e	b	a^w	b	c	d
Frame 0	→a/10	→a/10	→a/11	→a/11	→a/11	a/00*	a/00*	a/11	a/11	→a/11	a/00*
Frame 1	b/10	b/10	b/10	b/10	b/11	b/00*	b/10*	b/10*	b/10*	b/10*	d/10
Frame 2	c/10	c/10	c/10	c/10	c/10	e/10	e/10	e/10	e/10	e/10	→e/00
Frame 3	d/10	d/10	d/10	d/10	d/10	→d/00	→d/00	→d/00	→d/00	c/10	c/00
IN_t						e				c	d
OUT_t						c				d	b

At time 1, page c is read, resulting in no changes. At time 2, page a is written, resulting in the corresponding w bit to be set. At time 3, the read operation produces no change, whereas the write at time 4 sets the corresponding w of b. Note that the pointer has not moved because there were no page faults. At the time of the first page fault, the pointer is at page a. The algorithm scans the pages while resetting the u and w bits as follows: reset u bit of a; reset u bit b; reset u bit of c; reset u bit of d; reset w bit of a and remember that the page is dirty (asterisk). Reset w bit of b and remember that page as dirty. The next page c has now both bits equal to 0 and is replaced by the new page e, and the pointer is advanced to the next page d. Note that this search required almost two full passes of the pointer through the page frames.

The next three references (6 through 8) do not cause page faults but only modify the u and w bits of the pages a and b according to the reference type. (Note that the asterisk on page a is removed since the page has again been written into and thus its w bit is set.) The last two references replace pages d and b using the same principles, thus bringing the total number of page faults to 3.

CASE STUDY: PAGE REPLACEMENT IN UNIX

Berkeley UNIX uses a form of the second-chance algorithm presented above. The main difference is that the selection of a page to evict from memory is not done at the time of a page fault. Rather, a page fault always uses a frame from the list of currently free frames. If this list is empty, the process blocks until a free frame becomes available.

Creating free page frames is the responsibility of a dedicated process, called the **page daemon**. This process wakes up periodically to check if there are enough free frames, as defined by a system constant. If not, the daemon creates free frames using the second-chance algorithm as follows. During the first pass over all frames, the daemon sets the *use bit* of all frames to zero. During the second pass, it marks all frames whose use bit is still zero, i.e., those not referenced since their examination during the first pass, as tentatively free. Such frames may be used to service a page fault when no actually free frames exist. At the same time, if a tentatively free frame is referenced again by the process, it may be reclaimed without a page fault by removing it from the tentatively free frame list.

8.3.2 Local Page Replacement Algorithms

Measurements of paging behavior indicate that each process requires a certain minimum set of pages to be resident in memory at all times in order to run efficiently; otherwise, the page fault rate becomes unacceptably high. This condition, referred to as **thrashing**, will be discussed in the context of load control in Section 8.3.3. Furthermore, the size of this minimal set of resident pages changes dynamically as the process executes. These observations led to the development of several page replacement methods that attempt to maintain an *optimal* resident set of pages for each active process. These schemes are strictly local since the page replacement algorithm must distinguish between pages belonging to different processes. Thus, a page fault caused by a given process will never be resolved by reducing the resident set of any other process.

Optimal Page Replacement Algorithm (VMIN)

Similar to the optimal replacement algorithm MIN, used as a global page replacement algorithm (Section 8.3.1), there exists an optimal replacement algorithm, VMIN, which varies the number of frames according to the program's behavior (Prieve and Fabry 1976). As with MIN, it is unrealizable because it requires advance knowledge of the reference string.

VMIN employs the following page replacement rule, invoked after each reference. Consider a page reference at time t. If that page is currently not resident, it results in a page fault and the page is loaded into one of the free frames. Regardless of whether or not a page fault occurs, the algorithm then looks ahead in the reference string RS. If that page is *not* referenced again in the time interval $(t, t + \tau)$, where τ is a system constant, then the page is removed. Otherwise, it remains in the process resident set until it is referenced again. The interval $(t, t + \tau)$ is frequently referred to as a **sliding window**, since at any given time the resident set consists of those pages visible in that window. This contains the currently referenced page plus those pages referenced during the τ future memory accesses. Thus, the actual window size is $\tau + 1$.

EXAMPLE: VMIN Replacement

We use the reference string, $RS = ccdbcecead$. Let the size of the sliding window be defined by $\tau = 3$. Assume that there are enough free page frames to accommodate the set of pages that must be resident. We do not show which page resides in which frame, since this is not the concern of a local replacement policy; instead, we show, using check marks, the pages of RS that are resident in memory at each reference. At time 0, the only resident page is page d. The following table then shows the changes in the resident set.

Time t	0	1	2	3	4	5	6	7	8	9	10
RS	d	c	c	d	b	c	e	c	e	a	d
Page a	–	–	–	–	–	–	–	–	–	✓	–
Page b	–	–	–	–	✓	–	–	–	–	–	–
Page c	–	✓	✓	✓	✓	✓	✓	✓	–	–	–
Page d	✓	✓	✓	✓	–	–	–	–	–	–	✓
Page e	–	–	–	–	–	–	✓	✓	✓	–	–
IN_t		c			b		e			a	d
OUT_t					d	b			c	e	a

At time 0, page d is referenced. Since it is referenced again at time 3, which is within the interval $(0, 0 + \tau) = (0, 0 + 3) = (0, 3)$, it is not removed. The first page fault occurs at time 1, which causes the page c to be loaded into a free frame. The set of resident pages now consists of two pages, c and d. At time 2 and 3, both pages c and d are still retained because they are referenced again within the current window. Page d is removed from memory at time 4, since it is not referenced again within $(4, 4+3) = (4, 7)$. Instead, the faulting page b is loaded into one of the free frames. But b falls out of the current window at the very next time point 5 and is removed, whereas c continues to be resident. The next page fault at time 6 brings in page e, which remains resident until its next reference at time 8. The last two references bring in the pages a and d, respectively.

The total number of page faults for VMIN in this example is 5. The resident set size varies between 1 and 2 and at most two page frames are occupied at any time. By increasing τ, the number of page faults can arbitrarily be reduced, of course at the expense of using more page frames.

The Working Set Model (WS)

The working set model (Denning 1968, 1980) attempts a practical approximation to VMIN and employs a similar concept of a sliding window. However, the algorithm does not look *ahead* in the reference string (since this information is not available) but looks *behind*. It relies heavily on the principle of locality discussed previously, which implies that, at any given time, the amount of memory required by a process in the near future may be estimated by considering the process memory requirements during its recent past.

According to the model, each process at a given time t has a working set of pages $W(t, \tau)$, defined as the set of pages referenced by that process during the time interval $(t - \tau, t)$, where τ is again a system-defined constant.

The memory management strategy under the working set model is then governed by the following two rules:

1. At each reference, the current working set is determined and only those pages belonging to the working set are retained in memory.
2. A process may run if and only if its entire current working set is in memory.

EXAMPLE: WS Replacement

Let $RS = ccdbcecead$, $\tau = 3$, and the initial resident set at time 0 contain the pages a, d, and e, where a was referenced at time $t = 0$, d was referenced at time $t = -1$, and e was referenced at time $t = -2$. The following table shows the working set at each reference. As with the previous example of VMIN, we assume that a list of free page frames is available to accommodate the current working set. If not enough page frames were available, a load control mechanism, discussed in Section 8.3.3, would decide which process to deactivate to create more space.

Time t	0	1	2	3	4	5	6	7	8	9	10
RS	a	c	c	d	b	c	e	c	e	a	d
Page a	√	√	√	√	–	–	–	–	–	√	√
Page b	–	–	–	–	√	√	√	√	–	–	–
Page c	–	√	√	√	√	√	√	√	√	√	√
Page d	√	√	√	√	√	√	√	–	–	–	√
Page e	√	√	–	–	–	–	√	√	√	√	√
IN_t		c			b		e			a	d
OUT_t			e		a				d	b	

The first page fault occurs at time 1 and, as a result, the corresponding page c is loaded into one of the available page frames. The other three currently resident pages a, d, e are still visible in the window $(1 - 3, 1) = (-2, 1)$ and are retained. At time 2, page e falls out of the current window $(2 - 3, 2) = (-1, 2)$ and is removed. At time 4, the page fault brings in page b; this takes the place of page a, which fell out of the current window $(4 - 3, 4) = (1, 4)$. The next page fault at time 6 brings in page e, and the currently resident pages b, d, and c remain resident as part of the current working set defined by $(6 - 3, 6) = (3, 6)$. Over the next two references, the working set shrinks to only two pages e and c and grows again to four pages as a result of the last two-page faults at times 9 and 10.

The total number of page faults for this algorithm is also 5. The working set size fluctuates between two and four page frames as the reference string is processed.

While conceptually very attractive, the working set strategy is difficult to implement in its full generality. One problem is estimating the appropriate window size τ, which is a crucial parameter of the algorithm. This is usually performed empirically, by varying τ until the highest performance is achieved. Except for rare cases when anomalous behavior has been observed (Franklin, Graham, and Gupta 1978), increasing the window size reduces the paging activity of each process. The trade-off is, of course, a reduced number of processes that may be run concurrently.

A more serious problem with a pure working set approach is the large overhead in implementation since the current working set may change with each reference. To alleviate this problem, special hardware may be provided to keep track of the working set. Alternately, approximations of the working set algorithm have been developed which permit the working set to be reevaluated less frequently. These generally involve some combination of reference bits and/or time-stamps, which are examined and modified at fixed intervals determined by a periodic interrupt.

One such scheme uses aging registers similar to those used to approximate the LRU algorithm (Section 8.3.1). The left-most bit of an aging register is set to 1 whenever the corresponding page is referenced. Periodically, every δ memory references (where δ is a system constant), a timeout interrupt is generated and the contents of all aging registers are shifted to the right. Thus, an aging register gradually decreases in value unless the page is referenced. When the aging register reaches 0 (or some other system-defined threshold value), the page is removed from the working set of the process because it fell out of the sliding window. The size of the window is $\delta * n$, where n is the number of bits comprising the aging registers.

EXAMPLE: Approximating the WS Algorithm

Assume 3-bit aging registers and a timeout interval of 1000 references. The aging register of a page referenced at time t will be '100' at time t, '010' at time $t + 1000$, '001' at time $t + 2000$, and it will reach '000' at time $t + 3000$, at which time the page will be removed. This effectively approximates a working set with a window size $3 * 1000 = 3000$.

A similar approximation can be implemented with a single use bit and a time stamp associated with each frame. The use bit is turned on by the hardware whenever the page is accessed. The use bits and time-stamps are examined periodically at least every δ instructions using a timeout interrupt. When the use bit of the frame is found to be 1, it is reset and the time of this change is recorded with the frame as its time-stamp. When the bit is found 0, the time since it has been turned off, denoted as t_{off}, is computed by subtracting the value of the time-stamp from the current time. The t_{off} time keeps increasing with each timeout unless the page has been referenced again in the meantime, causing its use bit to be set to 1. The time t_{off} is compared against a system parameter, t_{max}. If $t_{off} > t_{max}$, the page is removed from the working set, i.e., the frame is released.

CASE STUDY: APPROXIMATING WS USING TIME-STAMPS

The virtual memory operating system (VMOS) employs the above scheme of time-stamps and use bits, but implements a further refinement of the basic scheme. It maintains two system thresholds, t_{max} and t_{min}. If $t_{off} > t_{max}$, the page is removed from the working set as before. If $t_{min} < t_{off} < t_{max}$, the page is removed *tentatively* from the working set by putting the frame on a special tentatively released list. When a new page frame is needed and there are no free frames available, one of the tentatively released pages is used. Otherwise, the faulting process (or some other process) must be swapped out and its page frames added to the free page frame list. This two-tier

---

CASE STUDY: APPROXIMATING WS USING TIME-STAMPS (*continued*)

system guarantees preferential treatment to pages which have not yet exceeded t_{max} but have not been used for a significant length of time (at least t_{min}).

Page Fault Frequency Replacement Algorithm (PFF)

One of the main objectives of any page replacement scheme must be to keep the number of page faults to a minimum. In the working set model described above, this objective was accomplished indirectly by adjusting the working set size. The page fault frequency algorithm takes a direct approach by actually measuring the page fault frequency in terms of time intervals between consecutive page faults. These times are then used to adjust the resident page set of a process at the time of each page fault. The faulting page is, of course, loaded into memory, increasing the size of the resident set of pages. The following rule then guarantees that the resident set does not grow unnecessarily large:

> *If the time between the current and the previous page fault exceeds a critical value τ, all pages not referenced during that time interval are removed from memory.*

Here is a more formal specification. Let t_c be the time of the current page fault and t_{c-1} the time of the previous page fault. Whenever $t_c - t_{c-1} > \tau$, where τ is a system parameter, all pages not referenced during the interval (t_{c-1}, t_c) are removed from memory. Consequently, the set of resident pages at time t_c is described as:

$$resident(t_c) = \begin{cases} RS(t_{c-1}, t_c), & \text{if } t_c - t_{c-1} > \tau \\ resident(t_{c-1}) + RS(t_c), & \text{otherwise} \end{cases}$$

where $RS(t_{c-1}, t_c)$ denotes the set of pages referenced during the interval (t_{c-1}, t_c) and $RS(t_c)$ is the page referenced at time t_c (and found missing from the resident set).

The main advantage of the page fault frequency algorithm over the working set model is efficiency in implementation. The resident set of pages is adjusted only at the time of a page fault instead of at each reference.

EXAMPLE: PFF Replacement

We use the same reference string, $RS = ccdbcecead$, as before and set the parameter τ to 2. Let the resident set at time 0 consist of the pages a, d, and e. The following table shows the set of resident pages at each reference.

Time t	0	1	2	3	4	5	6	7	8	9	10
RS		c	c	d	b	c	e	c	e	a	d
Page a	√	√	√	√	–	–	–	–	–	√	√
Page b	–	–	–	–	√	√	√	√	√	–	–
Page c	–	√	√	√	√	√	√	√	√	√	√
Page d	√	√	√	√	√	√	√	√	√	–	√
Page e	√	√	√	√	–	–	√	√	√	√	√
IN_t		c			b		e			a	d
OUT_t					a,e					b,d	

The first page fault occurs at time 1. Let us assume that the previous page fault occurred recently, so no pages are removed at this time. The next page fault occurs at time 4. Since $t_c = 4$ and $t_{c-1} = 1$, the condition $t_c - t_{c-1} > \tau$ is true, and all pages not referenced during the time interval (1,4) are removed; these are the pages a and e. The next page fault occurs at time 6. No pages are removed at this time because $6 - 4 = 2$ is not greater then τ. But pages b and d are removed at the next page fault at time 9, because the condition is again true. No pages are removed at the last page fault at time 10. The page fault frequency algorithm produces a total of five page faults for the given string RS, and the number of resident pages fluctuates between three and four.

CASE STUDY: PAGE REPLACEMENT IN WINDOWS 2000

Windows 2000 implements a page-replacement scheme that combines the features of several of the algorithms discussed above, notably, the working set model and the second-chance algorithm.

The replacement is *local* in that a page fault will not cause the eviction of a page belonging to another process. Thus, the system maintains a *current working set* for each process. The size of the working set, however, is not determined automatically using a sliding window. Instead, a *minimum* and a *maximum* size is assigned by the system. Typical values for the minimum are 20 to 50 page frames, depending on the size of physical memory. Typical values for the maximum are 45 to 345 page frames.

At each page fault, the working set of a process is increased by adding the referenced page to the set, until the maximum is reached. At that time (unless memory is plentiful, which is determined by a system constant), a page must be removed from the working set to accommodate the new page.

Whenever memory becomes scarce—which is measured by the number of free frames currently available—the working sets of some processes must be decreased. This is accomplished by a routine called the **working set manager**, which is invoked periodically (every second). It examines processes that have more than their minimum of pages and orders these processes according to their size, idle time, and other criteria to select the most suitable candidates for working set reduction.

Once a process has been selected, the system must choose which page(s) to remove. For this it uses a variation of the clock algorithm, which approximates the LRU policy. Each page frame has a use bit, u, and a counter, *cnt*. The use bit (called access bit in Windows 2000) is set by the hardware whenever the page is accessed. When looking for a page to evict from the working set, the working set manager scans the use bits of the pages within the working set. During each pass, it performs the following operations:

```
if (u == 1) {u = 0; cnt = 0 }
else cnt++
```

At the end of the pass it evicts the page with the highest values of *cnt*. Thus as long as a page is being referenced frequently, its *cnt* value will be low and it will not be evicted.

CASE STUDY: PAGE REPLACEMENT IN WINDOWS 2000   (*continued*)

Another interesting feature of the page replacement scheme is that the eviction of a page from a working set gradual. First, the selected page frame is placed on one of two lists: one holds the *tentatively* removed pages that have been modified; the other holds *tentatively* removed read-only pages. But the pages remain in memory and, if referenced again, can quickly be removed from the list, without causing a page fault. They are used to satisfy page faults only when the list of actually free pages is empty.

8.3.3   Load Control and Thrashing

When implementing a virtual memory management scheme, one of the main problems is to maintain a balance between the degree of multiprogramming and the amount of paging (i.e., page faults) that occurs. On the one hand, we would like to keep as many processes running concurrently as possible to keep CPU utilization high. On the other hand, since all active processes must compete for the same pool of memory frames, their resident page sets get smaller as the multiprogramming level increases, resulting in more page faults. **Load control** refers to the policy that determines the number and the type of processes that should be active concurrently, thus competing for memory, CPU time, and other critical resources. The goal is to maximize overall performance.

Three basic questions must be answered for a load control mechanism:

1. How to decide when to increase or decrease the degree of multiprogramming?
2. Which of the currently active tasks should be swapped out if the degree of multiprogramming must be reduced?
3. When a new process is created or a previously suspended process is reactivated, which of its pages should be loaded into memory as its current resident set?

The following sections address each of these questions in turn.

Choosing the Degree of Multiprogramming

In the case of local page replacement schemes, such as the working set model or the page fault frequency algorithm, the first question is answered by the replacement method itself. Since each process has a well-defined resident set, the system can increase the degree of multiprogramming only to the point where all memory is allocated. Only when the current resident sets shrink as a result of changing patterns in process behavior, or when one or more processes are deactivated, can new processes be added to the currently active set. Conversely, if a process resident set expands, it may be necessary to swap out one or more of the currently active processes to create the necessary space.

With global page replacement, the degree of multiprogramming is not determined automatically. Thus, explicit load control criteria must be provided to guarantee that each active process has some minimum number of resident pages. With too many active processes the page fault rate can increase to the point where most of the system's effort is expended on moving pages between main and secondary memory. Such a condition is termed **thrashing**.

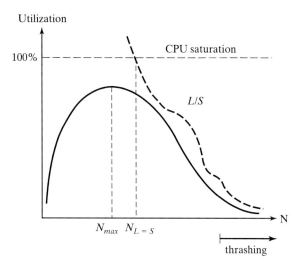

FIGURE 8-11. Processor utilization.

Figure 8-11 illustrates the problem of thrashing. The solid curve shows the effect of multiprogramming on CPU utilization for a given fixed size memory. The horizontal axis gives the degree of multiprogramming, N, i.e., the number of active processes sharing main memory. The vertical axis shows the corresponding CPU utilization. Initially, the curve rises rapidly toward high CPU utilization but it slows down as more processes are added. Eventually, it drops down again toward zero. It is this latter phase, that is referred to as thrashing and is the direct result of too many processes competing for a fixed number of frames. Since each process is able to execute only a few instructions before it encounters a nonresident page, all processes are blocked most of the time waiting for their page to be moved into main memory. As a result, the CPU is idle most of the time. Its main activity becomes the housekeeping related to paging, and the amount of useful work being accomplished is minimal.

The goal of an effective load control policy must then be to keep the level of multiprogramming at the point where the CPU utilization is highest, i.e., at point N_{max} in the figure. Unfortunately, CPU utilization varies at runtime due to a number of circumstances and is difficult to monitor accurately. Thus, we need some other measurable criterion that would tell us at any given point in time whether CPU utilization has reached its attainable peak.

A number of schemes have been proposed and studied to solve this problem. Since the main objective is to minimize the amount of paging, most criteria for determining the optimal degree of multiprogramming are based on the rate of paging. One example is the **L = S criterion**, where L is the mean time between faults and S is the mean page fault service time, i.e., the time it takes to replace a page in main memory. Intuitively, when L is much larger than S, the paging disk is underutilized. In contrast, when S exceeds L, there are more page faults than the paging disk can handle. When L approaches S, both the paging disk and CPU generally reach their maximum utilization.

The dashed curve in Figure 8-11 shows the L/S ratio—the utilization of the paging disk—which depresses the CPU utilization when the degree of multiprogramming is too high. Thus to achieve the highest overall performance, the **L = S criterion** criterion selects the point $N_{L=S}$ as the desired level of multiprogramming. Note that this is slightly higher than the optimum, N_{max}, but the deviation is usually tolerable for the purposes of load control. The curve is based on extensive measurements in actual computer systems and is valid under general conditions that apply to almost all real multiprogramming systems (Denning 1980).

Another basis for choosing the level of multiprogramming, referred to as the **50% criterion** (Denning et al. 1976), also relies on measuring the page fault rate. Using this criterion, the system maintains a level of multiprogramming such that the paging disk is busy 50% of the time. This is based on the observation that CPU utilization tends to be highest when the utilization of the paging device is approximately 50%. Both the $L = S$ and the 50% criteria are closely related.

Yet another criterion, called **clock load control**, has been proposed by Carr (1981). It is applicable to schemes which employ a pointer to scan the list of page frames, when searching for a page to be replaced. The method is based on the rate at which the pointer travels around the page frame list. If this rate is low, one of the following two conditions is true:

1. The page fault rate is low, resulting in few requests to advance the pointer.
2. The mean pointer travel between page faults is small, indicating that there are many resident pages that are not being referenced and are readily replaceable.

In both cases the level of multiprogramming might usefully be increased. Conversely, if the travel rate of the pointer increases past a certain threshold value, the level of multiprogramming should be decreased.

Choosing the Process to Deactivate

When the degree of multiprogramming must be decreased, the system must choose which of the currently active processes to deactivate. Some of the possible choices for selecting a process to evict are the following:

- The *lowest priority process*: follow the same rules as the process scheduler and thus try to maintain a consistent scheduling policy;

- The *faulting process*: eliminate the process that would be blocked anyway while waiting for its page to be loaded;

- The *last process activated*: the most recently activated process is considered the least important;

- The *smallest process*: the smallest process is the least expensive to swap in and out;

- The *largest process*: free up the largest number of frames.

In general, it is not possible to determine the superiority of one choice over another since each depends on many other policies and system parameters, including the scheduling methods used in a given system. Hence, the decision will rely upon the intuition and experience of the system designer, as well as the particular application.

Prepaging

In a system with static allocation, all pages belonging to an active process are loaded before the process is permitted to run. In a dynamically allocated system, pages are loaded only as a result of page faults. The latter method works well when the process already has some reasonable set of pages in memory since page faults do not occur too frequently. Before this set is established, however, the page fault rate will be high. This will be the case when a newly created process is started or when an existing process is reactivated as a result of a satisfied request.

The paging behavior can be captured by a process **lifetime curve**, which shows how the mean time between page faults increases with the mean set of pages resident in memory (Denning 1980). The shape of this lifetime curve, shown in Figure 8-12, is of particular interest. It shows that, as long as the resident set of pages is small, page faults occur frequently. When the set reaches a certain size, the page fault rate decreases dramatically and, consequently, the mean time between page faults increases accordingly. This continues until the curve reaches a *knee* beyond which the benefits of adding more pages to the resident set begin to diminish. This suggests that a process should not be started or reactivated with an empty or a very small resident set. Rather, a set of pages should be **prepaged** at the time of activation, which can be done more efficiently than loading one page at a time.

Theoretically, the optimal size of the prepaged set is given by the point at which the lifetime curve reaches its knee. In practice, however, this value is difficult to estimate. Thus, for a newly created process, prepaging is rarely used. In the case of an existing process, i.e., one that has been blocked temporarily when waiting for an I/O completion or some other event, the obvious choice is the set of pages that were resident just before the process was suspended. This is particularly attractive with schemes based on the working set model, where a list of currently resident pages is explicitly maintained.

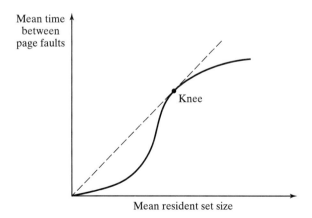

FIGURE 8-12. Lifetime curve of a process.

8.3.4 Evaluation of Paging

Systems that employ paging have two main advantages over nonpaged systems. The first is a very simple placement strategy. Since the basic unit of memory allocation is a fixed-size page, programs and data need not occupy contiguous areas of memory. Thus, if a request for k pages of memory is made and there are at least k free frames, the placement decision is straightforward—any frame may be allocated to any page.

The second advantage is the elimination of external fragmentation, which occurs with variable memory partitions. This is because page frames form a uniform sequence without any gaps. However, the problem of fragmentation does not disappear entirely. Because the sizes of programs and data are rarely multiples of the page size, the last page of each virtual memory space is generally only partially filled. This problem of **internal** fragmentation occurs with any scheme using fixed memory partitions, including paging. The magnitude of the problem depends on the page size relative to the size of the virtual memory spaces (e.g., segments) that are mapped onto these pages.

Many early experiments were carried out to study the dynamic behavior of programs under paging (Belady 1966; Coffman and Varian 1968; Baer and Sager 1972; Gelenbe, Tiberio and Boekhorst 1973; Rodriguez-Rosell 1973; Opderbeck and Chu 1974; Lenfant and Burgevin 1975; Sadeh 1975; Spirn 1977; Gupta and Franklin 1978). The most significant parameters that were varied were the page size and the amount of available memory. The results obtained from these independent studies were generally consistent with one another. They can be summarized by the diagrams shown in Figure 8-13; each illustrates the behavior of an individual process under different conditions.

1. Figure 8-13a shows how pages are referenced by a process over time. The curve rises sharply at the beginning, indicating that the process requires a certain percentage of its pages within a very short time period after activation. After a certain working set is established, additional pages are demanded at a much slower rate. For example, about 50% of a process total number of pages were referenced on the average during a single quantum in a typical time-sharing operation.

2. Usage within a page is illustrated in Figure 8-13b. It shows that a relatively small number of instructions within any page are executed before control moves to another page. For page sizes of 1024 words, less than 200 instructions were executed before another page was referenced in most of the samples investigated.

3. Figure 8-13c describes the effect of page size on the page fault rate. Given a fixed size of main memory, the number of page faults increases as the page size increases; i.e., a given memory within many small pages has fewer faults than the same memory filled with larger pages.

4. The effect of memory size on the page fault rate appears in Figure 8-13d. For a given fixed page size, the page fault rate rises exponentially as the amount of available memory decreases. The point labeled W represents a minimum amount of memory required to avoid thrashing, i.e., a page fault rate that causes CPU to be grossly underutilized as it must wait for pages to be transferred into memory.

These results provide important guidelines for the design of paging systems. Figure 8-13a, which is a direct consequence of the principle of locality, underscores

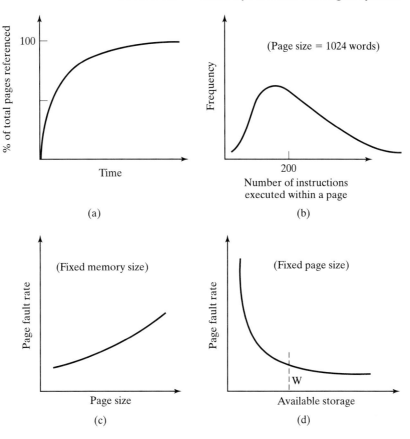

FIGURE 8-13. Qualitative program behavior under paging: (a) percentage of referenced pages; (b) portion of each page actually used; (c) effect of page size on page fault rate; and (d) effect of memory size on page fault rate.

the importance of prepaging. When a process is reactivated, for example, after an I/O completion, it should not be restarted with just the current page. This would cause it to generate a large number of page faults before it was able to reestablish its working set. Prepaging can load these pages much more efficiently than pure demand paging.

Figures 8-13b and c address the question of page size. Both suggest that page size should be *small*. In the case of (b), smaller page sizes would eliminate many of the instructions that arc not referenced, but must be brought into memory as part of the larger pages. An additional argument in favor of a small page size, not reflected in the figures, is that the amount of memory wasted due to internal fragmentation is also reduced. Smaller pages provide a finer resolution, and thus result in a closer fit for the variable size of program and data segments.

There are, however, important counterarguments in support of a relatively *large* page size. First, larger page sizes require smaller page tables to keep track of a given amount of virtual memory, which reduces memory overhead. Large pages also mean that main memory is divided into a smaller number of physical frames; thus, the cost of the hardware necessary to support paging is less. Finally, the performance of disks is dominated by the seek time and the rotational delay, whereas the actual data transfer time is negligible. As a result, transferring a contiguous block of data is much more efficient than transferring the same amount of data distributed over multiple smaller blocks. This, too, favors a larger page size.

In older systems, pages were generally in the range from 512 bytes to 4 KB (e.g., the IBM 360/370). Because of the increases in CPU speed and other technological advances, the trend has been toward increasingly larger page sizes. Many contemporary systems use page sizes of 16 KB or even as large as 64 KB.

Figure 8-13d underscores the importance of effective load control. It illustrates that there is a critical amount of memory a process must have to run efficiently; if this is not provided, the process' paging behavior deteriorates rapidly, resulting in thrashing, which only wastes the system resources.

CONCEPTS, TERMS, AND ABBREVIATIONS

The following concepts have been introduced in this chapter. Test yourself by defining and discussing each keyword or phrase.

Aging register	Page table register (PTR)
Associative memory	Placement
Clock load control	Prepaging
Clock replacement algorithm	Reference string (RS)
Demand paging	Replacement
Dirty page	Second-chance replacement
FIFO replacement	algorithm
Frame table	Segment
Global page replacement	Segment table
Inverted page table	Segment table register (STR)
Least recently used	Sliding window
replacement (LRU)	Third-chance replacement
Load control	algorithm
Locality principle	Thrashing
Local page replacement	Translation look-aside
MIN optimal replacement algorithm	buffer (TLB)
Page	Use bit
Page fault	Virtual address
Page fault frequency replacement	Virtual memory
algorithm (PFF)	VMIN replacement algorithm
Page frame	Working set model
Page table	Write bit

EXERCISES

1. Consider the following four paging systems A through D:

	A	B	C	D
Page size (in words)	512	512	1024	1024
Word size (in bits)	16	32	16	32

   Assume that each virtual address (p, d) occupies one word. For each system, determine:

   (a) the size of the page table (number of entries)

   (b) the size of the virtual memory (number of words)

2. Consider the following frame table in a paging system. Assuming page tables were used instead of the frame table, show the contents of the corresponding page tables.

0	3	1
1	7	4
2	3	0
3	3	2
4	7	1
5	7	2
6	7	0
7	7	3

3. A pure paging system has the page size of 512 words, a virtual memory of 512 pages numbered 0 through 511, and a physical memory of 16 page frames numbered 0 through 15. The current content of physical memory is as follows.

Physical Memory

0	free
1536	page 34
2048	page 9
	free
3072	page table
3584	page 65
	free
4608	page 10
	free

   (a) Assuming that page tables contain only the 4-bit frame numbers (rather than the full 13-bit physical memory addresses), show the current content of the page table.

   (b) Show the content of the page table after page 49 is loaded at location 0 and page 34 is replaced by page 12.

(c) What physical address is referenced by the virtual addresses 4608, 5119, 5120, 33300?

(d) What happens when the virtual address 33000 is referenced?

4. The following diagram is a snapshot of main memory in a paged system (no segmentation):

address	contents		address	contents			address	contents
0	6		12	0	Page table		24	5
1	15		13	−12	of p2		25	−3
2	3		14	24			26	−3
3	−2		15	−			27	2
4	−45	Page table	16	0			28	0
5	8	of p1	17	−12			29	1
6	28		18	−16			30	2
7	−2		19	−			31	3
8	9		20	0			⋮	⋮
9	−3		21	0				
10	8		22	0				
11	12		23	0				

Assume the following:
- The size of each page and page table is 4.
- Currently, there are two processes, p1 and p2. The page table of p1 begins at address 4; the page table of p2 begins at address 12.
- A dash (−) denotes a nonexistent page.
- The left-most bit of every page table entry indicates whether the page is currently in memory or on disk. Thus a negative number (whose left most bit—the sign bit—is 1) denotes an out-of-memory page, whereas a positive number gives the address of a resident page.

The two processes both reference the following virtual addresses:

$$0, 1, 4, 5, 8, 10, 12, 15$$

For each process, translate the virtual addresses into the corresponding physical address. If the translation is successful, read the content of the corresponding memory location. Otherwise, indicate whether a page fault or an error occurred.

(Hint: Translate each virtual address into a 4-bit binary number and interpret the first two bits as the page number and the last two bits as the page offset.)

5. Three functions, each of length 600 words, are to be linked together into one process and loaded into memory. Consider the following memory management schemes:

(a) paging (no segmentation):
   page size: 1024 words
   page table occupies 1 page

(b) segmentation (no paging):
   segment table size: 1024 words

(c) segmentation with paging (each function becomes a separate segment):
   page and segment size: 1024
   page and segment tables occupy 1 page each

(d) two-level paging (page table is paged):
   page size: 1024
   page table and page directory occupy 1 page each

Assume that all three functions as well as all tables are resident in memory. For each of the three systems, determine the total occupied memory space, i.e., the space that cannot be used by any other process. This includes the space occupied by the functions, and any page or segment tables. Determine also the amount of space wasted due to internal fragmentation.

6. You are given the following information about a virtual memory system that employs both paging and segmentation:

- Virtual addresses have the form $(s1, s2, p, w)$ where $|s1|$, $|s2|$, $|p|$, and $|w|$ denote the lengths (in bits) of each of the four address components;
- Virtual address size is 32 bits;
- Page size is 512 words;
- A page table occupies one page.

(a) What is the value of $|w|$?

(b) What is the maximum number of pages per segment and what is the corresponding value of $|p|$?

(c) Using the values of $|p|$ and $|w|$ determined above, which of the following choices for $|s1|$ and $|s2|$ is preferable? Explain.

    i. $|s1| = |w|$ and $|s2| = 32 - |s1| - |p| - |w|$

    ii. $|s2| = |w|$ and $|s1| = 32 - |s2| - |p| - |w|$

(d) Would either choice under part (c) result in a larger virtual address space? Explain.

7. Extend the *address_map* functions of Sections 8.2.3 and 8.2.4 to handle the following situations:

(a) segment and page tables are always resident but individual pages may not be

(b) only the segment table is permanently resident

(c) only the segment directory (Section 8.2.4 only) is permanently resident

8. The following diagram shows a portion of a virtual memory system that uses both paging and segmentation. The top portion is a snapshot of main memory; the bottom portion is a snapshot of the disk used for paging.

Main memory

address	contents						
0	4	16	52	32	28	48	16
1	8	17	−1	33	48	49	−
2	−2	18	−	34	−	50	−
3	−	19	−	35	60	51	36
4	17	20	−	36	56	52	120
5	16	21	−	37	−	53	16
6	100	22	−	38	−	54	16
7	3	23	−	39	−	55	27
8	−1	24	3	40	24	56	52
9	3	25	−2	41	−	57	47
10	16	26	36	42	−	58	−1
11	0	27	47	43	−	59	3
12	−	28	0	44	40	60	44
13	−	29	12	45	20	61	−
14	−	30	−	46	−	62	−
15	−	31	−	47	−	63	−

Disk

block #:	0	1	2	3	...
contents:	... 7 11 14 16	3 16 13 25	-11 4 -2 3	4 106 10 0	...

The following basic rules apply:

- The page size is four words; the size of each page table is also four words; the segment table is divided into four pages; the size of the segment directory is four words.
- There is only a single process in the system; its segment directory starts at address 32.
- A dash ($-$) denotes a nonexistent page.
- When a page or segment table entry contains a positive number, n, the page is currently resident in memory; it starts at address n. When an entry contains a negative number, $-n$, the page is currently not resident in memory, and must be loaded from the disk. The absolute value, n, denotes the disk block that contains the missing page. For example, a -2 in a page table entry indicates that the page is not in main memory and can be found in disk block 2.

(a) Starting with the segment directory at address 32, trace down the entire memory hierarchy, marking each page as one of the following: "page p of the segment table," "page table of segment s," or "page p of segment s," where p and s are the actual page and segment numbers. Note that some of the page frames will remain unmarked—those are the free page frames.

(b) Translate the virtual address 113 into a physical address and determine its content. (Hint: transform the decimal address into an equivalent 8-bit binary number and interpret each 2-bit component as the offsets $s1$, $s2$, p, and w.)

(c) Translate the virtual address 68 into a physical address and determine its content. In the case a page fault occurs, show all changes to the memory hierarchy.

(d) Assume that segment 7 is to be deleted. Show all changes to the memory hierarchy.

9. Suppose along with the diagrammed memory of the previous exercise, a TLB with the following contents is included:

$(s1, s2, p)$	frame address
0	4
16	52

(a) Which of the following virtual addresses will be translated using the buffer, i.e., bypass the page and segment table:

$$0, 1, 2, 3, 4, 9, 16, 17, 52, 64, 65, 68$$

(b) Which of these addresses cause a page fault? Which result in an error?

(c) Assume that each reference to main memory takes 1 microsecond. How long does it take to resolve a virtual address if, on the average, 60% of all program references find a match in the translation look-aside buffer. (Assume that access to the buffer is instantaneous.)

(d) Repeat the previous question for a match ratio of 85%.

10. In a system with paging and segmentation, each virtual address (s, p, w) requires three memory accesses. To speed up the address translation, a translation look-aside buffer holds the components (s, p) together with the corresponding frame number. If each memory access takes m ns and the access to the translation look-aside buffer takes $m/10$ ns, determine the hit ratio necessary to reduce the average access time to memory by 50%.

11. Consider the following sequence of virtual memory references generated by a single program in a pure paging system:

$$10, 11, 104, 170, 73, 309, 185, 245, 246, 434, 458, 364$$

Derive the corresponding reference string assuming a page size of (a) 100 words; (b) 200 words; and (c) 300 words.

12. A two-dimensional 512 x 512 array is stored in row major in a paged virtual memory system with page size 512. All elements of the array must be accessed sequentially. Initially, the entire array is on disk. There are 16 frames of physical memory available for processing the array.

    (a) For the FIFO page replacement discipline, how many page faults will be generated when accessing all elements of the array sequentially:

    i. in row major;

    ii. in column major.

    (b) Would the number of page faults be different under the LRU policy?

13. Assuming a physical memory of four page frames, give the number of page faults for the reference string *abgadeabadegde* for each of the following policies. (Initially, all frames are empty.)

    (a) MIN

    (b) FIFO

    (c) Second-chance algorithm

    (d) Third-chance algorithm (assume that all accesses to page *b* are write requests)

    (e) LRU

    (f) VMIN with $\tau = 2$

    (g) WS with $\tau = 2$

14. Consider the following reference string:

$$a\ b\ c\ d\ a\ b\ e\ a\ b\ c\ d\ e$$

Determine the number of page faults generated using a FIFO page replacement scheme for a number of frames ranging from 1 to 6. Illustrate Belady's anomaly by plotting the number of page faults against the number of frames.

15. Consider the working set model with $\tau = 3$. Given the following reference string of a process p:

$$y\ x\ x\ x\ x\ x\ x\ y\ y\ u\ x\ x\ x\ y\ z\ y\ z\ w\ w\ z\ x\ x\ w\ w$$

    (a) What is the largest working set process p will ever have?

    (b) What is the smallest working set process p will ever have (not counting the first τ references)?

16. Consider the reference string *abcdebcdcbddbddd*. Assuming the working set replacement strategy, determine the minimum window size such that the above string generates at most five page faults. Show which pages are in memory at each reference. Mark page faults with an asterisk.

CHAPTER 9

Sharing of Data and Code in Main Memory

The engineering of large software systems is greatly simplified if individual modules can be constructed separately and later linked together. This also permits the reuse of modules developed previously, and the use of libraries and other modules built by others, thus reducing the total software development cost. To facilitate the necessary cooperation, a flexible linking mechanism should be provided that does not require individual modules to be recompiled each time they are being included in a user address space. Important additional benefits are obtained if the same copy of a module can be linked into more than one address space at the same time, essentially *sharing* a single copy of the module in main memory among different processes. In addition to sharing code, many concurrent programs cooperate and must share common data areas to exchange partial results or other forms of information with each other.

The first part of the chapter presents the main techniques for the sharing of code and data in centralized architectures. Because the shared memory model has proven to be such a convenient abstraction, it has also been implemented on top of distributed systems. In the last sections of the chapter, we introduce the basic ideas underlying distributed shared memory.

9.1   SINGLE-COPY SHARING

Our general focus is on sharing a **single copy** of code or data in memory. We are not concerned with the sharing of software components for the purposes of reuse. The latter form of sharing can be accomplished easily by giving each process its own private copy of the shared object. The copy can be incorporated, either manually or by the linker, into other programs.

9.1.1   Reasons for Sharing

There are two main reasons for single-copy sharing. The first, which involves the sharing of **data**, is that some processes are designed to communicate, cooperate, and compete

274

for resources with each other through shared memory. This is a reason similar to that underlying the need for critical sections. For example, producer and consumer processes typically share a common buffer area through which data flows from one to the other. Other applications include those that select work from a common pool of tasks and those that access a common data structure representing the current state of the computation. For example, multiple processes could be engaged in a search or a divide-and-conquer computation, where a shared tree structure records the global state. Various systems resources also are accessed in a shared manner by multiple concurrent processes. File directories are notable examples of such common resources. To prevent inconsistencies due to concurrent updates, only a single copy must be in memory at any given time. A similar need for sharing arises with various system status databases, for example, those recording which resources are free and which are busy. Such information is continually being searched and updated by different OS processes, and must be maintained as a single consistent copy.

The second main reason for single-copy sharing is to better utilize main memory. This involves both **code** and **data**. It is frequently the case that several active processes use the same code or data. For example, many users in a time-sharing system may be running the same editor or debugger. If each process had its own copy, the need for main memory would increase dramatically. This, in turn, would reduce the number of users able to share the system at the same time. It also would increase the I/O overhead in loading the excess copies into memory; and in systems with demand paging, it would increase the page fault rate and thus the risk of thrashing. For these reasons, using a single copy of any heavily used software component is highly desirable. Such components generally include OS kernel routines, for example, the I/O drivers, which must be shared by all processes; and various utilities and system services, such as debuggers, file manipulation routines, and linkers and loaders. Finally, popular text editors and language processors, i.e., compilers, assemblers, and interpreters, are often maintained as a single shared copy in main memory.

Sharing of *user* level code and data also may be beneficial. An example is a shared-memory multiprocessing application where several processes execute the same code, such as the body of a parallel loop, with different data sets; here, a single copy of the common code could be shared in memory by the different processes.

9.1.2 Requirements for Sharing

Designating Resources as Shared

To allow some portion of code or data to be shared among processes, the system must provide some way of **expressing** what is to be shared and under what conditions or constraints. This can be done *statically* at the time of linking or loading, or *dynamically*, at runtime.

In the simplest case, all resources to be shared are known a priori. This is usually the approach taken when **systems** resources are shared, such as parts of the OS kernel, compilers, editors, and other widely used software components. These are designated as single-copy shared implicitly, i.e., by convention, at the time of systems design or initialization. Since all sharable resources are known, the OS can keep track of them and only load a copy if this does not already exist in memory. In some cases, a resource can be assigned permanently to a specific portion of memory. This is usually done with heavily used parts of the OS kernel, such interrupt handlers or I/O drivers. Other, less frequently used resources, such as compilers or editors, can be loaded on demand whenever one or more process needs to use them.

In systems that allow single-copy sharing at the **applications** level, the sharable resources are not known ahead of time. In this case, the system must provide some way for users to express which portions of their programs or data are to be shared and by which processes. To support this in its full generality would require a very complex set of commands and is rarely attempted. But some systems support various limited forms of application-level sharing.

CASE STUDY: SHARING MEMORY IN UNIX

UNIX allows a process to create a section of memory of a specified number of bytes using the command *shmget()* (shared memory get). The command returns a nonnegative integer representing a unique identifier of the shared memory area. Other processes can then map this portion of memory into their space with the command *shmat()* (shared memory attach). This command takes the identifier of the shared memory as a parameter and returns the starting address of the segment in the caller's virtual memory. Alternately, the caller can specify the starting address as another parameter. The original creator of the shared area and all processes that subsequently attach to it may read and write this area (subject to access restrictions specified as part of the *shmget* or *shmat* commands) to share arbitrary unstructured data.

Reentrant Code

When **code** is to be shared among processes, some precautions must be taken to ensure that multiple processes can execute different parts of the same code concurrently. In the early days of computing, instructions could be treated as data and vice versa, which allowed programs to modify their own code. This technique was necessary to implement loops and function calls. The invention of index and base registers made instruction self-modification unnecessary. Today's modern programming languages draw a sharp distinction between code and data, and although code modification is still possible with some languages, it is unnecessary and generally considered poor programming practice. It makes program logic very obscure and difficult to follow. It also makes it impossible to share code because the code keeps changing unpredictably at runtime.

To permit single-copy code sharing, all functions must be **reentrant** or **pure**. Such functions do not modify their own instructions and can be kept as read-only segments. All variable data associated with a process executing a pure function must be stored in separate areas private to the process, including, for example, its *stack* and its *data* area. The process stack stores parameters, return addresses, and local variables. The data area stores global variables and the *heap*, which is used for dynamically allocated memory.

The main challenge in code sharing is to guarantee that addresses generated by the shared code are translated correctly, depending on which process is currently executing the segment. Specifically, references to the segment itself (e.g., branch instructions within the shared code) must translate to the *same* physical addresses, regardless of which process runs. However, references to the stack, data area, or to other code sections must all translate to *different* physical addresses, corresponding to the areas belonging to the process under which the shared code currently executes.

EXAMPLE:　Simple Code Sharing

Figure 9-1 shows a code segment shared by two processes, p_1 and p_2. The target address of the *branch* instruction must be translated to the same physical location under both processes. The *load* instruction, on the other hand, must access data from different data areas, depending on which process is currently executing the shared code.

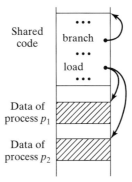

FIGURE 9-1. Addresses in shared code.

9.1.3　Linking and Sharing

Issues of sharing are closely related to linking, which is the process of combining several separately translated programs (object modules) into one load module. The main tasks are the relocation of individual object modules and the binding of external references to reflect the starting addresses assumed by the linker. In systems that do not support segmentation, all modules are linked into *one* contiguous load module. The address space assumed by the linker when generating this load module can be the actual physical address space, a contiguous relocatable space, or a paged virtual space, depending on the memory management scheme supported by the system. But from the linker's point of view, the task in all three cases is the same. For each external reference (M, w), where M is the name of an external module and w is an offset within that module, the linker determines the starting address, m, of M within the load module and adds the offset w to it. The resulting address $m + w$ then replaces all references (M, w).

In systems with segmentation, linking is conceptually simpler. Each segment to be linked is first assigned a segment number. All external references (S, w) to a segment named S are then simply replaced by a pair (s, w), where s is the segment number assigned to S and w is the offset within that segment.

If the linking process is completed, i.e., all symbolic external references are replaced by their corresponding load module addresses, before execution begins, the linking is referred to as *static*. If the linking is performed when execution is already in progress, it is called *dynamic*.

Let us now consider sharing. This may be viewed as the linking of the *same* copy of a module into *two* or more address spaces. If the links are resolved prior to execution, the sharing is called *static*. This is typically done by the *loader* just prior to program execution. The reason is that the linker does not know whether a shared component is already in memory or still on disk. Furthermore, the component's location can change before the new load module is loaded. Alternately, sharing can be done *dynamically*, where the external links are resolved at runtime. The remainder of this section discusses how sharing may be accomplished under different memory management schemes.

9.2   SHARING IN SYSTEMS WITHOUT VIRTUAL MEMORY

In the absence of any dynamic relocation mechanisms, or if there is only a single relocation register for the entire process, memory must be allocated to a process as a contiguous region at the time of linking or loading. In virtually all such systems, a sharp distinction is made between systems and user programs. Since space is contiguous, the only way for two processes to share any user components would be to partially overlap their memory spaces. Since this is very restrictive, sharing of user code or data is rarely supported.

Sharing of system components is more important and can be supported to some extent. Those system components that must be shared must be assigned specific *agreed-upon* memory addresses. The linker then uses these addresses when preparing a load module. It replaces each reference to a shared system module by its known memory address prior to loading the program. The main problem with this simple scenario is that the shared system component cannot easily differentiate between the different processes that invoke it. The identity of the invoking process or any other process-specific data can be made available to the shared component only via registers, which are saved and reloaded during each context switch.

Most processors provide more than one relocation register for the running process. Typically, a separate register is used for the code, the stack, and the data. This greatly simplifies the problem of sharing. To share the same code among two or more processes (system or user level), all that must be done is to load the code base register of any sharing process with the same address—the starting address of the shared code. The stack and data base registers point to different regions for each process, thus keeping them private.

EXAMPLE: Sharing of Code Using Relocation Registers

The two processes, p_1 and p_2, of Figure 9-2 share the same code but each has its own stack and data. Any reference to the (shared) code would use the code base register (*CBR*). For example, a branch instruction could have the form *branch x(CBR)* where x is the offset relative to *CBR*. Similarly, any reference to the stack, e.g., to access a local variable, or to the data segment, e.g., to access a variable on the heap, would use the current stack base register (*SBR*) or the data base register (*DBR*). For example, a load instruction could have the form *load x(SBR)* or *load x(DBR)*, where x is the offset for the desired variable relative to the given register. On a context switch to another process executing the same shared code, the content of *CBR* remains unchanged but the contents of the other base registers are changed to point to the stack and the data of the *new* process.

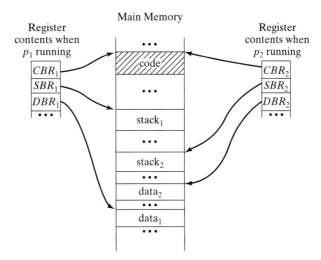

FIGURE 9-2. Sharing of code using relocation registers.

The sharing of data among processes is possible in a similar manner, assuming that additional base registers exist and are accessible by the sharing processes. Setting the base register of two or more processes to point to the same data address allows these processes to access the same region in memory.

9.3 SHARING IN PAGING SYSTEMS

Paging permits a noncontiguous allocation of main memory. Under a standard implementation, each page is referenced by an entry in the process's page table.

9.3.1 Sharing of Data

Sharing among several processes may be accomplished on a page basis by pointing to the same page frame from the different page tables. If the shared pages contain only *data* and no addresses—either to themselves or to other areas—the linker can assign arbitrary page numbers to the shared pages for each process and adjust the page tables to point to the appropriate page frames.

EXAMPLE: Sharing in Paged Systems

Consider two processes p_1 and p_2, whose virtual address spaces are represented by the two page tables PT_1 and PT_2, respectively (Fig. 9-3). Assume that page 0 of each process contains a reference to a shared data page. Under p_1, the shared page is assigned the number $n1$ and hence the corresponding reference is adjusted to $(n1, w)$, where w is the offset within the page. Under p_2, the same shared page is assigned the number $n2$ and thus the reference in p_2's page 0 is adjusted to $(n2, w)$. The page numbers $n1$ and $n2$ need not be the same as long as the shared page contains only data, i.e., the shared page is only read or written, but never executed. The memory mapping mechanism *(address_map)* guarantees that at runtime the correct page table is used.

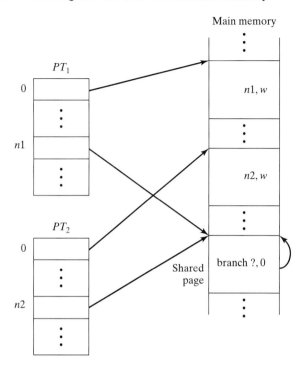

FIGURE 9-3. Sharing in paged systems.

CASE STUDIES: SHARING OF MAIN MEMORY DATA

1. *Linux.* Consider again the *shmget* and *shmat* primitives presented in Section 9.1.2, which allows two or more processes to dynamically declare a shared memory area. When a process performs a *shmget* operation, the system assigns the necessary number of page table entries to the shared area (based on the size of this area). When the process accesses the shared area, free memory pages are assigned and their addresses are entered into the page table. When another process attaches to the same area, using *shmat*, the system designates the same number of page table entries to this area; the caller may choose (using a parameter for *shmat*), whether the same page numbers must be assigned to the shared area as in the creator's page table. Regardless of which page table entries are selected, they are filled with the starting addresses of the same shared pages.

One difficulty with having different page tables pointing to shared pages is swapping. When a shared page is to be removed from memory, the system would have to find all page tables pointing to this page and mark the entries accordingly. To avoid this overhead, Linux keeps track of how many processes are currently attached to a given shared area. Only when a single process is attached is the page actually removed from memory and the (single) page table entry updated.

> **2.** *Windows 2000.* Windows 2000 uses the concept of **section objects** to support
> sharing of memory among processes. A section object is similar to the shared
> area obtained with *shmget/shmat* in Linux or UNIX. It is created by one process,
> which obtains a handle for it. The creator can pass this handle to other processes,
> which can open and access it. A section object has a size, access protection
> information, and a designation whether it must be mapped to the same virtual
> address for all processes sharing it or whether different addresses may be used.

9.3.2   Sharing of Code

Sharing of code requires more care since instructions contain addresses referring to other
instructions or data. For shared code pages to execute correctly under different processes,
they must be assigned the *same* page numbers in *all* virtual address spaces. To illustrate
why this is necessary, consider again the example in Figure 9-3. Assume that the shared
page is a function containing a branch instruction to some other location within itself,
say to the instruction 0. This instruction would have the form *branch n,0*, where n is the
page number of the shared function and 0 is the offset. The problem is that n depends on
the process executing the function. When executing under process p_1, the target address
must be $(n1, 0)$, and under p_2, it must be $(n2, 0)$. Since a memory cell can hold only one
value at any time, the two page numbers $n1$ and $n2$ must be the same. In other words,
the shared page must be assigned the same entries in *both* page tables. The potential
page number conflicts and wasted table space that can result when a new process must
share several already loaded modules limits the ability to share code in paged systems.

The problem can be avoided if the total set of sharable modules is known to the
system ahead of time. In that case, their page numbers can be permanently reserved to
eliminate conflicts, but such a priori knowledge is rarely available.

To make sharing of code more general, we must avoid using page numbers in the
shared code. Assume that the shared code is self-contained, i.e., it contains no external
references. Under this assumption, we can avoid the use of page numbers in the code
by using only base registers. All branch addresses are compiled relative to the code base
register. Similarly, all addresses of read/write instructions are compiled relative to the
data or stack register. A single copy of such a code area can be linked into any address
space, and it will execute correctly for all processes sharing it.

The only remaining problem is how to link a single copy of a code area into
multiple address spaces. First, the linker must assign page numbers to the area and
replace every reference to the area by the address (p, w), where p is the first page of
the shared area and w is the offset where execution should start. The linker must then
fill the corresponding page table entries with addresses of the pages belonging to the
shared code area. It is this second task that makes sharing difficult: the linker does not
know whether the shared area is still on disk or already used by some other process and
resident in memory. But even if the linker could find this information, it would not help,
because by the time the load module is loaded into memory, the location of the shared
module could have already changed many times.

To solve this problem, external references can be resolved by the *loader* just prior to
execution. But this task can be quite cumbersome, especially when the process specifies
a large number of potentially shared routines, most of which are never used. This is

typically the case when a process includes various system libraries but only uses a small fraction of them during execution. To reduce the overhead, the system can postpone the assignment of page numbers and locating the routines until runtime, when a particular function is actually being invoked. However, doing this for every external reference repeatedly would be wasteful. Instead, each external reference should be resolved *only once*, when it is first used. Subsequent references should use the actual address assigned.

To implement this form of **dynamic linking**, the linker sets up a special area within the process address space, called the **transfer vector**. Each entry of the transfer vector corresponds to a reference to a shared code segment. All references to a given code segment point to the corresponding entry in the transfer vector. Initially, each entry contains a piece of code, called the **stub**. When a reference is made to a shared segment for the first time, it executes the stub. This checks if the desired segment is currently resident in memory. If not, it loads it. Once the segment is loaded and its address is known, the stub replaces itself by a direct reference to this address. Thus, all future executions of this part of the code will go (indirectly via the transfer vector) to the specified library, without involving the OS.

EXAMPLE: Dynamic Linking Through Transfer Vector

Figure 9-4 illustrates the basic idea. Figure 9-4a shows the virtual memory of a process, where the instruction *bri* (branch indirectly) corresponds to a reference to a shared routine. It points to an entry in the transfer vector, which contains a stub. Figure 9-4b shows the memory after the first *bri* instruction executed. The stub found the corresponding routine in memory and replaced itself by a reference to this routine. Thus the next *bri* instruction, referring to the same shared routine, is able to invoke it without the overhead of linking.

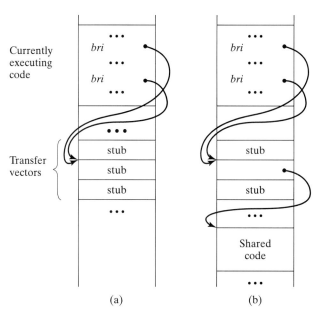

FIGURE 9-4. Dynamic linking through transfer vector.

CASE STUDY: DYNAMIC LINK LIBRARIES

Windows 2000 uses dynamic linking to implement all its application program inter-faces to the operating system, such as Win32 or POSIX. Each interface consists of code files, called **DLLs** (dynamic link libraries). There are several hundred different DLLs, each containing hundreds of library functions. Jointly, the DLLs provide the functionality of the system, from low-level operations on I/O devices to user-level functions to manipulate windows, menus, icons, fonts, cryptography, and many oth-ers. Because of the large numbers of DLLs each process could potentially include in its address space, the linker only sets up the transfer vector for the referenced DLLs, but the actual code is loaded and linked to the processes dynamically, only when actually needed.

9.4   SHARING IN SEGMENTED SYSTEMS

In general, sharing of segments is simpler and more elegant than sharing of pages because segments represent natural logical entities such as functions or data files, whereas page boundaries have no correlation with the program structure. The sharing of a segment in memory by two or more processes may be accomplished by pointing to that segment from entries in the different segment tables. These entries point to the absolute locations of the shared segments or, if the memory is also paged, to *shared* page tables.

9.4.1   Sharing of Code and Data

As in the case of paging, sharing of segments containing only *data* presents no serious problems. A shared data segment can have a different segment number assigned to it in each process segment table. The situation is analogous to that of Figure 9-3, but using segments instead of pages. With *code* segments, we face the same problem as with paging, where the shared segment must be able to reference itself correctly, while referring to dif-ferent stack and data segments, depending on the process under which the segment runs.

We can use the same basic approaches as with paging. The first is to require that all shared function segments have the *same* segment numbers in all virtual spaces. Different variants of this solution have been implemented in several contemporary systems.

CASE STUDY: SHARING OF SYSTEM SEGMENTS

The Intel Pentium processor supports a limited form of segment sharing based on designating a set of segment numbers as shared. The segment table of each process is divided into two halves, called LDT (local descriptor table) and GDT (global descriptor table). The entries in LDT corresponds to segments private to the process, whereas the entries in the GDT are shared among all processes in the system. The latter contain the OS and other sharable components. At runtime, one of the bits of the 14-bit segment number is used to choose between the two tables. The remaining 13 bits then select one of the 8K entries of the chosen table.

The second approach uses again different base registers. A code base register contains the segment number of the currently running process. All self-references by the shared segment are then relative to the current segment base register. For example, all branch addresses could have the form $w(CBR)$, where CBR designates the code base register, rather than (s, w), where s is the actual segment number. The offset w remains the same in both cases. In this way, the segment number is part of the invoking process state, rather than part of the code. Consequently, different processes may use different segment numbers for the same shared function.

Unfortunately, this still does not solve the sharing problem in its full generality. In particular, we must make the same assumption as with paging, namely that the shared segments are fully *self-contained*, i.e., they contain no references to other segments. To illustrate this restriction, consider the situation where a shared code segment, $C1$, must refer to another code segment, $C2$. Regardless of whether $C2$ also is shared or is private, $C1$ will refer to it by a segment number. This segment number must become part of the code since a base register cannot be used for an external reference. Consequently, all processes sharing $C1$, while able to use different segment numbers for $C1$, will have to use the same segment number for $C2$. This essentially limits the level of sharing to segments that are not nested, i.e., segments that do not invoke or access any other segments of their own.

9.4.2 Unrestricted Dynamic Linking

Unlike pure paging, segmentation lends itself to the implementation of a fully general scheme of *dynamic linking and sharing*, where *any* two processes (user or system) can share *any* portion of their spaces. Such a scheme was pioneered in the MULTICS operating system (Daley and Dennis 1968), and has subsequently been implemented in many different variations by other systems.

One of the main principles of dynamic linking is to give each segment its own *private* section, called the **linkage section**. This is similar to the transfer vector explained earlier, because it records the segment numbers of dynamically linked segments. Thus, no segment numbers appear directly in the code. This allows different processes to refer to the same segment using different segment numbers. But there is an important difference between linkage sections and the transfer vector: Each segment has its own linkage section while only a single transfer vector is provided for the entire process. The vector is set up statically by the linker; it contains an entry for every external segment (library) the process can ever access. In contrast, the linkage section of a segment records the external references for only that segment. Thus, as new segments are linked to a process, the process incrementally learns about new segments it may have to link to at future references. This allows shared segments to reference other segments of their own, which was not possible with the single static transfer vector.

To implement private linkage sections for each segment, base registers must be used for every process: A *code base register* always points to the beginning of the currently executing segment. All internal references (self-references) of the currently executing code segment are interpreted as offsets relative to this base register. A *linkage section base register* always points to the linkage section of the currently executing code segment. All external references are resolved using the contents of this linkage section. The contents of both of these registers change whenever the process transfers control to another code segment.

A *stack base register* is used for all references to the stack segment. For references to global data, a *data base register* could be used. Alternately, each code segment can reference various data segments using external references. Note that the contents of the base and data registers change only when the stack or data segments are relocated in memory (swapped out and reloaded at a different location) but otherwise remain unchanged for the lifetime of the process.

CASE STUDY: UNRESTRICTED DYNAMIC LINKING AND SHARING

The MULTICS system developed and implemented dynamic linking in its full generality. It allows code segments to reference other segments while avoiding the involvement of the OS at each external reference after it has been resolved for the first time.

Figure 9-5a illustrates the basic principles of this scheme. It shows a process, represented by its segment table. Segment i is the currently executing code segment C, and segment j is the linkage section associated with C. The linkage section was created originally by the compiler when segment C was compiled, and a private copy was made at the time the process linked to the segment C. The linkage section base register, LBR, points to this private copy, while the code base register, CBR, points to the code.

All self-references (i.e., branch instructions to within the current segment C) are relative to CBR. References to the stack segment are relative to SBR (not shown in the figure).

All external references by a segment remain in their *symbolic form* until they are actually needed during execution. At that time, they must be replaced by the corresponding virtual address of the referenced segment. The external references are kept in their symbolic form in a *symbol table*. In Figure 9-5a, we assume that the code C references another segment, S, at an offset W. Thus, the symbolic reference (S, W) is kept in C's symbol table.

The instruction that references this segment is set up by the compiler to point to the external reference via the linkage section. That means, the load instruction within C specifies the offset d. The l flag indicates that d is to be taken relative to the LBR, instead of one of the other base registers, and the star indicates that this is an indirect reference.

The entries in the linkage section consist of two parts: a reference to the symbolic name within the symbol table ((S, W) in the example), and a **trap bit**, initially set to one. When the load instruction is reached for the first time, it finds the trap bit set. The system traps to the OS. The OS invokes the dynamic linker which resolves the external reference as follows. It locates the segment using its symbolic name, S, and loads it into memory. Next it finds a free entry in the process segment table and assigns the corresponding segment number, s, to the new segment. It also translates the symbolic offset, W, into the corresponding numeric offset, w, using the process symbol table. The linker then replaces the entry in the linkage section with the virtual address (s, w) and turns off the trap bit.

Figure 9-5b shows the result of the above transformations. At this point, the segment C is ready to resume execution. The load instruction points to the same location within the linkage section as before. However, this location now contains a valid virtual address (s, w). Since the trap bit is off, the address is resolved by the normal

CASE STUDY: UNRESTRICTED DYNAMIC LINKING AND SHARING
(continued)

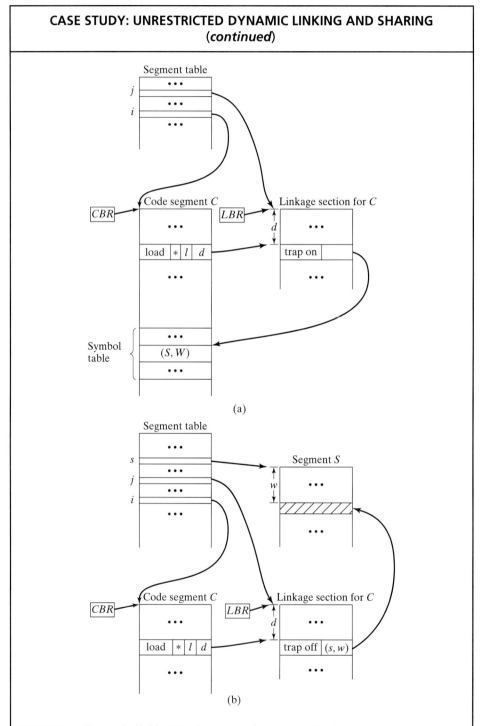

FIGURE 9-5. Dynamic linking/sharing: (a) before external references is executed; and
(b) after external references is executed.

> address translating mechanism using the segment table, which yields the desired location w within the segment s.

Note that the indirect addressing required by dynamic linking results in an additional memory access for every external reference. This is the price we must pay for supporting unrestricted sharing of segments among any subset of processes.

9.5   PRINCIPLES OF DISTRIBUTED SHARED MEMORY

The simplest computer architecture consists of a single processor and a single memory module. The previous sections of this chapter all assumed this type. The next level of complexity for a computer system is a multiprocessor, consisting of more than one processor, all sharing the same physical memory. The ability to run multiple programs at the same time complicates the scheduling and other tasks performed by the OS. It also results in a more complicated programming model, because individual applications can take advantage of multiprocessing to speed up their execution. But since they all share the same memory, programming for physical parallelism is no more difficult than programming for logical parallelism. In both the uniprocessor and multiprocessor cases, programs cannot make any assumptions about the sequence in which the various parallel components will be executed, and thus, must include adequate synchronization constructs to assure that CS and other dependencies are obeyed.

The level of complexity rises dramatically when the different processes do not share the same physical memory. In addition to synchronization, the user must now worry about the *location* of code and data in the different memory modules. In particular, any program or process must have all data it needs for its execution in the local memory of the processor on which it is executing. Since some pieces of data are needed by more than one process, the data must be sent between the processors when requested at runtime. This requires the use of message-passing, such as send/receive primitives, which is significantly more difficult and slower than just reading and writing memory directly.

Distributed Shared Memory (DSM) was proposed initially by Li (1986) and later refined by Li and Hudak (1989). The main objective of DSM is to alleviate the burden on the programmer by hiding the fact that physical memory is distributed and not accessible in its entirety to all processors. DSM creates the illusion of a single shared memory, much like a virtual memory creates the illusion of a memory that is larger than the available physical memory. This is accomplished in the following way. When a processor generates an address that maps into its own physical space, the referenced item is accessed locally. When it maps into a memory module belonging to another processor, the OS first transfers the needed data to the requesting processor's memory where it is then accessed locally. In general, the programmer does not have to be aware that data is being passed around using messages. However, given the great overhead of message-passing, sending individual words of data at each memory access would render this scheme too slow to be of any practical value.

To make the basic idea of DSM viable, the underlying data transfers must be done much more efficiently. Two possibilities have been suggested. One is to try to *optimize* the implementation, for example, by exploiting locality of reference or by using data replications. The other approach is to *restrict* the full generality of the DSM at the user level. Specifically, we can permit the sharing of only certain portions of the memory space, or we can relax the semantics of the DSM such that it does not mimic the behavior of a physically shared memory in its full generality. The following section discusses these options and trade-offs that make DSM a practical concept. It is convenient to introduce them from the viewpoint of the user or programmer.

9.5.1   The User's View of Distributed Shared Memory

Section 8.2 described the two principal schemes for presenting main memory to a user: The first is a single, linear address region, implemented as contiguous space in physical memory or as a collection of pages. The second method provides multiple segments to better reflect the program structure. The choice of memory structure has important implications for sharing. As was discussed in Section 9.4, sharing of segments is generally easier than the sharing of pages.

Since a DSM is by definition concerned with sharing, the choice of structure becomes even more important. The main questions are:

- Which portions of memory are shared and which portions are private among the different processors?

- Is the sharing fully transparent, i.e., does the logically shared portion of the memory behave exactly as if it was shared physically, or must the user do anything special to accomplish the sharing?

The choices are between a fully shared, unstructured memory and a partially shared, structured one.

Unstructured Distributed Shared Memory

The basic philosophy of this approach is to simulate the behavior of a single, physically shared memory. That means, from the user's point of view, there is only a single linear address space, and it is accessed by all processors in the system concurrently. Figure 9-6 illustrates this choice of memory structure. The shared memory is the union of the individual physical memories, MMi, belonging to the different processors, Pi. Under this scheme,

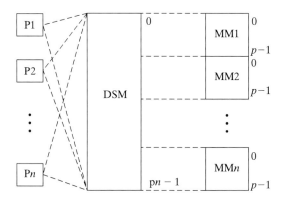

FIGURE 9-6. Unstructured DSM.

each processor can generate addresses in the range from 0 to $pn - 1$, where p is the size of each physical memory module (assumed all the same size here) and n is the number of modules. The underlying implementation translates these addresses to the appropriate physical memories. This creates the illusion of a virtual memory that is larger than the local physical memory, much like virtual memory implemented with paging. The main, and very important, difference between paging and this form of DSM is that the virtual space is not private with DSM but is accessible by all the other processors in the system.

The principal advantage of this unstructured organization is that the existence of physically disjoint memory modules is *fully transparent* to the user. That means, a concurrent program written for a system with a single physical memory can execute on a system using this form of DSM without any modifications. Concurrent computations also can communicate and coordinate their operations using this DSM. For example, semaphores can be used to synchronize access to CSs, and shared memory areas can be used to exchange data; there is no need to use any form of message-passing.

One drawback of such a fully transparent DSM, where the entire space is shared, is *efficiency*. Since each processor can access any address in the entire DSM, every instruction fetch or operand read/write potentially generates an access to a nonlocal memory module. Transferring each data item individually and on demand through the network is obviously not a viable approach. Section 9.6.1 outlines various ways to make this form of DSM practical.

Structured Distributed Shared Memory

Most programs are structured internally as collections of functions and data structures (variables). Those parts of a program to be shared with other objects usually coincide with the program's logical decomposition. In general, only specific functions and data structures must be shared. Since it is the programmer who decides what is to be shared and by whom, it is not unreasonable to require that the programmer specify this information explicitly. This can be done at the programming language level by defining some additional notations to indicate those functions or data structures that are private and those that are sharable.

Figure 9-7 illustrates this shift of paradigm. It shows a system of multiple processors, each with its own private physical memory. The logical address space available to the processor can be equal to the physical memory, or, if virtual memory is implemented locally, the logical space can be larger than the physical memory. The important fact is that some portion(s) of each of the logical spaces are shared among *all* processors. This shared portion is the DSM. When any of the processors writes into this portion of memory, the change becomes visible automatically and transparently by all the other processors, just as if the shared portion was implemented as a physically shared memory module.

This organization essentially segregates shared and nonshared variables, and is the first step toward a more efficient implementation of DSM. But it still requires too many data transfers between the processors. Thus, most systems impose additional restrictions on the use of the shared variables. The standard technique is to allow access to any shared variable only within CSs, which must be declared explicitly. Since CSs are by definition mutually exclusive, propagating the modifications of any of the shared variables can be limited to two well-defined points: either at the *beginning* or at the *end* of the CS. This idea leads to new forms of memory consistency, treated in Section 9.6.2, and results in greatly improved performance of the DSM.

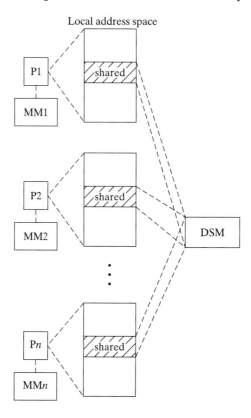

FIGURE 9-7. Structured DSM.

An attractive variant of the basic structured DSM is to use *objects* instead of just passive variables. Object-oriented programs are structured as collections of objects, whose functions are invoked from a main function or from other objects. This logical structuring provides a very natural basis for sharing. Whenever two processes execute the functions of a given object, they manipulate the same copy of the data; i.e., they are sharing the object.

This form of object sharing can be implemented transparently in an architecture where multiple processors do not share any physical memory. The resulting object-based DSM hides the fact that objects are distributed over multiple disjoint memory modules by providing the necessary mechanisms to access the remote objects.

9.6 IMPLEMENTATIONS OF DISTRIBUTED SHARED MEMORY

9.6.1 Implementing Unstructured Distributed Shared Memory

When a process references a data item that is not present in its local physical memory, it causes a fault. In response, the DSM runtime system must locate the missing data item and transfer it to the faulting process' local memory. There are several fundamental questions that lead to different schemes for building unstructured DSM. The key issues are the granularity of data transfers, replication of data, memory consistency, and keeping track of the data throughout the system.

Granularity of Data Transfers

It would be grossly inefficient to move each referenced data item individually through a network. Due to program locality, it is likely that a process will reference other data items in the vicinity of the currently accessed item. Thus, transferring a sequential block of data surrounding a missing data item is more efficient than transferring the data by itself.

The *size* of the data block is critical to performance, and its selection follows the same logic of that for choosing a page size (Section 8.3.4). In a memory system that uses paging, a natural choice for a DSM implementation is to use the existing page size as the granularity for transferring referenced data between processors. However, although transferring data through local networks is generally faster than from even local disks, the startup cost of a network transfer is very high. To amortize this overhead, some DSM systems choose multiple pages as the basic unit of transfer whenever a page fault occurs. Just like a larger page size, this increases network traffic. But, the more serious drawback of such increased granularity is a phenomenon called **false sharing**. It occurs when two unrelated variables, each accessed by a different process, end up on the same page or set of pages being transferred between memories. This causes a situation analogous to thrashing, where the pages are transferred back and forth as the two processes reference their respective variables. Obviously, the larger the unit of transfer, the greater the chance for unrelated variables to become transferred together.

Replication of Data

The second fundamental decision to be made when implementing a DSM concerns the possible **replication** of shared pages. That means, when a page fault occurs, should the requested page be actually *moved* from the remote to the requesting processor, or should only a *copy* of the page be transferred. The obvious advantages of maintaining multiple copies of a page are decreased network traffic, less thrashing, and reduced delays resulting from page faults, since any page only must be transferred once. The main problem is how to maintain consistency in the presence of multiple copies. Whenever a process modifies a shared page, the change must be made visible to all other processes using that page. The time at which the changes become visible is crucial to preserving the correctness of the programs. Figure 9-8 illustrates the problem. It shows two computations, p_1 and p_2, reading a shared variable x. Depending on the application, p_1 and p_2 could be independent processes or concurrent branches or threads of a common program.

At time $t1$, p_1 writes a 1 into x. At time $t2$, both processes read x. We would naturally expect that the values of $a1$ and $a2$ will both be 1, i.e., the most recently written value. Similarly, the values of $b1$ and $b2$ read by the processes at time $t4$ should both be 2, since this was the most recently written value written into x (by process p_1).

Ensuring that these expectations will be met in the case where each process is running on a different processor and the variable x is replicated in the corresponding local memories is a difficult problem. It is similar to the problem of maintaining cache

```
initial: x = 0
real time:    t1         t2          t3        t4
p1:      {    x = 1;     a1 = x;     x = 2;    b1 = x;}
p2:      {               a2 = x;               b2 = x;}
```

FIGURE 9-8. Example of strict consistency.

Operation	Page Location	Page Status	Actions Taken Before Local Read/Write
read	local	read-only	
write	local	read-only	invalidate remote copies; upgrade local copy to writable
read	remote	read-only	make local read-only copy
write	remote	read-only	invalidate remote copies; make local writable copy
read	local	writable	
write	local	writable	
read	remote	writable	downgrade page to read-only; make local read-only copy
write	remote	writable	transfer remote writable copy to local memory

FIGURE 9-9. Protocol for handling DSM pages.

coherence in a multiprocessor system, where each processor keeps copies of the most recently accessed data items in its local cache. The solution to the cache coherence problem is to broadcast all write operations performed by any processor to all others. The receivers of the broadcast then either **update** all copies of the same data item held in any of the caches, or they **invalidate** these entries so that the updated value needs to be reloaded from memory.

The solutions to cache coherence require a hardware broadcast that performs the updates or invalidation atomically. Unfortunately, DSMs are implemented in software, generally on top of existing OSs; and thus performing an atomic broadcast each time a variable is modified would render the DSM hopelessly inefficient. One practical method differentiates between **read-only** and **writable** pages. Consistency is preserved if only a single copy of any writable page is maintained, while allowing read-only pages to be replicated freely. Unfortunately, it is not always known in advance which pages will be modified and which will only be read, and thus we must permit pages to change their state between *read-only* and *writable* during execution. There are different protocols to assure consistency during such transitions. One popular representative is based on the rules given in Figure 9-9. This specifies the actions that must be taken, based on the current operation (*read* or *write*), the location of the page (*local* or *remote*), and the state of the page (*read-only* or *writable*). The following example illustrates the use of these rules.

EXAMPLE: Structured DSM Operations

Figure 9-10 shows two processors accessing two pages, A and B, in the DSM. Page A is writable and resides in P1's physical memory MM1. Page B is read-only, and each processor has a copy in its own physical memory. The following table shows certain operations performed by a processor and the corresponding actions taken by the system.

P1 reads A	operation is done locally
P1 writes A	operation is done locally (page is writable)
P1 writes B	invalidate copy in MM2; upgrade copy in MM1 to writable
P2 reads A	downgrade page in MM1 to read only; make copy in MM2
P2 writes A	transfer page from MM1 to MM2

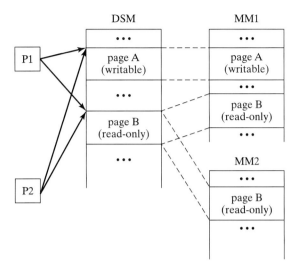

FIGURE 9-10. Example of page operations.

The above protocol treats the DSM coherence problem like the readers-writers problem in Section 3.3.1. That means, it allows multiple concurrent readers or a single writer to access the same data page. But in doing so, it must delay certain read/write operations until the intentions have been communicated to remote processors and the necessary changes prescribed by the rules of Figure 9-9 have been made. Specifically, when a read operation for a remote writable page has been issued, the current owner of the page will continue writing until it has been notified of the intended read. Consequently, the read operation will see a value that has been written later in real time. This could not occur if the memory was shared physically. Similarly, a write operation to a remote page will be delayed until all remote copies have been invalidated. In the meantime, the remote processes may be reading the current values. Again, a physically shared memory would automatically prevent any such delayed writes from occurring.

As a result, executing the same program on a system with physically shared memory could yield different results than executing it on a system with DSM. One way to make this behavior acceptable is to adopt a different model of memory consistency for the shared memory, that relaxes the requirements on how the DSM must behave with respect to real time yet still mirrors reality and intuition. We describe this **sequential consistency** model next.

Strict Versus Sequential Consistency

Most programs do not rely on real-time for their synchronization. When two branches of a program have been designated as concurrent, for example, using some of the constructs discussed in Chapter 2, the assumption is that these branches are independent. Consequently, they remain correct regardless of whether they are executed in parallel, in sequence (in either order), or by arbitrarily interleaving their instructions. When a particular ordering of instructions is required, it must be enforced explicitly by synchronization commands, such as semaphores or message-passing.

```
initial: x = 0
(a) p1:  {                        x = 1;    a1 = x;   x = 2;    b1 = x;}
    p2:  { a2 = x;      b2 = x;}

(b) p1:  {                        x = 1;    a1 = x;   x = 2;    b1 = x;}
    p2:  { a2 = x;                          b2 = x;}

(c) p1:  { x = 1;                 a1 = x;   x = 2;    b1 = x;}
    p2:  {                        a2 = x;                      b2 = x;}
```

FIGURE 9-11. Examples of possible instruction interleaving.

Consider the example of Figure 9-8. Except in very special situations of dedicated real-time systems, the two processes p_1 and p_2 should not rely on the fact that both perform the read operations at exactly the same point in real time. Thus, unless explicit synchronization constructs are included, the instructions of p_1 and p_2 could be interleaved in many different ways. Figure 9-11 shows examples of three possible interleavings. In all three cases, p_1 will see $a1 = 1$ and $b1 = 2$, since these were the values it wrote into x just prior to the reads. Any other behavior of the memory would not be acceptable. For p_2, however, the situation is different. In case (a), it will see $a2 = b2 = 0$ because p_1 has not yet overwritten the initial value. In case (b), p_2 will see $a2 = 0$ and $b2 = 1$. In case (c), it will see $a2 = 1$ and $b2 = 2$—the same values as read by p_1.

Based on the above observations, we can now formulate two different forms of memory consistency models for DSM (Lamport 1979):

- **Strict consistency:** A DSM is said to obey strict consistency if reading a variable x always returns the value written to x by the most recently executed write operation.

- **Sequential consistency:** A DSM is said to obey sequential consistency if the sequence of values read by the different processes corresponds to some sequential interleaved execution of the same processes.

To illustrate the difference, consider Figure 9-8 once again. Under strict consistency, both processes must see $x = 1$ with their first read operation and $x = 2$ with the second. The reason is that, for both processes, the first read operation (issued at real time $t2$) was executed after the write operation (issued at real time $t1$). In contrast, the same sequence of instructions executed under sequential consistency is considered correct as long as:

1. The two read operations of p_1 always return the values 1 and 2, respectively.
2. The two read operations of p_2 return any of the following combinations of values: 0 0, 0 1, 1 1, 1 2, 2 2.

The sequential consistency model is the most widely used model implemented for unstructured DSMs. It satisfies the intuitive expectations placed on memory for distributed programming. At the same time, it lends itself to a much more efficient implementation than the strict consistency model, since the results of write operations may be propagated to remote memories with delays and without compromising program correctness.

Finding Pages

When pages are allowed to migrate among the different processors, some mechanisms must be implemented to allow a processor to find the page it wishes to access. With replication, the problem is complicated further by the fact that multiple copies of the same page exists, all of which must be found when a write operation must invalidate them. The replication problem is usually solved by designating one of the processors as the **owner** of a given page and adopting the following policy.

When the page is writable, there is only one copy, and hence the processor currently holding the page is by default the owner. When a page is degraded to read-only, a copy is made for the requesting processor, but the ownership remains with the original owner. This owner keeps track of all the copies made of this page by maintaining a list, called the **copy set**, of all processors who requested a read-only copy. The page ownership is transferred to another processor only when a write request is received. In this case, all processors on the copy set are sent a message to invalidate their copies; this can be done by the original or the new owner. When this is completed, the new owner can write into the page. The owner also becomes responsible for maintaining the new copy set whenever another processor requests a read access to the page.

Several different schemes have been proposed for finding a page owner (Li and Hudak 1989). The simplest uses **broadcasting**. Whenever a processor must access a page that is currently not it its local memory, it broadcasts the request to all other processors in the system. The current owner then responds by transferring the page to the requesting processor. The main drawback of this method is the overhead resulting from the various broadcasts, each of which interrupts all processors.

Another simple technique designates one processor as a **central manager** to keep track of the current location of all pages. Unfortunately, the central manager is likely to become a bottleneck, rendering this solution not scalable. A **replicated manager** approach can alleviate the problem; here, several processors serve as managers, each responsible for a designated subset of the pages.

The last scheme is based on the concept of a **probable owner**. Each processor keeps track of all pages in the system using a data structure similar to a page table in a virtual memory system. For local pages, the corresponding entry in this table points to the page in local memory. When a page is transferred to another processor, say P, the table entry records P and the new owner of the page also becomes P. When the original processor must access the page again, it will send the request to the processor whose address it had recorded as the new owner. Unfortunately, the page may have migrated on to other processors in the meantime. Each migration would record the address of a new owner in its own table. A desired page can be found by following the chain of addresses, each pointing to the next probable owner. To make subsequent accesses to the same page less costly, the chain can be dissolved by making all probable-owner pointers point to the last node along the chain, i.e., the actual current owner.

Unstructured DSM implementations assume that all variables in the shared space are consistent at all times. This involves moving and/or invalidating pages whenever the access to a page changes from reading to writing or vice versa. Much network traffic can be generated, resulting in poor performance. The alternative, structured DSM, requires a new model of memory consistency.

9.6.2 Implementing Structured Distributed Shared Memory

Distributed Shared Memory with Weak Consistency

Weak consistency (Dubois et al. 1988) is based on the premise that the user knows and can identify those points in a distributed program where shared variables must be brought into a consistent state. To do this, a new type of variable, a **synchronization variable**, is introduced. Only when the concurrent processes access this shared variable are the effects of the various local write operations propagated to other processes, thereby bringing the shared memory into a consistent state. In other words, the DSM is guaranteed to be in a consistent state only immediately following the access to a synchronization variable.

EXAMPLE: Weak Memory Consistency

Figure 9-12 illustrates the principles using two concurrent processes p_1 and p_2, and a synchronization variable. Both processes independently modify a shared variable x, and subsequently read it. Since each process has its local copy of x (step 1 in Fig. 9-12), the modifications remain local until the shared memory is explicitly synchronized. Thus the value $a1$ (written by p_1) will be 1, whereas the value of $a2$ (written by p_2) will be 2. After both processes execute the synchronization S, the values of all shared variables are exchanged among the processes and a consistent state is established (step 2 in the figure). Therefore, the results of all read operations immediately following the synchronization will be identical in all processes. That means, both $b1$ and $b2$ will either contain the value 1 or the value 2, depending on the results of the consistency exchanges (step 2).

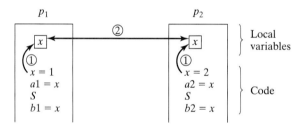

FIGURE 9-12. Weak memory consistency.

Distributed Shared Memory with Release or Entry Consistency

In many applications, the number of shared variables is small. By requiring the user to explicitly identify which variables are shared, we can dramatically reduce the amount of data that must be moved and/or invalidated by the DSM implementation. Furthermore, shared variables are typically accessed only within CSs. Since CSs are by definition mutually exclusive, only one process can read or write the shared data. Thus, there is no need to propagate any writes when the process is inside the CS. All we must guarantee is that such shared variables are consistent whenever a process is about to enter a CS. The exchanges can be performed at the **exit** or the **entry** point of a CS. The following example illustrates the first choice.

EXAMPLE: Release Memory Consistency

Figure 9-13 illustrates the first option. Assuming that p_1 enters the critical section before p_2 by executing the *lock* operation first (implemented, for example, using a spinning lock or a semaphore), it writes 1 into x (step 1) and then exits the critical section by executing *unlock*. The modified variables are exported to all other processes at the end of the CS (step 2). Then a is assigned the new value of 1 (step 3).

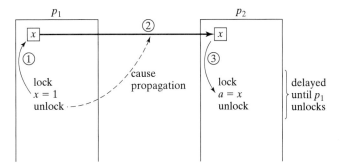

FIGURE 9-13. Release memory consistency.

This model, referred to as **release consistency** (Gharachorloo 1990) is straightforward but is wasteful in that the modifications are exported to all processes, regardless of which, if any, will be accessing them next. The unnecessary overhead can be eliminated by performing the exchange at the *entry* point to the CS, instead of the exit.

EXAMPLE: Entry Memory Consistency

Figure 9-14 illustrates this option. We again assume that p_1 executes the *lock* operation before p_2 and updates x (step 1). The *lock* operation of p_2 then causes the value of x to be brought up to date (step 2) prior to entering the CS and reading x (step 3).

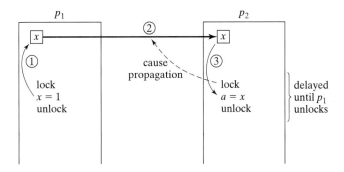

FIGURE 9-14. Entry memory consistency.

The above form of consistency comes in two forms: **lazy release consistency** (Keleher et al. 1992) or **entry consistency** (Bershad 1993). The difference between the two is that the former imports *all* shared variables whereas the latter associates each shared variable with a lock variable and imports only those shared variables pertaining to the current lock. In situations where a process repeatedly enters the same CS, no data is exchanged until another process wishes to enter the same CS.

Object-Based Distributed Shared Memory

Using especially designated variables as the basis for sharing reduces the amount of data that must be moved between processors. But for a shared variable to be accessible by a processor, it must be transferred or copied into the processor's local memory. With objects, the situation is different. There is no need to transfer a remote object into local memory to access the data it encapsulates. This is because the functions or methods that access the data are always part of the object. If the system provides the ability to perform *remote* methods invocation, similar to remote procedure calls as discussed in Chapter 3, then the DSM implementation can choose between moving an object, copying it, or accessing it remotely, to maximize performance.

When objects are replicated, maintaining consistency again becomes an issue. We can implement a scheme similar to that used for page-based DSMs, where read-only accesses can proceed concurrently while a write access invalidates all replicas of the corresponding object. Alternatively, because of the ability to invoke methods remotely, a write access can be sent and executed remotely at all replicas, rather than invalidating them. This corresponds to the update protocol implemented in some caches, but requires a reliable atomic broadcast capability, which is costly to implement.

CONCEPTS, TERMS, AND ABBREVIATIONS

The following concepts have been introduced in this chapter. Test yourself by defining and discussing each keyword or phrase.

Consistency in DSM	Replicated pages in DSM
Distributed shared memory (DSM)	Segmented systems sharing
Dynamic linking and sharing	Sequential consistency
Dynamic link libraries (DLL)	Single-copy sharing
Entry consistency	Static linking and sharing
False sharing	Strict consistency
Linkage section	Structured DSM
Object-based DSM	Unstructured DSM
Paged systems sharing	Weak consistency
Release consistency	

EXERCISES

1. Consider the problems of static sharing in a purely paged system. Assume a process p_a requires programs Q_1 and Q_2, temporary storage T_1, and data D_1, of size q_1, q_2, t_1, and d_1, respectively, in pages. These are combined and linked into a virtual space program of size $q_1 + q_2 + t_1 + d_1$ pages in the above order and loaded into memory.

While p_a is still active, another process p_b requests loading of information Q_1', Q_2, T_1', and D_1 with page sizes q_1', q_2, t_1', and d_1, respectively, where $q_1' \le q_1$ and $t_1' > t_1$. Q_2 and D_1 are to be shared between p_a and p_b.

(a) Show the page tables for the two processes.

(b) What problem arises if a new process p_c now enters the system and wants to share Q_1 and Q_1'?

2. Consider two processes p_1 and p_2 in a purely segmented system. Their current segment tables contain the following entries:

	ST1
0	4000
1	6000
2	9000
3	2000
4	7000

	ST2
0	2000
1	6000
2	9000

(a) Which segments are shared?

(b) Which of the following virtual addresses would be illegal in the segment at location 6000: (0,0) (1,0) (2,0) (3,0) (4,0) (5,0)?

(c) The segment at location 7000 is swapped out and later reloaded at location 8000. Similarly, segment at location 2000 is swapped out and reloaded at 1000. Show the new segment tables.

(d) A third process p_3 wishes to share the segments at locations 2000, 4000, and 5000. Which of these must be data segments (rather than code segments) to make this possible?

3. Consider a system with segmentation (no paging). Two processes, p_1 and p_2, are currently running. Their respective segment tables have the following contents:

	ST1
0	1251
1	0
2	810
3	145
4	2601
5	380

	ST2
0	512
1	1020
2	1477
3	145
4	1251
5	380
6	3500

Make the following assumptions:

- p_1 is currently executing in its segment 2;
- p_2 is currently executing in its segment 1;
- base registers are used for all self-references (references to the current segment).

Assume that both processes references the following virtual addresses, where "*BR, n*" denotes a self-reference (an offset n relative to base register BR):

$$(3, 0), (5, 20), (4, 5), (6, 10), (\text{BR}, 0), (\text{BR}, 10)$$

Translate each virtual address into the corresponding physical address for both processes p_1 and p_2. If an address is illegal, indicate so.

4. Consider a system with unrestricted dynamic linking. The memory snapshot below shows the various segments of a process p_1. Make the following assumptions:
   - The segment table of the process p_1 begins at address 1000. (The segment table is not paged.)
   - The process is currently executing inside segment 3, which is a code segment.
   - Segment 4 is the symbol table corresponding to segment 3.
   - Segment 5 is the current linkage section.
   - The segments named $D1$ and $D2$ are already in memory, residing at addresses 400 and 600, respectively.

```
        ┌─────────────────────────────┐
        │              ⋮              │
1000    ├─────────────────────────────┤
        │              ⋮              │
1003    │           5000              │
1004    │           8000              │
1005    │           9000              │
1006    │           free              │
1007    │           free              │
        │                             │
        │              ⋮              │
5000    ├──────────────────           │
        │              ⋮              │
        │  ┌──────┬───┬───┬───┐        │
        │  │ load │ * │ 1 │ 3 │        │
        │  └──────┴───┴───┴───┘        │
        │              ⋮              │
        │  ┌──────┬───┬───┬───┐        │
        │  │ store│ * │ 1 │ 0 │        │
        │  │ store│ * │ 1 │ 3 │        │
        │  └──────┴───┴───┴───┘        │
        │              ⋮              │
8000    │         D1,33               │
8001    │         D2,25               │
        │              ⋮              │
9000    │ trap-on          │    1     │
        │              ⋮              │
9003    │ trap-on          │    0     │
        │              ⋮              │
        └─────────────────────────────┘
```

(a) What are the current contents of the code base register (*CBR*), linkage pointer register (*LBR*), and segment table register (*STR*)?

(b) What other segments does the currently executing code segment reference? What are their symbolic names and entry point offsets?

(c) Show all changes to the memory after each of the three instructions (load, store, and store) are executed.

(d) Consider a second process p_2 wishing to share the code segment at address 5000 (and all other segments referenced by this segment). Assume that the segment table of p_2 begins at address 2000 and already contains 5 segment entries. Assume further that the linkage section of p_2 begins at address 3000. Show all changes to the memory *before* and *after* p_2 executes the code segment.

5. Consider two concurrent processes, p_1 and p_2, running on two different processors and sharing a two-dimensional array $A[n, n]$ kept in a page-based DSM. Make the following assumptions:
   - Each processor has enough memory to hold the entire array A.
   - Initially, the array is split evenly over the local memories of the two processors (processor 1 holds the first $n/2$ rows, processor 2 holds the remaining $n/2$ rows).
   - The page size used by the memory system is n.
   - The array is stored in row-major.
   - Each process must access every element of the array exactly once (reading or writing it).
   - A page is transferred instantaneously (no overhead) as soon as any element of that page is referenced.

   (a) Approximately how many pages will have to be transferred between the two processors in each of the following cases:
   - **i.** only one of the processes runs; it accesses A in row-major.
   - **ii.** both processes access A concurrently in row-major; both start with element $A[0, 0]$.
   - **iii.** both processes access A concurrently in row-major; both start with element $A[0, 0]$ but the execution of p_2 is delayed by n steps.
   - **iv.** both processes access A concurrently in row-major; p_1 starts with element $A[0, 0]$ while p_2 starts with element $A[n - 1, n - 1]$.
   - **v.** both processes access A concurrently in column-major; both start with element $A[0, 0]$.

   How would your answers to the preceding questions change if:
   (b) all accesses to the array A were read-only.
   (c) a larger or smaller page size was used.

6. Consider a page-based DSM that obeys the protocol of Figure 9-9. Assume there are three processes, p_1, p_2, and p_3, all accessing a single shared page. Give the actions carried out by the DSM implementation for the following sequence of operations. (Assume the page p is currently writable in p_1's local memory.)
   - p_1 writes p
   - p_2 reads p
   - p_3 reads p
   - p_1 reads p
   - p_2 writes p
   - p_3 writes p

7. Consider two processes p_1 and p_2 sharing a single variable x.
   (a) Give a sequence of read and write operations by the two processes that obeys sequential consistency but violates strict consistency.
   (b) Is it possible to construct such a sequence under the following assumptions:
   - **i.** process p_1 only reads while process p_2 only writes
   - **ii.** both processes only read
   - **iii.** both processes only write

8. Consider two concurrent processes, p_1 and p_2, performing the following operations on two shared variables, x and y:

```
initial: x = 0; y = 0;
p1: { x = 1; a1 = y; b1 = x; }
p2: { y = 1; a2 = x; b2 = y; }
```

At the end of the execution, the value of each of the local variables a_1, b_1, a_2, and b_2 can be zero or one. For the 16 possible combinations of these values, determine which ones are valid under sequential consistency.

9. Consider two concurrent processes, p_1 and p_2, performing the following operations on two shared variables, x and y:

```
initial: x = 0; y = 0;
p1: { x = 1; y = 1; }
p2: { a1 = x; a2 = y; S; a3 = x; a4 = y; }
```

At the end of the execution, the value of each of the local variables a_1, a_2, a_3, and a_4 can be zero or one. For the 16 possible combinations of these values, determine which ones are valid under weak consistency, where S is the synchronization statement.

PART THREE

FILE SYSTEMS AND INPUT/OUTPUT

CHAPTER 10

File Systems

Given that main memory is volatile, i.e., does not retain information when power is turned off, and is also limited in size, any computer system must be equipped with secondary memory on which the user and the system may keep information for indefinite periods of time. By far the most popular secondary memory devices are disks for random access purposes and magnetic tapes for sequential, archival storage. Since these devices are very complex to interact with, and, in multiuser systems are shared among different users, operating systems (OS) provide extensive services for managing data on secondary memory. These data are organized into *files*, which are collections of data elements grouped together for the purposes of access control, retrieval, and modification.

A *file system* is the part of the operating system that is responsible for managing files and the resources on which these reside. Without a file system, efficient computing would essentially be impossible. This chapter discusses the organization of file systems and the tasks performed by the different components. The first part is concerned with general user and implementation aspects of file management emphasizing centralized systems; the last sections consider extensions and methods for distributed systems.

10.1 BASIC FUNCTIONS OF FILE MANAGEMENT

The file system, in collaboration with the I/O system, has the following three basic functions:

1. Present a *logical* or *abstract view* of files and directories to the users by hiding the physical details of secondary storage devices and the I/O operations for communicating with the devices.

2. Facilitate *efficient use* of the underlying storage devices.

3. Support the *sharing of files* among different users and applications. This includes providing *protection* mechanisms to ensure that information is exchanged in a controlled and secure manner.

The first function exists because physical device interfaces are very complex. They also change frequently as new devices replace outdated ones. The I/O system, discussed in Chapter 11, provides the first level of abstraction on top of the hardware devices. It presents an interface where devices may be viewed as *collections or streams of logical blocks*, which can be accessed sequentially or directly, depending on the type of device.

This level of abstraction is still too low for most applications, which must manipulate data in terms of named collections of data records—**files**—and organize these into various hierarchical structures using **directories** (sometimes called **folders**). Thus, the role of the files system is to extend the logical I/O device abstraction to a file-level abstraction.

A file is defined as a set of related data items, called **logical records**. It is largely independent of the medium on which it is stored. The logical record is the smallest addressable unit within a file. The purpose of the file concept is to give users one simple uniform linear space for their code and data. Files and records within files then may be manipulated via a set of high-level operations defined by the **file system interface**, whose implementation is hidden from the user by the file system.

The second goal and function of a file system is the efficient use of storage devices on which files that may belong to many different users are kept. Unlike main memory, which has no moving parts and where access to any location takes the same amount of time, most secondary memory devices are electromechanical, are much slower than main memory, and have data access times that depend greatly on the data location on the device. For example, a disk access may or may not require a seek operation, i.e., the physical movement of the read/write head, depending on the head's current position. Since each seek is very time-consuming, the file system must strive for placing data items in such a way as to minimize the read/write head movements. As discussed in Chapter 11, the I/O system then may provide additional optimizations, for example by dynamically reordering the disk accesses to minimize the distance traveled by the read/write head. The situation is even more critical with tapes and other one-dimensional storage devices, where data can be accessed effectively only in the order in which they appear on the tape. The file system must ensure that a data placement appropriate for the underlying storage device is chosen for any given file.

The third reason for providing a file system is to facilitate file sharing. This is similar to the sharing of code and data in main memory, where two or more processes have simultaneous access to the same portion of main memory. The main difference is that files, unlike main memory information, generally persist in the secondary memory even when its owner or creator is not currently active, e.g., the owner may be logged out. Thus, sharing of files may not be concurrent. A process may wish to access a file written earlier by another process that no longer exists. The key issue is protection, i.e., controlling the type of access to a file permitted by a given process or user.

In this chapter, we are concerned primarily with the first two functions of a file system, which address the need for making details of the physical storage devices transparent to users and their programs. The problems of protection and security are treated separately in Chapters 12 and 13.

10.2   HIERARCHICAL MODEL OF A FILE SYSTEM

The file system, like any other complex software system, can be decomposed into several distinct parts according to primary function. We will adopt a hierarchical organization,

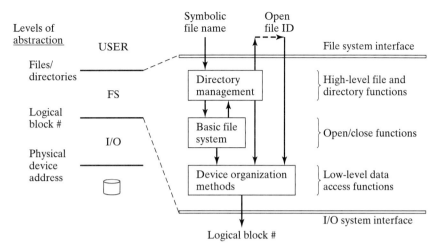

FIGURE 10-1. A hierarchical view of the file system.

where each level represents a successively more abstract machine in which a module at a given level may call upon the service of only modules at the same or lower levels. Although not all file systems are designed according to a strict hierarchy, this conceptual view is useful because it permits us to understand the complex functionalities of the file system and its interfaces to both the user and the I/O system by studying each level in isolation.

Figure 10-1 shows the organization. The left-hand side illustrates the file system's position as a layer between the user and the I/O system. For the user, it creates the abstraction of logical files, which can be manipulated and organized using various file and directory commands presented in Sections 10.3.4 and 10.4.2. It manages these on the underlying disks and other secondary memory devices by calling upon the services of the I/O system and exchanging data with it using logical block numbers. The responsibility of the I/O system is to translate the logical block numbers into actual disk or tape addresses.

The remainder of Figure 10-1 shows the file system subdivided into three main components in a hierarchy. Below, we briefly outline the tasks within each level, proceeding from the abstract user interface down to the file system and I/O interface. Succeeding sections describe the functions of each level in more detail.

The File System Interface

The file system presents the abstraction of a **logical file** to the user, and defines a set of operations to use and manipulate these. It also provides a way to organize individual files into groups and to keep track of them using **directories**. Typically, a file can be identified using two forms of names, depending on the operation to be performed on that file. A **symbolic name**, chosen by the user at file creation, is used to find a file in a directory. It also is used when manipulating the file as a whole, e.g., to rename or delete it. Symbolic names, however, are not convenient to use within programs, especially when used repeatedly. Thus, operations that access the file data (notably read and write operations) use a numeric identifier for the file. This is generated by lower levels of the file system. When a desired file is first opened by setting up data structures necessary to facilitate its access, an identifier, the **open file ID** (Fig. 10-1), is returned and used for subsequent read, write, and other data manipulation operations. Note that the symbolic name remains valid even when the file is not in use, whereas the open file ID is only temporary. It is valid only when the process that opened the file remains active or until the file is explicitly closed.

Directory Management

The primary function of this level is to use the symbolic file name to retrieve the **descriptive information** necessary to manipulate the file. This information is then passed to the basic file system module, which opens the file for access and returns the corresponding open file ID to the directory management module. Depending on the user-level command being processed, the open file ID may be returned to the user for subsequent read/write access to the file, or it may be used by the directory management module itself. For example, a search through the hierarchy structure requires that the directory management repeatedly opens and reads subdirectories to find a desired file. At each step of the search, the directory management routines must call upon the lower-level basic file system to open these subdirectories.

Basic File System

This part activates and deactivates files by invoking **opening** and **closing** routines. It is also responsible for verifying the **access rights** of the caller on each file request. The basic file system maintains information about all open files in main memory data structures called **open file tables** (OFT). The open file ID that is returned to the caller when a file is opened points directly to the corresponding entry in an open file table. Using this ID instead of the symbolic file name allows subsequent read and write operations to bypass the directory management and basic file system modules when accessing the file data.

Device Organization Methods

This module performs the mapping of the logical file to the underlying blocks on the secondary memory device. It receives read and write requests from the higher-level routines or the user interface. The device organization methods translate each request into the corresponding block numbers and pass these on to the underlying I/O system, which then carries out the actual data transfers between the device and the caller's main memory buffers. The allocation and deallocation of storage blocks and main memory buffers is also handled at this level.

CASE STUDY: HIERARCHY WITHIN THE UNIX FILE SYSTEM

To illustrate the above concepts, consider the UNIX file system. Before a file may be accessed, it must be opened using the following command:

$$fd = open(name, rw, ...)$$

where *name* is the symbolic file name and *rw* is a flag specifying whether the file is to be used for reading, writing, or both. The directory management routines verify that the named file exists and that the user is permitted to access it using the specified read/write mode. If this is the case, the file is opened by the routines corresponding to the basic file system, which create a new entry in the open file table. The index into this function is returned to the caller as the value of *fd*. This identifier is then used to read or write the file contents.

The read command has the following form:

$$stat = read(fd, buf, n)$$

where *fd* is the integer identified returned by the *open* command, *buf* is the pointer to an input buffer in the caller's main memory, and *n* is the number of characters to be read. When the operation completes, the value of *stat* indicates the status of the read operation. It returns the number of characters actually read or a -1 if an error occurred. The *read* (and the corresponding *write*) commands are performed by the level corresponding to the device organization methods of Figure 10-1.

10.3 THE USER'S VIEW OF FILES

From the user's point of view, a file is a named collection of data elements that have been grouped together for the purposes of access control, retrieval, and modification. At the most abstract, logical level, any file is characterized by its **name**, its **type**, its logical **organization**, and several additional **attributes**.

10.3.1 File Names and Types

What constitutes a legal file name varies between different file systems. In older systems, the name length was limited to a small number of characters. For example, MS-DOS allows up to eight characters, whereas older versions of UNIX support 14 characters. Certain special characters are frequently disallowed as part of the file name because they are reserved to serve a special role within the OS. This includes the blank, since this is usually a delimiter for separating commands, parameters, and other data items.

More recent systems have relaxed these restrictions, allowing file names to be arbitrary strings of characters found on most keyboards, and supporting name lengths that, for most practical purposes, are unlimited. For example, MS Windows allows up to 255 characters, including the blank and certain punctuation characters.

Many systems, including MS-DOS or Windows 95, do not differentiate between lower- and uppercase characters. Thus *MYFILE, Myfile, MyFile, myfile,* or any other combination of the upper- and lowercase letters all refer to the same file. In contrast, UNIX and Linux differentiate between lower- and uppercase; thus, the above names would each refer to a different file.

An important part of a file name is its **extension**, which is a short string of additional characters appended to the file name. In most systems, it is separated from the name by a period. File extensions are used to indicate the file **type**. For example, *myfile.txt* would indicate that the file is a text file, and *myprog.bin* would indicate that this file is an executable binary program (a load module). A typical file extension is between one and four characters in length. Older systems, e.g., MS-DOS, are more rigid, requiring an extension of one to three characters, while UNIX, Linux, and many other more recent systems allow more flexibility.

The file type implies the *internal format* and the *semantic meaning* of the file contents. In the simplest case, the file is a sequence of ASCII characters with no other format imposed on it. Such files are generally called *text* files and carry the extension *.txt*. A file containing a source program generally carries the extension indicating the programming language. For example, *main.c* might be a C program, whereas *main.f77* would be a Fortran 77 program. When compiled, the resulting files are object modules, denoted by the extension *.o* or *.obj*. A linker then takes an object module and produces the corresponding load module, a binary file, either annotated with the extension *.bin*, *.com*, or, as in the case of UNIX, left without an extension.

The file extension generally denotes the type of the file; the type, in turn, determines the kinds of operations that may be meaningfully performed on it by a program. Note, however, that it is the file type and *not* the extension that determines the file's semantic meaning. In most cases, the extension is only an annotation for the *convenience* of the user and the various applications using the files. That means, most systems allow the extension to be changed at will, but that does not change the type of the file, which is inherent to its internal format. A compiler could still process a source code file, even if its extension was changed. However, the compiler would fail when presented with an object module (even if this had the proper extension), since only a linker is able to correctly interpret the contents of an object module.

The file type is usually stored in the form of a file **header**. For example, any executable UNIX file must begin with a specific "magic number"—a code indicating that this is indeed an executable file. This is followed by information on how to find the code, the data, the stack, the symbol table areas, the starting point within the code, and other information needed to load and execute this file.

The number of file types supported and the strictness of enforcing the correspondence between the file type and the file name extension depends on the OS. Every system must support a minimal set of file types, including text files, object files, and load module files. In addition, the file system must be able to distinguish between ordinary files and file directories. Other utilities and applications establish and follow their own conventions regarding file types, their internal formats, and extensions. For example, a *.doc* file would normally be a formatted text document understandable by *MS Word*, *.ps* would be a file understandable by a *Postscript* printer, and *.html* would be a file containing information in the *Hypertext Markup Language* understandable by a *Web* browser.

CASE STUDY: ASSOCIATING FILE TYPES WITH APPLICATIONS

The MS Windows family of OSs allow a specific application to be associated (registered) with any file type. When the user double clicks on a file with an associated application, the file is automatically opened using that application. Some of the recognized file types are registered at the time the OS is installed. But none of these are hard-wired into the code. The user has the option to change the application associated with any file type, which allows the functionality of the system to be incrementally expanded. Many applications also will customize the file registration for their own purposes when they are installed. For example, the text processor *MS Word* will claim all files with the extension *.doc* as being in its format. All such files, which in the absence of *Word* would be open in *Windows'* simple text processor *WordPad*, are automatically opened in *Word*.

10.3.2   Logical File Organization

At the highest level, the file system is concerned with only two kinds of files, directories and ordinary (nondirectory) files. For directories, it maintains its own internal organization to facilitate efficient search and management of the directory contents. For ordinary files, the file system is concerned either with the delivery of the file contents to the calling programs, which can then interpret these according to their type, or with the writing of information to files. Traditionally, a file system views any file as a sequence of **logical records** that can be accessed one at a time using a set of specific operations. These operations also are referred to as **access methods**, since they determine how the logical records of a given file may be accessed.

A logical record in a file is the smallest unit of data that can read, written, or otherwise manipulated by one of the access method operations. Several different file organizations are possible, depending on the answers to the following questions:

1. What constitutes a logical record?
2. How does an operation address individual records?

Logical Records

Logical records may be of **fixed** or **variable length**. In the first case, a logical record can be a single byte, a word, or a structure of arbitrarily nested fixed-length components. Regardless of the complexity of each record, all records within a file must have the same length. In the second case, records may have different lengths; the size or length of a record is typically recorded as part of each record so that access method operations can conveniently locate the end of any given record. Fixed-length record files are easier to implement and are the most common form supported by modern OSs.

Record Addressing

To access a record within a file, the operation must address it in some way. This can be done either **implicitly** or **explicitly**. For implicit addressing, all records are accessed in the sequence in which they appear in the file. The system maintains an internal pointer to the current record that is incremented whenever a record is accessed. This **sequential** access is applicable to virtually all file types. Its main limitation is that a given record i can only be accessed by reading or scanning over all preceding records 0 through $i-1$.

Explicit addressing of records allows **direct** or random access to a file. It can be done either by specifying the record **position** within the file or by using a specific field within the record, called the **key**. In the first case, we assume that the file is a sequence of records such that each record is identified uniquely by an integer from 1 to n (or 0 to $n-1$), where n is the number of logical records comprising the file. An integer within that range then uniquely identifies a record. In the second case, the user must designate one of the fields within a record as the key. This can be a variable of any type, but all key values within a file must be unique. A typical example is a social security number. A record is then addressed by specifying its key value.

Figure 10-2 illustrates the four basic organizations graphically. Figure 10-2a shows a fixed-length record file. Figure 10-2b shows a variable-length record file, where the first field within each record indicates its size. Figures 10-2c and d show files where each record is identified by a unique key. The first consists of fixed-length records, and the

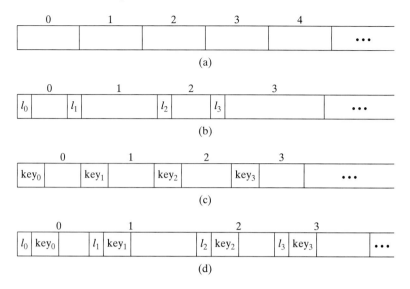

FIGURE 10-2. Record types (a) fixed length; (b) variable length; (c) fixed length with key; (d) variable length with key.

second permits variable-length records, where the record length is again recorded as the first field of each record.

Sequential access to records is equally easy in all four designs. However, only the fixed-length types allow efficient direct access, since the position of any given record can be computed given its index and the record length. For cases (b) and (d) in the figure, additional support structures, such as secondary indices, must be implemented to make direct access possible.

Although variable-size and key-based records are important for many commercial applications, few modern OSs support them at the file level. The reason is that such complex file organizations have been made obsolete by specialized **database systems** that are better equipped to manage organizing and presenting data in different ways and from different perspectives. The notable exceptions are file directories. These can be viewed as key-based record files, where the keys are the symbolic file names. The implementation of file directories is discussed in Section 10.4.3.

Memory-Mapped Files

The operations used to read or write files are usually very different in format and functionality from those used to read or write main memory. To eliminate these differences and simplify the task of programming, some systems allow files to be **mapped** directly into the process virtual memory. Memory-mapping a file involves first reserving a portion of the virtual memory for the file; then, instead of opening the file, the file contents are equated with the reserved virtual space.

For example, consider a file X, consisting of a sequence of n bytes. Assume it is mapped into a process virtual memory starting at a chosen virtual address va. Then, instead of using a special file access operation, such as $read(i, buf, n)$, where i is the open file index and n is the number of bytes to be moved into the virtual memory area *buf*, the user simply reads or writes the corresponding virtual memory locations directly. That means, accessing locations *va* through $va + n - 1$ corresponds to accessing bytes 0 through $n - 1$ of the file.

This more convenient view of files is implemented by dynamically linking the file into the process virtual address space. In systems with segmentation, the file becomes a new segment. In paged systems, the file is assigned one or more entries in the page table, depending on the file size. These pages are handled in the same way as any other pages belonging to the process. That means, each page table entry points to a page frame if the page is currently resident in main memory. It also points to a disk block from which the page is loaded when referenced and into which its contents are saved when the page is evicted from memory. For read-only code pages, the disk block belongs to the original binary code file. For data and stack pages, the disk block belongs to a special paging or swap file (or a dedicated area on disk). For memory-mapped files, the disk block belongs to the mapped file. Thus, accessing a memory-mapped file can be handled with exactly the same underlying mechanisms used for paging.

CASE STUDIES: MEMORY-MAPPED FILES

1. *Linux.* Linux (and UNIX) provides the system call *mmap()*, which allows a process to map a file into its virtual address space. The function takes the following parameters:

   - A file descriptor of the file to be mapped;
   - An offset within the file specifying the first byte to be mapped;
   - The number of bytes to be mapped;
   - A set of flags and access permissions.

   The function returns the starting address of the mapped file portion, which may then be accessed using regular virtual addresses. When the process no longer needs the file or wishes to change the size of the mapped area, it issues the call *munmap*. This takes the position of the first byte and the number of bytes to be unmapped, and changes/removes the mapping accordingly.

2. *Windows 2000.* In Section 9.3.1, we presented the idea of section objects, which may be used to share portions of virtual memory among different processes. The same mechanisms may be used to map files into the virtual address space. When the process creates a new section object, it specifies whether this object is associated with a file. If so, the specified file is located and its contents are mapped into the virtual address space. The file then is accessed as an array. When the process accesses an element in this array, a page fault is generated and the portion of the file corresponding to the page is loaded into memory. Similarly, when the process writes into the array, the data is stored in the file.

10.3.3 Other File Attributes

In addition to its name, type, and logical organization, a file also is characterized by a number of different attributes. Some of these are visible and readily accessible at the user level, whereas others are maintained and used by the file system for its various file and directory management functions. Each OS implements its own view of what specific attributes should be maintained. The following types of information are generally considered:

- **Ownership.** This records the name of the file owner. In most systems, the file creator is its owner. Access privileges are usually controlled by the owner, who may then grant them to others.

- **File Size.** The file system needs current file size information to effectively manage its blocks on disk. File size is also important for the user, and hence is readily available at the user level, typically as one of the results of a directory scan operation.

- **File Use.** For a variety of reasons, including security, recovery from failure, and performance monitoring, it is useful to maintain information about when and how the file has been used. This may include the time of its creation, the time of its last use, the time of its last modification, the number of times the file has been opened, and other statistical information.

- **File Disposition.** A file could be *temporary*, to be destroyed when it is closed, when a certain condition is satisfied, or at the termination of the process for which it was created; or it may be stored indefinitely as a *permanent* file.

- **Protection.** This information includes *who* can access a file and *how* a file can be accessed, i.e., the *type of operation*, such as read, write, or execute, that can be performed. Enforcing protection to files is one of the most important services provided by the file system. Chapters 12 and 13 are dedicated exclusively to issues of protection and security.

- **Location.** To access the data in a file, the file system must know which device blocks the file is stored in. This information is of no interest to most users and is generally not available at the abstract user interface. The different schemes for mapping a file onto disk blocks and keeping track of them affect performance crucially and are discussed in Section 10.6.

10.3.4 Operations on Files

The abstract user interface defines a set of operations that the user may invoke—either at the command level or from a program—to manipulate files and their contents. The specific set of operations depends on the OS. It also depends on the type of files that must be supported. Below we present an overview of the commonly provided classes of operations.

Create/Delete

Before a file can be used in any way, it must be created. The *create* command, which generally accepts a symbolic file name as one of its parameters, creates the file identity so that it can be referred to in other commands by its symbolic name. The *delete* or *destroy* command reverses the effect of the creation by eliminating the file and all its contents from the file system. Since deleting a file by mistake is a common problem with potentially serious consequences, most file systems will ask for confirmation before actually performing the operation. Another common safety measure is to delete any file only tentatively so that it can later be recovered if necessary. For example, the Windows OS will place a file to be deleted into a special directory called the *Recycle Bin*, where it remains indefinitely. Only when the *Recycle Bin* is explicitly emptied, e.g., to free up disk space, is the file deleted irrevocably.

Open/Close

A file must be opened before it can be used for reading or writing. The *open* command sets up data structures to facilitate the read and write access. An important role of the *open* command is to set up internal buffers for transferring the file data between the disk and main memory. The *close* command reverses the effect of *open*; it disconnects the file from the current process, releases its buffers, and updates any information maintained about the file.

Read/Write

A *read* operation transfers file data from disk to main memory, whereas a *write* operation transfers data in the opposite direction. The *read/write* operations come in two basic forms, *sequential* and *direct*, corresponding to the implicit and explicit forms of record addressing discussed in Section 10.3.2. A direct *read* or *write* will access a record that must be designated explicitly by its number (i.e., position within the file), or by its key. A sequential *read* or *write* assumes the existence of a logical pointer that is maintained by the system and always points to the record to be accessed next. Each time a sequential *read* operation is executed, it transfers the current record and advances the pointer to the next record. Thus, if the last record read was record i, issuing the same *read* command repeatedly will access a sequence of consecutive records $i+1$, $i+2$, and so on. Similarly, a sequential *write* command will place a new record at the position of the current pointer. If this position already contains a record, the operation overwrites it; if the pointer is at the end of the file, the write expands the file.

Seek/Rewind

Purely sequential access is too restrictive for many applications. To avoid having to read a file each time from the beginning, a *seek* command is frequently provided. It moves the current record pointer to an arbitrary position within the file. Thus a *seek* followed by a *read* or *write* essentially emulates the effect of a direct access. How the *seek* operation is implemented depends on how the file is organized internally, but it can usually be done much more efficiently than reading all records from the beginning. (Note that the *seek* operation discussed here is a high-level file operation, and should not be confused with a disk seek operation, which moves the disk's read/write head to a specified track.)

A *rewind* command resets the current record pointer to the beginning of the file. This is equivalent to a *seek* to the first record of the file.

10.4 FILE DIRECTORIES

An OS generally contains many different files. Similarly, every user often has many files. To help organize these in some systematic way, the file system provides **file directories**. Each directory is itself a file, but its sole purpose is to record information about other files, including possibly other directories.

The information in a directory associates symbolic names given to files by users with the data necessary to locate and use the files. This data consists of the various attributes discussed in Section 10.3.3, particularly the information necessary to locate the blocks comprising the file on the disk or other storage media. How this location information is organized and where is it kept is the subject of Section 10.6. In this section, we are concerned with the organization of file directories from the user's point of view, and with the operations defined at the user interface to locate and manipulate files.

The simplest possible form of a directory is a flat **list of files**, where all files are at the same level, with no further subdivisions. Such a directory is clearly inadequate for most applications. Thus, virtually all file systems support a multilevel **hierarchy**, where a directory may point to lower-level subdirectories, which, in turn, may point to yet lower-level subdirectories, and so on. Depending on the rules enforced when creating new files and file directories, or when changing the connections between existing ones, we can identify several specific organization within a general hierarchical structure.

10.4.1   Hierarchical Directory Organizations

Tree-Structured Directories

One of the most general practical directory organizations is a **tree** structure. In such a structure, there is exactly one **root** directory, and each file and each directory (except the root directory) has exactly one **parent** directory; the latter is the directory in which the file is listed. The **leaves** of the tree are the data and program files, and all intermediate nodes are directories, sometimes also referred to as **subdirectories**.

Figure 10-3 shows an example of a small tree-structured directory hierarchy. The root directory $D1$ contains two subdirectories, named a and b. Each of these in turn point to lower-level directories (shown as rectangles) or ordinary files (shown as circles.) For

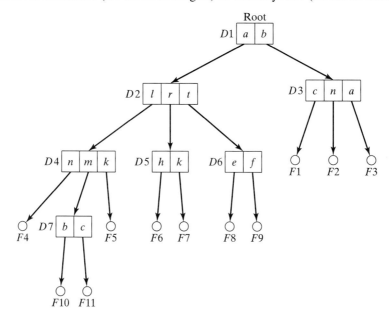

FIGURE 10-3. Tree-structured directory hierarchy.

example, b in $D1$ points to $D3$ containing c, n, and a; and n points to the file $F2$. The labels Di and Fi are not visible components of the directory structure. They correspond to unique internal identifiers that permit us to refer to directories and files regardless of their position within the directory hierarchy.

CASE STUDIES: TYPICAL DIRECTORY STRUCTURES

1. *UNIX.* Figure 10-4a shows the top portion of a typical directory structure in UNIX. The root directory usually contains a number of directories with agreed-upon names, that point to files where important systems information is kept. For example, */bin* contains executable binary programs corresponding to the various shell commands, such as *cd* (change directory), *ls* (list contents of directory), or *mkdir* (make directory). The directory */dev* refers to files describing specific devices, such as the disk, or the user terminal. The directory */etc* contains programs used primarily for systems administration. */home* is the starting point for all individual user home directories. */tmp* is used for temporary files. Finally, the directory */urs* contains several other subdirectories of executable programs, language libraries, and manuals. Each of the above directories generally contain many files and other subdirectories.

2. *MS Windows.* Figure 10-4b shows the top portion of a typical directory structure in the MS Windows OS. This structure reflects the fact that Windows has been designed for PCs, where each user is in control of local hardware devices, rather than for a shared multiuser system. The root of the file system is called the *Desktop* and corresponds to the initial user screen where icons for subdirectories or programs can be kept for easy access. One of the most important directories on the *Desktop* is *My Computer*, which contains subdirectories for different storage devices, such as the floppy disk drive (*A:*), the hard disk drive (*C:*), and the CD-ROM drive (*D:*). The *C:* directory, in turn, contains a number of subdirectories, including *Program Files* that store applications, and *Windows* which holds the OS itself. In addition to the storage device directories, *My Computer* generally contains several other directories for accessing and setting up printers, and for systems management tasks (the *Control Panel*). Other directories appearing on the *Desktop* include the *Network Neighborhood*, which describes other computers on the same network, the *Recycle Bin*, which holds deleted files until they are irrevocably purged from the system, and many other directories and/or programs.

The main attraction of the tree-structured hierarchy is that it is simple to search and maintain. An insertion creates a new entry in the specified directory, which then becomes the root of a new subtree. A *delete* operation removes the specified entry from the parent directory, with the corresponding subtree pointed to by the entry. For example, deleting the entry a from the root directory of Figure 10-3 would result in the removal of the entire subtree rooted at directory $D2$.

The main drawback of a strictly tree-structured directory is that *sharing* of files is always *asymmetric*. Any file must appear in exactly one parent directory, which

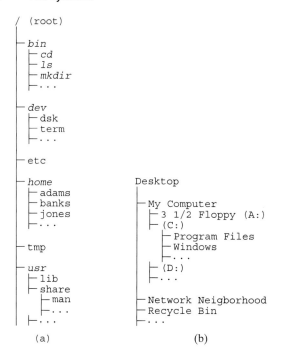

FIGURE 10-4. Sample directory hierarchy in (a) UNIX and (b) Windows.

effectively "owns" that file. It is up to the owner to grant or deny access to the file by other users, which must always access it through the owner's directory.

Directed Acyclic Graph-Structured Directories

Permitting files to have multiple parent directories destroys the tree property, but it allows sharing to be done in a symmetrical manner. That means, more than one directory, belonging possibly to different users, can point to the same file and use different symbolic names.

Figure 10-5 shows an example of a directory hierarchy structured as a **directed acyclic graph** (DAG) where any file can have multiple parents. Notably, file $F8$ has three parent directories ($D5$, $D6$, and $D3$), two of which refer to it by the same name (p). Directory $D6$ has two parent directories, each at a different level.

A directory hierarchy that allows multiple parent directories for any given file is more complex to maintain than a strictly tree-structured one. First, we must define the semantics of a *delete* operation. With only a single parent directory, the file can simply be deleted and the entry removed from that directory. With multiple parent directories, there is a choice. We can remove a file whenever a *delete* operation is applied to *any* of the parents. This policy is simple to implement, but unfortunately, leaves the references in the other parent directories pointing to a nonexistent file, possibly also causing unintended protection violations. The second choice is to remove a file only when it has a *single parent* directory. For this method, a **reference count** is maintained for each file; this keeps track of the number of parent directories the file appears in at any given time. A *delete* operation removes the file only when its reference count is one; otherwise, it only removes the entry from the parent directory.

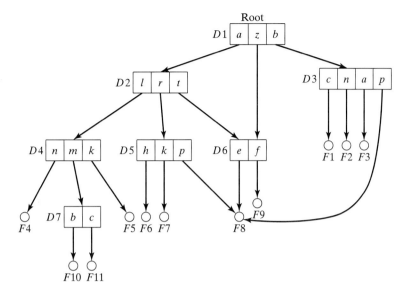

FIGURE 10-5. DAG-structured directory hierarchy.

For example, removing file $F8$ (Fig. 10-5) from one or two of the directories, say $D5$ and $D6$, would only remove the corresponding entries, p and e. Only when the file is deleted from the last directory $D3$ would both the entry p and the actual file be removed.

A second problem with allowing multiple parent directories is the possibility of forming **cycles** in the graph. Figure 10-6 shows a structure consisting of the same files and directories as Figure 10-5, but with an additional link from directory $D7$ to its

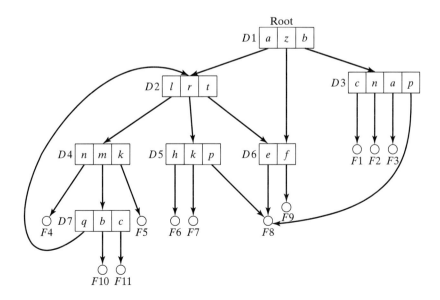

FIGURE 10-6. Directory hierarchy with a cycle.

grandparent directory $D2$; this last link completes a cycle in the graph. Cycles cause problems for many of the operations applied to directories. In particular, *searching* for a file may traverse the same portions of the directory structure multiple times, or, may even result in infinite loops. File *deletion* also becomes more difficult, because a simple reference count is not sufficient. The reason for this is that any file that is part of a cycle has a reference count of at least one and will not be deleted even if it becomes unreachable from outside of the cycle.

Consider, for example, the deletion of directory $D2$ from the root directory $D1$ in Figure 10-6. The reference count of directory $D2$ is two (it has two parents); thus, the deletion only removes the entry a from directory $D1$, but not $D2$ itself, even though $D2$, $D4$, and $D7$ are no longer reachable from the root or any other directory that is not part of the cycle.

To handle deletion in the case of a cyclic structure requires a **garbage collection** algorithm, which makes two passes over the entire directory structure. During the first pass, all components that have been reached are marked. During the second pass, all unmarked components are deleted.

Most file systems disallow cycles in the directory structure and enforce a DAG hierarchy, to eliminate the above problems with deletion and search. This can be accomplished by employing a cycle detection algorithm prior to inserting an existing file or directory in another existing directory. If this new connection forms a cycle, the insertion is disallowed. Regrettably, such algorithms are expensive to execute, since they may involve traversing large portions of the directory structure.

Symbolic Links

To satisfy the need for general file sharing and avoiding the problems with unrestricted directory structures, a compromise solution has been developed. The basic idea is to allow multiple parent directories but to designate one of them as the main (owner) parent. Other directories may refer to the same file but using only a secondary connection, called a **symbolic link**. Figure 10-7 shows a directory structure with the same files and directories as Figure 10-6, but it allows only one parent directory for any file; all other connections must be done by symbolic links, shown as dashed lines in the figure. Thus, the owner structure is a simple tree with real (nonsymbolic) links connecting the component parts.

Symbolic links behave differently for different file operations. For reading and writing purposes, the file looks the same regardless of whether it is accessed through the main parent directory or one containing only a symbolic link. For example, the name p in directory $D3$ refers to the same file $F8$ in both Figures 10-6 and 10-7. Deletions, however, have a different effect depending on the type of link. For symbolic links, only the link itself is deleted. Only when the *delete* operation is applied to the actual (nonsymbolic) link is the file itself removed. If the deleted file is a directory, the same operation is then applied recursively to all files reachable from the deleted directory.

Consider the deletion of the directory $D2$. Unlike in Figure 10-6, where an unreachable subgraph is created, deleting $D2$ in Figure 10-7 removes not only the entry a from $D1$ but also the directory $D2$ itself. In addition, it will remove all other files and directories reachable from $D2$ via actual (nonsymbolic) links. In comparison, removing the

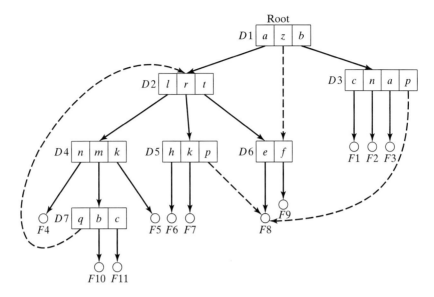

FIGURE 10-7. Directory hierarchy with symbolic links.

same directory $D2$ from $D7$, where it is recorded via a symbolic link, will only remove that link, i.e., the entry q.

CASE STUDIES: SYMBOLIC LINKS vs. MULTIPLE PARENTS

1. *MS Windows.* The MS Windows family of OSs implement a form of symbolic links called *shortcuts*. These are pointers to files or folders (directories) that may be arbitrarily copied and moved between different folders and menus. Deleting a shortcut simply discards the pointer.

2. *UNIX.* UNIX supports a combination of multiple parent directories and symbolic links. Multiple parents are permitted but only with nondirectory files. The shared child may be deleted equally from either parent directory. For all other cross-references, any number of symbolic links may be used. Notably, a directory can only have one parent directory, but it may be referred to by additional symbolic links from any number of other directories.

Path Names

All files and directories must be identified uniquely throughout the entire file system. This is usually done by concatenating the symbolic names along the path leading from the root to the desired file, producing a **path name**. The individual components are separated by a special delimiter, such as a period, a slash (/), or a backslash (\). Any path name uniquely identifies one file (or directory) in the file hierarchy. If the hierarchy is a tree, there is only one such path name for any file. With DAG-structured or general-graph-structured directories, multiple path names may exist for the same file, but, in all cases, a given path name uniquely identifies exactly one file.

For example, file $F9$ in Figure 10-7 can be identified by the two path names $/a/t/f$ and $/z/f$, where, following UNIX conventions, the leading slash indicates that the path begins with the root directory, and subsequent slashes separate the individual name components along the path.

Note that in the presence of cycles, all files along a cycle can be referred to by an unbounded number of path names. For example, file $F4$ in Figure 10-7 can be identified by the path names $/a/l/n$, $/a/l/m/q/l/n$, $/a/l/m/q/l/m/q/l/n$, and so on. The subpath $m/q/l$, which repeats one or more times in each path name except the first, is redundant.

Although path names uniquely identify any file within the directory structure, their use would be extremely tedious if the user had to specify the full path name each time a file was accessed. To alleviate this problem, the concept of a **current** or **working directory** has been adopted in most file systems. A process can designate, at runtime, any of its accessible directories as its current directory. Files can then be referenced relative to the current working directory. Such path names are referred to as **relative** path names, and those starting with the root of the file system hierarchy are called **absolute** path names.

For example, if the current directory in Figure 10-7 is $D4$ (identified by the path name a/l), using the relative path name m/b is equivalent to using the absolute path name $/a/l/m/b$; both refer to the same file $F10$.

To allow a path name to identify a file that is not within the subtree of the current directory, a component of the path name must be able to refer to its parent directory. Let us assume that the special notation ".." is used for this purpose. This notation, in conjunction with the path-naming conventions, allows the user to travel arbitrarily up or down the directory structure. For example, assuming $D4$ to be the current directory, the two path names $../t/f$ and $../../z/f$ both refer to the same file $F9$.

10.4.2 Operations on Directories

Similar to operations on files, the user interface specifies a set of operations that the user may invoke—either at the command level or from a program—to manipulate file directories. Some OSs will permit programs to open, read, write, and otherwise manipulate directories just as ordinary files. However, many operations are applicable only to directories. The specific set of operations that are defined depends on the OS and the structure of the particular file system hierarchy. Below, we present an overview of the commonly provided classes of operations.

Create/Delete

A directory must first be created before it can be assigned any contents. Generally, the *create* command for directories is different from that for ordinary files, since each file type has a different internal format. The difference is even more significant for the *delete* command. In the case of a directory, the question is what should happen with all the files reachable from this directory. The simplest choice is to allow the deletion of only an *empty* directory, which forces the user to explicitly delete all files listed in the directory to be deleted. The other extreme is to recursively delete all files reachable from the given directory. Many file systems, e.g., UNIX, give the user a choice between the different options as part of *delete* (called *rmdir* in UNIX).

List

This operation produces a listing of all files recorded in a directory. For example, listing the directory */b* of Figure 10-7 would show the file names *c*, *n*, *a* and *p*. Since the purpose of a directory is to keep track of a group of files, the *List* command is one of the most frequently needed operations. There are typically several parameters or preference settings through which the user can choose how the information should be displayed. In particular, the user may specify the order in which the files should be listed, e.g., sorted alphabetically by name, by size, or by some of the dates recorded with the file. The user can also specify how much information about each file should be displayed. In the simplest form, this could be just the lists of the file names, or it could include some or all of the other visible attributes. In most cases, the file type also determines whether the file is included in the directory listing.

Some OSs support a recursive version of the list command, which displays the contents of the entire subtree rooted at the selected directory. That means, the display shows the contents of the selected directory itself, followed by the contents of all directories reachable from the selected directory.

CASE STUDIES: LISTING FILES AND DIRECTORIES

1. *UNIX.* The UNIX *ls* command suppresses (by default) the display of files whose names begin with a period, as such files are considered system files. But they can be requested by including a parameter (*-a*) with the *ls* command. A number of other parameters are available to control the format of the display and the type of information displayed about each file. A recursive version is also available.

2. *Windows Explorer.* Windows OSs provide a special application, the *Windows Explorer*, to examine the contents of directories (folders). It consists of a split graphics window, where the left half allows the user to scroll through the directory structure while the right half displays the content of any particular directory selected in the left half. The format and type of information is controlled by specific menus associated with the window.

3. *Windows applications.* Many other Windows applications also display lists of files, e.g., those that can be opened or saved by that application. But they generally display only those files whose type is associated with the application. For example, the word processor *MS Word* will (by default) consider files with the extension *.doc*.

Change Directory

As explained in Section 10.4.1, most file systems support the concept of a current or working directory to eliminate the need for using absolute path names. The *change directory* command permits the user to set the current directory by specifying its absolute or relative path name.

In addition to the current directory, the file system also supports the concept of a **home directory**. This is usually the top-level directory associated with a given user, and is set (by default) as the current directory when the user logs in. A *change directory* command that does not explicitly name any directory also generally defaults to the home directory.

Move

Directory structures must frequently be reorganized. This requires moving files (and directories) between different parent directories. Moving a file between directories changes the file path name. For example, moving file $F11$ from directory $D7$ to directory $D5$, in Figure 10-7 changes its path name from */a/l/m/c* to */a/r/c*.

Rename

This command simply changes the name under which a file or directory is recorded in its parent directory. Thus, although the user thinks in terms of renaming a file, the operation is really applied to its parent directory. For example, renaming file $F1$ from */b/c* to */b/d* changes the entry in directory $D3$. If the *move* command allows a file to be moved to its new directory under a different name, then the *rename* command can be subsumed by *move*. The file is simply "moved" to the same directory under a different name.

Change Protection

This command allows the user (generally the owner) of a file to control who can access the file and which type of operation (e.g., read-only, execute-only, read/write) may be performed.

Link

The *Link* operation is applicable to directory structures that allow multiple parent directories for a given file or support symbolic links. In the first case, it creates a new link between a specified file and another existing directory. The new link becomes the additional parent. In the second case, only a symbolic link (Section 10.4.1) is created.

Assume that the *link* command for creating symbolic links has the format *SLink (parent, child)*, where *parent* and *child* are arbitrary path names referring to the new parent directory for the given child file, respectively. Then *SLink(/a/l/x, /b)* in Figure 10-7 would make a new entry, x, in the directory $D4$ (i.e., */a/l*), which would point (via a symbolic link) to the directory $D3$ (i.e, */b/*). From then on, the path names */a/l/x* and */b* would refer to the same directory $D3$.

Find

When the directory structure becomes large and complex, finding a specific file can become a challenge. Thus virtually all file systems support some form of a *find* command to facilitate this task. The user generally specifies the starting point for the search. This can be the current directory, the working directory, or any other directory. The possible search criteria include the file name, which could be specified using wild card characters for partial matches, and combinations of other visible attributes, such as the file size, type, and the various dates recorded with the file.

The *find* command may be invoked explicitly from the user interface or implicitly as part of various **search routines** invoked by the OS when a file must be located. Specifically, when the user names a program to be executed, the file system can follow a set of conventions in attempting to locate and invoke the program.

CASE STUDY: SEARCHING FOR PROGRAM FILES IN UNIX

UNIX allows the user to fully specify the directories to be searched when a program is to be invoked. The path names of these directories are listed in a special system file in the user's home directory containing various user preferences (the file *.cshrc*). These directories are examined in the given order until a match for the file name is found or the list of directories is exhausted (in which case the search has failed).

10.4.3 Implementation of File Directories

Directories must normally be stored on secondary memory because there is potentially a large number of them, and each can contain many entries. Most file systems treat file directories just like regular files for the purposes of reading and writing. However, their internal organization plays an important role in facilitating efficient access to files. Any directory contains a collection of entries, each corresponding to one file or subdirectory. The two most important questions that must be answered are:

1. What information should be maintained in each directory entry?
2. How should the individual entries be organized within a directory?

The minimal information that must be recorded within each entry is the file *symbolic name* and a pointer or *index* to additional descriptive information. At the other extreme, all attributes pertaining to a given file could appear in the directory entry. The disadvantage of the first method is that we need an additional disk operation to access the descriptive information. The disadvantage of the second is that directories could become very large and more difficult to manage. Furthermore, the entries could be variable in length. Thus, it would be necessary to support a file structure consisting of complex variable-size records.

Even with the first minimal approach, we face the problem of having to manage symbolic file names that can vary in length. If the length is limited to a small number of characters, each entry can reserve space for the maximum name length. This is the technique used by most older systems, where file names were limited to eight or another small number of characters. Reserving the maximum space for long name is wasteful. One possible solution is to reserve a relatively small fixed space for each name, followed by a pointer to an overflow heap for long names.

The second question above concerns the internal organization of file entries within a given directory file. First, the directory management routines must be able to delete and insert entries efficiently. Second, these entries are accessed associatively by the symbolic file name and must support search by content. The simplest approach organizes the entries as an unsorted **array** of fixed-size entries. When variable-size entries are required, an array of variable-size entries or **linked lists** can be used instead. Insertions and deletions are simple with both approaches, but searches require sequential scans for a given match. When the number of entries is small, this may be acceptable. But if the list of files is expected to be very long, a more efficient scheme is necessary to speed up searches. One alternative implements the directory as a **hash table**. Search, insertion, and deletion are then quite efficient. A difficulty here is deciding on an appropriate size for the hash table, a decision that depends on the number of file entries to be managed.

Another alternative is to implement directories as **B-trees** (Comer 1979). A B-tree is organized as follows. Every node may be viewed as containing s slots, each capable of holding one data entry, and $s + 1$ pointers to nodes at the next lower level of the tree. At any given time, each node must be at least half full, i.e., contain at least $s/2$ entries and the corresponding number of pointers. A data entry consists of a record **key**, such as a file name, and other information, for example, file attributes or pointers to them.

EXAMPLE: B-Tree

Figure 10-8a shows an example of a B-tree with $s = 2$. The nodes are organized according to the following rule: For any given data entry with key k, the subtree pointed to by the left-hand pointer contains only entries whose key values are *less* than k according to some chosen ordering, such as lexicographical; the subtree pointed to by the right-hand pointer contains only entries with key values *greater* than k. This determines a simple algorithm for locating a record given a key k. Starting with the root node, k is compared

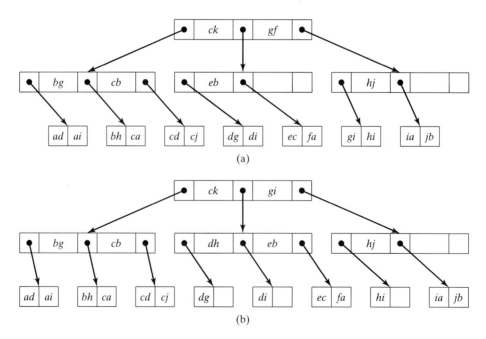

FIGURE 10-8. B-tree.

to the entries recorded in that node. If a match is found, the corresponding record is accessed. Otherwise, the search follows the pointer immediately succeeding the largest entry k' found in that node, such that $k' < k$. This is repeated until the desired record is found. The cost of the search operation is proportional to the depth of the tree, i.e., the logarithm of the file size. For example, to locate the record with $k = dg$, first the pointer to the right of entry ck is followed, and the pointer to the left of entry eb is followed. The desired entry dg is found in the leaf node.

An important property of B-trees is that they are balanced, i.e., the distance between the root and any leaf is a constant. The insertion and deletion operations defined on B-trees are guaranteed to preserve this property. Each of these operations may require the splitting or collapsing of nodes on the path between the root and the affected node. However, the cost of insertion or deletion is still proportional to the logarithm of the file size. Figure 10-8b shows the result of inserting the entry dh and deleting the entry gf in the tree of Figure 10-8a.

Unfortunately, the performance of *sequential* operations on the simple B-trees is not very satisfactory. This is because logically adjacent keys may be stored arbitrarily far apart in the tree structure, and there is no easy way to determine the location of the logically next key, given a key k. In fact, accessing the logically next key is as costly as performing a direct access.

To improve the performance of sequential access, variations of the simple B-tree have been proposed, the most popular of which are B^+-*trees*. The main distinction is that a B^+-tree keeps all the keys only in the leaf nodes, which are linked together using a simple linked list. The nonleaf nodes form a regular B-tree, whose sole purpose is to serve as an index for locating the desired leaf nodes. Search, insertion, and deletion in B^+-trees has the same logarithmic cost as with B-trees. Sequential access, however, is now also efficient: given a key k, the logical successor is found either in the same leaf node (immediately adjacent to the key k), or, if k is the right-most key in that node, by following the appropriate pointer to the neighboring leaf node.

CASE STUDIES: IMPLEMENTATION OF FILE DIRECTORIES

1. *UNIX.* The Berkeley Fast File System (BFS) allows file names of up to 255 characters. Each directory is organized as a variable-size array, where each element describes one file. It records the file name, the file type (directory or regular file), and a number (called the i-node number), which identifies the descriptive information about the file. Since the directory entries are of variable length, they will, over time, be interspersed with empty spaces (holes), which are also of variable length. The file system uses sequential search for both, finding a given file entry using the file name, and finding a hole to accommodate a new file entry.

   To avoid maintaining a separate list of holes, the file system uses the following convention: Every file entry is followed by a single hole (possibly of size zero). The hole size is recorded as part of each entry. This effectively turns each directory entry into a pair, consisting of the file information and an (optional)

CASE STUDIES: IMPLEMENTATION OF FILE DIRECTORIES (*continued*)

hole. Figure 10-9 illustrates the idea. It shows the entry for a file named *abc*. When searching for a given *file name*, say *abc*, the system sequentially scans all entries using the length indicators $l1$ and comparing the file name recorded in each entry with the string *abc*. When searching for a *hole* of a given size n, the system scans the entries using again $l1$, but instead of looking for a string match, it looks for an entry where $l1 - l2 \geq n$.

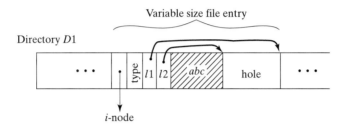

FIGURE 10-9. Organization of BFS directories.

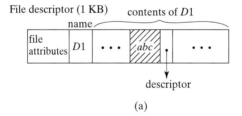

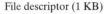

(a)

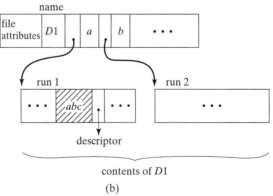

(b)

FIGURE 10-10. Organization of NTFS directories; (a) short directory; and (b) long directory.

> **2.** *Windows 2000.* The native file system, *NTFS*, of Windows 2000 describes each file and each directory using a descriptor of 1 KB. The contents of a directory may be organized in two different ways, depending on its length. For short directories, the file entries (each consisting of a file name and an index to a file descriptor) are kept inside the directory descriptor itself. Figure 10-10a illustrates the situation for a directory $D1$, which contains an entry for a file *abc*. When the number of file entries exceeds the length of the 1 KB descriptor, additional block sequences (called *runs*) are allocated to hold the file entries. These runs are organized in the form of a B^+-tree. Figure 10-10b illustrates the situation for a directory $D1$. File entries beginning with the letter a, including the file *abc*, are in the first additional run.

10.5   BASIC FILE SYSTEM

The main functions of the basic file system are to **open** and **close** files. Opening a file means to set it up for efficient access by subsequent read, write, or other data manipulation commands. Closing a file reverses the effect of the open command and occurs when a file is no longer needed. These and other operations require basic file data structures or descriptors.

10.5.1   File Descriptors

Section 10.3 introduced types of descriptive information associated with a file, including its name, type, internal organization, size, ownership and protection information, and its location on secondary memory. Where this information is kept is an important design decision. One extreme is to maintain the descriptive information dispersed throughout different data structures based on its use by different subsystems or applications. For example, some information can be kept in the parent directory, some on a dedicated portion of the disk, and some with the file itself. The other extreme—a cleaner solution—keeps all descriptive information about a file segregated in a separate data structure, pointed to from the parent directory. This data structure is generally referred to as the **file descriptor**.

CASE STUDIES: FILE DESCRIPTORS

1. *UNIX.* All versions of UNIX file systems provide a comprehensive descriptor for every file and directory in the system. This descriptor is famously, but somewhat obscurely, called an **i-node**. (The "i" stands for "index," as in "file index.") The information kept in each i-node includes the following:

- identification of the owner;
- file type (directory, regular file, special file);
- protection information;
- the mapping of logical file records onto disk blocks;
- time of creation, last use, and last modification;
- the number of directories sharing (pointing to) the file.

CASE STUDIES: FILE DESCRIPTORS   *(continued)*

All i-nodes are maintained in a dedicated table on disk. Directories then contain only the symbolic file names together with the number of the corresponding i-node. The number is used as an index into the table of i-nodes to retrieve the descriptive information. This convention permits the use of large descriptors and supports convenient file sharing by allowing multiple directory entries to point to the same i-node.

2. *Windows 2000.* The NTFS file system keeps all descriptors in a special file, called the **master file table (MFT)**, which may be located anywhere on the disk. Each MFT entry is a 1-KB record and describes one file or directory. The first 12 entries are reserved for special files (called *meta* files), such as the root directory, a bitmap to keep track of free and occupied disk blocks, a log file, and other files necessary to maintain the file system. The remaining entries are available for user files and directories. Each entry is organized as a collection of attribute/value pairs, one of which is the actual content of the file or directory. Other attributes include the file name (up to 255 characters), time-stamps, and access information. The location of the actual file content depends on its length, as has already been explained in the context of directories (Fig. 10-10b). For short files/directories, the content is kept within the descriptor itself. For longer files/directories, the descriptor contains a list of block numbers (runs) that contain the file/directory content. For extremely large files, i.e., when the number of runs exceeds the length of the descriptor, additional 1-KB descriptors can be allocated and chained to the first descriptor.

Opening and closing of files involve two components of the file descriptor: 1) protection information to verify the legality of the requested access; and 2) location information necessary to find the file data blocks on the secondary storage device.

10.5.2 Opening and Closing Files

Regardless of how the descriptive information about a file is organized, most of it is maintained on disk. When the file is to be used, relevant portions of this information is brought into main memory for efficient continued access to the file data. For that purpose, the file system maintains an **open file table** (OFT) to keep track of currently open files. Each entry in the OFT corresponds to one open file, i.e., a file being used by one or more processes.

The OFT is managed by the **open** and **close** functions. The *open* function is invoked whenever a process first wishes to access a file. The function finds and allocates a free entry in the OFT, fills it with relevant information about the file, and associates with it any resources, e.g., read/write buffers, necessary to access the file efficiently. Some systems do not require an explicit *open* command, in which case it is generated implicitly by the system at the time the file is accessed for the first time.

When a file is no longer needed, it is closed either by calling the *close* command, or implicitly as the result of a process termination. The *close* function frees all resources used for accessing the file, saves all modified information to the disk, and releases the OFT entry, thereby rendering the file inactive for the particular process.

The implementation of the *open* and *close* functions vary widely with different file systems, but the following list gives the typical tasks performed in some form as part of these functions.

Open

- Using the protection information in the file descriptor, verify that the process (user) has the right to access the file and perform the specified operations.

- Find and allocate a free entry in the OFT.

- Allocate read/write buffers in main memory and other resources as necessary for the given type of file access.

- Complete the components of the OFT entry. This includes initialization information, such as the current position (zero) of a sequentially accessed file. It also includes relevant information copied from the file descriptor, such as the file length and its location on the disk. Additional runtime information, such as the pointers to the allocated buffers or other resources, also is placed into the OFT entry.

- If all of the above operations are successful, return the index or the pointer to the allocated OFT entry to the calling process for subsequent access to the file.

Close

- Flush any modified main memory buffers by writing their contents to the corresponding disk blocks.

- Release all buffers and other allocated resources.

- Update the file descriptor using the current data in the OFT entry. This could include any changes to the file length, allocation of disk blocks, or use information (e.g., date of last access/modification).

- Free the OFT entry.

CASE STUDY: OPEN FILE TABLES IN UNIX

The UNIX OS has two levels of OFTs. A shared system-wide OFT is maintained by the kernel, and additional private OFTs are implemented for each user by the I/O libraries. The system-wide OFT supports unbuffered access to the file, whereas the private OFTs support buffered access. Figure 10-11 illustrates the relationship between the two types of OFTs, the file directories, and the table containing the file descriptors (the i-node list).

Consider first the command for opening a file for low-level, unbuffered access:

$$fd = open(name, rw, ...)$$

The *open* function first searches the file directory for the symbolic name, say F_j in Figure 10-11, and verifies that the requested type of accesses is permitted by reading

CASE STUDY: OPEN FILE TABLES IN UNIX   (*continued*)

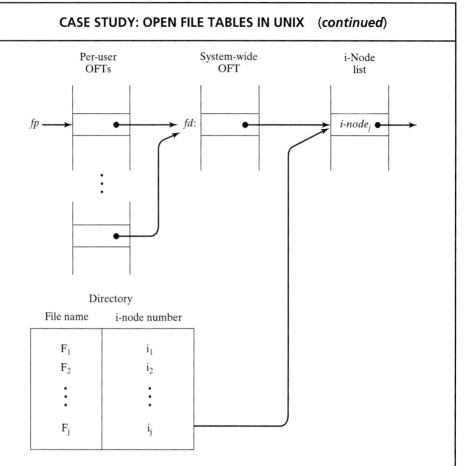

FIGURE 10-11. OFTs in UNIX.

the corresponding *i-node$_j$*. If this was successful, the function makes an entry in the system-wide OFT and returns the index of that entry, *fd*, to the caller. As already described in Section 10.2, the OFT entry contains the information necessary to locate the file and to read or write sequences of bytes using the commands:

```
stat = read(fd, buf, n)
stat = write(fd, buf, n)
```

These functions access the file's data via the system-wide OFT entry *fd*. They read/write *n* bytes of data to/from the memory location *buf*, and indicate how many bytes were successfully read/written in the variable *stat*. Both operations are unbuffered; consequently, each invocation results in a disk access (or disk cache access, if the block has already been accessed recently.)

Opening a file for buffered access is accomplished with the command:

```
fp = fopen(name, rwa)
```

where *name* is again the file symbolic name and *rwa* specifies whether the file is to be used for reading, writing, or appending of data.

The function *fopen* creates a new entry in the process private OFT and associates a read/write buffer with the entry. It calls the low-level *open* function, which creates a new entry in the system-wide OFT, or, if the file is already open by another user, it finds the corresponding entry in the system-wide table. In either case, the index *fd* is entered in the private OFT entry. Thus, each entry in the private OFT points to the corresponding file via an entry in the system-wide OFT.

fopen returns to the caller a pointer *fp* to the private OFT entry. This pointer is used to access the file using one of several functions to perform buffered data access. For example, the function:

$$c = \texttt{readc(fp)}$$

returns one character of that file in the variable *c* and advances the current file position to the next character. The operation is buffered in that the characters are copied from a main memory buffer, which is filled initially using a single low-level unbuffered *read* operation. Subsequent calls to *readc* require no disk access until the current file position moves past the end of the buffer. At that time, another unbuffered *read* operation is invoked to refill the buffer with the next set of characters from the file.

10.6 DEVICE ORGANIZATION METHODS

Space on secondary memory devices is organized into sequences of **physical blocks** (or physical records), where a block is typically the smallest amount of data that can be read or written using one I/O operation. The block size is determined by the characteristics of the storage medium. Several logical file records may be mapped onto one physical block, or, conversely, one logical file record may be spread over a number of physical blocks. This ratio is called the **blocking factor**. For the purposes of this section, we assume a blocking factor of one, i.e., each physical block holds exactly one logical file record.

Disks and tapes are the most frequently used secondary storage media. Although the blocks on tapes are by necessity arranged and addressed sequentially, disks are two-dimensional surfaces (sometimes with multiple surfaces), where each block is identified by a track number and a sector number within the track. Dealing with physical disk addresses is the task of the I/O system and is treated in Chapter 11. From the file system point of view, a disk is considered a *one-dimensional sequence of logical blocks* by simply numbering all disk blocks from 0 to $n - 1$, where n is the total number of blocks comprising the disk. This abstraction permits the file system to view both disks and tapes as linear sequences of blocks identified by their block numbers. In the remainder of this section, we are concerned primarily with disks and will use the term **disk blocks** to refer to the sequentially numbered logical blocks provided by the I/O system as the abstract interface to the file system.

The primary task of the device organization methods is to decide which disk blocks are to be allocated to which logical file records, and to facilitate access to these as required by the read, write, and other data manipulation operations. This information is recorded in the file descriptor introduced in the previous section.

10.6.1 Contiguous Organization

A file may be mapped onto a sequence of adjacent disk blocks. In this case, the information needed to locate the disk blocks, which is maintained in the file descriptor, is very simple. It consists of the number of the first block and the total number of blocks comprising the file. The mapping of a single file starting at block 6 and consisting of four blocks is shown in Figure 10-12a.

The main attraction of a contiguous organization is the simplicity with which both sequential and direct access (with fixed-length records) may be accomplished. In particular, sequential access becomes very efficient. That is because adjacent blocks are mapped to the same track or to neighboring tracks of the disk, thus minimizing both seek time, i.e., the need to move the read/write head, and the rotational delay of the disk. Contiguous mapping is particularly attractive for read-only (input) or write-only (output) files, where the entire file is sequentially read or written. In the case of devices that permit only sequential access (e.g., magnetic tapes), contiguous organization is the only scheme that may be implemented efficiently.

The major problem with contiguous allocation of disk blocks is its inflexibility in deleting and inserting records. For variable-length records, changing the length of a record is also problematic. In all these cases, it may be necessary to physically move all records following or preceding the location of the modification to preserve the contiguity of allocation. Alternatively, insertions and deletions may be permitted only at the end of a file.

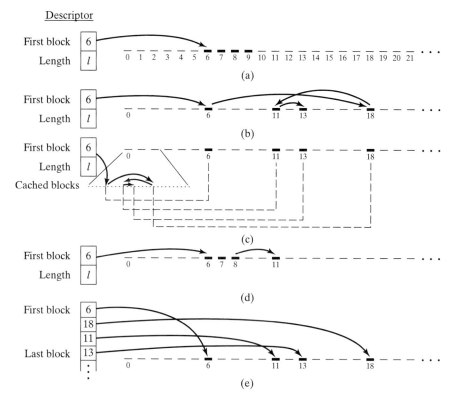

FIGURE 10-12. File organization on disk.

A related problem is how to cope with files that may expand in size due to insertions or appends of new records. One solution is to declare the maximum file length a priori. Unfortunately, if too little space is allocated, the file may not be able to expand, or it may have to be moved to another area of the disk where enough contiguous blocks are found. Too much space, on the other hand, results in wasted resources.

Finally, a contiguous allocation fragments the disk into sequences of free and occupied blocks. This is similar to the problem of managing variable-size partitions in main memory (Section 7.2.2). The file system must keep track of the available holes and allocate them to files using schemes similar to those for main memory management, such as first fit or best fit.

10.6.2   Linked Organization

With this organization, the logical file records may be scattered throughout the secondary storage device. Each block is linked to the logically next one by a forward pointer, as illustrated in Figure 10-12b, which again shows a file starting at block 6 and comprising a total of four blocks.

The main advantage of a linked organization is the ease with which records may be inserted or deleted, thus expanding or contracting the file without excessive copying of the data. There is also no need to impose an upper limit on the file size. With a linked organization, sequential access is easy but much less efficient than with a contiguous organization. The reason is that disk blocks must be read one at a time, since the number of any block is known only when its predecessor has been read. Thus, each block will experience the average rotational delay of the disk. Furthermore, each block may potentially reside on a different track and require a disk seek operation.

Another problem is that direct access is very inefficient. To access a given block requires that the read or write operation follows the chain of pointers from the start until the desired block is found. Yet another serious concern with the linked organization is reliability. If a disk block becomes damaged and cannot be read, the chain of pointers is broken; it is then difficult to find the remainder of the file.

Variations of the Linked List Organization

Many of the drawbacks of the simple linked organization can be alleviated by keeping the block pointers segregated in a separate area of the disk, rather than maintaining them as part of the disk blocks. This can be accomplished by setting up an array, say $PTRS[n]$, where n is the total number of blocks comprising the disk. Each entry $PTRS[i]$ corresponds to disk block i. If block j follows block i in the file, the entry $PTRS[i]$ contains the value j of the corresponding entry $PTRS[j]$.

The pointer array is maintained on a dedicated portion of the disk, e.g., the first k blocks of track zero. The number k depends on the total number of disk blocks n, and the number of bits used to represent each entry $PTRS[i]$. For example, assume that a four-byte integer is needed to record a block number. If the block size is 1024 bytes, $1024/4 = 256$ block numbers can be accommodated in each of the pointer blocks. With $k = 100$, the number of data blocks the $PTRS$ array can keep track of is 25,600. Thus, n would be $25,600 + k = 25,700$.

This organization has been adopted by a number of PC-based operating systems, including MS-DOS and OS-2. Figure 10-12c illustrates the idea. It shows the same file as Figure 10-12b but with the pointers segregated within the first three blocks of the disk. Thus, $PTRS[6] = 18$, $PTRS[18] = 11$, $PTRS[11] = 13$, $PTRS[13] = NULL$. One advantage of this scheme over the simple linked-list organization is that sequential access can be performed much more efficiently. All pointers that must be followed are concentrated within a small number of consecutive blocks containing the $PTRS[n]$ array, and can be read with a single read operation. Furthermore, these blocks can usually be cached in main memory, further improving the time to locate the blocks of a given file.

A serious limitation of the linked-list organization (Figs. 10-12b or c) is that the individual blocks are scattered throughout the entire disk. This unnecessarily increases the number and duration of disk seek operations. An *optimized* version of a linked-list organization tries to keep all blocks clustered close together, preferably on a single cylinder or a small number of adjacent cylinders. An additional optimization is achieved if sequences of adjacent blocks are linked together, rather than individual blocks. Figure 10-12d illustrates this idea. It shows the file allocated in two block groups linked together, one consisting of blocks 6 through 8, and the other consisting of the single block 11. This organization combines the advantages of the contiguous and the individually linked organizations.

10.6.3   Indexed Organization

The purpose of indexing is to permit direct access to file records while eliminating the problems of insertion and deletion inherent to schemes with contiguous allocation of storage. The records may be scattered throughout the secondary memory device just as with the linked organization. An **index table** keeps track of the disk blocks that make up a given file.

There are several forms of indexing, depending on how the index tables are organized and where they are kept. In the simplest case, each index table is just a sequence of the block numbers. Figure 10-12e is an example where the index is implemented as part of the file descriptor. It shows a file consisting of the same four blocks as the linked organizations (Figure 10-12b and c).

Since the size of the descriptor is significant, some file systems store the index table as a separate block. The table can reside anywhere on the disk just like any other block. The descriptor itself then only contains the number of the index block.

Variations of Indexing

The principal limitation of the simple index scheme is the fixed size of each index table. This size determines the maximum number of blocks a file can occupy. The problem can be alleviated by keeping track of **groups** of adjacent blocks, rather than individual blocks, as was done in the case of the linked organization of Figure 10-12d. Nevertheless, the number of possible entries remains fixed. Thus, the table must be large enough to accommodate the largest possible file. Consequently, much space is wasted on unused entries for smaller files. Several solutions exist for the problem. One is to organize the indices as a **multilevel hierarchy**. For example, in a two-level hierarchy, each of the entries of the root, or **primary index**, would point to a leaf, or **secondary index**. Entries in the secondary indices point to the actual file blocks. This makes the number of secondary indices, and hence the space needed to manage a file, variable, depending on the file size.

The disadvantage of the multilevel hierarchy is that the number of disk operations necessary to access a block increases with the depth of the hierarchy. An **incremental indexing** scheme minimizes this overhead while allowing the index to expand based on the file size. This scheme allocates a fixed number of entries at the top index level for actual file blocks. If this is not sufficient to accommodate a file, the index can be expanded by additional, successively larger indices. The first expansion is just another list of n additional blocks. The second expansion is a two-level tree, providing for n^2 additional blocks. The third expansion is a three-level tree, indexing n^3 additional blocks, and so on.

The main advantage of the technique is that the overhead in accessing a file is proportional to the file size. Small files, which constitute the majority of existing files, are accessed efficiently without indirection. At the same time, it is possible to construct extremely large files at the cost of additional indirect accesses.

CASE STUDIES: HIERARCHICAL FILE ORGANIZATION

1. *UNIX.* A three-level incremental indexing scheme has been implemented in the UNIX OS. Each file descriptor, or i-node in UNIX terminology, contains 13 entries describing the mapping of the logical file onto disk blocks (Fig. 10-13). The first 10 entries point directly to blocks holding the contents of the file; each block comprises 512 bytes. If more than 10 blocks are needed, the eleventh entry of the index table is used to point to an indirection block that contains up to 128 pointers to additional blocks of storage. This yields a total of $(10 + 128)$ blocks to hold the file content. If this is still insufficient, the twelfth entry of the index table points via a twofold indirection to additional 128^2 blocks of storage. Finally, for files exceeding the total of $(10 + 128 + 128^2)$ blocks, a threefold indirection starting in the thirteenth entry of the index table provides 128^3 blocks of additional storage to hold the file.

2. *Windows 2000.* The NTFS file system discussed in Section 10.4.3 implements a two-level hierarchy. The contents of short files (or directories) are kept directly in the file descriptor. For longer files, the descriptor contains lists of block numbers where the actual contents are kept (Fig. 10-10).

10.6.4 Management of Free Storage Space

When a file is created or when it expands, the file system must allocate new disk blocks to it. Deciding which blocks to allocate is important since the decision determines future disk access times. Similarly, when a file is deleted or shrinks in size, some blocks may be released and added to the pool of free disk space.

Allocating disk blocks and keeping track of the free space is one of the main functions of the device organization methods of the file system. The disk space is generally shared by many different files. Not surprisingly, some of the techniques for main memory administration described in Chapter 7 also are applicable here. There are two principal approaches to keeping track of available disk space.

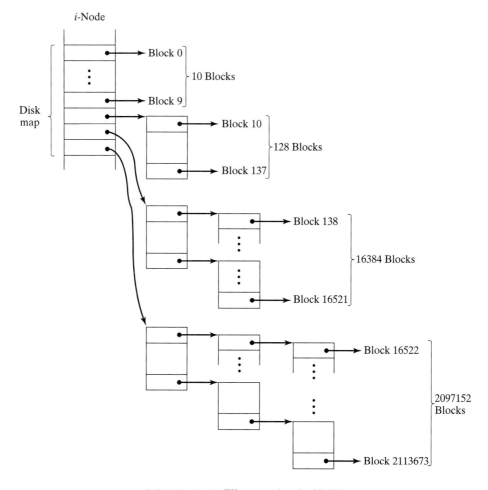

FIGURE 10-13. File mapping in UNIX.

Linked-List Organization

We can treat all free blocks as just another file. This file can be organized using the same techniques presented earlier in this section for keeping track of file blocks. In particular, the simple linked-list method (Fig. 10-12b or c) could be applied, where each free block contains a pointer to its successor on the linked list. The main drawback is that it does not facilitate block clustering. Furthermore, efficiency in allocating and releasing of blocks is also poor. It is frequently the case that multiple blocks must be allocated or released at the same time. The simple linked organization requires a separate disk access operation for each block. Similarly, adding several blocks to the free list requires that each is written separately.

A much better method is to link together **groups** of adjacent blocks instead of individual blocks. This is analogous to the modified linked-list approach of Figure 10-12d. The segregation of adjacent blocks not only shortens the linked list, but makes it much easier to allocate (and free) multiple blocks using a single disk access operation.

Bitmap Organization

Since disk space is allocated naturally in fixed-size blocks, the status of the disk space can be conveniently maintained as a bitmap where each bit represents the state (free or occupied). Because only one additional bit is required for each disk block, very little disk space is wasted. For example, if disk storage is allocated in blocks of 512 bytes, the bitmap overhead is only $100/(512 \times 8) = 0.024$ %.

Also, sequences of adjacent free blocks and occupied blocks are naturally segregated in the bitmap as groups of zeros and ones. Consequently, all operations, including finding free blocks in a given vicinity, allocating blocks, and releasing blocks, can be implemented efficiently using bit-manipulation operations, as developed in the context of main memory management (Section 7.2.2.)

10.7 PRINCIPLES OF DISTRIBUTED FILE SYSTEMS

In the previous sections, we assumed a single centralized file system. This system manages all files and directories on the underlying storage devices—typically a disk or a set of disks, and provides the user interface.

Networking makes it possible to connect many different computers together, each of which can have its own secondary storage subsystem. A typical environment is a local area network, consisting of some number of PCs and diskless workstations, as well as workstations with local disks. One function and goal of the file system in such a distributed environment is to present a unifying view of all files to the user and, as much as possible, to hide the fact that they reside on different machines. Another key function of a distributed file system is to support the sharing of files and directories in a controlled manner.

Most OSs will provide some utilities to share files *explicitly*, i.e., to copy them between different computers, each of which maintains its own (centralized) file system. One of the most common utilities to copy files between machines is *ftp* (file transfer program), which uses the Internet's standard file transfer protocol (FTP) to accomplish its task. *ftp* opens a dialog session between its invoking client and a server on a remote machine. It allows the user to execute a number of useful file and directory manipulation commands, including the transfer of files between the client and server machines.

Another common utility, supported on UNIX and Linux machines, is *rcp* (remote copy). Similar to the local file copy command (*cp*), *rcp* requires two parameters: the source and the destination of the file to be copied. The main difference between *cp* and *rcp* is that the source or destination parameter of the latter may be a local file or a remote file, specified as *m:path*, where *m* is the name of a remote machine and *path* is the file path name on that machine.

Such copying tools, although extremely useful, do not hide the distribution of files and require that users know about file locations and names. A **distributed file system** (DFS) makes this distribution transparent by presenting a single view of all files and providing easy access to them regardless of their present location.

10.7.1 Directory Structures and Sharing

Similar to centralized systems, a distributed file system must define a directory structure, together with a set of directory operations, to permit users to locate files. It also provides a high-level, abstract view of files, represented by a set of operations to read, write, and otherwise manipulate the file contents. However, a DFS must extend these structures, views, and services because files and directories can reside on more than one machine.

There are many ways to define a DFS, differentiated by how they handle the following important issues:

1. **Global vs. Local Naming.** Is there a single global directory structure seen by all users, or can each user have a different local view of the directory structure?

2. **Location Transparency.** Does the path name of a file reveal anything about the machine or server on which the file resides or is the file location completely transparent?

3. **Location Independence.** When a file is moved between machines, must its path name change or can it remain the same?

Let us examine these crucial points in more detail and consider the trade-offs between the possible options.

Global Directory Structure

From the user's point of view, the directory structure of a DFS should be indistinguishable from a directory structure on a centralized system. In such an ideal directory, all path names would be globally unique, i.e., a file would be referred to by the same name regardless of which machine the user was currently residing on, and would not change if the file was moved physically between different servers.

Unfortunately, such an ideal DFS is very uncommon. Less convenient and ideal systems are the norm for two important reasons. First, a DFS is rarely developed and populated with files from scratch. Rather, a set of preexisting file systems is combined into a common federation. The second reason is that there are usually certain files that must reside on specific machines. For example, workstation initialization programs or files that maintain some portion of the machine description or state may reside on that specific machine. Consequently, a DFS must leave certain aspects of distribution visible to the user.

The problems can be solved by sacrificing location transparency. In the simplest case, the path name of a remote file is simply prefixed by the name of the machine or server on which the file resides. A common notation for this approach is *m:path*, where *path* is a path name on the specific machine, *m*. A more elegant solution is to assign a unique name to the root of each local file system and unify them under a common global root.

To illustrate this approach, consider Figure 10-14a, which shows two file systems, each with its own root (/), and each residing on a different file server, *S*1 and *S*2. Figure 10-14b shows a federated directory structure resulting from combining the two local file systems under the names of their respective servers.

The new directory structure is global, resulting in path names that are equally valid on any machine. For example, the path name */S1/usr/u1* would identify the same file *u1*, regardless of whether it was used on server *S*1 or *S*2. The main problem with using such path names where the slash (/) refers to the new global directory is that path names that were used on the individual systems before they became federated would cease to work properly, since the slash was intended to refer to the *local* root directory. For example, */usr/u1* identifies the file *u1* on the local file system of server *S*1 but is invalid in the global structure (Fig. 10-14b).

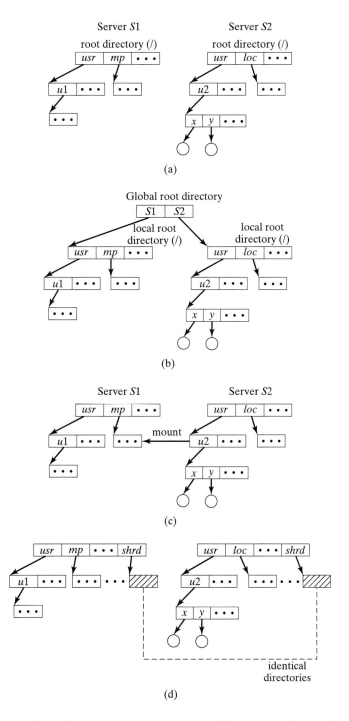

FIGURE 10-14. Unifying file systems: (a) two separate file systems; (b) creating a common root; (c) mounting; and (d) shared subdirectory.

To solve this naming dilemma, the following scheme was developed and implemented in the *UNIX United* distributed OS. The slash is retained as a reference to the *local* root directory, so that existing programs do not have to be modified. To access files above the local root, the same notation (..) is used as for referring to any other parent directory. Thus, a path name reveals clearly the boundary of the system, and it permits the user to reach any file within the global structure. For example, to reach the file *u1* from *u2*, either of the following path names could be used: *../../../S1/usr/u1* or */../S1/usr/u1*. The first is a relative path name, starting in the current directory *u2*, whereas the second is absolute, starting with the local root (/) of *u2* and moving up to the global root prior to descending down toward *u1*.

Note that combining the original file systems by simply merging their root directories, i.e., without introducing the new root directory, would be difficult due to name conflicts. For example, both file systems have the directory *usr*, each of which may contain files with the same names and could not simply be merged into one. The disadvantage of introducing the new directory names *S1* and *S2* is that file names are *not* location transparent. Choosing symbolic names for *S1* and *S2* can hide the identity of the underlying machines, but their position within the hierarchy, combined with the fact that each contains well-known system files such as *usr*, reveals information about the underlying physical file distribution.

Local Directory Structures

Another way to combine multiple existing files systems into one is by a **mounting** mechanism. Thereby, a user (with the necessary systems privileges) can temporarily attach any part of a file hierarchy residing on some remote machine to a directory within the local file system. The chosen local directory is called the **mount point**. After the mount operation is complete, the remote subdirectory becomes a subtree of the local directory, with the mount point as its root directory. Figure 10-14c illustrates this for the two structures of Figure 10-14a. The directory *mp* is the mount point, over which a user on server *S1* mounts the subtree identified by the name */usr*, residing on the remote server *S2*. Thereafter, all users on *S1* may use the path name */mp* to refer to the directory identified by */usr* on *S2*, and the path name */mp/...* to directly access any files under that directory as if they were local. For example, */mp/u2/x* on *S1* refers to the same file as */usr/u2/x* on *S2*. Note that the previous contents of *mp*, if any, are inaccessible when the remote subtree is mounted. Thus, mounting is typically done over special mount points, which are empty directories set up for just that purpose.

This approach provides complete location transparency since the path name does not reveal the actual location of any file. The main disadvantage is that different users may have different views of the file system hierarchy. As a consequence, path names are context sensitive; their meaning depends on which machine they are interpreted. For example, a program using the path name */mp/...* on machine *S1* would fail or possibly use a wrong file when moved and executed on machine *S2*.

Shared Directory Substructure

Because certain files often must reside on specific machines, the principles of location transparency and location independence can never be fully realized. An attractive compromise solution to this problem, pioneered by the *Andrew file system* (Howard et al.

1988; Satyanarayanan 1990), and adopted by its successor, the Coda file system (Satya-narayanan et al. 1990), specifies a two-part hierarchy for each machine. One part consists of local files, which are different for each machine. The other is a subtree of shared files; these are, of course, identical on all machines. Figure 10-14d shows the idea for the two file systems of Figure 10-14a. Each now has a new subdirectory, named *shrd* in this example, under which all files shared by the two systems are maintained. All other files are local. Thus, modifying the directory *usr* on either machine would affect only files on that machine, whereas modifying any portion of the *shrd* subtree would become visible by users on all participating machines.

This solution is a compromise in that it provides a single view of all shared files while permitting each subsystem to maintain its local files. It is also beneficial for performance since many files, such as temporary files, will never be shared and hence do not have to be subjected to the overhead resulting from file sharing.

10.7.2   Semantics of File Sharing

Files in a distributed environment are no different from files in a centralized system. They are characterized by their name, type, internal organization, and a number of other attributes, as discussed in Section 10.3.3. Distributed files are accessed and manipulated using the same operations as those used in a centralized environment. That means, a file can be created and deleted, opened and closed, and its contents can be accessed with read, write, and seek operations.

The main difference between centralized and distributed files is their semantics of sharing. Ideally, we would like files to behave the same way in both environments. Unfortunately, performance considerations make it necessary to sometimes relax this equivalence. This leads to the following possible types of file-sharing semantics:

- **UNIX semantics**. In most centralized file systems, including UNIX, sharing a file implies that all write operations become immediately visible to all users sharing that file. That means, a read operation will always see the data written by the last write operation. Implementing the same semantics in a distributed environment requires that all write operations are immediately propagated through the network to the corresponding file, resulting in much network traffic. Furthermore, since network delays are generally unpredictable, it is not always possible to guarantee that write operations are performed in the order in which they were issued on different machines. For these reasons, other forms of file-sharing semantics have been developed for DFSs.

- **Session semantics**. To avoid propagating all write operations to remote files immediately, a file opened under session semantics is treated as a private copy by each user for the duration of the session. Only when the file is closed are the changes propagated to the original file and visible to other users. This relaxed form of semantics has less overhead than the UNIX semantics, but is less appealing due to its increased unpredictability. Notably, when two processes simultaneously update a file, the file content will depend on which process closes the file last. The changes made by the first closing process are simply lost, i.e., they are overwritten by the values written by the last process.

- **Transaction semantics**. Under the session semantics discussed above, all modifications to a file performed by a user remain invisible until the file is closed. To reduce the time during which the changes are invisible, transaction semantics permits the user to designate specific portions of the code to be transactions, i.e., segments of code that can be considered indivisible. All modifications of a file performed during a transaction become immediately visible to all other processes sharing the file at the end of the transaction. In other words, a transaction can be used as an atomic operation, whose effects become immediately visible when it terminates.

- **Immutable-files semantics**. The problem of delayed file updates can be avoided entirely by simply disallowing any modifications of already existing files. That means, all files are treated as read-only. A write operation results in the creation of a new file, typically referred to as a new **version** of the file. The problem of file sharing then becomes a problem of version management, for which a number of solutions exist to maintain data consistency.

10.8 IMPLEMENTING DISTRIBUTED FILE SYSTEM

10.8.1 Basic Architecture

Most DFSs are organized as collections of servers and clients. Servers run on machines that contain portions of the file system, whereas clients run on machines that access the files and directories in response to user commands. The subdivision of machines into servers and clients, however, is not absolute; most machines can operate in either capacity, depending on the operations being performed.

Figure 10-15 shows a generic structure of a client/server-based DFS architecture, patterned after the popular Sun Microsystems **network file system**, commonly known as **NFS** (Callaghan 2000). The figure shows two machines, *A* and *B*, each of which contains a local disk and a portion of the file systems. Let us assume that machine *A* requests access to a given file. The request is presented to the top layer of the file system of *A*, called the *virtual file system* in the figure. This module determines whether the file is held locally or on a remote server. In the former case, it forwards the request to the

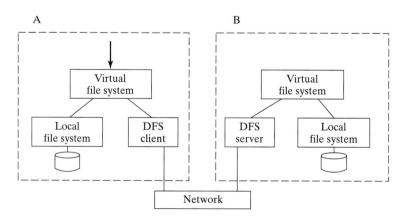

FIGURE 10-15. Client/server architecture of a DFS.

local file system, which accesses the file on the local disk. If the file is remote, machine *A* will play the role of a client. It will determine the appropriate server and send the request through the network to the corresponding machine. The server accesses the file via its local file system and returns the result back to the client.

Most existing DFSs are based on the basic client-server architecture. What differentiates the various types is how much functionality is implemented in the client and how much is implemented in the server. The most important issues are the forms of caching employed, the management of the state of open files, and the level of file data replication.

10.8.2 Caching

When a client accesses a remote file, it experiences two forms of overhead: a **network delay** and a **disk access delay** on the server. Both can greatly be diminished by caching. The main questions are whether the cache should be maintained on the server or on the client, and what information should be cached.

Server Caching

The disk access overhead can be eliminated on subsequent accesses to the same file if the server caches the file in its main memory. One approach caches the entire file. This can be wasteful if only a small portion of the file is being accessed; it also complicates the cache management since each file has a different length. A second option is to cache only the disk blocks that have been accessed. This technique results in a more structured and efficient cache, but requires a block replacement scheme, such as the LRU policy discussed in the context of paging (Section 8.3.1).

The main advantage of caching of file data in the server is that it is easy to implement and can be made totally transparent to the client. Both file-level and block-level caching reduce the need to access the disk and improve file access. The principal drawback is that the data still must be transferred through the network at each request.

Client Caching

To reduce the network overhead, caching also can be performed on the client. Similar to server caching, the client can either download the entire file into its own local memory or local disk, if one is available, or it can cache only those disk blocks it is accessing. Unfortunately, client caching is a source of potential inconsistencies. Whenever two clients share a file, updates performed to the locally cached data are not immediately visible to the server or to other process using the same file concurrently. We can subdivide this problem into two related issues: 1) when to update the original file on the server; and 2) when and how to inform other processes sharing the file of the changes that have been made. We examine these two issues in turn:

Write-through versus delayed writing

The simplest possible but least efficient solution to the problem of updating the original file on the server is to propagate each modification to the server immediately. This permits us to enforce UNIX semantics, but it greatly diminishes the benefits of client caching. The alternative is to adopt a weaker form of file-sharing semantics as discussed in the last section. For example, session semantics permits an update to be kept local and propagated to the file server only when the file is closed. Similarly, transaction semantics reduce the frequency with which updates must be propagated to the server. Thus, the basic trade-off is improved performance at the cost of less user-friendly file-sharing semantics.

Cache update schemes

Updating the file on the server is only the first part of the cache coherence problem. Once this is accomplished, other processes that have cached any portions of the file in their local space must be notified of the changes. This can be initiated by the server or clients. In the first case, the server keeps track of all processes that have opened the file for access, and it informs them automatically of any changes to the file. Unfortunately, the scheme violates the basic client-server model—the server, which should only respond to client requests, must in this case take the initiative to contact the client.

If the client is made responsible for validating its own cache, it must decide when to check with the server about any possible changes to the file. Doing so prior to every access would defeat the purpose of caching. On the other hand, checking less frequently increases the danger of reading out-of-date information. Relaxing the file-sharing semantics again alleviates the problem. For example, with session semantics, the client only must check with the server when opening the file.

10.8.3   Stateless Versus Stateful Servers

Before a file can be used for reading or writing, it must be opened. This causes a new entry in the open file table (OFT) to be created, which stores the current state of the file. The state typically consists of the current position within the file, the access mode in which the file has been opened, and location information to find the file contents on the disk. In the case of a centralized system, the OFT is maintained by the local file system. In a distributed system, the OFT can be maintained in the server or client. This leads to two possible forms of a server, referred to as *stateful* and *stateless*, respectively.

Stateful Servers

A *stateful* server maintains the OFTs for all its clients. When a client wishes to access a file, it sends an open command to the server. The server makes a new entry in the OFT and returns the index of this entry to the client. The index is used by the client for subsequent read or write operations to the file. This procedure is analogous to that for opening a file in a centralized file system.

Figure 10-16a outlines the basic interactions between a client and a stateful server. Assume that a user process wishes to open a file X and perform a series of sequential read operations on it. It first issues the command $i = open(X, ...)$. The client portion of the DFS passes the command to the corresponding server portion on the host holding file X. The server opens the file by making a new entry in its OFT. Part of this entry is the current position within the file, *pos*, which is initialized to zero. The server then returns the OFT index i to the user process via the client. Each of the subsequent *read* commands issued by the user also is passed to the server by the client. For each command, the server performs the operation, updates the OFT (notably the current file position), and returns the data (n bytes) to the client. The data are copied into the specified user buffer (*buf*).

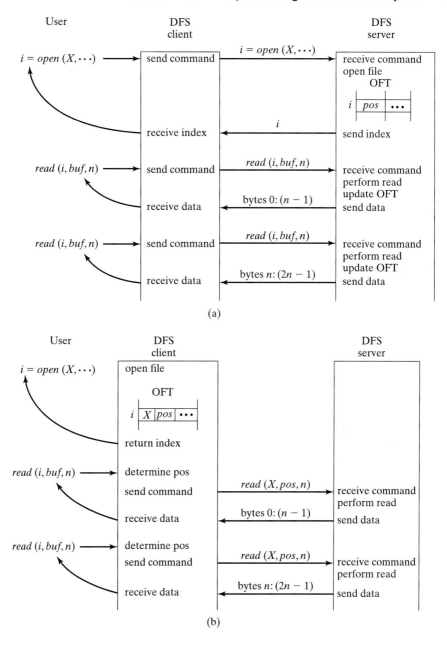

FIGURE 10-16. Interactions with: (a) a stateful server; (b) a stateless server.

The client's role is straightforward. It acts essentially as a conduit between the user process and the server by exchanging the commands and the results between them. The commands used to open and access the file are the same as in a centralized file system. The problem with the approach is reliability. Since the client and the server are on different machines, each can crash independently. All state information about open files is generally held in the server main memory. If the server crashes and sub-sequently recovers, this information is lost, including the current position within the file and any partially updated attributes, such as the file length or disk location. It is then up to the client to reopen the file and to restore the state of the file prior to the crash. When the client crashes with open files, the server is left with information in its OFTs that will not be claimed by the client after recovery and must be discarded through a recovery process.

Stateless Servers

A *stateless* server has no state information about any open files. Instead, each client is responsible for keeping its own OFT. Since the server does not accept any *open* or *close* commands, each access to the file by the client must contain all the information necessary to perform the operation. In particular, each command must contain the file symbolic name, which must be maintained as part of the OFT. Each *read* and *write* command also must specify the starting position within the file, in addition to the number of bytes to be transferred.

Figure 10-16b sketches the interactions between the client and the stateless server using the same sequence of user operations as in the stateful example. The *open* command causes the creation of a new OFT entry. This, however, is maintained by the client; the server is not aware of this operation. The OFT index (i) is returned to the user as before. The subsequent *read* operations cannot simply be forwarded to the server but must be transformed by the client into analogous *read* operations that do not rely on the existence of any state information in the server. In particular, each *read* must specify not only the number of bytes (n) but also the file symbolic name (X) and current starting position (pos), both of which are recorded in the OFT and maintained by the client.

Because the server has no current state information about any open files, it is possible to recover transparently after a crash; the server simply restarts and continues accepting commands from its clients. The commands are **idempotent**, meaning that they can be repeated any number of times and they always return the same data. The price to pay for this improved fault tolerance is the increased burden placed on the client; more information must be sent with every command than was the case with a stateful server.

CASE STUDY: NFS

Sun Microsystems network file system (NFS) implements a stateless server that clients use through a set of remote procedure calls. Most operations of the server, including reading and writing files and directories, are idempotent. Those that are not idempotent cause no inconsistencies in the stored data, but may generate error messages that can be confusing to clients. For example, deleting or renaming a file are not idempotent. If the server's reply to such a command is lost, the client generally retransmits the same command. Since the operation cannot be repeated, the server responds with an error message, such as "file does not exist," even though the operation has been performed successfully.

Caching is performed by both the server and clients. However, NFS also guarantees UNIX semantics, which interferes with client caching. To solve this dilemma, NFS allows client caching only for nonshared files and disables it when a file is shared by multiple clients. This, unfortunately, introduces some state into the "stateless" server, because the server must keep track of which client has cached which file. The popularity of NFS indicates that a successful DFS must make many important trade-off decisions in its design to satisfy a wide range of requirements.

10.8.4 File Replication

Keeping multiple copies of a file on different servers has several important benefits:

- **Availability**. When a server holding the only copy of a file crashes, the file becomes inaccessible. With additional replicas, users may continue accessing the file unimpeded.

- **Reliability**. When a file server crashes, some files may be left in an inconsistent state. Having multiple independent copies of a file is an important tool for the recovery process.

- **Performance**. Maintaining multiple copies of files at different locations increases the chances for a client to access a file locally, or at least on a server that is in its close proximity. This decreases network latency and improves the time to access the file. It also reduces the overall network traffic.

- **Scalability**. A single server can easily be overwhelmed by a number of concurrent accesses to a file. Maintaining multiple copies of the file defuses the bottleneck and permits the system to easily scale up to a larger numbers of users.

File replication is similar to file-level caching in the client. In both cases, multiple copies of a file are maintained on different machines. The main difference is that caching only maintains a *temporary* copy in the client when the file is being used. With file replication, the copy is *permanent*. Furthermore, a cached copy is often kept on the client's machine, and a replicated file is kept on a separate server that may be a different machine from the client's.

Again, the problem with file replication is consistency. Similar to caching, the system must guarantee that all update operations are applied to all replicas at the same time or the file semantics must be relaxed. There are two main protocols the file system can follow when reading and writing file replicas to keep them consistent:

Read-Any/Write-All Protocol

As the name suggests, this protocol allows a process to read any of the available replicas. An update, however, must be propagated to all replicas simultaneously. This latter requirement is difficult to implement. First, the update must be propagated atomically to all replicas so that it is not interleaved with other update requests, thus possibly introducing inconsistencies. Special group communication primitives can be used for that purpose. When the application domain allows interleaving, the propagation of the updates does not have to be atomic, but it must still be sent to all copies of the file. This raises the question of what should be done when one or more of the copies are currently unavailable, for example, due to a temporary server crash. Forcing the writing process to wait until all copies are available is not an acceptable solution. The alternative is to put the burden on the failed server. When it recovers, it must communicate with other servers and bring all its files up to date.

Quorum-Based Read/Write Protocol

The previous read-any/write-all protocol is only a special case of a more general class of protocols called *quorum-based protocols*. These avoid the need to always update all replicas of a file, but at the expense of having to read more than one copy each time. The number of replicas, w, that a process must write each time is referred to as the **write quorum**. The number of replicas, r, that a process must read each time is referred to as the **read quorum**. The two numbers r and w are chosen to obey the following constraints:

$$r + w > N$$

$$w > N/2$$

where N is the total number of replicas. The first rule guarantees that any read quorum intersects any write quorum. That means, any *read* operation will see at least one replica that has been updated by the latest *write* operation and represents the latest version of the file. The second rule prevents two processes from updating two disjoint subsets of the replicas, both of which could end up having the same version number or time-stamp. Subsequent *read* operations then could not differentiate between them.

EXAMPLE: A Quorum-Based Protocol

Consider a system of seven replicas of a given file, numbered $F1$ through $F7$. If we assume $r = 4$ and $w = 4$, then any *read* operation and any *write* operation must access at least four different replicas. Figure 10-17a shows an example where a *write*

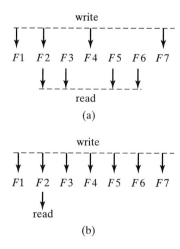

FIGURE 10-17. Accessing files using read/write quorum.

operation modified replicas $F1$, $F2$, $F4$, and $F5$, and the subsequent *read* operation read the replicas $F2$, $F3$, $F5$, and $F6$. The replica $F2$ is in both sets, thereby ensuring that the *read* operation will access the latest version of the file. Figure 10-17b illustrates the extreme case, where the size of the write quorum is 7, whereas the size of the read quorum is 1. In other words, a *write* operation must update *all* replicas, while a *read* operation may read *any* replica. This extreme example corresponds to the previous protocol, called read-any/write-all.

CONCEPTS, TERMS, AND ABBREVIATIONS

The following concepts have been introduced in this chapter. Test yourself by defining and discussing each keyword or phrase.

Access rights	Linked list organization
B-tree	Logical record
Caching of files	Memory-mapped file
Client caching	Mounting
Contiguous organization	Name extension
DAG-structured directory	Open file
Distributed file system (DFS)	Open file table (OFT)
Direct access	Path name
Directory	Quorum-based read/write protocol
File	Read-any/write-all protocol
File descriptor	Record addressing
File name	Replicating files
File protection	Rewind
File sharing	Seek
File system	Server caching
File transfer protocol (FTP)	Sequential access
File type	Sharing semantics
Free space management	Stateless and stateful servers
Hierarchical directory structure	Symbolic link
Hierarchical file system model	Transaction sharing semantics
Immutable file	Tree-structured directory
Indexed file organization	UNIX-sharing semantics
i-node	Working directory

EXERCISES

1. Consider the directory hierarchy in Figure 6-7.
    (a) What are the shortest absolute path names for the files $F4$ and $F8$?
    (b) What are the shortest relative path names for the same files $F1$ and $F8$ when the current working directory is $D3$?
    (c) What are the shortest relative path names for the same files $F1$ and $F8$ when the current working directory is $D7$?
    (d) Repeat the above three problems assuming that all symbolic links are eliminated.

2. The diagram below shows a portion of a tree-structured directory hierarchy.

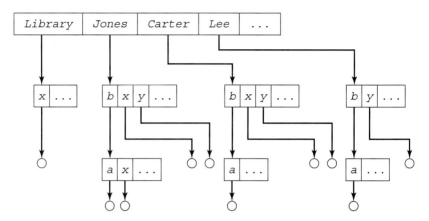

The file system maintains a *referenced file table* (RFT) for each session of each user. This contains the name of every file referenced during that session and its corresponding unique path name. The RFT is cleared when the user logs off. To locate a file, the following search rules are used:

1. search the RFT; if not found then
2. search the caller's parent directory; if not found then
3. search the current working directory; if not found then
4. search the library directory; if not found then fail

Each time a file is found using rules 2, 3, or 4, the corresponding new entry is made in the RFT.

Assume that each of the following path names identifies an executable file that references a file x. Determine which of the many possible files named x will be referenced in each case, and which rule will be used to make the selection. Assume that each line corresponds to a new login session, and the working directories of the three users are *Jones*, *Carter* and *Lee*, respectively.

(a) *Jones/b/a*

(b) *Jones/y*

(c) *Jones/b/a; Jones/y*

(d) *Carter/b/a*

(e) *Carter/y*

(f) *Carter/b/a; Carter/y*

(g) *Lee/b/a*

(h) *Lee/y*

(i) *Lee/b/a; Lee/y*

3. Consider the following file and directory commands: *create*, *delete*, *open*, *close*, *unbuffered read*, *unbuffered append (write)*, *seek*, *rename*, *list*, *move*, *link*, *find*.

Some of the following actions are taken as a result of each of the above operations:

- read a directory;
- write a directory;
- read the OFT;
- write the OFT;
- make new directory entry;
- make new OFT entry;

- read from disk;
- write to disk;
- free a directory entry;
- free an OFT entry;
- allocate new disk block;
- free disk block.

Construct a matrix showing which action(s) will in general be triggered by which command.

4. Consider a sequential file f of n characters. Write the pseudocode for a program that will double the length of such a file by copying and appending the file contents to the end of the file. The file system maintains the current read/write position, p, within the file, and supports the following operations: $seek(f, n)$ moves p to the n-th character of f; $ch=read(f)$ returns the character at position p and advances p; $write(f, ch)$ writes the character ch into the position p and advances p. The read and write operations are buffered, using an internal buffer of 512 characters. Write the routine to minimize the number of disk operations.

5. Consider a file system that supports no open or close operations on files. Instead, each read and write operation must specify the file's symbolic path name.
   (a) Assume block-oriented read/write operations each of which accesses a single fixed-length block. Which tasks normally performed by open/close commands would be performed by every read/write operation?
   (b) Could sequential read/write be supported, given that there is no OFT to keep track of the current position and the read/write buffer?

6. The following diagrams show portions of several data structures of a file system. These are organized as follows. Each entry in the *current directory* contains the symbolic name of a file, together with the index into the array of *file descriptors*. Each descriptor records the file length (in bytes) and the number of its first block on the *disk*. The disk blocks of a file are assigned contiguously on the disk; the block length is assumed to be 256 bytes. For example, the file *test* has a descriptor at index 19, which shows that the file comprises 280 bytes; it starts at disk block 8 and continues into block 9. The OFT keeps track of all open files. Each entry contains the index into the array of *file descriptors* and the current position within the file (for sequential access). Currently, file *abc* is open (descriptor index 16). Its current position is 55, which means the first 55 bytes of that file have already been read or written.

Current Directory:

symb. name	descr. index
...	...
free	
xx	20
abc	16
test	19
free	
...	...

File Descriptors:

	file length	disk block#
	...	...
15	free	
16	100	5
17	free	
18	free	
19	280	8
20	550	40
	...	...

Open File Table

	descr. index	curr. pos.
	...	...
7	free	
8	16	55
9	free	
	...	...

Disk:

	5	6	7	8	9	
	xxx	free	free	xxxxxxxx	xxx	

256 bytes

For each of the following operations, show all changes to the data structures:

(a) open the file *test*: *fd=open(test)*
(b) seek to position 60 of the open *test* file: *seek(fd,60)*
(c) create a new empty file called *new*: *create(new)*
(d) open the file *new*: *fd=open(new)*
(e) write 30 bytes into the file *new*: *write(fd,buf,30)*
(f) close the file *new*: *close(fd)*
(g) delete the file *new*: *delete(new)*

7. Consider a file consisting of three disk blocks. For each of the five file organizations in Figure 10-12, determine the total number of blocks that must be read from the disk to accomplish the following tasks. (Assume that the file descriptors are already in memory, and that only a single data block can be kept in memory at any point in time.)

    (a) Read the file sequentially first forward and then backward.
    (b) Read only the last byte of the file.

8. Consider a file consisting of eight logical blocks (numbered 0 through 7). Make the following assumptions:
    - the read/write head is currently at the beginning of block 4;
    - the following sequence of operations is performed:
      read block 3, read block 5, delete block 4, insert block 2A (i.e., between blocks 2 and 3).

    For each of the physical disk organizations shown in Figure 10-12, give the list of blocks that must be read from disk (if any) and the list of blocks that must be written to disk (if any) to perform each of the above four disk operations.

9. Consider a disk consisting of a total of 100,000 blocks of 512 bytes each. Assume that all descriptors are kept within file directories. A four-byte integer is necessary to address each disk block.

    (a) For the allocation strategy of Figure 10-12c, determine the number of blocks that must be reserved at the head of the disk to keep track of all the remaining file data blocks. What is the largest possible file that can be represented using this allocation strategy?
    (b) For the allocation strategy of Figure 10-12e, assume that a single block is used for each file index. Determine the largest possible file that can be represented using this allocation strategy?

10. Generally, the length of a file is not an exact multiple of the block size. Thus, a portion of the last block of every file is unused. This is analogous to internal fragmentation in main memory (Section 8.3.4).

    (a) Derive a formula that computes the space overhead due to internal fragmentation as a function of the average file length, l (in bytes), and disk block size, b (in bytes).
    (b) Compute the overhead for all combinations of the following file lengths and block lengths:
      b: 512, 1024, 2048 (bytes)
      l: 100, 1000, 10000 (bytes)

11. With a contiguous disk block allocation, the disk consists of a sequence of occupied and free blocks. A problem similar to external fragmentation in main memory occurs. But there is a difference: Main memory has either internal or external fragmentation, but never both, while a disk with a contiguous allocation has both. Why are the two situations different?

12. Consider the hierarchical organization shown in Figure 10-13 and assume that each block can hold 256 blocks instead of 128. What is the maximum file size?

13. Assume the hierarchical organization shown in Figure 10-13 is modified such that the first block of every file is part of the i-node data structure, and requires no disk access; all other blocks are accessed as before. Assume further that 80% of all files occupy less than one disk block, and the remaining 20% occupy an average of d blocks.
    (a) Determine by how much the modified scheme will reduce the number of disk accesses per file.
    (b) Compute the improvement for $d = 2$ and $d = 4$.

14. Consider a file system where the file descriptors of all files are kept in a dedicated portion of the disk. Make the following assumptions. Each file descriptor needs 64 bytes. The disk has 10,000 blocks, each of length 512 bytes. The average file lengths are distributed as follows:
    • 80% of all files occupy less than one block;
    • 10% of all files occupy two blocks;
    • 5% of all files occupy three blocks;
    • The remaining 5% of all files occupy an average of 10 blocks.
    (a) Determine the number of files that can be accommodated on this disk.
    (b) Determine the amount of space that must be reserved for the descriptors.

15. Consider a system that uses a bitmap to keep track of disk space allocation. Space is allocated in blocks of 512 bytes, i.e., one bit is needed in the bitmap for every 512 bytes. Assume that the disk is empty initially. Three files, A, B, and C, are written to the disk. The file sizes are 1040, 700, and 2650, respectively. File B is then deleted.
    (a) Show the beginning of the bitmap (covering the three files) before and after file B is deleted.
    (b) Repeat the above problem but assuming that the unit of space allocation are two blocks, i.e., a single bit is used for each pair of consecutive blocks.

16. In a system using a bitmap, what is the minimum block size such that the bitmap occupies less than 0.1% of the total disk space? (One bit is used for each block.)

17. Consider using a bitmap versus a linked list of free blocks. The disk contains a total of B blocks, F of which are free. A disk addresses requires d bits. The bitmap uses one bit for each block. The linked list is a data structure maintained in a dedicated portion of the disk. Each list element points to a single free block.
    (a) State the condition under which two methods use the same amount of disk space, assuming that the linked-list method connects all blocks individually.
    (b) For $d = 16$ bits, determine the fraction of the disk that must be free for the above condition to hold.
    (c) Repeat problems (a) and (b) above, assuming that the linked-list method connects groups of adjacent blocks, rather than individual blocks. That means, each list element points to the first block of a group, and contains a two-byte number indicating how many blocks are in the group. The average size of a group is five blocks.

18. Assume the directory shown in Figure 10-3 resides on a server S1. A user executing within the directory must access a file identified by the path name /a1/b1/c1 on a different server S2. The user is currently executing within file $F6$ and the current directory is $D2$.
    (a) Assume first the two file systems are combined under UNIX United. Give three possible path names the user could use to reach the file.
    (b) Assume now the two file systems are combined using mounting. The subtree identified by /a1 on S2 is mounted over the directory $D3$ on S1. Give again three possible path names the user could use to reach the file.

19. Assume a new directory, containing file names, x, y, and z is mounted over the directory $D6$ in Figure 10-7.
    (a) Which of the original legal path names become invalid when the new directory is mounted?
    (b) Which of the original files and directories become inaccessible?

CHAPTER 11

Input/Output Systems

11.1 BASIC ISSUES IN DEVICE MANAGEMENT
11.2 A HIERARCHICAL MODEL OF THE INPUT/OUTPUT SYSTEM
11.3 INPUT/OUTPUT DEVICES
11.4 DEVICE DRIVERS
11.5 DEVICE MANAGEMENT

All computer systems must communicate with the outside world. They use a variety of devices for this purpose, depending on whether the communication partner is human or another computer. Any computer system also must provide long-term nonvolatile storage. There are several types of devices for this purpose, varying greatly in storage capacity, speed of access, and cost. The I/O system is that part of the operating system (OS) that manages communication and storage devices. It is one of the most difficult parts of the OS to design and maintain in a systematic manner. One of the main reasons for this difficulty is the range of devices that require support. In addition, the I/O system must be able to handle new devices that were not available on the market when the OS was developed or installed.

After examining basic I/O issues and models, the chapter presents a brief survey of I/O devices. Some details of device drivers are described, followed by a treatment of device management, including buffering, caching, scheduling, and error handling.

11.1 BASIC ISSUES IN DEVICE MANAGEMENT

We differentiate roughly between two types of devices: **communication devices** and **storage devices**. The former can be subdivided further into **input** devices and **output** devices.

Input devices are those that accept data generated by an external agent (e.g., a human user, a biological or chemical process, a mechanical object, or another computer) and transform data into a binary format to be stored and processed in the computer memory. The most common ones include keyboards, scanners, pointing devices (e.g., a mouse, a joystick, or a light pen), and voice analyzers. Output devices accept binary data from a computer and transform these into other formats or media to make them available to an external agent (e.g., a human user, a physical process, or another computer). These include different types of printers, plotters, visual displays, and voice synthesizers. Many of these devices provide a human-computer interface. When a computer is connected to other computers by a network, it can view the network as a communication device that can both produce input data and accept output data in various formats.

Storage devices maintain internally some data in nonvolatile form, which may be accessed and utilized by the computer. We can classify storage devices into **input/output** devices and **input-only** devices. The most common I/O storage devices are magnetic disks and magnetic tapes; both are used for mass storage of data. Some forms of optical disks, termed CD-R or CD-RW, are also writable, but most fall into the read-only category. CD-ROMs (compact disks/read-only-memory) come with information already recorded on them by the manufacturer; the recorded data can be read with inexpensive CD-ROM drives.

All these types of communication and storage devices are considered **I/O devices**, and that part of the OS that interacts directly with these devices is the **I/O system**. A primary task of the I/O system is to make the devices usable by higher-level processes. It performs the following three basic functions:

1. presents a *logical* or *abstract view* of communication and storage devices to the users and to other high-level subsystems by hiding the details of the physical devices;

2. facilitates *efficient use* of communication and storage devices;

3. supports the convenient *sharing* of communication and storage devices.

These three functions are analogous to those formulated for file systems, which provide a high-level abstraction of secondary storage in the form of files. However, the I/O system must handle not only secondary storage, albeit at a lower level, but also all other types of communication and storage devices.

The first function addresses the fact that devices vary widely in many aspects, including the speed and granularity at which they accept or produce data, reliability, data representation, ability to be shared by multiple processes or users, and the direction of data transfer (input, output, or both). The differences are further accentuated because all devices are accessed and controlled through very low-level hardware interfaces. Each logical command issued by the user or application program must typically be decomposed into long sequences of low-level operations to trigger the actions to be performed by the I/O device and to supervise the progress of the operation by testing the device status. For example, to read a word from a disk, a sequence of instructions must be generated to move the read/write head to the track containing the desired word, await the rotational delay until the sector containing the desired word passes under the read/write head, transfer the data, and check for a number of possible error conditions. Each of these steps, in turn, consists of hundreds of instructions at the hardware device level. All such low-level details are of no interest to the processes wishing to use the I/O devices and are usually hidden from them by appropriate abstraction. Ideally, the I/O system will define only a small number of abstract device types or classes that can be accessed by a small set of read, write, and other high-level operations.

The second function above addresses performance. Most I/O devices are independent from one another and can operate concurrently with each other and with CPUs. Thus, one of the overall objectives of the I/O system is to optimize performance by *overlapping* the execution of the CPU and I/O devices as much as possible. To achieve that, the CPU must be highly responsive to the device needs so as to minimize their idle time, yet, at the same time, CPU overhead from servicing the devices cannot be too large. The task requires appropriate scheduling of I/O requests, buffering of data, and other specialized techniques.

The last point above reflects the fact that some devices can be shared concurrently by multiple processes, but other devices must be allocated exclusively to one process at a time for a large unit of work. A typical example of the former is a disk, where multiple processes can interleave their respective read/write operations without compromising correctness. A printer, on the other hand, must be allocated to only a single process for the duration of a print job to prevent the meaningless interleaving of output from different processes. Thus, controlling access to devices is not only a matter of adequate protection (Chapters 12 and 13), but also a matter of device allocation and scheduling.

11.2   A HIERARCHICAL MODEL OF THE INPUT/OUTPUT SYSTEM

The I/O system is the layer of software that resides between the low-level hardware interfaces of individual devices and the higher-level subsystems, including the file system, the virtual memory system, and the user processes that use the devices. Since the interfaces of most hardware devices are extremely cumbersome and also vary greatly between device classes and even individual device models, several layers of abstraction are used to bridge the gap to the high-level user and systems processes.

Figure 11-1 illustrates the relationships graphically. Each I/O device, e.g., a disk drive or a keyboard, is accessed by a special hardware device, called the **device controller**. Thus, the I/O software never communicates with any devices directly but only by issuing commands to and receiving responses from the appropriate controllers. These tasks are generally accomplished by reading and writing hardware registers provided by the controller. The set of these registers is the low-level interface between the I/O system and the controller, i.e., the **software-hardware interface**.

The I/O system can be subdivided into two layers, as indicated in the figure. The top layer consists of software that is largely independent of the specific devices being used, whereas the lower layer consists of device-specific software. Below, we briefly outline the responsibilities of each part of the I/O system.

- **Device Drivers.** Programs called *device drivers* constitute the lower layer of the I/O system. They embody specific knowledge of the devices they are to access. Given the wide variety of device types and models, device drivers must be supplied by the device manufacturers, rather than by the OS designer. Consequently, a new device driver must be installed whenever a new device is added to the system.

- **Device-Independent I/O Software.** Many functions that must be supported by the I/O system are general enough so that they apply to many types of devices and need not be modified each time a device is replaced or added. These include the tasks of data buffering, data caching, device scheduling, device naming, and others that can be provided in a device-independent manner.

User processes and other higher-level subsystems access all I/O services through a high-level *abstract* interface, which we will refer to as the **I/O system interface**.

11.2.1   The Input/Output System Interface

The I/O system typically provides only a small number of abstract device interfaces to the higher-level modules. Each such interface represents devices with similar characteristics, and provides a set of generic operations to access them. The three types shown in Figure 11-1 are representative of the possible choices.

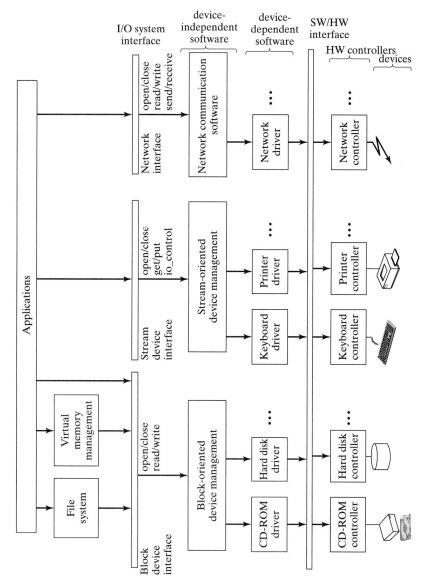

FIGURE 11-1. A hierarchical view of the I/O system.

The Block-Device Interface

The block-device interface reflects the essential characteristics of most direct-access mass-storage devices, such as magnetic or optical disks (e.g., CDs). These storage devices organize data in contiguous blocks, typically of fixed size, and support direct access to the blocks through a block number or address.

A block-device interface generally supports the following high-level operations: An ***open*** command verifies that the device is operational and prepares it for access. A ***read*** operation copies the content of the block specified by its logical block number into a region of main memory specified by an address. Similarly, a ***write*** operation overwrites the specified block with data copied from a region of main memory. A ***close*** operation releases the device if it was used exclusively or decrements the number of processes sharing it. The above high-level operations are mapped by the I/O system into lower-level operations supported by the device. For example, a read or write operation checks if the requested data is already in a disk cache in main memory. If so, it performs the access; otherwise, it initiates the necessary disk seek operation to the cylinder holding the desired block, followed by the actual data transfer operation.

Note that the block-device interface hides the fact that a disk is a two-dimensional structure consisting of cylinders and tracks within cylinders. It treats the disk as a linear sequence of blocks similar to a tape, but, unlike a tape, it makes them randomly accessible.

Some systems may permit application programs or certain system processes to access the disk directly via the block-device interface. However, since disks are typically shared, most programs are restricted to only the file system interface, which allows access to the disk only indirectly by reading and writing of files.

The **file system** uses the block-device interface to access the disk directly (Fig. 11-1). As discussed in Chapter 10, the file system translates the operations on files into the appropriate block-device commands (*read, write*) that use disk block numbers as parameters. The task of the I/O system is to translate the logical block numbers into actual disk addresses, and to initiate and supervise the transfer of the data blocks between the device and main memory.

The **virtual memory** system also uses the block-device interface. When invoked as the result of a page fault (Chapter 8), it must find the necessary page (represented as one or more data blocks on disk), and use the I/O system to read these blocks into main memory. If a page is evicted from main memory as part of the page fault, the virtual memory system must write this page back to disk by calling the appropriate *seek* and *write* commands of the I/O system.

The Stream-Device Interface

The second major interface is the **stream-device** interface, frequently also referred to as the **character-device** interface. It controls devices that produce or consume streams of characters, generally of arbitrary lengths. The individual characters must be processed in the order in which they appear in the stream and are not addressed directly. Instead, the interface supports a ***get*** and a ***put*** operation. The former returns the next character of an input stream to the caller, whereas the latter appends a new character to the output stream. This interface is representative of many communication devices, such as keyboards, pointing devices, display terminal, and printers.

In addition to the basic *get/put* operations, each device has a multitude of other functions it can perform, that vary greatly between different kinds of devices. For example, a terminal can ring the bell, toggle reverse video, or start flashing the cursor; a modem can be initialized or disconnected; and a printer can change its internal font tables and many other settings. To handle all these diverse functionalities in a uniform manner, the interface generally provides a generic *io_control* instruction that accepts many different parameters to express the many device-specific functions.

Finally, ***open*** and ***close*** operations are provided to reserve and release a device, since most stream-oriented devices cannot be shared but must be reserved by a process to prevent interleaving of different *read* or *write* operations.

Magnetic tapes present a special challenge. They are **block-oriented** in that each *read* or *write* operation transfers a block of data, where blocks can be of fixed or variable length. Unlike disks, however, tapes are inherently sequential in data access; their *read/write* commands do not specify the block number, which makes them **stream-oriented**. A preferred solution for tapes is to extend the stream-oriented interface so that the commands can request not only single characters one at a time (the *get/put* operations) but also read/write sequential blocks of data of arbitrary length. Other useful extensions generally also are added to the interface, for example, a ***rewind*** command to permit rereading or rewriting a tape from the beginning, or a (logical) ***seek*** command to skip over a number of blocks.

The Network Communication Interface

Increasingly, more computers are being connected to communication networks. This can be done via a **modem**, which uses telephone lines to transmit data, or specialized networks, such as an Ethernet, which is accessed via a corresponding Ethernet controller. Regardless of the connection, the network enables a computer to communicate with other computers or devices, including printers or terminals. This architecture offers great flexibility in configuring computer systems, since these devices are not dedicated to any specific computer but can be shared by many. In particular, it becomes economically feasible to provide expensive printers or other specialized devices that could not be justified for any single machine. Networking also makes it possible for users to access their computers from different locations and with different terminals. The **X terminal**, which is a sophisticated graphics terminal with its own internal processes, a keyboard, and a mouse, is a good example of a terminal that is not dedicated to any one specific computer but can communicate with different computers via the network.

To use a device that is not connected directly to a computer, the system must first establish a connection to the device. This requires that both the computer and the device name each other using network-wide identifiers, and that both express the desire to communicate with one another. A common abstraction for such a connection, supported in UNIX, Windows NT, and other systems, is the **socket**. A socket may be viewed as the endpoint of a connection from which data can be received or to which data can be sent. Thus, two processes—one on the host computer and the other on the device—that wish to communicate, each create a socket and **bind** it to each other's network address. The two commands, to create the socket and to bind it to actual addresses, are part of the high-level interface. Once a connection is established, the processes can use different communication protocols to exchange data with each other.

The two basic types of communication protocols are **connection-less** and **connection-based** protocols. In the first case, a process can simply *send* a message to the other process by writing it to the open socket. The other process can retrieve it from its socket using a corresponding *receive* command. A typical example of a connection-less protocol is UDP/IP (Universal Datagram Protocol/Internet Protocol), developed by the U.S. Department of Defense (DoD). Here, the messages are termed **datagrams**.

In connection-based communication, the two processes must first establish a higher-level connection. This is initiated by the process wishing to send data by issuing a *connect* command. The receiving process completes the connection by issuing an *accept* command. Establishing such a one-way connection is comparable to opening a shared file between the two processes. The sending process uses a *write* command, similar to a sequential file *write* command; the effect is to append the data to the "shared file." The receiving process uses an analogous sequential *read* command; the specified number of unread bytes are returned from the "shared file." The most common and widely used representative of a connection-based protocol is TCP/IP (Transmission Control Protocol/Internet Protocol), also originally developed by the U.S. DoD.

One of the main tasks of the I/O system is to translate the high-level operations that constitute its interface into low-level operations on the hardware devices. To better understand the specific tasks that the I/O system must perform at each level, we first describe the characteristics and the operating principles of the most common devices.

11.3   INPUT/OUTPUT DEVICES

11.3.1   User Terminals

The most basic user terminal consists of a keyboard for input and a visual display monitor for output. Most present-day systems also include a mouse as a pointing and selection device. Other common alternatives for user online interaction include joysticks or trackballs. Note that the word 'terminal' is frequently used to refer only to the display monitor. At other times, an entire PC that is connected to a network is said to be a terminal. In this chapter, we consider a terminal to be the combination of a monitor, a keyboard, and possibly a mouse.

Monitors

Monitors are similar to TV sets in that they display information dynamically on a visual screen. Most monitors use the same technology as TV sets. The inside of the screen is coated with a special chemical, which glows for a short period of time when activated by a stream of electrons. The screen is divided into image points or **pixels** (picture elements), each of which can be activated independently. A beam of electrons continuously scans the screen between 30 to 60 times a second. At each scan, it refreshes the image on the screen by activating the appropriate pixels, thus making the image visible by the human eye. Such monitors are also commonly called cathode ray tubes (CRTs) because of their underlying technology.

Laptop computers, as well as many new PCs, use **flat-panel monitors**. These are based on different technologies using LCD or plasma displays. Similar to CRTs, the flat-panel screen is divided into tiny cells, each representing a pixel. But instead of an electron beam, a mesh of horizontal and vertical wires is used to address individual rows and columns of pixels. An electric charge applied to one horizontal and one vertical wire activates the cell at the intersection of the two wires. In the case of LCDs, an activated cell blocks light passing through it, thus turning dark; in the case of plasma displays, an activated cell emits a burst of light.

The density or **resolution** of the pixels of a display determines the quality of the visible image. A typical 15-inch display has 800×600 pixels; a 21-inch display might have 1280×1024 pixels.

From the I/O system point of view, monitors may be subdivided into two basic types: character-oriented and graphics-oriented. Each requires a different type of interaction.

Character-oriented displays expect a **stream of characters** and process the stream one character at a time. Each character is either displayed on the screen at the current position of the cursor, or it is interpreted as a **control command**. The meaning of each control character (or a series of such characters) depends on the specific monitor type and the protocol used; typical commands include moving the cursor to the end or beginning of the current line, moving the cursor to the home position (top left of the screen), back-spacing the cursor, erasing the current line, performing a "carriage return" (moving cursor to the beginning of the next line), or toggle reverse video mode. The main limitation of character-oriented monitors is that the screen is subdivided into a small and fixed number of rows (lines) and columns (positions within each line), where each position can display only a single character chosen from a fixed set. A typical size of a character-oriented display is 25 lines of 80 characters each.

Figure 11-2a illustrates the principles of character-oriented monitors. It shows a character output buffer in the device controller—a single-character register—that the CPU can write. The register's content, the character t in the example, is copied to the display screen at the current cursor position.

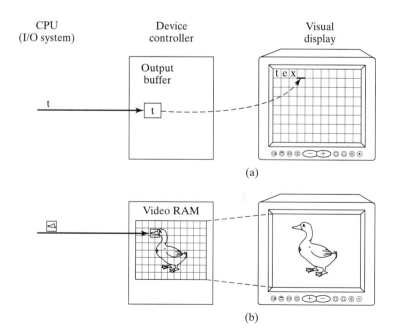

FIGURE 11-2. Display monitors (a) character-oriented; and (b) graphics-oriented.

Graphics-oriented displays use a separate **video RAM** memory to hold a copy of the entire image. Each pixel on the screen has a corresponding location in the video RAM. For a black-and-white screen, a single bit is sufficient to represent a pixel. For color displays, the number of bits determines the number of possible colors for each pixel. One byte allows $2^8 = 256$ different colors, and two bytes allow $2^{16} = 65,536$ different colors. The display hardware continuously reads the contents of the video RAM memory, the so-called **bitmap** of the image, and displays it on the screen.

Graphics-oriented displays have two advantages over character-oriented ones. First, each pixel is represented as a separate cell in the video RAM and hence the bitmap may represent an arbitrary image, restricted only by the display resolution. Second, the cells of the video RAM are randomly accessible by the CPU, and the displayed image may be changed arbitrarily by modifying the corresponding cells. Figure 11-2b illustrates the principles of graphics-oriented displays, showing the CPU updating a portion of the image.

Keyboards

Keyboards have been in existence long before the first computers emerged. In fact, the most common keyboard type still used today, the **QWERTY** keyboard, was designed in the second half of the 19th century for typewriters. Its name derives from the layout of the keys, where the top row of the nonnumeric characters starts with the characters Q, W, E, R, T, Y. Other key layouts have since been found more efficient for computer use and less prone to causing repetitive stress injury (e.g., carpal tunnel syndrome). Nevertheless, the pervasiveness of QWERTY keyboards perpetuates their use, since most people still acquire their typing skills with these keyboards and are reluctant to switch later.

Keyboards depend upon the speed of the human user and are among the slowest input devices. Even the most skilled typist will not be able to exceed a sustained rate of 10 characters per second. At the same time, each typed character generally requires some visible action to be taken, such as displaying the character on the screen. Thus, a keyboard is certainly a character-oriented device. When the user presses a key, the corresponding character is placed into an input buffer within the keyboard controller, from where it may be retrieved by the CPU. From the I/O system point of view, keyboards are similar to character-oriented displays. The main difference is the direction of the data flow; displays consume the characters produced by the CPU, whereas keyboards produce them.

Pointing Devices

Moving the cursor using keyboard keys is not very convenient. The movements are limited to the predefined lines and character positions of displayed text. With graphics-oriented monitors, the user should be able to point to arbitrary positions within the screen, e.g., to switch among applications, to select and move portions of text or images, or to draw line-oriented images. One of the most popular devices to achieve that is the **mouse**, invented in the early 1960s. The most common type, the **optical-mechanical** mouse, uses a small ball that protrudes through a hole at the bottom of the mouse. As the mouse is moved on a flat surface, traction causes the ball to roll. Any change in the horizontal or vertical position, as well as any buttons pressed or released, are detected by the hardware and translated into a stream of bytes. The I/O software retrieves this data from the input buffer and makes them available to the application software, which determines the corresponding cursor movement to be displayed on the monitor or any other actions resulting from pressing the mouse buttons.

A popular alternative to a mouse is a **trackball**. The hardware and software of a trackball are very similar to those of a mouse. The main difference is that the ball whose movement is being monitored is on top of the device; it is moved directly by the hand, and the device is stationary. Another alternative (or addition) to a mouse is a **joystick**. It is also used to control the cursor, but generally has more control buttons than a mouse or trackball.

Similar to a mouse, the trackball and the joystick report any changes in position or buttons pressed as a stream of events that must extracted from the hardware buffers by the I/O software. Like keyboards, pointing devices are character-oriented. They are also relatively slow, generating streams of data in the range of up to several hundred bytes per second.

11.3.2   Printers and Scanners

Printers convert **soft-copy** output, i.e., information stored in files or displayed on the monitor, into **hard-copy** output, i.e., information printed on paper. Scanners perform the reverse function, by generating digitized soft-copy data from hard copies.

Printers

There are several different technologies used to generate the hard-copy output. At the highest level, we can subdivide all printers into **impact** and **nonimpact** printers. The former include **line printers**, **daisy-wheel printers**, and **dot-matrix printers**. All three work just like typewriters by mechanically imprinting each character through an ink ribbon on the paper.

The simplest nonimpact printer is a **thermal printer**, which uses heated pins to burn images into special heat-sensitive paper. Thermal printers are inexpensive but produce low-quality output. They were used mainly in calculators and fax machines, but most have been displaced by more advanced technologies, including ink-jets and laser printers.

Ink-jet printers, developed by Cannon, have been very popular with PCs due to their relatively low cost, good copy quality, and the ability to produce not only text but arbitrary graphic images. The images are formed by spraying microscopic streams of fast-drying black or color ink on the paper as it passes under the ink jets.

Laser printers, and the related **LCD** and **LED printers**, use the same technology as copy machines. The image is created using laser light (or liquid crystal/light-emitting diodes in the case of LCD/LED printers) on a negatively charged drum. Powder ink (toner) is electrically charged, making it stick to the areas of the image. Next, the image is transferred to paper, which is heated to melt the ink and fuse with the paper.

The two key characteristics of printers are the **quality** of the output and their **speed**. The former is measured in dots per inch (DPI); the latter is given in characters per second or pages per minute. Dot-matrix devices can print several hundred characters per second. Speeds of ink jet and laser printers are in the range of 4 to 20 pages per minute.

Most printers are character-oriented devices; they accept output data in the form of a stream of control and printable characters. The stream is highly device-specific and must be hidden inside the specialized device drivers, generally supplied by the printer vendor.

Scanners

Most scanners use a charged-coupled device array, a tightly packed row of light receptors that can detect variations in light intensity and frequency. As the array passes over the presented image, the detected values are turned into a stream of bytes that the I/O software extracts from the device.

The most popular types of scanners are **flat-bed scanners** and **sheet-fed scanners**. The former are similar to copying machines in that the document to be scanned is placed on a stationary glass surface. Sheet-fed scanners are more like fax machines, where individual sheets of paper must be passed through the machine. Both types of scanner turn each presented page of text or graphics into a bitmap—a matrix of pixels. For black-and-white images, a single bit per pixel is sufficient; for color images, up to 24 bits per pixel are used to represent different colors.

11.3.3 Secondary Storage Devices

Secondary storage is necessary because main memory is volatile and limited in size. If the storage medium is removable, it also may be used to move programs and data between different computers. The most common forms of secondary storage are magnetic or optical disks and magnetic tapes.

Floppy Disks

Floppy disks or **diskettes** use soft magnetic disks to store information. Since their introduction in the late 1960s, floppy disks have been shrinking in size, from $8''$ to $5.25''$ to the presently most popular size of $3.5''$ in diameter.

The information on a floppy is organized into concentric rings or **tracks**. Each track is subdivided into **sectors**, where a sector is the unit of information (number of bytes) that can be read or written with a single operation. The reading and writing is performed by a movable **read/write head** that must be positioned over the track containing the desired sector. As the disk rotates under the read/write head, the contents of the specified sector are accessed.

To simplify the task of the file system or any other application using the disk, the sectors are numbered sequentially from 0 to $n - 1$, where n is the total number sectors comprising the disk. Numbering provides an abstract view of the disk as a linear sequence of sectors, rather than a two-dimensional structure where each sector is addressed by two numbers, a track number and a sector number within the track.

Figure 11-3 illustrates this concept. Figure 11-3a shows a disk surface subdivided into tracks with 18 sectors per track. The sectors are numbered 0 through 17 within each track. Figure 11-3b presents the logical view, where all sectors have been numbered sequentially. Numbering may be done in software, by the lowest level of the I/O system, but more frequently it is done by the disk controller in hardware. Thus, the I/O system only manages the more convenient abstract view of the disks. The hardware can then be optimized for best performance. For example, it may transparently skip defective sectors; it can use different numbers of sectors per track to account for the fact that the physical length of a track depends on its diameter; or it can number the sectors to optimize the seek time and rotational delay.

As an example of the last point, consider the sequential reading of sectors 17 and 18 in Figure 11-3b. It requires moving the read/write head from track 0 to track 1. Since

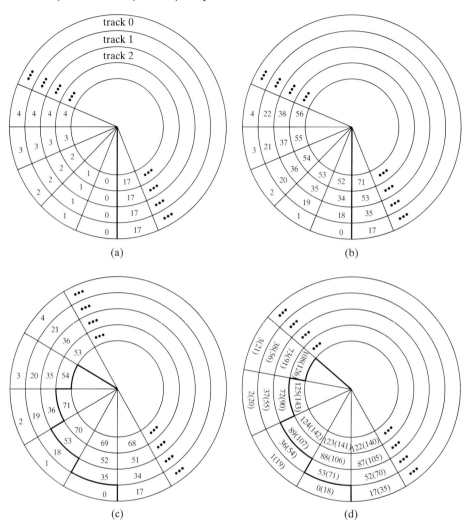

FIGURE 11-3. Numbering of disk sectors (a) physical; (b) logical; (c) with track skew; and (d) with double-sided disk.

this takes some time, sector 18 will already have passed by when the read/write head is in position. The system would then wait for a full rotation of the disk to access sector 18. To eliminate the problem, the sequential numbering of sectors on each track can be offset by one or more sectors to give the read/write arm sufficient time to get into position. Such an offset is termed **track skew**. The numbering in Figure 11-3c defines a track skew of one; this setting would be appropriate if the seek time between adjacent tracks took the same time (or less) as the reading of one sector. In the figure, the read/write head is moving from track 0 to track 1 when sector 35 is passing by, and will be ready to read sector 18 as soon as the head reaches the new track 1.

Some floppy disks use both sides to record information. As a result, there are always two tracks of the same diameter, one on each side of the disk. The number of sectors that can be accessed without moving the read/write head is essentially double that of the one-sided organization. Thus, when numbering the sectors sequentially, it is important to include sectors of both tracks before moving to the next pair of tracks, to minimize the read/write head movement. Figure 11-3d shows the numbering of the same disk as in Figure 11-3c but assuming both sides to hold information. The first number in each sector gives the logical number of the sector on the top surface of the disk, and the number in parentheses gives the number of the sector on the bottom surface. For example, logical sectors 0-17 are on track 0 (the outermost track) of the top surface, and the next set of sectors 18-35 is on track 0 of the bottom surface. Note that this example also uses a track skew of 1, as in Figure 11-3c.

Hard Disks

Hard disks are similar to floppies in that they also record information on rotating magnetic surfaces. Like floppies, they store this information on concentric tracks, each further subdivided into sectors. The main differences between hard disks and floppies are that the former are *not removable* and can hold much more data. Hard disks generally employ both surfaces of the rotating magnetic platter. Furthermore, many disks use more than one platter stacked on the same rotating axis. Each surface is accessed by its own read/write head, all of which are mounted on the same arm and move in unison. Figure 11-4 presents the basic idea of a multiplatter hard disk. With n double-sided platters, there are $2n$ tracks with the same diameter. Each set of such tracks is called a **cylinder** since the read/write heads are positioned to access one such set without movement and the physical arrangement resembles a hollow cylinder. Thus, a hard disk can be viewed from two different perspectives: as a collection of surfaces, each consisting of different-size tracks or as a collection of cylinders, each consisting of equal-size tracks.

    To provide an abstract view of the disk, all sectors of the disk are numbered sequentially. This numbering, generally performed by the controller hardware, is similar

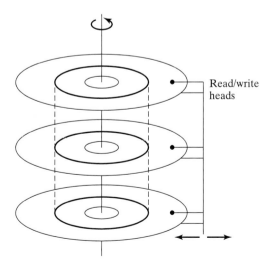

Read/write heads

FIGURE 11-4. Organization of a hard disk.

to that of a double-sided floppy; its purpose is to minimize the most time-consuming part of a disk access, which is the seek time between cylinders.

Optical Disks

Optical disks or CDs are different from magnetic disks in a number of important ways. Originally, they were designed to record music in digital form. As a result, information on such disks is not arranged in concentric tracks but along a **continuous spiral**. The individual bits are represented as a sequence of dots along this spiral that either reflect or absorb the light of a laser beam that tracks the spiral. In the early 1980s, the same technology was adapted to store computer data. Such disks are known as **CD-ROMs**. ROM stands for 'read-only-memory,' indicating that information on CD-ROMs, unlike information on magnetic disks, cannot be modified. Consequently, they only can be used for distribution of software or data; this information must be prerecorded on the CD-ROM using a complex process of burning the nonreflecting dots into the aluminum surface of the disk. CD-ROMs have a much higher density of information storage compared with magnetic disks. A double-sided, 4.72-inch CD-ROM can hold more than a gigabyte of digital data—a capacity equal to several hundred floppy disks.

CD-Rs are recordable CD-ROMs. Similar to ordinary CD-ROMs, their contents cannot be modified once written. However, the writing is done using a different technology, one that employs inexpensive CD recorders (CD burners). CR-Rs are also called **WORM**s (write-once/read-many-times). Yet another technology is used for **CD-RWs** that may be read or written multiple times, thus behaving like a magnetic disk. More recent developments in optical disks are **DVDs** (digital versatile disks) and **DVD-RAMs**. They have a different data format that increases their capacity to almost 3 GB per side.

The information on all optical disks is divided into sectors that are similar to magnetic disk sectors and directly accessible by the disk drive. Some drives also support a high-level grouping of sectors, called tracks, to mimic the concentric rings of magnetic disks. Thus, from the I/O software point of view, optical disks are operated using similar principles as magnetic disks: the software specifies the logical sector it wishes to read or write, and the disk controller hardware performs the necessary seek, rotational delay, and data transfer operations.

11.3.4 Performance Characteristics of Disks

Figure 11-5 compares hard disks, floppy disks, and CD-ROM disks in terms of their most important characteristics. Note that the CD-ROM characteristics differ somewhat from those of magnetic disks. This is due to the different technologies used and the intended use of the devices. First, because CD-ROMs store data along a single contiguous spiral, their capacities are given as the number of sectors for the entire surface, rather than broken into two components: sectors per track and tracks per surface. For the same reason, there are no "adjacent" tracks on a CR-ROM, and only the average seek time to an arbitrary sector on the surface is specified. Finally, the rotational speed of a CD-ROM, unlike that of a magnetic disk, is not constant. It varies with the position of the read/write head; the speed is slower when the head is near the center and faster when the head is near the outer edge. The reason for this is that CD-ROM have been designed originally

Characteristic	Floppy Disk	Hard Disk	CD-ROM Disk
Bytes per sector	512	512–4,096	2,048
Sectors per track	9, 15, 18, 36	100–400	333,000
Tracks per surface (number of cylinders)	40, 80, 160	1,000–10,000	(sectors/surface)
Number of surfaces	1–2	2–24	1–2
Seek time (adjacent tracks)	3–5 ms	0.5–1.5 ms	NA
Seek time (average)	30–100 ms	5–12 ms	80–400 ms
Rotational speed	400–700 rpm	3,600–10,000 rpm	$(200–530)*k$ rpm

FIGURE 11-5. Characteristics of floppy and hard disks.

to deliver music, which must be streamed at a constant rate. The basic rotational speed of a CD-ROM ranges from 200 to 530 rpm. The basic speed can be increased k-fold, where k is an even integer between 2 and as much as 40. Such CD-ROM drives are referred to as 2X, 4X, and so on, and their data transfer rates increase by the factor k.

There are two other important performance characteristics of rotating disks, which may be derived from those given in the table: **total storage capacity** and **data transfer rate**. The total capacity of a magnetic disk is obtained by simply multiplying the four values: number of surfaces × number of tracks per surface × number of sectors per track × number of bytes per sector. For example, the capacity of the smallest floppy disk listed in Figure 11-5 is $1 \times 40 \times 9 \times 512 = 184,320$ bytes or approximately 184 KB. The typical sizes of floppy disks today are 1.44 MB or 2.88 MB. A fairly large hard disk would have a total storage capacity of $12 \times 10,000 \times 300 \times 512 = 18,432,000,000$ bytes or approximately 18.5 GB.

For a CD-ROM, the total capacity is computed as the number of sectors per surface multiplied by the sector length. This is approximately $333,000 \times 2048 = 681,984,000$ bytes or 0.64 GB.

The data transfer rate may be interpreted in two different ways. A **peak** data transfer rate is the rate at which the data is streamed to or from the disk once the read/write head has been positioned at the beginning of the sector to be transferred. The peak transfer rate depends directly on the rotational speed of the disk and the number of sectors per track. For example, a disk that rotates at 7200 rpm requires $1/7200 = 0.0001388$ minutes per revolution. This is equivalent to 8.33 milliseconds per revolution. Assuming 300 sectors per track, all 300 sectors will pass under the read/write head in 8.33 milliseconds. Thus, it will take $8.33/300 = 0.028$ milliseconds for one block. Since each block consists of 512 bytes, the peak transfer rate is 512 bytes per 0.028 milliseconds, which corresponds to 17.43 MB per second. The peak data rate is used when determining the total access time to a given disk block or group of blocks, which consists of the seek time, the rotational delay, and the block-transfer time.

For a CD-ROM, the data transfer rate depends on its rotational speed. With a single-speed CD-ROM drive, the data rate is 150 KB/second, and it increases with the speed factor, k, to 300 KB/second for a 2X drive, 600 KB/second for a 2X drive, and so on.

A **sustained** data transfer rate is the rate at which the disk can transfer data continuously. This includes the seek times over multiple cylinders and other overheads in accessing the data over time. The sustained data transfer rate is an important performance characteristic used by many applications, especially those handling real-time data, to guarantee that they can meet the prescribed demands on delivering data that spans different surfaces and cylinders. The sustained data rate is typically several times lower than the peak data rate.

Magnetic Tapes

Due to their inherently sequential access, low cost, and large storage capacity, magnetic tapes are used mainly for long-term archival storage or for data backup. Magnetic tapes come in several different varieties, packaged as either individual **reels** or **cartridges**. The most common types are **DAT** (digital audio tape) and **DLT** (digital linear tape). DLTs segment the tape into multiple parallel tracks, which results in greater storage capacity and data transfer rate than with DATs.

The storage capacity of DATs ranges from a few hundred kilobytes to several gigabytes, and their data transfer rate is approximately 2 MB/sec. DLTs can store up to 40 GB, and achieve data transfer rates of 2.5 MB/sec.

Information on tapes is generally organized in sequences of bytes called *records* or *blocks*, which can be fixed or variable in length. The tape drive controller supports operations to read or write the next sequential block. I/O software extracts these blocks from or places them into input or output buffers, respectively. Thus, tape blocks are similar to disk sectors for the purpose of data access.

11.3.5 Networks

Networks allow two or more computers to exchange data with one another. There are many types of networks, differentiated by their size, speed, topology, protocols used to exchange data, and the hardware necessary to implement them. From each computer point of view, the network, including all other computers connected to it, is a source or a destination of data, i.e., an I/O device. Like all other devices, the computer has a hardware controller to interface to a network. This **network interface card** (NIC) accepts output data from the I/O software through registers and transmits these to their counterpart controllers in other computers. Similarly, the NIC also accepts input data from other controllers on the network and makes these available to the I/O software in registers.

The protocols used by the different controllers to communicate with each other depend on the network type. For example, an **Ethernet** uses a single common bus to which all controllers are connected. Each can place data on this bus, which all others can receive. A special protocol of rebroadcasting information is implemented by the controllers to solve the problem of collisions—the simultaneous output of data to the bus by two or more controllers. Other common network types are the **token ring** and the **slotted ring**. The former uses a special message (called token) that is circulated among all controllers arranged in a ring. Only the controller currently holding the token may transmit data to another controller on the ring, avoiding any collisions. (A higher-level version of a token ring protocol was developed in Section 3.2.3 to solve the distributed mutual exclusion problem.) Slotted rings continuously circulate data packet frames along the ring, each of which is marked as full or empty. When the controller receives an empty frame, it may fill it with data, mark it full, and pass it on along the ring to its destination controller.

The controller hardware takes care of the lowest layer of the communication protocol. At this level, the controllers have agreed upon the voltage to represent zeros and ones, the physical duration of each bit transmission, how many pins/wires are used to connect the controllers, and other low-level issues. The I/O software handles the high-level tasks, such as transmission errors, parceling of long messages into fixed-size data packets, routing of packets along different communication paths, assembling them at their final destinations, and many other high-level functions necessary to support different applications.

The **telephone network** also can be used by computers to exchange digital data. Since telephone lines were designed to carry continuous voice data, they use analog signals; these are generated as sine waves (the carrier). To transmit digital data, the amplitude, frequency, or phase of the sine wave is varied—a process called **modulation**. A **modem** (for modulator/demodulator) is a device that accepts a stream of bits as input and produces a modulated analog signal, or vice versa. Thus, to send data between two machines through a telephone network, both the sending and the receiving machines must have a modem. The sending modem transforms the digital data into analog signals, and the receiving modem restores the digital information after it has been passed through the telephone lines.

Telephone networks require that a number be dialed and a connection established. Consequently, any data exchange occurs only between two directly connected machines, greatly simplifying the protocols that must be provided by the I/O software. There is no need for packetizing messages, routing and assembly of packets, or any of the other high-level functions of general networks. Instead, the modem can be treated as a character-oriented device that produces and consumes a stream of characters. Thus, from the I/O software point of view, a modem looks more like a printer or a keyboard than a network.

11.4   DEVICE DRIVERS

The tasks of a device driver are to accept commands from the higher-level processes of the I/O system and to interact with the devices it is controlling to carry out these commands. For block-oriented devices, the most common requests are to *read* or *write* a block of data specified by its block number. For character-oriented devices, the most common requests are to *get* or *put* the next sequential character in the data stream. In the case of network drivers, high-level commands, such as those to use sockets, are translated into lower-level operations by the communications protocols. The commands issued to the drivers are to *send a packet* of data to another machine specified by a network address, or to *receive a packet* arriving on the network.

Each of the above requests must be translated further by the driver to the device-specific sequences of low-level operations that are issued to the device controller. The communication between the driver and the controller is accomplished by reading and writing specific **hardware registers** accessible in the device controller. These registers constitute the **software/hardware interface**. Figure 11-6 contains a typical interface for a device controller. The **opcode** register and **operand** registers are written by the driver to describe the operation it wishes the controller to carry out. The number of operands depends on the specific opcode. For example, a request to seek to a specific cylinder on a disk requires the cylinder number as the sole operand; a disk read operation, on the other hand, might require two operands: the track number within the current cylinder and the sector within the track.

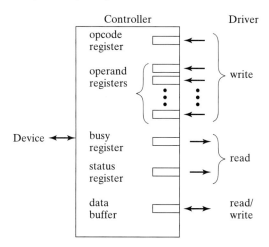

FIGURE 11-6. Device controller interface.

The hardware **data buffer** is used for operations that transfer data to or from the device. For output, the controller transmits the current content of the data buffer to the device. For input, the controller accepts data from the device and places it into the data buffer. The size of the data buffer can vary from a single byte (for character-oriented devices) to thousands of bytes (for fast block-oriented devices).

When the controller detects a new opcode in the register, it begins to work on the specified request. During this time, the **busy** register (which is just a Boolean flag) is set to true, indicating that the controller is busy and cannot accept any new requests. The outcome of a completed operation is reported in the **status** register. Possible outcomes, aside from normal completion, include a wide variety of potential problems or failures depending on the device type and the operation requested. The status register is usually read by the driver after the controller has indicated completion of its work by resetting the *busy* flag. If the operation completed successfully, the driver may issue the next operation, or, in the case of an input operation, it may access the data in the data buffer. If the operation failed, the driver must analyze the cause of the fault and either attempt to correct it (e.g., by retrying an operation that failed as the result of a transient fault), or report failure to the higher-level process that issued the request.

The controller shown in Figure 11-6 is quite complex. It is representative of fast block-oriented device controllers, such as those used for disks. The controllers for character-oriented devices generally have simpler interfaces, consisting of an input and/or an output character buffer, but no opcode or operand registers. An input device places individual characters into the input buffer, which the CPU retrieves using a simple "handshake" protocol of busy/ready signals or using interrupts. A stream of characters from the CPU to an output device is handled in an analogous fashion.

Many computers come from the factory already equipped with a set of generic controllers that may connect to a variety of devices. The most common controllers are the **serial port** and the **parallel port**. Both transmit individual characters to or from a device; the former sends the data one bit at time along a single wire, and the latter uses multiple parallel wires to send each character in one step.

11.4.1 Memory-Mapped Versus Explicit Device Interfaces

A driver specifies each I/O request to a controller using the register interface. One way to accomplish this is to provide *special I/O instructions* to read and write the controller's registers. Another method is to extend the address space of the main memory and to *map the controller registers* into the new memory addresses. Figure 11-7 illustrates the two approaches. In the first case (Fig. 11-7a), the CPU must distinguish between main memory and device addresses, using a different instruction format for each. For example, to store the content of a given CPU register (*cpu_reg*) into a given memory location (k), the following instruction could be used:

$$\texttt{store cpu\_reg, k}$$

In contrast, to copy the content of the same CPU register into a controller's register, an instruction with a different opcode and format would be used, for example:

$$\texttt{io\_store cpu\_reg, dev\_no, dev\_reg}$$

where *dev_no* specifies the device (i.e., its controller address), and *dev_reg* names the register within that controller.

The clear disadvantage of this approach is that two different types of instructions must be used for main memory addressing and device addressing. The second method, known as **memory-mapped I/O**, allows the same instruction format to be used for both

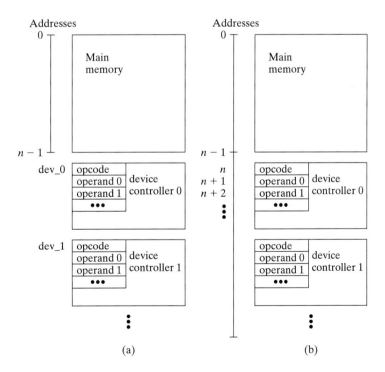

FIGURE 11-7. Forms of device addressing: (a) explicit; and (b) memory-mapped.

main memory and devices. For example, in (Fig. 11-7b), the instruction:

```
store cpu_reg, k
```

where k ranges from 0 to $n - 1$, would store the CPU register content into main memory locations as before. But with $k \geq n$, the same instruction stores the CPU register into one of the controller registers. For example, the opcode register of device 0 is mapped to address n in the figure. The instruction:

```
store   cpu_reg, n
```

stores the CPU register content into register 0 of device 0. This uniform view of main memory and devices greatly simplifies I/O programming. It is analogous to the simplification obtained by memory-mapped files, which were discussed in Section 10.3.2.

Having defined the register-based interface between the driver software and the controller hardware, we can now address two important issues, leading, in turn, to several different forms of I/O processing:

1. After an operation has been issued and the controller becomes busy with the I/O, how should operation completion be detected?
2. In the case of operations that input or output data, what should move the data between the controller data buffer and main memory?

11.4.2   Programmed Input/Output with Polling

In the simplest form of I/O processing, the CPU has complete responsibility for the job. That means, it explicitly detects when the device has completed an assigned operation and, in the case of a data I/O operation, it moves the data between the controller register and main memory. The first task is accomplished by repeatedly reading and testing the controller's busy flag—a task commonly referred to as **polling**. Once the flag becomes false, the CPU may access the data buffer. In the case of an input operation, it would copy the data to main memory; for an output operation, it would send data from memory to the buffer, prior to issuing the corresponding output operation.

Figure 11-8 illustrates the protocol for programmed I/O with polling for an input operation. It includes the following steps:

1. The CPU writes the operands required for the input operation into the appropriate operand registers. The number and type of operand required depends on the controller's sophistication and the operation type. A simple disk controller may require the track number and sector number to be specified for an input or output operation, assuming that the read/write head of the disk has already been positioned to the correct cylinder with a seek operation. A more advanced controller might accept a logical disk block number, from which it automatically derives the cylinder, track, and sector numbers, and performs the seek operation, if necessary. In contrast, getting the next character from a keyboard or another inherently sequential device requires no operands to be specified.

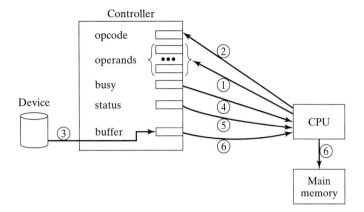

FIGURE 11-8. Programmed I/O with polling.

2. The CPU writes the opcode for the input operation, which triggers the controller to execute the operation. At that time, the busy flag is raised, indicating that the controller is busy and will ignore any other operations issued to it during that time.

3. The controller interacts with the device using the appropriate device-specific hardware protocols to carry out the requested operation. It transfers the input data extracted from the device to the data buffer.

4. While the controller/device are working, the CPU is polling the controller by repeatedly reading and testing the busy flag. (This is just another form of busy-waiting, as discussed in earlier chapters.)

5. Once the operation completes, the CPU reads the status register to detect any possible problems reported by the controller.

6. Provided no errors have been reported, the CPU copies the contents of the data buffer to main memory, where it is made available to the requesting process.

The protocol followed for an output operation is analogous. The main difference is that the driver, having detected that the device is not busy, places the data to be output into the controller data buffer. It then writes the necessary operands (as in step 1 above) and opcode (as in step 2), carries out the operation by transferring the data from the buffer to the device (step 3), polls the device for completion (step 4), and examines the status of the operation (step 5).

Let us examine the I/O programming necessary to implement this polling scheme. Assume that a sequence of characters is to be read from a sequential device (e.g., a modem) and written to another sequential device (e.g., a printer). To accomplish this I/O, the CPU repeatedly executes the above protocol of copying data between main memory and the controller buffer, writing the controller registers, and testing the busy flag and the status register. The following pseudocode describes the operation performed by the driver at a slightly higher level of abstraction than the register-based protocol:

```
Input:
    i = 0;
    do {
```

```
            write_reg(opcode, read);
            while (busy_flag == true) {...??...};
            mm_in_area[i] = data_buffer;
            increment i;
            compute;
        } while (data_available)

    Output:
        i = 0;
        do {
            compute;
            data_buffer = mm_out_area[i];
            increment i;
            write_reg(opcode, write);
            while (busy_flag == true) {...??...};
        } while (data_available)
```

The *write_reg* instruction represents the writing of the necessary registers; in this case, the *opcode* register that initiates the input operation. Thereafter, the driver program polls the busy flag by repeatedly executing the while-loop until *busy_flag* turns to false. (The meaning of the statement labeled "??" will be explained shortly.) Testing of the status register has been omitted in the code for simplicity. Assuming that the operation was successful, the driver copies the current character from the controller data buffer to main memory. The main memory area (i.e., the software buffer) is represented as a character array, *mm_in_area[]*, and *i* is the position to store the current character; this position is incremented each time a character has been deposited. The final statement of the loop, named *compute*, stands for any subsequent computation, such as processing the just-received character. The operations for the output loop are analogous.

The problem with polling is that it uses the CPU for both detection of the I/O completion and for moving of all data between the controller and main memory. Both tasks place a heavy burden on the CPU. The need for polling is especially bothersome in the case of slow character-oriented devices. The CPU may spend much of its time busy-waiting, i.e., executing the while-loop waiting for the busy flag to turn false.

There are several ways to address the looping problem, none of which is very satisfactory. One can simply accept the situation, letting the CPU idle while waiting for the I/O completion. This corresponds to turning the statement labeled "??" in the above pseudocode into a "no-op," i.e., an empty body of the while-loop. This waste of significant CPU time is not acceptable in most cases.

A better approach is to poll less frequently by performing other work during each iteration of the wait-loop. That means, the statement "??" can be replaced by another computation that does not need the current input or output. This improves CPU utilization by overlapping its execution with the I/O processing. The difficulty with this strategy is that a driver usually does not have anything else to do while waiting for an I/O operation to complete. Hence, the technique is only feasible in systems where the low-level I/O operations are visible at the application level. If an application is able to initiate an input operation (by writing the controller registers) and has access to the busy flag, it can explicitly interleave I/O with computing to maximize the performance of both.

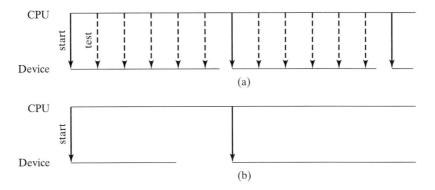

FIGURE 11-9. Frequency of polling: (a) too frequent; and (b) too sparse.

Unfortunately, such interleaving is extremely difficult to implement. The programs must be carefully organized with respect to the spacing of I/O commands and compute-only sections of code if a reasonable overlap of the two is to be obtained. If the busy flag is tested too infrequently, the device will be underutilized; testing it too frequently, on the other hand, results in wasted CPU time.

The diagram in Figure 11-9 illustrates the dilemma. Horizontal lines represent the time during which the CPU and the device are busy; each solid vertical arrow denotes the testing and subsequent starting of the device by writing the opcode register, and each dashed vertical arrow indicates the testing of the busy flag. In Figure 11-9a, the other extreme, the polls are issued too frequently, resulting in wasted CPU time. In Figure 11-9b, the polls are too sparse, resulting in device underutilization. Finding the right balance, especially when the busy times of the device may vary, is very difficult. The approach is also unsuitable for time-sharing environments, where the CPU is transparently switched between different processes and loses control over the real time in which the devices operate.

The third possible way to reduce CPU overhead caused by polling is to have a process voluntarily give up the CPU after issuing an I/O instruction. Other processes can use the CPU when the I/O operation is in progress. When the waiting process is restarted again as the result of normal process scheduling, it can test the busy flag. If the device is still busy, it again gives up the CPU; otherwise, it continues to execute. This guarantees good CPU utilization (provided there are other processes to run), but the device utilization is likely to be poor. That is because the process issuing the I/O command is not restarted *immediately* when the I/O completes. The busy flag is not tested until the process is resumed by the scheduler, resulting in delays of unpredictable length. Such delays are not only wasteful but also may lead to data loss. Many devices (e.g., modems) produce data at a fixed rate; if the data is not consumed in a timely manner, it is simply overwritten with new data.

11.4.3 Programmed Input/Output with Interrupts

From the above discussion of polling, we conclude that it is very difficult to find useful work of appropriate size that a process could perform when waiting for an I/O completion. A better solution is to suspend the process when the I/O is in progress and let other processes use the CPU in the meantime. In a multiprogramming environment, there are usually enough processes ready to run. The waiting process, however, should be restarted as soon as the I/O operation completes, to optimize the use of I/O devices. This can be achieved using **interrupts.** Recall from Sections 1.2.2 and 4.6 that an interrupt is a signal that causes the CPU to suspend execution of the current computation and transfer control to a special OS kernel code that determines the reason for the interrupt and invokes an appropriate routine (the interrupt handler) to address the event that triggered the interrupt.

When a device controller has completed an I/O operation, it triggers an interrupt. At this point, the next I/O instruction, if any, can be issued without delay. Thus, it is not necessary to continuously monitor the busy flag, which allows the CPU to devote its full attention to running other processes. Figure 11-10 sketches one common protocol for programmed I/O with interrupts for an input operation. The following steps are executed:

1. The CPU writes the operands required for the input operation into the appropriate registers in the controller.

2. The CPU writes the opcode for the input operation, which triggers the controller to start the operation. As in the case of polling, the busy flag is raised. This need not be tested explicitly to detect the I/O completion. Rather, it is only used initially to ascertain that the device is not busy (e.g., serving a request issued by another process) and is able to accept a new command. Once the operation has been initiated, the process blocks itself, giving up the CPU.

3. The device controller interacts with the device to carry out the current operation. In the case of an input operation, it transfers the data from the device to its data buffer. In the meantime, other processes may be running on the CPU.

4. When the operation is complete, the controller issues an interrupt. This causes the currently running process to be suspended and the CPU branches to the interrupt handler. This analyzes the cause of the interrupt and resumes the process waiting for the just-completed I/O operation.

5. The resumed process verifies that the operation has completed successfully by examining the status register.

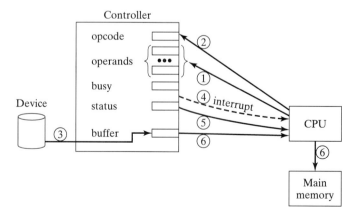

FIGURE 11-10. Programmed I/O with interrupts.

6. Assuming no errors have been detected, the process copies the data from the controller data buffer into main memory.

Note that the main conceptual difference between the two I/O protocols is in step 4. In the case of polling, the process requesting the I/O operation is also in charge of detecting its completion. In the case of interrupts, the requesting process is blocked, and other components of the OS, notably the interrupt handler, must be involved in detecting I/O completion.

Let us now examine the style of interrupt-driven I/O programming and compare it to the previous scheme of explicit polling. Assume a task that reads and writes a simple sequence of characters from/to a sequential device, as in the example of the last section. The following pseudocode describes the operations performed by the driver. This is essentially the interrupt service routine for the I/O interrupt.

```
Input:
    i = 0;
    do {
        write_reg(opcode, read);
        block to wait for interrupt;
        mm_in_area[i] = data_buffer;
        increment i;
        compute;
    } while (data_available)

Output:
    i = 0;
    do {
        compute;
        data_buffer = mm_out_area[i];
        increment i;
        write_reg(opcode, write);
        block to wait for interrupt;
    } while (data_available)
```

The code is similar to that of polling, with the main difference of no busy-wait loop testing the busy flag. Instead, the process blocks itself by giving up the CPU after initiating the I/O operation using the *write_reg* operation. When the process restarts as the result of the I/O completion interrupt, the data is ready to be copied from the data buffer (in the case of input) or to the data buffer (in the case of output). The *compute* operation in each of the loop again represents some processing that must be done for each character of input or output.

EXAMPLE: Keyboard Input

The following pseudocode implements the typical functions of a keyboard driver:

```
Keyboard_Input:
    i = 0;
    do {
```

```
                    block to wait for interrupt;
                    mm_in_area[i] = data_buffer;
                    increment i;
                    compute(mm_in_area[]);
              } while (data_buffer ≠ ENTER)
```

Note that this code is very similar to the interrupt-driven input sequence shown above, with only a few minor differences. First, there is no *write_reg* operation to start the input of a character. That is because the keyboard generates a character in its data buffer whenever a key is pressed or released by the user, without any explicit prompting. The driver's task is to copy this character into the appropriate area in main memory. The loop is repeated until the character in the buffer is the ENTER key (also called RETURN or CR, for carriage return, on some keyboards). This signals that the current line is complete and should be made available to the calling process.

The meaning of the statement *compute(mm_in_area[])* depends on the type of input desired by the process. In **character-oriented** input, all characters, including special characters, such as CONTROL, SHIFT, ALT, DELETE, or BACKSPACE, are copied to the memory area, and it is up to the process to interpret their meaning. This mode of input is usually called **raw input** and is of interest to sophisticated text editors that are able to interpret control characters according to the user's definitions. Most programs, however, do not need to see all characters. For example, when the user mistypes a character, and corrects it by pressing BACKSPACE or DELETE followed by the correct character, the process should see only the final complete line at the point when ENTER is pressed, rather than all the intermediate versions resulting from typing errors. Thus, it is up to the driver to perform all the intraline editing by interpreting special characters used for that purpose. Such **line-oriented** input mode is usually referred to as **canonical** or **cooked input**.

The timing diagram of Figure 11-11 shows the interactions between the CPU software and an I/O device for typical interrupt-driven input. Assume that a currently running user process issues a *read* operation. This is passed to the I/O system and eventually causes the appropriate device driver to be invoked to process the operation. The driver writes the necessary controller registers and starts the operation. At some time after the *read* and before or shortly after the device becomes busy, the current process is blocked. The process scheduler is invoked and selects the next ready process to run. As long as the device continues to be busy, other ready processes may be timeshared on the CPU. Eventually, the I/O operation completes and generates an interrupt, thereby suspending the currently running process and starting the interrupt handler. Determining that the interrupt was caused by I/O completion, the interrupt handler returns control to the driver in charge of the interrupting controller. The driver now analyzes the status of the just-completed read operation, and, if successful, transfers the data from the controller buffer to main memory. If more data are to be input, the driver immediately restarts the device, minimizing its idle time. When this is done, the process scheduler is invoked again to determine which process should continue executing. In the diagram, we assume resumption of the original user process, which now has the previously requested input data in its main memory area available for access.

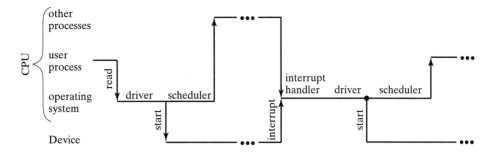

FIGURE 11-11. Timing of interrupt-driven I/O.

CASE STUDY: I/O PROCESSING IN UNIX

Device drivers in UNIX are divided into two parts, called the **top half** and **bottom half**, respectively. The top half is invoked **synchronously**, whenever a process requests an I/O operation. In Figure 11-11, the *read* operations would invoke the top half of the driver, which starts the device and terminates. The bottom half is invoked **asynchronously** by the interrupt when the device completes. The bottom half copies the data from/to the hardware buffer. Then, depending on the type of operation, it either terminates or invokes a portion of the top half, which restarts the device with the next operation.

In the case of terminal input (keyboard), the two halves are completely independent. The bottom half is invoked whenever a key is pressed on the keyboard (or mouse). It copies the corresponding character from the hardware buffer into a FIFO buffer, called C-list, in memory (see Section 11.5.1). A process retrieves characters from this buffer by invoking the top half of the driver. This automatically blocks the process when the FIFO buffer is empty.

With interrupts, the completion of an I/O operation is detected immediately and automatically. Thus, a process must not worry about testing the device flag at various intervals to optimize CPU and I/O device use. However, Figure 11-11 also illustrates that the flexibility gained by interrupt-driven processing over polling is not free of cost. The overhead caused by an interrupt is quite significant, involving the invocation of the interrupt handler and other OS routines. These can take thousands of CPU instructions to execute. Testing the busy flag, in contrast, can be done in just two machine instructions—a register read followed by a conditional branch. Nevertheless, polling is effective in only very special circumstances, e.g., with certain dedicated embedded systems or when a process must wait nondeterministically for multiple devices to complete. Virtually all general-purpose computers, including PCs, employ interrupts to manage I/O and other operations.

11.4.4   Direct Memory Access

With programmed I/O, either through polling or interrupts, the CPU carries the burden of physically moving all data between main memory and the controller data buffers. This

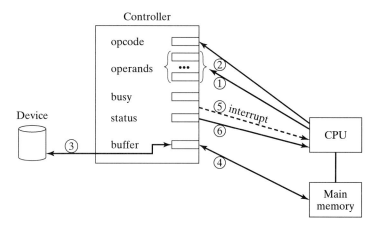

FIGURE 11-12. Direct memory access I/O (DMA).

is acceptable with slow, character-oriented devices, such as keyboards or printers, since the CPU is capable of executing thousands of instructions before a device completes the transfer of a single character. In the case of fast devices, however, the CPU overhead in initiating and monitoring each individual transfer of data between a device and main memory is too high. To alleviate this problem, **direct memory access** (DMA) hardware can be added to the system. It permits a device controller to transfer data directly to or from main memory. Using DMA, the CPU only commands the controller to perform the transfer of a block of data; the actual operation is carried out directly by the DMA controller. I/O completion can be detected, in principle, with polling as in the case of programmed I/O. However, interrupts are much more effective since the main objective of DMA is to liberate the CPU from as much overhead as possible.

The steps taken by the CPU when interacting with a DMA controller are marked in Figure 11-12. Although seemingly not much different than Figure 11-10, there are several significant changes in detail.

1. The CPU writes the operands relevant to the current I/O operation to the controller operand registers. This is generally more complex than with programmed I/O, since the DMA controller has more autonomy in executing I/O operations than a programmed one. In particular, the operands must include the starting location in main memory from or to which data should be transferred, and the number of bytes to transfer.

2. The CPU stores the opcode into the controller opcode register. This initiates the controller, which raises its busy flag to indicate that it will not accept any other commands in the meantime. When the controller is busy, the CPU is free to execute other computations.

3. The controller interacts with the device to carry out the data transfer to or from its data buffer.

4. The controller copies the data between its data buffer and the area in main memory specified as one of the operands. The steps 3 and 4 may be performed repeatedly to transfer a series of characters or blocks between the device and main memory.

5. When the operation is completed, the controller resets its busy flag and issues an interrupt to the CPU, indicating that it is ready for the next command.

6. The CPU reads and tests the controller status register to determine if the operation has been carried out successfully.

The CPU's involvement in I/O processing has been greatly reduced. Consider the task of reading or writing a stream of characters into/from main memory. The following pseudocode would accomplish this task:

```
Input or Output:
        write_reg(mm_buf, m);
        write_reg(count, n);
        write_reg(opcode, read/write);
        block to wait for interrupt;
```

Compare this simple code with the analogous code using programmed I/O (with interrupts), as shown in Section 11.4.3. Using the latter, the CPU must execute a loop, which inputs one character during each iteration. With DMA, the CPU only must write the opcode register and the appropriate operands, which include the starting address in main memory (m) and the number of characters to read or write (n). Thereafter, the CPU is free to execute other computations. It will be interrupted only after the controller has transferred *all* n characters into main memory (or has failed in some way).

One problem with DMA is that the DMA controller is interfering with the normal operation of the CPU—both compete for access to main memory. When the controller is in the process of reading or writing data in main memory, the CPU is momentarily delayed; this interference is known as **cycle stealing**, since the DMA has 'stolen' execution cycles from the CPU. Given that the use of DMA does not increase the total number of memory accesses in any way and that the CPU is frequently accessing data in its internal registers or in cache, thus bypassing main memory, the resulting conflicts are limited and well worth the gained benefits, i.e., a dramatic reduction in the CPU's involvement in I/O processing.

Although DMA liberates the CPU from directly performing data transfers, there is still a significant amount of work to be done by the CPU for each data transfer. In particular, it must analyze the status of each interrupting device to detect possible errors, attempt to correct or recover from discovered ones, and perform various device-specific code conversions and formatting functions. All these tasks may be delegated usefully to a specialized **I/O processor** or **channel**. This specialized device may be viewed as a more sophisticated form of a DMA controller, responsible for managing several devices simultaneously and supervising the data transfers between each of these devices and main memory.

Unlike a simple DMA controller, which only interprets the commands given to it via its register interface, an I/O processor has its own memory from which it can execute programs. Such programs can be complex sequences of specialized I/O instructions, logical and arithmetic operations, and control statements. Each I/O program is prepared and stored in the I/O processor executable memory by the CPU. The CPU then initiates the I/O processor, which executes its current program and interrupts the CPU only when it has completed its task. In this way, the I/O processor can be made responsible for transferring complex sequences of data, including all necessary error corrections or data conversions, without any assistance by the CPU.

11.5 DEVICE MANAGEMENT

Much of the I/O system is highly device-dependent, particularly individual device drivers. However, there are numerous functions that are common to many devices and that may be performed at a higher, device-independent level. This section discusses the general principles of several such functions, including buffering and caching, error handling, and device scheduling and sharing.

11.5.1 Buffering and Caching

A buffer is an area of storage, such as a dedicated hardware register or a portion of main memory, that is used to hold data placed there by a **producer** process until it is copied by a **consumer** process. We can distinguish two types of buffers, based on their organization and use: a FIFO buffer and a direct-access buffer.

Figure 11-13a shows the first type, a **FIFO buffer**. The key reason for using a FIFO buffer is to *decouple* the producer and consumer processes in time. Without a buffer, the two processes must tightly synchronize their executions such that the consumer is ready to receive the data while it is being generated by the producer. The use of a buffer allows concurrent asynchronous execution of the producer and the consumer.

Figure 11-13b shows a **direct-access buffer**, which is also referred to as a **buffer pool** or **buffer cache**. A direct-access buffer also decouples the execution of the producer and consumer. The key reason for its use is to avoid producing the same data *repeatedly* when it is accessed multiple times by the consumer. For example, when the file system (the consumer) accesses the same file block multiple times, the I/O system (the producer) should not have to read the block from disk repeatedly. Instead, it uses the buffer as a cache to keep the most recently accessed blocks ready for future use.

There are two other important reasons for using buffers, both FIFO and direct-access. The first is to handle any mismatches in **granularity** of the data exchanged between the producer and the consumer. If the producer's data granularity is smaller

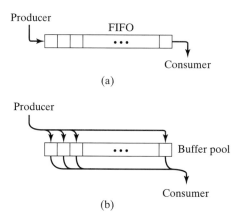

FIGURE 11-13. Buffer types: (a) FIFO buffer; and (b) direct-access buffer.

than the consumer's, the producer can deposit several of its data units in a buffer to make one large unit for the consumer. Conversely, if the producer's granularity is larger, the consumer can remove each data item from the buffer in several smaller units.

The second reason for buffering is to provide memory space that is not part of the producer or the consumer. This allows the consumer to be swapped out while it is waiting for data to be produced. Conversely, the producer can be swapped out while data is being consumed from the buffer. Both cases improve the use of main memory.

The number and organization of the slots within a buffer (characters or blocks, depending on the application) is critical for performance. Let us examine the common choices and their trade offs.

Single Buffer

A single buffer allows the producer to output data without waiting for the consumer to be ready. Such asynchronous transfer of data between processes is important for performance. However, the producer and consumer processes must still coordinate their operations to ensure the buffer is full when the consumer accesses it and "empty" (i.e., its contents have already been copied) before it is overwritten by new data.

A single buffer is employed typically with simple device controllers, as discussed in Sections 11.4.2 and 11.4.3. In the case of input devices, the controller is the producer, and the device driver is the consumer. In the case of output, the producer/consumer roles are reversed. In both situations, the data are exchanged one character or block at a time via the controller data buffer.

One drawback of a single buffer scheme—and a source of unnecessary loss of concurrency—is that the producer is idle when the consumer is copying the buffer and, conversely, the consumer is idle when the buffer is being filled.

Figure 11-14a shows the timeline for the loop with a single buffer. This corresponds to the input sequence using polling (Section 11.4.2), where the device is the producer and the CPU (the device driver) is the consumer. The CPU starts the device, and it repeatedly polls its busy flag. When the I/O is completed, the buffer is copied to main memory. The CPU is idle when the buffer is being filled, and the device is idle when the buffer is being copied to memory.

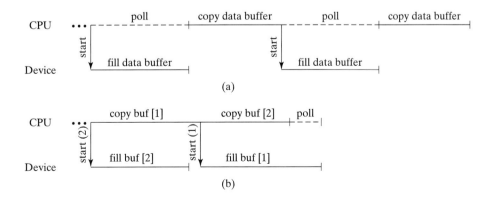

FIGURE 11-14. Buffering: (a) single buffer; and (b) buffer swapping.

Buffer Swapping

We can reduce the idle time resulting from the exclusive use of the buffer by employing two separate buffers, say *buf[1]* and *buf[2]*, in the controller. When the controller is filling *buf[1]*, the CPU may be copying *buf[2]*, and vice versa. The roles of the buffers are reversed at the completion of each I/O operation. The following code to input a sequence of characters illustrates the implementation of this **buffer-swapping** technique.

```
Input:
    i = 0;
    b = 1;
    write_reg(mm_buf, buf[2]);
    write_reg(opcode, read);
    do {
        while (busy_flag == true) ; /* busy-wait */
        write_reg(mm_buf, buf[b]);
        write_reg(opcode, read);
        if (b == 1) b = 2; else b = 1;
        mm_in_area[i] = buf[b];
        increment i;
        compute;
    } while (data_available)
```

The variable *b* indicates which of the two buffers is being used; initially, it is set to 1. This is followed by initial *write_reg* operations, which write the necessary opcode and operand registers. One of the operands is the buffer number (1 or 2) to be used for the next operation. The initial *write_reg* operations start the filling of *buf[2]*. The repeat loop alternates between the two buffers: Whenever it issues an operation with *buf[1]* as the operand, it changes *b* to 2, and vice versa. That way, the subsequent main memory copy always uses the other buffer, i.e., the one not being currently filled by the device.

Figure 11-14b illustrates the resulting overlap between the CPU and the input device. The time to input each character during each iteration is the maximum of the memory copy operation and the device input operation. Assuming these times are comparable, the technique of buffer swapping eliminates much of the idle time observed in Figure 11-14a.

Circular Buffer

Buffer swapping improves performance by increasing the overlap between the CPU and I/O, and, in fact, is optimal under the ideal condition where the data are produced and consumed at a constant rate. Unfortunately, timing sequences in real-world situations are rarely that simple. Programs usually contain bursts of I/O activity followed by periods of computing. Also, the times for consuming (copying) the data may depend on the data type and other circumstances, and vary from call to call. Similarly, the times that the controller is busy may vary because different physical records may be accessed on each call. For example, accessing a disk block that requires a seek operation is much slower than accessing a block on the current cylinder. Finally, in a multiprogramming environment, the speed with which a given process is executing and the current availability of devices are unpredictable. As a result, a user process frequently waits for I/O to complete, and a device frequently remains idle as a process copies the buffer.

The solution to this problem is to add more buffers to the system to further increase the asynchrony between the producer and the consumer. With n buffers, the producer can produce up to n data items before it must block and wait for the consumer to empty some or all of them. Conversely, when all n buffers are full, the consumer can execute up to n iterations before it must block to wait for the producer.

This solution corresponds to those given for the general bounded buffer problem in Chapters 2 and 3. All of the latter programs assumed a buffer capable of holding n data items and guaranteed that the producer would run up to n steps ahead of the consumer, without any loss of data. The buffer organization is referred to as a **circular buffer** because the producer and consumer both access the buffer sequentially modulo n.

EXAMPLE: Implementing a Circular Buffer

The circular buffer concept is outlined in Figure 4-2a. Whenever the producer continues, it fills the first empty buffer pointed to by the *front* pointer. Similarly, the next buffer accessed by the consumer is the one pointed to by the *read* pointer.

The following code demonstrates the use of the circular buffer monitor (Section 3.1.1) in an I/O application. The buffer resides between a user or file system process (the consumer) performing input and the driver of the corresponding input device (the producer).

```
User Process:
        do {
            buffer.remove(data);
            compute(data);
        } while (data_available)
```

```
Driver:
        do {
            write_reg(...);
            block to wait for interrupt;
            buffer.deposit(data_buffer);
        } while (data_available)
```

The user process repeatedly calls upon the buffer monitor to obtain the next data item and processes it using the subsequent *compute* statement. If it runs too far ahead of the driver so that all buffers become empty, the monitor guarantees that the user process blocks as part of the call; it resumes automatically when at least one buffer is filled.

The driver repeatedly obtains data from the input device by writing the appropriate registers of the device controller and blocking itself to await the I/O completion. When awakened by the interrupt, it places the new data copied from the controller *data buffer* into the circular buffer by calling the *deposit* function of the buffer monitor. In case the user process falls behind in consuming data and the circular buffer is completely full, the monitor blocks the driver as part of the call. It wakes it up again automatically when at least one buffer is free. Thus, the driver can be blocked for *two* different reasons: to wait for the device controller or to wait for the user process.

Buffer Queue

The circular buffer can be implemented efficiently as an array. But its main limitation is its fixed size, n, which is a very important parameter. If n is too large, memory space is wasted. If n is too small, the produce or the consumer process are blocked frequently. In some situations, no blocking of the consumer may be possible. For example, a modem delivering data cannot be stopped; if the data is not consumed at the rate is it produced, it is lost. Similarly, a user typing at a keyboard cannot be told to stop; the system must accept all characters as they are being delivered.

The problem can be solved by implementing an unbounded buffer in the form of a buffer queue, similar to that of Figure 4-2b. For each new data item to be inserted, the producer creates a new list element and inserts it at the front of the queue. The consumer removes elements from the rear of the queue. This allows the producer to run arbitrarily far ahead of the consumer. The main drawback of such a buffer queue is efficiency. Manipulating a linked list is time-consuming, because every operation requires dynamic memory management.

CASE STUDY: C-LISTS IN UNIX

UNIX implements a version of a buffer queue, referred to as a **C-list**, which is a compromise between a linked list and an array implementation. This is used for character input and output. The idea is to organize *arrays of characters*, rather than individual characters, in the form of a linked list. Figure 11-15 illustrates this concept. It shows a buffer queue containing 104 characters spread over three arrays of 64 characters each. The consumer (e.g., a user process) reads characters using and incrementing the rear pointer. When it reaches the end of the current array, it unlinks it from the queue and continues with the next array. Similarly, the producer (e.g., the keyboard driver) deposits characters using and incrementing the front pointer. When it reaches the end of the current array, it allocates a new one and adds it to the front of the queue.

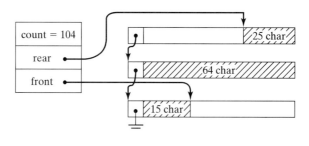

FIGURE 11-15. C-lists in UNIX.

Buffer Cache

FIFO buffers are most useful for stream-oriented devices (e.g., terminals and printers), where the data must be consumed sequentially in the order in which it is produced. For direct-access devices (e.g., disks), data items are accessed in a random order (determined by the program). Furthermore, the same data items may be accessed multiple times. Thus, the main role of the buffer is to serve as the cache of the recently accessed items to avoid generating them repeatedly.

A buffer cache is generally implemented as a pool of buffers. Each is identified by the disk block it is currently holding. The buffer cache implementation must satisfy the following two requirements. First, given a block number, it must be able to quickly check that this block currently exists in the cache and retrieve its contents. Second, it must facilitate the reuse of buffers that are no longer needed.

To implement the fist requirement, the buffers are generally accessed through a **hash table**, where each entry links together blocks identified by the same hash value. To satisfy the second requirement, the individual buffers are linked together according to a policy, typically least recently used (LRU), so that buffers that are least likely to be accessed again are reused first. This is analogous to the queue of main memory frames used with the LRU page-replacement policy (Section 8.3.1). Additional lists may be implemented to further improve the management or effectiveness of the buffer cache.

CASE STUDIES: DISK BLOCK CACHES

1. *UNIX.* BSD UNIX provides a disk block cache as part of the block-oriented device software layer (Fig. 11-1). This consists of between 100 and 1000 individual buffers. As a result, a large percentage (typically 85% or more) of all I/O requests by the file system and applications can be satisfied by accessing data in main memory rather than the disk. The virtual memory system uses a lower-level interface, which bypasses the buffer cache, but implements its own buffering scheme tailored specifically to its needs.

   Each buffer in the buffer cache is represented by a header, which points to the actual variable-size buffer area and records the buffer size, the descriptor of the file to which the data belongs, the offset within the file, and other information. It also contains two pointers to other buffers. The first implement the hash lists, and the second implements four other possible lists on which a buffer may reside.

   Figure 11-16 illustrates the concept. It shows an array of hash values, h_i, each pointing at a linked list of buffers whose identifier hashes to the same value h_i. For example, blocks $b71$ through $b75$ are all assumed to hash to the same value $h7$. This allows the system to find a buffer quickly, given its block number. In addition, each buffer is on one of four possible lists. The *locked* list (buffers $b11$ and $b51$ in the figure) contains buffers that cannot be flushed to disk; these are used internally by the file system. The *LRU* list (buffers $b21$, $b71$, and $b72$ in the figure) maintains the buffers sorted according to the LRU policy. A buffer at the end of the list (e.g., $b72$) is reused first, but only when the *Age* list is empty. This links together buffers that have been released, e.g., when a file is deleted, and are not expected to be accessed again. It also contains buffers that have been read in anticipation of future accesses (read-ahead of sequential files). The *empty* list contains buffers whose memory area is currently of size zero. These are only place holders for buffers—they cannot be used again until another buffer shrinks and generates free memory space.

CASE STUDIES: DISK BLOCK CACHES (*continued*)

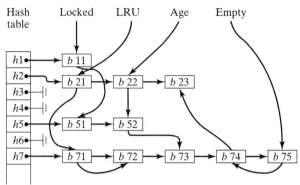

FIGURE 11-16. Buffer cache in UNIX.

2. *Linux.* Linux also uses hashing to find cached blocks. In addition, it segregates all buffers on three types of lists:

(a) Free buffers are kept on seven different lists, according to the buffer size; this starts with 512 bytes and doubles each time.

(b) Buffers containing valid blocks are kept on three different lists: *locked*, *clean* (i.e., read-only), and *dirty* (i.e., already modified); the distinction between clean and dirty avoids unnecessary disk writes when a buffer is evicted from the cache, which is governed by a time-stamp and a number of other system parameters.

(c) Temporary buffers used by the paging system when serving a page fault. These are freed as soon as the operation completes.

11.5.2 Error Handling

Most storage and communication devices contain mechanical moving parts, making them highly prone to error. Furthermore, devices are made by a variety of different manufacturers and may be replaced by newer models several times during the system's lifetime. It is a major challenge to assure a failure-free interaction with such devices.

Errors can be subdivided along different criteria. **Transient** errors or faults are those that occur only under very specific circumstances that are difficult to replicate, such as fluctuations in voltage or a particular timing of events. **Persistent** errors are those that occur consistently and predictably whenever the same program is repeated. A broken wire, a scratched storage disk surface, or a division by zero are examples of persistent faults.

We also can subdivide errors into **software** and **hardware** errors. Persistent software errors can be removed only by correcting and reinstalling the offending programs. Transient software errors also should be corrected in that way, but they are generally very difficult to trace and analyze, since they cannot be easily replicated. If these errors are not too frequent or disruptive, they are generally accepted as a necessary "fact of life." Some transient software faults are even expected to occur and special mechanisms are put into place to address them. A typical example is the transmission of data through a network. Unpredictable network delays, inadequate resources (e.g., buffers), or other circumstances beyond anyone's control frequently result in data packages being lost or damaged. It is then up to the communication protocols to perform the necessary **retransmissions** or attempt to correct some of the corrupt data using **error-correcting codes**. Such codes require redundant data bits that in some way reflect the data contents to be transmitted with the actual data. The number of redundant bits determine how many corrupt data bits can be detected or corrected.

Transient hardware errors, such as the failure of a disk drive to correctly position the read/write head over a specified cylinder, or a read failure due to a dust particle on a disk block, also can be corrected by **retrying** the operation. Only when the fault persists must it be reported to the higher-level processes. But there are certain types of persistent hardware errors that can effectively be handled by the OS, without involving the user or other high-level processes. The most common such errors are partial **storage media failures**, notably, the destruction of a block on a magnetic disk. These failures are quite frequent, since the magnetic coating on the disk surface is easily damaged. Replacing the entire disk to handle the failure of a single block is not an acceptable solution. Rather, the system must be able to detect failed blocks, generally called **bad blocks**, recover from the failure, and continue working with disks containing such blocks. Several possible solutions, sometimes in combination with one another, address different aspects of the media failure problem.

Bad Block Detection and Handling

Before a disk can be used to hold data, it must be formatted. This process divides the available disk space into blocks (sectors) of a specific size and, with each block, provides some amount of redundant information for the detection and correction of errors. A single parity bit (computed, for example, as the exclusive OR of all bits in the block) would allow the detection of a single failed bit. More generally, a multibit Hamming code attached to each block allows the detection and correction of more than one bit; the numbers depend on the size of code used.

The parity bit or error-correcting code is computed and written together with each disk block write, and it is checked during each disk block read. When an error is detected, the read is retried several times to handle any transient read failures. If the error persists, the block is marked as permanently damaged and all future accesses to it are avoided. This must be done transparently to the software to avoid any changes to the I/O system or application programs.

From the driver point of view, the disk is a continuously numbered sequence of n logical blocks, say $b[0], \ldots, b[n - 1]$. When a block $b[k]$ becomes damaged, simply marking it as unavailable would create a gap in the sequence and greatly complicate the I/O software. A more efficient solution is to let the disk controller handle all the mappings of logical to physical blocks internally and transparently to the I/O software. Specifically, when a block becomes inaccessible, the controller changes the mapping so that the software can continue using the same sequence of logical blocks without any gaps.

To make such remapping transparent, some blocks must be reserved initially as **spares**; otherwise, the loss of a physical block would reduce the number of logical blocks. Assume that the disk consists of a total of np physical blocks, where $np > n$.

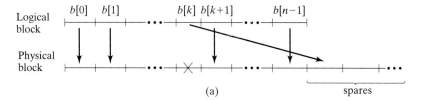

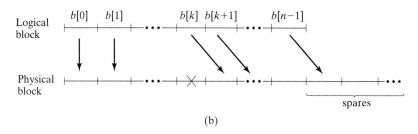

FIGURE 11-17. Handling of bad blocks: (a) remapping; and (b) shifting.

When the physical block holding logical $b[k]$ becomes damaged, the controller can remap the blocks either by allocating a spare to the block $b[k]$ or by shifting all blocks $b[k]$ through $b[n - 1]$ to the right by one block. Figure 11-17 shows the two schemes graphically.

The advantage of the first solution (Fig. 11-17a) is that only one block must be remapped, but it can lead to performance degradation if the spare block is on a different cylinder than the original failed block. Let us assume that blocks $b[k - 1]$, $b[k]$, and $b[k + 1]$ originally all reside on the same cylinder. To read the sequence of these three blocks requires a single seek operation. When $b[k]$ is remapped to a different cylinder, three seek operations are required to read the same sequence of blocks.

One way to minimize this problem is to allocate a number of spare blocks on every cylinder and attempt to always allocate spares from the same cylinder as the failed block. The method of Figure 11-17b shifts all blocks following the faulty one to the right. This requires more work to repair the disk, but it eliminates the problem of allocation noncontiguity.

Stable Storage

When a disk block become defective, some of the information it contains is unreadable. If error-correcting codes are used and the damage affects only as many bits as can be corrected, the information can be recovered and stored in a new block. But when the damage is more extensive, the information is simply lost. Another source of potential data loss is a system crash. If a crash occurs when a disk write operation is in progress, there is no guarantee that the operation was carried out successfully and completely. A partially updated block is generally incorrect and considered lost.

Loss of data is always undesirable but the consequences depend on the applications that use this data. In many instances, the application can be rerun and the lost data reproduced. In other cases, lost data may be recovered from backup files. However, many applications, such as continuously operating database systems or various time-critical systems logs, require data to be available, correct, and consistent at all times.

There is no system that can eliminate potential data loss with an absolute guarantee; no matter how many levels of backup a system chooses to provide, there is always a scenario that will defeat all safeguards. But we can reduce the risk to a level that is acceptable in any practical application. One way to achieve an extremely high level of data safety is with **stable storage**. This method uses multiple independent disks to store redundant copies of the critical data and enforces strict rules in accessing them.

Consider a stable storage with two disks, A and B. Under failure-free operations, the two disks contain exact replicas of each other. Assuming that both disks do not fail at the same time, one of them always contains the correct data, provided that the following protocols are obeyed by every read and write operation, and during recovery:

- **Write.** Write the block to disk A. If successful, write the same block to disk B. If either of the two writes fails, go to the recovery protocol.

- **Read.** Read the block from disk A and B. If different, go to the recovery protocol.

- **Recovery.** We must differentiate between two types of faults: 1) a spontaneous media failure, where one or more blocks (possibly the entire disk) become inaccessible; and 2) a system crash during one of the read or write operations:

  1. When a read or write operation fails, the block on one of the disks is defective. The data from the corresponding block on the other, still correct disk, are read and restored on a new block on both disks. The failed read/write operations then can be repeated.

     Figure 11-18a illustrates the situation where a block on disk B becomes damaged. The data, X, from the corresponding block on disk A are used to recover from this media failure.

  2. When the system crashes during a read operation, the read can simply be repeated after the system recovers. When the system crashes while writing to disk A, disk B's data are correct and can be used to restore disk A. Conversely,

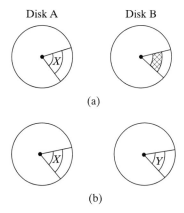

(a)

(b)

FIGURE 11-18. Stable storage: (a) bad block; and (b) block mismatch after system crash.

when the system crashed while writing disk B, disk A's data are correct and used to restore disk B.

Figure 11-18b shows that two corresponding blocks on the disks A and B contain different data, X and Y, respectively. This discrepancy is due to a system crash that occurred during the write operation. If this occurred before the write to disk A completed successfully, the data Y is correct and replaces the data X. If the crash occurred after disk A completed the write, X is correct and is used to replace Y. After recovery, both disks are again exact replicas of each other. Furthermore, the system knows whether the repaired block contains the old data that resided in the block prior to the write operation or the new data placed there by the write operation.

The assumption about the two disks failing independently is crucial for the stable storage concept to work. The probability of both disks failing at the same time is the product of the probabilities of the failures of each disk, which for all practical purposes is negligible. The addition of more disk replicas decreases the probability further, but it can never be made zero, especially when considering the possibility of catastrophic failures resulting from natural disasters (fires, floods, earthquakes), terrorism, or war.

Redundant Array of Independent Disks

The acronym RAID stands for **Redundant Array of Independent Disks**. Its purpose is increased **fault tolerance**, increased **performance**, or both. Fault tolerance is increased by maintaining redundant data on different disks. Performance, as measured by increased rate of data transfer, is increased by distributing the data across multiple disks. Because I/O can proceed in parallel over each disk, the total achievable data transfer rate of the RAID is the sum of the data transfer rates of the individual disks.

There are different types of RAIDs, depending on the level of data redundancy employed. The simplest form, shown in Figure 11-19a, is an extension of the stable storage concept. It provides an exact replica of each of the primary disks, such that for each block, b_i, there is a copy, b_i', on another disk. Such a RAID is highly fault-tolerant but also very wasteful, as it duplicates the amount of storage needed.

Figure 11-19b shows a RAID organization where only a limited amount of information, derived from the primary data, is kept on additional disks. This information,

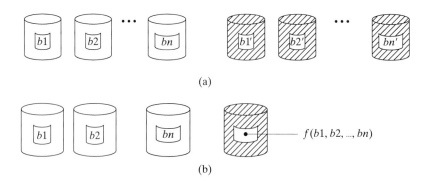

FIGURE 11-19. RAID: (a) fully replicated data; (b) derived recovery information.

denoted as $f(b_1, b_2, \ldots, b_n)$, could be simple parity computed across the corresponding bits or blocks of the primary disk, or it could be error-correcting code, capable of detecting and correcting the failure of a number of bits on the primary disks.

Within this basic organization, there are several different types of RAIDs. The basic trade offs are between the amount of redundant information (which increases the number of disks) and the achieved level of fault tolerance (i.e., number of bits that can be corrected). Redundant information can be segregated on separate dedicated disks or interspersed with the primary data. The placement plays a major role in performance; it determines the efficiency (access time and bandwidth) of data access during both normal operation and recovery from failure.

11.5.3   Disk Scheduling

The time to access a block on a rotating magnetic disks consists of three components. The **seek time** is the time to position the read/write head of the disk over the cylinder containing the desired block. The **rotational latency** is the time to wait for the desired block to pass under the read/write head. The **transfer time** is the time to copy the block to or from the disk.

The seek time requires mechanical movement of the read/write head and is the longest. It depends on the physical distance traveled, expressed by the number of cylinders that must be traversed. Seeking to an adjacent cylinder typically takes a few milliseconds; the average seek time to a random cylinder for a hard disk drive is approximately 10 ms and as much as 5 to 10 times that for a floppy disk drive. The rotational delay depends on the rotational speed of the disk, which ranges roughly between 5 to 15 ms per revolution for a hard disk. The rotational delay is, on average, half of that time. The actual data transfer time is the least costly, typically taking less than 0.1 ms for a sector on a hard disk, and less than 1 ms for a sector on a floppy disk. (See Figure 11-5 for typical ranges of disk performance characteristics.)

The above numbers show clearly that both the seek time and the rotational delay should be minimized to achieve good disk performance. This requires two levels of optimization. First, blocks that are likely to be accessed sequentially or as groups must be stored closely together, ideally, on the same cylinder. This is a matter of file allocation, which we have already discussed in Chapter 10. Keeping blocks belonging to the same file clustered within a small number of cylinders decreases the number of seek operations and their travel distance for any given process.

Unfortunately, requests to a disk may come from multiple processes concurrently. The interleaving of these requests would negate much of the locality of access. Thus, additional optimization techniques must be employed at runtime to continuously order the sequences of incoming requests; the ordering maintains the locality of reference, improving the disk performance.

Since both the seek time and the rotational delay are significant, we must order both, requests to different cylinders and requests to individual blocks within each cylinder. Let us first consider the ordering of requests for blocks within a single track. Since the disk always spins in one direction, the solution is straightforward. Assuming that the read/write head passes over the blocks on a track in ascending order, then, given a list of blocks to be accessed on the track, the list is also sorted in ascending order. In that way, all blocks on the list can be accessed during the same revolution of the disk.

With a multisurface disk, the same technique is applied sequentially to all tracks within the same cylinder. The list of blocks to be accessed on each track is sorted and accessed during a single revolution. Thus, it takes up to s revolutions to access all blocks within a given cylinder, where s is the number of surfaces (i.e., the number of tracks per cylinder.) The read/write head does not move during this time.

The ordering of accesses to different cylinders is a much more difficult problem because the read/write head moves back and forth across different cylinders. Thus, at any point in time, we must decide in which direction the read/write head should move next. The issue is complicated by the fact that requests to access different blocks arrive dynamically as an open-ended stream. They are placed into a queue where they await their turn. Whenever the disk completes the current operation, a process, called the **disk head scheduler**, must examine the current contents of the queue and decide which request to service next.

The scheduler can follow a number of different strategies in making its decision. The three most important factors to consider are: 1) the *overall performance* of the disk, which is reflected by the sustained data rate of the disk; 2) the *fairness* in treating processes accessing the disk concurrently; and 3) the *cost* of executing the scheduling algorithm.

To illustrate the different algorithms, assume the following scenario. The read/write head starts at cylinder 0. The scheduler moves it to satisfy a first request at cylinder 5, where it services all requests for blocks on that cylinder. After completing the latter, the queue contains a sequence of three new requests, to cylinders 12, 4, and 7, in that order. The following three algorithms show in which order these cylinders can be visited and the trade offs between the choices:

First-In/First-Out

The simplest approach to disk scheduling is to service the requests in the order of arrival in the queue, i.e., FIFO. For our example, the scheduler would move the read/write head from cylinder 5 to cylinder 12; then to cylinder 4, and finally to 7. Figure 11-20a tracks the movements of the read/write head. The total number of cylinders traversed is 23.

While very simple to implement, the main drawback of the FIFO algorithms is that it does not attempt to optimize the seek time in any way. It is suitable in systems where the disk is not a performance bottleneck. In such situations, the queue would contain only one or a very small number of requests most of the time. FIFO also may be adequate in single-programmed systems, where the sequences of block accesses already display a significant level of locality resulting from file-block clustering and sequential access.

Shortest Seek Time First

Multiprogrammed and time-shared systems generally place a heavy burden on the disk, and their access patterns show little locality because of the interleaving of requests from different processes. The **shortest seek time first** (SSTF) algorithms addresses the problem by always choosing the closest cylinder to access next, minimizing overall seek time. In the above example, the scheduler would reorder the three requests in the queue to access cylinder 4 first, since this is the closest one to the current cylinder 5. Next it would move to cylinder 7 and finally to 12. Figure 11-20b tracks the movement of the read/write head, which traverses a total of only 14 cylinders.

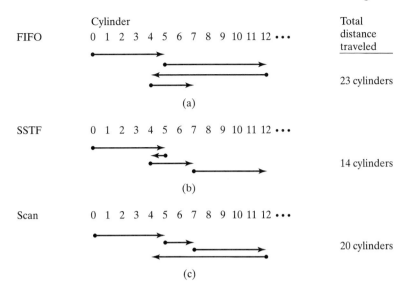

FIGURE 11-20. Disk scheduling algorithms: (a) FIFO; (b) SSTF; and (c) scan.

The SSTF algorithm minimizes the total seek time and maximizes the total bandwidth of the disk. Its main drawback is the unpredictability with which it services individual requests. Consider the following situation. When accessing cylinder 4, new requests for cylinders 3, 6, 2 arrive in the queue. The SSTF will service all of these before it gets to cylinder 12. In principle, an unbounded sequence of requests for cylinders in the general vicinity of cylinder 5 would delay the servicing of cylinder 12 indefinitely. Such unpredictability and possible starvation of outlying requests are not acceptable for a general time-sharing system that must guarantee some level of acceptable response for all users.

Elevator or Scan

A good compromise between the greedy nature of the SSTF and the need to maintain fairness in access is the elevator or scan algorithm presented in Section 3.3.3. Recall that the basic strategy is to continue to move the head in the same direction as far as possible and then change to the opposite direction. We can use the same *elevator* monitor for the disk head scheduler. The main difference is that with a real elevator, requests come from two distinct sources: call buttons at each floor and destination buttons inside the elevator cage. With a disk head scheduler, there is only a single stream of requests for different cylinders (destinations) issued by different processes. Thus, the I/O system translates each request for a particular cylinder into a call *elevator.request(dest)* where *dest* is the cylinder number. After it has read the corresponding blocks on that cylinder, it issues the call *elevator.release()*, which enables the next request to proceed.

Figure 11-20c tracks the movement of the read/write head under the scan algorithm. When it is on cylinder 5, its current direction is up and it does not reverse to service the closest cylinder 4, as in the case of SSTF. Instead, it continues in the same direction to service cylinders 7 and 12. Cylinder 4 is served on the down-sweep. The total number of cylinders traversed in this example is 20, which lies between the two previous extremes. The increase over SSTF is the price one pays for the greatly improved fairness in servicing individual requests—no request can be starved indefinitely.

There are several variations of the basic scan algorithm to further improve its behavior. The most important of these, **circular scan**, services requests only in one direction, say from lowest to highest. When it reaches the highest cylinder, the read/write head simply moves back to cylinder 0 and starts the next scan. This further equalizes the average access times to blocks; with the simple scan algorithms, tracks closer to the middle of the disk are serviced sooner on average than cylinders at the fringes.

11.5.4   Device Sharing

Some devices, such as disks, can be used concurrently by multiple processes. It is up to the scheduler to order the requests and present them to the driver, as discussed earlier. However, many devices, including keyboards, terminals, printers, or tape drives are only serially reusable. That means, they can be used by only one process at a time; otherwise, meaningless interleaving of data can occur.

To provide serial-reusability, most I/O systems have interface commands that permit processes to **request** and **release** individual devices. As already discussed in Section 11.2.1, some systems (notably UNIX/Linux) treat devices as streams of data similar to files. Thus, the same *open* and *close* commands used to request and release access to files are used to request and release devices. When a device is currently in use, the *open* command will block the requesting process, or it may return with a message indicating the state of the device. The use of *open/close* to control the sharing of devices provides for a uniform interface to access the file system and the I/O system.

Spooling, introduced briefly in Chapter 1, is frequently implemented for noninteractive output devices, such as printers. The output data of a process is not sent immediately to the printer as it is being generated but is written into a file instead. The file serves as a **virtual printer**. With this organization, multiple processes can output data concurrently without reserving the actual printer. The output files are kept in a special spooling directory. A dedicated server process then accesses these files sequentially and sends them to the printer one at a time. File transfers, email, and other communication through networks are handled in a similar way to optimize the use of underlying networks.

CONCEPTS, TERMS, AND ABBREVIATIONS

The following concepts have been introduced in this chapter. Test yourself by defining and discussing each keyword or phrase.

Bad block	Input-output (I/O)
Block-oriented device	Joystick
Buffer swapping	Laser printer
Buffering	LCD/LED printer
CD-ROM	Memory-mapped I/O
Circular buffer	Network communication interface
Circular scan	Network interface card (NIC)
Communications device	Optical disk

Connection-based and
   connection-less protocols
Consumer process
Cathode ray terminal (CRT)
Cycle stealing
Digital audio tape (DAT)
Device controller
Device driver
Device sharing
Direct memory access (DMA)
Disk cylinder
Disk scheduling
Disk sector
Disk track
Digital linear tape (DLT)
Dot-matrix printer
Ethernet
FIFO disk scheduling
Flat-panel monitor
Floppy disk
Hard disk
Hierarchical I/O systems model
Impact printer
Ink-jet printer
Interrupt-driven I/O
I/O device
I/O errors

Packet
Pixel
Polling
Producer process
Programmed I/O
Read/write head
Redundant array of independent
   disks (RAIDS)
Scan algorithm
Scanner
Seek time
Socket
Spooling
Shortest seek time first (SSTF)
Stable storage
Storage device
Stream-oriented device
Thermal printer
Track skew
Trackball
Transfer time
Transmission Control Protocol/Internet
   Protocol (TCP/IP)
Universal Datagram Protocol/Internet
   Protocol (UDP/IP)
Video RAM

EXERCISES

1. A fast laser printer produces up to 20 pages per minute, where a page consists of 4000 characters. The system uses interrupt-driven I/O, where processing each interrupt takes 50 μsec. How much overhead will the CPU experience if the output is sent to the printer one character at a time? Would it make sense to use polling instead of interrupts?

2. Consider a 56-Kbps modem. Transmitting each character generates an interrupt, which takes 50 μsec to service. Assuming each character requires the transmission of 10 bits, determine what fraction of the CPU will be spent on servicing the modem.

3. Assume a mouse generates an interrupt whenever its position changes by 0.1 mm. It reports each such change by placing a half-word (2 bytes) into a buffer accessible by the CPU. At what rate must the CPU retrieve the data if the mouse moves at a speed of 30 cm/second?

4. How much longer does it take to completely fill the screen of a color graphics monitor with 800×600 pixels and 256 colors than the screen of a character-oriented, black-and-white monitor with 25 lines of 80 characters? Repeat the calculation for a graphics monitor with double the resolution, i.e., 1600×1200 pixels.

5. Consider a two-sided floppy with 80 tracks per surface, 18 sectors per track, and 512 bytes per sector. Its average seek time between adjacent tracks is 2 ms, and it

rotates at 500 rpm. Determine the following:
   (a) The total storage capacity of this disk.
   (b) The number of seek operations that must be performed to sequentially read the
        entire content of the disk.
   (c) The peak data transfer rate.
   (d) The optimal amount of track skew.

6. Consider a single-sided floppy with 80 tracks, 18 sectors per track, 512 bytes per
    sector, an average seek time of 30 ms, a seek time between adjacent tracks of 3 ms,
    and a rotational speed of 360 rpm. A sequential linked file (Figure 10-12b) consisting
    of 12 blocks is stored on the disk in one of the following ways:
   (a) The 12 blocks are spread randomly over all tracks.
   (b) The file is clustered, such that the 12 blocks are spread randomly over only 2
        neighboring tracks.
   (c) The 12 blocks are stored in consecutive sectors on the same track.
    How long will it take to read the entire file in the three cases?

7. Consider a disk consisting of c cylinders, t tracks within each cylinder (i.e., t surfaces),
    and s sectors (blocks) within each track. Assume all sectors of a disk are numbered
    sequentially from 0 to $n-1$ starting with cylinder 0, track 0, sector 0. Derive the formu-
    las to compute the cylinder number, track number, and sector number corresponding
    to a given sequential block number k, $0 \leq k \leq n - 1$.

8. Two identical files, $f1$ and $f2$, of 100 KB each are stored on two different disks.
    The file blocks are spread randomly over the disk sectors. Both disks have an average
    seek time of 10 ms and a rotational delay of 5 ms. They differ in the organization of
    their tracks. Each track of disk 1 consists of 32 sectors of 1 KB each, and each track
    of disk 2 consists of eight sectors of 4 KB each. How long will it take to sequentially
    read the two files?

9. Consider a disk holding files with an average file length of 5 KB. Each file is allocated
    contiguously on adjacent sectors. To better utilize the disk space, it must be periodically
    compacted, which involves reading each file sequentially and writing it back to a new
    location. Assuming an average seek time of 50 ms, 100 sectors per track, and a
    rotational speed of 5000 rpm, estimate how long it will take to move 1000 files.

10. Consider a program that outputs a series of records and make the following assumptions:
    - It takes two units of CPU time to perform an I/O instruction; all other instructions
      take 0 units of time.
    - The device starts at the end of the I/O instruction, and it remains busy for 6 time
      units.
    - When polling is used, the CPU polls the device every 4 time units. The first poll
      occurs immediately after the I/O instruction. That means, if the I/O instruction
      ends at time i, the first poll occurs at time $i + 1$. Assume that a poll takes 0 units
      of CPU time.
    - When interrupts are used, the interrupt handler routine takes 5 time units
    - At time $t = 0$, the device is not busy and the CPU starts executing the program
    Draw a timing diagram showing when the CPU and the device are busy during the
    first 25 time units (a) with polling; and (b) with interrupts.

11. Section 11.4.2 shows the pseudocode for performing input and output using pro-
    grammed I/O with polling. Consider a process that must read a sequence of n char-
    acters and output a sequence of n other characters. Make the following assumptions:
    - The two character sequences are independent and thus may be processed concur-
      rently.
    - Two separate devices are used: one for input and one for output. The two devices
      are started using the instructions *write_reg(opcode1)* and *write_reg(opcode2)*,

respectively. Similarly, each device has its own busy flag and data buffer (referred to as 1 and 2).

Write the pseudocode for the process to work as fast as possible.

Hint: Combine the two separate code segments of Section 11.4.2 to achieve maximum overlap between the processor, the input device, and the output device.

12. Consider again the pseudocode of Section 11.4.2 (programmed I/O with polling). Make the following assumptions:

   - Each line of the code takes 1 unit of CPU time to execute.
   - The *write_reg()* function starts the I/O device. The device becomes busy at the end of this function and remains busy for 10 units of CPU time.

   (a) Draw a timing diagram for the input code, showing the sequence of instruction execution and the time the device is busy for the first 30 time units.

   (b) Draw a timing diagram for the output code, showing the sequence of instruction execution and the time the device is busy for the first 30 time units.

   (c) How long does it take to first input n characters and output n characters?

   (d) Draw a timing diagram for the combined I/O code of the previous exercise, showing the sequence of instruction execution and the time the two devices are busy for the first 40 time units.

   (e) How long does it take to concurrently input n characters and output n other characters using the program of the previous exercise?

13. Section 11.4.3 shows the pseudocode for performing input and output using programmed I/O with interrupts. Note that the device must remain idle during the memory copying operation, but it need not be idle during the *increment i* and *compute* operations. Assume that the compute statement has the form *compute(i)*, where i indicates the character to be processed. Rewrite the code for both input and output to achieve maximum overlap between the CPU and the device. That means, when the input devices reads character i, the CPU should be computing with character $i-1$. Similarly, when the output device writes character i, the CPU should be preparing character $i+1$.

14. Consider a single consumer process that communicates with n independent producers. Each producer uses a separate buffer to present data to the consumer. Assume that the time f to fill a buffer is larger than the time c to copy and process the buffer, i.e., $f = kc$, where $k \geq 1$ is an integer.

   (a) Draw a timing diagram (similar to Fig. 11-9) showing the concurrent operation of the consumer and the different producers (each filling one of the n buffers).

   (b) How many buffers can be used to keep the processor busy all the time, i.e., what is the optimal value of n?

   (c) What is the ideal number of buffers when $k = 1$, i.e., $f = p$? Does it still help to have multiple independent producers?

   (d) What is the ideal number of buffers when $k < 1$?

15. A RAID consisting of n disks uses a four-bit error correction code for each 512-byte disk block. The codes are not stored on a separate disk but are spread over the n disks, such that any disk i holds the codes of disk $i+1$ (modulo n). Determine what fraction of the total disk space is taken up by the error codes.

16. Consider a disk with n cylinders numbered sequentially $0, 1, 2, \ldots, n-1$. The unit has just finished servicing requests on cylinder 125 and has moved to cylinder 143. The queue of requests to be serviced is as follows:

$$143, 86, 1470, 913, 1774, 948, 1509, 1022, 1750, 130$$

where 143 is the oldest request and 130 is the latest arrival.

    (a) In which order will the cylinders be serviced under the following scheduling policies:

- FIFO
- SSTF
- Scan

    (b) What will be the distance (number of cylinders) traveled by the read/write head under each policy?

    (c) Consider a variant of the scan algorithm, where the read/write head services requests only in one direction, say during its up-sweep. When it reaches the request with the highest cylinder number, it moves down to the request with the lowest cylinder number, without servicing any requests on its down-sweep. The advantage of this strategy, referred to as *circular scan*, is that the disk distributes its service more uniformly over all cylinders. In comparison, the regular scan gives preferential treatment to cylinders closer to the center of the disk. Determine the number of cylinders the read/write head must traverse to service all the requests in the above queue using circular scan.

17. Simplify the code of the *elevator* monitor (Section 3.1.1) to follow the FIFO scheduling algorithm instead of the elevator algorithm.

18. Consider the following implementation of a disk head scheduler. It uses a single-priority wait queue, q; processes are placed into this queue based on their distance to the variable *headpos*, the current head position. Construct a scenario illustrating why this does *not* correctly enforce the SSTF algorithm.

```
monitor disk_head_scheduler {
  int headpos=0, busy=0;
  condition q;

request(int dest) {
  if (busy) q.wait(abs(dest - headpos));
  busy = 1;
  headpos = dest;
}

release() {
  busy = 0;
  q.signal;
}
}
```

PART FOUR

PROTECTION AND SECURITY

CHAPTER 12

The Protection and Security Interface

12.1 SECURITY THREATS
12.2 FUNCTIONS OF A PROTECTION SYSTEM
12.3 USER AUTHENTICATION
12.4 SECURE COMMUNICATION

The increasing dependence on computer systems in industrial corporations, financial institutions, government and administrative offices, education, health care, personal record-keeping, and in military installations has introduced a new set of problems related to their security. These problems result from two basic types of attacks—**malicious** and **incidental**. Malicious attacks attempt to intentionally read or destroy sensitive data, or to otherwise disrupt the system operation. In many cases, the culprit is a computer hacker who considers the penetration of a computer system a personal challenge; oftentimes, however, we are faced with acts of purposeful crime, resulting in great financial losses, injustice, or personal harm. Incidental attacks result from human error, hardware malfunctioning, and undetected errors in the operating system (OS) and other software components, or from natural disasters such as fires, earthquakes, and power blackouts. The consequences may be as serious as those of intentional crimes.

Similar to a military fort, a computer system must provide two types of protection **mechanisms** and **policies**: 1) those that govern the behavior of processes operating legally within the system; and 2) those that control the boundary of the system, i.e., govern who may enter the system. In this chapter, we address the second issue, which is concerned with the system protection and security interface to the outside world. After describing the types of potential threats to security, we examine the two problem areas that must be addressed to create an effective protection boundary around a system. The first is user authentication, the procedures that allow users to enter the system. The second is the protection of data that flows into the system from devices or other computers; cryptography is the principal technique used to protect this data from tampering or loss.

12.1 SECURITY THREATS

The terms *protection* and *security* do not have precise, widely accepted definitions in computer science. They encompass a broad spectrum of issues and applications. We define **protection** as the act or the state of defending or guarding from attack, invasion, loss, or annoyance. **Security**, on the other hand, is the freedom from danger, risk, doubt, or apprehension. Thus, protection may be viewed as the collection of mechanisms and policies necessary to achieve security; in other words, security is the *goal*, whereas protection is the *means* to attain it.

A computer system comprises collections of data that can be read or modified, and services that may be invoked; both of these are referred to as **resources**. Active components of the system, capable of performing the read and write operations or able to use a service, are called **subjects**. In most conventional systems, processes correspond to subjects, and data files, programs, or even processors are regarded as resources. Different subjects can coexist in a computer system and share its resources. Unfortunately, the ability to share poses a potential threat to security. Hence, one of the major objectives in designing secure computer systems is to provide mechanisms and policies to permit the sharing of data, services, and physical resources but only in a controlled manner according to well-defined policies.

12.1.1   Damage Types

We can divide the issues of protection and security into four basic categories, according to the type of security threat to be prevented.

- **Information disclosure** is concerned with unauthorized dissemination of information, either as a result of theft or through illegal actions on part of a user who has access to that information. Obvious examples of information disclosure are the reading of a forthcoming exam by a student, access to classified or secret military documents, or the theft of research results proprietary to a industrial enterprise. An important part of the problem is the enforcement of the right of **privacy**, a social policy defined as the ability of each individual to control the collection, storing and dissemination of information about himself. Failing to do so could result in substantial damage or harm to an individual or a social group. For example, monitoring an individual's financial transactions or personal activities could serve as the basis for subsequent blackmail.

- **Information destruction** is the problem of information loss, which can be the result of an error or an act of sabotage. An obvious example is the loss of an important OS data structure, such as a process or resource queue. Other examples are the destruction of the research or development results of an individual or an institution to eliminate unwanted competition, or the deletion of police or court records containing important evidence in a criminal charge. Information may be destroyed without being disclosed and vice versa.

- **Unauthorized use of services** is concerned with the problem of bypassing the system's accounting policies to make unauthorized use of some proprietary services or simply to obtain free computing time. Users of a computing facility often display a different attitude toward computer services than they would toward other resources. For example, a person who has been entrusted an object, such as a car, by the object's owner might hesitate to let a third party use it without the user's consent. On the other hand, letting a third party use an entrusted computer account or a software system could be viewed by the same person as quite acceptable. Especially if the proprietary package is "only" a computer game, few would hesitate to make a copy for a friend. In addressing this problem, we must realize that, although intangible, computer accounts, data files, or programs all represent valuable resources that might have been created as business assets. Consequently, their unauthorized use must be considered an act of crime.

- **Denial of service** is the problem of intentionally preventing an authorized user from using the system services in a timely manner. As the dependence of society on computers increases, timely response becomes an important issue. In many situations, any significant delay in service may have severe consequences. Such delays can be caused inadvertently, as a result of system malfunctioning, or deliberately, as an act of sabotage. In both cases, the resulting denial of service can be of temporary nature—an unexpected and intolerable delay—or it can result in permanent damage or loss of information. For example, a mechanical malfunctioning of a disk may require a service engineer to be called in to perform the necessary repairs. Even if no data are destroyed on the disk when its read/write arm stopped functioning and normal operation is resumed after the problem is eliminated, the unavailability of the system may result in serious damage. As another example, the system could be monitoring some real-time events or processes, whose uncontrolled behavior might pose a serious threat to human life or property. Substantial financial losses also may result from the unavailability of a computer system in many businesses; an airline reservation system is one such critical computer system. In many instances, hardware or software malfunctioning causes both denial of service and the destruction of information.

12.1.2   Vulnerable Resources

There are many possible ways that an attacker can choose to carry out any of the above threats. First consider the kinds of resources that the attacker may target.

- **Hardware resources** include the CPU, the main memory, secondary storage devices, and communication lines and devices. Illegally monopolizing the CPU can lead to unauthorized use or denial of service for other processes. Accessing the main memory or secondary storage devices can lead to information theft of destruction. Accessing communication lines and devices also can lead to information loss, but, in addition, it can be used to impersonate a user or a service and gain access to other information exchanged between users and their processes/services.

- **Software resources** include stored data files (or databases), programs, processes (both at the system and user level), virtual memory, and various system components, such as queues, tables, or ports. Reading or damaging stored program or data files has similar consequences as attacks on secondary storage devices; the main difference is the point of attack: The information is accessed via the file system, rather than the hardware devices directly. Similarly, attacks on virtual memory are analogous to attacks on main memory. The main difference is the level of abstraction at which is violation is carried out. Attacking executing processes, including various systems services, can lead to their destruction or malfunctioning (including denial of service). An imposter also may succeed in tricking a process to perform unauthorized services on his behalf. Finally, illegal access to system tables or other internal resources could be exploited to circumvent any protection mechanism the operating system has in place.

12.1.3 Attack Types

The possible attacks on both software and hardware resources can arise in a variety of ways, many of which are quite ingenious. The principal kinds of attacks are described below.

- **Attacks from within**

  - *Direct access as a valid process.* The attacker either becomes a bona-fide system user or assumes the identity of a bona-fide user. This allows him to establish a valid process (or thread), through which he abuses its privileges as a user by attempting to read, modify, or use other resources of the system, or to find additional security weaknesses.

  - *Indirect access via an agent.* The attacker succeeds in establishing a program within the system under attack, which performs illegal tasks on the attacker's behalf whenever it is invoked. The agent program executes as part of other user processes, so the attacker need not be present in the system during the attack.

- **Attacks from outside**

  - *Via legitimate channels.* Computers that are part of networks receive messages from other computers via communication lines. An attacker may be able to send messages to a remote computer via its legitimate network connections and thereby impersonate a valid service or a bona-fide user (client). This may lead to information theft or destruction. It also may lead to unauthorized use of a the service or possibly to service denial.

  - *Via illegitimate channels.* The attacker succeeds in establishing illegal communication channels by tapping into or physically modifying existing communication lines leading to a computer. The resulting security violations include those obtainable via legitimate connections. In addition, the attacker may be able to obtain or modify information exchanged between other remote users or servers and the computer under attack.

Within each of the above four categories, there are many instances of known attacks. This is illustrated in Figure 12-1, which subdivides the best known attacks into

Attacks from Within		Attacks from Outside	
Direct Access	Indirect Access	Legitimate Channels	Illegitimate Channels
• browsing • leaking of information	• Trojan horse • trap door	• virus • worm • remote execution	• wire tapping • searching of waste
• masquerading		• trial and error	

FIGURE 12-1. Classification of security attacks.

the above four classes. Note that some attacks, such as masquerading and trial and error, are very broad and may be applied to all four attack types. We now survey the various penetration attempts in more detail and suggest possible safeguards to counter them.

Browsing for Information

The term **browsing** refers to searching of storage for unauthorized information. When a portion of memory is allocated to a process, it may still contain some data that has remained there from previous computations. Browsing through this memory may compromise sensitive information belonging to other users or to the OS itself. This is true of both physical and virtual memory. Similarly, free space on disks or tapes, allocated previously to other users or the system, may still contain sensitive information when it is allocated to a process.

Browsing is a typical example of an attack from within the system that can be performed by any valid process executing legally within the constraints of the OS. The obvious protection against browsing is to always erase all memory areas and disk blocks prior to reallocating them to another process.

Information Leaking

All users depend on various services provided by the OS, commercial service providers, or other users. One common way to implement a service is in the form of a separate process (a server) with which the user communicates using message-passing or other forms of interprocess communication. To enable the service to perform its intended function, the user must generally extend some privileges to it. In particular, the service may require information that the user wishes to keep private. An untrusted service may—deliberately or accidentally—leak such information to its owner or to other parties by copying it to a file or memory area accessible by the unauthorized processes, or by sending it to them directly using interprocess communication.

Similar to browsing, information leaking is carried out from within a system by a legally established process. Preventing this from occurring is known as the **confinement problem**, and is one of the most difficult challenges to security, since the information being leaked has expressly been made accessible to the service process. As will be discussed in Section 13.4.1, the confinement problem in its full generality is unsolvable because of covert channels that a clever system may exploit.

Trojan Horse Attack

Many services are not implemented as separate processes but rather in the form of programs that users invoke as part of their environment. This includes most system software such as compilers and linkers, general utilities such as editors, specialized packages such as graphics or mathematical libraries, or any other application a user wishes to use. Like services that are constructed as separate processes, services implemented as programs may also require access to information belonging to the user. However, since the programs are invoked as part of the user's current process, they generally inherit all privileges of the invoking process. Thus, unlike separate processes, imported programs have access not only to the information supplied to them explicitly in a message or as parameters, but also to any information accessible to the calling program. Consequently, such programs can not only leak sensitive information to other parties, but also perform many malicious tasks, including modifying or destroying information within the user's domain, sending email in the user's name, initiating Internet purchases or other financial transaction's on the user's behalf, or abusing system resources.

A program that misuses the additional privileges gained by executing as part of an unsuspecting user process to perform unadvertised, illegal actions is known as a **Trojan horse** program. The name is based on Greek mythology: The Greek army, having unsuccessfully besieged the city of Troy for 10 years, left a large hollow wooden horse in front of the city gate upon their pretended abandonment of the siege. The Trojans, regarding the horse as a gift, pulled it into the city. At night, Greek soldiers concealed in the horse opened the city gates to the Greek army, thus causing the destruction of Troy.

A Trojan horse is a typical example of an indirect attack from within a system; the Trojan horse program is the agent, but its owner need not be present in the system. A Trojan horse also may be used for an attack from outside of the system by enticing a legitimate user to download and execute malicious programs (e.g., Java applets) through the Internet. Limiting the potential damage of a Trojan horse attack is largely a matter of access control to various resources, as will be discussed in Section 13.3.

Trap Doors

A **trap door** is an unspecified and undocumented feature of the system that may be exploited to perform subsequent unauthorized actions. A trap door can be the result of a flaw in the system design. For example, insufficient checking of parameters, the use of undefined opcodes, or an unusual and untested sequence of operations can result in an obscure system state that makes that system vulnerable to attack. More likely, a trap door has been implanted intentionally by a systems programmer for future use. Trap doors are a common practice and, sometimes a necessity, when developing certain types of programs. One example occurs when testing or debugging a login program or another authentication routine. The programmer may include a special command to bypass the very program being tested. Such a trap door can remain in the system—intentionally or by mere omission—after the development or testing has been completed, and can be misused in the future.

Trap doors are agents that attack the system from within. Detecting and eliminating them is very difficult, since each is implemented as an ad hoc feature of a legal program. Administrative policies that explicitly govern the use and subsequent removal of trap doors, are the only safeguard; these serve to some extent as a deterrent to negligent or malicious conduct.

Viruses

Viruses are malicious programs that are similar to biological viruses in three important aspects. First, a virus tries to *infect* as many systems as possible by actively replicating itself. Second, a virus cannot function on its own; it needs a *host* program to which it attaches itself and is executed whenever the host program is executed. Finally, viruses are *malicious* programs designed to cause damage to the systems they invade. Such damage can occur gradually as the virus spreads through different systems, or it may be scheduled to occur at a certain date or be triggered by a specific event. For example, the well-publicized Michelangelo virus was designed to erase the hard disks of all infected computers on March 6, 1992—the birthday of the Italian artist Michelangelo.

Viruses can spread via any executable programs shared among users via removable media (floppy disks or tapes), file transfers, email messages including executable attachments to email messages, or by downloading them from the Internet. Whenever an infected program is executed, the virus code first attempts to infect as many other programs within the user environment as possible. It does so by attaching a copy of itself to any such target program and modifying the program's starting instruction so that it executes the attached virus code prior to entering the original portion of the code.

Given the increasing pervasiveness of electronic communication media, viruses can now spread around the world within hours and cause major financial damage. For example, the Melissa virus, which spread in 1999 via email attachments worldwide within a few days, caused damage estimated in millions of dollars in denial of service and information destruction. An even more destructive virus, named the Love Letter virus because of the email subject heading it used when replicating itself, resulted in billions of dollars of loss within a few hours of its introduction.

The most effective protection against viruses is to avoid executing any programs of unknown or untrusted origin. But only a total isolation of the system from the outside world—not a practical solution for most users—could guarantee the absence of any viruses. Given the possibility of infection, many system employ various **virus detection** and **removal** software. Virus detection relies on the fact that a virus must in some way modify a host program. In the simplest form, the program length increases, which can be detected by virus detection software. To counter such measures, more sophisticated viruses attempt to hide their presence by ensuring that infected programs still pass the antivirus checks. For example, a virus can use data *compression* to preserve the original program size.

Another virus detection approach relies on the fact that a virus must somehow mark each infected program so that it does not become reinfected repeatedly, which would cause its length to grow indefinitely. The mark or **virus signature** is a specific bit pattern that characterizes the virus. The virus detection software can scan all programs for the presence of known virus signatures to detect infection. These attempts can be thwarted by advanced viruses that employ encryption to disguise their signature and make it unrecognizable by virus detection software. Such viruses can be detected by first interpreting the programs within a safe environment where they are periodically scanned for known virus signatures that would emerge as the virus gradually decrypts itself.

Once a virus is detected, it must be removed from the system. In a stand-alone system, this can be done by stopping all processes and restoring all programs to their original state prior to restarting them. The virus detection software must then be upgraded to prevent reinfection. In a network of computers with shared file systems, virus elimination is much more difficult because the virus must be removed from all machines at the same time to prevent repeated mutual reinfection.

A virus is an example of an attack carried out from outside of the system by exploiting existing legal communication channels used by other users for legitimate communication. Its main objective is the destruction of information or denial of service.

Worms

Similar to viruses, worms are programs that also replicate themselves to other computers. They are similar to viruses also in their purpose, which is the destruction of information or denial of service. Unlike viruses, however, worms do not need a host program to exist.

They are not code fragments but complete *self-contained* programs capable of executing as independent processes.

Worms spread by exploiting some weakness or flaw of the OS or other system software. Consequently, they are much less prevalent than viruses. A virus only must avoid detection as it propagates together with its infected host through legal communication channels. In contrast, each worm must find its own unique flaw in the system, which, when removed, disables the worm's ability to spread. Typical approaches involve remote login facilities, remote execution facilities, or design flaws of various services, such as email, provided by the system to remote users or hosts.

CASE STUDY: THE MORRIS WORM

To illustrate the functioning of a worm, we consider the well-known example of a worm created and released in 1988 by a graduate student at Cornell University. This worm, named the Morris worm after its creator, exploited three separate weaknesses of the UNIX system to spread itself to thousands of machines on the Internet, causing major damage in the form of denial of service.

The first method of spreading was to use the UNIX *rsh* facility, which allows one machine to spawn a remote process (shell) on another machine without having to provide a password. The *rsh* is intended for machines that mutually trust each other, and the list of trusted machines is specified in a configuration file. The Morris worm exploited this by spreading itself transitively from any machine it has already invaded to all others that allowed a remote shell to be spawned on them.

The second method took advantage of a bug in the *finger* utility that runs as a daemon process under most UNIX systems. This utility can be invoked remotely from any other system. It accepts a user login name as a parameter and returns information about the user to the caller, such as the user's real name, home directory, host name, idle time, and other information. When *finger* is invoked, the supplied parameter (user login name) is placed on the utility's runtime stack. The flaw exploited by the worm was that the string copying utility did not check for a maximum allowable length of the supplied parameter. The worm invoked *finger* with an argument that exceeded the maximum length, which caused the parameter buffer to overflow and overwrite a portion of the *finger*'s stack. As a result, the function did not return to its original caller, but to another address placed on the stack as part of the carefully crafted parameter.

Figure 12-2 illustrates this type of attack graphically. Let us assume that *finger* is invoked from within a currently executing function *foo*. Figure 12-2a shows the portion of the invocation stack prior to the invocation of *finger*. This consists of three parts: 1) the return address to which *foo* will return once it exits; 2) the local variables of the function *foo*; and 3) the parameters supplied to *foo* by its caller at the time of invocation. Figure 12-2b shows the stack after *finger* has been invoked with a valid parameter, *abc*. The stack has been extended by three components: 1) the return address (within *foo*) to which *finger* should return; 2) the local variables of *finger*; and 3) the parameter (*abc*) supplied to *finger* by *foo*. Figure 12-2c illustrates the attack, where the length of the supplied parameter exceeds the maximum length of the buffer. Consequently, the string *abcdefgh* overwrites a portion of the stack, including the return address of *finger*. Thus, when *finger* terminates, it will not be

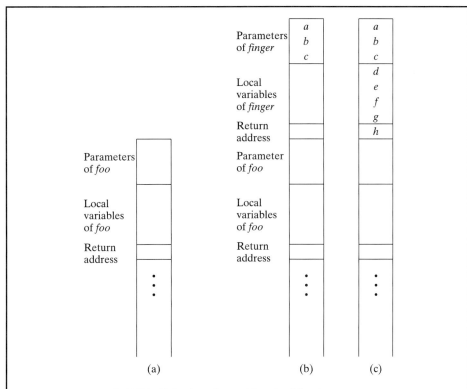

			a		a
Parameters of *finger*			b		b
			c		c
					d
Local variables of *finger*					e
					f
					g
Return address					h

Parameters of *foo*

Local variables of *foo*

Return address

Parameter of *foo*

Local variables of *foo*

Return address

(a)   (b)   (c)

FIGURE 12-2. Attack used by the Morris worm.

returning to *foo* but to whatever address, *h*, has been planted into the return address slot. Since this can be an arbitrary address chosen by the attacker, the worm can effectively take over the control of the entire process and established itself on the remote machine. From there, it continues its attack.

The third weakness exploited by the Morris worm was the debugging option in the email facility *sendmail*. It should be disabled when the system is in normal operating mode, but is frequently left operational to facilitate configuring the mail system. The debugging option supports commands that permitted the worm to mail itself to a remote host and to establish itself there as a new process.

Like a virus, a worm is an example of an attack from outside of the computer system. It uses legal communication channels to target servers operating legally within the system by tricking them into performing illegal actions on its behalf. The Morris worm employed three independent ways of spreading itself, as well as several other clever methods of disguising itself once established on a machine; it illustrates the difficulty of finding effective and general countermeasures against worms. Since each worm is likely to be unique, the best we can hope for is quick detection and elimination.

Remote Execution

A network, such as the Internet, may support several forms of code mobility. The best-known, already mentioned in the context of the Trojan horse attack, is the **downloading** of executable code from a remote machine. The opposite of downloading is **uploading**, where a user is able to send executable code from the local to a remote machine. If the user can cause the code to execute on the remote machine, the system is said to support **remote execution**. An even more advanced form of remote execution is provided by **mobile agents.** A mobile agent is a program that is capable of migrating among different machines at runtime (Bic et al. 1996). It does so by executing a special migration command, which instructs the system to package the agent's program and execution state into a message and send it to the machine specified by the migration command. The receiving machine reinstates the mobile agent in its own environment, where the agent continues its execution.

A mobile agent is similar to a worm in its ability to move or replicate itself among different machines. The main difference, however, is that a mobile agent operates legally within the system specifications. It does not exploit a system flaw to migrate but rather relies on specialized servers that support its mobility and its operation on the system. Thus, a mobile agent can only visit machines where such servers have been installed.

All forms of remote execution present opportunities for attacks from outside of the system. The system must guard itself against any illegal actions performed by the mobile agent or remotely executed code. One of the safest approaches is to use interpretation instead of direct execution in native mode. When code is interpreted, the interpreter, which is a trusted system, can verify each and every action taken by the migrated code. The main disadvantage is the degradation in performance resulting from code inter-pretation. For code executing in native mode, various forms of sandboxing may be used, which limit the scope and capabilities of the migrated code to minimize potential damage.

Wire Tapping

Communication lines connecting terminals and other devices to the host computer, or lines interconnecting nodes of a computer network cannot always be protected from physical access and constitute a vulnerable point for an attack. **Wire tapping**, defined as the act of establishing a physical connection to a communication line, can occur in two forms—**passive** or **active**. In the first case, the intruder is merely listening to the communication on the tapped line without altering its contents. It may be used to copy sensitive data, bypassing the user-authentication mechanisms, or it may be used to obtain information such as a password that would permit "legal" entry on subsequent occasions.

A method similar to and used for the same purpose as passive wire tapping is **electromagnetic pick-up**, which is the monitoring of electromagnetic signals emanating from the system or its components. This usually does not require any physical modifi-cation of the system hardware and consequently may be accomplished without leaving a trace. Communication lines as well as cathode ray terminals are susceptible to this type of attack. Even more vulnerable are wireless communications, where information is simply broadcast using radio waves of a certain frequency. Anyone within the broadcast radius is able to pick up this information using a simple radio receiver.

Active wire tapping occurs when the data being transmitted are modified by the intruder. Two special cases of active tapping are **between lines** transmission and **piggy-back** entry. The first refers to insertion of additional messages into the communication when the legitimate user is temporarily inactive, for example, between individual lines or characters transmitted via a terminal. The authentic massages themselves are not altered in any way. In piggyback entry, on the other hand, original messages are intercepted and modified or replaced by entirely new messages before reaching their destination. This is usually accomplished by breaking the communication line and letting all messages pass through a third computer that pretends to be the genuine source and destination of messages. A typical application of this technique is to intercept and discard a logoff command transmitted by a legitimate user and, after returning to that user a faked acknowledgment of the session termination, continue the session with the same privileges as the original legitimate user.

In general, the only effective means of preventing tapping is the use of encryption to make the transmitted information illegible to an intruder. Malicious disruption of communication, resulting in information loss or denial of service, cannot however be avoided by any means other than controlling physical access to all components of the system.

Waste Searching

Few people, or even organizations, pay much attention to what happens to the various forms of waste generated as part of everyday business. But, with a surprisingly high success ratio, the examination of old printer ribbons, listings, memory dumps, notes, discarded tapes and disks, and similar artifacts that are found conveniently in wastepaper baskets or other collection points, can yield information leading eventually to the penetration of a system.

Waste search is a prime example of an attack from outside the computer system and using unauthorized channels to gain information that might permit subsequent entry into the system (e.g., finding a valid password) or directly yield sensitive information maintained inside the system (e.g., on a discarded printout). The only effective safeguards against such attacks are administrative ones that regulate the management of waste, such as mandatory shredding of sensitive documents or the explicit destruction of potentially compromising artifacts.

Masquerading

Masquerading is the act of impersonating a user or process, and can be attempted from outside as well as from within a system. In the first case, an intruder could capture the login sequence of a valid user, for example, through passive wire tapping, and then attempt to enter the system by replaying the recorded sequence, impersonating the legitimate user. Alternately, the intruder could use active wire tapping to break the communication line between a user currently logged in the system, and effectively continue communicating with the system under the legitimate user identity.

Impersonating a service, commonly termed **spoofing**, is a masquerading attack from within the computer system. The unsuspecting user is tricked into believing that he is communicating with a bona-fide service and may reveal sensitive information to the imposter.

EXAMPLE: Masquerading as the System

A classic attack is the impersonation of a login program on a computer accessed by different users, such as a shared terminal in a public computer facility. Typically, any user wishing to login is first asked to type in a valid name, followed by a password. The attacker writes a program that mimics on the screen the same sequence of prompts displayed normally by the login routine. An unsuspecting user wishing to login will naturally type in the requested information, revealing it to the intruder's program. Having obtained the desired information, the program logs in the user through the genuine systems interface and exits, thus erasing any traces of its actions.

Trial and Error

Many authentication mechanisms rely on the low probability of guessing a valid string or other information items out of a vast space of potential choices. User passwords are the best-known example. Unfortunately, there are many ways to increase the likelihood of a successful guess in a trial-and-error attack. We discuss some of these, as well as appropriate countermeasures, as part of Section 12.3 on user authentication.

Some systems rely on this approach in generating unforgeable tickets, or capabilities, that permit the holder to perform certain tasks. One way to guarantee unforgeability is to generate the tickets as random bit sequences out of a very large space of possible choices. Guessing a valid sequence then becomes very unlikely.

12.2 FUNCTIONS OF A PROTECTION SYSTEM

The discussion and examples in the previous section make it clear that the issues in protection and security are multifaceted and that no single scheme can provide a completely safe computing environment. Rather, a spectrum of safeguards must be employed to achieve an overall level of system security. The interplay of these safeguards must be carefully balanced since any chain of policies and mechanisms is only as strong as its weakest link. Other factors to be considered are the *dollar cost* of providing protection mechanisms, which usually increases with the sophistication of the system, and, at the same time, a possible *degradation of performance* due to protection overheads.

We can distinguish several basic types of safeguards to be imposed on a system for the purpose of increasing its security level. These comprise the elements and functions of any complete protection system.

12.2.1 External Safeguards

The main purpose of external safeguards is to control **physical access** to a computing facility. For a single-user system such as a PC, external safeguards are limited to deciding who should be allowed to use the system. The choice is usually made and enforced by the owner, who also has the freedom to perform any modifications to the system hardware or software. Shared computer systems, on the other hand, are normally installed in buildings or rooms where entry is restricted to authorized personnel. These restrictions are subject to administrative policies and may be enforced through a variety of physical safeguards, such as locks, badges, sign-in procedures, or surveillance cameras. Inadequate control of physical access to any part of the computing facility can result in any of the security threats discussed earlier. For example, an intruder may read or modify information, employ some service, or cause a denial of service by using an administrator's terminal or by physically altering components of the system to bypass the protection mechanisms.

Assuming that sufficient external safeguards exist to stop a potential intruder from gaining entry into the system, the responsibility for the system security rests with the

OS. It must contain the necessary internal safeguards to prevent or at least reduce the risk of a possible security violation.

12.2.2 Verification of User Identity

When an authorized user executes a login procedure, a record of his presence in the system is created. Normally, this record has the form of a process that will be acting on behalf of the user. When such a process is created, we say that the user has successfully *entered* the system.

An essential task to be performed by any protection system is the verification of the user identity at the time of entry into the system. This **user-authentication** task is usually the first security check performed by the system internal safeguards. We survey a number of possible schemes in Section 12.3.

With computer networks, a problem related to user authentication is the authentication of remote processes attempting to communicate with a particular computer via communication lines. In particular, service providers must verify that any messages requesting service originated from a valid client and that all replies are delivered to only the legitimate client. Similarly, clients must verify that they are exchanging information with a valid service, rather than an imposter.

Given that both user login requests and requests for other services can be transmitted via communication lines that may not be physically secure from tampering, all messages transmitted along these lines must be protected. The only possible way to achieve that is by using **cryptography** to both hide the content of the transmitted information and to verify its authenticity once it is received. We describe various approaches in Section 12.4.

After a successful entry into the system, all actions taken by the user (represented by his process) are governed by internal protection mechanisms and policies enforced by the OS (Chapter 13). These can be subdivided into two classes, according to the type of problem to be solved: **access control** and **information flow control**.

Access Control

Access control is concerned with the ability of subjects to access resources. The fundamental question to be answered in a particular state of execution is: *Can subject S perform an operation f on a resource R?*

Most existing systems provide this type of control at the file-system level. Subjects are users or processes, confined to their own designated areas within main memory. They may request access to files stored on secondary storage devices by issuing appropriate commands to the file system. Depending on the sophistication of the file system, various degrees of access control may be provided. In the simplest case, the system does not distinguish between the operation types a process may perform on a file once access is granted. A more advanced scheme than this all-or-nothing policy recognizes operation types such as read, write, append, or execute, and grants or denies access based on the operation requested. The dissemination of access rights themselves is also controlled by the file system, which enforces the directives specified by the owner of each file. Access control also is required at the physical instruction level, where it is implemented primarily through hardware.

Information Flow Control

Access control mechanisms as described above are not sufficient to solve a number of important protection problems. In particular, they cannot be used to answer the question: *Is it possible for subject S to acquire the information contained in resource R?* It may not be necessary for the subject S to actually gain *access* to R; rather, the information could be transferred to it via other subjects or it could simply be copied into a resource that is accessible by S. Since such information transfers cannot, in general, be detected by access control mechanisms, different kinds of schemes which permit the specification and enforcement of policies to control the **flow of information** are necessary.

12.2.3 Communication Safeguards

All computer systems are connected to input and output devices. These can be attached directly to the system, but, frequently, they are located in different rooms or even buildings, and accessed via communication networks. Similarly, storage devices (e.g., file servers) are often accessed through networks. Most modern systems also support a variety of communication facilities that allow users to exchange information (email, programs, data files) with users on other machines, or to use a variety of remote services. All these interactions require information to be passed through communication lines, some of which may be public (e.g., telephone lines used by modems) and easily accessible by potential intruders. Increasingly, more information also is exchanged via wireless communication channels, which are readable by anyone with an appropriate receiver. To permit secure communication, a system must provide safeguards that guarantee the secrecy, integrity, and authenticity of the exchanged information; most of these safeguards are based on cryptography. A system also must have facilities to detect the presence of malicious software, such as viruses or worms, that typically enter the system from a network via legitimate communication channels.

12.2.4 Threat Monitoring

Despite the use of protection and security measures, it is not possible to prevent all possible attacks on a computer facility. To limit the damage from a successful attack and discourage future attempts, it is important to monitor the system security. The most common monitoring safeguards are *surveillance mechanisms* that automatically record all suspicious activities. Examples of such activities are unsuccessful login procedures, attempts to use privileged instructions, or invocation of protected internal system procedures. **Audit trails**, which are chronological sequences of these events, may be used in real-time to expose a potential intruder; they also may serve as the basis for subsequent external procedures that analyze potential threats. Threat monitoring also includes searches for the presence of unauthorized software, such as worms and viruses.

12.3 USER AUTHENTICATION

12.3.1 Approaches to Authentication

For any internal protection mechanisms to be effective, it is first necessary to guarantee that only authorized users are permitted to enter the system. Hence, any multiuser computer facility must have a means of verifying the user identity and establishing the connection to the appropriate internal record describing the user rights and privileges. This **user authentication** process is based on one or more of the following:

- knowledge of some information;

- possession of some artifact;

- physical characteristic of a person.

The most common instance in the first category is knowledge of a **password**. The likelihood of password guessing can be decreased by extending the scheme to a short dialog during which the user must answer a series of questions before entry is granted. This is similar to the security procedures employed by banks and other institutions, in which a client may be asked to give the mother's maiden name, date of birth, or similar information, before any client services are performed.

Another example of knowledge that must be possessed by a potential user may be a secret combination for a lock that is used to control physical access to the terminal room or to an individual terminal. Such physical safeguards are usually employed in addition to logical means of user authentication, such as passwords or dialogs.

The most prominent example of user authentication based on the possession of a unforgeable item is the use of plastic cards with **magnetic strips** containing **machine readable information**. To alleviate the threat of loss or theft, such items are usually employed in combination with a secret code or a password. For example, ATM machines permitting 24-hour access to a bank computer are controlled in this manner. Other common examples of unforgeable items are badges, used for visual inspection by a guard, or physical keys necessary to enter buildings, terminal rooms, or to operate terminals.

User-authentication methods in the third category are **biometric** methods, which rely on physical characteristics unique to an individual. Perhaps the best-known such characteristic, other than a person's appearance, is **fingerprints**. Unfortunately, their examination and comparison by a machine is difficult and costly to implement. Another scheme uses **hand geometry**, which measures the lengths of individual fingers or the length, width, and thickness of the hand. Similarly, **face geometry** measures the distances between features like chin, nose, and eyes, all of which yield patterns that are unique for each individual. **Voice patterns**, produced by measuring the frequencies and amplitudes of spoken phrases, and the patterns on the eye **retina** or **iris** offer other possibilities to verify the identity of an individual. Finally, the **dynamics of signatures**, i.e., the speed of writing and the pressure exercised when producing a signature, also have been employed successfully for user authentication.

In addition to being rather costly to implement, the main problem with the biometric methods is the uncertainty in the recognition process. This may lead to two types of error—rejection of an authorized user, known as a **false alarm**, and acceptance of an imposter. The relationship between these two error classes can be illuminated with a general example.

Assume that a given authentication mechanism returns a number n in a certain range, instead of a simple yes/no answer. Suppose that **genuine** attempts—those issued by authorized users—are clustered around 1, and **false** attempts—those originating from imposters—are clustered around 0. The probability of generating a value close to 0 or 1 typically follows a normal distribution. The problem is to choose an appropriate **threshold** that determines whether a given n represents a genuine or a false attempt.

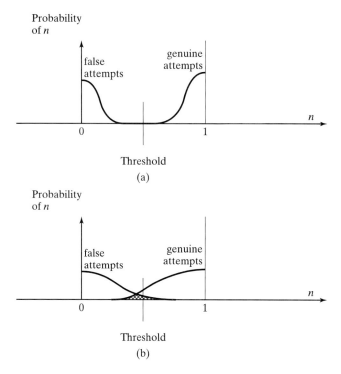

FIGURE 12-3. Sensitivity of user-authentication mechanisms.

Figure 12-3a illustrates the situation when the values of n are all close to either 0 or 1. Here, the obvious place for the threshold is at the midpoint between 0 and 1. Unfortunately, this neat separation is not always possible. In Figure 12-3b, a significant number of genuine attempts overlap with false attempts. The shaded area to the left of the threshold represents **rejected genuine attempts**, and the area to its right corresponds to **accepted imposter attempts**. By adjusting the threshold closer to 0 or closer to 1, we can reduce one type of error at the expense of increasing the other; the total number of erroneous recognitions cannot be decreased.

12.3.2 Passwords

Passwords are not only the most common means of user authentication in computer facilities but also they are the most likely target of a security attack. Successful password protection must guarantee the following:

1. Prevent unauthorized access to passwords stored and maintained within the system;
2. Prevent or at least minimize trial-and-error approaches at guessing passwords.

Possible solutions to these requirements are presented below.

Protecting Passwords from Illegal Access

Passwords are maintained by the system in the form of files. Each entry associates an authorized user with the appropriate password. There are two ways to protect the passwords from unauthorized access. The first is to rely on the file system's **access control** mechanisms: only authorized users, such as system administrators, are given read privileges to the password files. This approach has two limitations. First, the system administrators must be trusted not to misuse their access privileges. Second, should an intruder succeed in breaking into the system and gaining access to the password files, the passwords of *all* users would be compromised; new passwords would then be required from all users.

The second protection technique employs cryptography. Section 12.4.1 is devoted to the topic of cryptography in general. For the purposes of password protection, assume that we have a special hashing function H with two properties:

1. $H(P)$, where P is some text, produces a unique value C;
2. given C, such that $C = H(P)$, it is computationally infeasible to derive P, even when H is known.

Such a function is called a **one-way** function because its inverse is unknown, i.e., the function H^{-1} such that $P = H^{-1}(C) = H^{-1}(H(P))$ is unknown.

Using a one-way function H, passwords may be protected effectively by storing them in only their encrypted form. When a user U generates a new password, say PW, the system only records its hash value, $H(PW)$ in the password file. To authenticate the same user U at a later time, the function H is applied to the password, say PW', supplied by U. If the encrypted value $H(PW')$ matches the stored value $H(PW)$, then PW' must have been the correct password, i.e., $PW = PW'$, thus validating U's identity.

The main weakness of this approach is its vulnerability to computer-assisted trial-and-error approaches. That means, given an encrypted password C, an intruder tries a large number of possible passwords P' searching for a match $C = H(P')$. Since the password files do not need to be protected from reading, an intruder may examine and analyze them using various password-cracking programs. The password files may even be copied to other computers, where they can be subject to thorough analysis without any danger of being detected.

Preventing Password Guessing

Many systems permit a password to be an arbitrary sequence of alphanumeric (or even special) characters; the only possible restriction might be the maximum length of the resulting string. This permits very large numbers of distinct passwords to be created. For example, with an alphabet of 26 letters and 10 digits available on any keyboard, and a password length of only four characters, more than 1 million distinct passwords may be created. Thus, on the surface, the possibility of guessing a valid password might not seem likely. Unfortunately, studies of actual systems have shown that users tend to select passwords that are easily guessed, either because they are too short or because they are based on valid natural language words, which greatly reduces the potential name space. For example, a recent study that examined large numbers of UNIX password files revealed that nearly 25% of these could be guessed with relatively little effort because they were all based on information such as personal data, including the names, initials, or birth dates of the user or some immediate relatives; English words found in the system online dictionary or other sources; common first names; foreign words; or other word categories easily obtainable from online sources. Various modifications, such as adding a control or numeric character, or using various permutations of lower- and uppercase characters, also were easily discovered by exhaustive searches and simple heuristics.

Note also that, although guessing the passwords of a specific individual may be difficult, an intruder may be content with guessing *any* password that permits access to the system. Thus, from the system administrator point of view, even a single easily guessable password among the possibly thousands of valid passwords maintained by the system presents a serious threat. Several measures can be taken to reduce this danger:

- **System-generated passwords.** Passwords can be generated by the system as strings of characters consisting of random sequences of lower- and uppercase letters, digits, and control characters. This technique fully utilizes the available name space and lowers the probability of a successful guess. To alleviate the difficulty in managing such nonsense passwords, the system can make the generated strings pronounceable, thereby producing meaningless words that are easier to remember than completely random strings.

- **System-validated passwords.** A more user-friendly approach lets the user choose the password but accepts it only if it meets certain safety criteria. For example, it should have a minimum length, contain at least some number of control or numeric characters, and have both lower- and uppercase letters. The problem with this method is that the rules for forming valid passwords are generally known and may be used by a password-cracking program to limit the possible search space. A similar approach is to employ the same tools as an intruder, i.e., use a known password-cracking program to test every new password to see if it is vulnerable to guessing. Only if it passes the test is it accepted as a valid password; otherwise, the user is asked to try a different one.

- **Time-limited passwords.** Passwords are frequently limited by an expiration date or a number of uses to reduce the possible damage caused by a successful penetration. When the limit is reached, a new password must be obtained. Such restrictions are useful, for example, in preventing intruders from employing the system services free of charge over extensive periods of time. Their effectiveness in preventing theft or destruction of information, however, is limited.

- **One-time passwords.** The ultimate time-limited passwords are those that can only be used once. The problem is how to supply the user with an open-ended list of passwords, one for each session. Carrying a list of passwords is not only inconvenient but also potentially unsafe. One possible solution is to give the user a special-purpose calculator that generates new passwords on request, based on an an internal algorithm known and reproducible by the system. Such calculators can be manufactured in the from of plastic cards with an embedded computer chip. They are commonly referred to as **smart cards**. The use of such a card can itself be protected by a personal identification number (PIN), which is a form of a simple password.

Another approach produces passwords using a secret function, say f. To authenticate the user, the system presents to the user a random number, say n, known as a

challenge. The user returns the value $f(n)$, which is accepted as the password. Since $f(n)$ is different for each n, each password is valid only once. As a simple example, assume that $f(n) = 3*n/2$. Presented with a challenge of $n = 50$, the user would return 75 (i.e., $3*50/2$) as the password.

A third approach uses a one-way function, such as those used to protect password files stored on a computer, to allow a given password to be reused multiple times, without any danger of being misused. The idea is to encrypt a given password repeatedly with the same one-way function. Each encryption generates a different unique password, which can only be used once. Since the same sequence of encryptions may be performed by the system, it can verify each of the submitted passwords. However, the sequence of passwords must be used in the reverse order of their generation. That is because deriving the next password in the sequence, given the known one-way function, is easy; deriving the preceding password in the sequence, however, is not possible, because the inverse of the one-way function is not known (Lamport 1981).

EXAMPLE: One-Time Passwords

To illustrate this approach, assume that $H()$ is a one-way function. Assume that the user and the system know an initial password, pw, which is to be used to generate five unique one-time passwords. The user submits the following values: *H(H(H(H(pw)))),* *H(H(H(pw))), H(H(pw)), H(pw), pw*. Note that an intruder who captures any of the passwords can easily derive those that have already been used (and are by definition invalid), but cannot derive any of the future passwords.

One-time passwords are of particular interest in computer networks, where an intruder could obtain a copy of a password through wire tapping. Since any password is used only once, it cannot be misused by an intruder.

System-Extended Passwords

The system can expand each password internally and transparently to the user before storing it. This artificially increases its length and decreases the probability of a successful guess. The technique, so-called password "salting," has been implemented in UNIX, where passwords are kept only in encrypted form. When a new password, pw, is presented by the user, the system generates a random number, slt (the "salt"), that serves as the extension for the given password. The extension, slt, and the encrypted extended password, $H(slt, pw)$, are stored in the password file and associated with the given user. Figure 12-4a outlines the process graphically. The user identification, ID, is used to select the entry corresponding to the user; the values of slt and $H(slt, pw)$ are stored in this entry.

To later authenticate the user, the same entry is selected using the user ID. The password, pw', presented by the user, and the extension, slt, extracted from the entry, are encrypted using H. If the resulting value $H(slt, pw')$ matches the stored value $H(slt, pw)$, the user is accepted as legitimate.

Note that, although the extensions are stored within the password file in unencrypted form, they make password guessing much less likely, since the encrypted form $H(slt, pw)$ is now much longer than $H(pw)$ and a guess pw must be tried with every

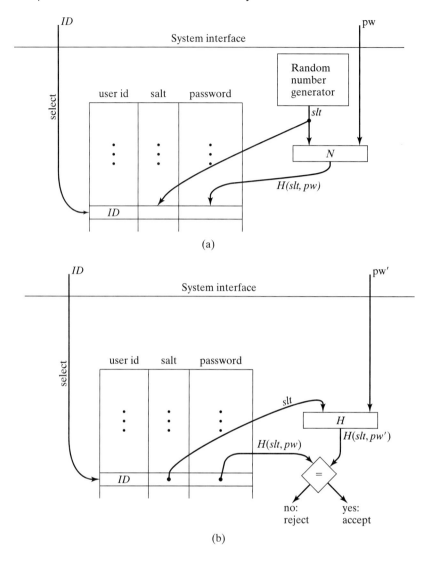

FIGURE 12-4. Salting of passwords in UNIX.

slt. Suppose that an intruder has a dictionary of *n* words and wants to test if any of these is a valid password. Without using the password extensions, the intruder would encrypt each of the *n* words and see if the encrypted form appears anywhere in the file. When random extensions are used, the intruder would have to try every word with every possible extension to see if their joint encrypted form appears in the file.

12.4 SECURE COMMUNICATION

12.4.1 Principles of Cryptography

Cryptography is the science of secret writing. It provides techniques to transform any text, called the **plain text**, into a **cipher text** that is unintelligible without some special knowledge. This transformation or **encryption** is generally implemented by a well-known function E that accepts the plain text P and a secret **encryption key** K^{encr} as arguments, and produces the cipher text C. That means:

$$C = E(P, K^{encr})$$

To transform the cipher text back into plain text, a **decryption** function D and a **decryption key** K^{decr} are employed. That means:

$$P = D(C, K^{decr}) = D(E(P, K^{encr}), K^{decr})$$

Cryptography is used for three main purposes: secrecy, integrity, and authenticity. We discuss these three concepts and how they are supported by cryptography.

Assume that a sender S transmits an encrypted message $C = E(P, K^{encr})$ to a receiver R, and that R is able to decrypt C back into P. The encryption key K^{encr} is known only to the sender and the decryption key is known only to the receiver. Under these assumptions, we can make the following guarantees:

- **Secrecy**. Secrecy addresses the problem of information disclosure. Both the sender S and the receiver R wish to prevent other parties from reading the contents of the transmitted message. As long as the keys of R and S remain secret, message secrecy is guaranteed, since only the receiver R will be able to transform C into the original plain text P and read its contents.

- **Integrity**. Integrity addresses the problem of information destruction or modification. Should the message be changed or damaged in any way (intentionally or accidentally) by a third party when in transit between S and R, the receiver R must be able to detect any modification upon receiving the message. The fact that R is able to successfully decrypt the message guarantees that the encrypted message C has not been modified; otherwise the decryption would yield a meaningless sequence of bits, rather that an intelligible plain text, P. The fact that the encryption and decryption keys are kept secret further guarantees that an intruder could not have modified the original plain text P, or substituted a different plain text.

- **Authenticity**. Authenticity is concerned with the message origin. It can be subdivided into two related problems, one addressing the message creator, and the second its sender:

    - *Authenticity of creator*. The receiver R of a message C needs a guarantee that the content of C was created by the sender S, i.e., C is not a forgery generated by a third party. As long as S and R trust each other, the authenticity of C's creator is guaranteed by the fact that the message was encrypted by the key K^{encr}. This is known to only S, and no other process is able to create a message that can successfully be decrypted using K^{decr}.

    Some applications cannot assume that R and S trust each other. It may be necessary to verify the authenticity of a message C even when S denies having created C. This requirement is generally referred to as **nonrepudiability**. It permits R to prove, not only to himself but to a third party, such as a judge, that S is indeed the creator of the received message C. That means, S cannot claim that C could have been created by a third party or even by the receiver R himself. Nonrepudiability can only be guaranteed when $K^{encr} \neq K^{decr}$, and one key cannot be derived from the other. This principle is the basis of digital signatures, to be discussed in Section 12.4.3.

- *Authenticity of Sender*: The fact that S created a given message C does not guarantee that S was the sender of C. An intruder could have intercepted a valid message sent from S and R and then replay (resend) it to R at a later time. Thus, authenticity of sender guarantees that S not only created but also sent the received copy of C. This cannot be guaranteed by encryption alone, since the valid encrypted message C can be copied and resent any number of times; the receiver will be able to decrypt each forged copy successfully. To solve this problem, S and R must obey a specific protocol to prevent message replay (Section 12.4.2).

12.4.2   Secret-Key Cryptosystems

Until recently, virtually all cryptosystems were **symmetric**, using the same key for both encryption and decryption. That is, $K^{encr} = K^{decr}$. The term **secret-key** indicates that there is only a single key for both senders and receivers. The encryption and decryption functions are also frequently identical, i.e., $E = D$, which greatly simplifies the implementation and use of such cryptosystems. All that is needed for a mutually secure communication is a common encryption/decryption function and a secret key.

Figure 12-5 illustrates the basic principles of a secret-key cryptosystem. It shows a sender process, S, and a receiver process, R, communicating via an insecure communication channel. Before sending any sensitive plain text, P, to R, the sender S first encrypts it using the function E and the secret key K. The encrypted message, $C = E(P, K)$ is transmitted to R, who decrypts it using the same key K and the function D, obtaining the original plain text P.

Enforcing Secrecy, Integrity, and Authenticity

Let us now use the scenario of Figure 12-5 to illustrate how various aspects of communication protection can be enforced. The **secrecy** of the transmitted information is guaranteed by the fact that C cannot be decrypted without the key K. The **integrity** of the transmitted information is guaranteed by the fact that no one can produce a valid encrypted message without the key K. In both cases, S and R must trust each other to keep the key K secret. Since secrecy and integrity are in the interest of both the sender and the receiver, we can generally assume that the key will not be compromised intentionally.

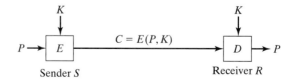

FIGURE 12-5. Principles of secret-key cryptography.

In contrast, **authenticity** is a more difficult matter to handle using secret-key cryptosystems. Authenticity of the message creator cannot be achieved if S chooses to deny it. S can claim that, since R knows the key K, R could have fabricated the message himself, or could have given the key to a third party to produce the counterfeit. (As shown in Section 12.4.3, this problem of nonrepudiability can be solved successfully with public-key cryptosystems.)

The second aspect—authenticity of the **sender**, which addresses the problem of who actually sent the current copy of C, also is not guaranteed by the fact that the message can successfully be decrypted by R. C could simply be a copy of an earlier message sent by S. Thus, although S is the original creator of information within C, its actual sender could be an imposter. This message **replay** attack can be used to trick the receiver to take some action that is not idempotent, i.e., an action that cannot be repeated multiple times without any consequences. For example, suppose that a valid sequence of commands exchanged between a server and an ATM machine to dispense cash is captured; the imposter can then withdraw cash from the victim's account repeatedly by replaying the valid sequence.

The problem of message replay can be solved by including with the message additional information that reveals its freshness. This information can take one of two forms: 1) a random number, referred to as a **nonce**; or 2) a **time-stamp**, which is the current value of the system clock.

The following protocol illustrates the use of a nonce to prevent the replay of a message sent from a process S to a process R.

	S	R
(1)	$\longleftarrow N$	
(2)	$C = E(\{P, N\}, K) \longrightarrow$	

In step (1), R sends to S a random number N as a nonce. This step is known as sending a **challenge** to S. The process S responds by combining N with the plain text P to be transmitted, for example, by simply concatenating the two. It then encodes the message $\{P, N\}$ with the secret key K and sends it to R. When R decodes the message, it obtains the plain text P and the nonce N'. If N' matches the original nonce N, R is assured that the received message is not a replay of some earlier message, but is a response to the last challenge.

Time-stamps are used in the following way to detect or limit replay of messages:

	S	R
	$C = E(\{P, T\}, K) \longrightarrow$	

T is the current time of the sender, and is combined with the plain text P in the same way as a nonce. The receiver can examine the value of T to determine the freshness of the message; it can reject it if T is too old. Note that this does not completely prevent message replay; it depends on the receiver's tolerance to accept old messages. The main advantage of time-stamps over nonces is that no challenge must be issued by the receiver. Time-stamps also are useful in limiting the validity of encrypted messages when these are used as unforgeable tickets (capabilities), which may be passed among different processes.

CASE STUDY: DES

One of the best-known secret-key cryptosystems is the **data encryption standard** (DES) adopted as the U.S. national standard for government and business applications (National Bureau of Standards 1977). DES divides the plain text into blocks of 64 bits that it encrypts using a 56-bit key. The encryption function has a sequence of 16 transformations, during each of which the text being encrypted is combined with the key using bit substitutions and permutations. Decryption reverses the process in 16 stages of analogous transformations.

With the steadily increasing speed of computers, the DES became vulnerable to brute-force attacks. In the late 1990s, it became possible to exhaustively search the space of the possible 2^{56} keys within several weeks of computation. The obvious solution is to increase the length of the key. Rather than developing new transformation algorithms to work with the longer key, the widely accepted solution is to apply the same DES algorithm successively multiple times. **Triple-DES** is one such approach. It employs up to three 56-bit keys, applied in sequence (ANSI 1985). That means:

$$C = DEA(DEA(DEA(P, K3), K2), K1)$$

where P is the plain text, C is the cipher text, and Ki are the three 56-bit keys. This effectively increases the key length to $3*56 = 168$ bits, which would require billions of years of brute-force computing for an exhaustive search with today's technology.

Key Distribution and Authentication

Before any two processes can communicate with each other using encryption, both must be in possession of the same secret key K. If the key is generated by one of the processes, the question is how to transmit it to the other process in a secure manner. We could send it manually, i.e., via channels outside of the computer system, such as through a courier service. This is very cumbersome, costly, and time-consuming for most applications. It also requires each process to maintain a separate key for all other processes with which it may ever need to communicate.

Most processes do not know all their potential communication partners a priori. Thus, we need a scheme that would allow different processes to establish a common key dynamically on an as-needed basis and discard it after the exchange is completed. A common way to establish such a short-term or **session** key between two processes is through a trusted server.

Trusted Server Approach

This method relies on a common trusted server, dedicated to the management and distribution of session key. The server, termed a **key distribution center** (*KDC*), shares a secret key K with every process in the system, a different key for each process. Initially, these keys are established outside of the system in a secure manner. This external task is much simpler than exchanging secret keys among individual processes. First, each process has only one secret key to maintain—the one for communicating with the *KDC*; only the *KDC* must maintain secret keys for all other processes. Second, the key is assigned to a process for its entire lifetime.

Under the above assumptions, two processes, A and B, can obtain a new secret session key by communicating with the KDC using the following protocol:

	KDC	A	B
(1)	$\longleftarrow A, B$		
(2)	$E(\{K_{AB}, B, ticket\}, K_A) \longrightarrow$		
(3)			$ticket \longrightarrow$

$ticket = E(\{K_{AB}, A\}, K_B)$

Assume that A initiates the exchange by sending its own identity (A) and the identity of the processes it wishes to communicate with (B) to the KDC. This information need not, in general, be encrypted. KDC replies to A by sending it the message $E(\{K_{AB}, B, ticket\}, K_A)$. This is encrypted using $A's$ secret key, K_A, which guarantees that it was generated by KDC. Upon its decryption, the message reveals three components: K_{AB} is the new session key; B is the identity of the process with which A is to communicate using the key K_{AB}; and **ticket** is an encrypted message to be passed on to B. Thus, at this point in the protocol, A is assured that it has a new valid session key (K_{AB}) for communicating with B.

The third step of the protocol requires A to send the ticket it obtained from KDC to B. The ticket has the form $E(\{K_{AB}, A\}, K_B)$. It is encrypted with B's secret key, K_B, and B is assured that the ticket was generated by KDC. Upon decryption, the ticket reveals the session key, K_{AB}, and the identity of the process (A) with which B may communicate using K_{AB}.

The above protocol is a simplified version of a general key distribution and authentication protocol (Needham/Schroeder 1978). The simplified version produces a unique session key for A and B, but is vulnerable to a replay attack. Consider, for example, a situation where a given key K_{AB} has been compromised and must be discarded. An intruder could trick B into communicating with it using the compromised key K_{AB} by replaying the old $ticket = E(\{K_{AB}, A\}, K_B)$ to it. B would interpret this as a new request for communication with A, that the intruder could impersonate by intercepting messages sent to and from B. Similarly, A could be tricked into communicating with an intruder by replaying to it the old message $E(\{K_{AB}, A, ticket\}, K_A)$ sent originally by KDC.

To protect against any replay, the original protocol uses two nonces: one for the exchange between A and KDC, which authenticates the KDC to A, and the second for the exchange between A and B, which authenticates A to B.

CASE STUDY: KERBEROS

One of the best-known key distribution and authentication systems, **Kerberos** (Steiner et al. 1988; Neuman and Ts'o 1994), is based on the above protocol but supports two important extensions to make it more usable in general client/server environments.

1. A session key, issued to a client for the purposes of communicating with a server, has limited validity. Recall that the session key is transmitted from the client to the server inside an unforgeable ticket generated by the KDC. Kerberos extends the concept of a ticket by including a time interval with it, defining the window during which the key remains valid.

CASE STUDY: KERBEROS   *(continued)*

2. A client must authenticate itself to the *KDC* before it is issued any tickets. This can be accomplished with passwords, but it would be too cumbersome to require *KDC* to provide the password for each new server. Kerberos solves the problem by dividing the client authentication into two levels. At login time, the client is authenticated using a password. It is then issued a ticket, valid for the duration of the login session, for accessing a special server whose task is to issue additional tickets for individual servers.

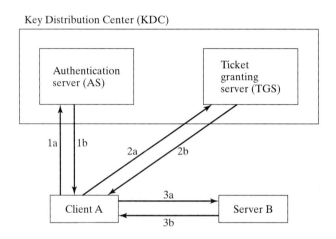

FIGURE 12-6. Organization of Kerberos.

Figure 12-6 shows the overall organization of Kerberos. The key distribution center is divided into two components: the **authentication server (AS)** and the **ticket granting server (TGS)**. A client *A* wishing to employ a server *B* must obey the following protocol. (To simplify the presentation, we have omitted the nonces, which are used to prevent any message replay.) The steps refer to the numbers on the arrows in the figure:

1. *A* obtains a ticket for the *TGS* from *AS*:

    (a) At login, the client *A* supplies a password to the *AS* to prove its identity.

    (b) *AS* returns to *A* the message $E(\{K_{AT}, tg\text{-}ticket\}, K_A)$, where K_{AT} is a session key for communicating with the *TGS*, and *tg-ticket* is a ticket-granting ticket. The message is encrypted using *A*'s secret key K_A and thus only *A* can obtain K_{AT} and *tg-ticket*.

2. *A* obtains a ticket for the server *B* from *TGS*:

    (a) *A* contacts *TGS*, requesting a ticket for the desired server *B*. As part of this request, *A* supplies the *tg-ticket* (obtained in step 1(b)) and an authenticator, AUT_{TGS}. The ticket-granting ticket has the form $tg\text{-}ticket$ $= E(\{A, TGS, T_{start1}, T_{end1}, K_{AT}\}, K_{TGS})$. It can only be decrypted by TGS and has the following meaning: A is allowed to get server tickets from TGS during the time from T_{start1} to T_{end1}, and it must authenticate itself using the key K_{AT}. The authenticator AUT_{TGS} accomplishes the latter; it has the form $AUT_{TGS} = E(A, K_{AT})$, which proves to TGS that A was the creator of the request.

(b) TGS returns to A the message $E(\{K_{AB}, sg\text{-}ticket\}, K_{AT})$, where K_{AB} is a session key for communicating with the server B, and $sg\text{-}ticket$ is a service-granting ticket for B. The message is encrypted using the session key K_{AT} and only A can obtain the K_{AB} and the $sg\text{-}ticket$.

3. A obtains service from the server B:

(a) A contacts B to obtain the desired service. As part of the request, A supplies the $sg\text{-}ticket$ (obtained in step 2(b)) and an authenticator, AUT_B. The service-granting ticket has the form $sg\text{-}ticket = E(\{A, B, T_{start2}, T_{end2}, K_{AB}\}, K_B)$. It can only be decrypted by B and has the following meaning: A is allowed to obtain service from B during the time interval (T_{start2}, T_{end2}), and it must authenticate itself using the key K_{AB}. The authenticator AUT_B performs this latter task: it has the form $AUT_B = E(A, K_{AB})$, which proves to B that A was the creator of the request.

(b) B performs the desired service and returns the results (encrypted using the session key K_{AB}, if desired) to A.

The two nonces omitted from the protocol are used to prevent any replay of messages between the client A and either the AS or the TGS.

12.4.3 Public-Key Cryptosystems

An **asymmetric** cryptosystem is one where different keys are used for encryption and decryption. If one key cannot be derived from the other using any computationally feasible means, then one of the two keys can be made public while the other is retained as secret. Such two key systems are called **public-key cryptosystems**.

The basic principles of a public-key cryptosystem are presented in Figure 12-7. It shows a sender process S and a receiver process R communicating via an insecure communication channel. Before sending any sensitive plain text P to R, the sender S first encrypts it. Unlike secret-key cryptosystems, the text is encrypted twice—once using S's private key, K_S^{priv}, and a second time using R's public key, K_R^{publ}. The receiver decrypts the received message $C = E(E(P, K_S^{priv}), K_R^{publ})$ first using R's private key and then S's public key, yielding the original text P. The order of the two encryptions/decryptions is usually not important.

Although generally more computationally intensive and more costly to use than secret-key cryptosystems, public-key cryptosystems offer a number of important advantages over secret-key cryptosystems, including the ability to enforce full authenticity of message contents (nonrepudiability).

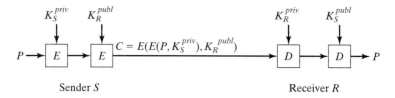

FIGURE 12-7. Principles of public-key cryptography.

Enforcing Secrecy, Integrity, and Authenticity

Let us now use the scenario of Figure 12-7 to illustrate how the aspects of communication protection can be enforced. The **secrecy** of the transmitted information is guaranteed in a manner similar to secret-key cryptosystems, since the transmitted cipher text $C = E(E(P, K_S^{priv}), K_R^{publ})$ is encrypted with R's public key, only R is able to decrypt it (using its private key).

The **integrity** of the message is guaranteed by the fact that R can successfully decrypt the inner portion of the message, $E(P, K_S^{priv})$, using S's public key; this implies that this portion of the message could not have been created by any other process but S.

The two aspects of authenticity are guaranteed as follows. Authenticity of the message **sender** can be determined using the protocol of Section 12.4.2, which employs nonces to prevent any replay attacks. Authenticity of the message **creator** is guaranteed in the same way as integrity: the inner portion of the message $(E(P, K_S^{priv}))$ is encrypted using S's private key, which is known to only S, and thus only S could have created it. Note that this can be proven even if S denies generating the message. That means, R is able to prove to a third party, for example a judge in the court of law, that S must have generated $E(P, K_S^{priv})$ and, consequently, the plaintext P itself. Recall that this was not possible with secret-key cryptosystems (Section 12.4.2), where both S and R share the same key, and either one could have created the message.

Encryption using private (nonshared) keys is also the basic principle underlying digital signatures, which will be discussed in Section 12.4.3.

CASE STUDY: RSA

One of the best-known public-key cryptosystems is RSA, named after its three inventors (Rivest, Shamir, and Adelman 1978). A message of arbitrary length is encrypted as follows. The message is first broken up into smaller blocks. Each of these is interpreted as an integer P, and encrypted independently of other blocks constituting the original message.

The encryption function has the form:

$$C = E(P) = P^e \bmod n$$

where the two integers e and n jointly are the **public** encryption key. The decryption function has the form:

$$P = D(C) = C^d \; mod \; n$$

where the two integers d and n jointly define the **private** decryption key.

The three integers e, d, and n must be chosen such that the following two conditions are satisfied:

1. $P = D(E(P)) = (P^e \; mod \; n)^d \; mod \; n$, i.e., the decryption function must be the inverse of the encryption function.
2. It must be computationally infeasible to derive the integer d from the two other integers, e and n, i.e., given the public key (e, n), it must not be possible to derive the corresponding private key (d, n).

The following rules yield three integers e, d, n, that satisfy the two conditions:

1. Choose two prime numbers, p and q, and compute their product $n = p * q$. For the purposes of illustration, we choose $p = 5$ and $q = 7$; $n = p * q = 35$. In general, p and q must be large, generally greater that 10^{100}.
2. Choose d to be a large prime number such that d has no common factors with $(p - 1) * (q - 1)$. That means, the greatest common divisor of d and $(p - 1) * (q - 1)$ is 1. For our example, $(5 - 1) * (7 - 1) = 24$. Thus, we could choose d to be 5, 7, 11, 13, $\ldots$, none of which is a factor of 24. Assume we choose $d = 11$.
3. Choose e such that the following condition is satisfied: $e * d \; mod \; (p - 1) * (q - 1) = 1$. For our toy example, we must find e such that $e * 11 \; mod \; 24 = 1$; the series of numbers 11, 35, 59, 83, 107, $\ldots$ all satisfy this equation. Let us choose $e = 59$.

The above choices of $n = 35$, $e = 59$, and $d = 11$ result in the encryption/decryption functions:

$$C = E(P) = P^{59} \; mod \; 35$$

$$P = D(C) = C^{11} \; mod \; 35$$

Note that e is derived using d and $(p - 1) * (q - 1)$. To reverse this process, i.e., to derive d from e, we also must know p and q. These are the two prime factors of n, which are kept secret. Since factorizing large numbers is computationally infeasible, it is not possible to derive p and q from n. Consequently, it is not possible to derive the private key (d, n) given the public key (e, n).

Public-Key Distribution and Authentication

With private keys, the main problem is how to establish the same secret key between a pair of processes wishing to communicate with each other. In particular, a secure channel is required for the initial transmission of the shared secret key. With public-key cryptosystems, each process generates a pair of keys; it makes one public and keeps the other secret. Since the public keys of all processes are freely available to any other process, there is no need to distribute them through secret channels. Instead, the problem is how to **authenticate** each public key. That means, when a process A claims a particular key K as its public key, all other processes must be able to verify that K is indeed A's public key and not that of some other process. Otherwise, an imposter C, claiming to be process A, could trick a sender into transmitting its messages encrypted with the key K_C^{publ} that he claims is A's public key.

Although the key authentication problem is different from the key distribution problem of secret-key cryptosystems, the solutions are similar. Both use a trusted server.

Trusted Server

The trusted server here plays the role of a *KDC*. It maintains the identities and the public keys of all processes. Processes communicate with the *KDC* in a secret manner using a single pair of keys: K_{KDC}^{priv} is the private key known only to the *KDC* and K_{KDC}^{publ} is the corresponding public key. This public key must itself be authenticated but, since all processes only manage a single key, this is much easier to achieve than the general problem of authenticating all possible public keys.

Using the *KDC*'s public key K_{KDC}^{publ}, any process can request and obtain an authentic public key of any other process. Assume that process A wishes to obtains the public key of a process B. The following protocol accomplishes that:

	KDC	*A*
(1)		$\longleftarrow A, B$
(2)	$E(\{B, K_B^{publ}\}, K_{KDC}^{priv}) \longrightarrow$	

Process A sends a request to *KDC*, consisting of its own identity (A) and the identity of the other process (B). This request may be sent unprotected. *KDC* returns to A a message encrypted with *KDC*'s private key, K_{KDC}^{priv}. This guarantees that only *KDC* could have generated the message contents, which state that B's public key is K_B^{publ}. A can now use this key to either encrypt messages sent to B, or to authenticate messages received from B.

Using Public-Key Cryptosystems for Digital Signatures

Public keys can be used to guarantee nonrepudiability of a message, as explained earlier. That means, by decrypting a message with a public key associated with a given process or user S, it can be proven to a third party that S was the creator of the original plaintext. The only way another process could have created that message would be for S to deliberately release its secret key to that process, which amounts to delegating one's signature authority.

Unfortunately, encrypting large documents with public-key cryptosystems is not practical because of the high cost of encryption. The concept of **digital signatures** was developed to solve this scaling problem, serving the same function of document authentication as does an encryption of a full document, but for a fraction of the cost. The basic idea is to reduce the plaintext document to be signed, say M, to a short sequence of bits, referred to as the document **digest**, d. This is accomplished using a special hashing function H:

$$d = H(M)$$

where H has the properties:

1. H is a one-way function. That means, given M, it is easy to compute $H(M)$; but given $H(M)$, it is computationally infeasible to derive M.
2. H is unlikely to lead to collisions. That means, given any $M \neq M'$, the probability of $H(M) = H(M')$ is extremely small.

Many such hashing functions have been developed and put to practical use. Among the most common representatives are **MD5** (Rivest, 1992) and **SHA** (NIST 1995). Both functions are applicable to text of arbitrary length, subdivided into blocks of 512 bytes. These blocks are repeatedly permuted and combined using bit-wise logical operations with various constants and with each other. MD5, one of the most efficient one-way functions available, generates a 128-bit digest. The result of SHA is a 160-bit digest. Although slower than MD5, SHA offers more protection against brute-force attacks, because of its greater digest length.

Figure 12-8 sketches the basic algorithm for generating and using digital signatures. Assume that the sender, S, wishes to send a digitally signed document, M, to the receiver R. S first generates a digest $d = H(M)$ of the message M using a one-way function H. It then encrypts d with its own private key, K_S^{priv}. The resulting ciphertext $SIG = E(d, K_S^{priv})$ is S's unique signature of the document M. S sends this signature together with the plaintext document M, to R.

Upon receiving the two pieces of data, R decrypts SIG using S's public key, thus obtaining the digest in plain text form: $d = D(E(d, K_S^{priv}), K_S^{publ})$. It then applies the same one-way function H to M, obtaining a digest $d' = H(M)$. If $d = d'$, R can conclude and prove the following:

1. The digest d contained in SIG could only have been generated from the document M, otherwise d would be different from d'; this links SIG to M in a nonrepudiable manner.

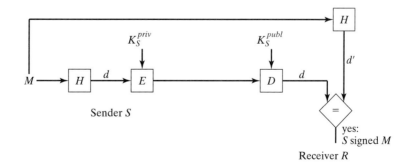

FIGURE 12-8. Principles of digital signatures.

2. Only S could have generated the signature SIG (due to the encryption using K_S^{priv}); this links S to SIG in a nonrepudiable manner.

3. By transitivity, S is linked to M in a nonrepudiable manner, i.e., S must have signed the original document M.

CONCEPTS, TERMS, AND ABBREVIATIONS

The following concepts have been introduced in this chapter. Test yourself by defining and discussing each keyword or phrase.

Access control	Key distribution center
Asymmetric server	Leaking of information
Attacks	Masquerading
Authentication	Message authenticity
Biometric authentication	Message integrity
Browsing	Message secrecy
Challenge	Nonce
Ciphertext	One-way function
Communication safeguard	Password
Confinement problem	Plain text
Cryptography	Protection
Cryptosystem	Public-key cryptosystem
Data encryption standard (DES)	Replay attack
Decryption	Secret-key cryptosystem
Decryption function	Security
Denial of service	Symmetric cryptosystem
Digital signature	Threat monitoring
Encryption	Trap door
Encryption function	Trial and error attack
Encryption or decryption key	Trojan horse
External safeguard	Trusted server
False alarm	Unauthorized use of services
Information destruction	Virus
Information disclosure	Wire tapping
Information flow control	Worm
Kerberos	

EXERCISES

1. Consider two users A and B with the following privileges: A can read and write a file f, and read, write, and execute a service program p; B can only read f and execute p. An intruder has managed to:
   (a) guess A's password.
   (b) guess B's password.

(c) place a passive tap on A's terminal line; however, the password transmission is protected through encryption (see Exercise 6 below).

(d) place an active tap on A's terminal line (password transmission is again protected using encryption).

For each of the above cases, describe a simple scenario (if one exists) that would lead to each of the following violations:

- information disclosure
- information destruction
- unauthorized use of services
- denial of service

2. Consider a biometric user-authentication system using fingerprints, which returns a value between 0 and 1 for each attempted match; 1 means perfect match, and 0 means perfect mismatch. The system was tested by presenting to it 1000 valid fingerprints and 1000 invalid fingerprints. The results were compiled into a histogram represented by the following table. That means, 192 of the 1000 genuine samples returned a value of n between 1 and 0.9; 188 of the 1000 genuine samples returned a value of n between 0.9 and 0.8, and so on. None of the invalid sample returned a value greater than 0.6, but one returned a value between 0.6 and 0.5, three returned a value between 0.5 and 0.4, and so on:

range of n	valid samples	invalid samples
$1 \geq n > 0.9$	192	0
$0.9 \geq n > 0.8$	188	0
$0.8 \geq n > 0.7$	176	0
$0.7 \geq n > 0.6$	158	0
$0.6 \geq n > 0.5$	133	1
$0.5 \geq n > 0.4$	88	3
$0.4 \geq n > 0.3$	49	5
$0.3 \geq n > 0.2$	15	29
$0.2 \geq n \geq 0.1$	1	319
$0.1 \geq n > 0$	0	643
Totals	1000	1000

(a) Determine the threshold value of n such that less than 1% of imposter attempts are accepted. How many false alarms will be generated as a result?

(b) Determine the threshold value of n such that less than 1% of genuine attempts are rejected. How many imposter attempts will be accepted as a result?

(c) Determine the threshold value of n such that no genuine attempts are rejected. How many imposter attempts will be accepted as a result?

3. Write the pseudocode for a login shell, which prompts the user for a name and a password, and reads those in. It invokes a function $valid(name, password)$, which returns a 1 if the name and password are valid, and a -1 otherwise. If the entry is valid, the login shell invokes a function $user\_shell()$; otherwise, it displays an error message and starts over. In addition, the login shell should contain a trap door that allows illegal entry whenever the user types "superman" as the user name.

4. At login time, every user must type in a user name and a password. Assume that the average length of the user name and the password is n characters each, and that all lowercase and uppercase letters, numbers, and special characters found on a standard

keyboard may be used. Consider the following three strategies followed by the system to reject invalid login attempts:

- It waits for the user name to be entered. If this is invalid, it displays the message "invalid user name;" otherwise, it proceeds by accepting and verifying the password.
- It waits for both the name and the password to be entered. If the name is invalid, it displays the message "invalid user name;" If the password is invalid, it displays the message "invalid password."
- It waits for both the name and the password to be entered. If either one is invalid, it displays the message "invalid entry."

(a) How many attempts will an intruder have to make to guess a valid combination of a user name and a password in each case?

(b) What are the numbers for $n = 5$?

5. Consider the scheme of encoding passwords using "salt" as shown in Figure 12-4. Assume that performing one encryption takes h microseconds and looking up and comparing a value in the password file takes c microseconds. The password file has n entries. An intruder is using a dictionary of 100,000 words to try to guess a password. Assuming no distinction is made between lower- and uppercase characters, determine the following:

(a) How long does it take to check if any of the dictionary words is a valid password of one specific user?

(b) How long does it take to check if any of the dictionary words is a valid password of any user?

(c) Repeat the above two problems for a system where no "salting" is used.

(d) Compute the actual values for the above four cases given the values $h = 0.1$ μs, $c = 0.02$ μs, and $n = 1000$ users.

6. Passwords may be stolen through wire tapping on the communication line between the system and a terminal. Assume that the system as well as each terminal are equipped with an encoding/decoding unit and each terminal has a secret key K known also to the system. Note that simply encoding the password in the terminal and decoding it in the system would not solve the problem. (Why?) Devise a scheme that will render passwords obtained through wire tapping useless. (Hint: Use a nonce to prevent message replay as discussed in Section 12.4.2.)

7. Repeat the previous problem using public-key encryption, where the system has a private key K_{sys}^{priv}, and the corresponding public key K_{sys}^{publ} is known to all users.

8. Consider the scheme for generating a sequence of one-time passwords using a one-way function, as described in Section 12.3.2. The user and the system both use the following one-way function: $H(c) = c^3 \bmod 100$, where c is the decimal value of an ASCII character. A given password is interpreted as a sequence of ASCII characters, and the function H is applied to each character separately. Assume the user's initial password is the string "Cat," and is to be used to generate a sequence of five distinct one-time passwords. Show the sequence of these passwords and the order of their use.

9. Consider the following simple encryption/decryption scheme for character strings in ASCII code:

- The plaintext and the ciphertext are divided into blocks of n ASCII characters.
- The encryption/decryption key K is a string of n ASCII characters.
- The encryption and decryption functions are both the bit-wise exclusive OR function applied to the ASCII codes, i.e., $E(P, K) = XOR(P, K)$ and $D(C, K) = XOR(C, K)$, where P is a block of n plaintext characters and C is a block of n ciphertext characters.

(a) Given the cipher text *TF%TO6QE5GEv* and the key *5$W*, generate the corresponding plaintext.

(b) Assume one encryption takes 0.01 μs. How long would it take to try all possible keys on a ciphertext of 30 characters?

(c) How long would the key have to be to increase this time to more than one month?

10. Modify the trusted server protocol for secret-key distribution (Section 12.4.2) to allow a session involving three processes, A, B, C, using a common secret session key K_{ABC}. Process A initiates the session by requesting two tickets from KDC, one for B and another for C.

11. Extend the trusted server protocol for secret-key distribution (Section 12.4.2) to prevent the replay of messages. Specifically, use one nonce to prevent the replay of the encrypted message sent from KDC to A, and another nonce to prevent the replay of the ticket set from A to B.

    Hint: For the first case, include a challenge with the original message sent by A. For the second case, B needs to verify the freshness of the received ticket by issuing a subsequent challenge to A.

12. Consider the following public-key encryption/decryption scheme for character strings in ASCII code:

    • The decryption function is $P = C^5 \bmod 35$. The corresponding encryption function $C = P^e \bmod 35$ is kept secret.

    • Each digit of the hexadecimal code corresponding to an ASCII character is viewed as one block and is encrypted separately using the above function. Thus, each character results in a pair of encrypted blocks. For example, the hexadecimal code for the ASCII character B is 42. This would be encoded as two blocks, ($4^e \bmod 35$, $2^e \bmod 35$).

    (a) Given the cipher text below, where each number corresponds to one encrypted block, generate the corresponding plaintext. (The parentheses and the commas are used only to increase readability; they are not part of the ciphertext):

    (9,4) (32,0) (6,15) (7,7) (6,10) (32,0) (7,4) (6,15) (7,10) (32,0) (32,9) (33,1) (32,17) (33,0) (33,0) (33,0) (32,17) (33,0) (33,0) (33,0) (32,1)

    (b) Break the above (simple) encryption scheme by finding the corresponding value of e. Verify this by reencoding the decoded plaintext back to the ciphertext.

13. Assume you receive the message "Let's be friends," along with a digital signature 23,6,17,6. The message was sent by a user U, whose public decryption function is $P = C^7 \bmod 35$. The signature was produced using the following known conventions:

    • The digest d of the message is produced by dividing the text into blocks of four characters. The decimal values corresponding to the four ASCII characters are added together modulo 10.

    • Each digit of the digest is encrypted with the sender's private function $C = P^e \bmod 35$, where e is secret.

    Prove that the received message is genuine, i.e., that it must have been signed by the user U.

CHAPTER 13

Internal Protection Mechanisms

13.1 THE ACCESS CONTROL ENVIRONMENT
13.2 INSTRUCTION-LEVEL ACCESS CONTROL
13.3 HIGH-LEVEL ACCESS CONTROL
13.4 INFORMATION FLOW CONTROL

The user-authentication mechanisms presented in the previous chapter govern who can enter the system as a valid user. Once established and represented by a legally created process, the user may access data maintained by the system and use its services. To prevent any security violation, the system must provide a set of protection mechanisms and policies to govern the behavior of all processes with respect to the system resources and to each other. In this chapter, we examine the two major problem domains that must be supported by the system. The first addresses the problem of controlling the access by a process to various system resources including programs, data files, or hardware devices. The second is concerned with controlling the flow of information between different entities within a system, such as processes or files.

13.1 THE ACCESS CONTROL ENVIRONMENT

In the course of its execution, a process must access various resources, both hardware and software. Hardware resources include the CPU, its status and data registers, main memory, and a variety of possible secondary storage and communication devices. Software resources include program and data files, system tables, runtime data structures, and other processes, each of which may reside in registers, main memory, or secondary storage. The collection of all resources—hardware and software—accessible to a process at a given time is defined as the process' **current execution environment**.

The current execution environment may be static, i.e., constant for the lifespan of a process, or it may vary dynamically during its execution. Dynamic execution environments are more difficult to implement but provide more flexibility in enforcing different protection policies. In particular, they can decrease the extent of damage a process may cause to itself or to other processes. Systems patterned after the "need-to-know" principle enforced by the military require that processes operate at all times in the smallest environment necessary to carry out the current tasks. Only a highly dynamic execution environment can satisfy this requirement.

We differentiate between two fundamental levels of access to the different resources of the current execution environment:

- **Instruction-level access:** Certain machine instructions use sensitive hardware resources, such as CPU registers, and must only be executed by authorized system processes. In addition, machine instructions that access memory (physical or virtual) must be prevented from specifying addresses that lie outside of the memory areas (partitions, pages, or segments) allocated to the process.

- **System-level access:** High-level abstract entities, e.g., files or logical devices, are accessed by issuing kernel calls to the OS. Controlling the use of such entities is the responsibility of the subsystems that handle the various kernel calls. In particular, the file system is responsible for enforcing legal accesses to files, as prescribed by the system policies.

Next, we explore the possible hardware and software mechanisms that support access control at the two different levels, and thus ensure that processes always remain confined to their respective execution environments.

13.2   INSTRUCTION-LEVEL ACCESS CONTROL

A machine instruction can access data in three types of memory: 1) hardware registers within the CPU; 2) hardware registers within I/O device controllers; and 3) main memory. We must prevent unauthorized access to data at each of the three levels to prevent different forms of security violations.

13.2.1   Register and Input/Output Protection

Central Processing Unit Registers

The CPU contains a number of hardware registers and flags. Some of these are read and written implicitly as part of instruction execution; these include various condition codes that reflect the result of the last operation, such as the sign bit or overflow. Others are accessed explicitly as operands of various machine instruction.

We can subdivide the directly accessible registers into two classes for the purposes of protection. The first includes registers that programs use to hold intermediate data or address values of the ongoing computation. These must be accessible to all programs. The second class includes registers that make up the CPU's *internal state* and must only be accessed by trusted system programs to prevent a variety of possible security violations. For example, the ability to explicitly set the program counter could give a process the ability to branch to any portion of memory. Altering the contents of timer registers used to generate time-sharing interrupts, or disabling interrupts altogether, would enable a process to illegally monopolize the CPU for its own purposes; this capability could result in unauthorized use of the computational resources or in the denial of service to others. In addition to the CPU registers, we also must prevent unauthorized access to I/O registers that comprise the interface to the various device controllers.

To support the necessary separation of user processes from authorized system processes, the instruction set of the processor is divided into two classes, **privileged** and **nonprivileged** instructions, respectively. The former include those that access and manipulate the CPU state, control I/O devices, or perform other sensitive operations, and may be executed only by authorized system programs. The remaining, nonprivileged instructions are used for general computation and are available to all programs.

The CPU hardware provides a special bit to differentiate between two distinct modes of execution: the **system** mode, also referred to as the **supervisor** or **kernel**

mode, and the **user** mode. When executing in the system mode, any instruction is valid. In the user mode, only the nonprivileged instructions may be executed; an attempt to invoke a privileged instruction causes an interrupt, which transfers control to the OS to take appropriate actions. Generally, the offending process is terminated and an error is reported.

The switching between different processor modes, which amounts to setting or resetting the special privilege bit in the CPU, must of course be controlled. Switching from the privileged system mode to the nonprivileged user mode can be done with a machine instruction that changes the mode bit. However, there can be no such instruction for switching from user to system mode; otherwise, any process could simply switch to the privileged mode, rendering the mechanism useless. The solution is a special instruction, generally called a **supervisor** or **kernel call**, that sets the bit to privileged mode and simultaneously transfers control to the OS. Thus, switching to system mode automatically takes control away from the invoking user process. When the OS decides to resume this process, it resets the bit to user mode prior to transferring control to it.

Some systems distinguish more than two modes. For example, the long-lasting VAX-11 architecture distinguished four processor states—kernel, executive, supervisor, and user—each capable of using a different subset of the existing instructions. This permits a finer subdivision of the OS into separate levels for further protection.

Note that the availability of two or more execution modes provides for a dynamic execution environment at the process level. The current execution of the process changes whenever it switches between different execution modes in that the set of usable machine instructions grows or shrinks with the current mode.

Input/Output Devices

Chapter 11 surveyed the many communication and storage devices that are attached to computer systems. To communicate with such I/O devices, the CPU must read and write various registers provided by the device controllers. Access to these registers may be through either a memory-mapped interface or a set of special I/O instructions. In the first case, access to devices may be controlled through the same mechanisms provided for memory protection. That means, only authorized system processes, such as the device drivers, are allowed to read or write the portion of memory corresponding to the device registers.

When special instructions are used for I/O, they must be made privileged to guarantee that I/O devices will not be accessed by user processes directly. Instead, a process that wishes to use a device issues a kernel call that transfers control to the OS in system mode. The appropriate parts of the OS, generally the device driver and the scheduler, carry out the I/O operation on behalf of the invoking user process. These programs have been specially designed to work with the devices in the most efficient and safe manner and are permitted to use the privileged I/O instructions. When the operation is completed, control is returned to the invoking process in user mode. Thus, from the user point of view, the kernel call is simply a single high-level I/O instruction.

13.2.2   Main Memory Protection

Memory protection facilities are required to control process access to both its own instructions and data, and to those belonging to other processes, i.e., processes must be protected from themselves and from others. This includes the OS, which needs protection from damage or unauthorized execution by user processes.

There are two main problems to be solved. First, processes must be **confined** to areas of main memory that have been assigned to them by the OS. Enforcement of such confinement depends greatly on the type of memory management scheme implemented in a given system. The second problem is concerned with the **type of access** by a process to different areas of main memory. Ideally, each process should have its own set of rights with respect to a given memory area.

EXAMPLE: Read/Write/Execute Access

The most common set of rights are read, write, and execute. If we represent the three rights as a triple *rwx* of Boolean values, then eight possible combinations of rights may be applied to a region of memory:

- 000   no access

- 100   read only

- 010   write only

- 110   read and write

- 001   execute only

- 101   read and execute

- 011   write and execute

- 111   unrestricted access

Note that write and execute (011) is of little practical value and is almost never used. Write only (010) is also rare. A possible scenario for this latter combination is when a designated memory area is being used to collect data from multiple processes, each process must be able to deposit its own data but not be able to read the data written by other processes.

Let us now distinguish between systems with and without virtual memory. For each, we examine the two problems of confining processes into specified memory areas and permitting different types of access to an area.

Systems with Static Relocation

In the absence of relocation registers, paging hardware, or segmentation facilities, programs address physical memory directly. To guarantee that processes remain within their own partitions, each physical address must be checked for its validity; it must refer to only the area assigned to the process. This can be enforced through: 1) **bounds registers** that specify the upper and lower addresses of a contiguous memory area; 2) **base and length indicators** containing the starting point and the size of a memory area; or 3) identification **locks and keys** associated with memory blocks and user processes.

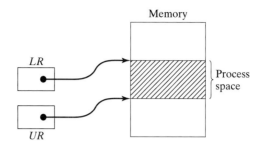

FIGURE 13-1. Bounds registers for main memory.

The use of bounds registers is illustrated in Figure 13-1. Each time a reference to a physical address *pa* is made, the hardware performs the check:

$$LR \le pa \le UR$$

where LR and UR point to the first (lower) and the last (upper) memory cell assigned to the process. Only if the check is successful is the reference carried out; otherwise, an error condition is signaled and the process is aborted. Instead of the upper-bound register, a length register, L, could be used. In this case, the check performed by the hardware is:

$$LR \le pa < LR + L.$$

The use of identification keys requires that memory be divided into blocks, usually of equal size. A combination of n bits is associated with each block as a *lock*. Each process has a pattern of n bits, the *key*, as part of its process state. Upon each reference, the hardware compares the current key with the lock of the block to be accessed; only if a match is found is the process permitted to proceed with the operation.

The use of bounds or length registers is the simplest form of access control; it permits only an "all-or-nothing" type of protection to a given area, without being able to distinguish different types of access. The use of memory locks and keys offers potentially greater flexibility in that each lock could incorporate the type of access permitted to the corresponding memory block. Associating protection information directly with physical memory, however, is very restrictive when programs or data regions are to be shared. A much greater flexibility is possible in systems with virtual memory, where protection is associated with the logical name spaces rather than physical memory.

Systems with Relocation Registers

In systems that employ simple relocation registers to implement dynamic address binding, the problem of confining processes to assigned areas is similar to that of systems with static relocation. A given logical address *la* is first transformed into the corresponding physical address by adding to it the content of the relocation register RR. The resulting physical address is then compared with the contents of the upper- and lower-bounds registers. The modified address mapping function has the following form:

```
address_map(la) {
    pa = la + RR;
    if (!((LR <= pa) && (pa <= UR))) error;
    return (pa);
}
```

Alternatively, a length indicator can be used instead of the upper-bound register *UR*. Both mechanisms prevent a process from accessing information outside its legal bounds. The problem of allowing different types of access to a given memory area, however, still persists. This can be solved by including the necessary access information with the process state. The address translation mechanisms perform the necessary checks as part of each memory access. This permits each process to have a different set of access rights for a given memory area.

Systems with Virtual Memory

A segment or a page of a virtual memory system is accessed indirectly via an entry in the page or segment table (or both). Such tables are private to a process; thus, by incorporating protection information into individual table entries, each process can have a different set of rights with respect to any segment or page (private or shared) accessible by that process. The necessary checks are performed at each address translation step as outlined below. Let us consider the general case of segmentation followed by paging, where each table occupies at most one page. Access information is specified on a per-segment basis and, therefore, it is kept in the segment table.

We extend the segment and page tables as shown in Figure 13-2. Each segment table entry, *s*, consists of the fields:

- *access* records the type of access (e.g., rwx) for the segment;

- *len* records the length of segment *s* (in bytes);

- *valid* indicates whether *s* is valid (i.e., exists);

- *resident* indicates whether the page table of *s* is currently in memory;

- *base* is a pointer to the beginning of the page table of segment *s*.

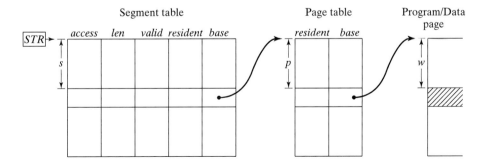

FIGURE 13-2. Memory protection through segment and page tables.

Similarly, each page table entry, p, consists of the fields:

- *resident* indicates whether the corresponding page p is currently in memory;

- *base* is a pointer to the beginning of p.

The physical address computation is extended as follows to ensure that every virtual address (s, p, w) remains confined within the legal memory space allocated to the process and that the type of access requested is allowed. We represent the type of access by an additional parameter, a.

```
address_map(s, p, w, a) {
    if (a not_element_of *(STR+s).access) invalid_access_type;
    if (*(STR+s).valid == false) invalid_segment_number;
    if (*(STR+s).resident == false) segment_fault;
    if (*(STR+s).len/pg_size < p) invalid_page_number;
    if (*(*(STR+s).base+p).resident == false) page_fault;
    if (*(STR+s).len % pg_size < w) invalid_displacement;
    return *(*(STR+s).base+p).base+w;
}
```

The first if-statement checks whether the requested access type a is recorded as a valid access for this segment; if not, an error condition is raised, and the computation terminates. The second if-statement checks whether the segment is valid; if not, a different error condition is raised, and the computation again terminates. The third if-statement ensures the segment's page table is resident before proceeding. The fourth if-statement determines the number of valid pages for the segment. This is done by dividing the segment length (kept in $^*(STR + s).len$) by the size of memory pages (pg_size). If the result is less than p, the page number is illegal. Assuming a valid page number, the next if-statement makes sure the page is resident before proceeding. The last if-statement checks the validity of the displacement: The modulo operation $^*(STR + s).len$ % pg_size computes the number of words the segment occupies on its last page. If the displacement is larger than this number, it would refer to data past the current extent of the segment.

Note that the last check is important to prevent illegal memory browsing. Since memory is always allocated in multiples of pages, the last page of every segment is, on average, only half occupied. The remaining portion does not belong to the segment, but, because it may contain sensitive information from previous computations, it should not be accessible to the process. If the check is not performed, an intruder could exploit this by systematically creating very small segments, say one byte each, and examining the contents of the allocated pages. Each segment would give the intruder nearly a full page of data left there by earlier computations. For a safer system, the contents of any page could be explicitly erased before the page is allocated to a process.

CASE STUDY: PAGE ACCESS CHECKS IN WINDOWS 2000

Windows 2000 uses paging without segmentation, so only security checks applicable to pages can be performed. The system distinguishes between several types of errors, which *abort* the process, and several types of page faults, which are *handled transparently* by the system.

Possible errors:

- The system distinguished between *kernel-mode* and *user-mode* pages. Kernel mode pages can be accessed only when executing in kernel mode and are used for system-wide data structures and other memory areas. A user process can access these only by invoking the appropriate kernel functions.
- The system (Win32 API) differentiates between the following types of pages: *no-access, read-only, read-write, execute-only, execute-read*, and *execute-read-write*. (Some architectures do not provide the hardware support to differentiate between a read and an execute access; in such cases, only the first three types are supported.) An attempt to access a page in an incompatible mode results in an error.
- Any page in a process address space is in one of three states: *free, reserved*, or *committed*. This is recorded in the corresponding page table entry. A free page is one that has *not* been allocated to the process, i.e., it is invalid. Any attempt to access such a page generates an invalid page number error. Accessing reserved or committed pages may result in different types of page faults, as explained below.

Possible page faults:

- A committed page is a regular valid page that has been allocated to the process and may be accessed by the process, subject to any read/write/execute or kernel-mode restrictions. If the page is not currently resident in memory, a page fault causes the page to be loaded.
- A process may reserve a number of pages for future use. Such pages have valid entries in the page table but no actual pages have yet been allocated; this is done only when the page is accessed for the first time. A special type of page fault first allocates a page and modifies its page table entry from reserved to committed. Reserved pages are used for dynamically expanding data structures (e.g., the user stack) that must occupy a contiguous area of the virtual memory. Initially, each process gets a single page for its stack, but additional neighboring pages are reserved and allocated as the stack grows beyond the current page.
- The memory manager employs a special optimization technique, called *copy-on-write*. When a page must be duplicated, e.g., as a result of a *fork* command, the page is only marked as *copy-on-write*, but both processes point to the same page. This allows the same copy of the page to be shared by multiple processes, but only as long as the page is not being modified. As soon as a process writes into the page, a special page fault is triggered, which creates a separate copy of the page for the process.

Sandboxing

In most systems, a function invoked by a process automatically inherits all access privileges of the invoking process. In particular, it has access to the entire virtual memory of the process. If the function cannot be trusted, as is frequently the case when an applet or service program is downloaded through the Internet or borrowed from another user, such unrestricted access is undesirable. The imported function could be a "Trojan horse" or simply contain errors that could be harmful to the invoking process. Similar concerns arise when programs may be sent to and started on a remote machine, or when a mobile agent hops to a different machine and continues its execution in a new environment.

To limit the scope of the potential damage caused by untrusted programs, the system may provide support to restrict the privileges to only a small subset of those granted to the invoking process. The reduced-access environment is generally referred to as a **sandbox**. One of the most important aspects of sandboxing is to confine the execution of the program to a small area of memory—a memory sandbox. Any attempt to access data outside of this sandbox or to branch to a location outside of this sandbox causes a trap to the OS, and the application is terminated.

A more powerful variant of memory sandboxing is to provide two separate sandboxes for each program—one for its code and the other for its data. The program is allowed only to read and write in the data sandbox, and to only execute in (fetch instructions from) the code sandbox. This prevents the program from modifying itself at runtime and circumventing certain validity checks that may have been performed on the code prior to loading it.

Memory sandboxing can be implemented in a manner similar to paging. The virtual address space is divided into equal-size regions, each corresponding to a different sandbox. This is accomplished by dividing every virtual address into two components, (b, w), where the number of bits allocated to b and w determine the number of sandboxes and the size of each sandbox, respectively. When a program is assigned to a given sandbox, s, the system can easily check the validity of any address (b, w) generated by the program by simply comparing b with s. If the two values do not match, the address is outside of the assigned sandbox, and the program is terminated.

13.3 HIGH-LEVEL ACCESS CONTROL

13.3.1 The Access Matrix Model

Information about who can access what in a computer system can be represented in the form of an **access matrix**. Each entry of the matrix records the rights that a given entity (e.g., a process) has to access a resource. This basic concept was developed into a formal model that allows the systems designer or administrator to reason about and prove protection properties of the system (Harrison et al. 1976). Specifically, the access matrix model tries to answer the most basic question concerning system **safety**: In a given situation, can a particular subject gain access to a particular resource? For this purpose, we must formally define the possible operations that can be performed on the matrix and prove whether or not there exists a sequence of operations that can modify the matrix in such as way as to give the subject the necessary rights for the resource.

We will use the access matrix only informally as a framework to discuss different implementations of access control mechanisms and their respective advantages and drawbacks. The access matrix model has the following main components:

- **Resources**: Each resource R_i represents an entity (e.g., a file or a device) that is to be protected, i.e., accessed in a controlled manner. (The literature frequently uses the term *object* instead of resource. We have chosen to use the latter to avoid any confusion with object-oriented programming and to maintain a consistent terminology throughout all chapters.)

- **Subjects**: Each subject S_j represents an active entity (e.g., a process) that can access resources.

- **Access rights**: Each right r_k represents an operation (e.g., read, write, or execute) that can be applied to a resource.

EXAMPLE: Access Matrix

Figure 13-3a shows the relationships between subjects, resources, and access rights in the form of a sample access matrix. Each column of the matrix represents a resource R_i, and each row represents a subject S_j. The intersection of the ith column with the jth row contains a (possibly empty) set of rights. These are the rights a subject S_j has with respect to the resource R_i. The letters r, w, and x stand for read, write, and execute rights, respectively. For example, subject S_1 is allowed to read and write resource R_1, and read, write, and execute resource R_2. Subject S_2 can only execute R_2, but it has all three rights for the resources R_3 and R_4. (The access and capability lists will be explained shortly.)

	R_1	R_2	R_3	R_4
S_1	rw	rwx		
S_2		x	rwx	rwx
S_3	rwx	r		r

(a)

Access lists:
R_1: $(S_1, rw), (S_3, rwx)$
R_2: $(S_1, rwx), (S_2, x), (S_3, r)$
R_3: (S_2, rwx)
R_4: $(S_2, rwx), (S_3, r)$

(b)

Capability lists:
S_1: $(R_1, rw), (R_2, rwx)$
S_2: $(R_2, x), (R_3, rwx), (R_4, rwx)$
S_3: $(R_1, rwx), (R_2, r), (R_4, r)$

(c)

FIGURE 13-3. (a) access matrix; (b) implemented as access lists; and (c) implemented as capability lists.

Having defined the basic structure of the access matrix, we now consider the operations that can be applied to use and manipulate it. In particular, it is necessary to add or remove the rows or columns of the matrix, and to enter or remove rights from the entries of the matrix. The techniques for performing these operations depend greatly on how the access matrix is implemented. The obvious way—storing the matrix as an actual two-dimensional data structure of n rows and m columns—is very wasteful. That is because n and m can be large, and yet the matrix is sparsely populated since a typical subject has access to only a small subset of the total set of resources. A more efficient scheme represents the matrix as a set of lists. These can take on two different forms, as discussed next.

13.3.2   Access Lists and Capability Lists

The access matrix maintains information about the rights of subjects to access resources. We can segregate this information along columns or rows. For the former, all nonempty entries of each column j form a list associated with the corresponding resource R_j. Each list is the **access list** of the resource. The second approach associates all nonempty entries of each row i with the corresponding subject S_i. This list is the **capability list** of the subject.

By analogy, a capability may be viewed as a ticket (e.g., a theater ticket) that entitles its holder to exercise certain privileges, such as entering a theater. An access list, on the other hand, is comparable to a reservation list (e.g., in a restaurant); only parties whose names appear on that list are permitted to enter the establishment.

EXAMPLE: Access List vs. Capability List

To illustrate the differences between access lists and capability lists, consider the access matrix in Figure 13-3a. Figure 13-3b shows the same matrix organized as a set of access lists, one for each resources. For example, the access list for R_1 consists of the two entries comprising the first column; this shows that S_1 is allowed to read or write R_1, and S_3 has all three access rights. Figure 13-3c shows the same matrix organized as a set of capability lists, one for each subject. For example, the capability list associated with S_1 gives it read and write access to R_1, and unrestricted access to R_2.

On the surface, there appears to be little difference between capability lists and access lists, since the same amount of information is recorded in both cases. However, because the information is segregated differently and is associated with different types of entities, there are fundamental differences in how each approach can manage a number of important problems in terms of both functionality and efficiency of implementation.

Granularity of Subjects

In principle, a subject could be a user, a process, or an individual procedure (function). Access lists rely on recording the identity of each subject within the access list. Consequently, it would not be practical for the creator of a resource to identify all possible procedures that could access the resource. Similarly, the creator cannot identify all possible processes, since these are generally created dynamically. Thus, the only choice for a subject in an access list is the *user*, whose identity must be verified at each access.

In contrast, capabilities are not associated with the resources being accessed but are viewed as unforgeable tickets held by the different subjects. The possession of a capability is taken as proof that the holder is allowed access to the corresponding resource. Thus, controlling the propagation of capabilities is the main issue, which must involve authentication, but there is no authentication of the holder at the time of access. Consequently, capabilities can be maintained at a *finer granularity* than access list entries. In particular, when a new resource is created, the capability may be associated with a user, a process, or an individual procedure.

EXAMPLE: Granularity of Subjects

The above important difference is illustrated in Figure 13-4. Assume that a process running on behalf of a user, U, executes two procedures, $P1$ and $P2$. Procedure $P1$ must read data from a file Q, whereas $P2$ does not. Figure 13-4a shows that the access list associated with Q contains U as a valid subject authorized to read Q. It would not be practical for the owner of Q to record individual procedures, like $P1$, as valid subjects. First, the owner would not know about all possible procedures that should access Q, but, more importantly, the individual procedure must somehow be authenticated at runtime for each access to Q. Since a system can generally authenticate the user process but no individual procedures, functions, or programs the process consists of, a procedure-level access granularity is not possible with access lists.

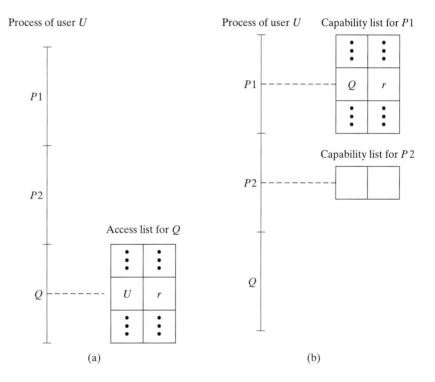

FIGURE 13-4. Granularity of subjects using: (a) access lists; and (b) capability lists.

Figure 13-4b shows the same scenario using capabilities. This allows the user U to distributed capabilities only to those portions of the process that actually need them and vary the extent of the current access environment dynamically. In this example, $P1$ holds a read capability for Q and may perform the access. $P2$, on the other hand, would be denied access to Q, because it lacks the necessary capability. As long as the capabilities are unforgeable, there is no need for any runtime authentication.

Static Versus Dynamic Environments

One of the main disadvantages of a user-level granularity of access lists is that the current execution environment of a process remains static during its entire execution. The process may, of course, switch to system mode by issuing a kernel call, in which case it is allowed to execute privileged instructions. However, its accesses will be subject to the same access lists as in user mode. For example, the process in Figure 13-4a is able to access Q regardless of which procedure it is executing in. To support a dynamic environment while keeping the subject granularity at the user level, the system may allow a process to *temporarily change its user identity*. This must be done in a highly controlled manner to prevent an imposter from assuming another user identity.

CASE STUDY: AMPLIFICATION OF PRIVILEGES IN UNIX

In UNIX, every process is assigned a user ID, which identifies the user responsible for the process. As a process invokes different programs (files) in the course of its execution, the user ID associated with the process may change. This is controlled by a special permission, called the *set-user-id* flag, which is associated with every executable file f. When this permission is turned off, a process invoking f will retain its current user ID. However, when the permission is turned on, the invoking process will temporarily inherit the user ID of f's owner. The original user ID is restored automatically when the process exits the file f.

This is a powerful mechanism that can be used to temporarily amplify the privileges of a process for the duration of a call to a service routine. Assume, for example, that a user U wishes to invoke a service program P that is provided by another user S. Assume further that P must access another file, D, to perform its function, but this file should not be accessible to U in general. This can be accomplished by excluding U from the access list of P, but enabling the *set-user-id* flag associated with P. When the process of user U invokes P, the user ID changes to that of user S, which gives P the necessary access privileges for D. Thus, the current execution environment of a process may change dynamically as it enters and exits different programs.

When a user process makes a kernel call, its current execution environment changes in two different ways. First, the processor is switched to system mode, which allows the process to execute privileged instructions. Second, if the *set-user-id* flag of the invoked system file is set, the process temporarily assumes the identity of the file owner, which is the OS itself (the root). This gives it greatly increased access privileges to systems resources.

List Sizes

Although a finer granularity of subjects results in more flexibility in expressing access constraints, a coarser granularity results in fewer entries and less space needed to maintain the lists. Reducing the number of entries in the lists is an important goal. Access lists lend themselves well to combining of subjects into groups, allowing a potentially large number of entries to be reduced to a few. For example, a file that should be generally readable by any user would include an entry for every possible user in its access list.

Providing a generic entry, "all users," which acts as a wild-card for matching purposes, reduces the number of entries to just one.

EXAMPLE: Grouping of Subjects

Figure 13-5 extends the matrix of Figure 13-3a by adding an extra row labeled "*", which is interpreted as a wild-card character. Thus, any subject, including newly created ones, automatically has all rights listed in this column. The matrix shows a new resource R_5, for which S_2 has read, write, and execution rights. In addition, the r right in the "*" row guarantees that all subjects, including those yet to be created, will be able to read the resource R_5.

	R_1	R_2	R_3	R_4	R_5
S_1	rw	rwx		r	
S_2		x	rwx	rwx	rwx
S_3	rwx	r		r	
*					r

FIGURE 13-5. Access matrix extended with a group subject.

When the matrix is implemented as an access list, adding such new rows is simple. The access list of the corresponding resource is extended to contain a new entry with "*" as the subject. In the above example, the extended access list for R_5 would have the form (S_2, rwx), $(*, r)$.

In contrast, implementing a group-access row in a capability-based system is more difficult. If the capability lists are maintained by the system, the new right could be entered into the capability lists of all subjects. Alternately, a separate capability list associated with the "*" could be maintained and included automatically with every subject capability list. However, when capabilities are implemented as unforgeable tickets maintained by their owners and dispersed throughout the system, there is no easy way to implement the new group-access row. The new right to be granted by default to all subjects needs to be explicitly propagated to all capability lists, but their owners and locations are unknown. Worse yet, newly created subjects would not automatically inherit such group rights as a default.

CASE STUDY: ACCESS LISTS IN UNIX

UNIX employs access lists to implement the access matrix and is able to conveniently support grouping of access rights. The following scheme has been adopted. A file access list distinguishes three types of subjects: 1) the file owner; 2) members of a specifically named group; and 3) all users. The first entry refers to the original creator of the file. The purpose of a group is to permit a selected team of users to access the file with rights different from those granted to the owner or to the general public. Every file belongs to one group, and every user belongs to one or more groups. Finally, all users are members of the general public; the group designated as "*" in the previous discussion. This gives all users a set of default rights with respect to a resource.

> **CASE STUDY: ACCESS LISTS IN UNIX   (*continued*)**
>
> Within each of the three user types, a file may be readable (*r*), writable (*w*), or executable (*x*). For example, a file designated as *rwxr-x--x* permits unrestricted access (*rwx*) by the owner, read and execute access by any member of the group (*r-x*), and execute-only access by all others (*--x*).

Combining subjects into a small number of groups also solves the problem of authentication in systems where subjects are individual procedures. Access lists only maintain information in terms of groups, rather than individual procedures. Thus, the maximum number of entries per access list is limited by the number of groups. Each entry records the rights that apply equally to all subjects (procedures) of a group. This permits the use of access lists with fine granularity of subjects and supports a dynamic execution environment. At the same time, authentication is necessary only when assigning a procedure to a given group.

> **CASE STUDY: RINGS OF PROTECTION IN MULTICS**
>
> The Multics OS pioneered the idea of grouping or levels of protection for access control (Schoeder and Saltzer 1972). Any segment, including executable segments and data segments, is assigned to one of *n* possible groups, numbered 0 to $n-1$. The groups are ordered so that segments in group 0 have the most access privileges, and segments in group $n-1$ have the least privileges. A convenient way to visualize the groups is as an arrangement of concentric **rings**, with the most protected ring 0 at the center.
>
> Figure 13-6 shows the initial ring assignments in Multics. The OS occupies the first three rings with the most critical part—the nucleus—occupying ring 0. Most of the system is in ring 1, and the remainder—the least sensitive segment of the OS—resides in ring 2. Rings 3 to $n-1$ may be employed by user processes.
>
> The rings control access to segments using this rule: When a process executing a program *S* in ring *i* attempts to read or write a segment *T* in ring *j*, the access is allowed to proceed only when $j \geq i$ and the access list of *T* contains the necessary read/write rights for the calling process.
>
> The rings also are used to limit transfer of control between segments, but the rules are more complicated. A call to a segment with the same or higher ring number is allowed (provided the caller has the execute right), but it may be necessary to copy the parameters passed from the calling segment *S* to a ring with lower protection to enable the called segment *T* to access them. A call to a segment with a lower ring number may or may not be allowed; this is determined by a special ring limit number prescribed as part of *T*. When the caller's current ring number is greater than this limit, the call is disallowed.

Only a very small number of the originally planned 64 Multics rings were implemented, indicating some problems with the scheme. One of the main constraints is the linearity of the ring-based protection mechanisms; resources must be ordered according

it contains a capability or another type of data. Only special privileged instructions, running in system mode, are allowed to create or modify memory locations tagged as capabilities.

If the architecture does not support memory tags, the capabilities may be **segregated** in an area inaccessible to user processes and managed by the OS. A subject can refer to its capabilities only indirectly, e.g., using an index into an array of capabilities. This is similar to managing memory pages or segments in virtual memory; the user specifies a page or segment by its page or segment number, and the system maintains the actual internal addresses.

In a distributed system, capabilities must be passed between different machines. One simple technique to prevent capabilities from being fabricated or tampered with applies an idea similar to that used for password protection: The capabilities are represented by unique strings or bit patterns chosen from a potentially large name space. This decreases the chances of an intruder guessing a valid capability by trial and error.

A second, and safer, method uses **cryptography**. For any newly created capability $(R, rights)$, where R is the resource and $rights$ is the list of applicable rights, the system generates a random number, N. The system records this number along with the capability and generates a ticket of the form $H(R, rights, N)$, where H is a one-way encryption function. This ticket is given to the subject and must be presented to the system along with the original capability to validate its authenticity. Assume a subject presents a capability $(R', rights')$ and a ticket t. The system looks up the number N' saved with the presented capability and computes the value $t' = H(R', rights', N')$. If t' matches the ticket t presented by the subject, the capability is valid and the requested operation is carried out, subject to the access rights; otherwise, the capability is rejected as a forgery.

Controlling Propagation of Capabilities

One of the advantages of capability lists over access lists is that the resource creator need not specify and manage a complete list of subjects that are allowed to access the resource. Instead, a capability for the newly created resource is passed to a subject, from which it propagates to other subjects as needed. To permit this, subjects must be able to move or copy capabilities to other subjects, but this must be done in a controlled manner to prevent protection violations.

For this task, some additional mechanism must exist that allows a subject to pass a capability to another subject, but restrict it in such a way that it cannot be propagated any further. In other words, the subject must be able to restrict the copying of a capability to only a one-time occurrence. We accomplish this by adding a special nonpropagation right to the capability. Unlike other rights, the nonpropagation right does not apply to the resource pointed to by the capability, but instead applies to the capability itself. A capability lacking this special right is prevented (by the OS) from being copied into any other capability list and is unable to propagate through the system.

Note that a capability can be propagated in one of two ways. First, a subject A holding the capability could copy it into the capability list of another subject, B, provided A has the necessary rights to write into B's capability list. Second, the subject B could copy the capability from A's capability list, provided B has the necessary rights to read from A's capability lists. The special nonpropagation right attached to a capability prevents both types of propagation.

CASE STUDY: CONTROLLING PROPAGATION OF CAPABILITIES

The Hydra OS (Cohen and Jefferson 1975) calls the nonpropagation right the **environment** right (*e*-right, for short). A capability can be copied only if it includes an *e*-right. Figure 13-8 shows how the lack of the *e*-right prevents a capability from being copied.

The figure shows five entities, *A*, *B*, *C*, *D*, and *E*. *A* has a capability for *C* with the *s*-right. This right, called the *store right*, permits a subject to copy capabilities from its own capability list to the capability list of the resource pointed to by the capability. Thus, *A* can store copies of its own capabilities into *C*'s capability list. In particular, *A* can copy the capability for *D* (including the *erw* rights) into *C*'s list; this transfer is possible because the capability being copied has the *e*-right. A capability lacking the *e*-right, such as *A*'s capability for the resource *E*, cannot be copied. Thus, *C* cannot be given access to *E*. Figure 13-8b shows the updated capability list of *C*, where the crossed-out dashed pointer represents the capability for *E* that could not be propagated to *C*. Note that *A* could have decided to remove the *e*-right from the capability given to *C*. This would allow *C* to read and write *D* as before, but would prevent it from propagating the capability for *D* any further.

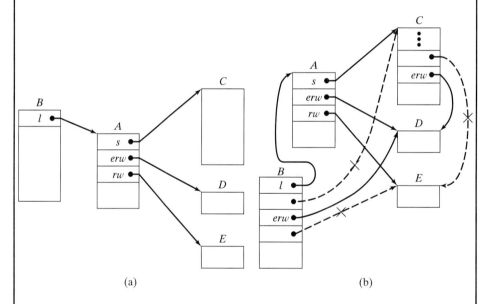

(a)   (b)

FIGURE 13-8. Propagation of capabilities: (a) initial state; (b) after transferring capabilities for *D* to *B* and *C*.

Figure 13-8a also shows that *B* has a capability for *A* with an *l*-right. This right, called the *load right*, enables its holder to load rights from the resource pointed to by the capability. Thus, *B* can read and copy capabilities from *A*'s capability list. In particular, it can copy the capability for *D* (including the *erw*-rights), but it is unable to copy the capabilities for either *C* or *E*, because both lack the *e*-right. Figure 13-8b shows the new capability list for *B*.

Revocation of Capabilities

Revocation of capabilities is the inverse of capability propagation. This concept is difficult to implement directly since many copies of the same capability may be dispersed throughout the system and may not be easy to find. Indirection can be used to eliminate this problem. A dummy or **alias** resource is created that contains the capability for a resource. Individual users are given capabilities for the alias instead of the resource itself (Fig. 13-9). When revocation of access to the resource is desired, the alias is simply destroyed, breaking all indirect connections to the resource. Note that with this approach, all users lose their capabilities to the resource; it is not possible to remove privileges from users on an individual basis.

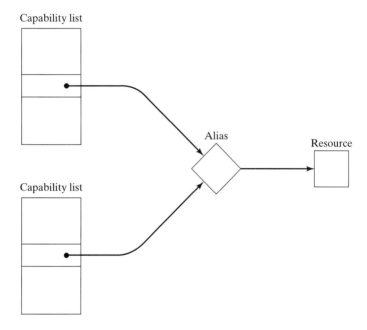

FIGURE 13-9. Use of alias for revocation of access rights.

13.3.3 A Comprehensive Example: Client/Server Protection

The majority of protection problems arise because various subsystems must cooperate. To illustrate the variety of potential problems and their solution, we consider a general client/server scenario, as shown in Figure 13-10. Assume that an owner offers a service program that may be called by legitimate users of the system. To do so, a user must supply information to the service in the form of parameters. After completing its work, the service returns the results of the computation to its caller. In addition, the service must communicate with its owner, e.g., it may report billing or performance data.

The owner and the user of the service have different concerns regarding their own security and the security of the service itself. The following requirements must be satisfied in general. The possible solutions depend on whether access lists or capability lists are employed:

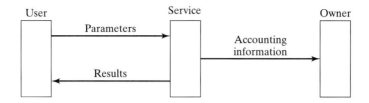

FIGURE 13-10. Example of mutually suspicious applications.

Requirement 1: *No user should be able to steal (obtain a copy) or damage the service in any way.*

Theft and destruction of information are solved through the enforcement of execute-only privileges for the resource, in this case, the service. These privileges are normally provided in both access list-oriented and capability list-oriented protection schemes.

Requirement 2: *No user should be able to employ the service without the owner's permission.*

Unauthorized use of the service is a problem of right propagation. With access lists, propagation is not possible since only the owner of a resource can extend any rights to it. With capabilities, specific mechanisms must be implemented, e.g., the *e*-right in the Hydra OS.

Requirement 3: *The owner should be able to revoke access to the service by an authorized user.*

This problem requires the removal of previously granted rights. With access lists, this is accomplished simply by modifying the list associated with the service. With capability lists, the reference to the service can be set up as an alias that can later be broken to deny further access. Otherwise, the only convenient way to ensure no further use is to destroy the service itself and recreate it with a new capability.

Requirement 4: *No user (authorized or not) should be able to prevent authorized users from employing the service.*

This addresses the problem of service denial. The simplest form of service denial results when the service is destroyed or damaged. Both access lists and capability lists provide means to prevent such actions by not granting write/modify rights to any user. A more subtle form of service denial occurs any time a legitimate user is impeded from making sufficient progress. This intuitive measure is, unfortunately, subjective since insufficient progress may not necessarily be caused by malicious actions on the part of a user or a system malfunction; it could simply be the result of an unexpectedly high demand on a shared resource or a general system overload. Hence, in general, it will not be possible to guarantee that denial of service does not occur. The best we can do is provide mechanisms to detect denial of service for specific critical resources and inform the user or a higher authority of such situations so that corrective actions can be initiated. The detection can be accomplished by associating a maximum service time with each service to be monitored. When this time limit is exceeded, the process is considered to be making insufficient progress, incurring denial of service.

Requirement 5: *The service should be able to access its own private files or other resources when performing the service, without granting the user access to these resources.*

Right amplification provides the desired control. When executing the service procedure, a user process is given additional access rights, in particular, permitting it to use resources needed by the service. The current execution environment must be dynamic for this solution to work.

With access list-based systems, right amplification can be done by allowing a process to temporarily change its user or group ID (as in Section 13.3.2) or to provide resource groupings such that the service would belong to a more privileged group (e.g., having a lower ring number in Multics.) With capabilities, this is accomplished elegantly by simply associating the capabilities for the private resources with the service but not with the user.

Requirement 6: *The service should not be able to steal, destroy, or otherwise compromise any information or services that the user did not explicitly supply to the service.*

This addresses the Trojan horse problem (Section 12.1.3), where the service could take unauthorized and unadvertised actions to harm the user. The problem cannot be solved in systems with static execution environments, since any borrowed program executes with the same privileges as the invoking process. In a dynamically changing environment, we could temporarily change the user ID to that of the service owner. Alternately, we could place the service in a group with lower privileges than the user. For example, Multics could assign a higher ring number to the service than to the user. In both cases, the service would be prevented from accessing *any* of the user resources. However, most services must be supplied with parameters or other resources belonging to the user to perform their tasks. To make any such parameters accessible to the service, they must be down-protected (at least temporarily) to the current level of the service. All these solutions to satisfy Requirement 6 are rather awkward to implement in systems using access lists.

Systems based on capabilities solve this problem in a more elegant manner. Since capabilities generally may be passed as parameters, the user can pass the necessary information to the service at the time of the call. This method gives the service the necessary rights, while preventing it from accessing any other resources not passed explicitly to it.

13.3.4 Combining Access Lists and Capability Lists

The more common way to organize protection information is in the form of access lists. However, capabilities also are used in many systems, frequently in conjunction with access lists to reap the benefits of both approaches.

A good example of a combined approach is with **files** (Section 10.3). In most file systems, a file must first be opened before its contents can be accessed. The *open* command verifies that the subject has the required type of access to the file by consulting the file access list. If the access is authorized, the *open* command returns a handle (pointer, or file descriptor in UNIX terminology) for the open file, that is subsequently used to read, write or otherwise access the file. The file handle represents an unforgeable capability for the open file, and is used without verifying the subject's identity upon every access to the file.

Another example is the dynamic linking of **segments** presented in Section 9.4. When a segment is referenced for the first time, the system verifies that the invoking process has the necessary rights by examining the access list associated with the segment and maintained by the file system. If the access is valid, a segment number s is assigned to the segment and its memory address is entered into the segment table with the valid access rights. Thus, the segment table may be viewed as the process capability list; each entry points to a valid resource (segment in memory) and records the valid rights for this segment. On subsequent accesses to the same segment, the segment number s is used as an index into the segment table to select the capability for the segment.

A third example is the use of the **tickets** in the Kerberos authentication system, discussed in Section 12.4.2. Initially, a client wishing to use a service must authenticate itself using a password. When this is successful, it is issued a *ticket-granting ticket*, which is a capability for the TGS. The capability is protected from tampering by being encrypted with a secret key known only to TGS. When presented to TGS, the capability enables the client to obtain other tickets (capabilities), also protected by encryption, which, in turn, enable the client to use the desired system services.

13.4 INFORMATION FLOW CONTROL

Consider the client/server scenario introduced in Section 13.3.3, and assume that the user of this service would like to impose the following additional requirement on the service: *The service must not be able to leak any information entrusted to it by the user to the owner or any other party.*

Such a breach of security can occur easily if the service is a Trojan horse program. Note that this is different from Requirement 6 of Section 13.3.3, which was concerned with protecting information *not* supplied to a service. The present concern is to prevent sensitive information actually entrusted to the service from being compromised. This is a matter of information flow control rather than access control.

Figure 13-11 illustrates the difference between the two problems. In Figure 13-11a, an unauthorized process is not permitted to read sensitive information—a problem of access control. In Figure 13-11b, a process is allowed to access the sensitive information but must be prevented from passing it to an unauthorized process.

13.4.1 The Confinement Problem

Information may be passed between processes in many ways without authorization, depending on the interprocess communication facilities available. In most instances, this involves copying data into an area that can be read by an unauthorized process. To prevent such illegal information flow through a service procedure, we must deny write access by the service to any areas accessible by other processes. This is the **confinement problem**, so-named because the service must be surrounded by a boundary beyond which it cannot pass any information. The challenge is how to define and enforce such a boundary.

In one method, the service is not allowed to modify any resource unless that resource was explicitly passed to it by the caller or client. This gives the caller complete control over which resources can be modified by the service, and stops the flow of any information beyond the modifiable resources.

Consider how this policy could be enforced using capabilities. The basic idea is to extend the procedure-calling mechanism such that the caller can disable all writing

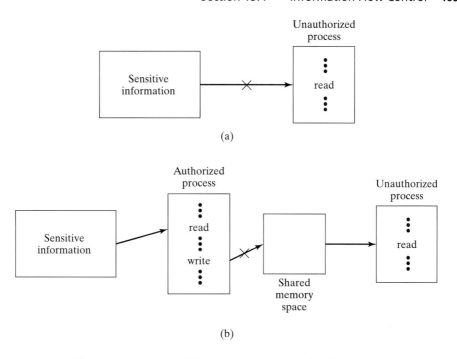

FIGURE 13-11. Flow of information (a) through direct read (b) via an authorized process.

capabilities of the service for the duration of the call, except those supplied explicitly as parameters. The Hydra OS implemented a special right for this purpose: the *modify* right or *m*-right for short. The *m*-right must be used in conjunction with a right that modifies a resource, such as a write or append right. Without the presence of the *m*-right, all such rights are automatically disabled. As part of the procedure call to a service, the caller may request that the *m*-right be masked out from all capabilities currently held by the service. At the same time, it may supply to the service capabilities as parameters; these may retain their *m*-rights and may be modified by the service.

CASE STUDY: CONFINEMENT OF A SERVICE

Figure 13-12 shows an example of the confinement of a service during its invocation by a user. We assume that the user capability list currently contains four capabilities: the first points to its own code segment; the second points to its own data segment; the third points to the service procedure to be called by the user code; and the fourth points to a data segment to be passed to the service procedure as a parameter. The latter may contain the caller's sensitive information, which must be passed to the service but must not be leaked to any other process, including the service owner.

The service procedure has a capability list containing three capabilities: one for its own code segments; one for its data segment; and the third for a resource labeled *common* that it shares with the service owner. The service intends to use this resource for

CASE STUDY: CONFINEMENT OF A SERVICE   (*continued*)

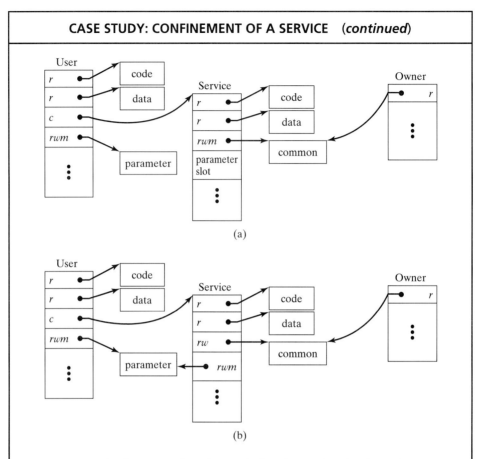

(a)

(b)

FIGURE 13-12. Confinement of service (a) before invocation (b) during invocation.

the illegal passing of information to its owner, who has read access to it. Figure 13-12a presents the processes before the call is issued.

At the invocation of the service, the caller requests that all m-rights be masked out from the service capability list. Figure 13-12b shows the capabilities that apply during the execution of the service. All previously held m-rights of the service are disabled, which renders all corresponding w-rights ineffective. Specifically, the service cannot write into the *common* resource, since the lack of the m-rights disables the w-right. The capability for the parameter resource, on the other hand, has been passed to the service with the m-right; hence, the w-right, as well as all other rights on that capability, are applicable. This confines the service such that it can read or execute any resources for which it had capabilities, but it can only modify those resources supplied by the caller as parameters.

Note that the m-right facility permits only a **total** confinement of the service; the service is unable to pass even nonsensitive information, e.g., billing or performance data, to its owner.

13.4.2   Hierarchical Information Flow

The security requirements of the U.S. DoD motivated much of the research into controlling the flow of information. The military, as well as a number of other institutions, base their information management policies on a hierarchy of **security classes**. Subjects may access resources in a given class only if they possess the corresponding clearance. One of the most important properties that must be enforced by such a hierarchical model is that all information flows only in one direction: from less sensitive to more sensitive security classes.

Security policies where access to resources is granted based on membership in security classes, rather than on the identity of subjects, are called **nondiscretionary**. These do not eliminate the need for **discretionary** policies, which grant privileges on an individual basis. Specifically, the military enforces the principle of "need to know," according to which each subject should be permitted to access only those resources that it needs to perform its duties. Such policies must be based on the subject's identity. A comprehensive security system must include both discretionary and nondiscretionary policies.

Most existing hierarchical security models are based on the fundamental principles formulated by Bell and LaPadula at the MITRE corporation (Bell and LaPadula, 1973a, b, c; 1984). Their model is one of the first attempts to formalize the problem of information flow control. The model extends the basic access matrix model (Section 13.3.1), which governs the discretionary policies, with levels of security, which govern the nondiscretionary policies. As before, each entry of the access matrix records the rights (e.g., read, write, or execute) that an individual subject has with respect to a given resource. In addition, each subject is assigned a security **clearance**, and each resource is assigned a **classification level**. Both security clearances and classification levels are taken from a fixed ordered set, such as unclassified, confidential, secret, top secret.

The requirement that information may flow only from lower to higher security levels is enforced by two important rules:

- **No Read Up**. A subject S may not read from a resource R unless the classification level of R is less than or equal to the clearance of S. That means, S may not read from any resource at a higher security level. For example, a subject cleared for secret documents also may read those classified as confidential or unclassified, but not top secret.

- **No Write Down**. A subject may not write a resource R unless the classification level of R is greater than or equal to the clearance of S. That means, S may not write into any resource at a lower security level. For example, a subject cleared for secret information may create documents with only secret or top-secret status, but not confidential or unclassified.

Figure 13-13 depicts graphically the legal flow of information enforced by the two rules. Consider a subject S with clearance i, $(1 \leq i \leq n)$. The possible flow of information due to *reading* by subject S is shown as dashed lines, and information flow due to *writing* by subject S is shown as solid lines. In all cases, the information flows only horizontally (i.e., between classes with equal security levels) or upward (i.e., from lower to higher security levels). Note that a subject requiring both read and write privileges to a resource must have a clearance equal to that resource classification level.

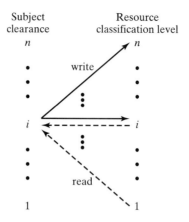

FIGURE 13-13. Legal flow of information in a multilevel system.

EXAMPLE: Using Hierarchical Information Flow

The hierarchical information flow model can, in principle, be used to solve the confinement problem. It requires that the user of a service suspected to be a Trojan horse possesses higher security clearance than either the service owner or any other subject to whom the service should not disclose information supplied to it by the caller. Assume that the user's clearance is i, and the owner's clearance is j, where $i > j$. Under such conditions, the user is able to invoke the service, which will execute at the user's current clearance, i. That permits the service to access any information belonging to the user

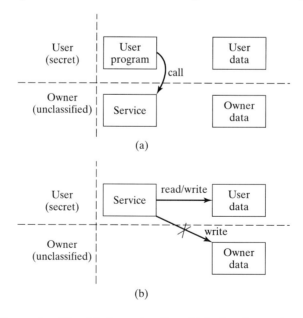

FIGURE 13-14. Preventing illegal information flow (a) before invocation (b) during invocation.

(subject to the discretionary read/write/execute rights of the access matrix). The service, however, is not able to pass any of this information down to its owner, due to the owner's lower security clearance.

Figure 13-14 contains an example of such a scenario. Operating at the secret level, the user wishes to invoke a service defined at the lower unclassified level. Figure 13-14a shows the situation prior to the call. In Figure 13-14b, the service is in use. During the execution of the service, it operates at the user's secret level, which permits it to access the user's data, but prevents it from writing into any files at the owner's unclassified level.

13.4.3 The Selective Confinement Problem

The objective of the confinement problem as discussed in the previous section is to prevent a service program from disclosing any information entrusted to it by its caller. This is a **total confinement**, since no information whatsoever may be leaked by the service to any other party, including the service owner. Such total confinement is only a special case of the more general and difficult problem of **selective confinement**, which distinguishes between sensitive and nonsensitive information. The objective of selective confinement is to prevent only the disclosure of sensitive data. For example, the service example presented in Section 13.3.3 should be able to send accounting and other information to its owner, based solely on nonsensitive information, such as the user's name and identity. It should not, however, be allowed to disclose any sensitive information.

Due to the difficulty of distinguishing between sensitive and nonsensitive information, and keeping these strictly segregated as part of the computation, few existing systems provide mechanisms that offer a satisfactory solution for the general case of selective confinement. In fact, it has been shown that, in its full generality, this problem is unsolvable (Fenton, 1974).

EXAMPLE: Limiting Information Flow

To illustrate the difficulty of tracking and limiting information flow, consider the following sequence of statements:

```
Z = 1;
Y = 2;
if (X == 0) Z = Y;
```

From the last assignment statement, it is clear that some information flows from Y to Z. Thus, by testing the value of Z at the end of the code fragment, we can deduce some information about Y. Such information flow is called *explicit*, since Y is used to compute Z.

Much less obvious is the fact that we also can deduce some information about the value of X at the end of the three statements. This can be done by testing the new value of Z. If Z is equal to 2, we know that X must be equal to zero. Thus, in addition to the explicit information from Y to Z, some information also flows from X to Z, regardless of whether the conditional statement is true or false. Such information flow is referred to as *implicit*.

The Lattice Model of Information Flow

To solve the selective confinement problem, the system must be able to restrict both explicit and implicit flow of information. The lattice model of information flow offers one approach to solve this difficult problem (Denning, 1976). The basic idea is similar to the hierarchical information flow model discussed in Section 13.4.2. A set of security classes is defined, and each subject and each resource is assigned to a class. The main difference is that the classes are not arranged according to a total ordering. Instead, a **flow relation** specifies the legal flow of information between any two security classes, and a **class-combining operator** specifies how any two security classes may be combined into a higher security class. The flow relation and the class-combining operator organize the security classes in a **lattice**, i.e., a partial order.

To enforce legal flow of information, any computation $RES = f(R_1, \ldots, R_n)$, where f may be an assignment or a conditional statement, may proceed only if the security class of the result RES is greater or equal to the security class of all the resources $R_1, \ldots, R_n$ used by that computation. This security class is derived using the class-combining operator. This policy guarantees that information flows only along the legal channels as defined by the flow relation.

EXAMPLE: Information Flow Lattice

Consider a system containing three types of records: medical, financial, and criminal. A resource can be classified as containing one or more of the three types of information, e.g., a resource could contain purely medical information, a combination of medical and criminal, or all three types. Information of a given type may flow only into resources classified as containing that information type. This can be expressed by the lattice of Figure 13-15. The lower bound of the lattice is the empty set (ϕ); the flow relation ($\rightarrow$) is the subset operator ($\subseteq$); the class-combining operator is the set union operator ($\cup$); and the resulting upper bound of the lattice is the set {*Medical, Financial, Criminal*}.

Assume that a given computation combines a medical and criminal record into a new record, R. The class-combining operator produces the class {*Medical*} $\cup$ {*Criminal*} = {*Medical, Criminal*} for the record R. The flow relation dictates that this record may

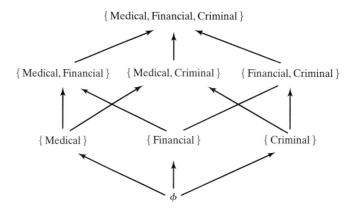

FIGURE 13-15. Information flow lattice.

be placed only into the class {*Medical, Criminal*} or {*Medical, Financial, Criminal*}; placement into any other class would violate the flow relation and would be disallowed.

Sneaky Signaling

The objective of confinement (both total and selective) is to prevent sensitive information from escaping out of the service program. Unfortunately, there is a number of possible implicit covert channels through which information may be conveyed to an observer. The use of such channels for information disclosure is called **sneaky signaling**. In principle, an element with two different states (representing zero and one) is sufficient to encode and transmit any amount of information when interrogated repeatedly over time.

There are many possible patterns of behavior that a service might display to signal binary information to an observer. For example, to signal a 1, a process S could open an agreed-upon file, say A; to signal a 0, it would open another file, B. An observer would then attempt to open the two files for writing. One of these *open* commands will fail because either A or B has already been opened by S. Depending on which file cannot be opened, the observer can deduce one bit of information signaled by S.

Other covert channels that can be employed in a similar manner for sneaky signaling include using different I/O devices or generating error messages that depend on the information content. Similarly, information may be encoded and passed by controlling the patterns of tape movement or of sound waves emanating from a printing device. The use of different time delays caused intentionally as a way to encode sensitive information is particularly difficult to detect and prevent. For example, the execution of a long loop could be initiated or suppressed based on some sensitive data, signaling one bit of information. Since such time delays are potentially unbounded; the problem of sneaky signaling and the confinement problem is quite impractical to solve, even when limiting assumptions about the system and its environment are made. In their full generality, confinement problems have proven to be unsolvable. Therefore, other means, particularly cryptography, are suggested for protecting sensitive and critical information.

CONCEPTS, TERMS, AND ABBREVIATIONS

The following concepts have been introduced in this chapter. Test yourself by defining and discussing each keyword or phrase.

Access control	Read right
Access list	Revocation of rights
Access matrix	Right amplification
Access rights	Rights
Capability	Rings of protection
Confinement problem	Safety
Environment right	Security classes
Hierarchical information flow	Security classification level
Information flow control	Security clearance
Instruction-level access control	Selective confinement
I/O protection	Sneaky signaling
Lattice model	Store right

Modify right	Subject
Memory protection	System mode
Owner right	Total confinement
Privileged instruction	User mode
Processor mode	Write right
Propagation of capabilities	Execute right
Protection	

EXERCISES

1. Consider a paging system that divides each page into four sandboxes.
   (a) Assuming a virtual memory occupies 32 bits and the page size is 1024 words, what is the total number sandboxes and how many bits are necessary to represent a box number?
   (b) The system enforces the confinement of a program to a sandbox b as follows. Any address (p, w) generated by the program is automatically transformed into a legal address using the following bit manipulations. The logical AND removes the current box number, and the logical OR provides the assigned box number:

   $$(p, w) \ \& \ mask \ | \ (b, x)$$

   Determine the structure and content of the *mask* and the field labeled x.

2. Consider a system using segmentation with paging. The virtual address has the form (s,p,w), where $|s| = 5$ bits, $|p| = 7$ bits, and $|w| = 9$ bits. Assume there are currently five segments (0 through 4) with the following respective lengths: 50, 515, 2048, 1200, and 2049.
   (a) The following three address are all invalid; for each, give the specific reason why:
   - $(9, 0, 0)$
   - $(4, 5, 6)$
   - $(1, 1, 15)$
   (b) For each of the five segments, give the valid range of p and w.

3. Consider the logical-to-physical address conversion function of systems with both segmentation and paging (Section 13.2.2). Simplify this function for systems with only segmentation. Show the new function and the corresponding segment table entry format.

4. Repeat the previous exercise for systems with only paging. Show the new function and the corresponding page table entry format.

5. Extend the logical-to-physical address conversion function (Section 13.2.2) to work with systems where:
   (a) the segment table is paged
   (b) each page table is paged
   Show the new functions and the corresponding table entry formats.

6. A list command in UNIX produced the following information about the current directory:

```
protection     owner     group    file name
----------------------------------------------
-rwxr-x---     smith     opsys    f1.txt
-rwxr-----     smith     comp     f2.txt
```

```
-rwxr-xr--        smith       comp     f3.txt
-rwxrwxrwx        richards    misc     f4.txt
-rwxrw----        smith       misc     f5.txt
```

Assume that *smith* is a member of all three groups, *opsys, comp*, and *misc*, and *richards* is a member of only *misc*.

(a) Show the above information in the form of an access matrix. (Hint: Represent the three groups, *opsys, comp*, and *misc*, as separate subjects.)

(b) Which files are accessible by *smith*? Which are accessible by *richards*?

(c) Show all changes to the matrix resulting from the following operations:

- *smith* performs: *chown richards f2*
- *smith* performs: *chgrp misc f3*
- *richards* performs: *chmod 750 f4*
- *smith* performs: *chmod 444 f1*

Which files are accessible by *smith* and by *richards* after all changes have been made?

(d) Consider the access matrix under (a) and assume it is to be implemented using capability lists. The OS keeps track of which users are members of which groups, but no capability lists are associated with groups. Instead, the corresponding capabilities must be replicated within each user list. Show the capability lists for *smith* and *richards*.

7. A system consists of two users, $U1$ and $U2$, and three resources, $R1$, $R2$, and $R3$. The process of $U1$ consists of two functions, $P1$ and $Q1$. The process of $U2$ consists of two other functions, $P2$ and $Q2$. The four different functions must access the resources as follows:

- $P1$ reads $R1$
- $Q1$ reads/writes $R1$ and $R2$
- $P2$ reads $R2$
- $Q2$ reads $R3$

Implement the above scheme using:

(a) access lists

(b) Multics protection rings

(c) capability list

In each case, give each subject the least amount of privileges necessary to do its job.

8. Consider five objects, A, B, $D1$, $D2$, and $D3$, in a capability-based system like Hydra.

(a) Show the graphical representation of the objects' capabilities such that the following operations may be performed:

- A can call B;
- B can read and write data from/to $D1$;
- B can give its capability for $D1$ to another object $D2$;
- A can read and write the capability list of $D1$;
- A can read data from $D3$;
- B can read and write data from/to $D3$.

(b) Answer the following questions based on your diagram. If the answer is yes, give a sequence of operations to accomplish the task:

- Can data from $D3$ ever get into $D1$?
- Can data from $D3$ ever get into $D2$?
- Can data from $D1$ ever get into A?
- Can data from $D2$ ever get into A?

9. Consider the following capability lists in a system like Hydra:

subject	capability for object	rights
$P1$	X	c
	$D3$	$emrw$
$P2$	$D1$	l
X	$D1$	$emws$
	$D2$	$emrws$

(a) Show a graphic representation of the above configuration.

(b) Assume $P1$ calls X and passes to it the capability for $D3$ as a parameter. Show the current capability list of X assuming the m-right was masked out during the call.

(c) During the call from $P1$ to X, which entities can X:

- read data from;
- load capabilities from;
- write data into;
- store capabilities into.

(d) Repeat the previous question for the state after X returns control to $P1$.

(e) Show a sequence of operations by which either of the two capabilities held by $P1$ propagates to $P2$.

10. Consider a system with two subjects, $S1$ and $S2$, and four resources, $R1$ through $R4$.

(a) Assign clearances to the subjects and classification levels to the resources according to the Bell-LaPadula model, such that the following conditions hold:

- $S1$ can write only into $R3$ and $R4$;
- $S2$ can write only into $R3$.

(b) Determine which resources can be *read* by which subjects under the assignment of part (a).

(c) Modify the assignment such that $S1$ *cannot* read $R4$.

11. Consider the set of security classes, $C = \{00, 01, 10, 11\}$, in the Lattice model of information flow. Define the flow relation "$\rightarrow$" and the class-combining operator to form the following four possible lattices:

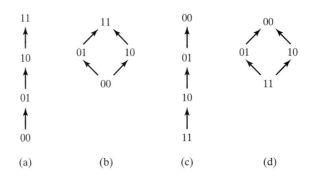

(a)   (b)   (c)   (d)

12. Consider the set of security classes, $C = \{(XYZ)|X, Y, Z \in \{0, 1\}\}$. Derive possible lattices analogous to those of the previous exercise. For each, specify the flow relation, the class-combining operator, and the lower and upper bounds.

PART FIVE

PROGRAMMING PROJECTS

P R O J E C T   1

Process/Thread Synchronization

---

1   PROJECT OVERVIEW

In this project, we will implement different solutions to the CS problem and the bounded-buffer problem. The first task is to set up two concurrent threads that access a shared resource. We will demonstrate that, without synchronization, some of the operations performed by the threads may get lost. We then implement two different solutions: 1) using *mutex* locks provided by Pthreads; and 2) using a software solution (Peterson). We compare the performance of these two solutions. Next, we develop two different implementations of the P and V operations on general semaphores: 1) using *mutex* locks and *condition* variables of Pthreads; and 2) using the software solution. We again compare the performance of the two versions. Finally, we implement a bounded buffer between two concurrent threads using the just-developed P and V operations.

2   SETTING UP A RACE CONDITION

We assume the use of POSIX Pthreads in this project, but other packages that provide multiple threads within a process may be used as well. The POSIX standard does not prescribe the exact concurrency requirements among threads. Let us assume first that our implementation supports concurrent threads with RR scheduling. That means, each thread is automatically preempted after it ran for some time and another thread is started. Thus, all threads within a process proceed concurrently at unpredictable speeds.

To set up a race condition, create two threads, *t1* and *t2*. The parent thread (*main*) defines two global variables, say *accnt1* and *accnt2*. Each variable represents a bank account; it contains a single value—the current balance—which is initially zero. Each thread emulates a banking transaction that transfers some amount of money from one account to another. That means, each thread reads values in the two accounts, generates a random number r, adds this number to one account, and subtracts it from the other. The following code skeleton illustrates the operation of each thread:

```
counter = 0;
do {
  tmp1 = accnt1;
  tmp2 = accnt2;
  r = rand();
  accnt1 = tmp1 + r;
  accnt2 = tmp2 - r;
  counter++;
} while ( accnt1 + accnt2 == 0 );
print(counter);
```

Both threads execute the same code. As long as the execution is not interleaved, the sum of the two balances should remain zero. However, if the threads are interleaved, one thread could read the old value of *accnt1* and the new value of *accnt2*, or vice versa, which results in the loss of one of the updates. When this is detected, the thread stops and prints the step (counter) at which this occurred.

An analogous program can be set up using files. Instead of the shared variables *accnt1* and *accnt2*, the main thread creates two shared files, $f1$ and $f2$, each of which contains a single value—the current account balance. The threads read and update the balances using a random number in the same way as the above program. (Note that the files must not be locked for exclusive access during the read/write sequence, otherwise no interleaving would be possible.)

Write the code for *main* and the two threads. Then measure how long it takes to generate a race condition, resulting in the loss of an update.

Note: In implementations that do not support RR scheduling of threads, you must emulate this behavior by forcing context switches between the threads explicitly. Insert a piece of code between the two update statement that performs the following: It generates a random number in a given range, say from 0 to 1. If this number is less than a threshold (e.g., 0.1), issue a *yield* statement to explicitly give up the CPU to the other thread. Thus, on average, one in 10 iterations will result in a context switch.

3   SOLUTIONS TO THE CRITICAL SECTION PROBLEM

The code within each thread represents a CS. There are two possible solutions to this problem. If the system provides a basic synchronization primitive, e.g., *mutexes*, those can be used to lock the CS for exclusive access. If the system does not provide any synchronization primitives, the software solution (developed by Peterson and presented in Chapter 2) can be used. We will consider and compare both options.

3.1   Solution Using *mutex* Locks

The Pthreads library provides a form of binary semaphores, called *mutexes*. A *mutex* can be locked and unlocked. Locking a *mutex* that is already locked by another thread causes the invoking thread to be blocked until the *mutex* is unlocked.

Using these primitives, it is easy to implement a CS. A *mutex* is locked prior to entering the CS, i.e., before the first read operation in our example. It is unlocked when leaving the CS, i.e., after the second update. The system takes care of the blocking (waiting) and unblocking of the threads.

3.2   Software Solution

Let us now assume that *mutex* or any other form of primitive synchronization is not provided. We must solve the CS problem using only standard programming language operations on conventional variables. The solution presented in Section 2.3.1 (Chapter 2) uses three variables, $c1$, $c2$, and *will_wait*, to solve the problem for two processes/threads. Each thread i indicates when it wishes to enter its CS by setting the variable c_i to 1. It also sets the variable *will_wait* to i to break any possible race conditions. The blocking is implemented as a busy-wait loop in front of the CS. When the thread exits the CS, it resets the c_i variable to 0.

Our CS is the code starting with the first read and ending with the second update. We can use the code of the software solution to enforce the mutual exclusion. To speed up the execution, the body of the busy-wait loop should contain the statement *sched_yield*. This gives up the CPU immediately, rather than continuing the empty loop until the quantum expires.

We are now ready to compare the efficiency of the two solutions to the CS problem. Simply repeat the same number of iterations using the two solutions and measure the execution time. To eliminate any possible external interferences, repeat the experiment several times and compute the average times.

4   IMPLEMENTING GENERAL SEMAPHORES

The P and V operations on general semaphores can be implemented conveniently using lower-level primitives, such as binary semaphores. Alternately, a solution using only conventional programming constructs can be attempted.

4.1   Solution Using *Mutex* Locks and *Condition* Variables

Section 4.5.1 (Chapter 4) discussed how the general P and V operations may be implemented using Pb and Vb operations on binary semaphores. This solution uses two binary semaphores, *sb* and *delay*, each for a different purpose. *sb* is used for mutual exclusion. Such a semaphore is analogous to a *mutex* lock of Pthreads. Thus, we can substitute the *mutex_lock* and *mutex_unlock* for $Pb(sb)$ and $Vb(sb)$, respectively. The binary semaphore *delay* is used to block a process inside P and to later release it (using a corresponding V operation). Such a binary semaphore may be emulated using a *condition* variable. The operations *pthread_cond_wait* and *pthread_cond_signal* then correspond to $Pb(delay)$ and $Vb(delay)$, respectively.

4.2   Software Solution

From the previous section, we already have a software solution (i.e., a solution that does not use any special synchronization instructions) for the CS problem. We can build the P and V operations using CS as follows:

1. Each semaphore s is implemented as an integer variable.
2. Any access to the shared variable s must be implemented as a CS.
3. When the P operation must block, it must enter a while-loop during which it repeatedly tests s (in a CS) until s becomes greater than 0; at that time, it decrements s and proceeds. During each iteration of the wait-loop, the thread should yield the

CPU to improve performance. (Note that the yield operation must not happen inside the CS. Otherwise, no other thread could perform a V operations and the system would deadlock!)

4. The V operation simply increments s (in a CS).

We are now ready to compare the efficiency of the two implementations of the P and V operations. Develop several test cases involving one or more threads performing different sequences of P and V operations. In particular, test the execution times of P and V in situations where no process is waiting inside a P operation and one or more processes are waiting inside P operations.

5 BOUNDED BUFFER

Implement the bounded buffer between a producer thread and a consumer thread, as discussed in Section 2.4.3 (Chapter 2). The producer repeatedly reads a value (e.g., an integer) from a file $f1$, until the end of the file is reached. It deposits each value into the bounded buffer, implemented as an array of size n, and shared between the two threads. The consumer repeatedly removes values from the buffer and writes them into another file, $f2$. When both threads finish, file $f2$ should be an exact copy of file $f1$.

Keep track of how many values are in the buffer during each iteration. Should the timing conditions be such that this value is either n or 0 most of the time then try to insert *sleep* statements of randomly chosen durations into the producer and consumer loops to emulate burst of consumption and production activity.

6 SUMMARY OF SPECIFIC TASKS

1. Set up two threads and get them to enter a race condition.
2. Solve the race condition using (a) *mutex* locks; and (b) Peterson's software solution; compare the performance of the two solutions.
3. Implement P and V operations on general semaphores using (a) *mutex* locks and *condition* variables; and (b) software solution to CS; compare the performance of the two solutions.
4. Implement a bounded buffer between a consumer and a producer thread; study the concurrency behavior of the two threads.
5. Document the results of your experiments in a report.

7 IDEAS FOR ADDITIONAL TASKS

1. Implement the basic monitor functionality using your P and V operations. This requires writing a precompiler, which replaces all *c.wait* and *s.signal* operations by the implementation code shown in Section 4.5.2 (Chapter 4) and inserts the mutual exclusion code to surround each monitor procedure (also shown in Section 4.5.2). Concurrent threads then may invoke the procedures to coordinate their use of a shared resource.

   To also model the encapsulation of procedures with the resource, the monitor can be implemented as a separate process. It communicates with other processes, which must use the monitor using UNIX pipes. When a process wishes to invoke a monitor procedure, it sends a request (containing the procedure name and the parameter) to the monitor process by writing to a request pipe. It then blocks itself by reading from a reply pipe. The monitor process repeatedly reads requests for procedure invocations from the request pipe. For each request, it invokes the corresponding procedure as a separate thread. This thread may use the *c.wait* operation to block itself and the *c.signal* operation to wake up other threads. When the thread terminates, the monitor process returns the results to the original calling process by writing into the reply pipe.

2. Extend the CS problem to more than two processes. Develop and compare solutions using the constructs provided by Pthreads and pure software solutions.

PROJECT 2

Process and Resource Management

1 PROJECT OVERVIEW

In this project, we will examine the portion of the kernel that addresses the management of processes and resources. We will develop a system that will allow us to create the data structures to represent processes and resources. We will also implement the operations invoked by processes to manipulate other processes or to request/release various resources. In the extended version of the manager, we will also implement operations that emulate the actions of hardware interrupts. The manager will be tested using a presentation shell developed as part of the project. This will allow us to test the manager without running the actual processes and using the machine's actual hardware interrupts. Instead, the presentation shell will play the role of both the currently running process and the hardware; it will accept commands typed in by the user, and will invoke the corresponding function of the manager.

2 BASIC PROCESS AND RESOURCE MANAGER

2.1 Process States

We assume there are only three process states: *ready, running, blocked*. The following table lists the possible operations a process may perform and the resulting state transitions.

Operation	old state		new state
Create	*(none)*	$\rightarrow$	*ready*
Request	*running*	$\rightarrow$	*blocked*
Release	*blocked*	$\rightarrow$	*ready*
Destroy	*any*	$\rightarrow$	*(none)*
Scheduler	*ready*	$\rightarrow$	*running*
	running	$\rightarrow$	*ready*

All of the above operations except the *Scheduler* are invoked directly by the currently running process—they represent *kernel calls*. The *Scheduler* is a function that is invoked automatically at the end of each of the operations.

2.2   Representation of Processes

Each process is represented by a data structure called the *process control block (PCB)*, as explained in Section 4.4.1 (Chapter 4). For this project, we use the following fields of the PCB:

ID
Memory
Other_Resources
Status
Creation_Tree
Priority

- *ID* is a unique process identifier by which the process may be referred to by other processes.

- *Memory* is a linked list of pointers to memory blocks requested by and currently allocated to the process. This field is used only if memory management is incorporated into this project (see Section 5, extension 2.)

- *Other_Resources* jointly represents all resources other than main memory that have been requested by and currently allocated to the process. It is implemented as a linked list.

- *Status* consists of two subfields, *Status.Type* and *Status.List*. Their meaning is explained in Section 4.4.1 (Chapter 4).

- *Creation_Tree* also consists of two subfields, *Creation_Tree.Parent* and *Creation_Tree. Child*. Their meaning also is explained in Section 4.4.1 (Chapter 4).

- *Priority* is the process priority and is used by the *Scheduler* to decide which process should be running next. We assume that priority is represented by an integer and is static.

Each PCB is created and destroyed dynamically using the operations *Create* and *Destroy* invoked by the currently running process. The only exception is the special *Init* process, whose PCB is created automatically when the system starts up, and destroyed when the system is shut down (see Section 2.5).

2.3   Representation of Resources

We assume that there is a set of resources a process may request, use, and later release. Examples of such resources are printers, terminals, other devices, or various software components or services. All resources are serially reusable, i.e., they can be used only by one process at a time. Each resource is represented by a data structure called the *resource control block (RCB)*. A RCB consists of the following fields:

| *RID* |
| *Status* |
| *Waiting_List* |

- *RID* is a unique resource identifier by which the resource may be referred to by processes.

- *Status* indicates whether the resource is currently free or allocated to other process.

- *Waiting_List* is a list of processes blocked on this resources. These are all the processes that have requested the resource but could not obtain it because it is currently being used by another process.

All resources are static and their RCBs are created by the system at start-up time.

2.4   Operations on Processes and Resources

The manager must support the four basic operations on processes: *Create, Destroy, Suspend*, and *Activate*. These have been outlined in Section 4.4.2 (Chapter 4). They may be simplified for this project because we are assuming only a single CPU, and because some of the fields have been omitted from the PCB.

The two operations on resources, *Request* and *Release*, are outlined in Section 4.5 (Chapter 4). The following algorithms present these operations at a more detailed level:

```
(1)   Request(RID) {
(2)      r = Get_RCB(RID);
(3)      if (r->Status == 'free') {
(4)         r->Status = 'allocated';
(5)         insert(self->Other_Resources, r);
(6)      } else {
(7)         self->Status.Type = 'blocked';
(8)         self->Status.List = r;
(9)         remove(RL, self);
(10)        insert(r->Waiting_List, self);
(11)     Scheduler();
(12) }
```

If the requested resource is currently available, the operation changes the resource status to *'allocated'* and makes it available to the calling process by entering a pointer to the RCB into the list of the process resources. If the requested resource is not currently available, the calling process is blocked. This includes changing the *Status.Type* to *'blocked'* and the *Status.List* to point to the RCB of the requested resource. The process also must be moved from the RL to the waiting list of the resource. Finally, the scheduler is called to select the process to run next.

```
(1)   Release(RID) {
(2)      r = Get_RCB(RID);
(3)      remove(self->Other_Resources, r);
```

```
(4)     if (r->Waiting_list == NIL} {
(5)       r->Status = 'free';
(6)     } else {
(7)       remove(r->Waiting_List, q);
(8)       q->Status.Type = 'ready';
(9)       q->Status.List = RL;
(10)      insert(RL, q); }
(11)    Scheduler();
(12) }
```

The operation first removes the resource from the process resource list. Then, if there is no process blocked on this resource (i.e., the *Waiting_List* is empty), the operation changes the status of the named resource to *free*. Otherwise, the process at the head the *Waiting_List* is removed, its status is changed to ready, and it is inserted on the RL. The scheduler is then called.

2.5   The Scheduler

We use a preemptive multilevel priority scheduler with fixed-priority levels. That means, the RL of processes maintained by the scheduler consists of n levels. Each level contains a queue of zero or more processes (pointers to their PCBs). Processes at level 0 have the lowest priority; processes at level $n - 1$ have the highest priority. The priority is assigned to a process at the time of its creation and remains unchanged for the duration of its lifetime. When a new process is created or an existing process is unblocked, it is inserted at the end of the list of processes for its priority level.

The scheduler services the RL in FIFO order, starting with the highest-priority level. That means, when asked to find the highest-priority ready process, it selects the process at the head of the highest nonempty queue. Note that this scheduling discipline can easily lead to starvation. A process at level q will get a chance to run only when all processes at levels higher than q have either terminated or blocked on a resource.

The organization of the scheduler is simplified if we know that there is always at least one process in the system ready to run. To guarantee this condition, we implement a special process, called *Init*. This process is created automatically when the system is started. It is assigned the lowest priority (0). The *Init* process plays two important roles. First, it acts as a "dummy" process that runs when no other process is ready to run. To ensure that, the *Init* process is not allowed to request any resources to prevent it from ever becoming blocked. Under this rule, the RL never becomes completely empty. Second, it is the very first process that runs when the system is started. It has no parent, but it may create other processes at higher priorities, which, in turn, may create other processes, and so on. Thus, the *Init* process is the root of the process creation tree.

The general structure of a priority scheduler was presented in Section 5.1.2 (Chapter 5). For this project, we simplify this as follows:

```
(1) Scheduler() {
(2)   find highest priority process p
(3)   if (self->priority < p->priority ||
(4)       self->Status.Type != 'running' ||
```

```
(5)         self == NIL)
(5)         preempt(p, self)
(6) }
```

The scheduler function is called at the end of any kernel call. Note that it is running as part of the current process, i.e., the process that issued the kernel call. The scheduler's task is to determine whether the current process continues to run or whether it should be preempted by another process. To make this decision, it finds the highest-priority ready process p (line 2). If p's priority is higher than the priority of the current process, i.e., the processes within which the scheduler is running (line 3), p must preempt the current process (line 5).

Note that the condition (*self->priority* < *p->priority*) may be satisfied in two situations:

(1) When the scheduler is called at the end of a *Release* operation, the priority of the process unblocked as a result of the *Release* operation may be higher than the priority of the current process;

(2) When the scheduler is called at the end of a *Create* operation, the priority of the new process may be higher than the priority of the current process.

In both cases, the current process must be preempted.

There are two other situations under which the newly selected process must preempt the current process:

(1) When the scheduler is called from a *Request* operation and the requested resource is not available, the state of the current process has already been changed to *'blocked'*. (This change has been made on line 5 of the request operation.) When the scheduler is called from a *Timeout* operation (see Section 3), the status of the current process has been changed to *'ready'*. (This change has been made on line 4 of the timeout operation.) In both of these cases, i.e., when the status of the current process is not *'running'*, the current process must stop running and the highest-priority process p must be resumed in its place.

(2) When the scheduler is called from a *Destroy* operation where the current process named itself to be destroyed, its PCB no longer exists when it reaches the scheduler. The PCB has been deleted by the *Destroy* operation. As in the previous cases, the highest-priority process p must be resumed instead.

The preempt operation consists of the following tasks. It changes the status of the selected process p to *'running'*. If the current process still exists and is not blocked, its status is changed to *'ready'* so that it would be resumed at a later time. Finally, the actual *context switch* takes place, which saves the state of the CPU (i.e., contents of all registers) in the PCB of the current process as the *CPU_State* and loads the *CPU_State* of process p.

In this project, we do not have access to the physical CPU to save and restore its registers. Thus, the task of the context switch is to display only on your terminal the name of the process that would now be running. At that point, the user terminal begins to play the role of the currently running process, as we describe next.

2.6   The Presentation Shell

If the process and resource manager described in the previous section were deployed in a real system, the kernel calls would be invoked by the currently running process. At the end of kernel call, the scheduler would either preempt the current process or resume its execution.

To be able to test and demonstrate the functionality of our manager, we develop a presentation shell, which repeatedly accepts commands from your terminal, invokes the corresponding function of the manager, and displays a reply message on the screen. The following diagram illustrates the basic structure:

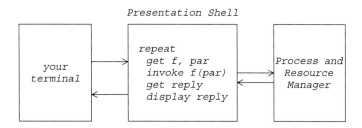

Using the above organization, your terminal represents the currently running process. That means, whenever you type in a command, it is interpreted as if the currently running process issued this command. The presentation shell invokes the corresponding function, f, of the process and resource manager, and passes to it any parameters (*par*) supplied from the terminal. The function invocation results in some changes in the PCB, RCB, and other data structures. When the execution reaches the scheduler, it decides which process is to execute next and makes the appropriate changes to the status fields of the affected processes. Then, instead of saving and loading the CPU state (since there is no actual CPU), the scheduler only displays a message on the screen, informing you of any changes in the system state. In particular, it will always tell you which process is currently running, i.e., which process your terminal and keyboard are currently representing. The function (f) also may return a value, e.g., an error code, which the shell also displays on your screen.

To simplify the interactions with the shell, we must devise a syntax similar to the UNIX shell, where each line starts with a short command name, followed by optional parameters separated by blanks. The shell interprets each line and invokes the corresponding manager function. For example, the command line *"cr A 1"* could be used to invoke the function *Create(A, 1)*, which creates a new process named A at the priority level 1. Similarly, *"rq R"* would result in the call *Request(R)*.

The following sequence illustrates the interaction with the shell. Lines preceded by the asterisk (*) are responses displayed by the shell; lines preceded by the prompt sign (>) are commands typed in:

```
. . .
* Process A is running
> cr B 2
* Process B is running
> cr C 1
```

```
* Process B is running
> req R1
* Process B is blocked; Process A is running
...
```

We assume that a process A with a priority 1 already exists and is currently running. You type in the command *"cr B 2"*, which is interpreted by the shell as "A creates a new process named B with a priority 2." The shell invokes the *Create* operation with the appropriate parameters, which makes all the appropriate changes to the data structures. Since B's priority is higher than A's, B is selected by the scheduler to run next; the message "Process B is running" informs you that you are now acting on behalf of process B. Thus, the next command, *"cr C 1"*, is interpreted as process B creating a new process C with a priority 1. Since C's priority is lower than B's, B continues running. The next command is a request (by B) to get the resource R1. Assuming R1 is currently not available, process B blocks and A, which is currently the highest-priority process, resumes its execution.

3   EXTENDED PROCESS AND RESOURCE MANAGER

In this section we extend the basic process and resource manager described in Section 2 to incorporate some aspects of the hardware. Notably, the extended manager will be able to handle hardware interrupts coming from a timeout generator and from I/O completion.

3.1   Timeout Interrupts

To implement time-sharing, assume that a hardware timer is provided, which periodically issues a timeout interrupt. This invokes a function, *Timeout()*, of the extended manager. This function performs the following task:

```
(1) Timeout() {
(2)     find running process q;
(3)     remove(RL, q);
(4)     q->Status.Type = 'ready';
(5)     insert(RL, q);
(6)     Scheduler();
(7) }
```

The function removes the currently running process q from the head of the RL, changes its status from *'running'* to *'ready'*, and inserts it back at the end of the RL. It then calls the scheduler, which changes the status of the currently highest-priority process p from *'ready'* to *'running'*.

Note that this function has no effect if there is only one process at that level. If there are multiple processes at that level, then repeated invocations of *Timeout* cycle through all processes in the queue in a RR fashion.

3.2 Input/Output Processing

We represent all I/O devices collectively as a resource named *IO*; the RCB of this resource has the following form:

This is analogous to the RCBs of other resources, except that the status field is omitted. A process wishing to perform I/O issues a request for the *IO* resource. The request has the following form:

```
(1) Request_IO() {
(2)     self->Status.Type = 'blocked';
(3)     self->Status.List = IO;
(4)     remove(RL, self);
(4)     insert(IO->Waiting_List, self);
(5)     Scheduler();
(6) }
```

Normally the caller would specify the details of the I/O request as parameters to the call; we will omit this in this project, since there are no actual I/O devices employed.

The *Request_IO* function blocks the calling process and moves its PCB from the RL to the tail of the waiting list associated with the IO resource. The scheduler is called to select another process to continue running.

A process blocked on I/O remains in the waiting list until an I/O interrupt is generated, indicating that the I/O request has been completed and the waiting process may be unblocked. We make the following simplifying assumption: all I/O requests complete in the order in which they were submitted (see Section 5, extension 3.) Under the simplifying assumption, the following function is invoked by an I/O completion interrupt:

```
(1) IO_completion() {
(2)     remove(IO->Waiting_List, p);
(3)     p->Status.Type = 'ready';
(4)     p->Status.List = RL;
(4)     insert(RL, p);
(5)     Scheduler();
(6) }
```

The function simply unblocks the first process on the waiting list of the IO resource and moves it to the RL. We assume again that *IO_completion* runs as part of a low-priority process such that the scheduler selects one of the other processes from the RL to run next.

3.3 The Extended Shell

In the extended form of the process and resource manager, the user terminal plays a dual role.

1. It continues representing the currently running process, as was the case with the basic manager version. Thus, typing any of the commands introduced in Section 2.6 will have the same effect as before. In addition, a process is now able to issue an additional call, *Request_IO()*.

2. The terminal also represents the hardware. Notably, the user is able to emulate the generation of the two types of interrupts—timeout and I/O completion—by triggering the corresponding functions of the manager.

To incorporate the above extensions into the shell, three new commands must be provided to invoke the functions *Request_IO()*, *IO_competion()*, and *Timeout()*. None of these functions require any parameters.

4 SUMMARY OF SPECIFIC TASKS

1. Design and implement the process and resource manager; the basic version includes the functions *Create()*, *Destroy()*, *Suspend()*, *Activate()*, *Request()*, and *Release()*, together with the underlying data structures; the extended version provides the additional functions *Request_IO()*, *IO_completion()*, and *Timeout()*.

2. Define a command language for the presentation shell. Then design and implement the shell so that you can test and demonstrate the functionality of your process and resource manager. For each command, the shell should respond by displaying the name of the currently running process, and any errors and other relevant system events that may have occurred.

3. Instantiate the manager to include the following at start-up:

   (a) A RL with at least three priorities.
   (b) A single process, called *Init*, that runs at the lowest-priority level and is always ready to run. This may create other processes at higher levels.
   (c) At least three fixed resources, say A, B, C, that processes can request and release.
   (d) An IO resource that processes may request and become blocked on until the next I/O completion interrupt.

4. Test the manager using a variety of command sequences to explore all aspects of its behavior. Demonstrate also a deadlock situation.

5 IDEAS FOR ADDITIONAL TASKS

1. Extend the concept of a resource to include multiple identical units. That is, each RCB represents a *class* of resources. Instead of the simple *Status* field, it has an "*inventory*" field that keeps track of which or how many units of the given resource are currently available. A process then may specify how many units of a resource class it needs. The request is granted when enough units are available; otherwise, the process is blocked. Similarly, a process may release some or all of the units it has previously acquired. This may now potentially unblock multiple processes at once.

2. Incorporate main memory as another resource class in the process and resource manager. That means, define a RCB for memory. The *Status* field is replaced by a

pointer to the list of holes, which represents the current inventory of the memory resource. Adapt and incorporate the memory *request* and *release* functions developed as part of Project 3 (Main Memory). Processes may request new memory blocks by specifying their size and later release them.

3. Remove the restriction that all I/O requests will complete in the order of their submission. This requires keeping track of which I/O completion interrupt corresponds to which I/O request, which a real system must do. In this project, the *Request_IO()* must be extended to record the ID of the calling process. The *IO_completion()* function then specifies the process whose request has been satisfied.

PROJECT 3

Main Memory Management

---

1   PROJECT OVERVIEW
2   THE MEMORY MANAGER
3   THE SIMULATION EXPERIMENT
4   SUMMARY OF SPECIFIC TASKS
5   IDEAS FOR ADDITIONAL TASKS

---

1   PROJECT OVERVIEW

In this project, we will examine main memory management in systems without virtual memory. The memory manager of such a system must maintain the list of free spaces, called holes. Processes can request and release blocks of variable sizes by invoking the appropriate functions of the memory manager.

Your tasks are the following:

- Design a memory manager that supports at least two different allocation strategies, such as first-fit, next-fit, best-fit, or worst-fit.

- Evaluate the different strategies by comparing how well they maintain the available memory.

2   THE MEMORY MANAGER

The memory manager is a set of functions that manage a hypothetical physical memory.

2.1   Main Memory

The memory manager is intended to manage a linear physical memory. While developing the manager, we need no access to the actual physical memory of the system. Instead, we can emulate physical memory by allocating a sequence of consecutive bytes, and develop all the necessary functions using this emulated main memory. The functions use pointers instead of physical addresses.

A main memory of size *mem_size* may be created in one of two ways:

1. By using a dynamic memory management function of the OS, such as $mm = malloc(mem\_size)$ in UNIX.

2. By declaring a character array, *mm[mem_size]*, that represents the physical memory.

In both cases, we obtain a sequence of *mem_size* consecutive bytes—the emulated main memory. The pointer *mm* corresponds to physical address 0 of the actual physical memory. All holes and allocated blocks are maintained by the memory manager within

492

this main memory array. (Note that type-casting must be used whenever the tag, size, and pointer fields, which are of different types, are written into or read from this memory.)

2.2   The User Interface

The memory manager must provide the following functions that can be invoked by other processes:

1. `void *mm_request(int n)`

   This function requests a block of *n* consecutive bytes of memory. If the request can be satisfied, it returns a pointer to the first usable byte of the allocated block. If the request cannot be specified—because there is no hole large enough or the parameter *n* is illegal (e.g., a negative number)—it returns NULL. (Note that this function is analogous to the *malloc* function of UNIX.)

2. `void mm_release(void *p)`

   This function releases a previously allocated block of memory, pointed to by the pointer *p*. If the released block is adjacent to another hole, the function must coalesce the holes to prevent the fragmentation of memory into increasingly smaller holes. If the released block is surrounded by allocated blocks, it is simply appended to the list of holes. (Note that this function is analogous to the *free* function of UNIX.)

3. `void *mm_init(int mem_size)`

   This function initializes the memory to become a single hole by creating the appropriate tag, size, and pointer fields. It returns the pointer *mm* introduced in Section 2.1.

3   THE SIMULATION EXPERIMENT

Implement two or more versions of the memory manager by varying the allocation strategy. The possible choices are first-fit, next-fit, best-fit, and worst-fit. Then design and carry out an experiment that will compare the performance of the chosen allocation strategies in terms of:

1. average memory utilization;
2. average number of steps needed to find an appropriate hole.

To set up the simulation experiment, let us make the following assumptions. Request and release calls arrive at the manager in two separate queues. Releases are always processed first. Since any release is immediately satisfiable, the queue of releases is always empty. A request may or may not be satisfiable, depending on whether there is a hole large enough to accommodate the request. If that is not the case, the request remains on the queue until adequate space has been freed by subsequent release operations. The request queue is processed in FIFO order; otherwise, starvation could occur.

Under these assumptions, we can model the behavior of the memory manager as follows. We start in a state where memory already consists of occupied blocks and holes; there is no release request, and the request at the head of the queue cannot be satisfied. At this point, the manager cannot do anything but wait for the next release. During this time, the memory allocation does not change. When a release is processed, the manager attempts to satisfy the request at the head of the queue. If this fails, the manager is again waiting for the next release. If the request succeeds, the manager immediately attempts to satisfy the next request in the queue, and so on. Thus, following every release, zero or more pending requests are satisfied, depending on the size of the released block and the sizes of the pending requests.

To evaluate the effectiveness of different allocation strategies, we must assume that memory is always filled to maximum capacity. That means, we assume that the stream of requests is unbounded, and the queue is never empty.

The following is a skeleton of the simulation experiment based on the above assumptions. It gathers the performance statistics for one chosen allocation strategy.

```
(1) for (i=0; i<sim_steps; i++) {
(2)    do {
(3)      get size n of next request    /* see Section 3.1 */
(4)      mm_request(n) }
(5)    while (request successful)
(6)    record memory utilization       /* see Section 3.2 */
(7)    select block p to be released   /* see Section 3.3 */
(8)    release(p)
(9) }
```

The program consists of a main loop (line 1), which is repeated for a number of simulation steps (*sim_steps*). For each iteration of the outer loop, the program performs the following tasks. The inner loop (lines 2–5) attempt to satisfy as many of the pending requests as possible. Each request is generated on the fly by getting a random number, n, to represent the request size (line 3).

Once a request fails, the memory manager must wait until a block is released. Until then, the current memory allocation does not change, and we can record the current memory use. (Note that we are making the implicit assumption that the time during which a block resides in memory is independent of the block size. Thus, each iteration of the outer loop represents a constant interval of time during which the memory use does not change.)

Next, one of the allocated blocks, p, is selected and released (lines 7–8). This frees some space and allows the simulation to proceed with the next iteration.

3.1 Generating Request Sizes

Let us assume that requests sizes can be approximated using a Gaussian distribution. Thus, we can generate each new requests size, n, using the function:

$$n = gauss(a, d)$$

where a is the average request size and d is the standard deviation. (Most math libraries will provide a set of such distribution functions.) Choosing a close to zero means that the average request will ask for just a few bytes of memory; a large a implies that processes typically request large blocks of memory. The standard deviation determines the shape of the Gaussian curve. A small d will result in a steep curve, implying that the majority of requests are clustered close to the mean; a large d implies that the distribution of sizes is more uniform.

Regardless of the values of a and d, the number n ranges from minus to plus infinity. Thus, we must truncate the range to reflect the physical size of memory. That means, whenever n exceeds *mem_size*, it is discarded, because a request that exceeds total memory size could never be satisfied. We must also discard all negative values of n (or use their absolute values) since all memory blocks are always greater than zero. (A block of size zero is, in principle, possible, but useless.)

3.2 Gathering Performance Data

There are two types of performance data we must gather. *Memory utilization* is expressed as the ratio of the allocated space to the total memory size. One such value is obtained during each iteration of the simulation loop. These values may be accumulated in a file and averaged at the end. Alternately, a running average may be computed during each simulation run.

The second performance value is the average *search time*, i.e., number of steps needed to satisfy a request. This may be gathered by instrumenting the *mm_request* function for each memory allocation strategy. It must keep track of the number of holes that must be examined for each request, and compute the average over the duration of the simulation run.

3.3 Choosing a Block to Release

If we assume that the time a given block stays in memory is independent of its size, we can select the block to be released during each iteration at random. The simulation program must keep track of all the allocated blocks; a linked list is the most appropriate data structure for that purpose. If there are k elements on the list of allocated blocks, we choose a random number, p, between one and k, and release the block at position p on the list.

4 SUMMARY OF SPECIFIC TASKS

1. Design and implement the three functions of the memory manager. Implement at least two different allocation strategies (i.e., first-fit, next-fit, best-fit, worst-fit).

2. Design and implement a driver program that allows you to test and demonstrate the functionality of your memory manager.

3. Evaluate the performance of the chosen allocation strategies using the simulation experiment. Generate families of curves that show how the average memory utilization and the average search time (number of steps to satisfy a request) vary with the average request size. Repeat the experiments for different choices of the parameters a and d of the *gauss* function.

5 IDEAS FOR ADDITIONAL TASKS

- Experiment with other allocation strategies, e.g., different versions of an optimal fit, that take into account the size of the remaining hole after an allocation.

- Use a different distribution of request sizes. For example, try a uniform distribution, where all request sizes are equally likely, or a bimodal distribution, where request sizes are clustered around two peaks (each represented by a Gaussian function.)

PROJECT 4

Page Replacement Algorithms

1   PROJECT OVERVIEW

In this project, we will implement different page replacement algorithms, both local and global. We will compare their relative performance using probabilistically generated reference strings.

2   GLOBAL PAGE REPLACEMENT ALGORITHMS

Global page replacement algorithms assume a fixed number of page frames. We consider a single-process system and make the following assumptions:

- The *virtual memory* of the process consists of P pages, numbered 0 through $P-1$.

- A reference string RS is a sequence of integers ranging from 0 to $P-1$. Each element, p, of RS represents one reference to page p.

- The *main memory* consists of F page frames, numbered 0 through $F-1$. This is represented as an array, $M[F]$. Each entry $M[f]$ contains the number p of the page currently residing in the frame f.

Section 8.3.1 (Chapter 8) describes several different global page-replacement algorithms. Each algorithm sequentially reads the elements of RS. For each element p of RS the algorithm searches the main memory array for a match, i.e., it tries to find an f such that $M[f] == p$. If no match is found, a page fault occurs. The algorithm must select a page frame $M[i]$ according to the policy it implements and replace the contents of that frame with p, i.e., $M[i] = p$.

Depending on the algorithm, additional data structures must be provided to implement it. The following list summarizes the needs of the different algorithms:

- *MIN* and *random replacement* require no additional data structures. In the case of MIN, the algorithm searches RS to find the page to replace. Random replacement must generate a random number between 0 and $F-1$ to choose the page to replace.

- *FIFO* only maintains a pointer (array index) pointing at the oldest page in memory. The pointer is incremented by one (modulo F) whenever the current page is replaced.

- *LRU* must maintain an additional array of size F, which implements the queue; this is reordered at each reference such that the referenced page is placed at the end of the queue.

- The *second-chance* algorithm must maintain a pointer similar to the FIFO algorithm. In addition, it needs an array of u-bits, one for each frame.

- The *third-chance* algorithm must maintain a pointer and three arrays; these represent the u-bits, the w-bits, and the *marker*-bits (the latter correspond to the asterisk in Table 8-1).

Once the algorithms are developed, they can be tested with various reference strings as described in Section 4.

3 LOCAL PAGE REPLACEMENT ALGORITHMS

With local page replacement algorithms (Section 8.3.2, Chapter 8), the number of page frames is not fixed. Instead, we must keep track of the *current working set* of the process. We consider a single process and represent its virtual memory as an array $VM[P]$, where P is the number of pages in the virtual memory. The information recorded as part of each element of VM depends on the algorithm:

- For the *working set* algorithm, *WS*, each element $VM[p]$ only records whether the page p is currently resident, i.e., a member of the working set. To keep track of the current sliding window, we implement another array, say $WIN[\tau + 1]$, where τ is a system constant. This array serves as a queue of constant length; at any point in time, it contains the pages references during the last $\tau + 1$ time steps. The *WS* algorithm uses the two arrays as follows. For each reference p in *RS*, it inserts p at the head of the queue *WIN*, and it removes the element, q, currently at the end of the queue. It then searches *WIN* for the occurrence of q; if this does not appear, the corresponding entry $VM[q]$ is set to zero, marking it as not resident. Next, the entry $VM[p]$ is checked; if this is not 1, the algorithm sets it to 1 and records a page fault.

- For the optimal page-replacement algorithm, *VMIN*, we use the same arrays *VM* and *WIN*. *VM* again records which pages are resident; *WIN* corresponds to the forward-looking window, i.e., it always contains the $\tau + 1$ pages that will be referenced next. At each reference, the page that will be referenced τ steps in the future replaces the currently referenced page p in *WIN*. If p is not resident ($VM[p] == 0$) at the time of the reference, $VM[p]$ is set to 1, and a page fault is recorded. In addition, all currently resident pages that do not appear in *WIN* are marked as nonresident in *VM*.

- For the *page fault frequency* algorithm, *PFF*, we extend the array *VM* such that each entry is a structure consisting of two fields. One of the fields, say $VM[p].res$, records whether page p is currently resident. The other field, say $VM[p].u$, corresponds to the use-bit of a page frame. The two fields are used as follows by the *PFF* algorithm. $VM[p].u$ is set to 1 at each reference to page p. At the time of a page fault, $VM[p].res$ of the referenced page p is set to 1 (making it a member of the resident set). Then, if the time between the current page fault and the last page fault (which the algorithm also must keep track of) is greater than the constant τ, the system finds all pages q with $VM[q].res == 1$ and $VM[q].u == 0$; these pages have not been referenced since the last page fault and are removed form the resident set ($VM[q].res$ is set to 0). Finally, $VM[*].u$ of all pages is set to 0; this is done at the end of every page fault, regardless of whether pages have been removed or not.

The three algorithms can be compared with each other and with global page replacement algorithms as described in Section 5.

4   GENERATING REFERENCE STRINGS

Recall that a reference string is a sequence of integers ranging from 0 to $P - 1$, where P is the total number of pages constituting the virtual memory of the process. We can generate reference strings with different properties using random number generators. The main property of a reference string is its degree of locality, which we can control in several different ways.

The simplest possible reference string is one that has *no locality*. This is a sequence of uniformly distributed random numbers in the range 0 through $P - 1$. Such a string is representative of an oversaturated system, where too many processes compete for the CPU; there is no locality of reference—the system is thrashing.

Most programs display a high degree of locality. That means, the same set of pages—the current working set—is being referenced repeatedly. We define the *current locus of reference* as a region in the virtual memory (not necessarily contiguous) from which addresses are currently being generated by the process.

A typical program behavior consists of periods during which the working set size is *stable*, punctuated by rapid *transitions* as the process changes its locus of reference. During each transition, the working set expands rapidly as pages in the new locus are being accessed. After a while, the working set shrinks to a new stable size as the pages of the previous locus are discarded from the working set.

We can model this behavior as follows. First, we assume that the current locus of reference consists of neighboring pages in the virtual memory. This is not the case in a real program, since pages from at least three regions (code, data, and stack) are being accessed. For studying page-replacement algorithms, however, we are interested only in the size of the working set and the frequency with which new pages are included and old ones are discarded. Thus, a contiguous locus of reference is adequate.

We make the simplifying assumption that references within the locus are distributed uniformly. Thus, a locus can be characterized by its starting address (page number p) and its extent (number of neighboring pages e). The following diagram illustrates the idea graphically.

The locus moves within the virtual memory as the process executes. The motion is gradual, with occasional transitions to new locations. To model the stable periods of gradual motion, we make another simplifying assumption: the locus is moving in the same direction at a constant rate, m, i.e., p is incremented by 1 every m references. To model the transition periods, we change the locus probabilistically. That means, each time we generate m references, the locus moves, with some chosen probability t, to a new location p.

Using the above assumptions, we can generate a reference string as follows:

```
- select a memory size (P), a starting location (p), an extent (e),
  a rate of  motion (m), and a probability of transition (t);
- repeat the following steps until a reference string of
  desired length is generated {
  - pick m random numbers in the range p through p+e and write
    them to a file (each number represents one reference);
  - generate a random number 0 <= r <= 1;
  - if (r < t) generate new p              /* transition */
    else increment p by 1 (modulo P); }    /* stable period */
```

The values of p in the above algorithm are chosen as uniformly distributed random numbers in the range $[0..P - 1]$. The values P, e, m, and t are constants that allow us to vary the properties of the generated reference strings. The value of P is the assumed size of the allocated virtual memory. When choosing values for e, keep in mind that the typical size of a working set is in the range of a few tens to perhaps 100 pages. When choosing values for m, keep in mind that a typical program references any page only a few hundred times, on average. When choosing the value of t, keep in mind that the stable periods typically last for thousands of instructions.

5 PERFORMANCE EVALUATIONS

The following is a suggested list of possible experiments that can be run using the different page replacement algorithms.

1. Using different reference strings and different memory sizes, answer the following questions:

    (a) How much is gained by using *FIFO* over a *random* replacement? How much is gained by using *LRU* over *FIFO*?

    (b) How close is *LRU* to the optimal (*MIN*)?

    (c) How effective are the *second-chance* and *third-chance* algorithms in approximating the *LRU* algorithm? For the third-chance algorithm, the reference string *RS* must differentiate between read and write accesses. This can be done during the generation of *RS* (e.g., by representing write accesses as negative numbers), or by augmenting the page-replacement algorithm itself. In either case, choose a constant $0 \geq W \geq 1$, and assume that, with probability W, any given request is a write operation.

    For all cases, present your results in terms of the average number of page faults for a given *RS*. For case (c), also estimate the overhead (in terms of numbers of operations) generated by different algorithms.

2. For the local page replacement algorithms, determine the following:

   (a) How close is *WS* to the optimal replacement *VMIN*?
   (b) How does the page fault rate (average number of page faults for a given reference string) vary with different values of τ for *WS, VMIN*, or *PFF*?
   (c) How close is *PFF* to *WS*?

   The main measure in all cases is again the average number of page faults for a given *RS*.

3. Compare a local page replacement algorithm with a global replacement algorithm. For this comparison, choose a local page replacement algorithms and a value for τ; determine:

   (a) the average number of frames, *nf*, needed to accommodate the working set
   (b) the average number of page faults, pf_{loc}

   Then use the number *nf* as the memory size for a *global* replacement algorithm, such as *LRU*; determine the number of page faults, pf_{glob}, for this algorithm and compare it with pf_{loc}.

6 SUMMARY OF SPECIFIC TASKS

1. Develop a set of page replacement algorithms (global, local, or a combination of both).
2. Develop a program to generate reference strings with different characteristics.
3. Compare the performance of the different algorithms using the reference strings.
4. Document the results of your experiments in a report.

7 IDEAS FOR ADDITIONAL TASKS

1. Implement the variation of the *LRU* that uses aging registers (emulated in software), as described in Section 8.3.1 (Chapter 8). Determine a suitable size of the registers for different scenarios. As a guideline, note that the registers should not all be zero at the time of a page fault to be of any use.
2. Extend the experiments to cover *multiprogramming* systems. Assume *n* processes, each maintaining its own locus of reference. Generate a reference string for each process. Assume all processes are to execute in a RR fashion. That means, during each quantum, the current process generates a number, *q*, of references from its reference string. After *q* references or whenever a page fault occurs, execution switches to the next process. References from the new process reference string are used until again *q* references have been used or a page fault occurs.

   Using the above scheme, study the effects of load control and thrashing. That means, assume a time, *s*, it takes to service a page fault. Thus, the faulting process remains blocked (cannot issue any references) for *s* number of steps following a page fault. Then vary *s*, *n*, and *q*; record and plot the frequency of page faults for a chosen algorithm as a function of these variables. Also record the periods of time during which the CPU is idle, i.e., when all processes are blocked waiting for their page fault to be serviced; when does thrashing occur?

PROJECT 5

File System

1   PROJECT OVERVIEW

This project develops a simple file system using an emulated I/O system. The following diagram shows the basic organization:

The user interacts with the file system using commands, such as *create, open*, or *read* file. The file system views the disk as a linear sequence of logical blocks numbered from 0 to $L - 1$. The I/O system uses a memory array to emulate the disk and presents the logical blocks abstraction to the file system as its interface.

2   THE INPUT/OUTPUT SYSTEM

The physical disk is a two-dimensional structure consisting of cylinders, tracks within cylinders, sectors within tracks, and bytes within sectors. The task of the I/O system is to hide the two-dimensional organization by presenting the disk as a linear sequence of logical blocks, numbered 0 through $L - 1$, where L is the total number of blocks on the physical disk.

We will model the disk as a character array $ldisk[L][B]$, where L is the number of logical blocks and B is the block length, i.e., the number of bytes per block. The task of the I/O system is to accept a logical block number from the file system and to read or write the corresponding block into a memory area specified by the command.

We define the interface between the file system and the I/O system by the following two functions invoked by the system whenever it must read or write a disk block:

- `read_block(int i, char *p);`

  This copies the logical block $ldisk[i]$ into main memory starting at the location specified by the pointer p. The number of characters copied corresponds to the block length, B.

- `write_block(int i, char *p);`

This copies the number of character corresponding to the block length, B, from main memory starting at the location specified by the pointer p, into the logical block $ldisk[i]$.

In addition, we implement two other functions: one to save the array $ldisk$ in a file and the other to restore it. This allows us to preserve the disk contents when not logged in.

3 THE FILE SYSTEM

The file system is built on top of the emulated I/O system described above.

3.1 Interface Between User and File System

The file system must support the following functions: *create, destroy, open, read, write, lseek*, and *directory*.

- *create(symbolic_file_name)*: create a new file with the specified name.

- *destroy(symbolic_file_name)*: destroy the named file.

- *open(symbolic_file_name)*: open the named file for reading and writing; return an index value which is used by subsequent *read, write, lseek*, or *close* operations.

- *close(index)*: close the specified file.

- *read(index, mem_area, count)*: sequentially read a number of bytes from the specified file into main memory. The number of bytes to be read is specified in count and the starting memory address in *mem_area*. The reading starts with the *current position* in the file.

- *write(index, mem_area, count)*: sequentially write a number of bytes from main memory starting at *mem_area* into the specified file. As with the read operation, the number of bytes is given in *count* and the writing begins with the current position in the file.

- *lseek(index, pos)*: move the current position of the file to *pos*, where *pos* is an integer specifying the number of bytes from the beginning of the file. When a file is initially opened, the current position is automatically set to zero. After each read or write operation, it points to the byte immediately following the one that was accessed last. *lseek* permits the position to be explicitly changed without reading or writing the data. Seeking to position 0 implements a reset command, so that the entire file can be reread or rewritten from the beginning.

- *directory*: list the names of all files and their lengths.

3.2 Organization of the File System

The first k blocks of the disk are reserved; they contain the following descriptive information:

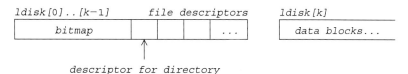

descriptor for directory

The *bitmap* describes which blocks of the disk are free and which are occupied by existing files. Each bit in the bitmap corresponds to one logical disk block. The bitmap is consulted by the file system whenever a file grows as the result of a write operation or when a file is destroyed. (Note that a file never shrinks. The only way to reduce its length is to copy the relevant portion into a new file and to destroy the original file.)

The remaining portion of the first k blocks contains an array of *file descriptors*. The maximum number of descriptors is determined by the block length and the number k. Each descriptor contains the following information:

- file length in bytes;

- an array of disk block numbers that hold the file contents. The length of this array is a system parameter. Set it to a small number, e.g., 3.

3.3 The Directory

There is only one directory file to keep track of all files. This is just like an ordinary file, except it is never explicitly created or destroyed. It corresponds to the very first file descriptor on the disk (see diagram). Initially, when there are no files, it contains length 0 and has no disk blocks allocated. As files are created, it expands.

The directory file is organized as an array of entries. Each entry contains the following information:

- symbolic file name;

- index of file descriptor.

3.4 Creating and Destroying a File

The main tasks performed by the *create* routine are as follows:

- Find a free file descriptor (read in and scan *ldisk [0]* through *ldisk [k − 1]*)

- Find a free entry in the directory (this is done by rewinding the directory and reading it until a free slot is found; recall that the directory is treated just like any other file). At the same time, verify that the file does not already exists. If it does, return error status.

- Enter the symbolic file name and the descriptor index into the found directory entry

- Return status

To *destroy* a file, the following tasks are performed (assume that a file will not be open when the destroy call is made):

- Find the file descriptor by searching the directory

- Remove the directory entry

- Update the bitmap to reflect the freed blocks

- Free the file descriptor

- Return status

3.5 Opening and Closing a File

There is an *open file table (OFT)* maintained by the file system. This is a fixed length array (declared as part of your file system), where each entry has the following form:

- Read/write buffer

- Current position

- File descriptor index

Whenever a file is opened, an entry in OFT is allocated. When a file a closed, the entry is freed. The first field is a buffer used by read and write operations. The buffer size is the size of one disk block. The second field contains the current byte position within the file for reading/writing; initially it is zero. The third field is an index pointing to the corresponding file descriptor on disk.

The tasks performed by the *open* routine are then as follows:

- Search the directory to find the index of the file descriptor

- Allocate a free OFT entry (if possible)

- Fill in the current position (zero) and the file descriptor index

- Read the first block of the file into the buffer (read-ahead)

- Return the OFT index (or error status)

The essential tasks performed by the *close* routine are as follows:

- Write the buffer to disk

- Update file length in descriptor

- Free the OFT entry

- Return status

3.6 Reading, Writing, and Seeking in a File

When a file is open, it can be *read* and *written*. The read operation performs the following tasks:

1. Compute the position within the read/write buffer that corresponds to the current position within the file (i.e., file length modulo buffer length)

2. Start copying bytes from the buffer into the specified main memory location until one of the following happens:

(a) the desired count or the end of the file is reached; in this case, update current position and return status

(b) the end of the buffer is reached; in this case,

- write the buffer into the appropriate block on disk (if modified),
- read the next sequential block from the disk into the buffer;
- continue with step 2.

Writing into a file is analogous; the data is transferred from main memory into the buffer until the desired byte count is satisfied or the end of the buffer is reached. In the latter case, the buffer is written to disk, the file descriptor and the bitmap are then updated to reflect the new block and the writing continues at the beginning of the buffer. If the file length expands past the last allocated block, a new block must be allocated;

The tasks of the *lseek* operation are as follows:

- If the new position is not within the current data block,

  - write the buffer into the appropriate block on disk

  - read the new data block from disk into the buffer

- Set current position to new position

- Return status

3.7 Listing the Directory

The tasks performed under this command are as follows:

- Read the directory file

- For each entry,

  - find file descriptor
  - print file name and file length

4 THE PRESENTATION SHELL

The functionality of the file system can be tested by developing a set of programs to exercise various functions provided by the file system. To demonstrate your project interactively, develop a presentation shell (similar to the one of the process and resource manager) that accepts commands from your terminal, invokes the corresponding functions of the file system, and displays the results on your terminal. For example, *cr* *<name>* creates a new file with the specified name; *op* *<name>* opens the named file for reading and writing and displays an index value on the screen; and *rd* *<index>* *<count>* reads the number of bytes specified as *<count>* from the open file *<index>* and displays them on the screen.

It also is very useful to develop two additional support functions: one to save the contents of the array *ldisk[]* in a file, and the other to restore it. This allows the emulated disk to retain its content between login sessions.

5   SUMMARY OF SPECIFIC TASKS

1. Design and implement the emulated I/O system, in particular, the two functions *read_block(int i, char *p)* and *write_block(int i, char *p)*.

2. Design and implement the file system on top of the I/O system. It should support the functions that define the user/file system interface.

3. Define a command language for the presentation shell. Then, design and implement the shell so that you can test and demonstrate the functionality of your file system interactively.

4. Test the file system using a variety of command sequences to explore all aspects of its behavior.

6   IDEAS FOR ADDITIONAL TASKS

1. Extend the directory management to allow the creation and use of tree-structured *subdirectories*. The naming of files and directories can be done using absolute path names or the concept of a current working directory.

2. Implement a multilevel indexing scheme for disk blocks such that a file may grow past the maximum of three blocks assumed in this project.

3. Implement the disk as a four-dimensional array $ldisk[C][T][S][B]$, where C is the number of cylinders, T is the number of tracks per cylinder, S is the number of sectors (physical blocks) per track, and B is the number of bytes per sector. Extend the emulated I/O system such that it accepts the same requests for logical block numbers as before, but it translates these into the actual disk addresses, consisting of cylinder, track, and sector numbers; these are used as indices to access the array $ldisk$.

Other Programming Projects

1 TIMER FACILITY

Objective: Use a single alarm facility to develop a system to generate multiple reminders.

Project Description: First develop the simple countdown timer *Delay(tdel)* described in Section 4.5.3 (Chapter 4). The *Set_Timer()* function of this timer can be implemented by calling the *alarm()* function in UNIX. This sends a SIGALRM signal to the invoking process when the time expires. The process can catch this signal and execute the function *Timeout()*, which wakes up the original process.

Next, extend the facility to allow multiple logical countdown timers. Implement the *Set_LTimer()* function using either the priority queue with absolute wakeup times or with time differences.

Finally, develop an interactive timer facility that functions as follows. It repeatedly accepts a time value (absolute or relative) from the user terminal and a brief message (character string). For each such call, it spawns a new thread, which invokes the *Delay()* function using the specified time value. This function blocks the thread (on *P(delsem)*); when the thread wakes up, it displays the corresponding message on the user terminal and terminates itself.

2 PROCESS SCHEDULING

Objective: Study the performance of RM scheduling.

Project Description: The rate monotonic (RM) scheduling algorithm is likely to fail if the CPU utilization rises above 0.7 (Section 5.2.3, Chapter 5). The use depends on three factors: 1) the number of concurrent processes, n; 2) the period d_i of each process i; and 3) the total service time t_i of each process i. That means:

$$U = \sum_{i=1}^{n} \frac{t_i}{d_i}$$

Determine experimentally which of the three factors is the most/least important. For example, given a fixed number of processes, n, is it better to have processes with longer average periods and shorter service times, or vice versa?

To perform these evaluations, write a program that accepts a series of values t_i and d_i for $1 \leq i \leq n$, and tries to generate a schedule using RM. Choose a fixed CPU utilization (greater than 0.7). Then, choose a number of processes n and the average values of t_i and d_i to match the chosen utilization. (The values of t_i and d_i can be chosen using a Gaussian distribution with a given mean and standard deviation.) Then, vary n, average t_i, and average d_i while maintaining the same utilization, and observe which variations are most significant. Then, repeat the experiments for higher values of CPU utilization.

3 THE BANKER'S ALGORITHM

Objective: Develop and demonstrate the functioning of the banker's algorithm for deadlock avoidance.

Project Description: Develop an interactive program that first reads the description of a system from a file; this includes the number of processes, the number of resource classes, numbers of units within each resource class, and the maximum claims of each process. Using this description, the program creates a current representation of the system, implemented as a set of arrays. For example, the total number of units of each resource can be represented as a one-dimensional array $R[m]$, where m is the number of resource classes and each entry $R[j]$ records the number of units of resource R_j. The maximum claims can be represented as a two-dimensional array $P[n][m]$ where each entry $P[i][j]$ contains an integer that records the maximum number of units of resource R_j that process p_i will ever request. The allocation edges and the request edges can be represented using similar arrays.

The program enters an interactive session with the user during which it accepts commands of the form *request(i, j, k)* or *release(i, j, k)*, where i is a process number, j is a resource class number, and k is the number of units of R_j process p_i is requesting or releasing. For each request operation, the program responds whether the request has been granted or denied. If denied, the process must retry at a later time.

Demonstrate the functioning of the banker's algorithm by presenting it a sequence of requests and releases that, without taking any precautions, would lead to a deadlock.

4 DISK SCHEDULING ALGORITHM

Objective: Compare the performance of the disk-scheduling algorithms FIFO, SSTF, and scan, as presented in Section 11.5.3 (Chapter 11).

Project Description: First implement the elevator monitor presented in Section 3.3.3 (Chapter 3). This implements the scan algorithm. Then, modify it to implement FIFO and SSTF. Write a driver program to test the algorithms. During each iteration, the driver calls the function *request(n)* or *release()* of the monitor; the choice is made at random using a 0.5 probability. If the operation is a request, the driver also generates the destination n as a uniformly distributed random number between 1 and T, where T is the number of tracks on the disk.

For each algorithm, compute the average distance (number of tracks) traveled by the read/write head to process a given series of requests and releases.

5   STABLE STORAGE

Objective: Develop and demonstrate the algorithms that make up stable storage, as defined in Section 11.5.2 (Chapter 11).

Project Description: Represent the two disks necessary to implement stable storage as two large arrays, $A[n]$ and $B[n]$. Initialize both arrays to contain a series of integers 1 through n. Implement the read and write functions of stable storage, including the recovery procedures invoked when a read or write operation detects a bad block or when the system crashes during a read or write operation.

Then, create two threads, $T1$ and $T2$, with the following functionalities. $T1$ repeatedly reads elements from the stable storage (both disks), reverses the sign of each element, and writes it back to the stable storage (both disks). $T2$ periodically wakes up and probabilistically takes one of the following actions: 1) it randomly selects an element on *one* of the disks and sets it to zero; or 2) it kills and restarts $T1$.

$T1$ must be able to recover from any damage done by $T2$ such that the stable storage always delivers the correct values of the stored integer sequence.

GLOSSARY

Access control Techniques for determining and enforcing the allowable operations on data objects.

Access list The list of subjects that can access a given object.

Access matrix A two-dimensional array whose elements describe the access rights of subjects to objects.

Access rights The permissible operations that a subject can perform on an object.

Address map The mapping of a logical or virtual memory address to a physical address.

Address space The series of addresses of a particular physical or virtual memory.

Alarm clock A software module that will send a wakeup signal to a client process or thread at a specified future time.

Associative memory A memory that is accessed by content rather than by address.

Asynchronous communications Nonblocking communications where sending and receiving operations are not synchronized but return immediately after they are invoked.

ATM Asynchronous transfer mode.

Authentication Verifying the identity of a computer user or the sender of a message.

B-tree A balanced search tree used to organize information on secondary storage.

Banker's algorithm A scheme for detecting deadlock in a system where the maximum claim for each resource is known in advance.

Batch processing Refers to systems, especially older ones, where jobs are entered, collected, and submitted in batches prior to execution.

Best-fit memory allocation A main memory allocation method that matches a request with the closest fitting available block.

Binary heap A binary tree structure, represented as an array, where the value at the root of a subtree is less than that of any nodes in the subtree.

Binding of addresses Assigning a physical address to a logical or a symbolic address.

Block-oriented device An I/O device that sends, receives, or stores data in fixed-size blocks.

Bootstrap A means of loading data into a computer, which uses part of the data itself to instruct the loading process.

Bounded buffer A fixed-size memory area used to efficiently smooth the flow of data between two or more processes.

Broadcast A communication mechanism where a transmitted message is available to all active receivers.

Busy-wait Waiting for a resource or event, not by releasing the CPU and blocking, but by looping and consuming CPU cycles.

Caching files Storing files temporarily in a local computer, where the files reside permanently in a remote node in a distributed system.

Capability An access priviledge of a subject to an object.

Checkpoint Saving the state of a computation or file for possible recovery if a crash occurs.

Ciphertext An encrypted message.

Circular buffer An n-slot buffer implemented as an array such that the ith element is logically followed by the element in position $(i + 1)$ modulo n.

Circular scan A disk cylinder access scheme, similar to the elevator algorithm, but accessing the cylinders only in one direction of travel, i.e., from 1 to n, for an n-cylinder disk.

Claim graph A directed graph used for deadlock analysis, which represents the maximum claims of each process for each resource, as well as the current allocation and request status.

Client-server A software architecture or framework that distinguishes between client processes, which request work, and server processes, which perform activities on behalf of clients.

Clock replacement A circular page replacement algorithm that approximates LRU.

Clock server A module that provides timer services.

Compacting memory Collecting unused noncontiguous blocks of memory and replacing them by a single contiguous block.

Condition variable A special type used for synchronization operations in monitors.

Confinement problem A security problem that is concerned with ensuring that the information supplied by a client to a service is not leaked.

Consistency in DSM Ensuring that multiple copies of data stored across a DSM are consistent.

Consumable resource A resource, such as an event or a message, which is consumed by the process that acquires it.

Consumer process A process that receives full buffers or messages and consumes the data contained in them.

Context switch The act of switching CPU control from one process, thread, or task to another.

Control block A data structure describing the state of some object, such as a process, a file, or an I/O device.

Countdown timer A timing device that decrements its value at each clock tick and generates an interrupt when the value reaches a predefined bound, usually zero.

CPU Central processing unit.

Critical section A section of code that must be executed in a logically indivisible manner with respect to similar sections in other processes, to maintain consistency.

CRT Cathode ray terminal.

Cryptography The art and science of deciphering and enciphering secret messages.

Cryptosystem A system for enciphering and deciphering secret messages.

CS Critical section.

CSP Communicating sequential processes programming language.

DAG Directed acyclic graph.

Data encryption standard The secret-key cryptosystem adopted by the U.S. government and business applications.

Deadline The time at which a computation must be completed.

Deadlock A system state where two or more processes are blocked forever on resource requests that can never be satisfied.

Deadlock avoidance Avoiding deadlock by dynamically delaying satisfiable resource requests.

Deadlock prevention Preventing deadlock through static schemes that restrict the order of resource requests.

Decryption Decoding a message.

Demand paging A paging policy that only loads a page when it is referenced.

Denial of service An undesirable security situation where an unauthorized user is deliberately denied a system service for an unreasonable amount of time.

DES Data encryption standard.

Descriptor A data structure representing the state of a process or resource.

Device controller A hardware interface for an I/O device, which controls the operation of the device.

Device driver A software module that controls the operation of an I/O device.

DFS Distributed file system.

Digital signature A short encoded message generated from a long message, which allows the authentication of the long message.

Dining philosophers problem A classical synchronization problem used to illustrate deadlock and starvation. (A group of philosophers are seated around a circular table set with one fork between each philosopher.)

Direct memory access An architectural feature that allows I/O devices to perform I/O directly to and from memory through a controller interface.

Dirty page A page in main memory that has been modified since it was loaded.

Disk head scheduler The software that schedules disk cylinder requests for a moving head disk.

Dispatcher A scheduling module that allocates a CPU to ready processes.

Distributed shared memory A shared-memory abstraction implemented in a physically distributed memory system.

Distributed system A computer system consisting of several computers connected through a communication network.

DMA Direct memory access.

DSM Distributed shared memory.

Dynamic linking and sharing Implementing the linking and sharing of software modules at the first reference during execution.

Earliest deadline first A scheduling policy that allocates the CPU to the ready process with the earliest deadline.

EDF Earliest deadline first.

Elevator algorithm A scheduling algorithm, used for disk head scheduling, which mimics the scheduling of an elevator.

Encryption Coding a message to ensure secure transmission.

Encryption key A parameter used by an encryption algorithm to code a message.

Entry guard or barrier A logical condition that must be satisfied before entry to a procedure is permitted.

Ethernet A broadcast-based communication mechanism and protocol for a LAN.

Event An instantaneous occurrence or happening that produces a signal.

Exception An unusual or error condition that occurs during program execution.

External safeguard Any method for controlling the physical access to a computing facility to improve or ensure security.

Feasible schedule A schedule that meets all constraints, normally timing constraints.

FIFO First-in, first-out.

FIFO replacement A page-replacement scheme that uses a FIFO strategy.

Fifty-percent rule A memory fragmentation result for nonpaged systems. The number of holes approaches 50% of the number of full blocks under equilibrium assumptions.

File descriptor A data structure containing all the relevant information about a file except its contents.

File system That part of an operating system concerned with storing, retrieving, organizing, protecting, and maintaining data files on long-term storage.

File type The type of data stored in a file, such as text, binary, figures, or program.

First-fit memory allocation A scheme for allocating main memory that selects the first free block that satisfies a request.

Forall statement A parallel programming statement that spawns a concurrent execution for each element in a list.

Fork-join statements Parallel programming statements that spawn new processes (fork) and wait for their termination before proceeding (join).

Fragmentation An undesirable state of memory where most of the free space is interspersed with allocated space.

Frame table A table in a paging system, one entry for each frame of memory, containing the correspondence between frames and the process pages residing therein.

FTP File transfer protocol.

Global page replacement Memory-management schemes with fixed numbers of frames that make page-replacement decisions based on the history of all pages in memory, rather than on just those associated with a faulting process.

Graph reduction A technique used for deadlock detection that simulates an ideal future behavior by eliminating edges of a graph representing the system state.

Guarded command A programming language construct where a statement or command is preceded by a guard that must evaluate to true for the command to be executable.

GUI Graphics user interface.

Hold-and-wait A necessary condition for deadlock where a process must both hold one resource and be waiting for another resource.

Holes in memory Free blocks of memory that are separated by used blocks.

IH Interrupt handler.

Immutable file A file that is never changed.

Indexed file organization A tabular method of keeping track of the location of file records so as to permit direct access to them.

Information flow control Security policies that control the transfer of information, directly or indirectly, from one object to another.

I-node The standard file descriptor originated in the UNIX OS.

Interrupt handler The code that directly interfaces and responds to an interrupt.

Interrupt-driven I/O Software for initiating, controlling, and responding to input and output, that is triggered by I/O interrupts.

Inverted page table Another name for a frame table.

I/O Input-output.

IPC Interprocess communication.

Kernel The lowest-level software in an operating system, residing entirely in main memory and interfacing directly to the most sensitive hardware facilities.

Knot A subgraph G of a directed graph where all paths from any node in G never leave G, and there is a path between any two nodes in G.

LAN Local area network.

Lattice model of information flow A protection model that uses a mathematical lattice structure to define the information flow among security classes.

Least recently used replacement A page-replacement strategy that selects the page that has not been used for the longest time.

Linking The process where interreferences among separately compiled software modules are bound to the real or logical addresses corresponding to the references.

Linking loader A software module that links other software modules together and loads them into main memory.

Livelock A system state involving several processes that never make any progress because each is executing a never-ending busy-wait.

Load balancing Spreading the computation load evenly over a set of available CPUs.

Load control A virtual memory management issue, concerned with how many concurrent processes should be competing for main memory at any point in time.

Load module A software module ready for loading into main memory and subsequent execution.

Local page replacement Memory-management schemes that maintain a variable-size resident set of pages for each process, and replace pages only from the faulting process resident set.

Locality principle The principle states that the next instruction/data address referenced by a program during execution is most likely to be the same as or close to those that were referenced recently.

Logical clock A counter that can be used to determine the potential causality of events: if event1 precedes event2, then the value of the counter at event1 should be less than that at event2.

Logical record A data record, independent of how or where it is stored.

LRU Least recently used.

Mailbox A message queue that may be used as a communication buffer by more than one sender or receiver.

Memory-mapped file A file that has its data bound to virtual memory locations so that file data are accessed directly using their virtual memory addresses.

Memory-mapped I/O An architecture that reserves some main memory addresses for one or more I/O controllers, allowing the same instruction formats to be used for accessing main memory and I/O devices.

Message authenticity Concerns associated with guaranteeing the identity of the creator or sender of a message.

Message port A message queue acting as a communication buffer between many senders and one receiver.

MIN Optimal page-replacement algorithm.

MLF Multilevel feedback scheduling policy.

Monitor, Hoare monitor, Java monitor, Mesa monitor An encapsulation scheme for resource management software, which incorporates CS protection, and provides wait and signal/notify synchronization primitives.

Multiprogramming Refers to a system that runs more than one program or job at the same time.

Mutual exclusion A property among code sections, called CSs, associated with different processes that run concurrently in general. The sections must not be executed in parallel or interleaved with each other.

Next-fit memory allocation A main memory allocation policy that selects the next block that satisfies a request from a list of free blocks.

Nonce A random number used in cryptographic protocols to prevent replay attacks.

Notify A signaling primitive defined in some monitor mechanisms, such as those in the Java and Mesa languages.

Nucleus Another name for an OS kernel.

Object module The relocatable code that is generated from a source program module by a compiler.

OFT Open file table.

One-way function A function with the property that, given its value, it is not feasible to compute its argument.

Open file A file that has been made ready for reading or writing.

Open file table A table that stores and maintains the state of all open files.

Optimal schedule A schedule that meets all constraints if it is possible to do so.

Ordered resource policy A deadlock prevention scheme requiring that resources be requested in a fixed order.

OS Operating system.

OSI Open systems interconnection reference model.

Overlaying A memory-management scheme that preplans the allocation and reuse of memory, with explicit overlays of the same memory area by different software modules.

P and V operations The basic waiting and signaling operations, respectively, which are part of the semaphore synchronization mechanism.

Packet The unit of data used in a network when transmitting messages.

Page A fixed-size unit of virtual memory, used for I/O and memory allocation.

Page fault The exception that occurs when a nonresident page is referenced during execution.

Page fault frequency replacement algorithm A page-replacement scheme that is triggered at each page fault and maintains a resident set based on the interval between page faults.

Page frame The unit of main memory in a paging system, having the same size as a virtual memory page.

Page table A data structure containing the mapping from logical pages to page frames.

Page table register A hardware register pointing to the page table of the currently executing process or thread.

Path name A file name obtained by tracing a path through a directory structure and concatenating the names of each branch of the path.

PC Personal computer.

PCB Process control block.

PFF Page fault frequency replacement algorithm.

Pixel A picture element. The lowest-level representation of an image in a computer, usually arranged in a matrix.

Prepaging Loading pages into main memory in advance of their use.

Priority ceiling A priority inversion prevention scheme with low worst case blocking times, which also prevents deadlock.

Priority inheritance A policy to prevent priority inversion which raises the priority of a process that blocks a higher-priority one.

Priority inversion The undesirable situation where a lower-priority process can be blocking a higher-priority one for an unpredictable length of time.

Priority queue A queue where the elements are removed in priority order.

Priority wait A monitor wait operation that associates a wakeup priority with the calling process or thread.

Privileged instruction A machine instruction that can be executed only when the CPU is in a privileged or protected mode.

Process A basic unit for resource allocation and also, frequently, of execution. Sometimes distinguished from a thread, which is a basic unit of execution.

Process descriptor A data structure containing the state, resource, and other attribute information of a process.

Process flow graph A directed graph representing the execution precedence constraints of a group of processes.

Process state The data needed by a CPU to start or continue the execution of a process.

Process status The status of a process with respect to CPU execution, minimally ready, running, or blocked.

Processor mode The status of a processor with respect to the instructions it can execute, minimally supervisor or user mode.

Producer process A process that generates messages or data elements and deposits them in buffers.

Producer-consumer A relationship among processes, some of which produce data that is consumed by others.

Programmed I/O   An I/O mechanism where the CPU is responsible for moving data between main memory and devices.

Protected type   A type of data object defined in the Ada language that ensures controlled access to the object by concurrent tasks, similar to monitors.

PTR   Page table register.

Public-key cryptosystem   A two-key cryptosystem where one of the keys can be made public.

Quorum-based read/write protocol   A file replication protocol that guarantees consistency, based on a minimum number of files that must be read or written.

RAID   Redundant array of independent disks.

Rate monotonic   A scheduling policy for periodic real-time processes, which assigns scheduling priorities inversely to period length.

Read-any/write-all protocol   A file replication protocol that guarantees consistency, based on propagation of writes to all replicas.

Readers/writers problem   A classical synchronization problem where reader processes may simultaneously be in a given section of code, and writer processes can be in their sections only one at a time and not concurrently with readers.

Ready list   The list of processes or threads that are logically ready to execute or continue executing but are waiting for an available CPU.

Real-time system   A computer system that monitors or responds to signals from an external environment and must meet the timing constraints defined by the environment.

Reducible graph   A process-resource graph that can be reduced to isolated nodes in a deadlock detection scenario.

Reference string   A list of successive page references made by an executing process or set of processes.

Release consistency   A consistency scheme for DSM that propagates changes of shared variables to all replicas at the end of a CS.

Relocatable program   A machine language program in a form that can be loaded by a relocating loader into an arbitrary sequence of contiguous locations in main memory.

Relocation constant   A constant offset defining the amount that an instruction or operand address must be incremented by to reflect its real location in memory.

Remote procedure call   A distributed communications mechanism where a client invokes a remote server procedure by calling it in a manner similar to a normal procedure call.

Rendezvous A synchronous communications scheme between two processes, resembling remote procedure call and defined particularly in the Ada language.

Replay attack A security violation involving resending copies of old messages.

Resource graph A directed graph representing the state of a system, and used for deadlock analyses.

Reusable resource A resource that can be used by only one process at a time and is permanently available.

Revocation of rights The ability to take back access rights that were previously granted.

Right amplification The temporary and dynamic expansion or addition of access rights to an object.

Rings of protection A protection scheme organized as concentric rings where the inner rings have more privileges than the outer ones. Originated in the Multics system.

RL Ready list.

RM Rate monotonic.

Round-robin A scheduling policy that allocates each ready process in FIFO order to the CPU for a short quantum of time, inserting a process at the end of the list after its quantum expires.

RPC Remote procedure call.

RR Relocation register.

RR Round-robin.

RS Reference string.

RSA A public-key cryptosystem abbreviated by the first letters of the names of its inventors: Rivest, Shamir, and Adelman.

Safe state A system state that is not a deadlock state and will never transition, directly or indirectly, to a deadlock state.

Scan algorithm Another name for the elevator algorithm, used for disk head scheduling.

Scheduler The software that allocates ready processes or threads to a CPU. Sometimes also called a dispatcher.

Second-chance replacement algorithm A page-replacement scheme that employs a use bit, ensuring that pages that have been referenced are not replaced until a second scan of the resident list.

Secret-key cryptosystem A traditional cryptosystem with a single secret key for both senders and receivers.

Security The freedom from danger, risk, doubt, or apprehension.

Security classification level The security classification assigned to a resource in a hierarchical system.

Seek time The time for the arm of a moving head disk to reach a given track or cylinder.

Segment A logical program or data unit.

Segment table A data structure containing the mapping from logical segments either to main memory or to page tables.

Segment table register A hardware register that points to the segment table of the currently executing process or thread.

Selective confinement The problem of preventing a server's disclosure of only part of the information—the most sensitive part—provided to it by a client.

Semaphore A synchronization object with two operations, a P that potentially blocks a calling process and a V that potentially wakes up a blocked process.

Sequential access The reading or writing of a file in the sequential order of its records or data elements.

Sequential consistency A consistency property of a DSM, where the values read by different processes correspond to those obtained by some sequential interleaved execution of the processes.

Shell The program that interprets the command language that acts as an interface between the user and an operating system, particularly in UNIX and its derivatives.

Shortest job first A batch-scheduling policy that gives highest priority to jobs with the smallest execution times.

Shortest remaining time A scheduling policy that gives highest CPU priority to jobs or processes having the smallest remaining execution times.

Single-copy sharing A situation where one copy of software is shared among more than one process or job.

Single-unit resource A resource class containing a single unit of the resource.

SJF Shortest job first.

Sneaky signaling The use of covert channels for information disclosures that violate security requirements.

Socket A common network interface defining the endpoints of a connection between a computer and an indirectly connected device.

Source module A software module in the form of a program in some source programming language.

Spinning lock A synchronization lock that waits by executing a busy-wait loop.

Spooling The technique of buffering output or input through secondary storage. The acronym "spool" stands for 'simultaneous peripheral operations on-line.'

SRT Shortest remaining time.

SSTF Shortest seek time first.

Stable storage Refers to a permanent and robust storage system that maintains its data even in unreliable environments, mainly through the clever use of redundancy.

Starvation A situation where one or more processes are prevented from making progress for a possibly unbounded period of time.

STR Segment table register.

Stream A string or sequence of characters, generally of arbitrary length.

Stream-device interface An interface that controls devices that produce or consume sequences of characters, called streams.

Stream-oriented device An I/O device that handles character streams.

Strict consistency A DSM property, where reading the value of a variable always returns the most recent (in real time) value of the variable.

Subject An entity in a security system, that has a given set of access priviledges or capabilities when active.

Swapping The act of removing a process from main memory, placing it on secondary storage, and replacing it by another process residing on secondary storage.

Symbolic link A symbolic identifier for an object in a software module, e.g., a file directory, that is defined in another module.

System mode The supervisor or kernel mode of a computer, that allows the execution of any machine instruction.

TCP/IP Transmission control protocol/internet protocol.

Test-and-set instruction A machine instruction that tests and sets a register indivisibly, permitting the convenient solution of CS and other synchronization problems.

Third-chance replacement algorithm A page-replacement scheme that employs both a use bit and a write bit, ensuring that written pages are not selected for replacement until a third scan of the resident list.

Thrashing An overload condition where the system is spending most of its time moving pages between main and disk storage, and not doing any useful work.

Thread An active software object that may share resources, especially main memory, with other such thread objects. Generally, the shared resources of a group of threads are managed by a process.

Time quantum An interval of CPU time given to an executing process in a time-sharing system.

Timeout An alarm signal that notifies a process after a specified time has elapsed or been reached.

Time-sharing system A computer system that handles multiple online users simultaneously by multiplexing CPU time among the users.

Time-stamp An addition to a message or other data item, consisting of the current time.

Token ring A LAN communication mechanism where a token circulates around a ring that is connected to each of the possible communicants.

Track skew The addressing offset of sectors on adjacent tracks of a disk, used to optimize access times of sequentially addressed sectors.

Transaction A sequence of actions that, when interleaved with another transaction, must produce the same results as if executed sequentially, in isolation.

Translation look-aside buffer A fast associative memory used to bypass the normal lengthy address translation mapping in a virtual memory system.

Trap An internal interrupt, either used by or caused by an executing program to immediately transfer control to an OS routine.

Trap door An unspecified feature of a system that may permit unauthorized access.

Trojan horse A security attack that involves passing a program containing a hidden means of breaching security to an unsuspecting subject.

TS Test-and-set instruction.

UDP/IP Universal datagram protocol/Internet protocol.

Use bit A bit associated with a page, which is set whenever the page is referenced.

User mode The normal execution mode of a user process, which has the least privileges.

Virtual address The address of a cell in a virtual memory.

Virtual memory The logical memory presented in a computer architecture, usually organized as pages or segments.

Virus A malicious program, attached to a host, which attempts to replicate itself and to inflict harm on the system it invades.

VMIN replacement algorithm An optimal page-replacement scheme where the number of resident pages for a process may vary.

WAN Wide area network.

Working directory The current file directory defined for a process or user.

Working set model A page-repacement strategy that attempts to approximate VMIN by looking backward over a window of time for referenced pages.

Worm A malicious program that replicates itself and inflicts harm on the system it invades.

Worst-fit memory allocation A main memory allocation method that satisfies a request for a contiguous block by allocating the largest available block.

Write bit A bit associated with a page, which is set whenever some part of the page is modified. Also called a dirty bit.

Bibliography

Accetta, M., Baron, R., Bolosky, W., Golub, D., Rashid, R., Tevanian, A., Young, M. 1986. Mach: A New Kernel Foundation for UNIX Development, Proc. 1986 Usenix Summer Conf. 93–112.

Ada. 1995. Annotated Ada Reference Manual, Version 6.0, ISO/IEC 8652:1995 (E), Intermetrics.

Aho, A.V., Denning, P.J., and Ullman, J.D. 1971. Principles of optimal page replacements. J. ACM 18, No. 1 (Jan.), 80–93

Andrews, G.R. 2000. Foundations of Multithreaded, Parallel, and Distributed Programming, Addison-Wesley.

American National Standard Institute. 1985. American national standard for financial institution key management, Standard X9.17.

Baer, J.L., and Sager, G.R. 1972. Measurement and improvement of program behavior under paging systems. In W. Freiberger (ed.), Statistical Computer Performance Evaluation, Academic Press, New York. 241–264.

Bal, H.E., Kaashoek, M.F., Tanenbaum, A.S. 1992. Orca: A Language for Parallel Programming of Distributed Systems. IEEE Trans. on Software Engineering. 18:190–205.

Bays, C. 1977. A Comparison of Next-fit, First-fit, and Best-fit. Communications of the ACM. 20(3):191–192.

Belady, L.A., Nelson, R.A., Shedler, G.S. 1969. An anomaly in space-time characteristics of certain programs running in a paging machine. CACM 12(6):349–353.

Belady, L.A. 1966. A study of replacement algorithms for a virtual storage computer. IBM Syst. J. 5(2):78–101.

Bell, D.E., LaPadula, L.J. 1973a. Secure Computer Systems: Mathematical Foundations. MTR-2547. Vol. 1. The MITRE Corp., Bedford, Mass.

Bell, D.E., LaPadula, L.J. 1973b. Secure Computer Systems: A Mathematical Model. MTR-2547. Vol. 2. The MITRE Corp., Bedford, Mass.

Bell, D.E., LaPadula, L.J. 1973c. Secure Computer Systems: A Refinement of the Mathematical Model. MTR-2547. Vol. 3. The MITRE Corp., Bedford, Mass.

Bell, D.E., LaPadula, L.J. 1974. Secure Computer Systems: Mathematical Foundations and Model. M74–244. Vol. 3. The MITRE Corp., Bedford, Mass.

Bernstein, A., Lewis, P. 1993. Concurrency in Programming and Database Systems. Jones & Bartlett. Sudbury, MA.

Bershad, B.N., Zekauskas, M.J., and Sawdon, W.A. 1993. The Midway Distributed Shared Memory System. IEEE Computer Conference (Compcon). 528–537.

Bic, L., Fukuda, M., Dillencourt, M. 1996. Distributed computing using Mobile Objects. IEEE Computer. Vol. 29, No. 8; 55–61.

Black, D. 1990. Scheduling Support for Concurrency and Parallelism in the Mach Operating System. IEEE Computer. Vol. 23. 35–43.

Bovet, D., Cesati, M. 2001. Understanding the Linux Kernel, O'Reilly & Associates. Sebastopol, CA.

Brinch Hansen, P. 1970. The Nucleus of a Multiprogramming System. Comm. ACM. 13(4): 238–241.

Brinch Hansen, P. 1973. Concurrent Programming Concepts. ACM Computing Surveys. 5(4): 223–245.

Brinch Hansen, P. 1973. Operating System Principles. Prentice-Hall. Englewood Cliffs, N.J.

Burns, A. 1988. Programming in occam 2. Addison-Wesley. Wokingham, England.

Burroughs Corporation. 1964. B5500 Information Processing Systems. Reference Manual. Detroit, MI.

Burroughs Corporation. 1967. B6500 Information Processing Systems. Characteristics Manual. Detroit, MI.

Callaghan, B. 2000. NFS Illustrated Addison-Wesley Professional Computing Series.

Carr, R.W. 1981. Virtual Memory Management. STAN-CS-81–873. Stanford Linear Accelerator Center. Stanford University.

Chandy, K.M., Misra, J., and Haas, L.M. 1983. Distributed Deadlock Detection. ACM Transactions on Computer Systems. 1:144–156.

Cheriton, D.R. 1988. The V Distributed System. Comm. ACM. 31(3):314–333.

Coffman, E.G., and Varian, L.C. 1968. Further experimental data on behavior of programs in a paging environment. Comm. ACM 11. 7:471–474.

Cohen, E., Jefferson, D. 1975. Protection in the HYDRA Operating System. Operating Systems Reviews. 9(5):141–160.

Comer, D. 1979. The Ubiquitous B-Tree. ACM Surveys. 11(2):121–138.

Conway, M.E. 1963. A Multiprocessor System Design. Proc. AFIPS Fall Joint Computer Conf. Las Vegas, Nevada. 139–146.

Courtois, P.J., Heymans, F., Parnas, D.L. 1971. Concurrent Control with Readers and Writers. Communications of the ACM. 14(10):667–668.

Daley, R.C., and Dennis, J.B. 1968. Virtual memory, processes, and sharing in MULTICS. Comm. ACM 11. 5:306–312.

Denning, P.J., Kahn, K.C., Leroudier, J., Potier, D., Suri, R. 1976. Optimal Multiprogramming. Acta Informatica. 7(2):197–216.

Denning, P.J. 1968. The working set model for program behavior. Comm. ACM 11. 5:323–333.

Denning, P.J. 1970. Virtual memory. Computing Surveys 2. 3:153–189.

Denning, P.J. 1980. Working Sets Past and Present. IEEE Trans. SE-6(1):64–84.

Denning, D.E. 1976. A Lattice Model of Secure Information Flow. CACM. 19(5): 236–243.

Dennis, J.B., Van Horn, E.C. 1966. Programming Semantics for Multiprogrammed Computations. Communications of the ACM. 9.

DIGITAL. 1982. VAX Software Handbook. Digital Equipment Corporation, Maynard, Mass.

Dijkstra, E.W. 1968. Co-operating sequential processes. In F. Genuys (ed.). Programming Languages. Academic Press, New York. 43–112.

Dijkstra, E.W. 1975. Guarded Commnads, Nondeterminacy, and Formal Derivation of Programs. CACM. 18(8):453–457.

Dubois, M., Scheurich, C., Briggs, F.A. 1988. Synchronization, Coherence, and Event Ordering in Multiprocessors. IEEE Computer. 21(2):9–21.

Fenton, J.S. 1974. Memoryless Subsystems. Computer Journal. 17(2).

Franklin, M.A., Graham, G.S., Gupta, R.K. 1978. Anomalies with Variable Partition Paging Algorithms. CACM. 21(3).

Gelenbe, E., Tiberio, P., Boeckhorst, J. 1973. Page Size in Demand Paging Systems. Acta Informatica. 3:1–24.

Gharachorloo, K., Lenoski, D., Laudon, J., Gibbons, P., Gupta, A., and Hennesy, J. 1990. Memory Consistency and Event Ordering in Scalable Shared Memory Multiprocessors. In Proceedings of the 17th Annual International Symposium on Computer Architecture. 15–26.

Gupta, R.K., Franklin, M.A. 1978. Working Set and Page Fault Frequency Replacement Algorithm: A Performance Comparison. IEEE TC. C-27:706–712.

Harrison, M.A., Ruzzo, W.L., Ullman, J.D. 1976. Protection in Operating Systems. CACM. 19(8): 461–471.

Havender, J.W. 1968. Avoiding deadlocks in multitasking systems. IBM Syst. 7(2):74–84.

Hoare, C.A.R. Toward a Theory of Parallel Programming. In C.A.R. Hoare and R.H. Perrott (Eds.). 1972. *Operating Systems Techniques*. Academic Press, New York. 61–71.

Hoare, C.A.R. 1974. Monitors: An Operating System Structuring Concept. Communications of the ACM. 17(10):549–557.

Hoare, C.A.R. 1978. Communicating Sequential Processes. Communications of the ACM. 21(8): 666–677.

Hoare, C. 1984. Communicating Sequential Processes. Prentice-Hall.

Holt, R.C. 1971. Comments on Prevention of System Deadlocks. CACM. 14(1): 36–38.

Holt, R.C. 1972. Some deadlock properties of computer systems. ACM Computing Surveys. 4(3):179–196.

Howard, J., Kazar, M., Menees, S., Nichols, D., Satyanarayanan, M., Sidebotham, R., and West, M. 1988. Scale and performance in a distributed file system ACM Trans. Computer Systems. 6(1).

Inmos. 1984. The Occam Programming Manual, Prentice-Hall.

Inmos. 1988. Occam 2 Reference Manual. C. Hoare (ed.). Prentice-Hall.

Keleher, P., Cox, A.L., and Zwaenepoel, W. 1992. Lazy Release Consistency for Software Distributed Shared Memory. Proc. of the 19th Annual Intl Symp. on Computer Architecture (ISCA92). 13–21.

Kilburn, T., et al. 1962. One-level storage system. IRE Trans. EC-11(2):223–235.

Knuth, D.E. 1968. The art of computer programming. Vol. 1. Addison-Wesley, Reading, MA.

Lamport, L. 1978. Time, Clocks, and the Ordering of Events in a Distributed System. Comm. ACM. 27(7):558–565.

Lamport, L. 1997. How to Make a Correct Multiprocess Program Execute Correctly on a Multiprocessor. IEEE Transactions on Computers. 46(7):779–782.

Lamport, L. 1981. Password authentication with insecure communication. Commun. ACM. 24(11).

Lampson, B.W., David D. Redell. 1980. Experience with Processes and Monitors in Mesa. CACM. 23(2):105–117.

Lea, D. 1997. Concurrent Programming in Java, Design Principles and Patterns. Addison-Wesley, Reading, Mass.

Leffler, S.J., McKusick, M.K., Karels, M.J., Quarterman, J.S. 1989. The Design and Implementation of the 4.3BSD UNIX Operating System. Addison-Wesley, Reading, Mass.

LeLann, G. 1977. Distributed Systems: Towards a Formal Approach. Proc. Information Processing 77, North Holland, Amsterdam. 155–160.

Lenfant, J., Burgevin, P. 1975. Empirical Data on Program Behavior. Proc. ACM Intl Symp. E. Gelenbe and D. Potier, Eds. Amsterdam, The Netherlands: North-Holland. 163–170.

Li, K., Hudak, P. 1989. Memory Coherence in Shared Virtual Memory Systems. ACM Transactions on Computer Systems. 7(4):321–359.

Li, K. 1986. Shared virtual memory on loosely coupled multiprocessors. PhD Thesis, Yale University.

Mattson, R.L., et al. 1970. Evaluation techniques for storage hierarchies. IBM Syst. 9(2):78–117.

National Bureau of Standards. 1977. Data encryption standard (DES). Federal information processing standard. FIPS publication 46–3 (reaffirmed 1999), Washington, DC.

Naughton, P., Schildt, H. 1997. Java: The Complete Reference. Osborne McGraw-Hill, Berkeley, Calif.

Needham, R.M. and Schoeder, M.D. 1978. Using encryption for authentication in large networks of computers. Comm. ACM. 21(12):993–999.

Neuman, C. and Tso, T. 1994. Kerberos: An Authentication Service for Computer Networks. IEEE Communications. 32(9):33–38.

Nichols, B., Farrell, J., Buttlar, D. 1996. Pthread Programming: Using POSIX Threads. O'Reilly & Associates.

National Institute of Standards and Technology. Secure hash standard. U.S. Department of Commerce. NIS FIPS PUP 180–1.

Opderbeck, H., Chu, W.W. 1974. Performance of the Page Fault Frequency Algorithm in a Multiprogramming Environment. Proc. IFIP Congr. 235–241.

Peterson, G.L. 1981. Myths About the Mutual Exclusion Problem. Information Processing Letters. 12(3):115–116.

POSIX. 1993. Portable Operating Systems Interface. POSIX P1003.4. IEEE.

Prieve, B.G., Fabry, R.S. 1976. VMIN — An Optimal Variable Space Page Replacement Algorithm. CACM. 19:295–297.

Redell, D., Dalal, Y., Horsely, T., Lauer, H., Lynch, W., McJones, P., Murray, H., Purcell, S. 1980. Pilot: An Operating System for a Personal Computer. Comm. ACM. 23(2):81–92.

Rivest, R.L., Shamir, A. and Adleman, L.M. 1978. A Method for Obtaining Digital Signatures and Public-Key Cryptosystems. Communications of the ACM. 21(2).

Rivest, R. 1992. The MD5 message digest algorithm. Internet RFC/STD/FYI/BCP Archives. RFC 1321.

Rodriguez-Rosell, J. 1973. Empirical Working Set Behavior. CACM. 16:556–560.

Ruschitzka, M., Fabry, R.S. 1977. A Unifying Approach to Scheduling, Comm. ACM. 20(7):469–476.

Sadeh, E. 1975. An Analysis of the Performance of the Page Fault Frequency (PFF) Replacement Algorithm. Proc. 5th ACM Symp. Operating Systems Principles. 6–13.

Schoeder, M.D. and Saltzer, J.H. 1972. A hardware architecture for implementing protection rings. Comm. ACM. 15(3):157–170.

Satyanarayanan, M. 1990. Scalable, Secure, and Highly Available Distributed File Access. IEEE Computer. 23(5).

Satyanarayanan, M., Kistler, J., Kumar, P., Okasaki, M., Siegel, E., and Steere, D. Coda. 1990. A Highly Available File System for a Distributed Workstation Environment. IEEE Trans. Comp. 39(4).

Sha, L., Rajkumar, R., Lehoczky, J. 1990. Priority Inheritance Protocols: An Approach to Ral-Time Synchronization. IEEE Trans. on Computers. 39(9):1175–1185.

Shatz, S.M. 1984. Communication Mechanisms for Programming Distributed Systems. COMPUTER. 17(6):21–28.

Shaw, A.C. 2001. Real-Time Systems and Software. John Wiley & Sons, New York.

Shore, J.E. 1975. On the External Storage Fragmentation Produced by First-Fit and Best-Fit Allocation Strategies. Communications of the ACM. 18:433–440.

Solomon, D.A. 1998. Inside Windows NT. 2nd Edition. Microsoft Press, Redmond, Wash.

Spirn, J.R. 1977. Program behavior: Models and Measurement. Elsevier/North-Holland, New York.

Steiner, J., Neuman, C. and Schiller, J.I. 1988. Kerberos: An Authentication Service for Open Network Systems. Proc. Winter Techn. Conf. USENIX.

Tanenbaum, A.S., Van Renesse, R., Van Staveren, H., Sharp, G.J., Mullender, S.J., Jansen, J., Van Rossum, G. 1990. Experiences with the Amoeba Distributed Operating System. Comm. ACM. 33(12):46–63.

Tanenbaum, A.S. 1995. Distributed Operating Systems. Prentice Hall, Englewood Cliffs, NJ.

Tanenbaum, A.S., Woodhull, A.S. 1997. Operating Systems, Design and Implementation. 2nd Edition. Prentice Hall, Upper Saddle River, NJ.

Weiss, M.A. 1993. Data Structures and Algorithm Analysis in C. Benjamin Cummings, Calif.

Author Index

Subject Index